ALSO BY PAUL HENDRICKSON

Seminary: A Search

Looking for the Light:
The Hidden Life and Art of Marion Post Wolcott

The Living and the Dead:
Robert McNamara and Five Lives of a Lost War

Sons of Mississippi:
A Story of Race and Its Legacy

HEMINGWAY'S BOAT

HEMINGWAY'S BOAT

Everything He Loved in Life, and Lost,
1934–1961

PAUL HENDRICKSON

ALFRED A. KNOPF   NEW YORK   2011

THIS IS A BORZOI BOOK
PUBLISHED BY ALFRED A. KNOPF

www.aaknopf.com

Portions of this work have appeared in different form in
The Washington Post, The New York Times, and *Town & Country.*

Owing to limitations of space, all acknowledgments for permission to
reprint previously published material may be found following the index.

Library of Congress Cataloging-in-Publication Data
Hendrickson, Paul, [date]
Hemingway's boat : everything he loved in life, and lost, 1934–1961 /
Paul Hendrickson. — 1st ed.
p. cm.
Includes bibliographical references and index.
ISBN 978-1-4000-4162-6
1. Hemingway, Ernest, 1899–1961.   2. Authors, American—20th
century—Biography. 3. Journalists—United States—Biography.
I. Title.
PS3515.E37Z628 2011
813'.52—dc22
[B]
2011003398

Jacket photographs courtesy of the Ernest Hemingway Collection/
John F. Kennedy Presidential Library and Museum, Boston
Jacket design by Carol Devine Carson

Manufactured in the United States of America
First Edition

For Jon Segal,
editor and friend of three decades

CONTENTS

Prologue: Amid So Much Ruin, Still the Beauty   6

PART ONE
GETTING HER

American Light   25
That Boat   47
Gone to Firewood   59
States of Rapture   72

PART TWO
WHEN SHE WAS NEW, 1934–1935

Home   94
Shadow Story   104
High Summer   146
Catching Fish   166
On Being Shot Again   201
Outside Worlds   220
Exuberating, and Then the Jackals of His Mind   245

PART THREE
BEFORE

Edens Lost and Darkness Visible   264

PART FOUR
OLD MEN AT THE EDGE OF THE SEA:
ERNEST/GIGI/WALTER HOUK, 1949–1952 AND AFTER

Moments Supreme   300
Facet of His Character   316
The Gallantry of an Aging Machine   345
Braver Than We Knew   381

CONTENTS

In Spite of Everything 389

"Necrotic" 405

What He Had 419

Reenactment 446

Epilogue: Hunger of Memory 455

Acknowledgments 467

Essay on Sources 471

Coda: On the Curious Afterlife of *Pilar* 503

Selected Bibliography 509

Index 515

HEMINGWAY'S BOAT

We have a wonderful current in the Gulf still in spite of the changes in weather and we have 29 good fish so far. Now they are all very big and each one is wonderful and different. I think you would like it very much; the leaving of the water and the entering into it of the huge fish moves me as much as the first time I ever saw it. I always told Mary that on the day I did not feel happy when I saw a flying fish leave the water I would quit fishing.

—ERNEST HEMINGWAY, in a letter, September 13, 1952

Then, astern of the boat and off to starboard, the calm of the ocean broke open and the great fish rose out of it, rising, shining dark blue and silver, seeming to come endlessly out of the water, unbelievable as his length and bulk rose out of the sea into the air and seemed to hang there until he fell with a splash that drove the water up high and white.

"Oh God," David said. "Did you see him?"

"His sword's as long as I am," Andrew said in awe.

"He's so beautiful," Tom said. "He's much better than the one I had in the dream."

—*Islands in the Stream*

The dark is different in Havana. It's lit in a kind of amber glow, as if every-thing's on low generator, weak wattage. If you come into Cuba for the first time at nighttime, this feeling of strange darkness is intensified. Even the plane must sense this—or at least the pilot—for it seems to hang forever in a low, back-powered glide, as if working through a tunnel, before hit-ting the runway with a smack at Aeropuerto Internacional José Martí La Habana. You emerge from the Jetway into a terminal with the complexion of tea water. In the customs and immigration area, soldiers in the olive drab of the Revolution are walking large dogs. If your papers are in order, a latch on a door clicks open. Like that, you're on the other side of a lost world that's always been so seductively near and simultaneously so far.

PROLOGUE
AMID SO MUCH RUIN, STILL THE BEAUTY

On *Pilar*, off Cuba, midsummer 1934

MAY 2005. I went to Havana partly for the reason that I suspect almost any American without a loved one there would wish to go: to drink in a place that's been forbidden to American eyes (at least mostly forbidden) for half a century. So I wanted to smoke a Cohiba cigar, an authentic one—and I did. I wanted to flag down one of those chromeless Studebaker taxis (or Edsels or Chevy Bel Airs, it didn't matter) that roll down the Prado at their comic off-kilter angles, amid plumes of choking smoke—and I did. I got in and told the cabbie: "*Nacional, por favor.*" I was headed to the faded and altogether wonderful Spanish Colonial monstrosity of a hotel where you're certain Nat King Cole and Durante are in the bar at the far end of the lobby (having just come in on Pan Am from Idlewild), and Meyer Lansky is plotting something malevolent in a poolside cabana while the trollop beside him rubies her nails. I also wanted to stand at dusk at the giant seawall called the Malecón that rings much of the city so I could watch the surf beat against it in phosphorescent hues while the sun went down like some enormous burning wafer. I wanted to walk those sewer-fetid and narrow cobbled streets in Habana Vieja and gaze up at those stunning colonial mansions, properties of the state, carved up now into multiple-family dwellings, with their cracked marble entryways and falling ceiling plaster and filigree balconies flying laundry on crisscrossses of clothesline.

Mostly, though, I went to Cuba to behold—in the flesh, so to speak—Ernest Hemingway's boat.

She was sitting up on concrete blocks, like some old and gasping browned-out whale, maybe a hundred yards from Hemingway's house, under a kind of gigantic carport with a corrugated-plastic roof, on what was once his tennis court, just down from the now-drained pool where Ava Gardner had reputedly swum nude. Even in her diminished, dry-docked, parts-plundered state, I knew *Pilar* would be beautiful, and she was. I knew she'd be threatened by the elements and the bell-tolls of time, in the same way much else at the hilltop farm on the outskirts of Havana—Finca Vigía was its name when Hemingway lived there—was seriously threatened, and she was. But I didn't expect to be so moved.

I walked round and round her. I took rolls and rolls of pictures of her long, low hull, of her slightly raked mahogany stern, of her nearly vertical bow. When the guards weren't looking, I reached over and touched her surface. The wood, marbled with hairline fissures, was dusty, porous, dry. It seemed almost scaly. It felt febrile. It was as if *Pilar* were dying from thirst. It was as if all she wanted was to get into water. But even if it were possible to hoist her with a crane off these blocks and to ease her onto a flatbed truck and to take her away from this steaming hillside and to set her gently into Havana Harbor, would Hemingway's boat go down like a stone, boiling and bubbling to the bottom, her insides having long ago been eaten out by termites and other barely visible critters?

A man who let his own insides get eaten out by the diseases of fame had dreamed new books on this boat. He'd taught his sons to reel in something that feels like Moby Dick on this boat. He'd accidentally shot himself in both legs on this boat. He'd fallen drunk from the flying bridge on this boat. He'd written achy, generous, uplifting, poetic letters on this boat. He'd propositioned women on this boat. He'd hunted German subs on this boat. He'd saved guests and family members from shark attack on this boat. He'd acted like a boor and a bully and an overly competitive jerk on this boat.

She'd been intimately his, and he hers, for twenty-seven years—which were his final twenty-seven years. She'd lasted through three wives, the Nobel Prize, and all his ruin. He'd owned her, fished her, worked her, rode her, from the waters of Key West to the Bahamas to the Dry Tortugas to the north coast and archipelagoes of Cuba. She wasn't a figment or a dream or a literary theory or somebody's psychosexual interpretation—she was actual. Onto her varnished decks, hauled in over her low-cut stern on a large wooden roller, had come uncounted marlin and broadbill swordfish, tuna, sailfish, kingfish, snook, wahoos, tarpon, horse-eye jacks, pompano, dolphinfish, barracuda, bonito, and mako sharks, which, as Hemingway once remarked, are the ones that smell oddly sweet and have those curved-in teeth that give them their Cuban name, *dentuso*.

He could make her do sixteen knots at full-out, and he could make her cut a corner like a midshipman at Annapolis. When she was up and moving, her prow smartly cutting the waves, it was as if she had a foaming white bone in her teeth—which is an expression old seamen sometimes use. When he had her loaded for a long cruise, she'd hold twenty-four hundred pounds of ice, for keeping cool the Hatuey beer and the daiquiris, the avocados and the Filipino mangoes, and, not least, the freshly landed monsters of the Gulf Stream, which Hemingway always thought of as "the great blue river." Who knew what was down there lurking in those fathomless bottoms—the skeletons of slave ships? Who'd ever caught what was possible to catch in those mile-deep waters of his imagination? "In hunting you know what you are after and the top you can get is an elephant," Hemingway once wrote in *Esquire* magazine. "But who can say what you will hook sometime when drifting in a hundred and fifty fathoms in the Gulf Stream? There are probably marlin and swordfish to which the fish we have seen caught are pygmies."

Pilar's master used to play Fats Waller records and "You're the Top" on a scratchy phonograph while his boat rocked in the Stream and he waited in his ladder-back fighting chair, which had leather-cushioned armrests and was bolted to the afterdeck and could swivel in a 360-degree circle. He said the tunes were good for bringing up the monsters. When the mood was upon him, he'd sing along in his lusty baritone.

In another piece for *Esquire,* also written in the mid-thirties, when he was still trying to decipher the mysteries of the Stream and escaping to it every chance he got, this most riddlesome of men wrote about the hooking of a marlin, always the blue river's greatest prize.

> He can see the slicing wake of a fin, if he cuts toward the bait,
> or the rising and lowering sickle of a tail if he is traveling, or if
> he comes from behind he can see the bulk of him under water,

great blue pectorals widespread like the wings of some huge, underwater bird, and the stripes around him like purple bands around a brown barrel, and then the sudden upthrust waggle of a bill. . . . To see that happen, to feel that fish in his rod, to feel that power and that great rush, to be a connected part of it and then to dominate it and master it and bring that fish to gaff, alone and with no one else touching rod, reel or leader, is something worth waiting many days for, sun and all.

And in a different mood, a few years later, no less in thrall:

Once you are out of sight of land and of the other boats you are more alone than you can ever be hunting and the sea is the same as it has been since men ever went on it in boats. In a season fishing you will see it oily flat as the becalmed galleons saw it while they drifted to the westward; white-capped with a fresh breeze as they saw it running with the trades; and in high, rolling blue hills, the tops blowing off them like snow. . . .

He had named her after a shrine and *feria* in Spain that commemorates Nuestra Señora del Pilar, Our Lady of the Pillar. It's in Saragossa, and he'd been to the bullfights there in 1926. But his boat's name was also meant to commemorate the secret nickname adopted by his second wife, Pauline, before she was his wife, when the two were still in adultery. It was the name he would have given his daughter, he once said, if he'd ever been blessed enough to have a daughter. *Pilar* could fit six in her sleeping compartments, two more in her open-air cockpit with its roll-down canvas sides and copper screens for warding off the nighttime bugs. In her prime, she'd been known among Gulf Stream anglers for her shiny black hull, for her snappy seafoam-green canvas roof and topside. A boat with a black hull, riding long and low in the water, can be extremely difficult to sight against a glaring tropical horizon—so, yes, something ghostly.

Her cabin sides and decks were crafted from Canadian fir and high-grade Honduras mahogany, with tight tolerances between the seams. But she wasn't a luxury craft—she was ever and always, her owner liked to say, a functional fishing machine, sturdy, reliant, built to take the heaviest weather, "sweet in any kind of sea." There's a term old boatmen sometimes use to describe a reassuring boat in a heaving ocean: "sea-kindly." That was *Pilar,* who'd come humbly out of a factory, and a shipbuilder's catalog, a "stock boat" of the 1930s, albeit with her owner's list of modifications and alterations for her. Over the decades Hemingway would add other modifications and innovations and alterations, further improving the well-built fishing machine that had already proved astonishingly durable and dependable.

After Hemingway's suicide, the pundits at *Time* wrote that conduct

> is a question of how the good professional behaves within the rules of a game or the limits of a craft. All the how-to passages—how to land a fish, how to handle guns, how to work with a bull—have behind them the professional's pride of skill. But the code is never anchored to anything except itself; life becomes a game of doing things in a certain style, a narcissistic ritual—which led Hemingway himself not only to some mechanical, self-consciously "Hemingway" writing, but to a self-conscious "Hemingway" style of life.

Yes, that was a piece of the truth about him.

He used to love standing up on his beauty's flying bridge and guiding her out of the harbor in the morning light. Sometimes, he'd be bare-chested. The flying bridge was his name for a top deck, and it wasn't added until 1937, just before he left for Spain to report on the Spanish Civil War (and—not unconsciously—to find a hugely successful novel about it). The sportfisherman, in his raggedy and beltless shorts—or, if he was wearing a belt, putting it not inside the loops but over top of them—would have his tanned, muscular legs planted several feet apart, like a heavyweight braced for a roundhouse or a golfer ready to slam his tee shot. He'd have his white visor pulled low over his blistering nose that was coated with zinc oxide or glazed with coconut oil. (One of the reasons Hemingway grew his iconic white Papa beard of the 1950s was because his fair midwestern facial skin could no longer take the harsh Cuban sun.) He'd be waving to people he recognized on the shore. The flying bridge had its own set of duplicate engine controls, throttles and levers, coming up via several pipes through the overhead of the cockpit. The steering wheel on the bridge— flat as a plate in front of him, the way steering wheels are on the back of hook-and-ladder fire trucks—was out of an old luxury car from a Key West junkyard, polished wood set into a steel casing.

From up there, when he wasn't manning the wheel, he could fight a decent-size fish—not a 450-pound marlin nor an Atlantic sailfish, but maybe a tarpon or a recalcitrant barracuda. On the way to the fishing grounds, he'd already have a line in the water, with a Japanese feather squid and a strip of pork rind on the hook, which in turn would be attached to a No. 10 piano-wire leader, which in turn would be knotted to a fifteen-thread line. This was for the smaller catches—good eating, good selling. Tarpon and kingfish liked to lie in close to shore and feed around the commercial fishing smacks. Hemingway was after almost any kind of fishing he could get, but he wouldn't get all four rods going on the boat until *Pilar* had reached the Stream. On going out—"running out" is how he sometimes said it, just as coming home was "running in"—he loved watching the motion of the Japanese squid bait skipping on the whitecaps. In 1949, in *Holiday* magazine, when he'd owned *Pilar* for fifteen years and had been living in Cuba for a decade, and was married to his fourth and last wife, who liked going out on the boat almost as much as he did, Hemingway described this feeling in a discursive, lore-filled reminiscence-cum-piece-of-fishing-reportage:

> Coming out of the harbor I will be on the flying bridge steering and watching the traffic and the line that is fishing the feather astern. As you go out, seeing friends along the water front . . . your feather jig is fishing all the time. Behind the boulevards are the parks and buildings of old Havana and on the other side you are passing the steep slopes and walls of the fortress of Cabanas, the stone weathered pink and yellow, where most of your friends have been political prisoners at one time or another. . . .
>
> Sometimes as you leave the gray-green harbor water and Pilar's bows dip into the dark blue water a covey of flying fish will rise from under her bows and you will hear the slithering, silk-tearing noise they make when they leave the water.

The "slithering, silk-tearing noise" was always a good sign—that the monsters might come that day.

And now Hemingway's boat sat beached and grime-coated and time-stunned in the Cuban sun. There were rips in her canvas topside; little hair-like pieces of fabric stuck up from the roof. Her brass and copper fastenings had gone green with corrosion, her bottom a hideous pink. Someone had reconfigured her power plant: instead of two propellers, there was just the big one, coming down the center of the boat. Where was the other screw? Anyone who's ever paid close attention to Hemingway's boat knows she ran two engines in her day—the big Chrysler seventy-five-horse Crown reduction gear engine for cruising; the little four-cylinder, forty-horse Lycoming motor for trolling. Many other things were discernibly, puzzlingly off about *Pilar* as well. But she was here, intact, beneath this awning, on this hill, sliced with midday heat and shadow.

When he got this boat—or, more precisely, when he placed the order for her and put down $3,000 toward the full purchase price, courtesy of a hastily arranged loan/advance from the editor of *Esquire* against future articles—on a spring day in 1934, at a shipyard in Brooklyn, just back from safari in east Africa, Ernest Miller Hemingway was not quite thirty-five years old. He was still living and writing in Key West, a sand-bitten and Depression-sagging outpost at the bottom of America. He was rugged, handsome, youthful, trim-waisted, owner of a killer grin and an even more killer ego, the reigning monarch of American literature, a sportsman and sensualist glorying in his life, in the external physical world. And when he lost *Pilar*? It was in that moment when he lost everything, on a summer Sunday in 1961, in a place where the mountains outside his three picture windows in the living room were as jagged as the teeth of a shredding saw. He was nineteen days shy of his sixty-second birthday: prematurely old, multidiseased, mentally bewildered, delusional, slurred of speech, in exile from Cuba, from the Stream, unable to compose so much as one true sentence a day, or so he'd wept on a sofa in his living room. Is it any wonder the most imitated writer of the twentieth century rose sometime after seven o'clock that morning, slipped a red silk dressing robe over blue pajamas, put on slippers, moved past the master bedroom where his wife was sleeping, padded down the red-carpeted stairs, crossed the length of the living room to the kitchen, retrieved the key to the locked storeroom where the weapons were (inexplicably, Mary Hemingway had left the ring of keys on the windowsill above the sink), went down to the basement, took shells from an ammo box, closed and relocked the door, came back upstairs, walked ten steps to the front-entry foyer (one sees him in this grainy mind-movie moving very fast but also methodically, teeth clenched and bared in that sickly smile that he often exhibited toward the end of his life), opened the foyer door, stepped inside, placed the butt of the gun on the linoleum tile, tore open the breech, slammed in the cartridges, snapped it shut, bent over, as you might bend over a water fountain, rested his fore-head against the blue steel, and blew away his entire cranial vault with the double-barreled, 12-gauge Boss shotgun with which he'd once shot pigeons?

In Havana, a thirty-eight-foot motorized fishing vessel, framed so long ago with steam-bent white oak and planked with white cedar, bobbed at anchor, ready to be gassed up, waiting.

This book is largely the story of the twenty-seven years and three months between the first week of April 1934 and the first week of July 1961. It's about the strange, sad distance from Wheeler Shipyard, Inc., at the foot of Cropsey Avenue in Brooklyn to a tight, oak-paneled entryway in a bunker-like house in Ketchum, Idaho, when the world went away from a suffering man in fractions of a second. But it isn't meant to be a Hemingway biography, not in any conventional sense, and much less is it meant to be the nautical history of a piece of floating wood. We've had far too many Hemingway biographies in the past fifty years, not to say daffy critical studies and even daffier psychological "explanations" of the man.

My aim, rather, is to try to lock together the words "Hemingway" and "boat" in the same way that the locked-together and equally American words "DiMaggio" and "bat," or "Satchmo" and "horn," will quickly mean something in the minds of most people, at least of a certain age.

So it's about such ideas as fishing, friendship, and fatherhood, and love of water, and what it means to be masculine in our culture (as that culture is now rapidly changing), and the notion of being "boatstruck" (a malady that seems to affect men more than women), and how the deep good in us is often matched only by the perverse bad in us, and—not least—about the damnable way our demons seem to end up always following us, even or especially when we think we've escaped them and are out cruising on the Stream.

But the narrative won't always stay between the bracketing and polar-opposite moments I identified above. No human history ever proceeds in a straight line, perhaps least of all Hemingway's. His prose was wonderfully rooted in geography and linear movement. And yet his life, like his boat, beat against so many crosscurrents. So there are more than a few purposeful zigzags and loop-arounds and time-bends and flashbacks and flash-forwards and other sorts of departures from the main frame here, but generally the story is on a trajectory from early spring 1934 to early summer 1961.

Ernest Hemingway has been examined by so many scholars and memoirists and respected biographers and hangers-on and pretenders and doctoral students desperate for a dissertation topic that I feel sometimes we have lost all sense of who the man really was. It's as if each new Hemingway book by each new Hemingway "expert" wishes to contradict the last, which is one reason why I have been determined to try to anchor a Hemingway narrative, to ground it, in something that had existed in his world—that still exists, in its way—just as he had once existed in the world. I felt that if I could somehow learn whatever was possible to learn about a possession that meant so much to its owner—if I could actually *touch* it, too—then I might be able to begin to understand things about Hemingway, and not only Hemingway, in ways that I had not previously been able to understand. Indeed, I hoped to find people who were once on that boat, who had had their own deep relationship with her, and tell their stories, too. And I have found them, both the living and the dead.

Actually, as far back as the summer of 1987, as a *Washington Post* reporter, I searched out and interviewed Hemingway's three sons. The series of articles that resulted was called "Papa's Boys." Their father had been dead for twenty-six years and the sons themselves were late-middle-aged men. What I recall so vividly about Jack and Patrick and Gregory Hemingway, in their deep psychic sibling pain, was their attempt to say how fine it had been to spend time with their father outdoors—in Idaho meadows, flushing quail; in the Stream, going for the monsters; in high Wyoming creeks, fighting rainbows. No one could ever take those feelings and experiences away. Past all their father's posing and public brawling, past all his posthumous critical whittling down, past all the intentional and unintentional psychic hurt he had inflicted on them, what each Hemingway son still possessed was the memory of the man when he was good. Patrick Hemingway, who is in Montana, the only one alive now (he is in his early eighties), the one whom his father had nicknamed Mouse, told me that it was as if some immense and wise Plains Indian, the head of a whole nation, was taking time out from warfare and buffalo hunts to instruct in the codes of manhood—of life itself. The chief taught his braves how to pee high and wide off rickety wooden bridges in the Florida Keys, how to crouch low and *whish-whish* through the back of their teeth for shore birds, how to enter pebble-clean rivers without spooking the cutthroat trout around their shoes. He taught them these things and a lot more besides, but in the end, which came sooner than later, everything changed. I recall each Hemingway son talking longingly about their father's boat, even amid stories about their retchings in the toilet down below when the seasickness overcame them; even amid stories about their inability to land the trophy fish that their dad—holding them by the waist and dousing them with pails of sea water to try to cool their bare bodies as they sat in the fighting chair at the stern of the boat, with their small arms giving out—so badly wished them to land, not for his sake as much as theirs. It wasn't that the sons loved going out on *Pilar* for a day or several days; it was that their father loved being out there so much on his boat with them. It was enough.

Gregory Hemingway—the most deeply scarred of the three, the most gifted athlete in the family, the one with the truest writing gift, the son who'd been given the nickname Gigi by his father—had grown up to be a doctor, like his paternal grandfather. Gigi (with a hard G sound, pronounced like "Wiggy") had also spent most of his adult life struggling— heroically seems not too strong a word—against the compulsion to adorn his squat, bulky body in hosiery, brassieres, wigs, girdles, makeup, spiked heels, fingernail polish, and then go out into public places talking to people in his deep-chested voice. He was fifty-five and in the Miami area when we met. Coarse gray hair fell in clumps over his face. His teeth were wrecked. Gigi was spending his days in public parks and libraries. He had no fixed address. He had been married and divorced several times. He was estranged from most of his children. The medical career had drained away. Sometimes, he said, he'd go out onto Biscayne Bay in a small rowboat to hand-fish over the side with a night crawler, to fall asleep in the sun until something below jerked him awake. Gigi said, and it was easy to believe, he'd undergone ninety-eight electroshock treatments. "I've taken every fucking pill there is," he said. "These horrible mixed-up feelings you have, the love and the hate," he said. We talked of yet another Hemingway biography that had recently come out, whose author, Jeffrey Meyers, had seemed to wish to put on view every nasty thing Hemingway had ever said or done in his life—so he had boatloads of material. Meyers described letters that a father had written about his troubled youngest son. These unpublished Hemingway letters of the 1950s, not well-known, had described Gigi, in the biographer's paraphrasing words, as "an exploded firecracker, worthless, no good, ruined by money, a macabre and mercenary mix of Charles Addams and the National City Bank, an absolute pathological shit, a son he would like to see hanged."

And in a way, it was as if none of it mattered, not finally. I can still hear the exact tone of fantasizing voice with which Gregory Hemingway— a very nice man, despite everything, with a doctorly sense of wanting to ease the pain of others—said: "I think I want to go over to Cuba and find a way to get that fucking boat off the hillside at the *finca* and bring her back over here to Florida. It's where she belongs, you know. It would be a way of honoring him. This is where my father first learned to take her out on the water and to sit in a chair and wait for a fish—when we were still living as a family in Key West. You know, there were periods when he didn't like to talk much on the boat. He'd just sit there and stare out over the water."

I have come to believe deeply that Ernest Hemingway, however unpost-modern it may sound, was on a lifelong quest for sainthood, and not just literary sainthood, and that at nearly every turn, he defeated himself. How? "By betrayals of himself, and what he believed in," as the dying writer, with the gangrene going up his leg, says so bitterly in "The Snows of Kiliman-jaro," one of Hemingway's greatest short stories. Why the self-defeating betrayal of high humanistic aspirations? The seductions of celebrity and the sin of pridefulness and the curses of megalomania and the wastings of booze and, not least, the onslaughts of bipolarism must amount to a large part of the answer. Hemingway once said in a letter to his closest friend in the last two decades of his life, General Buck Lanham, whom he had come to know on the battlefield as a correspondent in World War II: "I have always had the illusion it was more important, or as important, to be a good man as to be a great writer. May turn out to be neither. But would like to be both."

I also believe there was so much more fear inside Hemingway than he ever let on, that it was almost always present, by day and more so by night, and that his living with it for so long was ennobling. The thought of self-destruction trailed Hemingway for nearly his entire life, like the tiny wakes a child's hand will make when it is trailed behind a rowboat in calm water—say, up in Michigan.

Many years ago, Norman Mailer wrote a sentence about Hemingway that has always struck me as profound: "It may even be that the final judgment on his work may come to the notion that what he failed to do was tragic, but what he accomplished was heroic, for it is possible he carried a weight of anxiety within him from day to day which would have suffocated any man smaller than himself." The great twentieth-century critic Edmund Wilson, a contemporary of Hemingway's, who admired him early and had contempt for him late, wrote in his journals of the 1960s: "He had a high sense of honor, which he was always violating; he evidently had a permanent bad conscience." A writer named Ella Winter, one of the Lost Generation exiles of Paris in the twenties, said in a letter, seven months after the suicide:

I of course knew Hem as the big-broad-shouldered, dark-haired, most handsome "boy" who walked in that peculiar way not exactly limping but lurching, and who talked writing and ate and drank and dreamed and thought writing—only the boxing bouts and bicycle races and maybe skiing mattered besides—but you felt in him such a clean, clear strength. I know his legend caught up with him and all the beard and "Papas" and posing and drinking and publicity became part of the legend and the later man—I don't know how much he himself became the *persona* the legend created. But I've always felt there was the real human being, unphoney, unpublicized, caring like hell.

I think there's another truth here, too, and in a sense it doesn't even have to do with Hemingway; it has to do with *us:* namely, that his life, which is to say, the way he lived it, or our perception of the way he lived it, has always had the capacity to stir up complex things, to make us uneasy, defensive, secretly troubled about our own far less glamorous and more sedentary selves. Hemingway's fellow Chicagoan, the novelist Nelson Algren, to whom Hemingway was a hero, and who came along a literary generation behind him, once said of all the desk-bound critics who couldn't seem to bear the man in his own lifetime:

> It wasn't Hemingway's prose, but his life, which demanded "total and considered rejection." It wasn't his economy of language which made them feel small—it was his free-handedness. To men whose self-doubt put them in need of formal respect from others, the ease with which Hemingway earned the informal respect of workaday men and women felt like an accusation. . . . He flaunted a personality as poetic as Byron's and as challenging as Teddy Roosevelt's before timorous men whose lives were prosaic. It was necessary, no, absolutely *essential* to get his number.

He led a life of action in the physical world, all right. But underneath that was a bookish man in glasses trying to get his work done, and finding it harder with each passing year.

So what we have of this man are the irresolvable contradictions of the life and the glories of the work—some of it. The Hemingway myth, however much oversold and devalued, can still powerfully stand in a new century for a great many tensions unresolved in American males, or so I believe—and not only males. I also believe that all of Hemingway's writing, every bit of it, even at its most self-parodistic and Papa-cult worst, is seeking to be about the *living* of this life. The being of this life. The doing of this life. The engaging of this life. And in that sense, the work—and even, I am willing to say, so much of the coarsened personal history—can be thought of as something spiritual and indeed almost holy. In late April 1934, waiting in Key West with a schoolboy's excitement for his new boat to be shipped to him in Florida, Hemingway wrote to his beloved friend Sara Murphy: "Am working fine now—But I would rather had a good life than be a bloody great writer—(who says he's a b.g.w. Nobody) Have written *plenty* and will write *plenty* more. And I will be as good as I know and I'll know better all the time. But every day is a day and its *my* lousy life—not posterities. Oh well." That's such a characteristic Hemingway letter—the streams of loose syntax, the blunt emotion.

Loop backward seventeen days from his death—to June 15, 1961, at Rochester, Minnesota. A man in the psychiatric ward of Saint Marys Hospital at Mayo Clinic is writing a different kind of letter to a nine-year-old boy. The man writes it on two small sheets of notepaper, in his big, round, legible hand, with his trademark downhill slant. An irreversibly damaged Ernest Hemingway, his inner landscape now a paranoid's nightmare, has found within himself at the end of his life the kindness and courage and momentary lucidity—not to say literary grace—to write 210 beautiful words to a kid he likes very much. Whenever I begin to feel revulsion at Hemingway's ego and boorish behavior toward other human beings, I like to take out a copy of this letter. Two hundred and ten words, with so much emotion tucked below the surface of the prose, the sentences pile-driven by contained feeling and acute observation of the natural world, would have been a half-decent output for a workday, even in a master's prime.

The boy—his name is Frederick G. Saviers, although everyone, including Hemingway, calls him Fritz—has a congenital heart condition. He is the son of George Saviers, Hemingway's small-town doctor in Ketchum, who was also one of Hemingway's favorite duck-hunting companions. In these last weeks, Hemingway has been brought once more for treatment to Mayo. Not long after this note to Fritz, Hemingway will fool his foolish doctors at the world-famous clinic into believing he is well enough to go home to Idaho. And almost immediately the Boss shotgun will go off in the Sunday quiet of the house that sits a couple of hundred yards up the steep slope from the west bank of the Big Wood River.

The patient on the locked ward at Saint Marys on June 15, 1961, has just learned that Dr. Saviers's son is in a Denver hospital. In Idaho, Hemingway and Fritz and Fritz's father liked talking about the Yankees and rainbow trout. But none of that will ever be the same again.

> St. Mary's Hospital
> Rochester, Minn.
> June 15 1961

Dear Fritz

I was terribly sorry to hear this morning in a note from your father that you were laid up in Denver for a few days more and speed off this note to tell you how much I hope you'll be feeling better.

It has been very hot and muggy here in Rochester but the last two days it has turned cool and lovely with the nights wonderful for sleeping. The country is beautiful around here and I've had a chance to see some wonderful country along the Mississippi where they used to drive the logs in the old lumbering days and the trails where the pioneers came north. Saw some good bass jumping in the river. I never knew anything about the upper Mississippi before and it is really a very beautiful country and there are plenty of pheasants and ducks in the fall.

But not as many as in Idaho and I hope we'll both be back there shortly and can joke about our hospital experiences together.

Best always to you, old Timer from your good friend who misses you very much

> Mister) Papa.

Best to all the family. am feeling fine and very cheerful about things in general and hope to see you all soon.

> Papa

No one knows for sure, but these seem to be the last real sentences Ernest Hemingway set down on paper. Amid so much ruin, still the beauty.

PART ONE

GETTING HER

No one knows when the first boat was built, or where, or
by whom, or why. Boats began before history; boats are
part of our cultural memories. Why else do people gather
at the water's edge when tall ships appear?

—DICK WAGNER, founding director,
The Center for Wooden Boats, Seattle

In March 1929, Ernest Hemingway's mother, Grace Hall-Hemingway, a boat of a woman whose guts he famously hated, or claimed to, sent him a crate by Railway Express. The twenty-nine-year-old son, working on revisions of the World War I doomed-love story that would make him a literary figure on the world stage by the age of thirty, received the crate in Key West. For a week or so, it sat unopened in the corner. "Ernest, open the box," friends and family members said. Finally, Pauline Hemingway pried it open with a claw hammer. In the crate were some of Grace's recent mediocre paintings (she was hoping her writer-son might place them for her on his upcoming trip to Paris); a large chocolate cake that had gone runny and leaky through the crate's canvas packing; and the .32-caliber Smith & Wesson "Long John" Civil War revolver with which Hemingway's father, Dr. Clarence E. Hemingway, had killed himself several months earlier, on a weekday morning, shortly before Christmas, in an upstairs bedroom of the family home in Oak Park, Illinois. The gun had been impounded by the Cook County police department, but Grace had gotten it back. At his father's funeral, Hemingway had asked his mother for the gun. At first Grace seems to have resisted the idea. But then, a few months afterward, her son had written her a letter with some implied threats about maybe one day writing a novel concerning various members of his family now that his father, whom he had admired up until the suicide, was gone. The crate arrived in Florida not long afterward. Grace followed up with a letter saying that she would like the pistol back eventually. "I will take care of it for you," she said, which could be read as a loaded statement.

On page 337 of a later and even greater-selling novel, also about war, For Whom the Bell Tolls, Robert Jordan has taken the Civil War pistol with which his father killed himself and has leaned out over a rock in Wyoming and dropped it into a deep, high-mountain lake, where he "saw it go down making bubbles until it was just as big as a watch charm in that clear water, and then it was out of sight." Did Hemingway do that? He said he did, but that doesn't particularly mean anything. He liked to say that what makes literature is "inventing truly from honestly acquired knowledge, so that what you make up is truer than what you might remember." All the meanings of this story aren't clear. "I know why you did that with the old gun, Bob," a character in the novel says. "Well, then we don't have to talk about it," Jordan replies. As essayist Lance Morrow of Time once wrote, the fable of the gun and leaky cake and forgettable paintings is "minutely savage in its details and haunting in its outcome: perfect Hemingway. And of course, there is the water."

Ernest and Pauline Hemingway at the
rail of the SS *Paris*, New York City

APRIL 3, 1934. The temperature in Manhattan got into the high sixties.
G-men shot an accomplice of Dillinger's in Minnesota; the Nazis were
running guns to the Moors; Seminoles were reviving a tribal dance in
honor of alligators in Florida; Lou Gehrig had two homers in an exhibition game in Atlanta. And roughly the bottom third of America was out
of work.

According to "Steamship Movements in New York," a column that runs
daily in the business section of the *Evening Journal,* nine liners are to dock
today. The SS *Paris,* 34,500 tons, is just sliding in after a seven-day Atlantic
crossing, from Le Havre via Plymouth, at Pier 57 on the West Side of New
York City.

"Expected to dock: 5:00 P.M.," reports the newspaper. And she does.

If this were a Movietone News item about Hemingway the big-game hunter, arriving home after eight months abroad, and you were in a darkened movie palace of the thirties awaiting the feature, you'd see ropes being thrown off, gangplanks being lowered, steamer trunks being unloaded, and passengers starting gaily to stream off. You'd see the New York press boys with their rumpled suits and stained ties and skinny notebooks and Speed Graphic cameras clawing for position. The blocky white lettering superimposed on the flickering images would announce: "Back from Lion Hunt in East Africa!" They'd bring up the sound track—something stirring, to suggest the march of time. And then would come the voice-over—wouldn't it be Ed Herlihy's?—with its electric charge: "Famed author Mr. Ernest Hemingway, just back on the French liner *Paris* with Mrs. Hemingway from conquering the lion and the rhino and the wildebeest and the greater kudu, says that death in the afternoon is far less engrossing in a Spanish bull ring than on the African veldt."

The press boys clotted at the bottom of the gangplank badly want Hemingway, and they want Katharine Hepburn (she is on the boat, too, and makes wonderful copy, when she deigns to speak), but apparently none of them knows (for none of their papers will have it tomorrow) that an even bigger trophy has just berthed at Pier 57: Marlene Dietrich. She's going to give them the nifty slip. Publicity? Who needs it? Maybe Dietrich's hiding out in her stateroom. She might have registered under a different name—glamorous figures routinely do this. In fact, Hepburn is on the manifest as "Miss Katherine Ludlow." (Her husband is Ludlow Ogden Smith.) *She* has decided not to hide from the pack.

The famous and close and long-lasting Dietrich-Hemingway friendship dates from this Atlantic crossing. For the rest of his life, Hemingway mostly called her the Kraut, when he wasn't addressing her as "daughter," the latter being how he liked to address women younger than himself, famous or otherwise, whom he'd not—apparently—taken to bed. Dietrich was two and a half years younger. There is a well-traveled story about how she was stepping into the ship's dining room to join a dinner party. Every open-jawed man at the table rose to give her his chair, but just as she started to sit down, the international flame with the statuesque body and lusty voice counted the mouths and saw that there were twelve diners. "Oh. I'm the thirteenth. You will excuse me if I don't join you. I'm superstitious about thirteen at dinner," she said, starting to withdraw. But just then Hemingway blocked her way. "Excuse me," he said. "I don't mean to intrude. But I'd be glad to be the fourteenth."

Afterward, they supposedly strolled the decks arm in arm and told each other—maybe like Bogart and Claude Rains in *Casablanca*, except that the movie hadn't been made yet—that this was going to be the start of a beautiful friendship. At least this is the legend, and Dietrich herself greatly helped it along in 1955 in a first-person cover story in the Sunday supplement of the *New York Herald Tribune*. The piece was titled "The Most Fascinating Man I Know." She talked of how she and Hemingway had depended on each other through the years, how she'd protected his deeply personal letters to her in a strongbox. Actually, Dietrich may not have even written the piece—according to Mary Hemingway, it was ghosted by journalist and scriptwriter A. E. Hotchner, one of Hemingway's last confidants, or toadies, depending on your point of view, for the two-decades-younger Hotch, as Hemingway often called him, has been described as both in the vast, roily, envy-ridden sea of Hemingway studies. In any case, among smaller errors, Dietrich or her ghost got the name of the boat wrong; she said it was the other (even grander) star of the French line, the *Île de France*.

But this is a newsreel of the imagination. Hemingway's poised at the *Paris*'s rail with his spouse. He's intent on purchasing a boat, but right now he's allowing photographs to be made, and he's popping quotes. Freeze the frame. Stop time in a box.

Pauline Hemingway is in a zebra-striped suit and an almost dowdy hat, curled at the brim, tilting right to left. Her right shoulder touches her husband's left. She is so small beside him. Her hair is cropped like a boy's. She has a boyish physique and is known for her disinclination to use makeup. (It's true she likes to keep her fingernails and toenails manicured for her husband, often lacquering them in light pink.) Her body is turned a few degrees away from the rail, as if she might decide to walk off any second now. She's probably not getting a word in edgewise. She isn't a beautiful woman, but she isn't unattractive, either. She is four years and a day older than her husband, who is leaning forward, right into the middle of things, as if right into the middle of reporters' notebooks. Both his arms are on the rail, and his right hand is holding the brim of a fedora that has a wide, dark band. He's wearing a suit and tie and there's a sliver of handkerchief visible at the top of his vest pocket. No matter his dress, he's unmistakably a man of the outdoors, with the body of an athlete. His hair looks Brylcreemed and newly cut, although a strand or two at the back of his head are out of place. Around his seventeen-and-a-half-inch neck, inside his dress shirt, is a scapular: he's a convert to Catholicism, which is his wife's devoutly practiced faith. (She's a "cradle Catholic," while his on-again, off-again devotions are reputed to have arisen out of the shocks of World War I.) He's known to wear his scapular unfailingly in these years. It's got an image of Christ on it, suspended from a brown, shoestring-like loop. At home, in Key West, friends have observed him with the scapular, and how he'll make the sign of the cross before he goes in swimming.

That smile: hobnailed and hard-boiled all the way, just this side of aggressive. The more you study the photograph, however, the more you see that both Hemingways are holding a pose.

This picture, or versions of it, is going to get picked up and run in many hinterland places, including in the Twin Cities of Minnesota, where winter still has the earth in her grip, and where a young, self-styled, Hemingway-like character will see the photograph and tear it out of the *Pioneer Press* and fold it into his pocket and pack his knapsack and hop a freight to Florida, in hopes of meeting his writing idol. The young man's name is Arnold Morse Samuelson, and he is in for the ride of his life. But that's running out ahead.

Not every city editor in New York—there are something like nine dailies in the city in 1934—has sent a reporter to the docks today to shag quotes and to compose deathless passages on deadline about the return of the native. (In the old days of the news business, these pieces were often known as "brights." *Go get me a Hemingway bright,* some pale, overweight editor at the *Times* surely growled at a reporter on the city desk.) And what is the "fascinating man" saying to the press boys? He's telling them how he gives first honors to the leopards, "because they strike the fastest." But the lion is such a noble beast, too, he says. "He is not afraid or stupid. He does not want to fight, but sometimes man makes him, and then it is up to the man to shoot his way out of what he has got himself into." With the lion and the leopard, "you're either quick or you're dead. I saw a lion do one hundred yards in three seconds flat, which may give you an idea." The hunter saw ninety-six lions altogether and at one point he photographed twenty-nine lionesses "preening themselves like a group of finishing school girls." He made a moral bargain with himself to bring down only animals that were utter strangers to him; the lions that he'd stalked with his camera he could somehow not force himself to shoot. But now he intends to return to his home in Key West and resume his vocation. His season of intense writing, he hints, may or may not concern Africa.

The *World-Telegram* will have a seven-grapher tomorrow, page 11 ("Jungle Praised by Hemingway"). The lead:

> Ernest Hemingway, author ... is back home and "nearly broke" after eight months abroad, three of which he spent on the "dark continent." The trouble with bull-fighting, in the opinion of the man who admits he knows so little about it that he wrote a book on the subject, is simply that it's too formal. Like all invitation affairs, he holds, it has a plethora of rules. Out in the brush where the hunter fights for a clawhold with his prey as man to beast—and no rules committee in the offing—it's more fun.

The *Herald Tribune*'s subhead on its Hemingway bright (eleven paragraphs, page 4): "Author, Back from African Hunt, Says He Never Shot Beasts Trailed for Camera." The lead: "Ernest Hemingway, enthusiastic over the three months he had passed in East Africa stalking big game with rifle and camera, returned yesterday on the French liner Paris with Mrs. Hemingway, who shared his adventures. Mr. Hemingway was in such high spirits that he granted an interview, something unusual for him."

The subject's first quote: "It's hard to describe just what there is to killing big game. It's very exciting and—uh—it gives you a fine feeling. It's the sort of the same thing as any killing; that is, it's fine, if you do a clean job of it and it's lousy if there's bad sportsmanship." Toward the end: "The pursuit of game having renewed his enthusiasm for life, he returned home 'to work like hell and make enough money so that I can go back to Africa and really learn something about lions.'"

It must be the *Herald Trib*'s account that E. B. White of *The New Yorker* catches on his way to work on the morning of the fourth. The *Herald Trib* is the highbrow newspaper of choice in Manhattan, and these quotes are apparently just too much for a domesticated literary man. Because the following week, a three-stanza Hemingway send-up titled "The Law of the Jungle" appears on page 31 of *The New Yorker*. White's final lines:

> And who, in time of darkest danger
> Will only dominate a stranger.

Seventeen years from now, on the publication of Hemingway's weakest novel, *Across the River and into the Trees*, White, great American humorist, never a white hunter on the dark continent, will bring down Hemingway again in the magazine with a parody titled "Across the Street and into the Grill." By then parodying Hemingway will have become a cottage sport and pastime in America. White's piece will particularly enrage the author, perhaps because he instantly understands that it will get into anthologies and live way past his own death.

What was Ernest Hemingway's interior state when he stood at the *Paris* rail with his petite and affluent spouse on the eve of acquiring *Pilar*? (Pauline's uncle, Gus Pfeiffer—a New York businessman, part of whose fortune had been derived from his interests in a Paris and Manhattan perfumer named Richard Hudnut, and who liked Ernest a good deal, at least then—had staked the safari somewhere to the bottom line of about $30,000. The safari had lasted just a little over two months, not three, as was reported. Hemingway had been in Africa for nearly three months, but not in the bush for that long, and for about a week of the actual safari he was confined to a hospital bed in Nairobi, having suffered an attack of amoebic dysentery that necessitated evacuation by light plane.)

A whole lot of his state of mind can be glimpsed in his writing, not least his letter writing. Hemingway wrote somewhere between six and seven thousand letters in his life, by hand and by typewriter and by dictation, usually in free-associative bursts, often after a day's writing, to relieve tension, more or less in the way you'd speak in a conversation. This is particularly true of his letters to friends and to certain family members. "The desire to get to the man behind the work can be sometimes overwhelming. I always go back to the letters," Patrick Hemingway told me in 1987, a sentence that seems only truer with time.

Hemingway's momentary high spirits in early April 1934 must have had at least two prongs: he was back from his excellent safari adventure; and now, before heading home by train to Florida, he hoped to go to a Brooklyn boatyard and put in an order for his own longed-for fishing machine. And yet, what his letters, cojoined with verifiable facts of his life just then, suggest is that what might have seemed so clear in a photograph and in what he told some shipside reporters didn't nearly reflect what Hemingway was generally feeling inside. Every good photograph has a secret, a critic named Mark Stevens once wrote: "Something mysteriously and tantalizingly withheld, even when the world seems laid out as plainly as a corpse upon a table."

One verifiable truth is that the monarch of American letters had been riding through rough critical seas for the last few years—and much more rough going was up ahead. Somehow, nothing seemed quite as locked as it once did, and that included owning the reviewers. Not quite a year earlier—on June 13, 1933—the author for whom things had once seemed to come so effortlessly had written to his book editor: "I am tempted never to publish another damned thing. The swine arent worth writing for. I swear to Christ they're not. Every phase of the whole racket is so disgusting that it makes you feel like vomiting. . . . And it is a commonplace that I lack confidence that I am a man—What shit—And I'm supposed to go around with your good friends spreading that behind my back—And they imagine they will get away with it." He'd been referring specifically in this instance to his former friend Max Eastman (a fellow Scribners author), who'd just written a half-joking and belated review of *Death in the Afternoon* for *The New Republic* titled "Bull in the Afternoon." The Hemingway style, Eastman said, was that "of wearing false hair on the chest." In Hemingway's reading, and in the reading of some of his close friends, the piece wasn't trying to be humorous at all but rather was making overt suggestions to the effect that Hemingway must feel sexually inadequate. Well, he'd break Eastman's jaw the next time he saw him, and sell tickets to the event.

One way to read Ernest Hemingway's life is through the phenomenon of remarkable first luck. He'd become an international literary figure, specifically as a novelist, so quickly—in the second half of the 1920s, less than a decade from when he'd started out. He'd started out with stories—actually, sometimes just intensely felt imagistic fragments of stories. It was almost as if he'd had no real apprenticeship but had sprung full-blown into American consciousness as a serious writer. It wasn't true; it only seemed true. What is true is that, for nearly his whole life, Hemingway had a genius, among his many geniuses, for gathering knowledge inside of him with astonishing speed—lore, know-how, the names of streets in Kansas City. He seemed to learn everything and anything so early, almost as if to defy the word "learn." The statement can apply as much to the intricacies of big-game fishing as to the art of shaking daiquiris as to the craft of writing fiction: he simply found out, and lodged it inside him very fast. In so many instances, he seemed to mutate from eager novice to acknowledged expert with barely any larval stage in between. The pattern was to learn from his betters—betters at the time—and then to lap them on the track as if they were standing still.

The Sun Also Rises, Hemingway's slim and enduring first novel about world-weary expats doing the bullfights in Pamplona, sixty thousand lyric words, was published when he was twenty-seven. He completed the first draft in eight weeks—really, almost the whole novel was there in that first manic burst. It was as if the world had a new kind of writing on its hands— laconic, ironic, dialogue-driven, painterly in the way of an Impressionist canvas. Only the opening section was badly off in its tone, self-conscious and affected. ("This is a novel about a lady. Her name is Lady Ashley and when the story begins, she is living in Paris and it is Spring. That should be a good setting for a romantic but highly moral story.") His new friend, F. Scott Fitzgerald, three years older, convinced him to drop those open- ing pages, and Hemingway quickly did, and after that the pitch of the book was nearly perfect (that is, if you were willing to overlook its casual anti-Semitism), and possibly the extremely grateful author never quite for- gave Scott for his critical acuity. Certainly, he would begin condescending to him as a fellow artist almost the minute he was able to—another verifi- able fact.

Fitzgerald had gone out of his way to help bring Hemingway to the prestigious American publishing house of Charles Scribner's Sons, where he was a star. He'd written to his editor, the esteemed (if not yet quite leg- endary) Maxwell Perkins: "This is to tell you about a young man named Ernest Hemmingway, who lives in Paris (an American), writes for the transatlantic Review + has a brilliant future." That was early October 1924, even before Fitzgerald had met Hemingway. (Their first meeting came six months later, early spring 1925, at the Dingo Bar in Montparnasse, right after the publication of *The Great Gatsby*.)

Soon there would be a new Scribners star edited and soothed by Per- kins. You can pick up almost any page of *Sun* today, and at its center, the story of a war-wounded man, seeking to conceal his softness with cyni- cism, will seem as fresh in its language and feeling as it must have seemed to cognoscenti on both sides of the Atlantic in 1926. "It is awfully easy to be hardboiled about everything in the daytime," Jake Barnes confesses, "but at night it is another thing." The famously war-wounded man has been wounded in his genitals. He's incapable of making love.

As for the short stories, which Hemingway learned how to do before the long-form fiction: it was as if these, too, had sought their own level of near perfection without real apprenticeship. It only felt as if modernism in prose had begun with a young husband and father out of the Midwest— a rube, really, no matter that he'd glimpsed war and suffered wounds— sitting down at a table in La Closerie des Lilas in Paris in August 1924 and finishing a long "fish story" (in two parts) and, in the bargain, creating a new kind of American language. On the surface, nothing seems to be happening in the story. Its setting is the Upper Peninsula of Michigan. The stream he is fishing, as well as the title of the story, are given the musical-sounding name, "Big Two-Hearted River." A young man named Nick, who seems vaguely to be troubled, has gone camping alone. He leans over a railroad bridge in a burned-out town and watches trout far down through "the glassy convex surface of the pool." In a meadow, not far from the glinting river, he makes his camp, slitting off "a bright slab of pine" from a stump and chinking it into tent pegs. He fixes cheesecloth across the "open mouth of the tent." He crawls in and already there is "something mysterious and homelike." He climbs out. He places a wire grill over a fire and with his boot forces the four legs down into the ground. Now the beans and spaghetti are warming. They're "making little bubbles that rose with difficulty to the surface." " 'Chrise,' Nick said, 'Geezus Chrise,' he said happily." The story is proceeding in such inconsequential fashion, with attentions being paid to the smallest rituals of camping and fishing, as if this is all the story were about.

Many years later, no longer a young or well man, in a Paris memoir as elegant as it was often cruel, the author would say of that story, without naming it: "I sat in a corner with the afternoon light coming in over my shoulder and wrote in the notebook. The waiter brought me a café crème and I drank half of it when it cooled and left it on the table while I wrote. When I stopped writing I did not want to leave the river where I could see the trout in the pool, its surface pushing and swelling smooth against the resistance of the log-driven piles of the bridge. The story was about coming back from the war but there was no mention of the war in it." The author remembered that he wrote the story, with everything beneath the surface, at the café table in blue-backed notebooks, with two pencils and a dime-store sharpener beside him—to sharpen your writing instrument with a pocketknife was too profligate. When his so-called fish story was finished, the excited young husband and father, twenty-five years old, who lived with his wife and baby boy above the sawmill on rue Notre Dame des Champs, wrote to his bohemian literary friends, Gertrude Stein and Alice B. Toklas, sounding exactly like the rube of the middle border he essentially still was. He told them he'd been "trying to do the country like Cezanne and having a hell of a time and sometimes getting it a little bit. It is about 100 pages long and nothing happens and the country is swell, I made it all up, so I see it all and part of it comes out the way it ought to, it is swell about the fish, but isn't writing a hard job though?"

A Farewell to Arms, coming three years after *The Sun Also Rises,* a longer, more mature, more moving novel (Hemingway's finest sustained literary achievement, in my view), was published in September 1929, two months after he'd turned thirty. He'd started the novel in Paris, had worked on it in Key West; in Piggott, Arkansas; in Kansas City; on a ranch at Big Horn, Wyoming—other places, too. His wife gave birth to his second child by difficult cesarean section while he worked on it, and also his father killed himself. "I remember all these things happening and all the places we lived in and the fine times and the bad times we had in that year," he once said. "But much more vividly I remember living in the book and making up what happened in it every day. Making the country and the people and the things that happened I was happier than I had ever been." Living in that book, making the country, a man still so young had written a passage so immortal as this, about a retreat from a place called Caporetto:

> I was always embarrassed by the words sacred, glorious, and sacrifice and the expression in vain. We had heard them, sometimes standing in the rain almost out of earshot, so that only the shouted words came through, and had read them, on proclamations that were slapped up by billposters over other proclamations, now for a long time, and I had seen nothing sacred, and the things that were glorious had no glory and the sacrifices were like the stockyards at Chicago if nothing was done with the meat except to bury it. There were many words that you could not stand to hear and finally only the names of places had dignity.

From a beginner at long-form fiction to a master of it inside of three years—this was the impression that the world had formed of him, and it wasn't altogether wrong. "Veteran out of the wars before he was twenty: / Famous at twenty-five: thirty a master—" the poet Archibald MacLeish would say years later in a poem, but also saying, in the line immediately above: "And what became of him? Fame became of him."

But now it was the thirties, and *his* thirties, and suddenly the critical "swine" were attacking his books. It was as if the reviewers had secretly gotten together at a club in New York and voted to pile on—certainly in Hemingway's view. They'd done it firstly with his nonfiction meditation on bullfighting in Spain, *Death in the Afternoon,* published in 1932, and even more with his third volume of short stories, *Winner Take Nothing,* published on October 27, 1933, when Hemingway was in Europe, about a month before the trip to Africa. Individual stories in the fourteen-story work certainly had been admired—"A Clean, Well-Lighted Place," "Fathers and Sons," "A Way You'll Never Be," "Wine of Wyoming." But as an aesthetic whole, the book was judged by some of the country's most prestigious reviewers to be tedious and anti-intellectual and boorish in its subject matter. Louis Kronenberger of *The New York Times:* "One reads a story like the first and finest in the present book, a story called 'After the Storm,' and one regrets that in the main such incomparable equipment as Hemingway's goes off so many times with a proud and clean report—and hits nothing." T. S. Matthews of *The New Republic:* "Some of his current subjects are the kind of abnormalities that fascinate adolescence but really have very little to do with the price of our daily bread. . . . This may sound like an attack on Hemingway, and it is. I think he is one of the few exciting writers we have, and that consequently we ought to see, if we can, what all the excitement is about. And I think that what it is about is adolescence." H. S. Canby of the *Saturday Review of Literature:* "When you are bored by Hemingway, as I frankly am by a half dozen of these new stories, which are repetitive with the slow pound, pound of a hammer upon a single mood, there is nothing to revive you except flashes of excellent observation." Max Perkins had tried to send a pacifying letter to Hemingway in Paris, along with half a dozen of these reviews, while Hemingway was engaged in last-minute errands for the safari. He would not be pacified by his editor, even though the book was selling well enough.

Insult to injury, his onetime Paris mentor, Gertrude Stein, had also turned on him savagely in *The Autobiography of Alice B. Toklas.* Several installments had appeared in *The Atlantic.* Stein had actually called him "yellow." Well, just like Eastman, he'd get her back in spades. That old fat lesbian bitch.

It was in Paris, just before leaving for Africa, that this alternately gloomy and exhilarated and lashing-out man had written "A Paris Letter" for Arnold Gingrich's *Esquire.* He'd become a contributor to this new (and surprisingly successful) men's monthly, published out of his hometown,

Chicago. In "A Paris Letter"—it appeared in the February 1934 issue, while Hemingway was on safari—the author had talked about Paris not belonging to him any longer and, presciently, about the coming of another war in Europe. It was all very gloomy, he wrote. "This old friend shot himself. That old friend took an overdose of something. . . . People must be expected to kill themselves when they lose their money, I suppose, and drunkards get bad livers, and legendary people usually end by writing their memoirs."

And what of Hemingway's marital relationship with the boyish-looking woman in the zebra-striped suit and funny hat standing beside him in this held moment of Manhattan time?

Hemingway had been married to his second wife for seven years, the wedding having taken place within a month of his divorce from Hadley Richardson in April 1927, and there is evidence to suggest that the marriage was mostly over in Hemingway's mind by April 1934. He and the former Pauline Pfeiffer of Piggott, Arkansas, who were the parents of two young sons—and whom they'd been away from for months—would remain together, nominally, for the next five years, until 1939, but by then Hemingway's affair with his next wife-to-be, Martha Gellhorn, would be almost three years old.

In my view, Hemingway's staid, Protestant, suburban, midwestern roots—which he fought against all his life—could never allow him to reconcile his various adulteries and marriages past his first marriage, to Hadley, who was his truest love, or at least his truest marriage. In that sense, his subsequent marriages were doomed from the start. Also in that sense, Hemingway was much like another famous and onetime resident of Oak Park, Illinois: Frank Lloyd Wright. The two geniuses, who spent separate lifetimes flouting middle-class mores, even as they couldn't seem to escape them, overlapped for about a decade in that Republican community of churches and impressive houses and upright families located eight miles west of downtown Chicago. (Wright was born in rural Wisconsin in 1867, and his career in architecture lasted until his death in 1959. In seven decades of work, he designed, if not completed, over one thousand buildings. He was in his early thirties, residing in Oak Park, struggling for commissions, with a growing family, when Hemingway came into the world in the summer of 1899.)

There's no question Hemingway had great passion for his second wife, for a time. In the beginning of the affair, in Paris, and on the ski slopes of Austria, and at the summer bullfights in Spain, Pauline had made a covert play for him, betraying her friendship with Hadley, just as Martha would make a shameless play for him a decade later—and he would more than willingly, if not immediately, comply. After Hemingway's death, MacLeish—who had known him since the twenties in Paris and who, like almost all of Hemingway's closest friends, had an ugly falling-out with him that would never completely repair itself (the second of two major fights was aboard *Pilar*, or at least began there, when *Pilar* was very new)—said astutely: "I have always suspected that his subsequent detestation for her [he was speaking of Pauline] was in part the consequence of his own sense of disloyalty." At the close of *A Moveable Feast*—that aforementioned slender, wistful, posthumously published, and often gratuitously mean memoir of Paris in the early days—Hemingway talks so bitterly against Pauline and so tenderly of Hadley, with whom he'd had his first son, Jack, whom he liked to call Mr. Bumby, when Mr. Bumby was small:

> Before these rich had come [he was referring to the Murphys, Gerald and Sara], we had already been infiltrated by another rich using the oldest trick there is. It is that an unmarried young woman becomes the temporary best friend of another young woman who is married, goes to live with the husband and wife and then unknowingly, innocently and unrelentingly sets out to marry the husband. . . .
>
> When I saw my wife again standing by the tracks as the train came in by the piled logs of the station, I wished I had died before I ever loved anyone but her. She was smiling, the sun on her lovely face tanned by the snow and sun, beautifully built, her hair red gold in the sun, grown out all winter awkwardly and beautifully, and Mr. Bumby standing with her, blond and chunky and with winter cheeks looking like a good Vorarlberg boy.

In "The Snows of Kilimanjaro," which is fiction, not memoir, the dying writer, by turns self-pitying and accusatory, says of his older wife: "She shot very well this good, this rich bitch. . . . She had a great talent and appreciation for the bed, she was not pretty, but he liked her face." As in all his fiction, Hemingway was making things up from what he knew. His imagination was conflating and rearranging and transposing several women and different events from his life. But it's still hard to read parts of that story and not picture biographically the woman to whom the author was still married in the late summer of 1936, more than two years after the safari was over, when the story appeared for the first time in print, in *Esquire,* which was also about five months before Hemingway met Martha Gellhorn in the Key West bar named Sloppy Joe's.

Two letters, both written at sea, about a week apart, four months before this pictured moment in New York City, seem to say much about his state of mind. One letter is full of belligerence and prevarication and prideful-ness; the other is tender, loving, funny, and boy-adventuresome. The first letter was written late at night to one of his friendlier critics; the second was sent to his middle son. The first letter ran to more than eighteen hundred words and may have been typed (the original is apparently lost); the second was fairly brief and in longhand. The letters were written on a scow of a boat named the SS *General Metzinger,* part of the Messageries Mari-times line, on the front end of the African trip. The *Metzinger* had sailed from Marseille on November 22, 1933, bearing the Hemingway shooting party of three through the Mediterranean Sea toward Port Said, Egypt. The ship then navigated through the Suez Canal and into the Red Sea and the Gulf of Aden and the Indian Ocean, to its landing at Mombasa, East Africa, on December 8, 1933.

The shooting party of three bound for safari consisted of Hemingway, his wife, and Hemingway's close Key West friend, Charles Thompson, who sold fishing tackle and ran Thompson's Hardware store at the water-front. Thompson and Hemingway had known each other for close to six years, since the spring of 1928. Both he and Thompson were tall, outdoorsy men, with similar physiques and similar interests, born in the same year, 1899. Thompson, whose family were old-time Key Westers, had a boat, an old-fashioned nineteen-footer. Evenings, when he got off work, Charles would come by and collect Hemingway—who was living with the preg-nant Pauline in a sweatbox of temporary lodgings above a Ford Motor garage, working on *A Farewell to Arms*—and the two would troll into Jack Channel or over toward Stock Island to fish for grouper and snapper. They became fast friends. Charles wasn't in the least a literary man, or even a very educated man, but the more telling difference between them was that he had a very soft personality. He was a man you could dominate. Origi-nally, Hemingway had hoped that Archie MacLeish would go on the safari with him, and he had also invited other long-standing friends, including

Henry Strater, whom everyone called Mike, a painter and amateur boxer and graduate of Princeton, who'd known Hemingway since Paris sparring sessions in 1922. Both Strater and MacLeish had known better than to give in to the repeated invitations. Hemingway was a friend you might not be able to live without—as MacLeish would one day say—but he also was a friend with whom you wouldn't chance an extended shooting trip.

The critic to whom Hemingway sent his late-night diatribe was Clifton Fadiman of *The New Yorker,* known to friends as Kip. He'd done a long and serious review of the story collection *Winner Take Nothing* in the form of an open letter ("A Letter to Mr. Hemingway"), in which the reviewer was essentially entreating the author—it was obvious how he admired Hemingway's work—to go on to other themes if he wished to grow as an artist. Hemingway's reply, a month after the review had been published, was written four days after the *Metzinger* had left Marseille for Africa. He put at the top of the upper-right-hand corner on the first page: "A Bord du General Metzinger, le 26 Novembre 1933, One day out of Port Said." The letter got more rageful and scornful as it went on. It was as if Hemingway was writing to somebody whom he knew was both sympathetic and tough-minded toward his work—and yet couldn't stop himself from sounding immature and churlish. Besides, he told Fadiman lies. They were inconsequential, but they were lies, from a lifelong prevaricator. He said twice that he was thirty-five. (He was thirty-four.) He said he'd gone to war at seventeen. (He was eighteen, about to turn nineteen.)

He said: "You see, what is important, is that you write about what you know—the time is very short—for me especially—and because of having learned too much about too many things too early."

He also said: "Will be glad to have you come to lunch when I break max Eastman's jaw. Plan to have rather gala occasion."

He railed against turncoat friends like Gertrude Stein; against such stinking critics as "a merchant like T.S. (Chickenshit) Mathews [who] says it [the material in *Winner Take Nothing*] is all about the war and the others about lesbians, insomnia, castration, syphilis."

At 11:30 p.m., the steward came in to say that the writing room was closing for the night. The letter writer decided to write four postscripts at the bottom of the letter, one of which talked again of how "the time is short." Almost certainly he meant his life. The fourth postscript said:

> Look, I'm 35, I've had a damned fine life, have had every
> woman I ever wanted, have bred good kids, have seen every-

thing I believe in royally f——d to hell (for Scribner's sake
amen), have been wounded many times, decorated many
times, got over all wish for glory or a career before I was 20,
have always made a living in all times, staked my friends, written 3 books of stories, 2 novels, a comic book and one fairly
exhaustive treatise and every chickenshit prick who writes
about my stuff writes with a premature delight and hope that
I may be slipping. It's beautiful. But I will stick around and
write until I have ruined every one of them, and not go until
my time comes. So would not advise you to hedge yet.

The second letter was written to Patrick Hemingway, five years old. At
the top: "A Bord Du General Metzinger Le 2 December." It was as if
the letter writer was speaking to someone his own age—say, about eleven.
What boy wouldn't crave to get a letter like this from his dad? If you studied this letter years later and didn't think too much about anything else, it
might make you forget that Hemingway—and his spouse—were absentee
parents to very young children.

Dear Old Mex:
Well here we are almost at the southern end of the Red Sea.
Tomorrow we will be in the Indian ocean. The weather is just
like Key West on a nice day in winter. Yesterday we saw a big
school of big porpoises and many schools of small porpoises.
It was cold and rainy all the way down to Egypt. Then it
was hot and fine. Coming through the suez canal we went
right through the desert. We saw lots of Palm trees and Australian pines (like in our yard) whenever there was water. But
the rest was mountains and hills and plains of sand. We saw
a lot of camels and a soldier riding on a camel made it trot
alongside the ship almost as fast as the ship could go. In the
canal you have to stop and tie up to the side sometimes to let
other ships go by.
You would have liked to see the other ships go by and to see
the desert. The only birds we saw were some snipe and quite a
lot of hawks and a few cormorants and one old blue crane.
I miss you, old Mex, and will be glad to see you again. Will
have plenty of good stories to tell you when we come back.

The letter went for a few more sentences and finished with: "Go easy on the beer and lay off the hard liquor until I get back. Don't forget to blow your nose and turn around three times before you go to bed. Your affectionate papa, Papa."

In Hemingway, early in his life and late in his life, kindness and gentleness and understanding and probity seem never far from his most appalling behavior.

The man entertaining reporters and posing for pictures at the *Paris* disembarkation rail had come triumphantly back to America with his African trophies, all right (slain beasts were on their way to the taxidermist, and there were numerous Kodak exposures and also eight-millimeter film documenting the khaki-clad hunter kneeling beside his antlered or maned or horned prey), but it was hardly all one great adventure. The safari, a huge experience of an outdoor life thus far lived, had suffered its own huge tensions, owing mainly to competitive bile.

Green Hills of Africa, the loosely factual account that came out of the safari, published in 1935, is almost naked on the page in portraying Hemingway's jealousy at being largely outhunted by his easygoing friend Charles Thompson. Hemingway started writing the book almost immediately upon returning to Key West. He continued working on it through the spring, summer, and fall as he fished the Stream with his new boat in both Florida and Cuban waters. Parts of the book were written, or at least revised, aboard *Pilar*. Other parts got drafted in a hotel room in Havana, and still others—including all the early and late sections—were done in the writing studio above the garage at the author's home in Key West. But wherever he worked on the African book, as Hemingway referred to it, salt water was always close by.

About a quarter of the way into the story, two rhinos are taken. The narrator gets one. Charles Thompson—who's known as Karl in the story—gets one.

> We had tried, in all the shoot, never to be competitive. . . .
> I was, truly, very fond of him and he was entirely unselfish and
> altogether self-sacrificing. I knew I could outshoot him and I
> could always outwalk him and, steadily, he got trophies that
> made mine dwarfs in comparison. He had done some of the

worst shooting at game I had ever seen and . . . still he beat me on all the tangible things we had to show. For a while we had joked about it and I knew everything would even up. But it didn't even up. . . . We had not treated him badly, but we had not treated him too well, and still he had beaten me. Not only beaten, beaten was all right. He had made my rhino look so small that I could never keep him in the same small town where we lived.

On the last day of the hunt, Hemingway kills two huge kudu bulls. The horns are magnificent. He can't wait to get back to camp that evening to show his trophies. "Karl" (Charles Thompson had an older Key West brother whose name was Karl) has just gotten a greater kudu, too. He comes back into camp from a different stalking area.

"What did you get?" I asked Karl.
"Just another one of those. What do you call them? Tendalla."
"Swell," I said. I knew I had one no one could beat and I hoped he had a good one too. "How big was he?"
"Oh, fifty-seven," Karl said.
"Let's see him," I said, cold in the pit of my stomach.
"He's over there," Pop said, and we went over.
They were the biggest, widest, darkest, longest-curling, heaviest, most unbelievable pair of kudu horns in the world. Suddenly, poisoned with envy, I did not want to see mine again; never, never.

Two pages later: "But I was bitter and I was bitter all night long. In the morning, though, it was gone." Yes, by first light, the bile has passed off. "I had accepted the big one now and was happy to see him and that Karl had him. When you put them side by side they looked all right. They really did. They all were big."

I don't know whether Hemingway the artist understood precisely what he was doing in portraying his unsportsmanlike spirit so transparently— or if he somehow didn't get what many of his readers and reviewers saw so quickly. *Green Hills*—a work greatly undervalued by many Hemingway scholars; critically dismissed in its own day by such major critics as Edmund Wilson—will come up more fully in a later chapter of this narrative, at the chronological point when the author was working on the book; and when, still raging over Gertrude Stein's attacks on him, Hemingway would write, without naming his antagonist, nor needing to, and in another way just describing himself: " 'It's a damned shame, though, with all that talent gone to malice and nonsense and self-praise.' "

And so the safari had ended. Had the anger of recent months—toward hostile critics, former friends, a good-natured hunting partner who'd bettered him—passed? Yes and no. He did seem happy and relaxed. The hunting party had sailed back up to France, via some deep-sea fishing in the Indian Ocean. Charles Thompson's wife, Lorine, who'd come over on a liner from New York, had met them midway. She had showed Pauline pictures of the two young Hemingway sons bearing glum expressions. (Pauline kept a diary of her time on safari. There's no mention in it of missing her children.) In Paris, the Thompsons and Hemingways had checked in again at the Hotel Dinard, on the Left Bank, where the shooting party had stayed on the outward leg of the trip. But the Thompsons left for home quickly. The Hemingways stayed on for nine days. They had gone to dinner one night with James Joyce and his wife; on another day Hemingway had met the American novelist Katherine Anne Porter at the legendary bookshop Shakespeare and Company. On still another he'd visited Sylvia Beach, Shakespeare's proprietor. She showed him an essay about him by the critic Wyndham Lewis. It was titled "The Dumb Ox" and took him apart for his anti-intellectualism. Hemingway had become so enraged that he smashed a vase of tulips on Beach's table. All this has been told before, in other books about Hemingway.

But what hasn't been told quite as fully was how unsuspectingly decent and generous Hemingway was, in those days before sailing homeward, to a young journalist and novelist named Edgar "Ned" Calmer. The story is key to Hemingway's character, to the notion of when it was good with Papa— the writing, the fishing, the drinking, the eating, the talking, the palling around—few things on earth seemed better.

Ned Calmer was a reporter for the *Paris Herald*. He'd first come to Europe on the payroll of the *Chicago Tribune*. He and Hemingway met during the several weeks that Hemingway had spent in Paris before the safari. They'd been introduced by another Paris newsman and friend of Hemingway's, Guy Hickok of the *Brooklyn Daily Eagle*. Because Hemingway had been a Paris newspaperman himself, he was partial to those who toiled for lousy wages in exotic places and were trying at the same time to be more serious about their craft. But he was especially partial to Calmer, because the journalist had a chronically ill wife and an infant daughter to support. On the side, he'd been trying to write fiction. "From the beginning," Calmer remembered years later, "it was obvious in many ways that Ernest was generous and kind, with time and loans of money and patience, to other writers, of whom I was one." When they met, Calmer had just completed his first novel, *Beyond the Street.* Priscilla Calmer was in a sanitarium in Switzerland, being treated for lung disease. Hemingway wished to give her a book and had gone all over Paris until he finally found a copy of *Winner Take Nothing,* so that he might sign it.

After the safari, back in Paris, Hemingway called up Calmer to take him to lunch. He learned that Priscilla Calmer had been released from her Swiss sanitarium and was at home with her husband. He also discovered that their daughter, Alden, had not yet been baptized. As Calmer remembered years later: "Ernest . . . seemed genuinely concerned. The attitude was: this will never do! He came along to the church of St. Sulpice in Paris as sponsor at the ceremony."

One day he took the Calmers to eat at Chez Weber in the rue Royale. Hemingway knew that *Beyond the Street* had just been published by Harcourt, Brace in New York. At lunch, Hemingway "slipped a cheque across the table to me," Calmer recalled years later. The check was for $350. "It was the ship fare home for myself and my wife and little daughter—totally unsolicited. . . . Years later I was able to pay him back and he thereafter liked to refer to me as Honest Ned, remarking that few others he had helped had ever bothered. . . . After his death, the estate lawyer sent me one of my cheques made out to Ernest which he had never cashed."

That day at Weber's restaurant, the astonished and grateful newspaperman had presented Hemingway with a signed copy of *Beyond the Street.* Hemingway read it coming home on the *Paris.* He had agreed to read and react to some of Calmer's shorter fiction. On May 28, 1934, back in America, he wrote to Calmer about his novel, apologizing for the delay: "I've been working like a what the hell should you call it. . . . I read it on the Paris—so did Pauline. We both liked it. That was not quite two months ago. . . . The faults of it were the faults everybody has in the first one but the virtues of it were not first novel virtues i e glamour, freshness etc. No, bo. The virtues were understanding, sympathy and a certain cleanliness of handling." For the rest of his life, Calmer (who published a dozen or so novels and had a significant career in broadcasting for CBS Radio News) would remain grateful to Hemingway. The two renewed their friendship during World War II, when Calmer was reporting in war-blitzed London with Edward

R. Murrow and other CBS newsmen. If they were never intimate friends, they managed to stay loosely in touch. Calmer apparently never dined out on it. He came to know all four of Hemingway's wives, especially Martha Gellhorn. This was after her divorce from Hemingway, when she was living in Rome and he was working there as a correspondent. No bitter thing Marty Gellhorn could ever have said against her former husband—whom she liked to call Pig, and not only in response to his bathing habits—would have changed Calmer's estimation.

Priscilla Calmer died of emphysema in Charlottesville, Virginia, in 1955. Calmer wrote Hemingway a note about her death. He didn't hear back. The next time they saw each other, Hemingway blurted an apology: "I never was any good at wakes."

Ned Calmer died at age seventy-eight in 1986. He'd had three wives and two children. Several years ago, when I spoke at length to his son on the telephone about his father's relationship with Ernest Hemingway, Regan Calmer said: "I never heard a lot about it growing up—and I also never heard a bad word about it. Mostly, he kept it to himself. . . . I don't know, I guess it was just the fact that my father had such a high respect and even love for such a great writer like Hemingway who did him these unsolicited favors at a critical time. He could never forget it."

In late April 1934, Ned Calmer wrote to Hemingway. He was in America with his family. He was promoting his first novel. "It was a great thing you did for me," he said. "Hope you acquired that boat."

There's a passage in Green Hills of Africa: "If you looked away from the forest and the mountain side you could follow the watercourses and the hilly slope of the land down until the land flattened and the grass was brown and burned and, away, across a long sweep of country, was the brown Rift Valley and the shine of Lake Manyara." I've wondered: months before he composed this landscape-painting sentence, when he was actually staring at that blue shine of African lake, so far from the Gulf Stream, did Hemingway squint and see a thirty-eight-foot Wheeler skimming on it? Did Pilar already have her name? One pictures—I do, anyway— a hunter seated by a campfire in a canvas-back chair, a million stars out, wide-brimmed Stetson safari hat pushed back, bush trousers hiked up, sleeves of his sweat-soaked shirt rolled past his thick forearms. The fire gives his unshaven face a kind of orangy glow. His wife is sleeping under mosquito netting on a canvas cot in a tent a few feet away. He sips tin cups of whiskey and soda. Earlier, he'd dined on roast guinea hen. He's not bent on dominating man or animal. Somewhere in his mind is the greater kudu he might get to steal up on tomorrow at the salt lick. With his weak eyesight, the big-game hunter, who is even more of a big-game fisherman, is poring over fine print in a thumbed catalog for a twin-cabin cruiser, thirty-eight feet in length, offered by a manufacturer in Brooklyn. He's studying all the specs, calculating the various price arrangements. "If you are looking for a fine roomy cruiser with lots of comforts, and ability for long offshore cruising and fishing trips, we suggest that you look this boat over very carefully." In the price column: "Afloat at the plant. For rail or steamer deliveries add $175 for cradle and cover."

THAT BOAT

Pilar and master, before her flying bridge was built, circa 1935

IT'S VERY LIKELY that somewhere in Hemingway's dozen suitcases were catalogs and circulars and fold-over mailings from Wheeler Shipyard, Inc., whose listed address was "Foot of Cropsey Avenue, Brooklyn, N.Y." If Hemingway did have this clutch of boating literature with him, then it had traveled through Spain and France and Africa, through the Mediterranean and the Red Sea and the Gulf of Aden, through Babati and Kiunga and the Ngorongoro Crater.

A small, fold-over pamphlet had been mailed to him the previous summer from the Wheeler firm. It was postmarked July 14, 1933, which suggests Hemingway would have received it about three weeks before he left the States on his long journey, first to Europe, then to Africa. He may have had literature from other boat makers, too, since buying a motorized fishing cruiser had so long and lately preoccupied his thinking. (The brochure, with its still readable postmark, is among Hemingway's papers at the John F. Kennedy Presidential Library and Museum in Boston.) The founder of the company, Howard E. Wheeler, had Palmer-perfect handwriting, pork-chop sideburns, wild eyebrows, a walrus mustache, and five grown sons working by his side in the family enterprise in Brooklyn. Howard had addressed the mail-out himself to "Mr. Ernest Hemingway, Box 406, Key West, Florida." There was a one-and-a-half-cent stamp affixed to the document, which described in typical inflated advertising rhetoric the company's wares. It was a flyer for the 1933 model year, since catalogs for 1934 boats hadn't yet come off the presses.

The Wheeler firm designed and built cabin cruisers, sea skiffs, yachts, and motor sailers (a boat combining the features of both a motorboat and a sailboat). The company's signature model, known throughout the boating industry, was the Playmate, which came in many lengths and sleeping configurations and price arrangements—twin screw, single screw, diesel power, gasoline engine, sedan, twin cabin, stateroom cabin, enclosed bridge. For several years Hemingway had been studying such vessels in the cabin-cruiser style, and by the time he arrived back in America on the *Paris,* he seems to have known exactly the size of boat he wanted, and he wanted it from Wheeler.

As in the automotive business, the so-called new models from a boat-builder, along with their advertising wares, began to appear in the fall of the previous model year. That is, boats for the 1934 season were being readied by the major shipyards in the late summer and all through the autumn of 1933, and this is also when the new catalogs were mailed out to prospective customers and when ads began to show up in the press. The big event every year for showcasing new boats—and for taking orders—was the National Motor Boat Show, held in January at Grand Central Palace in New York. This is when the shipyards from across the country unveiled their beauties in the flesh, seeking to outdo one another with flashy exhibit spaces and giveaway trinkets and walk-through models. Sometimes chastely sexy girls were there to greet buyers on the foredeck. In other words, the New York boat show was just like a big car show, except that the motoring dreams were on water instead of the open road. Since he was in Africa, Hemingway was going to miss by roughly two months the gaudy 1934 show at which the Wheeler firm was one of the starring concerns.

Many American boat makers in the thirties were just trying to hang on, no matter the impression they were giving to would-be customers. By mid-Depression, some companies were down to a handful of employees. And their new models were often pretty much the old models—using the same hulls from prior years, but with different manufacturing numbers.

The 1934 Playmates—how Hemingway must have loathed the name—

ranged in size from twenty-eight to forty-six feet. The company produced mainly stock boats rather than custom-made craft, although if you were sufficiently well-heeled, the boatyard at the foot of Cropsey Avenue was glad to do custom work, starting either from absolute scratch or, more characteristically, from a stock Wheeler hull and constructing upward to your specifications. Mostly, though, Wheeler was known to yachting enthusiasts as a "production shipyard." The company had a reputation for good woodwork, inside and out, especially in its cabinetry. Its "brightwork" (what you see on the exterior) was known to be very solid, if not spectacular. Still, when you said "Wheeler," you tended to think of look-alike boats. To pure yachting snobs, for whom the Depression would have been an inconvenience, that term, "stock boat," no less than the term "production shipyard," would have had an odor.

And yet it's also true that the designers and old-school Scandinavian master shipwrights at Wheeler would produce some famed original boats in these years—a sixty-nine-footer, for instance, for a financier named Charles S. Payson, so that he might hydroplane to his office on Wall Street. These craft were known in the yachting world as "streamline commuters" or simply "commuters." Payson's custom Wheeler came out the year after *Pilar* and was christened *Saga*, with photographs of her in the boating journals, knifing the water with her V-12 Packards, this legend underneath: "Streamlining in Mahogany." Charlie Payson, known to be impeccable with his money, was married to the former Joan Whitney, and Joan was the sister of Jock Whitney, and Jock and Joan were the only children of Helen Hay Whitney and Payne Whitney, fabulously rich Americans and devotees of the sporting life. In the thirties, Jock Whitney and his spouse, and Charles Payson and his spouse, lived next to each other on Long Island's Gold Coast. It sounds so tight and clubby and Gatsbyesque, although apparently things were competitive, too, in a sporting way. *Saga* is said to have come about in the first place out of Payson's need to outrun Jock Whitney's mahogany commuter, *Aphrodite*. The brothers-in-law wished to race toward their money in the city, and whoever got there first could make more.

If you went past forty-six feet in length for your Wheeler watery dream, you were really talking about a yacht, not a motor cruiser. So technically speaking, Ernest Hemingway never owned a yacht, even though that phrase is often thrown around in connection with the history of his boat. The 1934 Wheeler catalog on the stock thirty-eight-foot cabin cruisers said:

Do not forget that a WHEELER "38" is practically a 40 footer and with its wide beam, semi Vee bottom form and wide flaring bow this boat provides more comfort, more room, better sea-going qualities, more headroom and runs steadier and smoother than any other boat of its size on the market today. Before considering any boat in this size you owe it to yourself to look over the fine specifications and complete equipment list offered in the new WHEELER PLAYMATES. We offer SEVEN fine arrangements, each with features very far in advance of competitive models and best of all at the VERY LOWEST possible PRICES. . . . Forward deck is fitted with monkey rails of varnished oak, anchor windglass, chocks, side cleats, etc. . . . Center of main cabin has large modern galley on starboard side fitted with three burner alcohol stove, large sink, chromium flashed drain board, refrigerator, dish and glass racks and plenty of food and locker space. Port side fitted with a toilet room, which has marine type toilet, large sink, mirror, shelves and other fittings complete.

The '34 catalog offered an endorsement from Vincent Astor himself. He'd recently bought a Wheeler thirty-eight. He was the son of Colonel John Jacob Astor IV, robber baron supreme. Vincent Astor could have afforded any kind of yacht or yacht maker he wanted. And he came to Brooklyn for a Wheeler—well, not literally. The hull of his *Little Nourmahal* was white and she was a little more upright as she churned the water, but still: Astor's custom Wheeler looked remarkably similar to the production Wheeler that, in about six months, was going to come off the wooden ways at Cropsey Avenue, with her five-character Spanish name lettered neatly in white on her dark stern.

On March 24, in Paris, four days before boarding an ocean liner with the same name (it's the day he punches the vase of tulips at Sylvia Beach's Shakespeare and Company), Hemingway wrote to Arnold Gingrich at *Esquire*. Much of the letter was taken up with instructions regarding his next contribution to the magazine, which would be about the safari. "You may also use the photo of me and lion," he wrote. "But under no circumstances run this picture with the group of pictures or any single picture of live lions. It would be very bad taste and give people the impression that we photographed lions and then shot them." Further on:

> I hope to hell your finances are on the wax rather than the bloody wane as I am broke (after fashion) and it is a pain in the jaw to be writing stuff for nearly enough money to pay the postage when I could put it in a slightly different form and get 10 times as much for it.
>
> Cosmop paid 5500 for that story ["One Trip Across"]—think I told you—I want to buy a boat that costs $7,000 and have only $3500. Once I get the boat am set. But have been within a grand of enough to buy it with twice and both times the money has peed away.
>
> Must send this now—Bremen boat train leaving.

The letter of the twenty-fourth had a postscript: "Please acknowlege pictures to Scribners and mark letter PLEASE HOLD. Will be there in about a week or 8 days." He had addressed the envelope: "Arnold gingritch Esq." (Inside, in the greeting, he had used the same spelling and lower-case *g*.) Hemingway's spelling, not least the spelling of people's names, was often erratic, and sometimes had a kind of deliberate facetiousness about it, but it seemed to take him a particularly long while to get this one down, even though Gingrich had been his acquaintance for a little more than a year. It would be a good while before Gingrich, like so many others, would begin to register his public contempt for Hemingway. Years later, for *Playboy*, he'd write a biting memoir called "Horsing Them in with Hemingway." By then Gingrich was not only a legendary American magazine editor, he was a world-class fly-fisherman. He was also the fourth husband of Jane Mason, a lifelong, high-maintenance, oval-faced American beauty who, for a time, back in the early thirties, when she was still youthful and blond and high-strung and high-sexed and wed to an old Yale clubman and high executive of Pan American Airways in Cuba, was Hemingway's wild-assed drinking partner and fishing companion and, probably, his lover. (No one's ever been able to establish this as an indisputable fact, although many Hemingway chroniclers have assumed it for fact.) "Ernest was a meat fisherman," Gingrich would write in "Horsing Them in with Hemingway." For a true sportsman, that's about the unkindest cut of all. By then, the famous editor seemed to take special delight in the posthumous decline of Hemingway's literary fortunes.

But not in 1933 and 1934 and 1935, when his magazine was trying to get traction and badly needed Hemingway's name on its covers. Gingrich, a native midwesterner still in his late twenties, of Pennsylvania Dutch extraction, a collector of first editions, had met Hemingway at a rare-book shop in New York City called The House of Books in January 1933. Ever since, the young editor had been doing whatever he possibly could do to stay on Hemingway's good side and to get him to write for the magazine. The first issue of *Esquire,* on stands in late August 1933, with that fishing contribution by Hemingway, had sold one hundred thousand copies at fifty cents apiece. All told through the years, he'd publish twenty-five essays and six stories in Gingrich's magazine—"letters," he and the editor decided to call his fishing and hunting reports. After Hemingway's suicide, Gingrich wrote in his editor's column:

> It is not too much to say that, at the very earliest point, he was [*Esquire's*] principal asset. . . . We were going around New York with a checkbook, calling on writers and artists all and sundry, trying to make them believe that we were actually going to come out with a luxury magazine, "devoted to the art of living and the new leisure," at the very moment when the banks had just reopened. . . . [O]ur gentlemen's agreement with Hemingway was that we would pay him twice as much as we paid anybody else, and that, while we hoped to pay more, if and as the magazine succeeded, we were still honor-bound to preserve that ratio. Such was the stature of the man that even then (Spring of '33), nobody objected.

Gingrich was exaggerating—or more likely remembering wrong—when he said he had paid Hemingway twice as much as anybody else in the beginning, although it's true that F. Scott Fitzgerald, John Dos Passos, Sinclair Lewis, and Theodore Dreiser, all of whom were early and famous contributors, had to get in line behind both Hemingway's pay and ego. Gingrich had also promised not to tamper with so much as a comma of Hemingway's copy.

In the letter mailed from France on the twenty-fourth, a hook had been set. *I want to buy a boat that costs $7,000 and have only $3500. Once I get the boat am set.* On April 3, 1934, the big-boned 210-pounder in suit and tie popping quotes at Pier 57 beside the small and zebra-suited woman couldn't know for certain his hook-setting had worked. Couldn't know that the magazine editor in Illinois had fairly hopped to it and already mailed

him, in care of Scribners, a nine-page, handwritten, semi-sycophantic letter that began: "The enclosed, or attached, represents a couple of blood
vessels. You'll have to scratch another $500 somehow, and then we all stand
up and call you skipper." (A week later, after he was home in Key West,
Hemingway wrote to Gingrich and said, "Thanks for raising the 3G. . . .
You were a good guy to send the money.") Hemingway wouldn't know his
hook-setting had worked until he'd opened an envelope at his publishing
house. The letter and the check, written on April 2 in Chicago and posted
the next day via air mail, were there waiting, on either April 4 or April
5, in Max Perkins's office, when the biggest horse in the Scribners stable
went to visit his editor at 597 Fifth Avenue. And immediately afterward,
a jubilant man, suppressing his demons, with dough in hand, spouse on
arm, glorying in his life, in his luck, in the new possibilities of the physical
world, taxied to Brooklyn, to buy his boat.

Several weeks later, while *Pilar* was still being outfitted and altered to her
owner's wishes, some official documents were filled out and signed and sent
to the Department of Commerce, in its Bureau of Navigation, in Washington, DC: the master carpenter's certificate, the certificate of admeasurement, the application for registration. If you went to the right archive, you
could pore over the originals of these papers, like this document, certificate
No. 1261, dated April 23, 1934, with its unconscious poetry of form:

> *I,* E. Lawrence Wheeler, master *carpenter*
> *of* Wheeler Shipyard, Inc., *do certify that*
> *the* gas screw yacht
> *called* the "Pilar"
> *was built* by the Wheeler Shipyard, Inc.
> *during the year* 1934
> *at* Brooklyn, N.Y.
> *State of* New York
> *of* wood
> *for* Mr. Ernest Hemingway, P.O. Box 406, Key West, Florida

Six days afterward, in its Sunday sports pages, in a roundup of boating
news, *The New York Times* ran a twelve-line item: "Back from writing about
picadors in Spain and ambulance drivers in Italy, Ernest Hemingway, who
has gone to his home at Key West, has taken up motorboating and last
week bought a 42-foot cruiser at the Wheeler shipyard in Brooklyn. White

paint is now being burned off to comply with Hemingway's preference for a black hull and the boat will be shipped to a Southern port for delivery at Key West." The twelve lines contained only four or five errors of fact, which, considering the oceans of misinformation already attending this coveted life, wasn't half bad.

He'd dreamed of having his own seagoing boat for about as long as he'd been an ocean fisherman and had fished from other people's boats—which is to say for about six years. Hemingway first saw Key West in the first week of April 1928, and in a sense this is a way of demarcating the beginning of his serious saltwater life, which eventually superseded all other kinds of fishing he'd ever done or would do again. From boyhood on, he'd been a passionate fisherman, and from infancy on—literally—he'd been around steamers and launches and rowboats and other small craft plying the summer waters of Walloon Lake in northern Michigan. When he was eleven, his mother had taken him on a nearly monthlong trip by rail and steamer to Cape Cod and Nantucket Island, where he experienced the ocean for the first time and where he fished for sea bass and mackerel. But up until the Key West years, roughly 1928 to 1939, his fishing obsessions had been primarily of a freshwater and landlocked kind. Wild trout taken in waded streams on delicate equipment, using worms or hand-tied flies—these had seized Hemingway's angling imagination until his late twenties. Even after he owned Pilar, he still liked going for trout, in the big mountain streams of the West, but more and more that kind of fishing and those kinds of fish, no matter their wildness and fragile beauty, became too small for his imagination. He needed expanses of water where you couldn't see the other side. He needed fish whose size was theoretically illimitable and which could be triumphed over and brought into shore and strung upside down for documenting with cameras. He needed an environment far less sheltered than a trout stream could afford, an environment where there was implicit danger. As for boats themselves: when you look through Hemingway's letters in the half-dozen years before he got Pilar, it's instructive to see how often the noun "boat" comes up. Boats and fishing and salt water, not to say other kinds of fluids: it's as if these overlapping dreams and preoccupations and pastimes frame Hemingway's correspondence in his early Key West years, the more so when he is in some kind of pain and seeks escape.

For instance, there's the letter—profane, funny, bigoted, homophobic, anxious, watery—he wrote to Thornton Wilder in late May 1929, roughly two months after his mother had mailed the suicide weapon, roughly five years before he boated his first broadbill aboard Pilar. Hemingway had lately arrived in Paris with his wife and children and one sister. The first serial installment of A Farewell to Arms had appeared in Scribner's Magazine. Wilder had written to say how much he liked it. Hemingway was obsessively reworking the ending of the novel—which would come out in the fall—and he was also reading page proofs for the next magazine excerpt. Wilder, two years older, was the bigger literary name. Like Hemingway with the publication of The Sun Also Rises in 1926, he'd become a suddenly famous man with the publication, in 1927, of his second novel, The Bridge of San Luis Rey (for which he won the first of his three Pulitzer Prizes). He was an unlikely celebrity—reserved, schoolteacherish. As a closeted homosexual, he was also an unlikely Hemingway friend.

Hemingway typed the letter and added in things by hand.

Damned good to hear from you. . . . I'm awfully glad if you like the book but hate to have you read it in chunks and possibly bowdlerized. . . . Were in America about 14 months and at no time encountered anyone who had read anything of mine but by judicious use of your name acquired quite a reputation as a literary gent.

All I did was work like a convict on this book for a year—then laid off and fished and shot and took grand trips with Pauline and Dos and old Waldo Pierce. Wrote it everywhere—Paris—Key West—Arkansas—K.C. Wyoming—back in Key West—Drove 17,000 miles in a new Ford. Now can't write a damned thing. It always seems like that—either working and not speaking to anyone and afraid each day you will get out of it and living like a damned monk for it—then a fine time after it's done then hellish depression until you get into it again. My father went in for shooting himself and leaving a family and etc. on my hands to support. . . . If you ever hear I'm dead don't believe a word of it as will turn up in blackface having changed name or something to get rid of economic pressure. . . . Paris is going to pot. Seems awfully lousy. More traffic than N.Y. Everybody has too much money and it's expensive as hell and after where we've been and what seen and how felt this last year there's no damn fun in drinking at a café with a lot of hard faced lesbians (converted ones not even real ones) and all the little fairies when you-ve been out day after day on the carribean in a small boat with

57

people you like and black as a nigger from the sun and never any
shoes nor any underwear and champagne in the water butt covered
over with a chunk of ice and a wet sack—dove for the champagne
out on the reef where a rum boat went aground—flying fish instead
of fairies—and with only so long to live why come back to cafes and
all the little snivelling shit of literary politics.

What the hell does success get you? (Money of course but I
~~*always*~~ *dont get that) All it gets is that people treat you snottily*
because they think you must have a swelled head. That's the lousi-
est thing of all. I may quit the whole business and buy a boat with
what dough I can get together and shove off.

He wouldn't have shoved off, even if he'd been able to acquire Pilar on
the spot, because the bite of fame had already chomped down too hard.

GONE TO FIREWOOD

Docks of Bimini, 1935

IF YOU MADE YOUR WAY now to the hemmed-in wedge of metropolitan New York still referred to as the foot of Cropsey Avenue, you wouldn't find a trace, not a wooden shaving, of Wheeler Shipyard, Inc. So much craftsmanship in oak and pine and fir and cypress and cedar and mahogany—gone from this ground. So much timber that once got bent on this ground, lovingly curved and steamed and hammered and milled and sawed and planed and joined and otherwise coaxed toward improbable shapes and watertight angles on these premises—vanished. Where has it all gone? Oh, say to firewood, collectors of vintage boats, a museum or two, buzzards, a hillside in Cuba, the sludgy bottoms of coastal waterways, the photo albums of Wheeler descendants, the posthumous pages of *Islands in the Stream*, which, true enough, may be one of Ernest Hemingway's lesser novels but is nonetheless incredibly rich for any student of *Pilar*. "The mate shrugged his shoulders and bent down to the second anchor and Thomas Hudson eased her ahead against the tide, watching the grass from the banks riding by in the current. He came astern until his second anchor was well dug in. The boat lay with her bow into the wind and the tide running past her. There was much wind even in this lee and he knew that when the tide changed she would swing broadside to the swell."

There's a Pathmark Super Center at Cropsey's foot now. It shares a pocked parking lot with a diner. (I ventured in, and my server said, in response to my question, "Sorry, darlin', never heard of a boat business around here, and I've been a waitress in crappy joints in this neighborhood for a long time.") Coney Island Creek, where they used to put in the new boats, for their virgin launches, is still here, but these days the creek is an imperceptibly moving slit of diseased-looking water that hardly seems big enough to hold a flotilla of toy boats. But even in Wheeler's boatbuilding days, Coney Island Creek—which flows into Gravesend Bay, which in turn flows out into the Atlantic—was known to be a pretty narrow and impure thing, not something you would have chosen to sit beside for a Sunday picnic with your sweetheart. One of the reasons they stopped making boats at this site after World War II (there were lots of reasons, not least economic) was because there was too much mud in the launching water.

In the middle of the Depression, New Yorkers thronged to the national boat show every January at Grand Central Palace. They wished to gape at the new models: cruisers, streamliners, racers, V-bottoms, hard-chines, runabouts, sedans, cigarette boats, sea skiffs, salons, sportfishermen, twin-cabins, bridge-cabins, trawlers, luxury yachts.

It seems like such a historical disconnect. How did the companies making these luxuries manage to stay in business? The short answer is that many didn't. The more complex answer is that even in terrified times, life goes on, weekend leisure goes on. No question that pickings were far slimmer for Depression boat manufacturers than in the previous decade—or than they would be, in the years following the war, when the idea of a modest-priced boat sitting on a trailer in a suburban garage seemed part of the middle-class dream and bargain. (This was part of Chris-Craft's marketing genius and strategy in the 1950s.) But even, or especially, in the Depression, there were still boat dreamers who wanted to be out on water, beyond sight of shore and its anxieties, and some of them even had the means to negotiate that dream.

Dream. You could be in rags and still dream. In the Sunday paper, you'd see a picture of a beautiful girl, her hands gripping an enormous steering wheel, her hair streaming back, her head tilted toward the wind in what looked like sexual pleasure. She was churning through open water in a nineteen-foot runabout. Where was this—Lake George? Northern Wisconsin? That part didn't matter; it was the feeling that you got from looking at the girl making whitecaps in the boat that she was piloting alone. Her racer, with its long inlaid snout, had a windshield that looked like something on a British convertible sports car. There was a flag whipping at the stern. The leather seat that the girl sat on looked as plush as a banquette at a Hollywood restaurant. You saw this photograph in the depths of winter, with its goofy caption ("All Hands on Deck"), and all you wished was to pull on your ratty old overcoat and woolen hat with the earflaps and go out the door to catch the first subway or bus or streetcar you could find to the Palace. Maybe you barely had carfare and gate admission. Maybe you'd left the snarling missus and the bawling kids behind. But there was that picture in your brain of the girl in the nineteen-foot runabout. (I am describing an actual newspaper photograph published in *The New York Times* in the Depression. It's in the Chris-Craft collection at the Mariners' Museum in Newport News, Virginia.)

Some of the staying-in-business had to have been accomplished with smoke and mirrors. The Gar Wood firm in Marysville, Michigan, liked to promote itself in advertisements as "The Greatest Name in Motor Boating." According to C. Philip Moore's *Yachts in a Hurry,* Gar Wood's boats "were considered the Buicks of Jazz Age mahogany runabouts, with Chris-Craft products being the Chevrolets." In the summer of 1929, a couple of months before the stock market crashed, Gar Wood employed something like 150 master carpenters. By 1933, the company was down to three employees—but you wouldn't have known that from looking at its ads in the boating journals. Gar Wood's major biographer is a cultural and boating historian named Anthony Mollica Jr. For both Moore and Mollica, the study of boats, not just in the Depression, is a kind of social lens on America itself. "I had no idea when I started out my research that they had shrunk like that," Mollica told me. "It's really what happened to a lot of those venerable companies. . . . You see, when a boat business goes bad, when it dies, the owners just walk off. It's the failure of it all. I think it's even more true for boat companies than for other companies."

One Wheeler offspring I tracked down, in his upper seventies now, never wanted anything else for himself but a career in boats and marine engineering. He got it, too. His name is Wesley D. Wheeler, and he is the son of Wesley L. Wheeler, and is the grandson of company founder Howard E. Wheeler. He was born the year before Ernest and Pauline Hemingway came to his grandpop's boatyard. His own dad, who was close in age to Hemingway, was, for many years, the firm's chief naval architect—so he's the man who would have designed *Pilar* and so many other Wheeler pleasure craft. "You could ask anybody, Wheelers were known as the Cadillac of the industry," Wes Wheeler told me, with understandable pride if not razor accuracy. "The World's Finest Yacht Construction" was the corporate slogan Wheeler used to run on its catalogs in the fifties. When I asked Anthony Mollica (along with some other boating historians) what he thought a Wheeler was closest to in automobile paradigms, he said without hesitation: "A Wheeler is a Packard. A prewar Packard. Big and strong and comfortable and sturdy. Beamy. Sea-kindly. Very well thought out. Extremely well made. Some sly, deceptive speed. Its own form of beauty. In other words, not a tug, but not a racing boat, either. It's got eye appeal, but of a subtler kind. The price structure would be right, too."

Some of that almost sounds like a description of Hemingway's own body mass: the lumbering athlete who could surprise you with his quick feints. Once more, how intuitively Hemingway had chosen. He'd found a boat, located a company, in synch with himself, probably much more than he ever knew. Call it again the phenomenon of easy first luck—built, of course, on all the hard work of looking, investigating, intuiting.

The majority of Depression boat manufacturers in America had their yards in the Northeast or in the Great Lakes region or along the Atlantic Seaboard—it remains pretty much true today. (There was another boat-building community on the West Coast, and Canada also had its clot of wooden-boat makers.) Then as now, boat sales tended to follow the wealth of the country, so the greatest concentration of manufacturers was in the New York metropolitan area. But it's both pleasurable and instructive to pick up old boating magazines and chart the place-name geography of North American boatbuilding.

As with most thirties manufacturers, Wheeler didn't have its own dealer network. (Chris-Craft, the General Motors of the industry, was the great exception.) Wheeler had a few distributors around the country, but mostly it sold its products—certainly in the thirties—either at the annual boat show in New York or straight from the factory floor. Wheeler never went to its customers so much as its customers came to Cropsey Avenue. For a brief time, after World War II, the company had its own showroom on Park Avenue—one of the things that helped take Wheeler down.

The "factory floor" at the foot of Cropsey was really a jerry-built collection of wooden building berths and tin-roof assembly sheds, some of which hung out precariously over the unprepossessing stream, next to a drawbridge. Just across that drawbridge, with its scrolled ironwork, on Coney Island itself, were some five-cent Depression thrills named the Cyclone and the Thunderbolt and the Loop-O-Plane: Wheeler's artisans built their wares in the shadow of Coney's amusement dreams. When they built boats on the north side of this creek and slid them into the water, a drawbridge was crucial, so that the bigger Wheelers could get through and out into the bay.

When they launched the new boats in this water, the idea was to get them out of it as quickly as possible. "If you left them there a week or ten days, the hulls would start to turn purple," Wes Wheeler told me. Nonetheless, if it could talk, this maligned channel of once-navigable water (minimally navigable, it is said by New York historians) would have its tales. Today, all that exists of the historical strait between the two bays is the little ribbon of pollution on the creek's western edge, running perpendicular to the foot of Cropsey. On the snow-crusted winter afternoon when I stood at the edge of the supermarket's parking lot and stared at the water, trying to see a just-wet *Pilar* bobbing in it, seven decades past, Coney Island Creek had a grocery cart without wheels washed up on its trash-strewn bank. The water looked swollen, pea green.

The phone number here used to be Esplanade 2-5900.

They used to have planking races here. They'd put the Swedes on one side of a hull, the Norwegians on the other.

When you're building a boat, the keel gets laid down the middle. The frames come up the side, vertically, then the horizontal planking, over top of the ribbing. The Egyptians were doing this—planking on framing— five thousand years ago. At Cropsey, the oak frames sometimes got bent hot right on the boat—the boards were grabbed piping hot by the artisans from the portable steam boxes that had been pulled up alongside the hulls. Whether you're in the framing or planking stage of boat construction, you're essentially trying to follow the natural inclination of an organic material, something that has its own specific grain, its unique anatomy. (In Japan, when sawyers are examining a tree trunk, they speak of "reading the wood.") It's true that a new shape is being willed and forced by the shipwright, but in an even truer sense the shape has already grown into the

boards before they're in the shipwright's hands. So the shape is predeter-
mined, you might say, and the true builder must respect this idea and work
with it, not go against the nature of things. He seeks to be guided by the
inclination of the wood itself as he creates the curvy, swooping, shadowy
angles and shapes.

They used to squash bananas on the launching rails here. It was easier this way to get the finished boats into the water. The rails, made of
wood, ran from the shop floors down the bank and into the creek. The
banana-squishing was a cheap and ingenious Depression way of greasing
skids. Even so, Wheeler must have used up a ton of bananas, because it's
a fact that this nearly always financially threatened company produced a
lot of boats in its gaudy, roller-coaster, roughly half-a-century history. No
one seems to have a precise count of how many boats got built, but three
thousand is a figure that Wheeler descendants like to cite. And it should
also be noted quickly that not every Wheeler, whether a pleasure boat or
some type of military craft during war years, was produced at the Brooklyn
plant. Every time the boating world wrote off the company, the company
seemed to find a way of coming back, in a slightly different incarnation,
with a slightly different legal variant on its well-known name. At least
once, after a bankruptcy, the Wheeler family, or members of that family,
took over another boatyard and just started in again. In this regard, and
some others, too, you could compare the bounce-back and up-and-down
commercial and legal fortunes of Wheeler boats to the bounce-back and
up-and-down life and literary fortunes of the man who bought *Pilar*.

At Cropsey, its mother yard, Wheeler had a furniture shop, a machin-
ing shop, an upholstery shop, a sawmill, and a four-room hospital with a
full-time doctor and nurse. For a time, during World War II, this company
had its own fifty-six-piece marching band, made up largely of employees
who wore uniforms embroidered with corporate insignia. A day or two a
week, the band would saw away on a stage in the middle of the yard while
the rest of the workforce—in metal hats and coveralls with "Wheeler"
stenciled on the back—ate lunch out of black pails. Sometimes the programs went out over the radio—Wheeler had its own broadcasting operation for a few years. Actually, this part of the Wheeler legend isn't directly
connected to Cropsey Avenue, but to a second and larger yard, which got
thrown up on the eve of war, at Whitestone, Long Island, on the East
River. Almost overnight the company payroll had leaped from a few score
prewar master boatbuilders making pleasure craft in Brooklyn to a workforce of six thousand, round-the-clock shifts, seven days a week, at two

sites. The company had ceased all private-boat production so that it could produce 83-foot wooden Coast Guard cutters at Cropsey and 136-foot wooden YMS antimagnetic navy mine sweepers at the Whitestone facility. Sometimes, as the band played, and before everybody turned back to the work, the progenitor and founder—he of the Palmer-perfect penmanship and wild hair and outlandish mustache and absurd pork-chop sideburns— would pass through, handing out watches to the boys who'd soon be going overseas.

Howard E.—which is how he was addressed when he wasn't being called Pop Wheeler—was married to Edith Berentha Clayton Wheeler. She was a vital part of this company, too, in on all major decisions, known to keep an eye on the books and personally sign checks. Judging by photographs and family recollections, the matriarch, at least in middle age, was great-bosomed and tended to dark clothes and bomber hats with stickpins in them that must have scared the bejesus out of her many grandchildren. She was easily the sternest Methodist of them all in this close-knit clan of boat-making Methodists who'd come out of English Methodism, and who'd settled, in the early years of the century, in Bensonhurst, Brooklyn, and who'd later moved to Flatbush.

Everybody in the extended family had something or other to do with the advancement of the boatyard, even if it was only showing up at banquets during World War II when the navy or the Coast Guard or the army was awarding another "E" pennant for production excellence. Mother Wheeler was known to tolerate no drinking or smoking in her presence—even Coca-Cola was sinful. It sounds a little like the repressive, God-fearing, Oak Park household presided over by the bomberish Grace Hall-Hemingway in the first and second decades of the century, when her recalcitrant first son was straining for escape.

In 1961, outsiders took control of the business and sent the Wheelers into exile. Some family members tried to start things anew, unsuccessfully. But in the hot heart of it, from, say, the mid-twenties to the late fifties, the Wheeler story, which is first and last a family story, seems so, well, *American,* meaning that it was ever boom to bust and back to boom again, its highs so high, its lows so low.

First and last, the old man seems to have been a salesman, so maybe it wouldn't have truly mattered whether the product was frying pans or toasters. He was born in 1869. The family myth is that he'd started out in his newly married adulthood, before the turn of the century, building houses with a brother-in-law in Bay Ridge, Brooklyn. He is said to have owned one of the first gas stations in Brooklyn. He got interested in boats and bought a small piece of property at Twenty-third Avenue on Gravesend Bay in Bensonhurst. World War I came along, and America's entry into it, and the salesman-visionary caught a train to Washington and bid on a contract for 110-foot wooden submarine chasers. He'd never really built a big boat before, but he ended up building nine chasers—and when six of those were finished ahead of time, he got contracts on four more, as well as commissions on tugs for both the army and the navy. All the Wheelers lived at the family boatyard. As the younger sons finished school at Erasmus Hall, they joined their father in the business, putting on the apron and getting knee deep in shavings in the mold loft, taking college classes at night for engineering or drafting or naval design.

In the postwar economy, Howard E. was making large plans for his little company. "War Plant Builds Pleasure Boats" was the headline in the *Brooklyn Daily Eagle* in May 1919, six months after the armistice had been signed. Under the headline was a nice one-column feature on the boatyard. Not even two months later, Wheeler had suddenly gone into receivership. The founder made an arrangement with his creditors, though, and stayed in business; part of his brilliance. In 1921, there was a terrible fire. He had no insurance. But since he had nowhere to go but on, he borrowed money, mortgaged whatever else he had, convinced an acquaintance to stake him.

For the next several years, the Wheeler company—essentially the Wheeler family—built and sold rowboats and small sea skiffs. In 1924, the yard exhibited its first boat in a national motorboat show—a twenty-foot launch. By 1928, the yard at the foot of Cropsey was producing and selling between fifty and sixty pleasure boats a year. Its name was growing in the field. By 1930: seventy-five boats. The business was always short of working capital, but this fact didn't hurt its reputation in the industry. By 1938, Wheeler was producing the fattest sales catalog in the national boating industry. By 1939, the company's production and sale of motor cruisers in the thirty-eight-foot range was said to number 225 boats.

Another war was looming. There were more trips to Washington, DC, by the builder (and the builder's sons) to secure contracts: picket boats, cutters, minesweepers, rescue tugs. To satisfy the banks, whose officers had made large loans for the construction of the Whitestone yard, a new company was formed—Wheeler Shipbuilding Corporation. Soon admirals were journeying from the capital to both plants to present pennants and to read telegrams of congratulation from Secretary of the Navy Frank Knox. The Wheeler women, black-gloved, wearing huge corsages, exploded bottles of champagne at the bows of the new boats—and these pictures get prominent display in the *Eagle* and the *Herald Tribune*. There were black-tie dinner-dances attended by military brass. Mayor Fiorello LaGuardia appeared at christenings, jawing with the old man—Howard E. was now in his seventies—on flag-draped podiums in the middle of the yard, making speeches that defied syntax and went out live over WNYC.

But if you live by fat government contracts, you can die by them, too. What happens when the war is won and six thousand people are on the payroll and your federal contracts are shutting off like water from a spigot? Wheeler tried to seize the postwar public's imagination with a sleek new pleasure craft called the Sunlounge. Howard E. opened a showroom right around the corner from the Waldorf, an expensive dare. Other boat companies were doing it, too. Think of plate-glass showrooms on Park Avenue with gleaming yachts inside and people on the sidewalk staring at them with bewildered expressions: it's a *New Yorker* cartoon. For the launch of the boat that would save the company, Wheeler brought in B-list movie stars and Broadway folk and local broadcast personalities. A fifteen-minute program on April 24, 1946, went out over the local affiliate of the American Broadcasting Company, WJZ. Reading a transcript of this old radio show—a copy is in Wes Wheeler's basement in Stamford, Connecticut— you can sense the great giddiness of a country returning to leisure. You can also sense how Wheeler had bet the ranch.

> Good evening, everyone, this is Gene Kirby, speaking to you from the after cockpit or deck of the magnificent new Wheeler Sunlounge, as beautiful a boat as I've ever been aboard or seen. . . . We are in the beautiful new showroom of the Wheeler Shipbuilding Corporation, here at Park Avenue and 46th Street, 241 Park Avenue, to be exact, taking part in the gala ceremonies attending the first postwar showing of the new Wheeler Sunlounge Cruiser, in which I am standing. It's been an exciting afternoon here, with stars of the entertainment, sports and boating world, dropping in to be thrilled by this spectacle of the forty-foot boat on Park Avenue. We're gonna have many of these celebrities talk with us on this broadcast during the next thirteen minutes or so. . . . I could go on talking about this Wheeler Sunlounge for hours, but I don't believe words could

really do it justice. Let me just say it's the dream of anyone from a small boy to the Ancient Mariner.

The Sunlounge didn't work. From court documents: "About December 13, 1946, Wheeler Shipbuilding, by its president, Wesley, filed a petition under Chapter XI of the Bankruptcy Act in which petition it admitted that it was unable to pay its debts." The Cropsey Avenue property had been sold by then. Family members had to be hauled into tax court for alleged "deficiencies in income taxes determined for the calendar years 1946 and 1947" (quoting again from legal documents). The reports of these legal problems made the papers. In the end, the Wheeler family, individually, collectively, corporately, lost to the government and the banks and nearly everyone else. And still they somehow managed to stay in the boat business, or some of the family did.

After the 1946 failure, several of the sons had reincorporated and taken over the property of Dawn Cruisers. There were new display ads in the papers to the effect that Wheeler boats were up and running once again at the foot of Patterson Avenue, Clason Point, the Bronx. But toward the late fifties, into the early sixties, the numbers on the books seemed desperate once more. Family members had quit the business, the eldest son was dead, others were no longer on speaking terms. There had been charges of embezzlement in the civil war that had broken out in the churchgoing and close-knit Methodist family. And yet, if you were reading the papers in this period, you'd form an impression distinctly otherwise. On the second to last day of the 1959 motorboat show, by then being convened annually at the New York Coliseum, the *Times* wrote:

> [T]he National Motor Boat Show, is drawing to a close at the Coliseum. . . . The three Wheelers [sic] brothers, Wesley, Eugene and Robert, who are manning the annual display of the Clason Point, the Bronx, concern with their octogenarian father, Howard [Howard E. was shortly to be ninety], reported sales this week of $1,181,000. This comprised firm orders for one 43-footer at $70,000, three 34-footers at $23,000 each, one 37-footer at $30,000, and forty orders from dealers for spring deliveries.

Within two and a half years, the company was dead, at least in terms of involvement by any Wheeler family members. "In a year that has seen two other boat-manufacturing companies acquire new ownership, still a third boat-building firm has changed hands," the *Times* wrote on August 26, 1961. "The famous Wheeler Yacht Company, now on Clason Point, Bronx, on Patterson Avenue and formerly with yards on Coney Island Creek and during World War II in Whitestone, has been taken over by the Rimbach family of Flushing, Queens." Wheeler had been seized for debt by a father-son firm of certified public accountants with German connections. The new owners said that they intended to keep the marquee name. Howard E. didn't live to see this final insult. He'd died in Florida, five months earlier, on March 23, 1961. But in some sense he had to have known it was all behind him, the wooden, watery dream obsessing him since 1910.

Howard E. died three months before Hemingway died. He is said to have suffered a short final illness, a quick reversal that seems in perfect keeping with his life and the history of his company. The salesman-builder-dreamer-visionary, who'd made it into his ninety-third year, was survived by twenty-one grandchildren and thirty great-grandchildren. In his last years, with his physical health still strong, the emotionally distraught patriarch, only semi-involved with the business, still possessed of his flaring brows and untamed hair and pork-chop sideburns, all of it gone shock white, had tried to distract himself by building a house on a canal in Fort Lauderdale. He'd go to the ocean and sit fully clad on the sand in a porkpie hat and a dress shirt and a tie with miniature Wheeler flags on it. In the same season that some landlubberly CPAs in Queens were getting ready to dispossess the progenitor's business, another distraught man, in Idaho, absent of both physical and mental health, stared at his shotgun. I wonder if Hemingway even knew Howard Wheeler's name.

There's a Bruce Springsteen song called "Atlantic City" with this line: "Well now everything dies, baby that's a fact / But maybe everything that dies someday comes back." So I can report this happy fact: a Wheeler rising yet again. A great-grandson of Howard E.'s, Wesley Wheeler, who is Wes Wheeler's son, and so has pleasure boats in his blood, has sought to remake Wheeler Yacht Company on a small scale at a shipyard in North Carolina.

He was a world-class pack rat and kept all kinds of pieces of paper, uncounted numbers of which have passed down to posterity. These receipts and tickets and bills of sale—from trains, steamship lines, hotels, hardware stores, laundries, bullfights, barbershops, taxidermists, automobile dealerships, heavyweight championship bouts, rod-and-reel outfitters—along with his letters, Western Union telegrams, journals, fishing logs, and list-makings on the front and back of envelopes, translate to manna from heaven for anyone trying to grasp a life. And yet at other times, Ernest Hemingway has a canny way of disappearing from sight, like Houdini doing a trunk trick. Documentation for a significant moment, event, incident, or day just goes missing. Maybe he's having a great horse laugh about it now from wherever he is.

The sad fact is we know next to nothing about the day he went to Cropsey Avenue. I am convinced the date was Thursday, April 5, no matter that others have fixed it as April 4. (You can consult the endnotes for my argument.) Did he and Pauline flag down the first taxi they saw outside Scribners? What time of day—early afternoon? What was the route to Brooklyn? How long did they stay at the boatyard, and with whom did they shake hands there, and what did they do afterward, when they'd motored back into the city? (There had to have been magnums of champagne involved.) Biographer Carlos Baker, in his 1969 pioneering study, *Ernest Hemingway: A Life Story*, has him coming back to his hotel "in a state of rapture"—and who'd want to disagree?

What we do have are some excited Hemingway descriptions of the boat in letters to friends and business associates in the days and weeks and months afterward, and two documents from the company. The first is a postdated purchase order, the second a bill of sale (which shows the date that the balance was paid off, in Key West, on the day after the boat had arrived). The purchase order, dated April 18, 1934, states the price (which ended up changing by a modest amount, reflected in the subsequent bill of sale); provides a description of Pilar's power plant; gives an anticipated delivery date (which wasn't far off from the actual delivery date); and lists the agreed-on modifications and alterations to "one 38-foot twin cabin Playmate cruiser." This one-page document on legal-size paper tells us nothing, though, about the emotional texture of that day in Brooklyn. That you have to make up almost entirely in your mind.

STATES OF RAPTURE

At sea, that first or second summer

I HAVE NO PROOF that the boat-owner-to-be, with Gingrich's wad in his pocket, took the elevator (or maybe the stairs) from Max Perkins's fifth-floor office down to the street and grabbed the first taxi he saw. Maybe he went to his hotel and changed into different clothes. Maybe he went straight to his bank and deposited the check. Maybe he and Pauline, feeling flush, had an expensive lunch on *Esquire*. But what I picture (guided by the maps and hunches of the reference assistants at the Brooklyn Public Library) is that at some soon-after point a cabbie conveyed husband and wife over the Manhattan Bridge, got onto Flatbush Avenue, negotiated around Prospect Park, connected to Ocean Parkway, and then followed that down through the spine of the borough before turning back west and taking several side streets over to Cropsey and then to Cropsey's foot.

Was the old man waiting to greet them when they arrived? He must have been. He loved taking people through, making personal introductions, the more so if they were somebodies. Wouldn't they have hit it right off, the monarch of literature, the purveyor of pleasure boats, both sharing the name Ernest?

As noted, the purchase order has the date April 18 on it, but surely that's the date the document was typed up and mailed to Hemingway in Key West for his executing signature. This piece of paper was the formal sealing of the bargain that had been made two weeks before in person at the ship-yard. The modifications Hemingway ordered for *Pilar* at Wheeler raised the cost by $455 from the $7,000 catalog price that he had fixed in his mind and had been contemplating since Africa. But Hemingway wouldn't know the "final" price (it wasn't) until he received the purchase order in the mail.

ORDER

For: One 38-foot twin cabin Playmate cruiser
Power: One Chrysler Crown reduction gear engine, and troll-ing motor (see below)
Equipment: Complete as per catalogue.
Special Details:
* Gas tanks to be four 75-gallon galv.
* Two copper lined fish boxes to be built in after deck
* Sheer for approximately 10' from transom to be lowered about 12"
* A live fish well to be installed in boat with proper valves for filling and emptying
* A settee to be built on portside similar to one now on starboard side
* Hull to be painted black
* A 4-cylinder Lycoming straight drive engine to be installed for trolling purposes. This motor to be installed as a unit entirely independent of main power plant, and all controls and instruments are to be at steering posi-tion
* Name to be "Pilar" of Key West
* Builder to furnish shipping cradle, pay for insurance, and deliver to purchaser complete afloat at Miami, Florida, for the amount set forth below.

The amount "set forth below" was $7,455. That figure would grow to $7,495 after the purchaser decided—apparently after he'd studied the specs some more at home—that he wanted part of *Pilar*'s cockpit to be enclosed with copper screens. This *was* the final price, and it got reflected on the bill of sale, a one-page document dated May 5, 1934, and executed with a company signature in Key West on May 12, 1934, after the balance was paid, and following the two-day shakedown cruise from Miami.

The bill of sale helps establish the chronology of events. The purchase order of April 18 stated the terms at "$3,000.00 with order." This suggests Hemingway had turned over Gingrich's money—or at least his own bank check—on the day he and Pauline went to the factory and put in the order. (I couldn't find a paper trail.) It's possible Hemingway could have sent the down payment after he put in the order. But that doesn't seem like it would have been sound business practice on Wheeler's part, nor does it seem in keeping with what I know about Hemingway. He liked to pay as he went.

The estimated delivery date was "About two weeks. Subject to steamer sailings." That turned out to be reasonably accurate: by April 18, when the document was typed up and mailed to Florida, the builders at Wheeler had been at work on Hemingway's boat for approximately two weeks; in three more weeks, she'd arrive in Miami.

Roughly seven weeks after the day he went to Cropsey—and roughly two weeks after *Pilar* was in his possession—on May 25, 1934, Hemingway, wrote a letter to Gingrich succinctly describing what he'd just acquired: "The boat is marvelous. Wheeler, 38 footer, cut down to my design. 75 horse Chrysler and a 40 h. Lycoming. Low stern for fishing. Fish well, 300 gal gas tanks. 100 gal water. Sleeps six in cabin and two in cockpit. Can turn on its own tail burns less than three gals an hour trolling and four at cruising speed with the big engine. Will do sixteen with the two motors. The little one will do five hooked up."

He wrote that at the beginning of his first summer with *Pilar*. Toward the end of that fishing season, on September 27, Hemingway described his boat again in a letter to his old boxing and painting and fishing pal from Paris days, Mike Strater:

> This boat is a marvel for fishing. Takes any sea comfortably and can turn on her tail to chase a fish. Can literally turn in her own length. Comfortable to live on board, big galley, five big beds, damned roomy and a wonderful fishing machine. With the reduction gear on the big motor we can troll ten hours a day on less than twenty gallons and can speed up to do sixteen miles when we need to head a fish. Had two of those major chairs made here for 23 bucks apiece.

He wrote that from the Ambos Mundos Hotel in Cuba, on stationery monogrammed with "Atlantic Refining Company of Cuba." He started the letter, "Dear Mike. This note paper doesn't mean old hem has sold out to the oil boys. . . . Just picked it up in the hall."

The man in a rapture came back into Manhattan from Brooklyn. Pauline left for home by rail. For the next several days Hemingway made the rounds of in-laws and close friends and, one wouldn't doubt, New York saloons. He saw the Murphys. He saw Waldo Peirce and Sydney Franklin. (The first was a painter and outdoorsman; the second an American bullfighter from Brooklyn, son of a Flatbush cop, whom Hemingway had celebrated and profiled in *Death in the Afternoon.*)

That Friday night, the sixth, he went to Uncle Gus Pfeiffer's apartment and showed a roomful of guests three reels of home movies from the safari. Sometime that weekend, he saw Edwin Balmer, the editor of *Redbook* magazine. Balmer, a native Chicagoan, fifteen years older, had gone out of his way a decade and a half before to try to help twenty-year-old Hemingway get published. Hemingway was the famous man now, and the veteran editor was the one with awe in his eye and eagerness in his voice, hoping to snare some new piece of Hemingway fiction. Hemingway hadn't forgotten Balmer's earlier kindness, when he was so raw, back in Illinois and up in Michigan. "I am too grateful to you for the trouble you took with me when my stuff was worthless and for encouragement and good advice you gave me," Hemingway wrote from Key West, four months after they'd met in New York, addressing him still as "Mr. Balmer."

Editors of *The Saturday Evening Post* also tried to woo him—they'd be eager to pay $4,000 for a piece of fiction and up to $2,500 for any article he'd like to write.

The wooed man also saw—abortively—a sad, anxious, apparently potted F. Scott Fitzgerald, who'd come up to New York from Baltimore for the publication of *Tender Is the Night*, the novel that both Fitzgerald and Max Perkins were praying would resuscitate a fading reputation. Fitzgerald was not quite seven years from his early death in the screenwriting mills of Hollywood. *Tender*, of course, is the story of an impossibly charmed couple, the Divers, Dick and Nicole, whose lives are charmed no longer. Doctor Diver is mysteriously going down; he's lost some essence of himself, some indefinable emotional vitality. The pride and discipline are draining away. Just as mysteriously, his emotionally ill spouse is regaining her health.

The creator of this beautifully written but structurally difficult-to-follow fable hadn't published a novel since *The Great Gatsby*. That was nine years before. In between had come Zelda Fitzgerald's breakdowns and institutionalizations, and the collapse of the world's economy. The twenties were over, and the poet of the Jazz Age feared in his bones his book would fail. As critic Alfred Kazin once wrote, Fitzgerald had labored over *Tender* while "struggling against a mountain of debt, his notoriety as a drunk and a has-been, and his despair over his schizophrenic wife." So there is a way to think about Fitzgerald's achievement in heroic terms, even if so much of his ruin was self-inflicted. He feared for his book's failure even as the friend and fellow author who'd supplanted him at Scribners—and who'd just bought a new boat, and before whom the supplanted man was apparently behaving like a pathetic drunk—seemed to do little else but succeed, at least insofar as Scott's blurred vision could register. I say "apparently" behaving like a drunk because we have no one else's word for what happened that weekend but Hemingway's, and it is so brief that it's hardly word at all (though there are other accounts of how badly Scott was behaving in general, waiting for his book to appear).

Fifteen months earlier, in January 1933, also in New York, Scott had met Ernest in a drunken state, and that time, too, things had gone badly. Edmund Wilson was present and recorded the night in his journal:

> Scott with his head down on the table between us like the dormouse at the Mad Tea Party—lay down on floor, went to can and puked—alternately made us hold his hand and asked us whether we liked him and insulted us.... Hemingway told him he oughtn't to let Zelda's psychoanalysis ball him up about himself—he was yellow if he didn't write.... When Scott was lying in the corner on the floor, Hemingway said, Scott thinks that his penis is too small.

According to the late critic-biographer Matthew Bruccoli, who wrote acutely about Hemingway and Fitzgerald for decades, the 1933 encounter possibly prompted the following entry from Fitzgerald in his notebooks: "I talk with the authority of failure—Ernest with the authority of success. We could never sit across the table again." But they did, a year later, on that April weekend in New York. What survives is an oft-quoted letter from Hemingway to Fitzgerald, written about eight weeks later, from Key West, after Hemingway had read and made his thumbs-down critical judgments about *Tender*. (By then, however, Hemingway had slowly begun to revise his first opinions of the novel, albeit grudgingly.) Fitzgerald ached to know what Hemingway felt. He had allowed himself almost to grovel for Hemingway's response. "For God's sake drop me a line and tell me one way or another. You can't hurt my feelings," Scott had written on May 10, a month after their meeting. It was a brief note. What he got back was a long letter dated May 28 from a supposed friend who knew he had every psychological advantage; a friend who by turns bullied and lectured and counseled and pitied and forgave him: pure Hemingway. It couldn't have helped matters that the letter contained brilliant and offhand turns of phrase. "I'd like to see you and talk about things with you sober," Hemingway wrote. "You were so damned stinking in N.Y. we didn't get anywhere." (More on that later.)

Tender Is the Night, published at $2.50 a copy and contracted to earn its author thirty-seven-and-a-half cents a copy in royalties, went through three small printings and sold about fifteen thousand copies in all, a disappointment, but not an out-and-out commercial failure, as has often been said. It netted its strapped author an eventual $5,104.65. But what the novel has come to represent in American literature obviously has no price.

Something else apparently happened to Hemingway that weekend, involving a woman who, so far as I know, has never been identified in print. That is close to astonishing considering this long-dead woman's claimed importance—by Hemingway himself—as the principal inspiration for what is one of his two or three greatest short fictions, "The Snows of Kilimanjaro." The extravagantly wealthy Manhattan society matron, according to Hemingway, invited him to tea and presented him with an alluring offer. (You might also call it provocative.) She would foot the bill for a return trip to Africa, apparently whenever he wished, as soon as he wished, as long as she could go along, accompanying Pauline. Carlos Baker says briefly of this incident: "As Ernest later told the story, he considered the lady's offer and politely declined." Baker doesn't say her name, either in his text or notes, and neither will her name be found among his archived papers in Firestone Library at Princeton.

I believe, however, that Hemingway left behind enough clues, in both life and art, some deliberate, some inadvertent, to allow us to identify her. The deliberate ones he inserted into "The Snows of Kilimanjaro," a parable about many things, but perhaps most centrally about the corruptions of wealth, and about what those corruptions have done to a kept man who once saw himself as the possessor of a true writing gift but is now dying bitterly from gangrene on the African plain. The man in the fiction wishes to blame his fate as a failed writer on his rich bitch of a wife, whom he has never loved, not really.

The real-life woman breathing behind this work, or so I believe, controlled a fortune in the neighborhood of $179 million. Hers was one of the greatest and best-known surnames in America. The name stood for money, for sport, for art, for philanthropy, for noblesse oblige. She would have been twenty-three years older than the not quite thirty-five-year-old author who came to call on an April day before he entrained home to Key West. She was a big-boned, middle-aged widow, well preserved, with high flair, with noted cheek, with literary abilities of her own (she'd published a lot of poetry in her youth, some of it quite erotic for its time), whose financier husband had died seven years before of an attack of acute indigestion, leaving her the owner of one of the finest racing stables in America. Her name was Helen Hay Whitney, who'd won the Kentucky Derby, with Twenty Grand three years earlier, and she very much intrigued her guest.

I believe Hemingway both wanted and didn't want us to know her name. It's almost as if Hemingway was baiting his future chroniclers with hints, not to say courting libel in his own day. What a dangerous game, dangerous down to the point of giving the "made-up" woman in your story the same first name as that of the person with whom you'd been to tea in the enraptured afterglow of buying your boat. (According to Hemingway, "tea" was a few knock-backs of whiskey.) When the story was published, Helen Hay Whitney, with all her wealth, would have been very much and litigiously alive. But that's not why the incident is worth pausing to think about. Rather, it's because it goes straight to the heart of Hemingway's method of creation: telling terrific lies about real people, rearranging and transposing and conjoining, so that what he made up was somehow truer than if it had actually happened.

"Stop it. Harry, why do you have to turn into a devil now?" pleads the woman in the story whose name is Helen.

"I don't like to leave anything," answers her husband. "I don't like to leave things behind."

What happened, apparently, is that the widow of Payne Whitney had read about Hemingway in the papers, had seen his photograph. She saw the papers of April 4 in which the author stood beside his wife and held his banded fedora and told the ship-news reporters of his intention to return home to Florida "to work like hell and make enough money so that I can go back to Africa and really learn something about lions."

She sent him a note. Please come by. Hemingway doesn't say where the visit took place. Were just the two of them present? His couched words in subsequent years seem to suggest that. According to Hemingway, his hostess told him there'd be no need to worry about making more money for Africa because she had all the money required, and would be pleased to share some of it, since money was something only to be used well by those who possessed it.

Was she propositioning him with her money? Certainly you could construe that from what Hemingway later said, when he was spinning it all into myth, even though he also seemed to go out of his way in his several written accounts (there are only the written ones to go on, although Hemingway is said to have told the story more than once to friends) to say how "sincere" her offer was, how truly "nice" a person she was. It's possible her offer was no more and no less than what it purported to be on the surface. Where does the truth reside?

Here's Hemingway writing of the incident in a January 1, 1947, letter, a decade after "The Snows" was published, to General Buck Lanham:

> I put what I thought about the very rich (on a very limited scale) into The Snows of Kilimanjaro. Probably told you the story of that one. When I came back from Africa where I had been happier than I ever was in my life some reporter asked me what I was going to do and I said earn enough money to go back to Africa. So that was in the paper and the next day one of the richest (and nicest) women in US. wrote me a note and asked me to have tea (Bourbon was tea) with her and told me she had read what I said in the paper and that I didn't need to make money to go to Africa. She had all the money that was needed for that. There was a lot more to the story but I wrote the Snows as a study of what would or could have happened to me if I had accepted the offer.

Where is that note she supposedly sent to him? I wish I knew.

The dying man in the fiction is filling with gangrene, while his spouse, the good and rich bitch, "this kindly caretaker and destroyer of his talent," waits with him for an evacuation plane from Nairobi. The story takes place over the course of most of one day and that night. The rescue plane doesn't arrive in time. Harry dies because he has done something so simple as to fail to use iodine two weeks previously when a thorn had scratched his knee, as he and his wife had crouched closer with their cameras to a herd of waterbuck. And so he goes in and out of his dreams and deliriums and acid accusations while the rot rises and the hyenas inch closer. "Now he would never write the things that he had saved to write until he knew enough to write them well." The things he'd never get to write are presented in the form of five italicized and intensely poetic flashbacks.

But it's really himself Harry hates. "He had destroyed his talent himself. Why should he blame this woman because she kept him well? He had destroyed his talent by not using it . . . by drinking so much that he blunted the edge of his perceptions, by laziness, by sloth, and by snobbery, by pride and by prejudice, by hook and by crook."

As I have said, there's no question that Hemingway's imagination is conflating and rearranging and transposing and upending several women and different events from his life in the service of his art. He's amalgamating two wives, one a former, one a current, both older than himself, both of whom, in one way or another, in lesser or greater ways, had kept him. At the time he wrote "The Snows," Hemingway had been married just twice. If he'd had four wives by the mid-thirties, perhaps each would have made it in, in one rearranged and unflattering way or another. There are clearly disquieting messages for Pauline Hemingway, but there's no question that Hadley is a rearranged presence, too, and so also Agnes von Kurowsky, the Red Cross nurse for whom the young volunteer ambulance driver had fallen, so headlong, during his recovery from shrapnel wounds in a Milan hospital in World War I.

"The Snows" is the story in which Hemingway makes the famous crack about his friend Fitzgerald and his "romantic awe of them and how he had started a story once that began, 'The very rich are different from you and me.' And how someone had said to Scott, Yes, they have more money. But that was not humorous to Scott." When Fitzgerald saw that passage on page 200 of the August 1936 *Esquire,* he wrote to his friend and asked him to lay off in print. Hemingway apparently wrote a nasty letter back, which we don't have. For republished editions of the story, Hemingway changed Fitzgerald's name to Julian. But there was no chance any serious Hemingway student could have missed the true target of his scorn.

"The Snows" is the fiction in which the verbally abused older wife says, "You don't have to destroy me. Do you? I'm only a middle-aged woman who loves you and wants to do what you want to do." Harry's wife has a great house on Long Island. She has a "well-known, well loved face" from magazines like *Spur* and *Town & Country*. She isn't what you'd call pretty, although Harry does appreciate her face. Harry's wife has a great gift for the bedroom. She is fond of drink. She has a daughter who made a debut. She has survived the tragedy of a husband's early death. Things had commenced easily enough between the widowed Helen and Harry. "She liked what he wrote and she had always envied the life he led. She thought he did exactly what he wanted to. The steps by which she had acquired him and the way in which she had finally fallen in love with him were all part of a regular progression in which she had built herself a new life and he had traded away what remained of his old life."

In the spring of 1934, Helen Hay Whitney was fifty-eight years old. Although she was matronly looking, and had sort of a mannish face, the First Lady of the American Turf, as the sports pages liked to call her, still had piercing eyes and a way with long-trailing leopard-print scarves. She lived at 972 Fifth Avenue, that is, when she wasn't living at the family's 438-acre Greentree, in Manhasset, Long Island. It was one of the greatest houses on Long Island—twenty-one servants, stables, kennels, three grass tennis courts, its own nine-hole golf course, baseball diamond, indoor and outdoor pools, four Rolls-Royces in the garage.

She'd gotten married in 1902, in a Washington wedding attended by Theodore Roosevelt and all of his cabinet and the justices of the Supreme Court. Her father, John Hay, had once been President Lincoln's private secretary, and then President McKinley's secretary of state, and then TR's secretary of state. She was the mother of two adult children, Joan Whitney and John Hay Whitney, better known to the world as Jock.

In the fiction, the woman named Helen had lost her husband "when she was still a comparatively young woman and for awhile she had devoted herself to her two just-grown children, who did not need her and were embarrassed at having her about, to her stable of horses, to books, and to bottles."

When Payne Whitney died, his wife was fifty-one. Their two just-grown children, Jock and Joan, respectively, were twenty-three and twenty-four.

Jock Whitney was destined to become a much more famous Whitney than either his mother or sister. Among other things he was a financier, sportsman, philanthropist, and would become the last owner of the *New York Herald Tribune,* in whose editions of April 4, 1934 (this would have been three decades before Jock controlled the *Trib*), on page 4, Ernest Hemingway's photograph appeared beside this headline: "Stalking Lions Was 'Exciting' to Hemingway."

As for Jock's only sibling: by the spring of 1934, Joan Whitney was Joan Whitney Payson, whose Wall Street husband, Charles Shipman Payson, was waiting for the Wheeler boatyard in Brooklyn to complete his custom-built yacht, already named *Saga*. Not that Hemingway—in whose unfathomable head an idea for a story seems to have grown, following a spot of tea and spirits with a rich society lady—might have even known of that watery connection.

"The Snows" is almost nine thousand words long. Hemingway had first worked on the story in the late summer and early fall of 1935, after a season of great fishing on Bimini with *Pilar*, and had then put it away and didn't come back to it until the spring of 1936 in Cuba. In the early draft, the dying writer's name is Henry Walden, but by the time the story appeared in print the main character is just Harry. If Hemingway had kept to his earlier plan, the initials of his protagonist, no less than those of Harry's wife, would have been HW. (Hemingway doesn't say the name of Harry's wife until late in the piece. Only then does he begin calling her Helen, whereas earlier she'd been "the woman" or "she." It's almost as if he was daring himself. In for a dime, in for a dollar.)

Literary critics have argued for years whether Harry's dream of flight to Kilimanjaro at the end of the story represents moral redemption. But apart from that, and separate from the beauty of the language itself, the real power of "The Snows of Kilimanjaro" is that an author still so young and in seeming control of his life and craft was able so vividly to foresee his own doom. There's a school of critics and biographers who contend that, by the early 1930s—roughly around the time he got his boat—the arc of Hemingway's creative life had crested and was on its way down. I think it's far more complex than that. I think it's a sine curve, like most of our lives.

"The Snows" had been off the stands about a month when Hemingway wrote to MacLeish from Cooke City, Montana: "Me I like life very much. So much it will be a big disgust when have to shoot myself."

But listen again. This is Hemingway writing of the "tea-taking" in a posthumously published 1981 essay in *The Paris Review* titled "The Art of the Short Story." He wrote it in 1959, when the journey to shotgun destruction had reached the point of no exit. As Hemingway himself might have said, 1959 marked the end of the beginning of all that. "The Art of the Short Story" is a terrible piece of writing—mawkish, boastful, truculent, almost incoherent in places. But there are paragraphs less embarrassing and more coherent than others, and that includes those in which he writes about the origin of "The Snows":

> Anyway we came home from Africa, which is a place you stay until the money runs out or you get smacked, one year and at quarantine I said to the ship news reporters when somebody asked me what my projects were that I was going to work and when I had some more money go back to Africa. . . . Well it was in the papers and a really nice and really fine and really rich woman invited me to tea and we had a few drinks as well and she had read in the papers about this project, and why should I have to wait to go back for any lack of money? She and my wife and I could go to Africa any time and money was only some-thing to be used intelligently for the best enjoyment of good people and so forth. It was a sincere and fine and good offer and I liked her very much and I turned down the offer.
>
> So I get down to Key West and I start to think what would happen to a character like me whose defects I know, if I had accepted that offer. So I start to invent and I make myself a guy who would do what I invent. . . . So I invent how someone I know who cannot sue me—that is me—would turn out. . . . I am not gambling with it. Or maybe I am. Who knows? Real gamblers don't gamble. . . . So I make up the man and the woman as well as I can and I put all the true stuff in and with all the load, the most load any short story ever carried, it still takes off and it flies.

How someone I know who cannot sue me. I am not gambling with it. Or maybe I am. Who knows?

I spoke earlier of hints left inadvertently behind, and of clues outside the story. I believe that Hemingway left a telltale sign on an envelope that weekend—Arnold Gingrich's envelope, the one mailed from Chicago with the cash. The word I am referring to is partially obscured by a tiny brown blot. But what I believe is written on its front, along with "Wire Philadelphia" and "go to Museum" and "guy at 11:45 at Scribner," is: "write Mrs. Whitney." The last letter of "Whitney," if it is Whitney, has the little dab of brown. I believe this was Hemingway's notation to himself to drop her a note of thanks for having him over. Thanks, but no thanks, Mrs. Whitney.

No correspondence between Hemingway and Whitney has ever surfaced, or vice versa. Which isn't the same as saying it didn't once exist.

One more clue: *Jock: The Life and Times of John Hay Whitney,* by the
late *New Yorker* writer E. J. Kahn Jr., was published thirty years ago and
is the only full-length biography of Jock Whitney. In its opening pages,
there is this passage about Jock's mother: "Helen herself, though she all
but stopped writing about the time that a third child was born to her in
1912 and died in infancy, never lost her interest in literature. It pleased her
when people like Ernest Hemingway came to call. The story goes that she
told him his works were mostly potboilers, and that he concurred." There
are no endnotes in Kahn's book to pin down when such a visit might have
taken place. But if the real Helen Hay Whitney did indeed have the real
Ernest Hemingway to a private séance in her salon, and if she did indeed
make him an intriguing offer, and if she did indeed tell him that his stuff
wasn't pure literature, and that he should try to do better, did her much
younger guest take it all in with a predatory grin and ingrained midwestern
politeness, knowing that he'd soon enough fix her up in print?

The woman named Helen in "The Snows of Kilimanjaro" is not Helen
Hay Whitney, any more than the dying author named Harry is Ernest
Hemingway. But there are just enough seeming allusions and parallels
and associations to make clear that Hemingway knew exactly what he was
doing and had some part of her in mind and some part of himself in mind
when he sat down and began to tell lies terrifically, almost recklessly, in the
way of a beautiful gambler.

"There was a lot more to the story," Hemingway wrote to Buck Lanham.

But never mind. Because a boat-happy man is on his way home, full of
benevolence and momentary good feeling toward humanity, in the wool
overcoat he can't wait to shed. The April balminess of the Keys is two rail
nights away.

Hemingway departed New York on Monday the ninth, by rail, in the
early afternoon, ticketed through to Key West, but with a stopover in
still-chilly Philadelphia to meet the "scientificos" of an institution that
liked to bill itself as "the oldest continuously operating natural history
museum in the western hemisphere." Their names were Charles Cadwalader and Henry Fowler, and they were high officials of the Academy
of Natural Sciences. (For the rest of his life, Hemingway could never quite
get the name right.) Later that summer, these easterners, stiff in their per-

sonalities and dress, both a good deal older than Hemingway, would take him up on his renewed invitation to go fishing with him in Cuban waters aboard his new boat. It was to be a month's expedition, but in the bargain they'd have something like the adventure of their lives, not to say something for their obituaries some decades hence: that they'd once fished big game with Hemingway.

Homeward on the *Paris*, one day out of New York harbor, Hemingway had answered a letter from Cadwalader, the museum's managing director. The letter had been forwarded to France by Scribners. Cadwalader inquired whether Hemingway might be interested in helping the academy's naturalists conduct research in the Gulf Stream on sailfish, marlin, tuna, and other game fishes, "in order that our knowledge of these fish may be advanced." Hemingway's reply of April 2—one week before he and Cadwalader met—was written in longhand in blue ink, on a small piece of manila stationery folded in half, thus giving him four sides. "On Board" Hemingway wrote over the sepia typescript of "S.S. Paris." He followed with the old flooding graciousness: "I would be very happy to co-operate with you in any way. . . . It would be very interesting to have a complete collection of these fish and determine scientifically which are truly different species and which are merely sexual and age variations of the same fish. No one has studied them as they should be studied."

Hemingway's father, Clarence E. (friends and relatives knew him as Ed, which is how I'll refer to him through the rest of this book), the deeply troubled physician, had an eye for detail, an interest in science and the natural world. He loved microscope slides even as he loved the life of the outdoors. Grace Hall-Hemingway, for all her crushing will, was artistic and refined and highly intelligent. It makes whole sense that the son of Grace and Ed Hemingway would have been drawn to the academy's proposition.

Cadwalader received Hemingway's shipboard reply on the fifth, the day—I feel certain—Ernest and Pauline were at the foot of Cropsey Avenue securing *Pilar*. The scientifico, who hadn't yet been awarded that word as his Hemingway nickname, cabled the author immediately, and then followed it up with his own letter, inviting him to be his houseguest in the Philadelphia suburbs. On the sixth (the day he showed home movies to envious friends), Hemingway cabled back at 1:35 p.m.: CAN COME PHILADELPHIA MONDAY AFTERNOON ENROUTE KEYWEST SAME NIGHT WILL WIRE TIME ARRIVAL MUSEUM MONDAY THANKS INVITATION REGRET HURRY UNABLE ACCEPT HEMINGWAY.

For all his adult life, Hemingway was in love with and expert at the economic art of cable-ese. Economic in more senses than one. The pull and sport of telegram expression, in which the sender seeks to relay as much information as possible in as few words as possible, went back for him to at least 1922, when, having just been elevated to a staff reporter, he was wiring dispatches about the Greco-Turkish war from Constantinople to his penny-pinching bosses at the *Toronto Star*. As the great literary historian Malcolm Cowley once wrote, cable-ese for Hemingway "was an exercise in omitting everything that can be taken for granted," which is another way of understanding how he arrived at his literary method.

On Monday, he sent another telegram from New York to Philadelphia at 11:50 a.m., an hour or so before boarding a train: ARRIVING MUSEUM THREE FIFTEEN HEMINGWAY. Ten minutes later, the cable was logged in at a Western Union office at 2111 Market Street in Philadelphia. (It would have come over the wire within a minute or so—somebody at the receiving end must have been out for a smoke or busy with other wires.) The words were taken off the teletype paper and glued in narrow strips onto a half sheet. The teletype paper was of the cheap, brownish colored, newsprint kind. The half sheet that the words were pasted onto was inserted into a Western Union envelope, and the envelope was hustled over to Nineteenth and Parkway, about six blocks distant, where it was likely handed to a receptionist at the museum's front desk, in return for a casually flipped coin. Somebody would have then quick-stepped the wire upstairs to Director Cadwalader's office, where its throat—the envelope's—would have been slit with a sterling-silver opener in just the way they always do it in old black-and-white movies. That nearly eight-decade-old wire, with its slit envelope, with its logged-in times, with its raised and glue-crusted strip of words on the cheap teletype paper, can still be fingered in a high-vaulted room in the academy's turn-of-the-century library on Logan Square in Philadelphia.

There's no documentary record of what transpired at the museum, but things had to have gone well, judging from subsequent correspondence. Surely the celebrity in their midst would have taken a little time out to look at mounted fish, at beetles and shells and minerals in glass cases, at the recently installed dioramas of wildlife. That would have brought back memories of Saturday boyhood outings to The Field Museum of Natural History on Lake Shore Drive in downtown Chicago.

Late that night: he's hurtling through blackness on the Havana Special, proudest train name of the Florida East Coast Railway. At the end of the nineteenth century, industrialist Henry Flagler invented South Florida as a world-class tourist destination. Then, in the first years of the twentieth, the empire builder sought to polish his myth by erecting the Key West Extension: 157 miles of track, over trestles and bridges and viaducts, across coral and mangrove swamps and limestone outcrops and spits of sand, to the southernmost town in the continental United States. (On a meridian, it lies 755 miles farther south than Los Angeles.) As you go down, the Gulf's on your right, the deep-blue Atlantic on your left. Flagler's Key West Extension, completed in 1912, never made a profit; now, in the mid-Depression, passenger traffic on the line is down to one train a day in each direction. The extension's in receivership. Seventeen months hence—September 1935—the "Railroad that Went to Sea" will be wiped away by a murderous hurricane, and afterward the remains of its bridges, viaducts, and roadbeds would be used by the government to construct highway U.S. 1. By 1938, travelers by land will be able to go to the bottom of the Keys via a two-lane without having to drive their car onto a ferry between some of the islands.

The Havana Special is so named because of the way it connects at the end of the line with six-hour steamer service to Cuba. The waiting boats anchor at the town's old seaport, out at Trumbo Point. The trains chug in along the north side of the island and pull up to the piers alongside the boats. The passengers walk down the steps of their Pullman car and up the gangplank of the Peninsular & Occidental Steamship Company.

The rest of this has to be conjured, the train rolling through the dull electric glow of cities and towns on the other side of a Pullman glass, Perryville and Baltimore and Washington and Richmond and Savannah and Jacksonville and St. Augustine and East Palatka and Daytona and West Palm Beach; the deeply satisfied man going in and out of dining cars and lounge cars with their white-jacketed Filipino waiters and silver-stand ashtrays. By morning light of the second day, Wednesday, April 11, 1934, Hemingway's on the five-hour leg out of Miami: Homestead, Florida City, Key Largo, Rock Harbor, Plantation, Islamorada, Marathon, Big Pine, Pirates Cove, Boca Chica, and, at last, at almost exactly noon, end of the line, end of the continent, the little water-encircled town of 11,600 "conchs." Locals amuse themselves here by cultivating orchids in the forks of trees, tying them in with nylon hosiery, so that their white, twisty, spindly-legged roots will work down the sides of the trees, embedding themselves in the bark like bulged veins in a grotesque leg. Almost all the cigar factories have closed down. The average income is seven dollars a month. Civic government operates like a lazy Latin palace, and the city council will soon declare municipal bankruptcy. A Negro orchestra plays in a downtown hotel every Saturday night and balcony seats at the picture show go for a dime (fifteen cents in the orchestra). Turtle is one of the local delicacies. The evening sky can bleed from pink to red to purple into the deepest azures, and the sailor bars along the wharves are like dank caves of sin. Maybe best of all, mornings are glassy and cool, raked with the sea's quiet. Ernest Hemingway is going to continue to live and work and sink himself deeply into the offerings of the sensual world in this subtropical offshore place for about another five years before upending everything again and expatriating himself and his boat and his not-yet-third wife more or less permanently to Cuba, an even more exotic locale for a writer.

Thirty-six hours after boarding in Philadelphia, he's stepping down from his Pullman car to cheers and a jazz band. *The Key West Citizen* has a reporter on hand to take notes and to get it semi-accurately. The story will be on page one tomorrow, a one-column news feature, alongside a larger piece about FDR having just concluded a fishing trip in the Bahamas.

> Ernest Hemingway, famed writer, adventurer and big game hunter, who was absent from Key West on a big game hunt since last summer, returned home on the Havana Special from New York yesterday and was given one of the most enthusiastic ovations ever accorded a celebrity. Mrs. Hemingway, son, Pat, a group of artists and writers, Mr. and Mrs. Charles Thompson and other Key West friends were waiting with a jazz band to give a vociferous welcome to the returning author. When the train was pulling into the terminals the group gathered near the tracks and just as it was slowing down the band started a thrilling march accompanied by shouts of welcome as Mr. Hemingway stepped down from the Pullman.

After eight months away, with a new boat coming, with a new book brewing, with two of your boys and your wife and John and Katy Dos Passos and half a dozen other friends waiting for you at the bottom of the steps, with live jazz, in the sunshine, you're home.

PART TWO

WHEN SHE WAS NEW, 1934–1935

If I had a boat
I'd go out on the ocean
And if I had a pony
I'd ride him on my boat
And we could all together
Go out on the ocean
Me upon my pony on my boat.

—LYLE LOVETT,
from "If I Had a Boat"

There's a small park in Old Havana called the Plaza de Armas where you can sit on cracked marble early in the morning, before the heat gets up. It's a block from Hemingway's hotel. The park dates from the 1600s. It's shaded by immense trees, with a fountain in the middle. A crew of elderly women, in their blue smocks, their heads turbaned in towels, come to clean the park every morning. They work with stiff brooms and dustpans connected to long swivel handles. They inch along. It might take half an hour to make a ten-by-fifteen-foot section pristine again from the cigarette butts and gum wrappers and condoms of the night before. They'll even comb the dirt around the protruding roots of the royal palms and Chinese banyan trees. They jabber in Spanish.

By nine or so, the park is filling up with locals and tourists—Spaniards who've been disgorged the night before from Iberia 747s, Germans, South Americans. By then, too, the booksellers, who set up their portable wooden stalls every day on the perimeter of the park, are hard at their hawking—postcards of Che, last year's calendars, Marxist manifestos, water-swollen baseball guides from the Cuban pro leagues of, say, 1946, bookmarks of Fidel and Hemingway shaking hands the one time they ever met. It's something like the booksellers along the Seine in Paris. Presently, cartoonists materialize to produce ten-second likenesses with Flair pens on sheets of slick paper, hoping for the illicit Yankee buck in your pocket. Afro-Cuban women in flowing Technicolor garb, with firetruck-red lipstick, are coming over to plant huge stencil-like kisses on your cheek, hoping for the same payday. Vendors selling peanuts in skinny white paper cones are also passing by. The music makers are best, though. With their gourds and guitars and homemade instruments, they begin writhing around, their bodies transforming into S curves. They'll laugh and pull you from your seat and try to get you to dance with them. (It'll make you think of Hemingway, who famously couldn't dance a lick. On the dance floor, he was said to be like a trained bear in a bad circus.) Meanwhile, the old women who've put the park new again have slipped from sight. They must be home, in their airless apartments, rich with Cuban aromas.

The Plaza de Armas is situated almost exactly halfway between the hotel room where Hemingway drove his thoughts and memory-sensations into literature and the docks where he nightly secured his boat, in that first summer of Pilar's history, after he'd brought her over to Havana for the striped marlin runs. If you've ever read anything about Hemingway in Cuba, before his permanent relocation there at the end of the 1930s, you know that the Ambos Mundos was his favorite hotel. The name means "both worlds," new and old, Cuban and Spanish. Room 511 is a Hemingway shrine—maybe Fidel himself wouldn't be allowed to sleep in it. The room is claimed to have the best view and cross-ventilation in the hotel and possibly in the city. It's a large corner room, in a triangle shape. When you take the state-run tour of the room, it'll make you remember all over again what a gift and sense and intuition he had for locating himself in the best symbolic place. The great critic Alfred Kazin once said that. For so many years, that luck and art and intuition held.

In 1934, a room at the Ambos Mundos cost Hemingway two dollars a day. The hotel boasted one hundred rooms—with one hundred baths.

On one side of 511 there are three floor-to-ceiling windows with white louvered shutters opening onto a balcony. The bed, low to the floor, is in an alcove, giving it a protected feeling. There's an old hulking black phone in the room and also a black typewriter on a wooden desk. In the carriage of the typewriter is a blank page. On a wall is a framed photocopy of the purchase order for Pilar. Hemingway couldn't glimpse his boat from his balcony, but he must have been happy knowing she was down there, waiting for what big fish and fight the next day might bring.

He once described room 511 in Esquire.

> The rooms on the northeast corner of the Ambos Mundos Hotel in Havana look out, to the north, over the old cathedral, the entrance to the harbor, and the sea, and to the east to Casablanca peninsula, the roofs of all houses in between and the width of the harbor. . . . You look out the north window past the Morro and see that the smooth morning sheen is rippling over and you know the trade wind is coming up early. You take a shower, pull on an old pair of khaki pants and a shirt, take the pair of moccasins that are dry, put the other pair in the window so they will be dry next night, walk to the elevator, ride down, get a paper at the desk, walk across the corner to the café and have breakfast.

The elevator he speaks of is still operating—a 1926 Otis, with a black wire cage.

Sitting in the Plaza de Armas, on one of the smooth slabs on the south side of the square, resting your back against the iron grillwork, you can look to your left, up Calle Obispo, and make out the entryway to the Ambos Mundos. And if you turn your head in the other direction and crane your neck, you can catch the sun's glare glinting off the harbor between the buildings. You can feel yourself, with some imagination, secretly and privately suspended between the San Francisco wharf, where Pilar slept, and the room where her owner slept and where pages of Green Hills of Africa got shined like stones.

So imagine him, on mornings he didn't go out in the boat, on the fifth floor, behind the white balcony, the windows open, the curtains billowing inward, after having read the papers, after a glass of Vichy water and maybe a tumbler of cold milk and a piece of hard Cuban bread, seated now in a straight-backed chair, working in longhand, the intense concentration, advancing the book he'd begun back in his Key West workroom, right after getting home from Africa. By the time he came over to Cuba in the third week of July, he was three months into it and had more than two hundred manuscript pages. In the beginning he hadn't even known it was a book—perhaps only a long short story. The original sheets of the 491-page handwritten manuscript of Green Hills—the copy that Hemingway gave over to a typist in late 1934—are preserved in a maroon-colored, acid-free slipcase in a belowground room in a special collections library at the University of Virginia in Charlottesville. It's thrilling to untie the ribbon and lift out the first sheet and peer at the several strike-throughs and one circled insertion of his simple, declarative, action-starting, opening sentence: "We were sitting in the blind that Wanderobo hunters had built of twigs and branches at the edge of the salt lick when we heard the truck coming."

Could he have anticipated the degree to which some writers and critics in New York and elsewhere would be lying in wait for this book? Maybe, for he called them—in the book itself—"angleworms." He said that critics were the lice crawling on literature. The following year, fall of '35, he'd go up to Manhattan for the book's launch, only to slink back home in rage when it was clear the reviews were starting to turn against him—the "black ass," Hemingway used to call these rages, which could last for weeks, cause stark-awake insomnia, prompt not just new expressions but seeming promises, guarantees, of self-destruction.

HOME

Key West, 1934 or 1935

THE NEXT DAY he was writing—at least letters, which had always tuned him up, cooled him down. His writing studio was directly behind the main house, and its second floor was reached via a curved iron stairway. It didn't have its catwalk built yet, which, when finished, would run right off the master bedroom.

The house (Uncle Gus Pfeiffer had bought it for Pauline and her husband for $8,000) was one of the grandest in Key West—two-storied, Spanish Colonial, set back from the street, on not quite an acre of ground. It had been built in 1851 from white pine brought in from Georgia and also from coral rocks quarried right on the premises. The house had wide, wraparound verandas, with iron railings on the second floor, giving it a touch of New Orleans. Each side of the house featured four arched windows, with hurricane shutters, and these symmetrical windows were so tall that they were like doors in and of themselves.

Pauline must have been somewhere about. And great-bosomed Isabelle, the cook, and Jimmy, the yardman, and Lewis, who brought whiskeys when the writing was done. At times there were as many as five servants for the four people residing in this house.

Shading the grounds were weeping figs, African tulips, royal poinciana, and an aged sapodilla tree. Not quite two and a half years before, during the move-in, on a December afternoon, the head of the house had taken a spade and planted coconut trees.

"Dear Mr. G.," Hemingway began to Arnold Gingrich on the twelfth, while his townsmen were reading about him on the front page of the *Citizen*. Immediately, he took up the matter of the $3,000 loan/advance. He typed the letter, apparently fast, with his usual erratic spacing (going to single to double and back to single), and occasional uncorrected misspelling, and made-up words, and abrupt shifts of thought. "As I understand it you want to be covered in case I bump off without writing ten articles without a raise in price on same. O.K. If I bump off (which gord forbid) owing you money my wife will pay you what is due." In the seventh paragraph: "I saw Balmer in N.Y. The little skiff is costing 7 G without putting anything in that I really want or any bloody luxuries. But is going to have eveything a fishing machine needs. You better come down sometime this summer and get some use out of it." Two paragraphs from the close: "Never had a better time in my life than in Africa, never felt in better shape in spite of that damned amoebic recurring all the time, and feel so bloody removed from all that literary crap that was getting on my nerves."

The following day, April 13, his second full day back, he wrote a penny postcard to a young fiction writer just out of college named Prudencio de Pereda, who'd been born in Brooklyn, but whose Spanish ancestry traced back to an Old Castilian family. The two hadn't met yet (they'd meet in Spain, several years hence, during the Spanish Civil War, and would collaborate on two important film projects), but de Pereda was hoping that Hemingway might agree to look at some of his work. The postcard writer crammed in the words in a small, neat hand, finishing in the margins. He invited de Pereda down to Key West, suggesting alternatively that they might meet in New York in the fall. "[A]bout looking at stuff I can read it and talk to you about it better than I can write letters as am working like hell and with the best intentions in the world to write a letter always end by not doing it. The only thing, anyway, is to keep on working. If the stuff is good it always comes through."

"Am working like hell" suggests Hemingway was already sweating out, or his subconscious was, the first scenes and sentences of what would turn out to be his next book-length work. Maybe sentences or fragments of sentences had already been written, at least in his head, back there somewhere, in Africa, or on the boat coming home, or in that long weekend in New York.

Within four days of arriving home, possibly even before that, he was back out on the Stream. In the way that it must have felt so good to reclaim the old morning rhythms in the room above the garage, it must also have felt so good for a lifelong fisherman to reclaim the afternoon rhythms of home waters. Once again, we can be grateful for the density of his documentary detail:

"April 15," he wrote, under *Date,* in his fishing log. "Boca grande, Turtle Channel," he wrote under *Waters.* "5 grouper—2 mutton fish—1 mackerel, 1 Jack—1 Barracuda," he wrote under *Catch.*

He made notes of the weather conditions, and listed the names of the people in his fishing party. (John Dos Passos and his wife, Katy, who were renting a large "conch" house at 1401 Pine Street in Key West, were on board on the fifteenth, and so were Pauline, Sara Murphy, and Archibald MacLeish's wife, Ada.) Since Hemingway didn't yet have his own boat, he was enlisting, as he'd done numerous times in the past few years, the boat of his friend Bra Saunders, a lean, leathery, white Bahamian from Green Turtle Cay. Bra knew all the fishing grounds from Bimini to Key West and out to the Tortugas.

"April 17," the fisherman wrote in the log, "gave Bra 6.00 for gas."

Hemingway doesn't note what fishing tackle he was using, but it can be safely assumed that one of the rods and one of the reels he'd reclaimed from storage was his six-inch "Zane Grey" Hardy nickel-plated reel and his No. 5 Hardy hickory rod with the twenty-ounce tip. It was one of his favorite rigs—fast, not too heavy, able to handle very large fish but good enough for medium-size ones as well. Whether you're angling for rainbows in freestone mountain streams or for big game in the Atlantic, a fishing rod has to be sized to its reel, and the same goes for the line, or "thread"—all three components must work together in their improbable, fragile way if they're going to succeed against something so wild and alive and furious at being fooled.

If you turn back to the first page of the prologue to this book, you'll be able to see a portion of the No. 5 Hardy rod and the Zane Grey six-inch reel, with the heavy line going through the first guide. Hardy fishing tackle, crafted in Alnwick, England, was generally regarded as the finest in the business, outfitting serious sportsmen since 1879. This stubby well-wrapped rod was a little under seven feet in length, and Hemingway probably got it at Abercrombie & Fitch in New York City or by mail order from England. We know from his writings in *Esquire* and other places that Hemingway liked using this particular big-game rig when going for marlin off Cuba, and that he often fished it with a trolled cero mackerel bait, on a 12/0 Pflueger swordfish hook and a No. 13 piano-wire leader, with five hundred yards of No. 39 thread. He was inclined to put such technical information into journalistic pieces written for general audiences. Even in his fiction he'll work into the plot his proven method, say, of how to affix live bait to the hook so that it won't come off. This, on baiting up, from "One Trip Across," a tale about fishing and murder and smuggling and Cuba, just out in *Cosmopolitan* magazine, earning him his biggest paycheck to date for a short story: "The nigger came on board with the bait and we cast off and started out of the harbor, the nigger fixing on a couple of mackerel; passing the hook through their mouth, out the gills, slitting the side and then putting the hook through the other side and out, trying the mouth shut on the wire leader and tying the hook good so it couldn't slip and so that bait would troll smooth without spinning."

Maybe it was a reporter's instinct to include such lore, maybe it was damnable perversity, maybe it was an inability to resist showing off to other anglers what he knew. Perhaps he thought to himself: If I bore the ass off of nonfishermen, so what? Real fishermen will appreciate the piece more. The editor of *Esquire* (himself a serious fisherman, as already noted) may not have liked the inclusion of technical details in Hemingway's hunting and fishing letters, but, as we know, Gingrich had promised not to tamper with the copy. (In the letter mailed to New York in which he'd enclosed the $3,000, Gingrich had made sure to tell Hemingway of having cut an upcoming Theodore Dreiser story by one-third—and battling with Dreiser about it, and to boot paying him $50 less than he was paying the uncuttable Hemingway.)

A man both happily and not happily back home, at 907 Whitehead Street in Key West, did this, did that, over the next four weeks, while awaiting the arrival of his new boat, while seeking the storytelling channel of his new book. (On that—Hemingway wrote to Max Perkins on April 30: "Am going well but it is hard going. Have 20 good pages now on a story and 30 bad ones discarded. Some are certainly easier to write than others.") Then, on May 9, in the *Citizen*, page 4, there was this in the Personal Mention column: "Ernest Hemingway left on the afternoon train yesterday and will return to Key West in a launch which he will use for fishing and recreation." Of such small notices are momentous occasions sometimes made.

Just as he was leaving, his nineteen-year-old kid brother, Leicester, known to Hemingway as the Baron, arrived in town with a companion on a homemade sloop. Les Hemingway of Oak Park and Al Dudek of Petoskey, Michigan, had spent the winter in Mobile, Alabama, building a top-heavy sailboat named *Hawkshaw*. The plan was to stop over in Key West for a few weeks, visiting the sibling Les Hemingway barely knew (the two were almost sixteen years apart, and Hemingway was essentially gone from Oak Park when the Baron was still in short pants), and then to work their way down the coast of South America. Early in April, they had started out across the Gulf of Mexico with thirty gallons of fresh water and rations for a couple weeks and also with a one-cylinder backup motor. The Florida leg was supposed to take about ten days in their rudimentary seventeen-footer, but bad storms came up and for something like a week they were thought to be lost at sea. This made the papers. They got within forty miles of Key West before turning back. Regrouping, they started out again across the Gulf and this time made it to Fort Myers, Florida, and from there sailed down to the bottom of the Keys, apparently coming through the front gate on Whitehead on May 8 at about the time big brother and his wife were heading out the door. "Our mishaps had been comical and the fact that we had survived on a diet of wormy water and half a potato a day won genuine admiration from Ernest," remembered the Baron, many years later, in a worshipful, fanciful, factually unreliable, but nonetheless engaging and surprisingly well-written biography-memoir titled *My Brother, Ernest Hemingway*. The book came out within months of the suicide, its lock on best-seller lists assured. I once met Les Hemingway, a hearty and likable and generous and essentially sad man, wreathed in his great Hemingway beard and stomach. We spent part of a weekend together. The meeting was entirely by chance, on the island of Bimini, a few years before the Baron, like the sibling he idolized and never quite got enough back from, shot himself with a borrowed pistol.

In Miami, on the morning of the ninth, Hemingway met his boat and the Wheeler representative who'd accompanied *Pilar* south on a steamer. Two days later, *Pilar* strutted into her new home port for the first time, a vision of fresh paint and gleaming varnish. They came down via the old Hawk Channel, with Captain Bra doing most of the piloting through the markers, but with the new owner getting his hand on the wheel, too.

Assembled that afternoon on the docks at the largely deactivated Key West Navy Yard was another small crowd of waving and horn-tooting friends and family, including the Baron, Pauline, and the two children. (She, or her husband, had apparently decided it was best not to be part of the tryout trip, and so she'd returned home by land.) The *Citizen* wasn't there to cover this Hemingway arrival (or at least there wasn't a story in the paper the next day), nor was there a jazz band. The boat herself was the jazz.

The next day he paid off the balance of $4,495. Inked across the typed bill of sale was the signature of the boatyard official who'd helped out on the shakedown cruise and was now handing over *Pilar* to her owner before heading back to Brooklyn by rail: "Rec. May 12. Rep. Charles Johnson. Wheeler Shipyard Inc." Hemingway had his boat.

Over the next few weeks would come uncounted hours of fishing and cruising and picnicking on the open water aboard what must have seemed the shiniest prize in town—at Cosgrove shoal, out at the Western Dry Rocks, in the kingfish flats above Little Sand Key. Many guests would be invited aboard. Many noses would get coated with the zinc oil and end up getting sun-cracked anyway. Many cases of beer would bead with sweat against diamonds of melting ice kept in the shade of the cockpit or down in the galley. The trays of deviled eggs, the hampers of baked chicken, the stacks of fried yellowtail sandwiches slathered with mayo and onions (kept fresh in double thicknesses of wax paper) would get consumed by the ravenous salt-air eaters, trying to balance paper plates in their laps while sitting in wicker chairs on the afterdeck or on the long cushioned seats on either side of the cockpit. (The afterdeck chairs, brought from home as makeshift fishing chairs, slid their occupants all over the afterdeck as the boat bucked the swells.)

"Mr. H. is like a wild thing with his boat," Pauline will say in a letter to Sara Murphy on May 17, when *Pilar* has been in his possession for eight days. "I see him at ten minute intervals, hours apart and from notes on doors saying why he cant get home until 3 instead of 12:30."

Six days later, a Jesuit priest, Father McGrath, down from Miami, who has more or less invited himself aboard for an afternoon's fishing, hooks into a record Atlantic sailfish in a place called the Ten Fathom Bar, about eight miles from Key West. But a dockside angler more than an oceangoing one, the priest can't land the fish because of bad arthritis in his left arm. So *Pilar*'s captain takes over and finishes the job, in forty-odd minutes of slacking and pumping the line, until the defeated beauty is gaffed and hauled over the stern by several hands in all its oily slickness. That night, the prize is officially weighed in front of eight witnesses on tested scales at Charles Thompson's icehouse at the foot of Margaret Street and then sliced open: a female, 119½ pounds in weight; 9 feet, ¾ inches in length. She's round and thick, thirty-five inches in girth, beautifully proportioned, not slab-sided like the big sails of the Pacific. But the largest sailfish ever known to be caught on a rod and reel in the Atlantic Ocean will have to have an asterisk beside it in record books of the day: hooked by Thomas J. S. McGrath of the Southern Jesuit Mission Band, landed by Ernest Hemingway of Key West. It's a coclaiming, which really is no claiming at all.

Archibald MacLeish, to mention only one long-standing if wary friend and fellow athlete, will come on board a handful of times in these first days, only to end up in a row with *Pilar*'s captain, provoking the captain to say of the poet in a letter to their mutual artist friend Waldo Peirce: "He's gotten, between ourselves . . . a goddamned bore. Righteous, fussy, and a bloody bore. Strange mixture of puerility and senility. What the hell do American writers turn into?"

Yes.

The Maestro—that was Arnold Morse Samuelson's Hemingway-bequeathed nickname, which got shortened soon enough to the Mice. During dead calms on Pilar, the quiet evening drifts of that first (and largely disappointing) summer and fall of the fishing, when most of the marlin trophies had seemed to desert the Stream, or hang at the bottom, the Mice used to take out his battered violin and send Mozart and Beethoven out across the waves, not so well, but with great exuberance.

Arnold Samuelson was the twenty-two-year-old aspiring writer and self-styled Hemingway character who tore from a Minneapolis newspaper Hemingway's photograph (yes, the one at the rail of the Paris), stuck it in his rucksack, and rode his hitchhiking thumb and the top of boxcars straight into his hero's life and right onto his new boat. For something like nine months, from late spring of 1934 to late winter of 1935, the Mice got to serve as the night watchman and deckhand and writing acolyte at the master's knee, making a dollar a day to boot.

For the bulk of the nearly five decades he lived on the earth after stepping off Hemingway's boat, Samuelson, who'd once so badly wished to make it as a serious fiction writer, lived a socially outcast existence on the edge of a little jackrabbit crossroads in Coke County, Texas, called Robert Lee. Found among his scattered possessions, upon his death, was a three-hundred-page typed nonfiction manuscript about his long-ago time with Hemingway. Most of it he had drafted on Pilar, under Hemingway's guidance. But every now and then, through the decades, he would take out the fly-specked pages of his memoir and look at them by lamplight, adding, subtracting, rewriting, shifting around sentences and paragraphs, wondering—as he once wrote in a scrambled note to himself that was discovered by his family after his death—if he could turn the work into literature. That's only one of the sadder ironies—it was literature. He just could never see it.

I can't really say, even now, why, nearly from the start, I felt myself pulled toward this eclipsed and footnoted and shadowed life, although I suspect the pulling must have had something to do with a daughter's brief and eloquent preface to her father's posthumously published and largely ignored work (which came out in 1984, three years after Samuelson was dead), but also something to do with the photographs themselves. You see, there's something so appealing in that lank, boyish, midwestern face, in that bony frame, in the way bars of Gulf light swath across his back as he sits at Pilar's stern in her virgin newness, holding one of the deep-sea rods, feet propped against the live-fish box, long-billed swordfisherman's hat pulled low, nose coated with coconut oil, turning at this instant to share in some joke or inside story with his literary idol, who's seated right beside him. Who could be so fortunate?

But of course the gypsies have that curse: may your fondest fortune come true.

Other book-length chroniclers of Ernest Hemingway have either ignored Arnold Samuelson's life altogether or else dealt with it in not much more than a couple of dismissive (and often inaccurate) paragraphs. But might a deeper look at his story reveal important Hemingway truths from oblique angles? "Tell all the Truth but tell it slant" is the way Emily Dickinson started a poem. "If you go, it'll happen," an old mentor from The Washington Post used to say. So I went, in search of the Maestro.

SHADOW STORY

Ernest and Arnold, summer 1934

He could be chilling in the pulpit and indescribably cruel in his personal life and he was certainly the most bitter man I have ever met; yet it must be said that there was something else in him, buried in him, which lent him his tremendous power and, even, a rather crushing charm.

—JAMES BALDWIN, writing of his father, in *Notes of a Native Son*

I was just somebody else, some stranger, and my whole life was a haunted life, the life of a ghost. I was halfway across America, at the dividing line between the East of my youth and the West of my future, and maybe that's why it happened right there and then, that strange red afternoon.

—JACK KEROUAC, *On the Road*

Any man's life, told truly, is a novel . . .

—ERNEST HEMINGWAY, *Death in the Afternoon*

WITH HEMINGWAY: A YEAR IN KEY WEST AND CUBA begins with
an importuning knock at the front door of 907 Whitehead Street. The
"importuning nobody" (as a Hemingway essayist in an academic journal
once wrote of Arnold Samuelson, accurately if a little meanly) has just
come through the iron gate and up the walk and past the brown patches in
Hemingway's front yard. He's swallowing his spit, shifting from one foot
to the other, twisting his woolen hobo's cap like a man trying to get water
out of a rag. Keep him here for a moment on Hemingway's doorstep, with
his arm raised, in the dozen or so heartbeats between his knock and the
crowding of the other side of the doorway with a sizable shadow. Think
of Hemingway coming toward his front door from somewhere inside the
house, wondering who the hell this is. Think of the knocker fighting off
the urge to do a pivot and hotfoot it to the curb.

When exactly is this knock? The author of *With Hemingway* places
the moment in late April 1934—but he's incorrect. Samuelson isn't really
good at pinning down dates, and he's also prone to mangle certain easily checked facts and names. (At other times, he gets the chronologies
and smaller facts exactly right.) But that's okay; he's far more interested
in—and very good at—rendering the texture of experiences, not least
his own.

It's really toward the end of the first week of May, two or three days
before the Wednesday news item in the Personal Mention column of the
Citizen that Hemingway has departed on the train to Miami the day before
to collect his new fishing machine. This would mean it's either Sunday or
Monday, May 6 or 7, 1934. Hemingway himself touched on the moment
in a semi-famous piece in *Esquire* in 1935 titled "Monologue to the Maestro" (more on this later). He said the knock occurred right after he'd gotten back, on May 5, from a quick reconnaissance trip to Cuba. He'd gone
over to politically turbulent Havana on the ferry with John Dos Passos to
watch the May Day festivities, and to do some casual fishing, and to check
personally on the upcoming summer's marlin prospects, and, not least, to
secure the necessary forms and bureaucratic signatures for a good docking
site when he'd return with his boat in July. Dos and his wife were leaving
within the hour for the north, and Hemingway wished to see them off at
the Key West rail depot. There were some letters he needed to get written
and in the mail. And goddamn it here was somebody at the door. "[T]he
road brings in every son of a bitch I ever knew or who ever read a line I
wrote," Hemingway once said in a letter.

This interrupter—who has written many first lines of would-be novels and stories, all of them, he's now decided, being bunk and junk—could probably pass for somebody still in his teens. He's all elbows and big feet and has a former farm boy's blunt hands. He's about six foot and weighs maybe 175 dripping wet. He's got a "porcupine hair-cut" (as Hemingway will say in *Esquire* the following year). Mostly, he's got a look about him of extreme earnestness and seriousness.

Last night, as the night before, he lodged at the Key West city jail, where the mosquitoes were big as bombers. On his first night in town, he'd tried sleeping on the rough planking of the turtling dock, lying on his back, against his knapsack and violin case, to ease the pressure on his hip bones. A night cop had shaken him awake and taken him off to the hoosegow, where he promised him he'd be safer and even have a cot, or at least a hammock. He hadn't mentioned anything about the bugs.

This stranger, who's been wandering in America for much of the last two years, is down to a squashed loaf of bread and about eight bucks. Ever since he got out of college in the spring of 1932, he's been living on not much more than his wits. He's worked as a cub at a Minnesota newspaper, cut alfalfa in Iowa, slept all night in Los Angeles movie theaters, barbered with a pair of hardware-store shears. He's hitched and walked and ridden rails in his lace-up lumberjack boots with a fellow college-educated "tramp" (it's how he generally refers to himself) and together they've made it through the Pacific Northwest, down into Texas, across the middle border. He's awakened in his bedroll to April snowfalls of cherry blossoms in the state of Washington, speared salmon near the Pacific Coast with the bent-back tines of a pitchfork, panned for nuggets in sluicing California streams, decorated his Christmas tree (fetched illicitly from a nearby national forest) with cigarette butts and the tinfoil of gum wrappers, made himself into a half-assed roofer and a not-at-all-bad carpenter. He has set it all down in his notebooks, hoping to convert the base metal of raw sensory American experience into literary gold.

Some of it, in fact, has already been penned into long-winded journalistic travel accounts and mailed back to the *Minneapolis Tribune*, where he'd worked on and off through college—running copy down to the printers, subbing for the beat reporters, filling in on "late cops." (It's an old newspaper expression, meaning that you hang around police headquarters to sop up whatever local crimes get logged onto that night's blotter.) The *Trib*, which didn't give him a full-time job after college, has published his road stories in an occasional Sunday series, headlining them "Letters from a Forgotten Boy." So far, he's done nine pieces, and the editors have paid him a total of fifteen bucks. He knows they're just Depression filler, nothing like the serious writing he feels called to do.

College was the University of Minnesota. He'd concentrated in journalism, hated it all the way through, refused formal graduation and a degree—a life of contrariness was already showing itself. On June 20, 1932, in a little hard-backed, marbleized notebook, the adventurer-to-be had set down the first journal entry of his newly escaped life: "Never have I spent my days in greater tedium. Graduation exercises took place without my participation. The fee is $10. The money will take me farther bumming than will the diploma. The only ambition that was predominant during the windup of school was to get out of town, never to view the interior of a university of any kind again." He was already on the road when he recorded that. His older brother Sam—a Twin Cities doctor, who'd removed his tonsils free of charge as a kind of graduation gift and then shoved a few bucks in his pocket—had dropped him off on the outskirts of Minneapolis. There were a lot of hitchhikers that day, but none able to score rides in the way he scored them: by taking out his violin and turning his back to the oncoming traffic and starting to saw away. For instance, there was that farmer named Morica Rashin, from Detroit Lakes, Minnesota, whose curiosity got the best of him—he slowed up, put it in reverse, backed up, and apparently said something like, *Get in, bub.*

This stranger—who was raised in a frontier-like place called White Earth, North Dakota, youngest child of severely religious immigrant Norwegians—has been spending eighteen-hour days of late at his writing. This past winter, having returned to Minneapolis, where much of his family now was, he'd toiled from the moment he got up until long past dark, forgetting sometimes even to eat, falling into bed exhausted only to wake up again and go over to the desk and pick up the sheets and see how truly bad his cooled-off prose was. So far he's written something like two unpublished novels and twenty short stories, and in the worst of his despair, about three weeks ago, he'd come across Ernest Hemingway's story in *Cosmopolitan*, "One Trip Across." It was the most convincing piece of literature he'd ever read. There wasn't a fifty-cent word in it. He felt himself right there, on Harry Morgan's charter boat, in the glow of the binnacle light, off Havana, when the whole smuggling plot turns foul. That scene where Harry, a decent guy driven to desperate acts because of money, gets Mr. Sing down on his knees and then uses his thumbs to crack open the guy's talk box from behind—hell, he could hear that crack coming straight out of the ink on the printed page. And so an educated tramp in a rented room in unthawed Minnesota had begun to think, dream, that if he could just have a conversation with Ernest Hemingway about the craft of fiction, even if it lasted five minutes, he might yet have a fighting chance with his own bad stuff. Which basically explains why and how he's come to be fidgeting here on Hemingway's doorstep in this moist morning heat; why and how he's made his own trip, not across but down, something like eighteen hundred miles, on his luck and spit, to the dividing line between the east of his youth and the west of his future.

A few days ago, on the roof of a middle boxcar, his rags turning sooty with coal smoke, but feeling kingly and free as air, he'd looked down over the side and saw the sun lighting the clear shallows of the ocean floor. Schools of fish were sunning themselves. He'd watched their dark shadows. He'd wondered if they were sharks. He was on his rackety perch forty feet above the Atlantic and the Gulf, and the trainmen weren't after him with their headache sticks. After eighty miles or so, as he would later write in his memoir, "I could see a patch of land floating on the water up ahead. It looked bigger than the other keys and there were buildings on it, far off but coming closer." He'd made it to Hemingway's town.

How does he know Hemingway's even in town? He doesn't. What he's going on is a photograph from a newspaper along with the accompanying story that quoted the subject of the piece as saying he was on his way home to Florida to start a season of intensive writing. It's enough.

There's one more fact, a pretty sad one, you need to know about Arnold Morse Samuelson's life just now. On October 16, 1931, Samuelson's older sister—she was twenty-four and her name was Hedvig, though everybody called her Sammy—was murdered, along with another woman, in her lounging pajamas in a female love triangle gone wrong. It happened in Arizona. Sammy was shot in the head at close range, and her hacked-apart body was stuffed into a trunk and a suitcase and shipped to Los Angeles.

The little brother, in his last year of college, was working for his keep in a Twin Cities fire department barn, and he was also moonlighting for the *Tribune*. He was in a corner of the newsroom, hunched over a story, when the first late-night dispatches began to come in. "News Wires Tell Student Reporter His Sister's Slain" was a headline the next day, followed by this subhead: "You'll Want Pictures, I Suppose, He Says to City Editor As He Stifles Grief." From its first moment, the tabloids and even America's mainstream press couldn't get enough of the story.

Minot was the closest North Dakota city to the Samuelson farm. The day after the bodies were found, the *Minot Daily News* sent a reporter out to White Earth to try to speak to Sammy Samuelson's parents. The reporter's paper had already published its first story, with "Mutilated Bodies" in the headline. The reporter knew that pieces of Sammy had been put into one of the trunks and other pieces of her into the suitcase—but he couldn't bring himself to say that to seventy-one-year-old Anders Samuelson and fifty-nine-year-old Marie Samuelson. It was the family pastor, from the next town over, who'd delivered the news to the parents that their daughter was dead, but he, too, couldn't say the worst: "A representative of the News, calling at the Samuelson home in company with the Stanley minister, was pressed for further details, but the parents still are unaware that their daughter's body had been dismembered and mutilated by the slayer."

The person eventually convicted of this double homicide was a soft-spoken, five-foot-two, blue-eyed, one-hundred-pound woman named Winnie Ruth Judd. All around the slaying have swirled unproven tales of adultery, abortion rings, narcotics, lesbianism.

If you understood your vocation as that of a serious writer, and if one of the hacked-apart bodies in a foul-smelling metal trunk and leaky suitcase that got opened and peered into on a train platform in LA by railway dicks holding handkerchiefs to their noses, if this corpse turned out to be your own sibling, wouldn't you have to face it in a piece of writing, fiction or otherwise, if not now, someday?

On October 16, 1931, Ernest Hemingway and his much-pregnant wife were newly arrived in Kansas City by train, where they planned to wait out the birth of their second son. (Gregory Hancock Hemingway was born, by cesarean, on November 12, 1931.) Fourteen Octobers before, in 1917, an unknown and impecunious Ernest Hemingway, newly graduated from Oak Park High, had come to this city and signed on as a reporting cub at *The Kansas City Star.* He'd worked at the paper for seven months, a crucial apprenticeship to the writer he'd become. His old paper, which Hemingway would almost certainly have been reading as Pauline's time neared, put the murder on page 1 on October 20. The following day, the *Star* devoted four columns to it on page 3.

Thoughts not only of birth but death as well would have been much on Hemingway's mind, for the thirty-two-year-old author was just then working on the final chapters of his documentary-like bullfight book, *Death in the Afternoon.* There were two chapters left to write, plus a glossary and some back matter, but before going ahead, he wanted to tighten what he'd already written. Near the end of chapter 18 in the finished work, Hemingway writes of making the mistake of telling his three-year-old son

Patrick about the gory death of a small bullfighter that he'd recently witnessed in the ring.

"I don't like it that he's dead," the boy said.

The next day he said, "I can't stop thinking about that man who was killed because he was so small."

"Don't think about it," I said, wishing for the thousandth time in my life that I could wipe out words that I'd said. "It's silly to think about that."

"I don't try to think about it, but I wish you hadn't told me because every time I shut my eyes I see it."

"Think about Pinky," I said. Pinky is a horse in Wyoming.

In chapter 19, which Hemingway worked on while awaiting his son's delivery, and while Winnie Ruth Judd was helping to sell newspapers in America, the word "kill" or "killed" or "killing" occurs seven times in the first three sentences.

Arnold Samuelson was just one of maybe five hundred people, famous and otherwise, who stepped down onto Hemingway's boat in the twenty-seven years he owned her. In very many of those first photographs aboard *Pilar*, he appears so uncomplicated and carefree. Photographs lie, or often do. Samuelson couldn't really have been those things—or, better said, he had to have been so many other things in addition. There must have been deep wells of grief and melancholia inside him, not unlike the nearly lifelong melancholy stuffed down inside the man into whose employ he'd lucked himself. At nineteen, in Minnesota, on a late night in October, Hemingway's eventual apprentice had to have suffered an acute shock to his central nervous system. Anyone who knows anything about the life of Ernest Hemingway would know of the even greater shock, to both his body and spirit, that he suffered, on July 8, 1918 (it was thirteen days before his nineteenth birthday; he'd quit the *Star* a few months previous), shortly past midnight, at the Piave front, in a forward listening post near a village called Fossalta, while passing out tobacco and chocolate bars and other canteen supplies to Italian troops under the auspices of the American Red Cross. It was an Austrian trench mortar shell, and when the shrapnel from the canister exploded into his legs and scrotum, it was as if he was wearing rubber boots filling with warm water.

The screened double doorway at 907 Whitehead has just filled with Ernest Hemingway's bulk. From *With Hemingway:*

[H]e came out and stood squarely in front of me, squinting with annoyance, waiting for me to speak. I had nothing to say. I couldn't recall a word of my prepared speech. He was a big man, tall, narrow-hipped, wide-shouldered, and he stood with his feet spread apart, his arms hanging at his sides. He was crouched forward slightly with his weight on his toes, in the instinctive poise of a fighter ready to hit. He had a heavy jaw and a full black mustache, and his dark eyes, which were almost closed, looked me over the way a boxer measures his opponent for the knockout punch.

It was obvious he needed no bouncer to keep tramps off his property. He could handle that job himself.

"What do you want?" he asked.

"I bummed down from Minneapolis to see you," I said, very ill at ease.

"What about?"

"I just want to visit."

You can almost guess what happens next. Far from getting clocked, the nobody seems to have struck some kind of unwitting and almost instant chord. But he's busy now, Hemingway says—could you come around tomorrow about one thirty? The door-knocker starts to step backward.

"Wait. I'll drive you downtown."

Oh, he can walk.

" 'I was going down for the mail anyway,' " he said, falling into step beside me. " 'Wait a minute. I forgot my keys.' "

In the Model A Ford roadster (it's bright yellow, with oaken running boards), there is already talk about writing, advice about writing. Even advice about life. The man at the wheel keeps peppering the nobody with questions. Where would Samuelson like to be let off? How's he fixed for dough?

We shook hands and I watched him drive off to the post office. He left me with that damned marvelous feeling you can have only once in a lifetime if you are a young man who wants to become a writer and you have just met the man you admire as the greatest writer alive and you know instinctively he is already your friend.

The next day. E.H. is in bedroom slippers and khaki pants, drinking whiskey and going through *The New York Times*. He's leading the nobody to a shady spot on the north porch. The hobo takes a seat in a padded wicker chair. He watches the peacocks pluming their tails out by the fence, sticking their heads through the bars, trying to get out. Again, Hemingway offers fatherly-cum-brotherly writing counsel.

"The most important thing I've learned about writing is never write too much at a time," Hemingway said, tapping my arm with his finger. "Never pump yourself dry. Leave a little for the next day. The main thing is to know when to stop. Don't wait till you've written yourself out. When you're still going good and you come to an interesting place and you know what's going to happen next, that's the time to stop. Then leave it alone and don't think about it; let your subconscious mind do the work."

They go up to the studio. It's got a tile floor and shuttered windows and its own bathroom and shelves of books. Hemingway takes a seat at a big antique flat-topped desk in the middle of the room. He's writing on a sheet of paper.

"It's hard for me to tell, but you seem to be serious," E.H. said at last. "Seriousness is one thing you've got to have. Big-time writing is the most serious business there is, and imaginative writing is the peak of the art. Another thing you've got to have is talent. Some people never can write fiction. What would you do if you found out you couldn't write fiction?"

"I don't know. How can a man know if he's got talent?"

"You can't. Sometimes you can go on writing for years before it shows. If a man's got it in him, it will come out sometime."

The sheet Hemingway has been writing on contains a personal reading list—the essential books any serious fiction writer must read, works by Joyce, Flaubert, Stephen Crane, Stendhal, Tolstoy, Henry James. Hemingway hands it over. The bottom of it is signed "Ernest Hemingway." From a shelf Hemingway pulls down a collection of Crane's stories and a personal copy of *A Farewell to Arms*. He hands them over, but says he'd like them back, especially *Farewell*, since it's his last copy of that particular edition.

What explains the way Hemingway took to him—was it some vision of his own earlier, Nick Adams, alter-ego, midwestern self? Perhaps. More likely, it was the seriousness that won the hobo the day, without his quite knowing it. Hemingway suggested as much a year later, in *Esquire,* in "Monologue to the Maestro," which is a piece far less about Samuelson than it is a treatise on the craft of writing, with Samuelson employed as the organizing principle and gently mocked storytelling foil. Hemingway never identifies Samuelson by his real name, but "Monologue to the Maestro," published in October 1935, about eight months after he'd departed *Pilar* and Hemingway's company, assured the luck-struck boy of his wee place in American literary history.

Hemingway tells the reader of how he'd been "both flattered and appalled" at the prospect of someone having come all the way from Minnesota to ask "a few questions about writing." He writes of how he gave Samuelson his nickname and his dollar-a-day job. He pokes fun at his apprentice's slow-footedness and general clumsiness, calling him a "calamity" at sea. He speaks of his "incurable tendency toward sea-sickness and a peasant reluctance to take orders." But Hemingway also says:

> He was a tall, very serious young man. . . . It seemed that all his life he had wanted to be a writer. . . . He wanted to be a writer and he had good stories to write. He told them very badly but you could see that there was something there if he could get it out. He was so entirely serious about writing that it seemed that seriousness would overcome all obstacles. . . . I thought, perhaps, that this was modesty until he showed me a piece he had published in one of the Minneapolis papers. It was abominably written. Still, I thought, many other people write badly at the start and this boy is so extremely serious that he must have something; real seriousness in regard to writing being one of the two absolute necessities. The other, unfortunately, is talent.

The day after Hemingway loans him a personal copy of *A Farewell to Arms,* the tramp is at the door again. His intention is to drop off the books (he has read them, or at least read *in* them, overnight) and to thank Hemingway and then to hop a freight north—he cannot possibly expect any more largesse. Hemingway is down getting the mail and the papers on Duval Street. Pauline asks him to wait. Shortly, Hemingway appears.

" 'I've got a boat being shipped from New York. I'll have to go up to Miami Tuesday and run her down and then I'll have to have someone on board. There wouldn't be much work.' " Would Samuelson like the job?

" 'That would be swell.' "

He can work on his writing when he isn't scrubbing a deck or standing watch. He'd be fishing, serving a seaman's apprenticeship, learning both craft and trade.

> "Of course, I don't know you very well, but you seem to be the sort of person that can be trusted. Do you drink?"
> "Not much. Just a little moonshine when I was a kid."
> "That's good. The owner is the only person who can get drunk on board a boat."

There's something endearing about the dialogue corniness of *With Hemingway*—in and amid its literate cunning. Much of the voice sounds just like the voice of that former rube of the middle border, living in Paris with his wife and baby boy, who wrote excitedly in 1924 to Gertrude Stein and Alice B. Toklas with the news of having finished a long fish story set in Michigan and "trying to do the country like Cezanne" and how he "made it all up," and how "it is swell about the fish, but isn't writing a hard job though?"

Hemingway drives him downtown to the jail to get his stuff. He advances him ten dollars against future wages. A cot is fixed up for him in the garage. Isabel the cook brings him a meal that comes out on a tray. Is he living in some kind of hobo dream?

A few days later, Friday afternoon, May 11, Hemingway's boat struts into town, and Arnold Samuelson is at the Key West Navy Yard, along with some of the other greeters, stepping aboard his new home:

> I took my shoes off in order not to scratch the varnished deck. . . . The cockpit was twelve feet wide and sixteen feet long with leather-cushioned bunks on each side; the cabins below . . . [had] two compartments with bunks to sleep six people. . . . She was a fine boat, the most valuable property E.H. owned, and I began to think the responsibility of taking care of her might be too big for me, a young fellow who had never been on board a ship before.

If you were born in a sod hut, and were raised on a homesteading wheat farm in the upper Midwest, and had never been to sea, and had ridden horses bareback to school, wouldn't you think to call the thirty-eight-foot shiny new floating thing that you'd just stepped down into a "ship"?

The crowd goes off. The new hire is there alone. That night "I had a soft bunk with clean sheets and a clean blanket, and the cool salt air came through a screen that kept out the mosquitoes. In the morning, I dove off the stern and had a swim between the piers in the clear green water." These are Samuelson sentences, but you can instantly hear the Hemingway echoes. It's how any serious-minded writer learns to write—by imitation.

In the morning, Hemingway's roadster "with the sun shining through the block of ice on the rear bumper" rattles over the rough planking of the dock. Captain Bra arrives. Pauline and Charles and Lorine Thompson will be aboard. Here's Archie MacLeish in his big cotton athletic sweater. They're all handing down chairs and the boxes of beer and the lunch baskets and the mullet bait wrapped in yesterday's *Citizen*. The men are aiding the women aboard. Now they've cast off and are purring past the town. Hemingway's at the wheel. "The sea was green and flat over the reef and the boat ran along smoothly"—again, you know where that sentence found its imagistic, economical stroke.

> "It's a bloody marvelous day, isn't it?" he said to Pauline.
> "It's lovely," she said.
> "How do you feel, Mummy?"
> "Fine. I couldn't feel any better."
> "Are you quite comfortable?"
> "This is splendid."
> "You won't get seasick today, Mummy. It'll be even better when we get out past the tide rip."
> "Oh, I think this is grand."

And right from the first, the master seems to be paying special attention to his pupil, pointing out markers, explaining why the colors are different on the water: " 'That's the edge of the stream, that darker water. See that glossy path? That's made by the current flowing against the tide from the reef. It's filled with patches of seaweed.' "

That afternoon, hundreds of dolphins appear. Hemingway, almost frantic, is throwing out teasers and bait to try to keep them close to the boat. "When there was no mullet left, he threw out pieces of newspaper wiped in fish slime and they struck at the floating papers." But as quickly as the dolphins come, they are gone. This is the first recorded day of fishing in *Pilar*'s history: Saturday, May 12, 1934, documented by a writer whom virtually nobody in America has ever heard of.

One more recording. It's high summer; *Pilar* and crew have come to Cuba. Things are still very new for a landlubber, but in another way not so. Pauline has ridden over on the ferry from Key West to join her husband for a brief stay. The day before, with his wife aboard, Hemingway had reeled in a shark—a "big shark, yellow and ugly-looking in the water, uglier than anything else in the sea, giving you the same feeling you have when you see a snake on land." When the thing got close, Hemingway had instructed Samuelson to bring him his pistol. "I got the automatic out of its holster in the rubber bag, handed it to E.H. and held his rod while he shot his initials into the top of the shark's head." The shark was thrashing wildly. When they gaffed and pulled it aboard, blood was everywhere. The hook was so far down the fish's throat that it had to be cut out of its side. They threw the dead animal overboard and then dipped bucket after bucket into the sea to wash away the blood and guts on the decks.

This was yesterday, after Ernest and Pauline had attended Sunday Mass and the deckhand had gone for a walk by himself. Today is not a good day for marlin fishing. It's cloudy and dark, the current is weak, the sea too becalmed. Harsh sunlight's generally best when you're hunting marlin, that and a stiff breeze out of the east or northeast to oil up the sea. The fishing party, small today, has given up on getting a trophy fish and has reeled in most of the baits. A couple of rods with feather jigs on them are still out, but those are for tarpon or whatever else small might come along. Suddenly—

> We looked ahead and saw that the sea had become black with the backs of an incredible herd of rolling porpoises traveling against the current. From the boat to the shore, a mile away, the water was covered with them and they were rolling as far as we could see on the other side toward the stream. The school was at least two miles wide and there seemed to be no end to the run ahead. There were thousands of porpoises everywhere in sight, and those we saw at any one time coming up for air and rolling with a slow, wheel-like motion were only a few of the number near the surface. They were passing under the boat four layers deep, everywhere side by side as thick as a herd of stampeding cattle, and we were in the middle of that great stampede, moving against it, wedging through and over them untouched. . . . They were jumping higher and higher, their big round bodies and flat horizontal tails making long graceful curves over the water. . . . I danced on the deck in a delirious ecstasy, yelling in a high-pitched voice whenever I saw a porpoise and seeing them all the time.

"Yi! Yi! Yi! Three of them at a time! Lookit! Oh, boy! Oh boy! Wow! Eeeeyi! Yi!"

When his rapture is over, the Maestro asks his teacher, "How many would you say there were?"

"Maybe ten thousand" is the answer. "They were spread out two miles wide and at least six miles long and you saw how thick they were."

The student says, "Do you think we'll ever see anything like that again?"

The answer, "No, and it may be nobody ever will."

The porpoise ecstasy comes in the middle of *With Hemingway*. About ninety pages later, in the last chapter, back in Key West, in the late winter of 1935, the luck-struck boy, about to turn twenty-three, is getting set to say good-bye. The February issue of *Motor Boating* magazine is out, and he has a story in it—his first-ever piece in a national magazine. It's a journalistic account of some of the events of the summer and fall. He's written the story on the boat, with his mentor's guidance and personal edits, even as he's worked on his other and more serious fiction writing. Hemingway seems almost as proud of the piece as if it were his own. Those crisply printed words on the smooth paper bearing your name at the top of the first page—do you ever really get complacent about such a feeling?

> "Well, Maestro," he said. "Now you are a writer. Why don't you stick around and go with us to Bimini next summer? You might get something for the *Saturday Evening Post*."

But the protégé knows in his bones he must move on. On his last morning, he's putting away the blankets, locking the boat, gathering his things. He goes up to the house to find Hemingway. Hemingway leads him up to the workshop. They sit facing each other, just as they had ten months previous. Hemingway tells him that he must find a way to keep up his courage, his moral courage. He's too inclined to get discouraged. There'll be so many times up ahead when he'll feel incapable of writing a single word. In terms of his fiction efforts, which Hemingway has been looking over as the months have passed, well, frankly, he has to tell him that he may be as far behind right now as he was in journalism when he first showed up. But for crissakes, don't get downhearted, E.H. says. Just keep going. And, listen, try not ever to worry about the writing when you're not actually doing it, because that'll only tire you out and make you impotent. either man can know that they'll never see each other again.

We went down to say goodbye to Pauline and when I went through the iron gate they waved, standing together by one of the palm trees beside the house. I waved back and I felt a sore lump in my throat growing bigger as I struck off on Duval Street toward the highway.

It's page 181. A book, as we will posthumously know it, is over. Except that a man's actual life has forty-six and a half years remaining to it.

The hitcher and rail rider left town somewhere around the end of the first week of February. He kept notes all the way, hoping for stories. When he wasn't making notes, he struggled with *The Brothers Karamozov*—the mentor had put it on the reading list. After he reached Minnesota, Arnold sent a letter to Key West, and on February 26 Hemingway answered: "Glad to hear you got home all right. Ten days was good time." He filled him in on the latest news, which included getting a new exhaust pipe for the boat and doing a minor repair and paint job on the engines. "[S]he looks swell and we have discovered how to fix a black paint that won't blister."

The returnee worked on a fishing piece that turned out badly, and then spent two weeks writing another fishing piece that he felt was good enough to send out—but it was quickly sent back by two sporting magazines. "When you don't look it over the stuff doesn't seem to go so hot," he told Hemingway in a letter that May. But in the same letter Samuelson had some good news: another fishing piece, with his mentor at the center, had been accepted by *Outdoor Life*. The editors said they'd pay him one hundred dollars and publish it that June. He could scarcely believe it. (When he saw the piece in print, he could scarcely believe how much they'd changed some of his sweated-out sentences.)

He went out to North Dakota and built a dugout tar-paper shack into the side of a hill. When the doors and windows were closed, the shack smelled like a dirt cellar, but it was a place to be alone and think and try to write. He came back to the Twin Cities and worked on construction projects for his brother, the Minneapolis doctor who'd dropped him off at the north side of town four years before. It was summer now, and in the mail came sixty dollars from Key West—payment on an old promise. "Dear Ernest," he replied, "The maestro is always happy a long time after he gets a letter from you, and for the last one with the check in it I'm especially grateful. I'm sitting pretty now. I had left fifty bucks out of the other dough, after a couple months dissipation like a rich nigger in Minneapolis, building the shack, buying a rifle and a few months of good living in the country. The hundred and ten I have now will carry me through very comfortably until next summer. . . . It is damned marvelous being able to live the way you want to live and doing the work you like even if it doesn't sell." He was going to Dakota again, to try to get the writing started again. Eleven days later, from White Earth, he wrote: "I couldn't get at ease in the city where most of the people I knew thought a great deal about making money and spending it." He added, "I'll start writing again tomorrow on some new stuff." He added, "Out here a fellow can write a little every day and if you keep visiting with the neighbors you don't feel like you're going dry."

In the fall, Arnold rode the rails down to Arizona and on to Mexico. He kept filling up the notebooks, hoping to find stories. Once, he played the fiddle over a Mexican radio station. In the spring, he came back to Minnesota, bringing some horsehair ropes and belts and two rawhide lariats. "Just blew in yesterday in a cold wintery rain," he wrote to Hemingway on April 28, 1936. "Wish to hell I could be down there chewing the fat with you now."

The trip into Mexico did yield up a piece, and he was able to sell it to *Esquire.* It can't be said whether Hemingway midwifed it into the magazine, which by now was considered by writers to be one of the top publishing venues in the country. "Dear Mr. Samuelson," wrote Gingrich's secretary. "Enclosed is our check for $125 in payment for North American rights on your manuscript, MEXICO FOR TRAMPS, including pocket size digest rights for which you will be given additional compensation, if and when sold." The story appeared in the November 1937 issue of the magazine and was labeled "Article," although some of it sounded made up. It had a snappy beginning and the usual clear Hemingway echoes: "When they saw me yawn and knew I was getting sleepy the cook led me through the kitchen out the back door to a shed built of shipping boxes, the thin boards shrunk so there were half-inch air spaces between them for the wind to blow through."

Late in that same summer, 1936, having been back and forth across the country twice since leaving Key West, he wrote: "The hell of it is you can't write or even try to when you've got a ten hour a day job in this goddamned heat. . . . My brother has made a respectable, hardworking fellow out of me; I have got a job now, a 1931 ford coupe that looks like new and a redheaded mistress with a pretty face and broad hips." He said he had just read "the gangrene story" in *Esquire*. He meant "The Snows of Kiliman-jaro." In August, when the letter caught up to Hemingway, the headlines in the world's papers were about Franco and his fascist troops launching war against Republican Spain.

Arnold got married. Her name was Vivian Stettler. She came up to his shoulder blades and had rolls of curly dark hair and a sense of adventure nearly to match his own. The two took off to see the continent again on a rebuilt Indian motorcycle. He liked going with his shirt off, head low, his beloved clinging to his belt loops with the wind rushing past their ears. Sometimes he rode with a ridiculous-looking Abe Lincoln stovepipe hat pulled down tight. Sometimes he worked all night at his writing notes by campfire light.

There was a temporary job down in Texas, breaking wild broncos. Arnold had been around horses for most of his life. He took the job and then came back to the Midwest, where he helped his physician-brother, who didn't want to be beholden to other people's rules, build his own hospital. When that was over, there were other construction projects. These always got in the way of the writing intentions. "Dear Maestro," Hemingway wrote on April 24, 1942. "It was good to get a letter from you and to know that you are okay. After all, the building trade is quite a lot like writing, when you boil it all down, and I know you will get back to the other too."

With world war on, the Samuelsons went to Alaska, up near the Arctic Circle, where they found work as civil servants on a government construction project. After the war, yearning for warmer weather and what he thought of as a Thoreau-like existence, Arnold convinced his spouse to go back down to Texas. Robert Lee, the place where they settled, was the seat of Coke County, named for the man who'd led the South against the North in the Civil War. It was on the remote edge of the great Sonoran Desert, at the confluence of Mountain Creek and the Colorado River, in the valley of what is called the Edwards Plateau. The whole of Coke County had a population of barely three thousand people, making it one of the most sparsely populated counties in America. Robert Lee was its tumbleweed metropolis. A wealthy and ex-Olympic polo player named Fred Roe, native of those West Texas parts, gave Arnold a job of retraining his polo ponies for ranch work.

He fell in love with his new home—the bluebonnets in the spring, the sun going cloudlessly toward noon for seven or eight months of the year. Things black as the ocean at night and a red sky at morning. Husband and wife scrounged savings and bought property on the outskirts of town, at the south end, in what was thought of as Mexican Town. They built a small, tin-roofed, cinder-block house back in the brush, off a dirt road, a house that for the next four decades would be a kind of Rube Goldberg work ever in progress. In their front yard, they began Mesquite Lumber Company, constructing inexpensive, well-made, ready-built houses at the rate of about one every six months. It was a little hard to run a lumber company without a telephone, but the head of the household vowed he'd never have one.

After the move to Robert Lee, Arnold rarely traveled again. When he did venture out after 1946, it was for temporary construction jobs on bridges in other parts of the state. Those damp fields blurring by in moonlight from the rackety doorway of boxcars were history, and so was that kid dancing on a boat over a porpoise sighting, crying "Yi! Yi! Yi! Oh, boy! Oh boy! Wow! Eeeeyi! Yi!" That had been only little more than a decade ago.

A daughter was born in 1947, a son three years later. Correspondence with Ernest Hemingway grew sparser.

In 1955, his mother died. "Dear Arnold," his closest sibling wrote on May 5 of that year.

> As you know mother is no more with us. I stayed with her all night the last 3 nights. She would not let go of my hands. She would give me messages to everyone. I tried to call you but they said you would not come to the phone [he means a neighbor's phone]. I told her you would not be coming and that I had tried to get you. She was satisfied that it was impossible. . . . Enclosed you will find a bank draft with $1,000 of her money for you. . . . Your brother, Sam.

That same year, an ex-hobo, who must still have been carrying somewhere inside dreams of becoming a recognized writer, sold a second story to *Esquire*. It was called "One Too Many," and it picked up some of the old Mexico adventures. He wrote about its acceptance to his mentor, and from Cuba came a wire of congratulation, care of Mesquite Lumber Company: HAPPIEST YOUR SALE ESQUIRE VERY PROUD SURE YOULL SELL OTHERS IF STORES AS GOOD AS YOUR LETTERS BEST LUCK ERNEST. That December, in his Christmas card, Hemingway wrote: "Dear Maestro: Love to you and your family and congratulations on all the good work this year. Best always. Ernest." But for whatever reason, "One Too Many" didn't get published.

The "abused share cropper of the high seas"—as Hemingway had once mocked him in a letter to a mutual acquaintance—was in his mid-forties by now, still fit, with a goatee. Late at night, he'd sit with his shoes and socks off in his favorite corner, next to the immense fireplace that he'd set into mortar, rock by rock. He'd be reading, or playing his violin, or studying Russian, or recording things onto cassette tapes, or making journal entries, or just puffing on a homemade pipe. His family was aware of a long-ago manuscript he'd drafted in the company of Ernest Hemingway—that's about all they knew. He'd grown increasingly reticent around them, especially his children.

But in other ways, his eccentricities raged. He enjoyed dressing like the rag-picker's son. He carved his sandals from rubber tires. He wore his belt over top of the loops—he'd learned to do that on *Pilar*. He'd show up in Robert Lee on a Saturday wearing three and four hats stacked on top of one another. He'd drive through town in his beat-up pickup with his beloved horse Bozo in the rear and then let the nag out to graze on the courthouse lawn—where was the city ordinance that prohibited it? He walked through the streets sawing away on his violin, acknowledging no one. He'd sit in the back of the Baptist church and sing loudly and off-key and out of synch with the rest of the congregation—and stay afterward to offer a point-by-point critique of the pastor's sermon. He'd start arguments with the Ford dealer or the guy who had the hardware store, and then quote to them arcane points of tort law, for he'd become something of a self-taught lawyer, having scrounged out-of-date Texas law books at garage sales. Still, most of it seemed harmless enough, the various actings-out of a Coke County crank.

Harmless? There's a cartoon of him that his daughter drew—she might have been perhaps seven or eight at the time, so this would have meant the early fifties. It's of a figure with horns and huge teeth and menacing eyes and a pointy tail and freakish-looking ears and an ugly stubble of whiskers. The caption bubbles surrounding the monster: "Ears that hear everything." "I am boss." "Fool." "Take your bath."

If that was the scary father, there was the good one, too, only you never quite knew when *he* would show. Sometimes in the summer, Arnold would tell his daughter to fetch her playmate Lois Eubanks (the Eubankses were the Samuelsons' closest neighbors), and Arnold would spend the afternoon towing the two, squealing, on an old rubber raft through the floatable parts of the Colorado.

In 1956, he made the papers again when he stole his own horse from the town pound. He said that Bozo, who was fourteen years old and fairly broken down, had been taken from him illegally and wasn't being properly fed and watered and so he had every moral right to take him back without permission. About one hundred spectators crowded into city hall for the comic horse-opera trial. Even out-of-town reporters showed. "I'm appearing," he announced, "as an attorney for the defendant and not as the defendant." The county prosecutor wouldn't let him operate a popcorn stand during recess. He was found guilty of the theft and fined one hundred dollars. "They think I'm crazy," he told a reporter. Vivian Samuelson and the two children had stayed home.

Could such behavior have been masking something else? Could it have represented some form of redirected rage and plowed-under bitterness? "A writer not writing is practically a maniac within himself," F. Scott Fitzgerald once said.

"My father kept a journal and wrote constantly, but he was never satisfied with his efforts," Arnold's daughter would write, many years hence, in the quiet introduction to the book her father wouldn't live to see published.

Another telegram arrived, with another family shock: PLANE CRASH SAM AND BOYS BILLED. It was August 26, 1957. "Billed" was supposed to be "killed." Dr. Sam Samuelson and his young sons had gone down in a light plane that the physician was piloting. I wonder how long Dr. Sam's brother might have stared at the crazy word "billed."

In the early summer of 1961, after getting the news on the radio of another death (not yet termed a suicide), Arnold wrote to Arnold Gingrich. Gingrich had published him once in almost three decades, but the two had kept in sporadic touch because of the Hemingway connection, just as Hemingway and Samuelson had kept sporadically in touch. Gingrich's Publisher's Page column of that October, addressing the suicide and the magazine's long association with Hemingway, was titled "E.H. A Coda from the Maestro." He wrote: "We'll let the Maestro end this. His name is Arnold Samuelson and we heard from him, right after the event, from Texas. 'Ernest lived as long as he could. His last act was the most deliberate of his life. He had never written about his own suffering. He said it all without words in the language any man can understand.'" In a handwritten note to Samuelson, Gingrich said: "I was more moved by your letter, written on those sheets of that same old yellow paper from Whitehead Street, than I was by any other single thing connected with Ernest's death."

Every now and then, a librarian or Hemingway scholar from some far place would send a letter to Robert Lee, making inquiries about the long-ago, chance relationship. Arnold wasn't interested.

Years later, the town fathers wouldn't let him have a part in a historical pageant called "Old Coke County." It was held at Mountain Creek Amphitheater. In the middle of the performance, the local agitator came up through the audience, playing his violin, halting things onstage.

After the local paper stopped publishing his rants to the editor, Arnold began taking out his own paid announcements. You can read them now and envision rage disguised as humor: "Vote for Cheap at Half Price Samuelson. Community Candidate for County Judge. . . . If elected, I will be available at all times to commissioners desirous of voting themselves another raise. I'll show 'em how to get both front feet in the trough and make room for me, too." Even the ads for his lumber-and-housing business were a hoot: "Mesquite Lumber Company. Arnold Samuelson, Janitor in Charge. Special Notice: I'm not setting any price on the two bedroom house now under construction. When it's finished the highest bidder gets it. The main thing is to get it out of here. If we can't do anything else we might at least be able to clean up the yard."

In 1973, a book about the long-ago trunk murders and Winnie Ruth Judd (who was still alive, in California) was published. In Minnesota, one of the grown daughters of the late Dr. Sam Samuelson reviewed *Winnie Ruth Judd: The Trunk Murders* for her book club. Hearing about this, her uncle in West Texas became outraged. He sent a cassette tape to his niece filled with ramblings, labeling her activities bloodthirsty, shameful.

Joan Davis, justice of the peace, lifelong Robert Lee–ite, was something of a Samuelson family friend:

> A strange man. I think they were prisoners of each other, Arnold and his wife. People get to doing that to each other. His joke was, the joke is on everybody else. He thought he was so far above everybody else. Of course when you come here as a Yankee, you've got one strike against you right there. I think those kids were ashamed of him. He might do or say anything. I think they felt people avoided them because of their father. He could be insulting to people, rude. You never knew how he was going to react. His daughter used to baby-sit my kids— I wasn't sure Arnold would ever allow it, but he did. I go to a lot of deaths here. They can't move the body till I get there. I can't imagine the effect of something like that trunk murder

on him when he was so young. Your sister chopped into pieces. Even if you never saw it, you saw it in your mind. You know, toward the end of his life, after Vivian had left him, carloads of kids would drive in the gate and heckle him. I am ashamed to say that my own children were part of that. He'd run out of the house with a revolver over his head, shouting at the kids to go away. He never would have fired it at them. I was always more fond of him than angry at him. Here's something. No one ever mentioned his book about Hemingway to me. I don't know a single person in this whole town who ever mentioned it to me when it came out after he was dead. I do have a copy, though. I read it and liked it a good deal. His daughter sent me one.

Joan Burns, Robert Lee–ite for most of her life:

I can't recall any real exchanges with him. He'd sort of have his head down if you passed him. I could never figure out what was eating him. It was as if he was just continually angry about something, frustrated. We always looked forward to what he was going to put in the paper. I did know he was abusive to his family. I'm not sure how I knew this. Maybe from my own children. I guess I would say of his own children, for lack of a better word, they were just . . . *cowed.* They went around looking not very good, you know, old clothes and cast-down faces. It was almost as if he wanted to keep his family out of town, as if he didn't want them to mix with anyone. The Hemingway connection was kind of a rumor around Robert Lee. Probably a lot of people didn't believe it. Maybe they never gave a hoot about Ernest Hemingway in the first place. I do remember certain things all these years later that stick—his daughter, for instance, she had the most beautiful blue eyes. Whatever happened to her?

That daughter, Diane Samuelson, had left home in 1964, at seventeen, on the day she graduated from Robert Lee's high school. She didn't come back until her father's death. She attended college in Lubbock, Texas, and studied communications and lived for a long while on the West Coast, going through divorces and name changes.

Arnold's son, Eric, a brilliant kid, or so nearly everyone in Robert Lee remembers of him, had become by the late sixties a troubled teenager, although destined to become an even more troubled and unwell adult.

Once, in their upper years of school in Robert Lee, their father had stomped to town and claimed that the people who ran the school were trying to poison his children.

Arnold's daughter got the Betty Crocker Award. She was on the Pep Squad in junior year. She made Miss Citizenship. Under her portrait, this self-description: "Why aren't they contented like me?" Like photographs, yearbooks can bald-facedly lie.

A single sheet of paper, typed and handwritten. There's no date on it. But Samuelson's daughter, who retrieved it from among his things after her father died, feels it was a journal entry of some kind and that it might have dated from the mid-sixties and perhaps from as early as the fifties, although it also could have been written in the seventies. Some of the sentences on the sheet don't syntactically track. There are scratch-outs and write-ins. Words and phrases are hard to make out. It's as if an emotionally tortured man can't get out what he aims to say, or at least can't get it out in any way that pleases him. Arnold isn't telling a story on this sheet, although in another way you might say he's telling the whole story.

He's trying to parse his thinking on something.

> My problem is that I have a year of Ernest Hemingway's life [the word is mangled] locked up in my head. . . . I have everything to work with . . . the diary, the log dictated by Ernest during the quiet intervals as we fished, a three hundred page manuscript outlining the conversations and the action that I wrote when the events were fresh in my mind. But the manuscript was badly written and never worked over. and is in no shape for publication. Much was left out and I am the only one who can put it back in. . . . If I do nothing to the Hemingway diary and the 300 page manuscript, when I am dead. it will have no value to anyone. On the other hand if I can fix it up so that it can be read, who knows, it might be literature. . . . I was lucky enough to have that experience, and now I would like to put it out on paper and give it to others. It happened to me, now let me see if I can make it happen to you.

Vivian Samuelson left her husband and went to live with her daughter in California in the late 1970s. Arnold's spouse of forty years told her children she would put up with any amount of verbal abuse, but not his violence. After he hit her, that was it.

Alone, he went around naked on his property. His beard—not quite the full wreath of a Hemingway beard—turned white. He collected old fiddles and repaired them. He'd now walked off from Mesquite Lumber Company, abandoned houses he was in the middle of constructing. Sometimes he'd stay up for twenty-four hours straight, making tape recordings and sending them to members of his family. He was bald and no longer had his teeth and ate his dinner by candlelight, mashing the food with his tongue against the roof of his mouth before swallowing—"like a snake," he reported. The photograph on his driver's license is almost scary—a man looking deeply medicated. (He apparently wasn't, but the pattern of bipolar behavior, especially on the manic side, now seems overwhelmingly clear.)

One Christmas, he stared at the TV all day with the sound off. It was pro football, which he could have cared less about. He was down to three dogs, and he said that they were good enough company. (Once, a pack of dogs had roamed among the stacks of lumber and ready-builts.) He still found great solace in music. Sometimes on Friday afternoons he'd meet for an hour of playing with a friend named Josephine Bird. She was a pianist and the postmistress of a small town nearby. She and her husband, Ulmer, a Texas poet and newspaperman and cultivated man, had always seemed to understand Arnold, befriending him when almost everyone else wished to ridicule.

His letters of this period make grim, if riveting, reading. To his estranged wife, he wrote: "Have been burning personal effects, so no strangers can root through our private lives, hauling books to the library and junk of no value to others to the city dump."

To his only daughter, who'd never really given up on him, no matter how he'd hurt her, hurt them all, he wrote: "I've been swimming twice a day, listening to music that is good and loud and so far there has been nobody down except the west Texas utilities man.... No use putting on pants for him." In another letter to Diane, he said: "Life here fairly simple. Keep wearing the same clothes and when they get stinko swim with them. Floor never needs sweeping, and it doesn't matter if the roof leaks." In another to Diane, he said: "Sorry to hear about Eric passing the bar. Shows our local judicial system going to pot. You'd think they'd have some way of weeding out the misfits." Another: "As usual keep studying music all day every day with very slow progress. Now through all the available violin solo books and into ten concertos.... This hole and the isolation are perfect for studying music and I've been taking full advantage of it." Another:

I have been like a lone survivor having to dispose of the contaminated effects after everybody has died off in a village plague. Getting rid of forty years of accumulation is no fast job for the one who is left. . . . The keepsakes once of value are now the things we want most to get rid of so no strangers will be snooping through our private lives when I leave here. Your teddy bear, dancing shoes, letters and cards etc etc once kept so carefully have now gone up in smoke. Less personal stuff has been hauled off to the city dump. Fifteen pickup loads so far.

And one final letter to Diane: "Have reconsidered your suggestion that I get another woman. If I ever leave my solitude and go out into the social world I will try to find a suitable mate that likes to get screwed to the ground."

This is worth quoting because perhaps the most bizarre behavior of all had taken hold: the father had fallen headlong for his son's former girlfriend. "Every animal has to go through its own existence in its own way separate from all others and the next turn is never predictable," Arnold wrote to this woman, years younger than himself. Eric had apparently brought her to Robert Lee to meet his father. Whether Eric's father actually did have some kind of fleeting physical relationship with her isn't clear. The letters, and there are piles of them, are often addressed to some variant of the word "Desired" and are often signed "Antonio Bazar." They amount to unnerving, manic mash notes, and sometimes they go on for pages. It was as if an impotent writer was no longer impotent. For her, he pledges to give up "my dirty hermit routine." For her, he promises "to move over and make room for you in my bed and in my life, as simple as that, so you see it was not the temporary thing of a strong moment." All he can think of is that "I want your lips, our strawberries, your hands on me, and our bodies crushed together, naked waist up and waist down night and day." In one cracked letter to "Desireee," he says of his son: "I'm not responsible for his confusion. It is caused by self-inflicted chemical brain damage. A lifetime of counseling wouldn't help."

That son: no matter how hard he'd sought his father's approval, Eric Samuelson had rarely ever gotten it—or this is what his sister will say, as well as others who glimpsed the family from the outside. In the middle of high school, he'd been jerked out of class by his dad and put into a job corps center in another part of Texas. (Arnold believed his son had stolen something from his truck.) Eric, with a GED certificate, somehow made himself into a champion debater in junior college in California. He could beat practically anybody at chess. He attended the University of Southern California and then earned his law degree from the University of Texas (where he was on the prizewinning moot court team). And yet this same brilliant Eric Anders Samuelson, in the years following these uphill achievements, following a divorce and various other emotional reversals, would sever almost all communication with anyone to whom he was related by blood. Gradually, he would transform himself from practicing attorney into conspiracy theorist of the World Wide Web. There, he'd post offers for "conspiracy scholar training programs." There, he'd claim to other like-minded souls that he possessed the true gen on America's "elite secret groups": the Bilderbergers, the Council on Foreign Relations, the Knights of the Garter, the 33rd Degree Masons, Skull and Bones, the Knights of Malta, the Trilateral Commission, Rhodes Scholars.

The terrible things we do and hand to our children, wittingly and unwittingly.

But long before this, on September 11, 1981, the naked body of Eric Samuelson's dad was discovered on his property by his friend Ulmer Bird. (When Arnold hadn't shown up at their home for a standing music date, Bird, who lived with his wife in another part of the county, drove to Robert Lee to check on him.) It was late in the day, and Arnold was stretched out on his back, as if taking a nap. Apparently, it was a heart attack. He'd just returned from San Angelo on his new motorcycle, the first new mechanical thing he'd bought for himself in decades. A box of groceries was roped to the back of the still-warm bike. He was sixty-nine.

The death certificate, in a book on a shelf in the Coke County courthouse, got the date of birth wrong. Under *Usual Occupation,* somebody stroked in: "Carpenter." The body was taken to San Antonio for cremation. The *Robert Lee Observer* ran a small story. Before Samuelson's daughter was able to get there from California, vandals broke into the house and trashed it—drawers pulled out, closets ransacked. But they didn't take a yellowed heap of manuscript with scribbles all over it about a long-ago sojourn on a boat with a famous writer. In that manuscript, the famous writer, up in his workroom, says to the kid who knocked at his door the day before: "Another thing you've got to have is talent. Some people never can write fiction. What would you do if you found out you couldn't write fiction?" And the kid replies: "I don't know."

Once, on his boat, in that first summer of their fishing, the master had crowed about his student: "'Arnold Samuelson! The coming American novelist.'"

Once, in a letter to a mutual acquaintance, about a month after the Mice was gone, the master wrote: "[W]e shipped back [Arnold] to wherever or whatever strange pastures he came from (never hire a son of a bitch because you are sorry for him)."

I think the turn—my own slow turn toward a softer feeling—began once I traveled to Austin, Texas, and met Arnold Samuelson's daughter, Dian Darby (who some years ago legally changed the spelling of her first name). It's unlikely *With Hemingway: A Year in Key West and Cuba* would exist at all, at least as a published work, had it not been for her will and energy and love. Dian won't quite come out and say that getting the book accepted by a publisher was a way of seeking to honor and validate a life of so much seeming failure—but that's the way it seems to me. It was only after the first two or three visits to Dian's home that I think I could begin to perceive that most of her father's life, after Hemingway and *Pilar,* must have added up to one long inward scream of desperation: the scream of not being able to write, or at least to write well enough to satisfy your own standards, when writing well and writing seriously had once been the most important thing to you on earth. "Serious" is the word that Arnold Samuelson's mentor had used to describe his character. Any person's existence is a novel of riddles within riddles, and how much more so when it's a closed-off existence. But this—the soundless inner cry over your inability to find the right words, or any words—must be a very large part of the Samuelson story, even as it's a core part of the Ernest Hemingway story, the eventual Ernest Hemingway story.

Arnold's daughter, now in her mid-sixties, a doctor of Oriental medicine, a decent and kindly person with a patina of weariness about her, said to me one night, in a voice that kept rising to a series of question marks: "He definitely withdrew. I don't know. You could speculate and speculate about it. . . . He never really left Robert Lee, except that one time when we were small and he went back up to Minnesota to build that lake house for his brother. I mean, before that he had traveled everywhere. He took off on his motorcycle. He had my mother on the back. Was being with Hemingway too powerful an experience for him? Is that it? Is this what caught up with him as the years went on? I don't know. Could he never recover from Hemingway? I don't know. Did he feel he could never live up to what he wanted for himself as a writer, after being on *Pilar*?" She paused. "What I think I know about him is that his whole life was overwhelmed by that year with Hemingway. Nothing was ever the same."

One night I said: "Did your father ever talk about Hemingway when you grew up?" She answered, "Well, first, he almost never talked to me, period. He never talked to any of us. He never talked about his own family. He never talked about his murdered sister. He never talked about his brother, Sam. He lived inside his mind."

Another night, I asked: "What were some of the good things about him?" She answered, "Well, he was very honorable, in his own way. He was a clean liver, in his own way. He loved my mother, and in his way he loved us. I think what I figured out about my father eventually was that he resented his kids. They took his wife's attention from him. He wanted her all to himself."

"Why aren't you more bitter?" Her answer: "You can't miss what you never had."

I remember the first evening I knocked on her door. A wild barking took up on the other side of the door. "Pilar, get down, get down!" I could hear a voice commanding. Pilar was a purebred Chesapeake. "What else did you expect me to name him?" Dian said, laughing, holding back the dog.

We spent some of that evening paging through old family photo albums and scrapbooks. White Earth, North Dakota, looked like a nineteenth-century town with false storefronts. "His mother, just like Hemingway's, was the strong one," she said. "Four kids on a farm, miles from anywhere, and she somehow made sure they all went to college." She pulled down from a high shelf one of her father's old violins. It was in a battered leather case with red-velvet lining. The strings were a fist of broken wires. Hemingway used to tell friends that the violin case made Arnold look like an underfed gangster.

On another night, Dian talked of a high school letter jacket she had badly wanted as a teenager. "I hadn't played enough on the girls' basketball team to earn a letter. The jacket was leather and wool. I think it must have cost twenty-five dollars. There's no way in hell we could afford that. But he came into my room and woke me up and said kind of roughly, 'The jacket's yours.' I think he'd been up all night thinking about it."

Had any of Arnold's apparently failed efforts at fiction or other pieces of serious writing ever been found? "No. I don't know how much he tried after a certain point, or whether he burned it all, or took it to the dump, or whether he kept on, or just gave up and stopped years before. We don't know. Only the Hemingway manuscript and the fishing logs from the boat.

Well, a few other things. But when I found that sheet of paper where he's talking about wanting to get the book out, but can't, I knew I had to try."

A carbon copy of the incomplete *Pilar* fishing logs from the summer and fall of 1934 in Cuba now resides in the Hemingway archives at the JFK Presidential Library in Boston, an intensely valuable documentary resource. Nearly all the log was dictated aboard the boat by Hemingway to Arnold, who took down the words in longhand, and who then, apparently, once he was back in Key West, not long before he left Hemingway's company, transcribed the pages to type. (He must have done so at his mentor's request.) This, from page 141 of *With Hemingway:*

> I went for the heavy notebook with the silver pencil marking the place. I spent a few minutes every day taking his dictations in the log. It was the one thing I could do better than anybody else on board. . . . "Where did we leave off yesterday?" E.H. asked. "Went into the cove for lunch," I said.

Dian took a year off to work on her father's manuscript. She and her mother spent many hours deciphering crabbed handwriting written in over faded lines of type. She gave the book its unassuming title. From her foreword: "I whipped the manuscript into shape in much the same way my father was taught to whip big fish: by giving myself plenty of slack, striking some parts and pumping up others, reeling all the while, and finally mastering it." She sent the book around to various publishers, including Scribners, which sent it back. She found an agent who believed in it and who got the manuscript accepted by an esteemed editor, Robert Loomis, at Random House, with a modest contract and a small printing. When it appeared, in the fall of 1984, *With Hemingway* died very quickly, although the book received some admiring critical notices. In *The Washington Post,* Jonathan Yardley wrote: "This brief account of a year spent hanging around with Ernest Hemingway is an unexpected literary discovery, one of no particular moment but quite considerable charm." The book won an overseas literary award. But it never made it into tiny Robert Lee's tiny public library, not until a handful of years ago, when perhaps some late-blooming local consciences began to awaken.

In the final pages of *With Hemingway,* the author has his mentor telling him, "The best stuff you've got is from your farm life in North Dakota and your sister's murder. That's something nobody else can write and nobody can ever take it away from you, but you don't want to use it for a long time. Save your best stuff until you've learned how to handle it." In *Islands in the*

Stream, there's a passage in which the main character, the painter Thomas Hudson—Hemingway in faint disguise—is talking about the creative process to his writer friend, Roger Davis (again, Hemingway, or certainly parts of Hemingway). Davis's brother had drowned in a Maine lake when they were boys. Their canoe had tipped over. Davis, unable to save his brother, and haunted by that fact ever since, wonders if he can find a novel in the trauma. "You never will if you don't try," Thomas Hudson tells him. "Just start with the canoe—"

"And end it how?"

"Make it up after the canoe." And a minute later: "You could just make the canoe and the cold lake and your kid brother—"

But Arnold Samuelson never did make the canoe.

So *was* he the boy who flew too close to the sun and got melted by his own daring? "Icarus": that's the title of an article written by Hemingway essayist Robert Lacy, a handful of years ago in a university journal. It's one of the few useful, if relatively brief, things ever written about the Maestro. Otherwise it's just the scattered and often inaccurate mentions in the standard biographical texts, and the handful of critical notices in book review sections after *With Hemingway* was published.

In truth, the one slim book Arnold Samuelson accomplished in his youth, the bulk of it done under Hemingway's eye, wasn't just good; it was fine. It didn't need to be compared to anything Hemingway had ever written, or that anybody else had ever written. But its author couldn't see that. As he wrote in that scrambled, undated note to himself: "On the other hand if I can fix it up so that it can be read, who knows, it might be literature." But he could never fix it up, not to his satisfaction. No wonder, as the decades piled on, he turned increasingly to his silences and hostilities. His rage was directed primarily at himself, at his inability to complete a page of prose—and this, too, has its tragic Hemingway echoes. So many writing dreams ended up dying inside both men. In *Papa Hemingway,* A. E. Hotchner's highly controversial book about Hemingway and his last days, Hotchner has Hemingway asking, "What do you think happens to a man going on sixty-two when he realizes that he can never write the books and stories he promised himself?" On the next page, Hemingway says: "Because—look, it doesn't matter that I don't write for a day or a year or ten years as long as the knowledge that I *can* write is solid inside me. But a day without that knowledge, or not being sure of it, is eternity." Earlier,

Hotchner quotes a dead-voiced Hemingway saying: "I've got it all and I know what I want it to be but I can't get it down. . . . I *can't*."

The summer after he finished college, before bumming through America, Arnold Samuelson hitched 560 miles from the Twin Cities back to the family farm in White Earth. His sister had been dead eight months. The homestead was abandoned—his bewildered parents, unable to face their grief alone, had packed up and gone to Minneapolis to be with their son the doctor and other family members. Weeds spiked the yard; rooms were furred with dust. The twenty-year-old pitched a tent and lived with his horse, Dude, and his dog, Pup, down in a "coulee" (a kind of steep ravine, by a streambed). The Maestro kept an extensive diary, and reading it now is to see so many of the themes in his life that would later develop in sadder and bolder relief: incipient mood swings, fights with a neighbor, the need to be left alone, even as he yearns for companionship, especially female companionship. At one point, he says: "Alone and incapacitated, I found in myself the sensations a wounded animal must feel when he lies alone in his den." At another point: "The moon was full in a clear sky spangled with stars and graying northern lights alternating in the north." At another: "I enjoy solitude in the woods and on the prairie as I can enjoy nothing else. It is supreme." At another: "He makes many friends and keeps them, while I lose the few friendships that I contrive." At another: "Parental tyranny I believe is the most despicable tendency, but it is tolerated more than cruelty to animals." At the end of that summer, back in the city, ready to head out: "My attitude toward life is that it doesn't seem worth while, when one considers the great proportion of tedium and dissatisfaction as compared with the few ecstatic moments which are too short lived to really compensate for the vast amount of boredom and displeasure we humans endure. One may fairly doubt the worthwhileness of life."

In this fifty-thousand-word document, some of it empurpled and other of it poetic, the diarist never mentions the murder of his sister—but its subtext is on almost every page. I now know that it was a deeply fatalistic and prone-to-depression "serious" young man who came knocking at 907 Whitehead in the spring of 1934. *They killed my sister, maybe they'll end up killing me.* Such fatalism only gives the instant lie to all those sunny-seeming pictures aboard *Pilar*. Such fatalism only links him up intimately with the deeply fatalistic and prone-to-depression man into whose good graces he'd improbably stepped, no matter how polar opposite their stories would always be in other ways. In *For Whom the Bell Tolls,* the hero Robert Jordan, who has volunteered his services to the Loyalists in the Spanish Civil War, who has gotten over all wish for personal ambition as well as hope for his own survival, wonders if he can live "as full a life in seventy hours as in seventy years." He is free from his fear and discovers that a full union with another human being is possible. Let come what will come. Here's another expression of the underground river of Hemingway fatalism: not long after Arnold Samuelson knocked at his door—about three months later, by my calculations—in Cuba, with his boat, remembering Africa, remembering Spain, remembering a car wreck and a fractured arm out West, remembering a forward listening post on the Piave front in World War I when he was a teenager, the mentor wrote: "I did nothing that had not been done to me. I had been shot and I had been crippled and gotten away. I expected, always, to be killed by one thing or another and I, truly, did not mind that any more." That determinism comes at the start of chapter 8 in *Green Hills of Africa,* just ahead of the lengthiest and one of the most stream-of-conscious sentences Ernest Hemingway would ever commit to paper.

Echoes from the shadows. Not long ago, as I was writing this, I found buried in an archive a seven-page letter Samuelson wrote to Hemingway not quite a year after he had given up his job on *Pilar.* Basically, it's a guilt-ridden confession about getting a girl pregnant aboard Hemingway's boat. The impregnating happened after Samuelson and Hemingway had come back from their summer in Havana, perhaps three or four weeks before Samuelson had said good-bye to the Hemingway family and turned down Duval Street to ride the freights north toward home. It had happened late one night at the navy yard. The letter is undated but he wrote it in either late October or early November of 1935. He mailed it from Des Moines, Iowa.

"Dear Ernest," he began, in his smooth penmanship. "Please read this. I've got a confession to make that may not be very important to you, but it means a hell of a lot to me." He told how he had invited the girl onto the boat. He gave her name, said how young she was. It was clear from the start that she wanted to have sex, and that she had sought him out at the navy yard that night for that purpose. "It was a cold blooded sexual affair and when she was satisfied she left and I did not ask her to come back or tell her to stay away." A little while later, she came back. "I let her on board.

The rubber was irritating, a lousy brand sold downtown, and she asked me to throw it away." She went home and then some weeks later came back to the boat to tell him she was pregnant. For a long time he couldn't go to sleep, stumbled through his boat chores.

> I felt damned sorry for the girl and gave her my name and told her that my mail would be forwarded from Key West if I went away, and I'd help her all I could with money if she needed any, or in any other way I could. She wasn't after money or a husband, and she didn't seem to be worried. . . . It was the first time I'd ever been involved in that sort of trouble, she was only seventeen and, not knowing a damned thing about what they can do to fellows who knock up young girls, I imagined the worst, I was afraid of having my folks find it out and what bothered me most was the fear there would be a scandal on your boat. The only thing I could give you was absolute loyalty and I hadn't even given you that. I wanted to tell you about it but I didn't have the courage. I knew I would have to quit and go up north, and the meantime I couldn't tell anybody and every day I expected her old man to come down raising hell. . . . It damned near drove me crazy and I had been thinking about it till my mind was a blank. . . . I was conscious only of some inevitable force blowing up everything, and I felt like a miserable dog that had suddenly turned and bit the hand of a master that he loved. . . . The way all that happened isn't very clear to me even now, but I have told you the truth as I know it. . . . You were always frank with me, but I wasn't big enough to be candid at the time. If this story makes a difference to you and if you ever let me see you again I hope I'll be able to tell you everything you ought to know, and not try to conceal anything.

He said he'd not heard from the girl since he'd left town.

Yes, he needed to get on his own, to try to make it by himself as a writer. But in a far more crucial and immediate sense, Arnold Samuelson was fleeing Key West in February 1935, and in a cowardly fashion. And yet I am moved by the letter. It's the honesty, his shame, the bad conscience, the wanting to repair, those not-faint notes of midwestern, boyish innocence, in spite of everything. Call them atavistic Hemingway notes. Lost Hemingway notes. Amid so much ruin, still the beauty.

Beauty. She shines on the back of his eyeball every time he stands up from his writing desk to stretch his aching muscles. It's mid-July 1934, and he's had his boat for two months. A few days from now Ernest Hemingway will take Pilar across to Cuba for the remainder of the summer and fall's marlin season. He intends to be in place for the first quarter of the new moon, by which time the striped marlin will have commenced their yearly run, down from Bimini. No one knows why the big fish always appear off Bimini, on the western edge of the British-held Bahamas, a couple of months before they decide to run in Cuba. But they do. As Captain Harry put it in that recently published story, "One Trip Across" (payment for which has helped pay for Pilar): "They aren't here until they come. But when they come there's plenty of them. And they've always come. If they don't come now they're never coming. The moon is right. There's a good stream and we're going to get a good breeze. . . . The small ones thin out and stop before the big ones come." Sweet Jesus, though, if this hasn't been a queer year in the Stream for marlin. Haven't the big boys taken their own time in getting down? Something like his work in progress, at least some days.

Every part of his fishing machine still has a kind of factory gleam. He's been keeping her at the sleepy Key West Navy Yard. (Captain Jackson, the commanding officer, who's been out on the boat as a guest a Sunday or two, is opening the facility to private boats, since nothing much is going on there anyway.) This means she's at anchor not even ten minutes by foot from his front gate, ten minutes from the second-floor room behind the main house where pages of his new and experimental Africa book are filling up almost daily. The work, which hasn't yet found its true title (he'll have to go through the usual list making), is going across with him, of course. The title for now is "The Highlands of Africa."

Like the sentences that made him famous, the beauty of his boat is of the spare, clean, serviceable kind. She's been written, you could say, in the deceptively plain American idiom. She's long, low-slung, sexy, a black hull, a green and canvas-cladding topside, and butternut-colored decks and side panels. Her heat-reflecting green—which is what you'd mainly see if you were looking at her from the air—is not quite turquoise, not quite jade, not quite emerald, but something blending all three. As for her mahogany brightwork—on the decks and cabin sides and transom—well, it's almost as if you're gazing at the insides of a lit jack-o'-lantern.

If you stood away from her, at about thirty paces, and gave her a level look, she'd strike you as something tubular. Tied up at the dock, nodding in the wash like a thoroughbred aching to go, she's apt to put you in mind of one of those classic open-cockpit racing cars at Indy, whose drivers climb in wearing skintight aviator caps and outsize goggles. A large part of the sleekness is owed to the way her curved and raked stern has been cut so low—a whole foot lower, the better for bringing over, on a large wooden roller bar that projects slightly aft of the transom, the thousand-pounders of her master's deep-sea imagination.

When she's out on the water, starting to move at a good clip, slicing through whitecaps, with both engines hooked up—the big seventy-five-horse Chrysler, the little four-cylinder Lycoming—she'll appear a little less submariney. Three years from now, when her flying bridge is constructed over top of the cockpit, she'll become even more of an upright-looking craft. But even then, her lines will still be quite aesthetic. Like her owner's prose, there will always be something linear about her.

If she'll never be a speedboat on the high seas, the lady's got some surprising wheels. As noted, she can do sixteen knots at top speed, and do it almost without breaking a sweat. It's true you get a pretty strong vibration at that level. When he cuts off the little engine, the ride goes much smoother, mainly because the big Chrysler beneath the floorboards is rubber mounted. Typically, he has her at about ten knots. This saves on gas. In addition to her three-hundred-gallon-capacity fuel tanks, he can store another one hundred gallons in portable drums in her forward compartment, and carry an extra one hundred gallons of drinking water up there, too. He can troll her all day on ten gallons, using the little guy. The big guy will use up about fifteen gallons in a day's trolling, but at low speeds Pilar runs quiet as a watch, or at least this is how the captain brags about her.

She's got a twelve-foot beam and a three-and-a-half-foot draft. Her cockpit is both an open-air and enclosed sedan-like structure on the back third of the boat. Seven or eight people can fit into this space without feeling suffocated. It's the vessel's nerve center and the place where you'll most often see him, port side, at the helm, unless he's taking a nap or fighting a fish astern from his high-rigged and slat-back swivel fishing chair. Several of the cockpit windows are screened, and others have roll-down canvas curtains, providing a tent-like, house-like, feeling. (The curtains can also be swung out—awnings on his summer porch.) The middle window in the cockpit on the port side swings inward and can be latched to the wainscotted overhead (there aren't any "roofs" at sea; rather overheads) with a hook-and-eye screw, in the same way a screen door latches to a doorjamb. So the ventilation throughout is generally superb, even on the fiercest Gulf Stream days, when "the sun gives you something to remember him by," which is how the owner put it in his latest Esquire dispatch, out on stands that very week.

There's a bell in the cockpit, and he loves to clang it loudly with a loop of cord.

Her name, his favorite Spanish feminine name, is painted in handsome lettering at the center of her stern, along with the name of her home port. Like this:

PILAR

KEY WEST

FLA

The name appears again, in smaller font, below the cockpit window, out of which her master, standing at the wheel, can often be seen leaning and waving to folks on shore as he's easing off. ("Pilar" is lettered in the same place on the starboard side, too.)

One of Arnold Samuelson's jobs every morning is to swab the dew off the green cladding on the top of the cockpit. In these two months of his employment, the Maestro, the Mice, has been learning to sleep in a sway, a different kind of hobo's lullaby.

She's got no ship-to-shore radio. Basically what she's got is a lighted binnacle holding a compass, a wheel, various engine controls. The throttles for the two engines look like handlebars on a bicycle. There's a dashboard with gauges and switches for monitoring such things as oil levels and engine temperatures, and for turning on the bilge pumps and running lights. (The port-side running light is red, the starboard green—any seaman knows this.) But, really, this whole cockpit lash-up seems almost as elementary as what you'd encounter on the dash of a Ford tractor. And yet everything's here to navigate in and around and through the shoals of surprise, if you just keep your nautical wits.

Consider the helm: again, elegant simplicity. Many parts of Pilar will get replaced over the next three decades, but never her wheel. It's made of wood, with six tapered knobs, built on three shafts, each shaft running to a hub. Set into the wood, flush with it, is a circular plate bearing the manufacturer's name in raised brass lettering: "Wheeler Shipyard, Brooklyn, New York."

Inside the cockpit, on either side, are two long cushioned bunks, for general lounging, as well as for seating at meals. At the factory, they've custom built the starboard-side bunk to be a foot wider than the one on the other side, the better to accommodate the bulk of Pilar's master when he's taking a siesta or using it as his nighttime bed. At mealtime, a table gets put in place and secured on two outer legs from its stowed position a few feet behind the wheel. Presto, a stable space for four diners, maybe more if they're willing to get elbow to elbow. Presto, a cockpit becomes an open-air dining salon, with two banquettes, with the food and the wine brought up from the galley below. When Mrs. Hemingway's aboard, a tablecloth gets spread, and real dishes and silverware will get put out— well, not always. Sometimes things go grungy.

Forward of the cockpit, on a lower deck level, is the main sleeping compartment. You step into it through a varnished half door. (The in-between space is referred to in the catalog literature as the "companionway.") There are upper and lower berths down here, a tight toilet, a cubbyhole galley. Also down here, forward of the main sleeping compartment, is a smaller compartment, which gets used for storage as well as bunking. On a boat you never have enough storage room. Belowdecks is its own little universe.

On the topside, in the middle of Pilar's long snout, is a hinged hatch cover, which serves as an air scoop for the main sleeping compartment. At the bow is another hinged hatch and a small sliding doorway, which provides access to the two interior compartments as well as to the bow and which also helps with air flow. Everything about her design feels artful, tidy, crafted, efficient, thought out.

The forward cockpit—really just a small, triangular, walk-around and open-air space at the bow—is where the anchors and winches and ropes and throw-off lines and "fenders" get stowed. Fenders are those cushioned pads—sometimes old tires are employed—that protect the sides of the boat from getting cut up when she's settling in at the dock. When the boat is under way, the fenders get hauled up and stowed with the ropes and anchors. A boat with her fenders showing is a damn sloppy boat.

Pilar's captain has been so devoted to learning her quirks and tics and little running secrets that he's been more or less willing to leave the actual fishing of late to his guests. The fact is, on this side of the Gulf Stream, the Florida side, the fish aren't big enough. He needs marlin, and they're over there, across the Straits of Florida, off Cuba's north coast. Meantime, on this side, waiting to go, he's been practicing his swivel maneuver. With one engine pushing forward, the other in reverse, Pilar can turn in her own literal length. You couldn't hope to do this on a one-screw boat. The swivel maneuver is both tricky and crucial when it comes to chasing a large fish. The enraged, terrified animal wants to dive beneath you, tangle your line in the other fishing lines, drag you and your thirty-eight-foot machine around the sea as if she were a toy boat.

You're adjusting the throttles and listening for the pulse of the engines as they start to synchronize. You're eyeing the tachometers. This swivel skill is about your ear as much as your eye, and you learn in roughly the same way that a student pilot learns to shoot approaches on a runway: by putting aside the manuals and strapping on a chute and going up with the instructor and then just practicing over and over. Pilar's master has been serving as his own instructor, learning by the seat of his pants, not that he's yet got her eating out of his hand, turning on a nickel and returning him some change. But soon.

Hilariously, he's ordered custom-made sailor suits for his "crew." They're in both navy blue and summer-dress white. They have his boat's name stitched across the breast. He's sent them on ahead to Cuba. You'll forgive him this bombast. In a year or so, the monogrammed uniforms will get ditched.

Pilar, as I said, snoozes at night less than ten minutes by foot from where her master's been toiling on his new book from about 8:30 in the morning until 1:30 in the afternoon. In April he'd begun this work, not really knowing where it was taking him, on rustle-free onionskin sheets, and the slanted sentences were then getting written in a small, concentrated hand: it was as if you could sense the torture of the start just by the size of the words. At page 91—that was early June—he'd switched over to newsprint, cheaper even than onionskin, the kind on which he used to pound out his copy in Kansas City and Toronto and Paris. Now, three months in, the words quite round and large and fewer of them per page, the old newshound is at 201 sheets. It's Bastille weekend. On page 201 he'd evoked a shady little hotel porch in Africa, and his wife dancing with the manager to a scratchy gramophone, and the emetine with which they'd shot him through for his amoebic dysentery, and the wind that blew like a gale, and, not least, the smoking-hot teal and fresh vegetables that the waiters had brought to the table on that cold night. You render something like that on the page and it's as if you've earned your afternoon on the boat, rid of everything mental, just the blessed life of action once more.

So picture him getting up from his desk, going down the stairs, grabbing a few things from the main house, and saying good-bye to his wife and calling to the kids to behave themselves and promising to be home by supper and then exiting by the front gate and making a sharp right on Whitehead Street. It's in the vicinity of two o'clock. He walks in a west-by-northwesterly direction, cutting through the old Afro-Bahamian quarter, which abuts his own estate-like home. He angles past the raw-board houses, the roosters roaming with the freedom of sacred cows, the curbside food stalls, the hair-straightening parlors, the female cyclists pedaling lazily along with their dresses provocatively hiked up. He moves through the white glare of a Key West afternoon in that curious, rolling, cantilevered, ball-of-the-foot, and just-off-kilter gait that suggests a kind of subtle menace. He's on dense and narrow and aromatic streets bearing people's first names—Olivia, Petronia, Thomas, Emma, Angela, Geraldine. He's Tom Sawyer on a Saturday in Hannibal, tooting like a steamboat, rid now of Aunt Polly's clutches, left to his own devices, not to show back home until the sun is slanting in long bars. He's Jake Barnes on a spring morning in Paris, when the horse chestnut trees are in bloom in the Luxembourg gardens. Jake is expert at shortcutting down the Boul'Mich' to the rue Soufflot, where he hops on the back platform of an S bus, and rides it to the Madeleine, and then jumps off and strolls along the boulevard des Capucines to l'Opéra, where he then turns in at his building and rides the elevator up to his office to read the mail and sit at the typewriter and prepare a few cables for his newspaper across the Atlantic. "There was the pleasant early-morning feel of a hot day," is the way Jake's creator, living in this different region of light, had said it at the start of chapter 5 of The Sun Also Rises.

Jake's creator has been to cockfights in this quarter. He knows where the second-floor bordellos are in this quarter. He has refereed boxing matches in one-bulb arenas on dirt flooring scuffed smooth as talc in this quarter. (The local fighters, a few of whom he's sparred with, have wonderful monikers: Shine Forbes, Iron Baby Roberts, Black Pie Colebrooks. Even the venue for a lot of the weekend fights has a wonderful name: the Blue Goose. They set up the ring beneath a huge Spanish lime tree.) And now, having angled and shortcutted and cantilevered his way to the waterfront, Jake's creator is heaving into the yard, through the main gate, across the corduroy planking, and he sees her, the first goose-bumping glimpse, right ahead, bobbing in the sparkle of a deep body of water known by the locals as the submarine pens. He spies her registration number painted on a wooden plaque toward the tip of her angled nose: K 26761.

For the last several books and years, Ernest Hemingway's world-famous prose style has been discernibly if subtly altering, but no more so than just now, on the eve of crossing over. What explains this evolving artistic change, which the critics have begun to take notice of but don't especially like and can't quite seem to reconcile with the writer whom they've fixed in their parsimonious imaginations? This is the modernist who wrote all of those not-quite-duplicable Dick-and-Jane-go-up-the-hill-seeming sentences, so evocatively free of the subordinate clause, yoking his strange declarative music with the simple conjunctive "and," sans any commas. Sentences such as: "I saw the faces of the first two. They were ruddy and healthy-looking. Their helmets came low down over their foreheads and the side of their faces. Their carbines were clipped to the frame of the bicycles. Stick bombs hung handle down from their belts." That's from A Farewell to Arms, in the extended and magnificent account of the retreat from Caporetto. But now, as a prose innovator seeks to marry the morning landscapes of Africa to the afternoon pleasures of the Gulf Stream, something new and exhilarating is occurring. Ernest Hemingway's prose line is filling up, is growing much more expansive, and there are many subordinate clauses. The pattern has been in evidence for the last several years, but never more freeingly than just now. The critics aren't privy.

Could the artistic change have something to do with getting out of those tight, damp streets of Europe, away from those repressive, four-square enclosures of Oak Park so bulwarked against nature and the cold? Could his fuller prose line, his more complex sentence structure, have to do with a kind of literal and metaphorical thawing out, a throwing open of all the windows and doors? In the decades to come, there will be any number of scholarly explanations and interpretations and theories and analyses of this loosening. "Loosening": that's a word the artist himself employed a couple of weeks earlier in a letter. "[H]ave gotten to like writing again," he'd said. "Was about through with it for a while but am getting the old 4th dimension back in the landscape again and loosening up in the rest of it and believe I'll make a writer yet."

I believe Pilar was a key part of the change, allowing him to go farther out, where you don't see shoreline.

HIGH SUMMER

A 420-pound blue marlin, photographed in an evening drizzle,
Havana, August 6, 1934

ON JULY 19, 1934, with a motley crew of two, with guns in sheepskin cases, with a big, boxy Graflex camera and much film, with thirty-two cases of canned vegetables and thirty-five gallons of motor oil, with heavy Hardy reels and marlin-ready rods and hundreds of yards of fishing line in various thread sizes, with boxes of catgut and swivels and gigantic Pflueger hooks and piano-wire leaders, with four shelves of books (both pleasure reading and reference tomes), Ernest Hemingway took his boat across that mythical ninety-mile wedge of fast-moving blue water between the United States and Cuba. In point of fact, the distance on navigational charts from Key West to Havana is closer to ninety-nine nautical miles, one nautical mile equaling 1.15 statute miles, so that ninety-nine nautical would translate to nearly 115 statute. But all this is technical quibbling, because in both common vernacular and popular myth, the distance is still and will always be ninety miles.

It took *Pilar* most of the day to get over, beating almost perpendicularly against a current whose surface velocity can reach five knots. If that doesn't sound like much, then consider that the volume of flow in the passageway known as the Straits of Florida has been measured at more than a million cubic feet per second—or many hundreds of times the current of the Mississippi River.

They started out early. Arnold Samuelson was green and excited and prone to seasickness. The other crew member was a picked-up, twenty-eight-year-old mate named Charles J. Lunn, who, as a pilot on the Havana–Key West ferry run (the P&O Line), knew these waters well and would help man the wheel. Lunn wasn't going to figure in the coming summer's plans; he'd get paid off and catch a ferry back after they were safely across the Straits. The day before, Hemingway had signed clearance and oath-of-manifest papers, listing himself as "master," Samuelson as "engineer," Lunn as "seaman." He had put down addresses and next-of-kin names. The engineer's address was given as 2940 Vincent Street in Minneapolis, and his mom, who must still have been grieving over her terrible loss, was listed as his nearest relative.

Within an hour, the boat had "dropped" the Key West government radio towers, and in another hour the Sand Key lighthouse was gone from the horizon, and then there were only the cerulean Straits. Their course was almost due south. On a plumb line, or any decent map, Havana would fall a few degrees to the left of Key West. Since the stream is coursing eastward at its variable rates, you cross to Cuba at what is essentially a right angle to the current. At an average speed of ten knots, Havana is roughly a day away, assuming nothing goes awry.

The engineer was bidden by the master to church-key the tops off three bottles of beer, and when the bottles were empty, the master threw them over the side for target practice with a .22 Colt Woodsman automatic. The beer and the heat and the bucking swells began to have a queasy effect on the engineer, and so he lay wanly on the cushioned settee opposite the master, who, feeling dandy, took turns at the wheel with the seaman. When he wasn't at the wheel, Hemingway trolled a feather rig, but there was too much rolling and the boat was moving too fast. In early afternoon, the trio spotted purple anthills on the horizon: the sugarloaf mountains of La Cabaña. After a while, Hemingway, through his field glasses, could see the low, green shoreline. Havana, dead ahead. Their course had been true. They'd make port by six o'clock, the captain thought, in time to be cleared by customs, and maybe go out on the town, the thought of which brought awake the horny engineer—he'd heard about how those hot Cuban *señoritas* would give you a "three-way."

It all seemed so propitious, and then it wasn't. "Something's burning," the captain said. They were about three miles off the coast. Hemingway pulled open the gull-wing doors in the floorboard above the engine pit. The big motor was so hot that paint was blistering off its cylinder head. The water pump that cooled the Chrysler had busted. They had to go the rest of the way in on the little guy, the Lycoming, and what should have taken twenty minutes ended up taking two hours. The four-cylinder motor was barely able to hold the boat against the current.

They entered the harbor between the old fortress of Morro Castle and the Havana waterfront. A gunboat full of khaki-clothed and carbine-bearing *federales* ran up alongside them. (The guards in the Morro's tower, watching the boat come slowly, must have suspected *Pilar* was smuggling cargoes of munitions for the local revolutionaries, waiting to make land under cover of darkness.) The owner kept shouting to the soldiers in his pretty fluent Spanish that they were a fishing craft from the States with an engine problem. The troops were about to come aboard when a small launch appeared out of the dusk and a voice called, "El Hemingway!" It was Carlos Gutiérrez, a Havana commercial fishing-smack captain, in his fifties, whom Hemingway had engaged to be his boat's first mate for the remainder of the summer. Gutiérrez had first gone to sea in the bows of skiffs with his father at about age six and had been keeping detailed records of his large catches since at least 1912. He'd been described by Hemingway in the pages of *Esquire* the year before as "the best marlin and swordfisherman around Cuba." For weeks, he had been sending reports to Key West by wire regarding the mysterious lateness of the season's striped marlin run.

Carlos saved the moment. The *federales* moved off. *Pilar* limped in the rest of the way, past the fishing smacks and the splashing stone seawall where Havana lovers have always sat and spooned. The trio, unable to be cleared till morning (unless they were willing to pay an extra twenty-five dollars), slept on board. But that burning smell beneath the floorboards and the broken water pump and the contretemps with the gunboat and the twilight crawling-in seemed only harbingers of the kind of luck that was going to plague Hemingway's Cuban marlin dreams for the next three months. Not that he'd go fishless.

On the weekend before Hemingway made his troubled crossing, he wrote back-to-back letters to the editor of *Esquire*. He wrote them up in his workroom. Typing the date of the first letter in the upper-right corner of the sheet, he must suddenly have realized what day it was: "Sat. July 14 (my God le quatorze Juillet and me sober.)" The old debauching Bastille Days in Paris, were just that, the old days.

He said, "Am getting stale writing and no bloody exercise. On my tail out here in the workhouse five hours a day now since early April. Haven't made a trip except up to Miami to get the boat." It was a somewhat true statement, and within it you could detect defensiveness about getting set to leave home for another lengthy period (when he was only three months back from Africa), and also rationalization about interrupting the flow of work on his book—which would keep getting worked on in Cuba, best it could, fits and starts, if nothing close to the disciplined morning writing schedule of Key West.

One of the rituals, before ascending to the workhouse, was to turn on the garden hose and aim it in a desultory way at one of the parched spots in the yard. At length he'd go on up the stairs. He'd sharpen pencils. He'd walk around. He'd unfold his wire glasses and begin to read over what he'd written the day before. He'd go as far back as he could before resigning himself to trying to take the story forward.

The man who wrote his telegram-like sentences in his letter to Gingrich on Bastille Day probably knew as much or more about marlin fishing—and the habits of marlin—as any angler alive, as any ichthyologist or natural scientist, including a highly esteemed one from the Academy of Natural Sciences in Philadelphia who'd shortly join him on his boat. Perhaps that claim doesn't sound like much. But Hemingway had been a marlin fisherman for barely two years, and in that time he'd managed to catch and examine, by his record keeping, ninety-one marlin, many of them trophy size. A big-game fisherman might have counted himself blessed to have landed two or three good-size marlin in a season's fishing. In one month alone, May 1932, right after he'd begun, Hemingway had landed nineteen marlin on a rod and reel. The following year, fishing again on the north coast of Cuba, from mid-April to mid-July, Hemingway brought in fifty-two marlin. The largest of these, a black marlin, went 468 pounds and nearly thirteen feet, a Cuban record.

The acknowledged pioneer of Cuban fishing grounds was a proper little man named H. L. Woodward, who worked for Havana Electric. He'd begun his saltwater fishing career in 1915 and had averaged maybe six or seven good fish a year through the twenties. Once, he'd landed a 459-pound blue. By the early thirties, when Hemingway fished with this older dapper gentleman (gleaning whatever he could), Woodward had boated somewhere between seventy-five and a hundred marlin. It took three years for the upstart to overlap the pioneer.

As I noted, a handy demarcation point for Hemingway's life as an ocean fisherman is the year 1928—when he first spied Key West with his spouse. But it took him another four years, until 1932, to discover the sport, the spectacle, the art form, the ritual of testing and manhood that somehow seemed to have been designed by the Creator just for him. Once he'd found marlin, all bets were off; it was as if nearly every other creature in the sea was just guppy sport. Yes, giant bluefin tuna and broadbill swordfish and, to some extent, mako shark off Bimini in the mid-thirties would have their obsessions. But for the rest of his life, marlin reigned supreme, most especially the blue marlin: *Makaira nigricans,* a trophy that could go to fifteen feet, could go from fifty pounds to twelve hundred.

His Key West saloonkeeper pal, Joe Russell, known by Hemingway as Josie Grunts, did the marlin introducing. Russell, about a decade older than Hemingway, owned a thirty-four-foot cabin cruiser named the *Anita,* a little clunky-looking but very able, with plenty of speed. According to the myth (partly promulgated by Hemingway), Russell is said to have made something like 150 rum-running trips from Havana to the States since the start of Prohibition in 1920. In December 1933, when the ban ended (the ban had never quite been recognized in Key West), Russell set about acquiring a lease on a "blind-pig" bar in a rickety wood-frame building at 428 Greene Street that quickly got on the map of every sailor in port. He'd added a room for dancing and named it the Silver Slipper. Sometime in 1934 he renamed the bar Sloppy Joe's, supposedly at the suggestion of Hemingway, and in a bow to the saloon of the same name in Havana. The owner kept a sawed-off pool cue behind the bar for banging heads. After the fights were over, his barmen would swab the blood off the floor with a mop and bucket—so goes an *Esquire* account in the fall of 1934 by Hemingway, lamenting that Josie Grunts, who had to make it while he could off the drunk sailors, hadn't been able to join him that summer at the helm of his new boat. (In 1937, Russell would relocate Sloppy Joe's once more, to 201 Duval Street. The former Greene Street address— the bar Hemingway calls Freddy's in *To Have and Have Not,* and also the spot where he met the leggy blond much his junior whom he'd eventually marry—became Captain Tony's Saloon.)

In April 1932, Russell had taken Hemingway and Charles Thompson (the easygoing hardware store owner) and Hemingway's Kansas City cousin Bud White and one or two others across to Cuba. What was supposed to have been a two-week holiday with some big-game fishing thrown in turned into a two-month marlin marathon. Pauline came over twice, but Hemingway was there for the duration, wild in his new passion. He kept a log in a book of Western Union cable blanks. During this trip, Hemingway met Carlos Gutiérrez for the first time and gathered in every-thing he could about the ways of marlin. On May 30, to his pal Dos Passos, he wrote: "Well, you played it wrong not to make this trip. Damn I wish you could have made it. . . . You ought to see them strike, Dos. Jump more than tarpon and fast as light—one jumped 23 times. . . . Have had 17 strikes in a day—never less than 3."

In *Esquire*'s inaugural issue, Autumn 1933, in his first contribution to the magazine, Hemingway speaks of marlin "traveling along the edge of the dark, swirling current from a quarter of a mile to four miles off shore; all going in the same direction like cars along on a highway." Finest life you could ever know.

During that Saturday morning in his workroom, on the eve of cross-ing over for the third campaign, Hemingway's oldest son, Bumby—his child by Hadley, who was down for his summer visit with his dad and half brothers—came in with the mail. There was the new issue of *Esquire*, the August edition, about to hit newsstands, with his latest piece, "Out in the Stream: A Cuban Letter," featured at the front of the magazine. He'd writ-ten it in May in anticipation of the summer's fishing season. A couple of days before he sent it off, Hemingway had written to *Esquire*'s editor: "It seems to be about fish and is I'm afraid a little bit scientific. Will try to ease off the science and let a good gust of shit blow over it in the re-writing." He'd also said in that letter, dated May 25, "Am on the 59th page of a long story in which am very interested. Looks as if it would be considerably longer." Here is the first sentence on manuscript page 59 of *Green Hills of Africa*, as it exists, after changes, on page 50 of the published book: "[In] the glasses it was a rhino, showing very clear and minute at the distance, red-colored in the sun, moving with a quick waterbug-like motion across the hill." And here is more from that page: "So we went back to the camp, down the hill in the dark, edging down on our shoes and then feeling the trail smooth under foot, walking along that deep trail, that wound through the dark hills, until we saw the firelight in the trees." Again, that's how the sentence appears in its published form. Hemingway had made about a half-dozen edits, simplifying, streamlining, crossing out, inserting, replacing seven words ("under the rubber of our shoe soles") with just two ("under foot"). In all, he seems to have taken his story forward by about one manuscript page in what I am guessing was four or five hours of effort. And the next day, judging from his correspondence, same thing: one more page, less than two hundred words. This was the day, May 26, Hemingway wrote to his angler friend Waldo Peirce, in Maine, and said he now had about sixty pages done on a long story, and that their mutual friend, Archie MacLeish, who had been down visiting, was one of the great poet–nose pickers of all time and wondering, by the way, Waldo, what the hell is it that American writers turn into?

If the magazine piece that ten-year-old John Hadley Nicanor Hemingway brought to his dad's workroom on July 14 was only perishable journalism, it was also a piece seeking to be serious in its own way, in and amid its boasting, in and amid its gratuitous cracks about movie actresses and homosexuals. Edmund Wilson, were he alive, would probably be jeering at this statement. He believed Hemingway helped ruin himself as an artist with his "rubbishy" articles "for a men's-wear magazine."

Hemingway tells his readers it's his hedging belief that almost every known variety of marlin, the white, the silver, the striped, the black, maybe even the blue, are only color and sex and age variations of the same fish. The different colors represent different growth stages, not different marlin species. The white is the first stage and the black is the last stage. The black marlin is always a female even if in its earlier life it had been male. "The jewfish becomes a female in the last of its life no matter how it starts and I believe the marlin does the same thing," he writes. "Now you prove me wrong" is the article's last sentence. Black marlin are very old fish, he explains, and you can always tell by the coarseness of their hide and bill, but above all by the way they tire, after the initial struggle, which you'd swear is going to crack your back when they sound. Except that the phrase "the way they tire" had come out as "the way they live." The typo was infuriating.

The self-taught naturalist, son of a physician-naturalist, writes of having a lot of time to think out on the water, while the sun slants in like molten lead, as the teasers dip and dive in the wake. If he's caught ninety-one marlin in the last two years, he'll have to land and open up several hundred more before any serious conclusions can be drawn. In the meantime, he has his questions, about many kinds of fish, although especially marlin: Why is it that they always travel from east to west against the current? Where do marlin go after they reach Cape San Antonio at the western tip of Cuba? What makes them decide to migrate down from the Bahamas in the first place? Could there be a countercurrent hundreds of fathoms below the surface current—and do they return working against that? Do they make a circle through the entire Caribbean? Why, in the years of abundance of marlin off the California coast, have the fish been equally plentiful off Cuba? Is it possible that all marlin are following all the warm currents of all the oceans on the earth? Why does the south wind keep marlin from biting off the coast of Cuba when the same wind makes far lesser fish bite off the Florida Keys? And as for a striped marlin, with its "small head, heavily rounded body, rapier-like spear," with its broad lavender stripes that encircle its body from gills to tail like bands on a barrel, well, the market fishermen of Havana would swear to you the striped are all males. And yet: "This time last year we caught a striped marlin with a roe in it. It wasn't much of a roe it is true. It was the sort of roe you would expect to find in certain moving picture actresses if they had roe, or in many actors."

Hemingway's marlin theories, advanced with seriousness and some low humor, have been proven wrong by time and natural scientists. But he had the theories, he had the bent of scientific mind—that seems the point to appreciate.

The next afternoon, Sunday, July 15, home from Mass with Pauline and his sons, again up in his workroom, the congenitally restless man wrote another letter to *Esquire*'s editor.

How many pieces do I have to write after this one before I am paid up? The only thing I have had to be proud about this year due to the failure of the cuban marlin season, the arkansas quail season etc. has been the fact that owe-ing you pieces and money I have steadily written you goddamned good or even swell pieces on time or a little ahead of time no matter how badly have needed dough or how easy to make it writing something else. Or perhaps I simply have the braggies. But what I want now is dough in a sufficient sum safe somewhere so I can get out to africa. Because really Mr. G. I do not give a shit for anything except to get out to Africa again and especially on this Sunday afternoon. . . . As far as I know I have only one life to live and I have worked hard and written good stories, pieces etc. and by Jesus I want to live it where it interests me; and I have no romantic feeling about the American scene. Also pretty soon I will be a long time dead and outside of writing I have two well developed talents; for sea fishing where there is current and migratory fish and shooting with a rifle on targets at unknown ranges where the vital spots are not marked but have to be understood to be hit and for Christ sake why not go where I can use them instead of go out here and play around with chicken shit sailfish that I feel sorry for interrupting when I catch and never put my hand to a rifle from one year's end to the other. Also why not take kids out there and let them die or have fun rather than grow up in this F.E.R.A. Jew administered phony of a town.

"Out there" in the last sentence refers to Africa. The "F.E.R.A. Jew administered phony of a town" is the place he's about to be shed of for the next several months. On July 2, 1934, Key West's city council and the board of commissioners of Monroe County had declared a state of local emergency. They petitioned the governor to take over the city. What had once been close to the richest little town in the United States in the late 1800s was now at the edge of financial collapse. The Mallory Steamship line, the cigar industry (which in its prime had twenty-nine local factories going), the sponging business, the sea-freight business, the pineapple business, the commercial fishing business: all kaput, or mostly so. Governor David Sholtz had called Commissioner Julius F. Stone, FDR's federal fund agent for the state of Florida. The New Deal's Federal Emergency Relief Administration (FERA) would now be in control of Key West's immediate future, minus one of its most prominent citizens.

"Chicken shit sailfish"? Back in May, you'll remember, twelve days after he'd brought *Pilar* down from Miami, a record-busting sail of 119 (and one-half) pounds was a lot of cheese to the man who'd caught it—well, co-caught it, along with that hooky-playing Jesuit. But that was May. Around Key West, you could expect to take kingfish, tarpon, bonito, sharks, amberjacks, dolphinfish, permits, snook, wahoos, groupers, yellowtail, bonefish, barracuda, sails—but what were they next to marlin?

The priest and the writer and several others had departed the navy yard at 2:30 that afternoon. There'd been an earlier sailfish on Father McGrath's line, not nearly as big, but a shark got hold of that one after forty-five minutes and fifteen jumps. About 4:30 p.m., they were fishing on a flood tide in ten fathoms of heavy, dark water. They'd put on a new strip of mullet bait, and the 119-pounder came smashing at it. After a few minutes, the arm-aching cleric shouted for Hemingway to take the rod; Hemingway resisted. When he did take over, he was certain that the fish was foul-hooked, because no sailfish could pull that hard on twenty-one-thread line. But it was a sail. A 50-pound sail, Hemingway afterward enthused, was a good fish. A 75-pound sail was a hell of a fish. But a 119-pound sail? Six times they got the creature close to the boat, and each time the fish eluded the gaff. At twilight, they tooted in with her to the submarine pens (they didn't know she was a female until they'd cut her open), loaded her onto the rear bumper of Charles Thompson's roadster, drove her across town to the Thompson icehouse, made many pictures at the dock, uncorked the whiskey and the champagne. Father McGrath stayed out of the pictures, although not out of the champagne. Later that night came the official weighing before a horde of inebriated witnesses.

Two days later, on the front page of the *Citizen*: "Ernest Hemingway, the author, is anxious to know the record catch for sailfish in the Atlantic Ocean, as he has just made a catch which he thinks is near, if not the record. While out trolling Tuesday afternoon [sic] in his Cabin Cruiser 'Pilar,' he caught one of the finest specimens he has ever seen. The fish was perfect in every way." The celebrity of Whitehead Street must have spoon-fed the words to the reporter. And yet, almost immediately, the egoist began refusing credit for the catch, perhaps the flawed conscience of an honorable sportsman doing the pricking. On the day the *Citizen* ministory appeared, Hemingway wrote to Gingrich and described the fish and misspelled the priest's name and also momentarily forgot the fish's sex. "He was so beautifully proportioned he didn't show his weight. I won't claim him because I didn't hook him so am trying to get Father MacGrath to claim him. Anyway will enter him for the Atlantic record as a fish." The priest went back to Miami and wrote up an anonymous account, which he hoped to place in *The Miami Herald,* under the byline "Eye Witness." Hemingway sent him a cable: "Story and picture ok with me provided story states Hemingway has steadily refused to make any claim to the record for himself since another person handled the fish but claims Atlantic record for the fish since it was weighed on tested scales before eight witnesses. Stop. Thanks pictures. Send bill. Regards."

Yes, Hemingway was "congenitally restless," but is it possible he had set out purposely in this high moment of his life (new boat, new book ticking along, a father reunited with his boys) to destroy some of his closest friendships? Did Hemingway want "a wholly different kind of human associa-tion—one he could dominate as a matter of course?" Those are Archibald MacLeish's words, in a letter, four years after Hemingway's suicide, speak-ing for himself and his spouse, Ada. What is inarguable is that so many of Hemingway's deepest relationships, especially literary friendships, going back to Paris, and even before Paris, would never be the same after the 1930s. One by one he'd lose them all—well, if not lose, exactly, estrange them all, in lesser and greater ways: F. Scott Fitzgerald (never mind the mentally broken Zelda, who'd pretty much always despised him, and vice versa); both MacLeishes; John Dos Passos and his wife, Katy (whom Hemingway had introduced to Dos Passos, and whom he had known and loved since teenage summers up in Michigan); Mike Strater; Gerald and Sara Murphy. The losing, or at least dropping off, happened with Gingrich, too, although he had never been a member of their expat Paris life. There's no question that Hemingway knew what he had done—it's remorsefully there in the letters. In 1943, by then living in Cuba, his third marriage all but finished, he'd write to MacLeish: "Why don't you come down here sometime. . . . I could take you to some odd places and you could have a change. I will promise absolutely not to be self righteous, no-good and bastardly as in my great 37–38 epoch when alienated all my friends (who I miss like hell) (not to mention my sonofabitching epoch of 1934 when was even worse). How is my lovely Ada?" That double parenthesis, that quick switch of thought, speaks gulf streams.

He and MacLeish had been friends since the summer of 1924. (They met at La Closerie des Lilas in Montparnasse.) They went to Pamplona, to Saragossa, to the snow slopes of Gstaad, where Hemingway became devoted to the MacLeishes' young son Kenny, and vice versa. When Hemingway's marriage to Hadley fell apart, the MacLeishes took him in, kept his "god damned head working" (Hemingway's words) all through that emotional Paris winter of 1926–27. Archie and Ada were living then in an expensive borrowed apartment on avenue du Bois, and he and Heming-way kept their bicycles in the ornate front entrance, which disgusted the butlers of the other tenants.

The Depression forced the MacLeishes home—"Exile's return," to use critic Malcolm Cowley's phrase and book title about the Left Bank lives that had to be reinvented back in America in the thirties. MacLeish went to work for Henry Luce's *Fortune*. This brought rebuke from Hemingway about selling out, which made Ada cry.

In November 1930, when Hemingway suffered a compound spiral fracture of his right arm in an auto accident near Billings, Montana, MacLeish flew to his side (on a wind-flapping Northwest Orient airliner), only to be accused later by his friend of having come out to see him die so he could make literary jack out of it for some crappy magazine. Hemingway spent seven weeks recovering in a Montana hospital, growing a silky black beard, and here is some of what that accident had felt like:

> my right arm broken off short between the elbow and the shoulder, the back of the hand having hung down against my back, the points of the bone having cut up the flesh of the biceps until it finally rotted, swelled, burst, and sloughed off into pus. Alone with the pain in the night in the fifth week of not sleeping I thought suddenly how a bull elk must feel if you break a shoulder and he gets away and in that night I lay and felt it all, the whole thing as it would happen from the shock of the bullet to the end of the business. . . .

That's from *Green Hills*, in a passage written not quite four years removed from the accident, after the crossing to Cuba for the season that was going to disappoint severely.

If the pattern through much of the thirties was for Hemingway to brutalize a friendship, and then to feel terrible about it, the pattern for MacLeish was to feel rage—then to swallow it and come back. There are two well-known fights between Hemingway and MacLeish worth describing. Both incidents involved fishing, and one was on his new boat. The first: March 1932, right before Josie Russell took Hemingway over to Havana on the *Anita* for marlin. Hemingway and Bra Saunders (the Key West and Bahamian fishing captain) and Mike Strater (painter pal from Paris, via Princeton) and Uncle Gus Pfeiffer went to the Dry Tortugas on a fishing holiday (Uncle Gus probably financed the whole thing). They got marooned by a norther; tempers frayed. After they were back in Key West, MacLeish told Hemingway that somebody should prick his ego balloon; Hemingway said MacLeish's prick wasn't big enough. The poet walked out of Whitehead Street and moved into a hotel and then flew back to New York.

The second rupture came around the third week of May 1934 (*Pilar* would have been in Hemingway's possession for about two weeks). MacLeish, feeling seasick, but trying to hide it, hooked into a sail. *Pilar*'s master started screaming commands, while Arnold Samuelson watched open-jawed and took his mental notes: "Hi. A sailfish! He's after you,

Archie. . . . Get ready to slack to him. Don't strike until I tell you. There! He hit! Slack to him. *Slack to him!!* Shit! Why the hell didn't you slack to him? He's spooked now and he will never come back." Enraged that he wasn't heeded, Hemingway took out a shotgun and began killing seabirds. "Ernest took to shooting terns, taking one on one barrel and the grieving mate on the other. He was fed up with the world and I was fed up with him," MacLeish remembered years later, in a letter to Carlos Baker. (He seemed to be confusing the earlier fight in the Tortugas with the '34 humiliation on *Pilar*. No matter. What had burned itself in was the sight of the birds plopping in the water, two by two.) In an earlier letter to Baker, MacLeish had said: "It would be so abundantly easy to describe Ernest in terms, all of which would be historically correct, which would present him as a completely insufferable human being. Actually, he was one of the most profoundly human and spiritually powerful creatures I have ever known." The one other person he'd ever met who could suck up all the air in a room just by entering it was FDR.

Not long after the ugliness aboard *Pilar*, Hemingway, up in his workroom, wrote to Waldo Peirce and said what he said about MacLeish: nose picker, bloody bore, weird combination of senility and puerility. Maybe his bile had something to do with the single page of prose produced that day. Maybe, as others have speculated, he was still nursing a grudge against Archie for declining to go on safari with him. He typed the letter, writing in sentences by hand, and to me it is all a Hemingway Rorschach test. He typed, "It's too bloody pompous." He wrote in (does this mean it was entered later?): "I shouldn't write this. So forget it. But he kept asking for it and asking for it. I only like the people I like. Not the bastards that like me." He was out of space, so he turned the sheet sideways and wrote in the right-hand margin: "I wouldn't want to hurt his bloody feelings for anything. So tear this part out and burn it."

In the last pages of the manuscript copy of *Green Hills*, there's a long meditation about cowardice. Hemingway's father, Fitzgerald, Dos Passos, and MacLeish, among others, are in this passage, which was ultimately deleted from the published book. Archie had the most charm of any of his friends, the narrator muses, they'd had wonderful times together, but, you see, "he was really a coward so you were never completely comfortable with him just as he was never completely comfortable with himself."

In the late 1950s, the MacLeishes stopped off in Cuba on their way north from a vacation in Antigua to see Mary and Ernest Hemingway.

The welcome was so wistful and touching. It was as if Hemingway couldn't do or say enough.

And what of "poor Scott," as Hemingway was ever wont to put him down, once he'd superseded him? On May 28, 1934, two days after the Waldo Peirce letter, Hemingway answered Fitzgerald's almost pathetic plea of three weeks before regarding Hemingway's opinion of *Tender Is the Night*. This is the letter where he reminds Fitzgerald that he'd been too damned stinko for any real conversation when they'd seen each other in New York on the weekend that he'd purchased *Pilar*.

> Goddamn it you took liberties with peoples' pasts and futures that produced not people but damned marvellously faked case histories. You, who can write better than anybody can, who are so lousy with talent that you have to—the hell with it. . . . Forget your personal tragedy. We are all bitched from the start and you especially have to hurt like hell before you can write seriously. But when you get the damned hurt use it—don't cheat with it. Be as faithful to it as a scientist. . . . You see, Bo, you're not a tragic character. Neither am I. All we are is writers and what we should do is write. . . . Anyway I'm damned fond of you and I'd like to have a chance to talk sometimes. . . . We have a fine boat. Am going good on a very long story. Hard one to write. Always your friend Ernest.

He postscripts: "What about The Sun also and the movies? Any chance?"

And that very long story he was now going good on, that had crested two hundred manuscript pages? His letters from May to July show his continuing surprise at the way his book seems to want to grow—as if it has its own mind and refuses to be only a "story." Always, no matter what else is being said, there is the preoccupation with word counts, page counts. Here he is on June 10, writing to his friends Grant and Jane Mason, who live in Havana: "Am on page 100 and think it will run maybe another hundred. Maybe less." Here he is nine days later, writing to his wife, who's gone to Arkansas with the children to visit her parents: "Worked hard yest. Am on page 137. Going to write this morning and then go out in the boat this pm. . . . Sunday went sleepy as hell after getting to sleep on a hot night . . . to 7 a.m. Mass—then fished in the gulf. . . . I watered good yest p.m. It hasn't rained since about 6 or 7 days now." Here he is, next day, June 20, in a letter to Max Perkins: "Am on page 141 of the mss. (something over 20,000 words of the triply re-written shit-removed mss. so far. Will run another 10,000 it looks.) Am not troubled by the lack of confidence, what will the critics say, general impotence jeebies that seem to be driving the boys to religion. . . . Get out in the boat in the afternoons when my work is finished and keep my mind off it." Here he is, the day after that, writing to Gingrich: "Then I've been in a damned fine epoch going well on this thing (up to page 147 on the triple re-written shitremoved now and going fine). . . . You shouldn't fish blindly in the ocean any more than in a stream. You can know the damned gulf stream like a trout stream. The holes, the eddies, the shallows are all there. Only you can't see them." This is the letter in which he speaks of "loosening," of getting back "the old 4th dimension," of becoming a writer yet.

That loosening: it's as if an imagination is intermingling salt water with desert, sea with plain, creatures of the deep with creatures of the bush. He's writing a book about Africa, but with the soundings and color shadings of the Stream. There are phrases and sentences and whole passages that would make you think of *Pilar,* even though *Pilar* is nowhere physically present. It's almost as if he's summoning Africa every morning through the mnemonic "trick" of getting on his boat and hauling in fish every afternoon. Hemingway was one of the most efficient writers who ever lived—he used everything. *Green Hills,* like nearly all his work, is about the experience of living your life, and sometimes he'll state this credo in nearly religious terms.

> I was completely happy. I had been quite ill and had that pleasant feeling of getting stronger each day. I was underweight, had a great appetite for meat, and could eat all I wanted without feeling stuffy. Each day I sweated out whatever we drank sitting at the fire at night, and in the heat of the day, now, I lay in the shade with a breeze in the trees and read with no obligation and no compulsion to write, happy in knowing that at four o'clock we would be starting out to hunt again. . . . The only person I really cared about, except the children, was with me and I had no wish to share this life with any one who was not there, only to live it, being completely happy and quite tired.

Only to live it. He wrote this passage in the period when he'd humiliated Archie and then attacked him in a letter and then hectored and counseled and lectured Scott in another letter, two days after.

Three weeks after, on June 21 (the day he writes to Gingrich of his belle epoque and of his general "loosening up"), he completes a six-page burst, concluding with:

> It was cool in the shade, but if you stirred into the sun, or as the sun shifted the shadow while you read so that any part of you was out of the shadow, the sun was heavy. Droopy [one of the trackers] had gone on down the stream to have a look and as we lay there reading, I could smell the heat of the day coming, the drying up of the dew, the heat on the leaves, and the heaviness of the sun over the stream.

The word "stream" appears twice here. The word will keep finding its way into his text—which can be almost unbearable to read in places: all that macho killing, all that unnecessary ego—but never more mystically than in the greatest Stream sentence in American literature. That sentence, with its 497 diagram-defying words, won't be about Africa at all, even though it appears in a story about Africa. It'll get itself onto paper at some point within the first month after the crossing to Havana, when his general progress on the book—because of his nearly nonstop fishing; because of how many people are crowding both his boat and life—has narrowed to a trickle.

The art of slacking, of holding back before you try to set the hook, is counterintuitive, counterreflexive, which is probably why Hemingway was so damn good at it—in both fishing and literature. This immense thing is coming at you, his back projecting out of the water like a submarine, a submarine with wings, and then he hits it, smashes at the bait, explodes and boils the sea around him, and all you can think to do—against every instruction and mental reminder—is to jerk back on the rod. The most natural impulse in the world. But if you do this, if you sock without first trying to slack, almost certainly you'll lose the fish—and maybe your line as well. You'll horse the bait right out of his mouth, or, worse, you'll snap your line like a matchstick.

There's so much to remember, in split seconds of timing, and all of it's apt to go out the window at the instant of the thrill and the strike.

Once the fish has got it in his mouth, but realizes what's up, what's off, and has started his run, it's important to screw down lightly on the drag—but not too much. Too much tension drag on the reel and it's over. The line won't bear it.

Sometimes the immense thing will only be rolling and lolling the bait around inside that cavernous gullet, gumming it, finning slowly away, as if trying to know whether there's something a little bit off here, as if trying to decide, even as the taste of the meat is quite satisfactory, whether there's another kind of taste mixed in here, something foreign, something hard and bitter, iron-like, although I realize that this will sound far-fetched to a nonfisherman. It presupposes that something as dumb as a fish could reason, could know what alloys of metal taste like. Yet it has often seemed that way to me, when I've got a rainbow trout tethered to the other end of my fly line, but not yet firmly hooked, and his intelligence is about to outshine mine once more.

Sometimes a rainbow will just instantly spit out the fly, knowing it's a fake, an imitation, and then there's nothing you can do but reel in, and start your hopes over, start your loops over, arcing your line back and forth across the stream.

"One Trip Across" could be read almost as much for its marlin instructions as for its taut drama: "If you don't give them line when they hook up like that they break it. There isn't any line will hold them. When they want it you've got to give it to them. . . . What we have to do is use the boat to chase them so they don't take it all when they make their run. After they make their run they'll sound and you can tighten up the drag and get it back." If you could remember that, you'd likely have your fish.

At an earlier point in the tale, Harry Morgan is providing more instruction to his wealthy and ignorant and thieving client, whose name is Johnson, and who has booked Harry's charter boat for the day. Harry's at the wheel.

He put on his belt and his harness and put out the big rod with the Hardy reel with six hundred yards of thirty-six thread. I looked back and his bait was trolling nice, just bouncing along on the swell and the two teasers were diving and jumping. . . . "Keep the rod butt in the socket on the chair," I told him. "Then the rod won't be as heavy. Keep the drag off so you can slack to him when he hits. If one ever hits with the drag on he'll jerk you overboard."

But Johnson doesn't keep the drag off—he screws it down too tight. And he takes the rod out of the chair socket. And he gets out of his leather harness and foolishly places the rod across his knees because he's grown tired of holding it steady in an upright position in the socket. A few minutes later, when the fish hits, Harry sees Johnson "rise up in the air off the chair as though he was being derricked."

The finest fishing passage from the story may be this:

Then I saw a splash like a depth bomb and the sword and eye and open lower jaw and huge purple-black head of a black marlin. The whole top fin was up out of water looking as high as a full-rigged ship, and the whole scythe tail was out. . . . The bill was as big around as a baseball bat and he slanted up, and as he grabbed the bait he sliced the ocean wide open. He was solid purple-black and he had an eye as big as a soup bowl.

To try to land the thousand-pounder of your saltwater dreams, you sit in a ladder-back swivel chair with your feet braced against footrests and with somebody pouring ice water on your wrists and with your shoulders encased in a leather harness that almost looks like something from an electric chair. (The straps of the harness, which goes around your shoulders, are buckled to the sides of the giant reel. A lot of the weight is thus directed to your shoulders and back and legs. This takes the pressure off your arms. The bolted-down chair is supporting the weight of the rod, which is in the socket, sometimes referred to by fishermen as the "gimble socket," or just the "gimble." You see that expression in Hemingway. The word is said to be a corruption of "gimbal," which in nautical terms refers to a device that allows an object—such as a ship's compass, mounted in or on it—to remain suspended in a horizontal plane. A gimble socket on a fishing chair is just an iron cavity built into the middle of the seat.)

In almost forty years of wedging fast, pure water in many beautiful mountain places in obsessive search of rainbows and browns and brookies and cutthroats, I've probably landed and released (most of the time) several thousand trout in the ten-inch and half-pound range—and I've lost, in the same period, probably five times, ten times, twenty times that many fish. Why? Well, for many reasons, but not least because I came back too fast. Because I tried to implant the hook before I'd sufficiently slacked. All my experience and self-reminding as I stepped into the stream couldn't stop me at the instant of the hit and thrill from jerking backward. The fragile thing came darting out of the shadows of some gorgeous pool, striking the little blow-away wad of hackle and glue affixed to the end of my two-ounce Sage graphite rod and Orvis reel and tapered, lime-colored, weight-forward, high-floating line. And what did I do? I reflexively pumped, jerked, socked. I hauled the fly right out of his mouth.

When you've actually had him on the hook and have been fighting him for a minute or two or five; have been edging him, in between his various deep runs and spray-filmed leaps, ever closer to your net, and he then suddenly gets off, wriggles free, is gone, disappeared, vanished, well, the loss feels monumental. You want to go bawling and trembling in your waders to the closest boulder to sit down and try to get your life back—or I do. Damn, you lost him. Oh, you would have set him free anyway. But he beat you. Again. On bad winter days, when I'm up to my knees in the trout pools of memory, I usually wind up thinking—even laughing—about all the times I have failed at this wretched and exquisite sport, which, like writing, you could work at for the rest of your life and never come close to mastering.

"One Trip Across" is both a taut story and a marvelous instruction manual—and yet perhaps surpassed by Hemingway's account of David Hudson's six-hour losing battle with the giant broadbill swordfish in Islands in the Stream. David is transparently Ernest Hemingway's middle son, Patrick.

Davy's broadbill battle goes on for pages. It's in the "Bimini" section, which opens that wobbly-connected, three-part, autobiographical, posthumous novel. The account of the battle is almost breathtaking for its tension and utter fishing authenticity, not the least of which is the prayer of a ten-year-old once he knows the living thing is on the other end of his line.

"Hit him now, Dave, and really hit him," says Roger Davis, who, as I have already noted, is partly Hemingway, just as the novel's central character, Thomas Hudson—Davy's father—is even more unambiguously Hemingway.

" 'Do you think he's had it long enough?' David asked. 'You don't think he's just carrying it in his mouth and swimming with it?' "

" 'I think you better hit him before he spits it out.' "

The boy's father, narrating the fight, says: "David braced his feet, tightened the drag well down with his right hand, and struck back hard against the great weight. He struck again and again bending the rod like a bow. The line moved out steadily. He had made no impression on the fish.

" 'Hit him again, Dave,' Roger said. 'Really put it into him.' "

Davy does. Then, " 'Oh God,' he said devoutly. 'I think I've got it into him.' "

And three paragraphs later: " 'I'm wonderful, papa,' Dave said. 'Oh God, if I can catch this fish.' "

CATCHING FISH

At a café off the Prado, July 21, 1934, Ernest's birthday

SO THEY'RE IN CUBA.

The quarantine people have come and gone. The immigration officers, in their casually insolent way, have opened a few lockers and poked in a few drawers. Had they been more intent, they might have found the 12-gauge pump, and the 1903 Austrian Mannlicher Schoenauer hunting rifle, and the Colt Woodsman automatic revolver with its extra-long barrel, all of which, with their rounds, were hidden in sheepskin cases under the bunk mattresses, saturated with Fiend oil so the salt air wouldn't rust them. When the doctor left the boat and the yellow flag was hauled down, Carlos Gutiérrez, waiting in a dinghy with "Bumby" painted on the bow, clad in his spanking white sailor suit with "Pilar" stitched on the breast, oared up alongside. The owner went ashore to send a cable to his wife and to hunt with Carlos for a mechanic for the busted water pump, while the Mice kept watch over the boat and looked across in the middle distance at "the dark faces and white suits of Cubans riding past the gray apartment buildings in small street cars and open automobiles on the waterfront boulevard."

A cook-cum-mate named Juan got hired. He was about thirty, "hungry-looking, with high cheekbones, hollow cheeks and shoes that were cracked open" (again, Samuelson's description), and his one major flaw, apparently, was that he talked way too much. In the photographs, he looks lecherous and wears sleeveless undershirts and smokes little penny cigars only a little less skinny than he is. But it turned out that he could prepare marlin steaks five ways. Also, in the coming days Juan, who spoke a pure and old form of Spanish, would prove himself more adept at handling the wheel (when Hemingway was in his chair, fighting a fish) than the excitable Carlos. Carlos could gaff and scout and bait better than anyone around, but he had little experience at piloting a cabin cruiser. There are times when it seems as if everybody's running in circles in the small space of the boat, yelling at the top of his lungs.

The busted pump got attended to. The mechanic's Spanish nickname was Cojo, which means "cripple," and he was a round little Cuban, who, like Juan and Carlos, would come in and out of photographs and log entries of the next several months. Cojo was missing his toes and so walked stiff-legged and pitched back on his heels. He told Hemingway he knew of Havana metalworkers who could replace the brass on the interior parts of the pump without having to send the pump to the factory in the States, and that he'd see to it that the motor was back in operation by the next midday. He kept his word, and to boot refused to take payment. For the rest of the summer, this chubby government employee, longing for a wife, was good for all the liquor he could down on the afterdeck when *Pilar* was in for the night and the owner hadn't yet headed to his hotel, with or without company.

That evening, while the boat was under repair, Pauline crossed over. Her husband met her at the ferry slip, and together they went off to room 511 at the Ambos Mundos. Early the next morning, the Hemingways came down to the wharf to see about progress on the engine. They retrieved Arnold, and the trio toured town, walking single file through the tight and still-cool streets of the old quarter, with Hemingway in the lead. "I don't care if I ever see the United States again," the deckhand announced to the air. They left Habana Vieja and came toward Centro Habana, turning up the Prado, with its wide marble promenade in the middle, its overhanging trees, its lovers' benches, its lanes of darting traffic on either side. The Prado is Havana's Fifth Avenue, or maybe its Champs-Élysées. The tourists sat down at an outdoor café, near the Capitolio Nacional, across the Prado, while a nameless street photographer, nameless to history, came up and stopped time in a box. It's the photograph at the start of this chapter.

The instant survives in its original form on the front of a small postcard in a white folder in an acid-free box at the JFK Presidential Library in Boston. It survives in soft brown hues, a surprisingly clear printed image on what had to have been ready-made photographic stock, handy for mailing by *turistas*. Dian Darby has a copy of this photograph on her living room wall, and the photograph is also on the dust jacket of her father's memoir. (Pauline is cropped out—it's just Hemingway and his protégé—but you can see part of her arm hanging at the edge of the frame.) What's revelatory is how much there is to see and muse on when you're holding the cheap-cum-glorious original in your hand.

A cloudless July morning in Havana, temperature mid-seventies. (I checked.) Most likely the three are sitting at the Hotel Inglaterra, a Havana landmark, close by the Gran Teatro de La Habana, an even greater architectural landmark. (It was built to be one of the world's largest opera houses.) Samuelson doesn't name the place—he just says a café off the Prado, where "they served beer on the sidewalk in the shade."

Beggars pass by and importune the people at the tables. Pedicabs go up and down. Foreign correspondents trade their rumors. Dogs seek shade up against the hotel's walls, until the white-jacketed waiters curse them off. In a way, it's like being in the heart of Montparnasse—or maybe at Rick's in Casablanca. Across the street is Parque Central, a leafy, open space, with its throngs of all-day debaters, arguing baseball, politics. There's a statue in the park of José Martí, Apostle of Independence, poet-revolutionary.

Three *norteamericanos,* in their light-colored and loose-fitting clothing, in the Saturday sun, at their glass-topped wicker table (actually, they seem to have taken over two tables), the table space strewn with saucers and cloth napkins and stemware and three bottles, the dark contents of which have been partially consumed, each bottle with a cork stopper in it. Look more carefully: isn't that a folded-over newspaper on the back of the table, between Hemingway and Samuelson? Part of another newspaper is just behind Pauline's arm. In the background are stacked chairs and curtained panels of glass, an upright piano with the lid down.

The plain-looking woman in the striped sleeveless sundress has on her usual thin smile. (Pauline, who once worked for *Vogue,* had a knack for wearing simple clothes that made her look stylish.) The dress is tied at her shoulders with little string loops. In the coming months, in an effort to please her husband, she'll bleach her hair and grow out the close-cropped cut into an entirely new look. Something about her body language seems just slightly pulled back. By contrast, her husband (who knew next to nothing about clothes), with his thick right leg crossed over his left, in his Basque sandals without socks, with his left arm resting on the table, is gazing straight into the camera. His coal-dark mustache is neatly parted at the middle. He looks to have gotten a recent haircut—possibly last week, before coming across. He's at ease, but isn't there something poised, ready, almost coiled?

Between the older man and woman, as if he could be their son: the luck-struck apprentice with the porcupine hair, from the Twin Cities via White Earth, North Dakota.

Up in the States, a midwestern heat wave has taken 206 lives in three days. Tomorrow, John Dillinger, ace badman of the world (as the pulps like to say), will buy it on the sidewalk outside a Chicago movie house. Roughly seventeen million Americans are on relief. But down here a threesome is about to go out on the Stream, hoping to christen *Pilar* with her first-ever marlin.

July 21, 1934: his thirty-fifth birthday. On page one of today's *Havana Post*—the only English-language morning newspaper in Cuba—there's a two-column feature by a staffer named Jack O'Brine. The headline: "Ernest Hemingway Returns to Cuban Fishing Grounds." Twenty-some stories are crammed onto A-1. O'Brine, who must have gone enterprisingly down to the docks yesterday, has outdone himself, beating even those hyperventilated accounts from the New York press boys clotted at the bottom of the gangplank at Pier 57 three months ago.

> The lure of deep sea fishing, coupled with the desire of a master fisherman to top his formidable records of past seasons, has again brought Ernest Hemingway into Cuban waters. . . . So quietly and unheralded, however, did Mr. Hemingway make his return to Havana this year that only a few were aware of his presence yesterday morning when he put in for the clearance papers on his piping new motor yacht Pilar, in which he entered Havana Bay Thursday night.

The start of the third paragraph: "Designed by Mr. Hemingway, the trim 38-foot yacht is specially equipped for the quest of marlin and other big fish. It is named after his daughter."

Piping right along, two paragraphs down:

> With the arrival of Mrs. Hemingway, it was recalled that the writer of "Death in the Afternoon," and other novels, chalked up the remarkable record of 54 marlin during the mornings and

afternoons he spent in the quest of the "big ones" along Cuba's palm-fringed coasts last year. His 468-pound catch is registered as the largest swordfish ever landed on the Atlantic side of the North American continent.

In the sixth paragraph:

Despite the writer's prominence in the literary world, scores along the waterfront of the Cuban capital know him only as a good sport and an extraordinarily good fisherman. During his previous visits, Mr. Hemingway supplied hundreds of families with marlin steaks. Once his trophies are recorded the food part of them always goes to the "boys" at the docks.*

On page 74 of *With Hemingway,* the man in the middle of the frame is remembering this café-idling moment. The Maestro doesn't say it's Hemingway's birthday. He doesn't mention the feature in the *Havana Post,* which may be folded over on the table in front of them. He just says, "It was a very marvelous life, I thought, when you can make a business of living for the pleasure there is to be got out of it, and I was having a fine time." An undeniable Hemingway truth.

They took a taxi back to the waterfront. They got bonged on the fare.

Pump working, noses coated against the sun, baits in the fish box, food and drink cooling in the galley, *Pilar* and company got away from the dock at 11:35 a.m. The current was strong to the east. They puttered out into the purple-looking Stream and turned right with the current. Often, in Cuba or Key West or Bimini, it's possible to look out and see the belt of blue or black or purple just a couple hundred yards offshore: the tide has pushed it in close. In *Islands in the Stream,* Thomas Hudson is talking to his eldest

---

*Who could live up to this kind of self-mythologizing? It went on through his twenties, thirties, forties, fifties, and two years of his sixties, aided and abetted always by his unwitting, too-willing, hack journalistic accomplices. Yes, as the decades wore on, many of the hacks and those who didn't think of themselves as hacks grew all too eager to slay Hemingway, but there were always others ready to do his bidding. It had to have been the charismatic force of his personality. This is not meant to sound harsh about Jack O'Brine, who just must have been trying to earn twenty bucks a week in a limp seersucker suit, and who has to be long dead, even as his newspaper is long out of business. In fact, I found myself growing suddenly curious: Who *was* he? I didn't find out much. In the forties he apparently went to work as a foreign correspondent for the *International Herald Tribune* and translated a Trotsky manifesto when he was in Mexico.

son, Tommy (Bumby Hemingway, in real life), who's just asked his father, "What makes the Gulf water so blue?"

"It's a different density of water. It's an altogether different type of water."

"The depth makes it darker, though."

"Only when you look down into it. Sometimes the plankton in it make it almost purple."

"Why?"

"Because they add red to the blue I think. I know they call the Red Sea red because the plankton make it look really red."

Hemingway shut down the engines and coasted across the piles of garbage that were hauled out and dumped wholesale into the ocean every day by the Havana scows. Carlos baited up Pauline's rod, spitting for luck on the two-pound cero mackerel. Almost immediately she had a fish. From *With Hemingway:* "She slacked, screwed the drag and struck into something alive that bent her rod and ran the vibrating line off her spool in long jerks." From the first surviving log entry of that Cuban summer: "Raised a small marlin five minutes off Morro. Pauline hooked him on third slack."

The core rhythm and mechanics, as you're trying to work the fish toward you, is to pump on the way up, wind on the way down. Meaning: if you're right-handed, you pull the rod backward with your right as you wind the reel with your left (and vice versa if you're left-handed). Pump on the way up, wind on the way down, this strange waltz with your hooked partner. In the great broadbill fight in *Stream*, the author writes: "David was lifting and reeling as he lowered, lifting and reeling as he lowered, as regularly as a machine, and was getting back a good quantity of line onto his reel."

This animal, it turned out, was very small, but it was a marlin all right, a striped. "Yi! Yi! A marlin! He's after you, Mummy! He'll take it!" Hemingway had shouted, even before the first slack. In the twelve-minute fight that followed (was someone keeping a stopwatch?), the fish made several jumps. It went on a deep run. It tried to sound. Pauline kept pumping and winding. They got it to the boat and rolled it over.

Despite the quick luck, there were no more catches on Hemingway's birthday afternoon, only a couple of strikes. Later, they anchored the boat at Playa Bacuranao, a cove at the mouth of the Río Bacuranao, where the British had first landed three centuries before, when they'd come to conquer Cuba. The beaches east of Havana are famously soft and white as pancake mix. Arnold and Ernest and Pauline climbed an old watch-tower, swam in the bath-like waters, while Juan and Carlos tended the boat. Back on board, the captain poured Castilian wine into tumblers filled with chopped ice. He toasted his wife. Juan brought up a meal from the galley and stood in the companionway admiring his efforts. The group sang along with Jimmy Durante—something about "hot potatas"—whose *a-dink-a-do* voice was scratching from the portable phonograph propped on a shelf in the cockpit next to the wheel. They trolled westward, back toward Havana, past the harborside village of Cojimar. They steered into the early evening sun, feeling little of its blister, since they were fishing off the back of the boat and were protected by the long shade of the cockpit. They were at the dock by six. After a birthday dinner in town at El Pacífico with Jane and Grant Mason, the Hemingways came back to sleep on the boat, drifting into dreams in the main cabin, while the pupil stretched out on one of the long cushions in the cockpit. Thus, *Pilar*'s first-ever angling day in Cuban waters, with a marlin in the bargain—her first.

Two days later, Samuelson saw the sea turning black with porpoises and was *yi-yi*-ing. Apparently, Hemingway's reaction was only a little less religious. When he'd recovered, he'd tried to take pictures with the big Graflex while the Maestro was all thumbs with the Kodak.

A fishless day followed. The next day Pauline left for Key West on the ferry. Then, on Thursday, July 26 (with Jane Mason on board), about an hour before sunset, a *real* marlin, of at least several hundred pounds, came up, showing purple on the surface, fins spread out on either side like gull wings. Throughout that afternoon, the wind, out of the northeast, had been kicking up the sea. Quickly, the crew pulled in the teasers—the fish had been chasing the teaser on the starboard side. Perhaps this confused the fish, because he planed the water and charged the stern until his sword was inches from the propellers. Hemingway, standing atop the live fish well and holding his rod out for as far as he could reach, practically dangled the bait into the fish's mouth. Without slacking, Hemingway pumped. Samuelson's description rises to the poetic:

> The fish suddenly disappeared, tearing line off the reel with a scream of metallic brakes straining against a terrific burst of speed, bending the rod like a buggy whip. Then he came up less than ten feet from the stern, flinging himself clear out of the water, dancing erect on his tail, shaking his head with his pointed jaws wide open, trying to throw the hook, his striped sides glistening silver.... He turned a somersault, went down

in a splash of spray, came up again and again, throwing white spray in a rapid succession of somersaults. Every jump was a picture lost. I was paralyzed by the action. My bait was still out and by the time I had reeled in and opened the Graflex, the marlin sounded and headed for Havana in a run that kept the reel at a high-pitched shriek. E.H., sitting in the fishing chair with his feet braced against the side, screwed down the drag as tight as he could without snapping the line and tried to stop him.

"Get me the harness! The harness!" he said.

"Where is it?"

"In the locker, for chrissake!" Then to Carlos in Spanish, "Turn around! Turn around! Head toward Cojimar!"

In the middle of it, Hemingway's glasses got fogged. His clothes soaked through. The crew kept holding the back of his chair and bringing him ice water to rinse his mouth. He kept screaming orders to swing the boat around, but Carlos, perhaps in panic, didn't heed. At one point he had nearly five hundred yards of thirty-six-thread line out. Toward the last, when he'd gotten the fish close to the boat, Hemingway held the rod with one hand and fired the Mannlicher with the other, trying to fight off the circling sharks. The Mannlicher had an extraordinarily long eighteen-inch barrel—maybe he felt something like General Custer at the Little Big-horn. One of the fins from one of the sharks came up and sliced the line close to the leader swivel. That ended the battle. The fisherman cursed and slowly reeled in and went below to change and rub himself down with alcohol. As Samuelson would put it tersely in his piece in *Motor Boating:* "We ran back to Havana in the dark." As he'd write in *With Hemingway:* "I pondered all the cussing and excitement over a fish. I couldn't see it."

The scientificos had come—those Philadelphians from the Academy of Natural Sciences whom Hemingway had met back in April. Charles Meigs Biddle Cadwalader, the museum's chief officer, and Henry Weed Fowler, its head ichthyologist, had sailed on the Ward Line, arriving early on July 24, when the phone lines on the island went dead from a work stoppage. The *Post* put the arrival at the top of page one the next day: "Two American Scientists Here to Join Hemingway in Search for Rare Fish." For the next month, the pair lodged at the Ambos Mundos and most days went out with Hemingway on the boat. In fact, Hemingway got them out on the day they arrived. They hit Havana at eight, were aboard *Pilar* by eleven.

It isn't hard to squint and see them disembarking from their New York steamship, in their suits and ties and pasteboard suitcases, stepping lightly among the whores and garbage of Havana. Samuelson wishes from the start to make them into a WASP cartoon, probably because they represented in his mind everything he was not. And yet, for all his caricature and instant dislike (especially of Cadwalader, the genuine blueblood of the two), he manages to convey essential truths.

Cadwalader, forty-nine then (fourteen years older than Hemingway), was a short, thick, pontificating, bull-necked figure with a pipe that seemed fixed on the right side of his jaw (judging from the many surviving photographs). He wasn't a trained scientist. His main work at his museum—which was far older than the better-known and deeper-pocketed American Museum of Natural History in New York—was separating other wealthy Philadelphians like himself from their money so that the underfunded institution could go forward with its mission. From *With Hemingway:*

> Cadwalader, short-legged, slightly pot-bellied, always wore the same club-room conversationalist expression on his freckled face. . . . I had not yet been told [he] was the last of a distinguished line of money-making, money-hoarding Cadwaladers. . . . This was the first man I had run into who had so many ancestors and so much money, and I had difficulty understanding him. He would not drink vermouth with us before dinner or wine with his meals or whiskey in the evenings, but would only drink bottled mineral water, and half the mornings he forgot to bring his mineral water and E.H. would have to send Juan ashore for it before we could leave. Cadwalader never gave Juan any money. He must be worried about his investments, I thought.

Samuelson has Cadwalader announcing, on the first morning he steps aboard, "I venture to say that we will encounter a marlin today." Maybe he really said that.

Cadwalader *was* known back in Philadelphia to have that unctuous and almost unaware attitude of certain patricians who believe their inferiors exist to serve them. Besides, he was from a Quaker city, where being a tightwad with your boodles of money is a high value. On the other hand, he served without salary and at his death in 1959 he left a wad of cash to the academy. But the real reason that C. M. B. Cadwalader—whose people went back nearly to the *Mayflower;* and who never married; and who lived on an estate called Stonedge, where there were said to be ribbons across the chairs in the parlor so that you couldn't sit down—drank only mineral water aboard the boat was because he was a recovering alcoholic.

"You ought to be nicer to Cadwalader," Hemingway says to Samuelson, and Samuelson answers, "I haven't said anything to him." Hemingway: "That's just it. You might talk to him a little and make him feel welcome. He can't help it if he's a stuffed shirt." Hemingway adds, "We might get him to finance an expedition to Africa." The ache to get back to Africa is in so many Hemingway letters.

The other half of this Philly duo, come to Cuba for sport and maritime research, is a far more compelling figure. Henry Fowler—older by two decades than Hemingway; who never learned to drive; deeply allergic to formaldehyde; who'd once played violin in the Philadelphia Orchestra; who was keeping field notes of crustaceans, amphibians, reptiles, and birds by age seven; who helped found the American Society of Ichthyologists and Herpetologists and served for a time as its president; who used to go on his Sunday collecting expeditions in the wilds of New Jersey wearing a watch fob, three-piece suit, and pith helmet—was fifty-six then. Astoundingly, the full bibliography of this man's scientific writings runs to more than six hundred titles and nearly nineteen thousand pages of printed text. His career as a student of the natural world began in 1897, with his first monograph, and ended in 1962, when a stroke incapacitated him and kept him from finishing *A Catalog of World Fishes.* Altogether, he was associated with his museum for seventy-one years. Among his tomes: *A Collection of Fishes from Sumatra, The Marine Fishes of West Africa, The Fishes of Oceania.* That last one was published in 1928, and is the size of the Manhattan phonebook and is bound in red leather.

In Fowler's time, almost everybody in the science part of the fish world had heard of him. He is thought to have illustrated more species of fish than any other person in the history of ichthyology. (He was famed among his counterparts not only for his natural drawing ability and the precision of his renderings, but for his uniquely stippled style that contained elements of pointillism: the Georges Seurat of marine life.) When he died, at eighty-seven, on June 21, 1965, the *Philadelphia Evening Bulletin* wrote: "Dr. Fowler, who for many years hunted fish in oceans all around the globe, was a friend of the late novelist Ernest Hemingway and a frequent passenger aboard the Hemingway yacht." (He wasn't a doctor, and he was never again on Hemingway's boat.)

From *With Hemingway:*

> The white-haired ichthyologist brought out the pieces of a net and screwed the segments of the handle together. He dipped up patches of seaweed and shook out little fish half-an-inch long, which he dropped in a jar of alcohol. Juan thought that was a lot of fun. He asked to try . . . when he made a catch he would come running with the quarter-inch fish flipping in the palm of his hand, shouting, "*Mira!* Look at the scientific fish!"

Mira! In the metroplex sprawl of suburban Dallas–Fort Worth, a kindly, upper-middle-aged woman, whose surname is Fowler, is bringing out of a closet shards of a life, not just some of the books, but quills, compasses, paperweights, glycerin bottles, beakers, his personal seal and stamp, bow ties, magnifying glasses, microscopes, his round wire spectacles. Bonnie Fowler is Henry Fowler's daughter-in-law, not that she ever knew him. She's the widow of Henry W. Fowler Jr., who was the only offspring of HFW the elder. By the time she joined this family—in the early 1990s—her father-in-law had been dead for almost three decades; and her husband, who'd never had children, upper-aged himself, couldn't see the point of hanging on to what seemed like little more than junk.

"I'm the last one there is," she's saying. "No more Fowlers, not in this line. It stops here. It's going to die out with me. I wasn't even related. I came in by marriage. But how could I throw this stuff away? To me, it was like throwing a life away."

She reaches into one of the boxes and pulls out a crusted bottle with a rubber nozzle on it. It looks like something you'd see in the Smithsonian. "Do you know what this is? It's an atomizer. For his allergies and asthmas, I suppose. I bet this dates from the twenties. The man used to travel with his own drugstore. He had a specially made wooden case for all his ointments and pills." She pauses. "This is what I mean. Wouldn't somebody be interested in this life?"

For about a year after the scientificos were in Cuba, they would correspond with Hemingway. The fisherman would send northward to the museum iced specimens of fish that he'd caught in Cuba and Bimini and Key West. Some of these specimens—tuna, marlin, swordfish—remain in the academy's collections. Long past their intersection with Hemingway, the scientificos would state, in conversation and letters and published remarks, that he had significantly helped to advance the knowledge of marine life in the Atlantic Ocean. In February 1935, in partial gratitude, the chief ichthyologist named a small and previously unclassified scorpion fish that had been caught by a market fisherman in the waters off southern Jersey. He named it *Neomerinthe hemingway*. Pretty ugly fish. But still.

The *Pilar* logs. There seems little doubt that Hemingway would have started them on the day his boat weighed anchor at Key West—it's just that the first two days of entries haven't survived. What we have, as noted earlier, is a typed log, and a poor carbon at that, of one hundred–plus pages, with gaps. This raises a sticky scholarly question: since we don't possess the original document, and since that original document wouldn't have been in Hemingway's hand anyway, how do we know for certain that what's in the logs are exactly the words as he dictated them, rather than a pupil's typed approximation several months later? The answer is: we don't know. But Hemingway scholars tend to believe that except for where otherwise noted in the entries themselves, the words, or maybe 99 percent of them, are Hemingway's, and that Samuelson took them down faithfully, and then just as faithfully typed them out, in Key West, before he left Hemingway's company and headed home. (There are several places in the logs where you see a parenthetical note: "Log by Arnold.") In 1989, the JFK Presidential Library—or, more precisely, the Friends of the Hemingway Collection at the JFK Presidential Library—acquired the logs from the Samuelson estate.

What distinguishes this record from earlier and also some later Hemingway fishing logs is its fullness. He's writing, in the third person, in the usual telegramese, but in another way he's crowding the margins, filling up his prose line, recording far more than what the weather was, or what equipment was being used, or who was aboard. There is always that data, but a kind of emotional texture, too. It's as if he's creating a raw, immediate, documentary novel within the larger novel of his life, a work with its own storytelling arc. A small wooden boat is daily tossing on a large sea, and here is some of what it tastes and looks and feels like. Somewhere in the background you can hear the revolutionary turmoil in the streets of Havana. If there's the occasional fishing victory, there's more often the palpable disappointment. A Hemingway expert named Linda Patterson Miller, whose scholarship is much to be admired, and who has studied these logs in depth, has said that, in effect, two Hemingway manuscripts were evolving simultaneously in Cuba: *Green Hills* and a ship's diary. As Professor Miller has demonstrated, one manuscript synergistically reinforces the other. There are distinct parallels in terms of structure and theme. Essentially, they're both about one thing: the hunt. You can read these logs and imagine a man composing his book up in the fifth-floor room—or trying to, if only he could find more time, if only there weren't so many people to be looking after, to be playing host to, both friends and near strangers. As with all of Hemingway's work, you end up feeling more than you necessarily understand: another core Hemingway writing value.

The fullness and richness of the thirty-four logs are partially explained by the presence of Samuelson himself. The teacher is dictating to the novice, who's taking it down with the silver pencil in the big notebook. Hemingway intends to show how a writer must observe it all.

"Out at 8:10," he notes on July 28. Water is clear and cool, barometric pressure at 30.10. On the lunch menu: corn beef hash, good salad (shrimp and cucumbers), custard pudding. Alas, there will be no caught fish, hardly a strike, nothing the whole afternoon. On the way home, they troll for tarpon—no strikes. To add to the insult, *Pilar* runs out of gas in her port tank at the harbor, but the captain cuts in another tank. Dinner is on board, with some good talk beforehand. The leftover hash, beans, an avocado salad, more of the pudding. There's a letter from Pauline. Also a message from "Mrs. [Jane] Mason" that, alas, she's headed out of town and can't join the fishing party tomorrow.

Next morning: At 11:05 (they've gotten away from the dock by 9:40), Cadwalader has "a marlin strike which he failed to hook, possibly by not slacking freely. . . . Was a big bait for small fish." Lunch is in a cove. Three other fishing boats are anchored there and all the fishermen are lamenting the poor luck. Coming back in at 6, the head scientifico snags a horse-eye jack just outside the harbor. The log writer doesn't note whether Cadwalader is thrilled. (Must be.)

Three days onward: Away from shore at 8:30. Barometer's at 30.02. Things look propitious. But no: "Sheared pin in pump. Found engine heating badly. Pump not functioning." They come back in and Cojo supposedly fixes the problem and they're right back out. Damn thing still isn't working. They glide in on the small engine and send the pump to be fixed. "Promised for 7 a.m. Thursday." We'll see, you can almost hear Hemingway saying.

The next day (this is Thursday, August 2): "On board at seven thirty, waiting for pump. . . . The day looks very good for marlin. Water the darkest it has been. First time we have seen fish traveling on the surface since

Pauline's marlin." Once again the day doesn't prove to be good for marlin. On the following day, this terse entry: "Yesterday a very disappointing day. Saw nothing all afternoon. . . ."

Seven weeks hence, on September 24, when the year's fishing pattern is too painfully clear (he's lately been over to Key West on the ferry for eight days of intense book-writing and family-visiting and is now back, piling up pages in the hotel room in the morning and hoping for luck in the afternoon), he'll write: "Nine days since we've seen a fish on top of the water or had a strike trolling. . . . A sooty tern flew toward us from the stern passing close over the boat, looking like a flying symbol of bad luck."

In rare moments, you hear the simplicity and serenity—the hell with this obsession for monsters. This entry, from August 29: "Awake early. Pauline and Bumby slept on until seven while Carlos was swabbing down. Had breakfast out on the cockpit . . . with the tide and the early morning sun on the bay and the hills."

Your stomach could start to growl from reading passages in this document, just as it could from reading passages of *Green Hills*. Hemingway scholar Matthew Bruccoli, in writing about Hemingway's "pleasures of the senses," once said something to the effect that, had the boy from Oak Park not turned into an immortal novelist, he might have made a decent living as a restaurant critic for his hometown paper. The novelist E. L. Doctorow once wondered whether "Hemingway's real achievement in the early great novels was that of a travel writer who taught a provincial American audience what dishes to order, what drinks to prefer and how to deal with the European servant class."

From manuscript page 151 of *Green Hills* (Hemingway worked on this page in the third week of June, not quite a month before he crossed): "When they woke up we had lunch of cold sliced tenderloin, bread, and mustard, and a can of plums, and drank the third, and last, bottle of beer." He's waking up ravenous in the parch of Africa, but you can imagine him just as easily waking up starved after a nap on one of the cushioned settees on *Pilar*. On the previous manuscript page, sounding almost like a second-rate film star in the thirties shilling for a product in a radio commercial: "[F]rom the chop box one of the natives . . . produced, in its straw casing, a bottle of German beer. . . . Its neck was wrapped in silver foil and on its black and yellow label there was a horseman in armor. It was still cool from the night and opened by the tin opener it creamed into three cups, thick-foamed, full bodied."

In Key West, in the first weeks of the boat, it seemed as if the whole world was coming aboard—opera singers, prizefighters, fellow writers, in-laws, kid brothers, navy brass, local wharf rats. Still, he'd managed to advance the work in the second-floor room. Now, in Havana, he's entertaining avant-garde artists, Venezuelan sportsmen, Cuban sportsmen, Havana social figures, correspondents for stateside papers, a bullfighter, consular folk, employees at the Ambos Mundos—not to say a pair of prim Philadelphians, whom he's grown quite fond of and is seeking to loosen up a little. Hemingway's dandified fellow egotist Sidney Franklin was down from Brooklyn for something like three weeks, arriving the week after the scientificos, partly to promote bullfighting and partly to visit with Hemingway. Uncounted numbers were on the dock after *Pilar* was in, when the bottles were being unstopped, when a dead-on-his-feet fisherman must have felt caught between wishing to be hospitable and wanting only to go to bed, whether bed on that particular night would have been down below or two blocks away in room 511 at the Ambos Mundos, where his neglected manuscript sat on a desk in the middle of the room. But Hemingway, a man in a solitary profession, could barely stand to be alone, no matter how he'd curse at the world for not leaving him alone.

August 6, 1934: a fishing day to remember.

It starts out with no portents. The sea is "lumpy"—to use Samuelson's word in the piece he'll soon write for *Outdoor Life*. There's ten gallons of fresh gas in a lower tank; the barometer reading is good. The owner slept on board last night. Yesterday he went to Sunday Mass. Six people are going out with Hemingway, including the head scientifico. (Fowler has stayed in to organize his notes.) They get away from the dock by 9:50 and plan to troll in the blue water about three miles off Cojimar. In town today, three Americans, including a soldier of fortune known for fomenting revolutions, will be arrested on suspicion of smuggling in a shipment of arms. Tomorrow Pauline's due here on the ferry, bringing along her young Arkansas cousin Ward Pfeiffer Merner, one more landlubber to whom he'll need to try to explain the basics of deep-sea fishing. On the society page of the *Post* this morning is an item reminding local matrons that the Book and Thimble Society meets at 3:00 p.m. at the home of Mrs. Guillermo Arguedas.

Shortly before noon, Arnold has a strike, but doesn't sufficiently slack. In the next instant, though, everything has changed, because that same fish has crossed over to attack one of the other lines. From the logs: "Something hit E.H. bait and he slacked, missed, slacked again and hooked a big marlin, blue and silver color." Samuelson, in his *Motor Boating* piece: "E.H. stood up, let out fifty yards of line, struck three times hard, missed and slacked again. The next time he struck the fish was solidly hooked." From his piece in *Outdoor Life:* "Hemingway stood up between his chair and the fish box, feet wide apart. . . . Pressing his finger tips lightly against the spinning spool to prevent a backlash, he let out fifty yards of line." From the logs: "[The fish] jumped four or five more times and waggled his spear, showing parts of his wow out. . . . Carlos turned tiller over to Juan and took gaff. Cojo held chair and exerted calming influence on Carlos and Juan. Lopez Mendez got water and held chair. Arnold took pictures."

When the fish jumped, he "shot upward, stiff as a ramrod, blue on top and silver below, the two colors divided sharply by a line down his body," Samuelson wrote. The fish came down on its tail and shot up again. It seemed to hang there, a blue vision against a blue horizon with the blue water below.

"Harness," Hemingway has commanded. He's now got the butt of the rod in the chair socket. Earlier, he'd been steadying the rod in a leather crotch cup affixed to his belt—but you don't want to fight a fish of this size with a crotch cup. The fish is liable to break your back, or haul you over.

In about thirty minutes, he brings it close enough to gaff. But the fish breaks free and carries away the gaff. The gaff floats to the surface and is retrieved by two market fishermen, who are watching the fight from a small skiff. The fish, still hooked, is pulling desperately for the bottom. Six times Hemingway gets it close, but for all his strength, he can't raise it. Then suddenly the animal is at the surface, an apparition. It's terrifying. From Samuelson's piece in *Motor Boating:* "Carlos buried the gaff into the marlin's head and we all took hold of the gaff handle and pulled him over the stern roller. When the marlin was well up it came forward so fast that its spear narrowly missed going through my middle before he flopped down on the deck."

In a drizzle, the boat and occupants ran back to Havana. They weighed the fish at Casa Blanca, the village underneath La Cabaña fortress across the harbor from the city: 420 pounds. "Took pictures in rain. Hope we got something," writes the log keeper.

The big Graflex gets positioned on a barrel. Dick Armstrong—an American correspondent for the Hearst chain, who lives at the Ambos Mundos and has been out on the boat often—is taking the pictures. (They've sent for him because he's a pro with a camera.) He keeps shooing away the local urchins, but they keep peeking back into the frame. There must be twenty-odd Cubans, young and old, in and amid the recognizable faces, trying to line up for a posterity snap. Cadwalader, shirt collar open, pipe in place, is crowding in close, as if he's the one who's caught it. Arnold, the lank of bone and hank of hair, has his hands in his pockets. Carlos is squatting in front of the catch, with a rain parka over top of his sailor suit that's got "Pilar" on the front. Bullfighter Sid Franklin is duded up in a suit and tie and dark beret. And not least, here's the fisherman, in one frame looking predatory, in another relaxed, in another punch-drunk with fatigue. His white trousers are rolled at the cuff. Hanging down between his legs, resting against his fly, is his leather fishing belt and crotch cup. He's got his rod and reel in one hand, and in his other is his long-billed cap, and with this same hand he's reaching up and holding out the pelvic fin of the fish, in the center of everything, hung upside down by block and tackle, the great mouth open, the tip of his sword two inches from the slick pavement, that eye looking big as a soup bowl. Pictures and more pictures. And here's a funny thing: the man with the rage for data will write the wrong date on many of them, consternating his future chroniclers.

Later, Henry Fowler draws sketches and helps Hemingway with the steel-tape measurements. Later, too, Arnold is sent for an extra quart of whiskey. From *With Hemingway:*

> [W]hen I got back the boat was full of people. Everybody we knew was on board drinking and admiring the marlin lying on the fish box, and when it became dark we turned on the cockpit dome light so they could still see the fish. When it got late, Carlos sawed off the marlin's sword and tail for E.H. to keep as trophies, cut a few pieces for his friends, saved a slice and ten pounds of roe for the ice box and cut the rest of it into chunks small enough to row ashore and cart to the market, where he would sell it for ten cents a pound.

The cutting up of the fish into chunks will keep the fisherman from coming back to the dock later in the evening, when everyone has cleared away, to punch the dead thing into further oblivion. But in Bimini, year after next, Hemingway will famously do just that: show up at the dock close to midnight in a jubilant drunk to find his 514-pound giant bluefin tuna that he'd fought for seven hours (sweating off something like a pound an hour), and pound his fists over and over into the strung-up raw meat in moonlight the way prizefighters in the gym slam at the heavy bag.

Three days later, Cadwalader hooks into an even bigger fish, a monster black marlin. Carlos, standing on the roof of the cockpit when it strikes, swears the fish would have gone six or seven hundred pounds, maybe more. From *With Hemingway:* "E.H. would have traded the whole fishing season for such a strike."

On August 13, a week after his blue marlin, Hemingway stayed in to write. He wanted to work on his book, but there was an odious magazine deadline to honor. That day he also answered a letter from MacLeish. They were both trying to patch up their most recent feud. "Was awfully glad to hear from you," he wrote to Archie. "Had your letter on top of the desk to answer every day but fishing with all these scientificos no could do. Up every morning at—and too pooped at night. Scientificos, very good guys. . . . [W]e landed (E.H.) a $fuck that dollar sign 420 lb marlin in one hour and twelve minutes." Half a dozen stream-of-consciousness paragraphs later:

> Am a pretty good Man. Probably, as you suggested justly, consider myself even better Man than am but still can unman several of them and write the pants off all. Modestly. Need I add. . . . Big postoffice strike here. Maybe no can mail. Had to stay in today and write my Desquire piece. Feenish thank god. Much love from all. Scientificos agree completely with my marlin theories. Whoopee. Pappy.

Another distraction: Les Hemingway, with his seeming need to get attention, particularly his big brother's, has gone missing at sea—again—with a new sailing companion. The pair had shoved off from Key West on Saturday at midnight, trying for Havana. Now it's Tuesday (the day after Hemingway's letter to Archie), and they still haven't shown. So far, everybody's keeping a calm face. Jack O'Brine is covering the story for the *Post.* Two more days elapse, and then Hemingway himself is out searching for the "youthful mariners." Late on Thursday, he finds them, twelve miles off the coast. He escorts them in, and for the last mile or so, as they're trying to make the harbor, he has to throw out a line and tow them in behind his own boat. In O'Brine's page-one account the next day, Les is popping quotes to the Havana press corps as his boat settles at the dock. Nah, he wasn't scared. Anybody got a smoke? "By the way, what day is it?" He's flashing the old Hemingway grin. Whatever tongue-lashing his brother gave him that night hasn't been recorded, but in plenty of letters between the two in later years Hemingway speaks to his sibling in the way you might speak to an irksome dog. (There are also letters through the years in which Hemingway sounds generous, solicitous, and big brotherly, even though the thinly veiled contempt never seems far away.)

In the middle of the Lester-the-Pester fiasco, Hemingway wrote a letter to his mother-in-law in rural Arkansas. "Dear Mother: Thank you and Pauline's father very much for the birthday present. It was the largest looking fifty dollars I ever saw," he began. He and Mary Pfeiffer were so totally different—she was a strict Catholic, conservative, provincial, a well-bred upper-class mid-South woman whose main obligation was to keep her home going smoothly—but he'd won her over and, as with the scientificos, enjoyed loosening her up. He railed at the way FDR's New Deal was ruining the country. He said that he now had about twenty-three thousand words done "on this thing I am writing on." He couldn't stop himself from getting a little dig in at the relatives. "It was something of a blow to learn that an unknown cousin had been invited to spend two or three weeks with me at a time when I was hoping to finish a book but have found Ward no strain at all and very good company on the boat."

A few days later he wrote to Gingrich, who was trying to edit a magazine by day and to write a novel by night. Can't be done, Hemingway told him. If you're serious about your craft, you need four to five hours at it every day. "What makes it is when you go over the whole piece each day from the start to where you go on from rewriting it really and then going on. Even then the actual writing is probably only about an hour and a half. Of course lots of times you can't write but nearly always you do. Each day you throw away what turned out to be shit in the stuff you did the day before." Eight or ten paragraphs later: "Have to get out on the wasser now. . . . [T]his looks like a bad year. We may hang a huge one but so far they aren't running and it is hard work finding them."

He wrote again to his mother-in-law, the second time in six days, and it's clear what's eating him. He said he had torn up two earlier letters to her because they were full of political invective. He thanked her again for the cash gift. He reported that Pauline had just been over and had gone back to Key West but was coming back on the ferry tomorrow. And then he said: "When I am writing a novel I am making nothing and am probably regarded by the family intelligence service as a loafer. On the other hand when I am all through with a novel I make plenty of money and then, while I am loafing, am regarded with respect as a Money Maker. Have

23,000 words done on this." It was the second time in less than a week he'd mentioned that number.

Hemingway had said on Bastille Day, five days before crossing, that he had 201 manuscript pages. Not quite a month before that, on June 20, he had told Max Perkins he had "20,000 words of triply re-written shit-removed mss. so far." So if he had twenty-three thousand keeper words by August 20—one month after crossing—he had written damn little in Cuba, even allowing for some overly generous estimates back in June.

But the sentence—*The Sentence*—had to have been part of the damn little. If it's an amazing sentence, it's also an entirely absurd and ill-fitting sentence to the book itself. It's not known whether it was written on *Pilar* or at a Havana café or up in the white-curtained fifth-floor room of the hotel whose name means "both worlds." What can be said is that the sentence begins five lines down on manuscript page 223 in the acid-free archival box in Charlottesville and isn't over until the third line of sheet 228. Immediately before, the author is talking about trying to make yourself responsible only to yourself, and the feeling that comes of that when you're a writer. He starts out arrogantly and defensively but along the way seems to catch up to himself to say what he really wants to say. Was he even fully aware of what he was doing, or, as with the best of all writing, had his subconscious done its work in his sleep, so that in the actual writing a kind of autodidacticism, a sort of trancelike state, had taken over? Ostensibly, the sentence (*The Sentence*), which has very few cross-outs and revisions, is about the Gulf Stream, that mythic warm current named by Ben Franklin two centuries ago, deep as the bottom itself in places, sixty to eighty nautical miles wide in places, which forms in the western Caribbean Sea, flows into the Gulf of Mexico, courses through the Straits of Florida, hooks left, and moves up the southern coast of America to Cape Hatteras, before switching directions again, to the northeast, and breaking up into several other currents and crosscurrents of the Atlantic system.

He starts out so calmly, in the middle of a paragraph with the words "That something."

> That something I cannot yet define completely but the feeling comes when you write well and truly of something and know impersonally you have written in that way and those who are paid to read it and report on it do not like the subject so

they say it is all a fake, yet you know its value absolutely; or when you do something which people do not consider a serious occupation and yet you know, truly, that it is as important and has always been as important as all the things that are in fashion, and when, on the sea, you are alone with it and know that this Gulf Stream you are living with, knowing, learning about, and loving, has moved, as it moves, since before man and that it has gone by the shoreline of that long, beautiful, unhappy island since before Columbus sighted it and that the things you find out about it, and those that have always lived in it are permanent and of value because that stream will flow, as it has flowed, after the Indians, after the Spaniards, after the British, after the Americans and after all the Cubans and all the systems of governments, the richness, the poverty, the martyrdom, the sacrifice and the venality and the cruelty are all gone as the high-piled scow of garbage, bright-colored, white-flecked, ill-smelling, now tilted on its side, spills off its load into the blue water, turning it a pale green to a depth of four or five fathoms as the load spreads across the surface, the sinkable part going down and the flotsam of palm fronds, corks, bottles, and used electric light globes, seasoned with an occasional condom or a deep floating corset, the torn leaves of a student's exercise book, a well-inflated dog, the occasional rat, the no-longer-distinguished cat; well shepherded by the boats of the garbage pickers who pluck their prizes with long poles, as interested, as intelligent, and as accurate as historians; they have the viewpoint; the stream, with no visible flow, takes five loads of this a day when things are going well in La Habana and in ten miles along the coast it is as clear and blue and unimpressed as it was ever before the tug hauled out the scow; and the palm fronds of our victories, the worn light bulbs of our discoveries and the empty condoms of our great loves float with no significance against one single, lasting thing—the stream.

On September 5, Hemingway went over to Key West to see the family and now the book caught fire. (In Havana, Carlos and Arnold had put *Pilar* in dry dock to scrape and paint her bottom.) In three days, he piled up seventy-two manuscript pages. Carlos sent a wire that he should come back as quickly as possible, because it seemed as if the big ones would run at last. The new moon was up. On the fourteenth, the fisherman rode back on the car ferry with his satchel of burning prose only to encounter the same lousy fishing luck. The bad luck even extended to the crew: while he was away, Juan had to be taken to the hospital with a perforated ulcer, and *Pilar*'s new cook, Bollo, was one step up from disaster. And yet writing, when it's going, will cure everything, anything. To the Murphys, Gerald and Sara, he writes, on September 30:

> We (I) have caught 10 of these fish—420—324—243—228— etc etc—down to 104 pounds. The weather is still good and there are no hurricanes yet—Have gotten through fifteen days of the bad hurricane weather and if we get through next 20 are all right. . . . Hope to get a big fish at 900–1200 lbs. Boat has been lovely—comfortable and a marvelous sea boat—all we hoped for and more. . . . Have been working hard on this long thing and now have 50,000 words done—

Three days later, he wrote to Perkins:

> Dear Max.
> We have had a good summer—Have 50,000 words done on this long thing—Have caught 11 big marlin (none over 420 lb. though) and done a hell of a lot of work for and with the Philadelphia Museum—Cadwalader, their director and Fowler, the ichthyologist, were down for a month. . . . I went to Key West for two weeks early in Sept to write on this thing and with so much juice went very well.

If his word count was accurate, he'd more than doubled the size of "this long thing" in less than six weeks, from August 20, when he wrote to his mother-in-law and for the second time used the figure twenty-three thousand. *So much juice.* It's the writing mystery itself, of course: how for weeks and months nothing, or almost nothing, seems to be happening, and then you locate the storytelling groove, get the juice, and suddenly it's as if you're highballing on Interstate 80 in Iowa in the middle of the night in an eighteen-wheeler, not a state trooper in sight. Christ, you'll make Los Angeles by morning. It's anybody's guess what kicked the Hemingway rig into fifth gear, but at least part of the juicing might have been his belief that the scientificos wished him to lead a gorilla expedition to Africa. (He mentions the prospect in his letter to Max.) But who cares what it was? The second wind had kicked in.

He fished on, wrote on, for three more weeks, sustaining in the process a small cut on his index finger that swelled into a bad infection. (From *With Hemingway:* "Then his whole fist swelled so that it was smooth across the knuckles with red streaks spreading up along the veins of his arm.") Even without that mishap, it was clear the Cuban fishing year was done. He filed exit papers with the American vice consul, testifying that he was bringing no infectious diseases back to the States, that his boat had remained thirty yards from shore while he'd been a three-month guest in Cuba. (It's why they needed to use the dinghy named *Bumby* to get to and from *Pilar* every morning and evening.) Well before dawn on October 26, Hemingway and his apprentice puttered out of Havana Harbor and took *Pilar* across. As Hemingway wrote to the Murphys a couple weeks later:

> We picked a good night to come across as soon as the hurricane warnings were down and before a norther should start and raised sandkey in nine hours forty minutes lead on the shipchannel buoy. Pretty good with a five knot current to figure and it rough as hell in the middle of the gulf with a beam sea. . . . I had an infected finger then hand for about a month so didn't write. Wrote on my book mornings then kept it in a sling and now is o.k.

Sometimes Hemingway will contradict himself in successive sentences: he didn't write at all, he wrote every morning. Postscripting to the Murphys: "It is lovely indian summer weather here now—Place looks beautiful—Have lots of pep for working—"

From *With Hemingway:* "We only went out in good weather half days and, after the marlin, catching sailfish and dolphin was more like play than a sport."

One day when they're out, the apprentice asks, "Do you think I'll ever make a writer?" The teacher: "You're getting better. Much better. If you have talent, it will show up later." The pupil presses a little more. "I was thinking about a few years from now if I find out for sure I don't have any talent." Just keep working, the teacher says.

On November 16, Hemingway proclaimed his book done. (He'd continue to obsess on it, naturally, up until its publication the following October.) He immediately wrote to various friends. To Gingrich: "Finished the long book this morning, 492 pages of my handwriting. Going to start a story tomorrow. Might as well take advantage of a belle époque while I'm in one." To Perkins: "I finished the long bitch this morning, 492 msspages, average, I suppose, something over a hundred and twenty words to the page." To the Murphys: "The weather here is perfect now, cool and fresh and swell for working. I finished my long thing, 492 pages, today." Writing well is the surest revenge.

Four days later, he wrote again to his book editor, having made exact word counts of sixteen random pages. He decided that the work averaged out to 150 words per page—some, because of narrative, had a lot more words, while other pages, straight dialogue, added up to only eighty or ninety words per page. "There are 491 pages which would make it 73,650 words—" he wrote. In the counting, you can get a sense of what the cost of 73,650 words had been.

New Masses, the Communist-leaning weekly, which had never been hesitant to attack his work, took off the gloves in a signed piece by Robert Forsythe. (It was a pseudonym.) It was titled "In This Corner, Mr. Hemingway" and was all about how he couldn't take it. "Quite the most delicate thing in the world is an author and quite the most delicate of all authors is Mr. Hemingway," it began. "He is, for example, the most honest man alive in telling the truth about a friend. He will not shirk his duty, he will hide no grisly detail even if it ruin the friend, but art will be served and literature will be enriched." The piece, so entertainingly written, so close to the mark, kept up its body blows:

> The suspicion that Mr. Hemingway may have slipped slightly south of genius is calculated to throw the great man into furious exercises on the punching bag. . . . [H]e has since enjoyed himself on various occasions in slitting the throats of his hated ones, but he will tremble in rage if a reviewer on the Tuscaloosa (Ala.) Times so much as mentions him without reverence. As a prize fighter, he must have been a spectacle. . . . [I]t may be said that Mr. Hemingway so cherishes a lukewarm review that he will be in a mood to resent it physically ten years later. Like an elephant and a Bourbon, he forgets nothing. As for learning anything, Mr. Hemingway quite scorns the notion. I have been

told by Mr. Hemingway's friends, and his works bear out the rumor, that he will not read a book for fear of the effect on his art. What he does is go about masquerading as a photographic plate, acquiring impressions and giving them off like a tin-type man at a fair. As a general thing he uses the personal tragedies of his friends for his fictional masterpieces and his hatred for his enemies for his non-fiction works.

And there was plenty more.

But our devils are the gauge of our angels. If Hemingway went around the house in a fury following that, he was only kindness when first-time novelist Irving Stone and his wife appeared at his doorstep. Stone, four years younger, had read *The Sun Also Rises* in 1926 in close to one sitting and felt there was now a whole new written language for Americans. Eight years later, *Lust for Life*—his biographical novel about Vincent van Gogh, based on van Gogh's letters to his brother Theo—had just been published. He used the occasion to write to Hemingway to ask if he could stop by and present him a signed copy. Hemingway led them through the airy, high-ceilinged rooms of 907 Whitehead, past the Juan Gris canvases and big-game skins on the tile floor. He poured tumblers of whiskey. "Are you having any fun?" he asked several times. The visitors stayed two hours and in the middle of it Hemingway's children came into the room in their robes and pajamas to say good night. Their papa horsed around with each, shook hands formally with each. At the door, saying good-bye, the mag-nanimous host offered to take his fellow writer out on *Pilar* the next day.

But the weather was bad the following day, so the two sat on the up-turned bottom of a small boat down at the submarine pens and talked about writing. Thirty-two years later, in 1966, in a letter to Carlos Baker, Stone could seem to remember every bit of it, in the same way that Ned Calmer, Hemingway's friend from Paris days, could remember for the rest of his life how fine and gentle and generous Hemingway had acted toward him and his ill wife just as Hemingway was crossing the Atlantic to acquire *Pilar*. In 1966, Stone lived in a big house in Beverly Hills, his commercial novels having been made into big-budget movies. But to read his letter to Baker is to get the idea that he would have given up nearly everything to write the kind of books Hemingway had written. "I remember when Ernest joined the backs of his hands to make a point, I saw that they were covered with cuts and scratches from fish hooks and lines and all the other bruises one gets hunting big game fish. Ernest looked down at the cuts and scars and said proudly: 'Fisherman's hands.' . . . I think he expressed those two words with as much pride as anything he said about any of his books."

Several years ago, on a sultrifying June evening, I went out for a boat ride in Key West with Toby Bruce's son. His name is Benjamin Bruce, but around Key West everyone knows him as Dink Bruce. Like his father, who knew Hemingway intimately for almost three decades, Dink's a small, compact figure with a taciturn air. Dink's dad, T. Otto Bruce, who died of lung cancer in 1984, and whom everyone called Toby, was originally from Pauline's hometown, Piggott, Arkansas, which is tucked up into the northeast corner of the state, close to the Missouri border.

Toby Bruce was twelve years younger than Hemingway and less than half his size. He was the ultimate fix-it man. He met Hemingway in the late twenties but didn't get to know him until a few years later, when Hemingway had come to Piggott with his family for Christmas. The friendship is said to have cemented itself when Toby proved himself a good thrower of skeet targets for Hemingway behind the Pfeiffer barn. Toby had remodeled the barn, had built it into a kind of studio to give Hemingway a place to write on visits to his in-laws. "I knew how to throw a trap for clay pigeons," he once said. "I'd give him the business. A low one, then a high one, then a skimmer." Eventually, Hemingway convinced Toby to come to Key West. For the last three decades of Hemingway's life, Toby was the ever-ready secretary, cross-country driving companion, drinking and hunting mate, surrogate parent to Patrick and Gigi, money holder, property manager, fixer-upper, listening post for the newest round of injustices and grievances. After the breakup with Pauline, Toby lived for a time in Cuba with Hemingway and Martha Gellhorn. Then he said he was going back to Key West. Still, the skimmer was seldom more than a wire or phone call or letter away. Toby's the one who, in 1935, not long after first coming to Key West (he'd hitchhiked down from Piggott), built a chain-link fence for Hemingway around 907 Whitehead. Two years later, Pauline got Toby to tear down the unsightly chain-link and put up a more privacy-providing brick wall. She wangled bricks from the city at an absurdly cheap price (later to be the subject of a city council inquiry). Toby borrowed a pickup truck and began transporting nineteen thousand bricks from the navy yard—three thousand at a time. He'd not tried to lay a nearly six-foot-high brick wall in his handyman career. But Toby's wall, with its uneven bricks spaced at odd intervals, bulging out from their mortar here and there, stands today.

On the evening that Toby's son, who was then sixty-one, took me out in his new boat, he'd been cruising Key West waters for something like fifty years. His boat had been constructed as a replica of a thirties Elco and had that instant classic wooden-boat look. She was tubular but she also sat upright, like *Pilar*. All her wooden parts had a kind of pumpkin gleam. Other parts were trimmed out in a rich green canvas nautical cloth. She could have been a pint-size *Pilar* in her prime. As he minded his business going out, Dink said that as a child he'd known Hemingway, although not well, since by then Hemingway was living in Cuba and didn't get over to Key West that much. Once, in elementary school, he was doing a book report on *The Old Man and the Sea,* and, when the teacher didn't especially like what he wrote, he got to ask the author himself some questions about the story. He got a good mark.

We were out about two hours, and it was a great relief from the Calcutta-like humidity on shore. Standing at the wheel, Dink called out the names of different cays and spits and rocks and channels—but it was hard for me to hear the names above the engine noise, so I put away the notebook and just enjoyed the ride. He was barefoot, in brown shorts and a white cotton shirt. His Beatlesque mop of gray hair was blown back. "This is what Hemingway was seeing and hearing all those years ago," he said. "It's the same sand, the same light, the same water hitting the sides of the boat." By the time we were headed back, the sky had grown purple, the water blue-black. The town was winking on like a Christmas set. Dink negotiated us skillfully through the pilings of an old wooden bridge, where the current swirled against the sides of the boat in circles and cross-circles. I trailed my hand in the wake. I felt a shiver. Dink put her into the slip neat as you please. "Do you feel you know your new boat?" I asked. He laughed. "Hell, no. Not yet. Just like I still don't really know these waters yet. But I'm getting the boatman's hands."

Like the big brother he wished only to copy, like his father, like one of his four sisters, Leicester Hemingway, the Baron, the baby of the family, went one September day in 1982 to the foyer of his ill-tended Spanish Colonial stucco home on San Marino Island on Biscayne Bay in Miami Beach and ended his life. He was sixty-seven. He'd become depressed after a string of surgeries. He had diabetes and other ailments. He was convinced they were going to take off his legs, even as his own paranoid and depressed and diabetic father, fifty-four years before, had been convinced of a leg amputation and other horrors on the winter midday when he sat on his marriage bed in Oak Park and put a Smith & Wesson behind his right ear.

Two and a half years before he shot himself—so it would have been either late February or early March of 1980—there was Les Hemingway early one morning, for all the world Ernest Hemingway himself. He was standing off to the side at the Chalk's International Airlines seaplane ramp at Watson Island in the Port of Miami, waiting, as were the rest of us, for the pilot to give a signal to board the plane for the hop over to Bimini. He had that instantly recognizable square-jawed and leathery Hemingway face; the massive upper body of Hemingway males; the requisite white Papa beard. He wore ratty clothes and sneakers without laces, and beneath one arm was a folded-over grocery bag: the never-quite-measuring-up kid brother who'd tried to be a serious writer, and who'd known some success. The one who'd kicked around in the newspaper and magazine worlds, in government service, in boatbuilding and commercial fishing. There are Hemingway letters in which the older sibling is saying things like For crissakes, Baron, take a bath, will you, and get your hair cut, and wash your face good before you go for that job interview, because as we both know one of your worst habits is your goddamn sloppiness.

Les Hemingway had been haunting Bimini for years. He genuinely cared for the place, and the place genuinely cared for him back. In the folded-over grocery sack were a hundred or so copies of the latest edition of the Bimini News, of which Les was editor, reporter, distributor, and proprietor. His custom, once each new issue was ready, was to fly over on the seaplane and then go up and down Bimini's main street—essentially Bimini's only street—pressing free copies on locals and tourists. He'd retrieve them from the grocery sack with his big hearty wave and hello and, often, a handshake. "Smallest newspaper in the world, takes two editions to wrap a bonefish," he liked to say. I watched him do that all weekend. This was seven years before Ernest Hemingway's eldest son, Jack, told me, "Well, I've decided what works for me is not going deep." Before the in-between son, Patrick, said, "I have stared ambition in the face and decided I don't wish it." Before the youngest, Gregory, told me: "The 'Papa' cult. Just think what it means to be one of the three of us in this goddamn 'Papa' cult."

The pilot signaled, and the ten or twelve of us got on. Les boarded toward the last. As he strapped himself in, he nodded and smiled. I leaned forward and asked, "Are you by any chance Leicester Hemingway?" The instant reply through a bared-teeth grin: "Yeah, and if you're lucky, it might get you a cup of coffee somewhere."

The World War II–era Grumman Goose seaplane duck-walked into the harbor and took off, spraying water everywhere. Its frame rattled and shook. Twenty minutes later, we whooshed into Bimini Harbor, taxied in the sun past pastel-colored buildings and coconut palms, waddled up a ramp, onto the lower end of King's Highway. Island boys helped the pilots put chocks under the wheels. There was a commotion of unloading. Everybody went into a one-story cement-block customs office. Les got waved through.

There was defiance in things he said that weekend, some stiffening pride. There were moments of bombast and goofy statement. He seemed willing to share an astonishing number of family secrets. (Much later I'd learn from other family members about his great generosity, helping to rear various Hemingways who weren't his own children.) He talked of Pilar, and of how he'd been in Key West on that day in 1934 when she first came in, sparkling in her new varnish. He said he was the founder of a nation called New Atlantis. He'd established it on a reef off Jamaica. He'd issued his own stamps, minted his own coins.

When Ed Hemingway killed himself, on December 6, 1928, at fifty-seven, trying to get away from his diabetes and angina and frozen mind, his youngest child was thirteen—and in the house. Les hadn't gone to school because of a cold. The doctor came home at noontime, burned papers in the basement, told his wife he felt tired and would lie down before lunch. He went upstairs and closed the door. In his 1953 autobiographical novel, The Sound of the Trumpet, Les recounted the moment, as he must have been recounting and fictionalizing it all his life:

195

"It sounded like a shot." He knocked at the door. "Daddy!" He tried the door. It opened, and in the darkened room, all shades drawn except one, there on the bed lay his father, making hoarse breathing noises. His eyes were closed, and in that first instant as he saw him there in the half-dark, nothing looked wrong. He put his hand under his father's head. His hand slipped under easily and when he brought it out again, it was wet-arm with blood.

Grace, who had to be sedated, said she was too grief stricken to appear at the coroner's inquest. She sent the thirteen-year-old to report what he knew.

Critics were thinly condescending about Les's novel, which was a war novel. The cruelest words came from the clever fellows at Time, a two-paragraph notice:

> Many a novelist has tried to be another Hemingway. A 38-year-old ex-newspaperman has long held this distinction without trying: Leicester Hemingway is Ernest Hemingway's younger brother. A commercial fisherman and builder of boats, he looks like Ernest and, like Ernest, has gone to war and written about it.
>
> His first novel, The Sound of the Trumpet, is a fictionalized report of his G.I. experience between D-Day and the end of the war. It focuses on Danforth Granham, a G.I. cameraman in a documentary film unit, later an infantry photographer. . . . The result of all this picture-taking is a series of dramatically unrelated clichés which add up to a minor war document disguised as a novel. What Leicester Hemingway chiefly demonstrates is the importance of being Ernest.

Hemingway himself was in Tanganyika, on five-month safari, when he saw the Time review in late 1953. He was the most famous writer in the world. Six months before, he'd won the Pulitzer Prize; the next year, he'd get the Nobel. Two months hence, in January 1954, he and his wife Mary would survive a pair of surreal plane crashes on successive days in Africa—and he'd stumble from them to read his own obituaries and stoke his myth. Half a dozen years later, in a letter to his brother, Hemingway said of that witty two-graph cut in Time, "It was the most unjust and dirty review that I have ever read." He told Les that he'd written a letter to Time's editors, blasting them, and that he'd had it in the car ready to mail, when he received a copy of the novel itself. The novel, inscribed by Les, had caught up with Hemingway in Nairobi. He didn't take to some things in it that his brother had written about the family, about him, about his army pal, Buck Lanham. "You could hang and rattle on what you wrote about Buck," he told Les. After he saw the novel, Hemingway never bothered to mail his angry letter to Time.

Once, aboard Pilar, Hemingway had said to his little brother, yelling at him, holding in his hand a letter from Grace Hemingway:

> Listen, Baron, will you, for Christ's sake, stop writing those wild letters to your mother? You want to scare her to death with a bunch of wild exaggerations? Sure, you're kidding. But for Christ's sake stop writing that kind of bullshit to your mother. Here's something about a fucking boa constrictor you supposedly fought with. Will you please stop this kind of crap before you give the woman a heart attack.

Les proved a wonderful Bimini tour guide, taking me to room 1 on the second floor of the Compleat Angler Hotel, with its wide veranda and tropical flowers curling through the railings, so that I could see where Hemingway worked and sometimes slept (when he wasn't sleeping on the topside of his boat or elsewhere). He walked me down onto Radio Beach. He arranged for me to get inside the two-story clapboard house, with its overhanging porches, that had inspired the opening paragraph of Islands in the Stream:

> The house was built on the highest part of the narrow tongue of land between the harbor and the open sea. It had lasted through three hurricanes and it was built solid as a ship. It was shaded by tall coconut palms that were bent by the trade wind and on the ocean side you could walk out of the door and down the bluff across the white sand and into the Gulf Stream. The water of the Stream was usually a dark blue when you looked out at it when there was no wind. But when you walked out into it there was just the green light of the water over that floury white sand and you could see the shadow of any big fish a long time before he could ever come in close to the beach.

You can fault hell out of that heavily edited and stitched-together novel (the cleaver work was done principally by Hemingway's widow and publisher nine years after his death), but not a word in that lapidary opening paragraph.

I remember asking Les where he stayed on Bimini, when he came every fortnight or so with his newspaper, which, judging from the several issues I saw, had many typos and a haphazard layout. (He told me he did the writing and editing out of his Florida home.) "Oh, I never worry about that," Les said. "I sleep on the beach. Sometimes I'll sleep in a chair on the porch at the Angler."

We had lunch in the Angler's dark, cool bar, and he didn't object when I offered to pay. Maybe he had plenty of money, but I guessed otherwise. The proprietor of the hotel, a wiry, amiable Biminite named Ossie Brown, whose own father, Harcourt Brown, had been around in Hemingway's time, seemed to enjoy Les, but I thought I could detect a small contempt.

There was no sign of lacerating rage at having been consigned a life—like practically every Hemingway after Ernest—under the shadow of the volcano. Indeed, as the weekend went on, it was Les's decency, in and amid all the apparent neediness, loneliness, that stood out. He'd made what he could of his life.

On August 12, 1982, thirty-one days before his suicide, Les Hemingway mailed a mimeographed letter to his subscribers. It seems so character-istic of what he must have wished to project to the world. "Dear Friend and Subscriber. I've been hospitalized four times in the past five months. Three serious leg operations, two in the last 40 days. Now I can no longer drive a car, or go in a boat or airplane. So the Bimini News is having to suspend publication. Am sorry, but this is life. Cheers, Les."

In the months after the funeral, Les's family helped put together a memorial edition of his best-selling 1962 book about his brother, which had made Les a semi-wealthy man, at least for a time. In the appendix of the 1982 commemorative edition, Jack Hemingway wrote:

> He was a fine writer who was forced into the ring too early against a tough pro and made to suffer the inevitable comparisons. He and his brother came out of the same nest and both had fine quali-ties as human beings. Somewhere along the line, success and other things killed a lot of the finest qualities in Papa. Leicester remained unspoiled.

One of Les's daughters, Anne E. J. Hemingway Feurer, wrote:

> After the first few operations last Spring, he periodically lost sight of his reasons for living. He was extremely irritable, but this allowed

me to see through his cheerful shell, and I was finally able to talk seriously with him a few times before he died. The thing he wanted least in life to do was to commit suicide. He hated the idea that the world could corner him into that choice—of dying slowly, without dignity, while medicine tried futilely to repair him. He made his choice at the end of a very hot August, becoming cheerful, and eagerly participating in discussions for another week and a half.

The cover and inside flap of the commemorative edition of My Brother, Ernest Hemingway narrate so much of Les's story. In the jacket photograph, Les, in his late twenties, is looking eagerly at his brother, who's now in his forties, and who isn't looking at Les, but at the camera. They're on a sailboat. It's as if all Les desires, still desires, is approval. On the inside flap is an author's picture of Les, now in late-middle age, in full Papa mock-up, hunched at a typewriter, hunting and pecking. It's a mimic of the celebrated photograph of Hemingway on the jacket of For Whom the Bell Tolls. That picture, which took up the entire back cover, was shot in a hotel room at Sun Valley in December 1939. There he is, the real thing, sleeves rolled, hair licked down, one-day growth of black whiskers, the thick hairy arms, the laser concentration, hunting and pecking on his portable.

Hemingway refused to allow Les to publish My Brother, Ernest Hemingway while he was alive. Les had been working on the book in semi-secret for five or six years before the Boss shotgun went off in Ketchum. After a time, Les let his brother know he was writing it. There's a 1959 exchange of letters between them in which Hemingway says:

As of today I forbid absolutely any such publication. If you are short of dough let me know by return mail. . . . Sorry to be so stuffy and formal about something in the family but privacy is more limited each day and I want to keep what I have and it is damned little as it is and if your brother starts invading it things could be, should we say, semi-intolerable and I was never one to refuse to put in the counter attack when it is called for.

Six months after Hemingway was dead, there was Les, back in the limelight, entertaining the New York press about his just-published work.

I remember something he said during that weekend on Bimini, a line so seemingly right about Ernest Hemingway: "He loved everything up to a certain point, and then nothing was any good any more." Les stole the line from himself. The sentence is on page 169 of his book. He was writing of a spring Sunday in 1934 when they'd been out on Pilar, off Key West, in all her newness, and had caught eight dolphinfish, nine bonito, some barracuda. They'd had seven sailfish strikes. It just wasn't enough.

ON BEING SHOT AGAIN

Ernest with his sons, Bimini, July 20, 1935

But now am cured, I think, and want to wash myself out clean with the Gulf and the best soap I know—which is excitement or whatever you call it.

—ERNEST HEMINGWAY, in a letter,
two days before setting out for Bimini

. . . head her across the stream toward a new place where we've never been.

—ERNEST HEMINGWAY, *Esquire*, May 1935

IN *ISLANDS IN THE STREAM*—that botch of a sometimes beautiful book that Ernest Hemingway took up in the fall of 1945, about seven months after returning from World War II—he speaks of raising Bimini out of the sea. He means from the helm of his boat. First, you'd see the line of tall casuarina trees. (They're still there.) Then the house that sat on the highest part of the narrow tongue of land between the open ocean and the protected harbor. "Then, as you came closer, you raised the whole length of the island with the coconut palms, the clapboarded houses, the white line of the beach, and the green of the South Island stretching beyond it." That must have been exactly what it was like from *Pilar's* wheel: raising Bimini, like a green Lazarus, from limitless sea.

Even on maps of the Bahamas, never mind of the western Atlantic, it looks almost like an afterthought, like a mistaken daub of cartographer's ink. Consider: about seven hundred islands and cays and about two thousand rock formations, reaching across one hundred thousand square miles of ocean, from Florida to Haiti, make up the independent archipelago of what's formally known as the Commonwealth of the Bahamas; depending on how you count, little Bimini is about six of those. It seems to hang out there by itself, about fifty miles on the other side of the Gulf Stream, pretty much a straight shot due east of Miami. It amounts to less than ten square miles of landmass. When you first glimpse it from the air, it looks like a belt of trees sitting in a bottle-green lagoon. Some portions of the main strip of land—North Bimini—are so narrow that you can get across it, harbor side to the ocean side, in less than a minute. Its highest rocky point is about twenty feet above sea level—it seems almost as much part of the sea as of the land. But despite its microscopic size, or maybe partly because of it, the place has long had great allure for yachtsmen and sailors, and even more so for big-game fishermen. Only with mild exaggeration does Bimini like to promote itself as the game-fishing capital of the world. It possesses some of the clearest and most colorful and deep-dropping-off water in the world. You can wade right out into the warm water, on a seven-mile-long bathing beach, but before long, that water can go a half-mile deep, and then deeper. When Hemingway first saw it, he said it felt to him like something out of the South Seas, not that he'd ever been to the South Seas. Even today, Bimini will strike you like that, as if it has cheated time. And it's so close to the American mainland, closer even than Cuba.*

Hemingway knew it obsessively, exuberantly, seeming to inhale it whole, for parts of three consecutive fishing seasons, 1935–1937, each stay a little briefer than the previous, and then, for complex reasons, he never saw

*"Bimini Island" is a misnomer. It's a tiny island chain within the Bahamas themselves. Bimini should be called "The Biminis." Some do call it that, actually. The name itself is said to mean "two/small." The natives like to speak of North Bimini, South Bimini, East Bimini, although the last is mostly uninhabited mangroves and sandbars and occasional outcroppings of limestone.

Bimini again. It was almost as if he used it up, spent it through, in the way he used up and spent through so many other things and places and human beings in his life. *He loved everything up to a certain point, and then nothing was any good any more.* In 1935, he spent his longest period there, from mid-April to mid-August, and about four weeks of it were in the company of his wife and children, who'd come over to join him after he'd established his Bimini beachhead. It's curious that we think of Bimini as one of the iconic Hemingway places—and it is, no question—and yet it's also a fact that he passed only about six and a half months there in total. Which of course only speaks to the way he could powerfully imprint himself. You go to the island now, and it's his picture on the cover of the island history book, his legend that seems to be bobbing in every boat slip.

First, though, a semi-famous story about what happened the first time Hemingway tried to take his boat to Bimini (which from Key West was about 230 curving nautical miles to the northeast). Gertrude Stein's even in the story.

Roughly twenty miles out into the Stream, on that spring Sunday morning, in a moderately choppy sea, he looked down at a mess of blood on both his lower legs and said something like *Jesus Christ, I'll be a dirty sonofabitch, I shot myself.* But you couldn't say this in the pages of *Esquire* in 1935. And so, in a curious piece titled "On Being Shot Again: A Gulf Stream Letter," Hemingway wrote of a self-inflicted if not life-endangering pistol wound: " 'I'll be of unsavoury parentage,' remarked your correspondent. 'I'm shot.' " He wrote the piece very fast, as he did all his *Esquire* contributions, this one within five days, when he was back home in Key West, in bed, recuperating, licking his wounds in more senses than one.

It happened on April 7, 1935, about two hours after *Pilar* had pulled away from the navy yard dock with either five or six adults and two months of canned goods and other survival rations on board. (Also, with some expensive new fishing gear that Hemingway intended to try out, as well as with a newly purchased and nifty-looking thirteen-foot sea skiff he was bringing to Bimini.) It happened near a place called American Shoal, when they were trolling along a heavy and dark current of Stream. It happened right at the tail end of a nasty fight with a shark, as they were trying to get the thrashing beast, with its brown back and milky white belly and fearsome teeth, into the boat. It happened when the greased, hollow-point, soft-nosed, lead bullet from Hemingway's .22 caliber Colt Woodsman automatic ricocheted off the brass strip that ran along the top of the coaming at *Pilar*'s stern. The shot, which had gone off involuntarily and whose report no one on board had apparently heard, made a "starry splash" in the metal. From there it caromed into Hemingway's legs.

Hemingway had a long and queer history with queer mishaps. They started early in his life and never really let up. It was as if something was always waiting to poke him in the eye or fall from a bathroom skylight in the middle of the night to gash him in the forehead and send him to the hospital for stitches. That freakish accident was in Paris in March 1928; he'd just gotten over a bout with influenza. In London, in World War II, at three in the morning, he'd smash his forehead into the windshield of a car that had rammed into a steel water tank: fifty-seven stitches at St. George's Hospital. In Jeffrey Meyers's *Hemingway: A Biography*, there's a three-page appendix of Hemingway's accidents and illnesses, starting with a stick in the throat in childhood.

At least once, in the chaotic several seconds before the unheard shot and unseen ricochet, Hemingway had fired into the brainpan of the fish, hoping to kill it. But the shark—which had some new and costly leaders and hooks in its mouth that Hemingway by damn intended to get back—didn't want to be killed. They'd been trying to bring the animal close enough to the boat so they could gaff it, and so that Hemingway could shoot it again and then club it into senselessness and finally haul it aboard.

The shark was a *galano,* or this was Hemingway's name for it. It was a word he'd picked up in Cuba. Hemingway hated almost all sharks, because they were thieves and cannibalizers of the sporting trophies he was trying to get into his boat. (Soon, on Bimini, he'd be tommy-gunning sharks with a Thompson submachine gun, spattering the waves, turning the foam red, like a mad gangster, trying to keep count of how many he'd killed.) But he seems to have had special venom for *galanos,* which are known for their shovel-shaped head, large triangular fin, bad odor, and, not least, by the way they'll go after anything—even the side of your boat, or your rudder—when they're hungry. Seven times in his *Esquire* piece Hemingway uses the word, setting it off with italics.

"Fuck the bastard," he apparently said, which came out a little too cutely in Arnold Gingrich's middlebrow men's magazine as "Fornicate the illegitimate." He'd said that the first time the *galano* had popped his line, which was wound around a new reel he'd ordered by mail over the winter from Abercrombie & Fitch at Forty-Fifth and Madison in New York. It was a "Commander Ross" 14/0 Vom Hofe model, and it could hold up to one thousand yards of thirty-nine-thread line, and it weighed nine and a half pounds before the line was on, and its seven-inch side plate was surfaced with a hard vulcanized rubber so that the reel wouldn't heat up when a big fish began sizzling out the line, and it had cost him $250, not counting the parcel post.

Big-game reels are measured by the diameter of their side plates. A seven-incher was *big*.

Hemingway was counting on it for his coming battles with tuna. All winter he'd daydreamed of giant bluefins off Bimini weighing up to a ton— not that any angler had ever been able to come close to landing such a fish on a rod and reel. But the one-tonners were claimed to exist, were claimed to come highballing along "Tuna Alley" off Bimini each year around the middle of May. How would you land a two-thousand-pound fish? Even if you could get the thing aboard before the sharks got to it, wouldn't it make a hole the size of a torpedo through the floorboards, or stand your boat on end? But Hemingway had a plan, altogether loony sounding. It had to do with that little sea skiff he was taking along.

In addition to the Vom Hofe, he'd also bought a seven-inch Zane Grey reel, crafted by the House of Hardy in Great Britain. Its interior parts were made of Monel, "the strongest non-ferrous metal known . . . guaranteed to be absolutely immune to the action of sea water and air in any part of the world"—that's from 1935 Hardy Brothers catalog copy. For the last three years, Hemingway had been fishing with Zane Grey reels, and up until now a five-and-a-half-inch Zane Grey and a six-inch Zane Grey were all that he'd really needed. His six-inch marlin reel (it's the one previously mentioned, pictured on the first page of the prologue of this book) was a beautiful piece of tackle. Its spool spindle was encased in seize-free ball bearings. It weighed seven and three-quarters pounds—without any line.

Hemingway slacked out another bait on the same line, and goddamn if the illegitimate didn't pop that one, too. Now the fish had a "length of double line streaming out of his mouth like one whisker on a catfish," Hemingway wrote in *Esquire*. It was on the third slack, with yet a third bait on a different line and different equipment, that they'd managed to get the fish close—and he'd managed to get the gaff in, even as he was struggling to keep the line taut against the fish. He was out of his fighting chair, standing nearly atop the shark, holding the hickory-tipped rod as far out from him as he could. And right at what must have been the instant of greatest strain between animal and man and fishing line, with the gaff hanging from its side, with two lengths of popped double line in its whiskered mouth, the fish went into what seemed a convulsing fit of epilepsy. There was this huge cracking sound. The shaft on the gaff splintered, and a piece of it came flying at Hemingway's right hand. That's the hand that held the .22.

All this was happening in several square feet of spraying space at the boat's stern. It was happening while another fisherman, fishing amidships (Mike Strater, his close friend but also his athletic rival), was battling his own *galano*. There were sharks in the water in the first place because they'd come after the school of dolphinfish into which *Pilar* had trolled just a little while earlier. Once the sharks had shown, the dolphins began to flash silver above the waves, terrified at what was freight-training up from below to tear huge chunks from their sides at a single bite. Dolphins are small, toothed whales. There's something almost innocent, playful, about them. You don't associate them with the word "savage." But like almost any blindly attacked thing, they can seem savage in their terror.

And even before the dolphins had come, there had been the giant green turtle. It had come close to the boat, scudding—to use Hemingway's word—under the surface. The turtle would make good eating for the trip; they could fillet the meat and salt it down in layers in a keg. They had rigged the harpoon to get the turtle when the dolphins appeared. And after the dolphins, the *galanos*.

Up on the overhead of the cockpit, John Dos Passos, who was much more of a Sunday kind of fisherman than a competitive one, was trying to make eight-millimeter black-and-white home movies. He'd been the first one to hook into a twenty-pound dolphin, but once the sharks were at the boat, he handed off his rod and went for the movie camera. The camera jerked wildly.

The footage is thrilling, blurring stuff, although only ten seconds of the actual fight have been preserved. You see the fisherman climbing into his leather harness as the battle begins. You see the fish thrashing in the water. You see various hands trying to bring it aboard. You see the fit of epilepsy. Then, suddenly, in the next sequence, Hemingway is back on shore, limping around with his second son, grinning, mugging for the camera, pulling up his striped pajama pant leg to show off his bandaged wounds, clowning with Dos Passos. It's a couple days later, and he's in the yard of the big fine house at Key West with all those strutting peacocks and airy verandas. He surely looks like someone overcompensating for a recent humiliation.

There's a surprising amount of Hemingway film footage around, from the thirties through the fifties. It brings him back to human scale. It reduces him, so to speak, rescues him from his insupportable myths. Even when he's doing things that the rest of us wouldn't try, Hemingway in home movies seems far less of a Hollywood invention, somehow. He seems almost ordinary, somebody who could almost be your show-offy neighbor. Here he is, at the dock that morning as they're getting set to go. He's picking up Pauline as if he's a bridegroom carrying his beloved across a threshold. He's clowning with a captain's hat, as if he's the admiral of the ocean sea. He's shaking hands with his fishing partners. Hardware-store proprietor Charles Thompson has come down with his wife, Lorine, to say good-bye. Hemingway's so hungry for the hungry eye of the camera. How very tall he seems in the old thirties footage—somehow you get it on film far more than in the photographs. He looks rangy as a tight end, and there is about his physical movements a likable schoolboy gawkiness, even allowing for the cinematic jumpiness, even allowing for the voracious ego and competitive infighter that lived inside the schoolboy. The old movies will also reveal how radically his looks changed, once they began to change. The internal must have been devouring the external. Somehow, he had turned into an elderly man before he'd even hit sixty, and the transformation from what he looks like on this fine Sunday in 1935 to what he'll look like by the middle and late fifties seems to have had, once again, very little in-between stage. But such thoughts are too gloomy to linger on when someone, not yet thirty-six years old, is making the world new on a piece of paper.

He looked down. A mess of blood. A discrete hole about three inches below his kneecap. A second discrete hole, more ragged than the first, "bigger than your thumb," as he put it in *Esquire*. Plus, any number of birdshot-like small lacerations on the calves of both legs. "Could I have pulled the trigger twice or three times without knowing it the way former mistresses did in the testimony regarding Love Nest Killings. Hell, no, thought your correspondent." Again, that's from "On Being Shot Again."

Apparently, he fired just once. The bulk of that bullet was in his left calf and the fragments of it in both legs. This would become clear once he was back on land and Dr. William Warren at the Key West U.S. Marine Hospital was extracting many of the fragments, although not the largest piece. That one was too far in. To take out the big chunk would have meant removing too much muscle. Doctor Warren gave the patient a shot against tetanus and told Hemingway to go to bed. None of it was particularly serious, he said, as long as no infections set in. And to keep that from happening, he needed rest. The wounds would heal over quickly.

There wasn't any pain, or not initially, or so Hemingway would tell his readers. Soon after *Pilar* had been turned around and headed back to Key West, soon after someone had boiled water and scrubbed the wounds with antiseptic soap and had poured a lot of iodine into the two holes, he would retch his lunch into a bucket. This, too, he would report.

Back home (or even on the way home), as John Dos Passos wrote in his 1966 memoir, *The Best Times*, Katy was "so mad she would hardly speak to him." This line has been much evoked by Hemingway chroniclers to support the view that Hemingway had recklessly endangered the lives of others. (Dos Passos's account has several errors of both fact and chronology. For instance, he claimed Hemingway had shot himself with a rifle.) Maybe Katy, who'd known and loved Hemingway ambivalently since his northern Michigan years, was rageful in the way of parents or older siblings once an endangering event is over: you are so relieved that no serious harm has come to your loved one that you end up showing it by turning unspeakably angry at him. Katy, nearly eight years older than Hemingway, often reproached him like a kid brother. What happened aboard *Pilar* isn't so much emblematic of Hemingway's carelessness—he was never known to be careless with weapons—as of his ego: he needed once again to be the whole show. Perhaps if the fisherman hadn't been trying to land the fish and gaff it and shoot it in the head all at once, the accident would never have occurred. So you could say he'd hoisted himself, not for the last time, on his own petard.*

On Monday, April 8, at home, he wrote to Gingrich. "Am staying in bed today and tomorrow. Will get up Wednesday and leave Thursday if all o.k.—if had to get shot couldn't have been shot in better place." He didn't

---

*At the beginning of this paragraph, I put in parentheses the words "or even on the way home" because I don't know for sure if Katy was aboard on the first try for Bimini. Many Hemingway chroniclers and chronologists have assumed she was. But Dos Passos's text doesn't explicitly say that, and neither Hemingway's letters nor his wife's letters confirm it, and indeed the film footage seems to suggest otherwise: all the women look to be waving from shore as *Pilar* leaves the dock. I know for certain that Katy was aboard with her husband a week later, when the party set out for Bimini again. Does such a trivial fact matter one way or the other? Only to the extent that it seems to reveal unwittingly the animus of those latter-day experts who wish to seize on practically any Hemingway negative they can find—and God knows, there are so many. Kenneth S. Lynn, in his unforgiving 1987 biography—which is often as absurd in its psychosexual interpretations of Hemingway as it is brilliant in its critical analyses of the work—wrote: "Katy was so mad at Hemingway that she barely spoke to him the whole way." Well, maybe.

get away on Thursday, nor did he leave for Bimini on Saturday—the second try would be pushed back three times, until the following Monday. A writer's mind is working. Suddenly, Hemingway has a story to tell. He knows he owes Gingrich a piece on his $3,000 boat loan, and he's late with it. "I can write you a piece," he says, proceeding to set up typographically on the page the suggested title. He centers the words and skips down several spaces on his stationery.

On Being Shot Again
a Gulf Stream Letter

By that Friday, the story is in hand. "Here is the piece," he says in a covering letter. As to that fuck-the-bastard business, which he's made into fornicate-the-illegitimate, he asks Gingrich: "If you can't say fornicate can you say copulate or if not can you say co-habit? If not that would have to say consumate I suppose." Going on: "Wound perfectly clean so far and should be healed tight in another couple of days. Very little pain."

"On Being Shot Again" appeared in the June 1935 *Esquire*. This is how it disconcertingly—you'd almost want to say gleefully—opens:

> If you ever have to shoot a horse stand so close to him that you cannot miss and shoot him in the forehead at the exact point where a line drawn from his left ear to his right eye and another line drawn from his right ear to his left eye would intersect. A bullet there from a .22 caliber pistol will kill him instantly and without pain and all of him will race all the rest of him to the ground and he will never move except to stiffen his legs out so he falls like a tree.

The beginning of the second paragraph: "If you ever have to shoot a shark shoot him anywhere along a straight line down the center of his head, flat, running from the tip of his nose to a foot behind his eyes." The piece goes on like this for about another thirty lines, providing instructions on the right bones to sever in the neck or the spinal column when you wish to take down large creatures cleanly.

And how does Gertrude Stein fit into all this? With her own taking down. Not razor-clean, but a wounding for sure.

In the fall of 1934, and through the winter and spring of 1935, Hemingway's onetime Paris mentor and godparent to his oldest child, now a sworn enemy, along with her sour, diminutive secretary-lover, Alice B. Toklas, had crisscrossed and barnstormed America. It was Stein's first time back in thirty-one years. They had left Le Havre on the SS *Champlain* in October in their crocheted hats and heavy coats, and they didn't return to the badly heated comforts of 27, rue de Fleurus—where those avant-garde canvasses shimmered in the hallways and above the mantels—until May 11, 1935. Stein had said that she wished to experience the land of her birth from coast to coast, which is just what she did. As she later wrote, "People always had been nice to me because I am pleasing but now this was going to be a different thing. We were on the Champlain and we were coming." That seemed a limpid enough thought, unlike this one: "I will be well welcome when I come. Because I am coming. Certain I come having come."

In America, the seer with the obscure flashes of something or other had belted into an airplane for the first time. She had lectured at something like thirty colleges and universities, among them Harvard, Princeton, the University of Chicago, Bryn Mawr. Pathé News produced a newsreel—they nearly had to get in line. On NBC radio and at the Museum of Modern Art, she had made many literary pronouncements, not all of which were immediately clear (headline in *The New York Times:* "Miss Stein Speaks to Bewildered 500"). In New Orleans, she had dined with Sherwood Anderson. In Chicago, she had stayed at Thornton Wilder's apartment on Drexel Avenue. In California, she had driven a rental car through Yosemite. In Monterey, she had sat like a stone contemplating the Pacific. At Berkeley, a University of California student had asked her why her prose was so much more difficult to comprehend than her spoken words. She'd replied: "If they invited Keats for lunch, and they asked him an ordinary question would they expect him to answer with the 'Ode to the Nightingale'?"

Oh, how this boatload of press coverage must have galled Hemingway. At a dinner party in Beverly Hills (the guest of honor got to choose her own guests), she'd had a séance with Dashiell Hammett, Charlie Chaplin, Lillian Hellman, Anita Loos, and Paulette Goddard. She'd declined a movie offer from Warner Brothers—Hollywood didn't interest her except as a passing spasm of contemporary life. Finally, the summer having almost come, having patchworked and crisscrossed America to her satisfaction for nearly seven months, shed of those coarse-nap woolens designed for dank French winters, longing only to get back to the other side of the ocean (where she had once strolled Bumby Hemingway in a big black pram in the Jardin du Luxembourg), she and Alice had returned to New York.

On Friday, May 3, 1935, the day before the pair had sailed again for Le

Havre on the *Champlain,* Stein had granted one last stateside interview. By then the ex-acolyte and his boat had been on Bimini for something like two weeks. He hadn't been able to fish yet, not for big ones out in the Stream, just some small stuff around the docks. But he was a happy man, even if he was still a little wobbly on his feet. His wife had just been over on a brief visit, and other friends were shortly due. His wounds, as he'd just reported to Max Perkins in a letter, had all but stopped "suppurating," which was a word his physician-father would have appreciated. In Chicago, "On Being Shot Again" was set in type—subscribers would have the story in their hands in another twelve or thirteen days. In New York, *Scribner's Magazine* had just come out with the first installment of its serialization of *Green Hills of Africa,* which would appear as a book in the fall, containing some tart comments about Miss Stein. (Through that summer, and into the early fall, Max Perkins would try to get him to remove, or soften, some of the Stein passages—with mixed results. Hemingway did relinquish on the word "bitch" in one passage.)

Stein's interlocutor on the third was John Hyde Preston, a semi-obscure Canadian writer who was almost as pretentious-sounding as she was. Most of the talk was in Stein's suite at the Algonquin Hotel, although some of it took place while they were out marching on Madison Avenue. "Walk on my left," she commanded, above the traffic, "because my right ear is broken." The "conversation," as the piece was titled when it appeared in print several months later, was about the terrible thing that happens to American writers: how they feel they must create a new literature; how they get to be thirty-five or forty and the juices dry up, and then what happens? They stop writing altogether or they begin to repeat themselves formulaically. It was all so sad and tragic.

You could almost hear what was coming next. "What about Hemingway?" the interviewer asks, venturing his own opinion that Hemingway was good merely until after *A Farewell to Arms*—say, into the first years of the 1930s.

Oh no, Stein says, he wasn't really any good after 1925. In the early short stories, he had it, but then he betrayed himself. You see, she said,

> When I first met Hemingway he had a truly sensitive capacity for emotion, and that was the stuff of the first stories; but he was shy of himself and he began to develop, as a shield, a big Kansas City-boy brutality about it, and so he was "tough" because he was really sensitive and ashamed that he was. Then

it happened. I saw it happening and tried to save what was fine there, but it was too late. He went the way so many other Americans have gone before, the way they are still going. He became obsessed by sex and violent death.

She elaborated, testing a stubby finger in Manhattan hotel-room air.

It wasn't just to find out what these things were; it was the disguise for the thing that was really gentle and fine in him, and then his agonizing shyness escaped into brutality. No, now wait—not real brutality, because the truly brutal man wants something more than bullfighting and deep-sea fishing and elephant killing or whatever it is now, and perhaps if Hemingway were truly brutal he could make a real literature out of those things; but he is not, and I doubt if he will ever again write truly about anything. He is skillful, yes, but that is the writer; the other half is the man.

Obsessed by sex and violence. Developing, as a shield, your big Kansas City–boy brutality, because your sensitivity to life deeply shames you. A mask for the thing in you that's really gentle and fine.

I've always wondered if at least part of the reason that Ernest Hemingway so grew to revile Gertrude Stein was because he understood how close to the bone she could scrape. A writer and Hemingway friend named Prudencio de Pereda (mentioned earlier) once used a baseball analogy to describe some of the better psychological tries by Hemingway's detractors: the ball looks beautiful from the instant it leaves the bat, seemingly headed straight for the upper deck, clear homer, only to veer off in the last seconds to just this side of the foul pole. It ends up only another strike on the batter, but, damn, wasn't it fine watching that thing fly?

Pilar departed the Key West docks again early on April 15 and this time the fishing party made it fine. The two newly hired crewmen, who'd been aboard the week before, were again along, and of course they had their nicknames. They were Albert "Old Bread" Pinder (engineer and pilot) and Richard "Saca Ham" Adams (cook and mate); both were both longtime Key West hands. Hemingway's Cuban mate, Carlos Gutiérrez, wasn't making this trip, but Hemingway planned to send for him later in the summer, if things on Bimini turned out to be as good as he hoped. All winter Carlos had hung the cleaned fishing lines in loose coils in a muslin bag from a rafter in his Havana home where he knew the sun wouldn't hit them but the breezes would. Both Dos Passoses were aboard. But in place of Mike Strater—who'd gone back to his winter residence in West Palm Beach and intended to fly over early in May—was Charles Thompson.

They trolled well out into the current and rode the Stream in the way of an airliner catching a tail wind, letting it carry them eastward and northward along the Keys, for the first leg, which is to say about 150 north-by-northeast miles, past Molasses Reef and French Reef and Dixie Shoal and what's known on nautical charts as the Elbow. They caught some small yellowfin tuna and some dolphinfish with rainbow-colored tails. At night they came inside the coastal barrier reef for safe anchorage in Hawk Channel, which runs all the way up on the Atlantic side of the Keys. The year before, when Hemingway and the Wheeler rep from Brooklyn and Captain Bra Saunders had first steered *Pilar* down from Miami, they'd come via the protected Hawk Channel passage, staying close in to shore. Now he was a much more confident captain.

They slept on board and cooked up what they caught. On the morning of the third day, when they were up near Key Largo, Hemingway cut his boat directly across the Stream, taking his bearing from Carysfort Light (which is how it's listed on nautical charts), steering east-northeast for Gun Cay, and then on up to Bimini itself.

Within days, he was inhaling it whole, claiming it for his own. Within days, he was junking his original plan, which was to stay for only a couple weeks on this first visit. No, he'd probably stay right on through and send for the family later in the summer. Maybe Cuba would have to wait this year until late summer or even the fall. He wouldn't catch up to Gertrude Stein's near-miss of a homer until he'd gotten back home and had unwrapped several months' worth of magazines and newspapers. (The piece appeared in the August 1935 *Atlantic*.) It isn't known whether he read her piece up in his writing studio with the door closed and began suppurating all over again. (The medical definition means to form or discharge pus.)

Now and again in the years ahead, he'd claim he'd not turned around and gone back to Key West after he'd shot himself, but had wadded up his wounds and taken shots of whiskey and gone on fishing and steaming toward that speck of British-held soil on the eastern side of the Stream whose original settlers (somewhere around AD 500) were said to be seafaring Indians from South America called Lucayo. Maybe Hemingway forgot he'd written "On Being Shot Again." More likely, he didn't care.

Go back for a moment to the photograph at the start of the previous chapter. He had been on Bimini three months when it was taken. The following day he'd turn thirty-six. That's Pilar flying her American colors in this back-of-the-moon Crown Colony, where there's one policeman; where two-thirds of the population is black; where the native kids go to school barefoot but also in clean white uniforms; where drinking water and ice and the fresh vegetables and mail for the visiting anglers arrive every Tuesday on the pilot boat from Miami; where the slattern little waterside bars are so inviting and dark when you've ducked in from the glare of the white coral road; where wedding parties strut and jive through the center of town to calypso beats, with the whole island taking a holiday; where it's an almost unheard-of thing for a house or a school or one of the Protestant missionary clapboard churches to have glass in its windows—they have wooden hurricane shutters instead. They get propped outward with a stick, so that the light refracts in at a cooling slant.

In this early-evening Bahamian light, the fisherman stands proudly, victoriously, with his three boys, ages seven, eleven, and three. This is at Brown's Dock, which is where he usually parks Pilar after her labors. Just out of sight is a pole with a saggy wind sock, and close by a sign with large block lettering: ENTRANCE DOCK GAS AND OIL. In wider shots, you get the pleasing ricketiness.

The four beaten things in the background are blue marlin. They'd been caught by three fishermen in three boats within several hours of each other. The two at the left are Hemingway's, smallest of the four, which must have agitated deeply. One weighed 362 pounds, the other 330. They were his tenth and eleventh big-game catches of the season. All four fish were taken by rod and reel, and each was fought solo to the boat by the fisherman who'd hooked it, thus honoring the codes of the sport.

Perhaps an hour before, Hemingway had brought in his two marlin, maneuvering Pilar through the shallow, narrow channel that separates North Bimini from South Bimini, flying the victory flag, clanging the bell, hauling the prizes up onto the dock, winching them into place along with the other two, getting the native boys to scrub them down with soapy pails of water so that they'd properly glisten in the photographs. Later in the evening he got very drunk. Soon after, possibly the next day, when he was sober, he wrote down some notes about his catches—they may, in fact, be several days' worth of cryptic notes. He was using for a logbook the title page of his 1932 Modern Library edition of Thomas Mann's The Magic Mountain, which is one of the fifty or so books that had come across the Gulf Stream in Pilar's hold back in April. Using a pencil, he wrote around and through the publisher's logo, around and through the name of the translator, around and through the large type of the title itself.

Hemingway noted that he was using his new Vom Hofe, with thirty-nine-thread line, and that one of his fish had "jumped 3 times straight toward boat—then ran about 350—got him alongside boat—He hooked up and jumped 33 times against the current," and that once they'd gotten the other fish "on board alive" he managed to jump "20 times or more in cockpit." Such minutiae, even if they defy credulity, help bring the day that much more alive. (How could he know in the midst of all that watery chaos his fish jumped thirty-three times against the current? Sure it wasn't thirty-four? Never mind, that's being a literalist, and this is a fabulist, inventing his life even as he's living it.)

But all of what I've said thus far has little to do with the real reason why I asked you to turn back and gaze again at the image at the start of the previous chapter. What I wanted to dwell on is the terrifying and unwitting but no less destructive influence of a man's unconscious on those whom he deeply loved. That's an idea, not possible to prove, that the youngest child of Ernest Hemingway spoke about at length when I met him in Miami in 1987. In a sense, that's all that Gregory Hemingway spoke of in a surreal conversation that started in the evening, before it was dark, and didn't end until close to midnight. I had this photograph in my hand that night.

Here they are, the Hemingway kids, day of the four blue marlin, July 20, 1935, standing with their windblown and barefoot and newly bearded specimen of a dad:

Patrick, the Mexican Mouse, in his dorky sunsuit and black tennies, sans socks. He often poses with hands on hips, as if to say to the world, as if to imitate his own father as a child: ain't afraid of nothin'. You might gaze on him and form the word "mouthy."

Jack, in his knickers and webbed Boy Scout belt and canvas espadrilles, with their ribbon loops knotted at his ankles. He could almost be a dainty Parisian kid. His characteristic shyness has forced his head down in the instant before the snap. Schatz, as his dad calls him, when he's not calling him the Bum or Mr. Bumby or some derivation thereof, has been fetched from St. Louis by his stepmother for this monthlong stay in the British West Indies sun with his half brothers, with whom he does and does not get along.

Gregory, the Gig, Mr. Gigi, fitting himself neatly in the space between his protector's spread-apart legs. Isn't he the most innocent of the three, just a dopey little guy with pudgy fingers and rolls of baby fat? He'll be four in November.

In the real-time space that existed on either side of this rectangle, the things of childhood had to have been happening. Can't you see Patrick taking his right arm off his hip and beginning to pick his nose? Or Bumby starting to bang Gigi on the top of his head? And Gigi scrunching up his face and bursting into tears? As the poet and critic Mark Strand, who has written eloquently about the power of family album photographs, once said, as he looked at a snapshot of his mother and his sister and his four-year-old long-ago self, and in so doing felt a great and terrible rush of sadness: "[I]t is so much about the moment in which it was taken. Like childhood itself, it is innocent of the future."

In Islands in the Stream, one of the characters says: " 'And the meanest is Andy.' " Many pages later, after the broadbill swordfish fight that serves as the climax of the "Bimini" section, Thomas Hudson muses about his youngest boy: "But there was something about him that you could not trust." This is Hemingway's next sentence: "What a miserable, selfish way to be thinking about people that you love, he thought."

Islands is the only novel into which Hemingway directly and unambiguously inserted his three children: Bumby as young Tom, Patrick as David, Gregory as Andrew. Each son is a minor-major character in the "Bimini" section. Islands is also a book that Hemingway didn't believe in enough artistically to publish in his lifetime, and the first fact may well have something to do with the second. Furthermore, Islands is a book that Hemingway had once envisioned as part of a mammoth trilogy of war novels about the sea, the land, the air. As many chroniclers have said, the dream never came close to reality. The land part ultimately got reduced and siphoned off into Across the River and into the Trees. The air part died aborning. And the "Sea Book," or the "Sea Novel," as Hemingway often capitalized it in letters and shadowy conversation, is what we know today as Islands in the Stream and The Old Man and the Sea. It's all pretty confusing, and the academics are still trying to sort out exact time frames of composition. In the summer of 1951, Hemingway put a microfilm copy of sixteen hundred pages of the unfinished Sea Book into a lockbox at the Banco Nacional of Havana, keeping the original for revisions, but apparently he didn't work on it again after December 1951—or so scholars have concluded. Nonetheless he had to have known that one day, when he wasn't around, those pages would be taken up and retrofitted into a so-called finished work of art by the Hemingway merchants, one of the chief merchants in this instance being his fourth wife, whose six-line disingenuous note to readers at the front of the 1970 publication of Islands in the Stream said, in part: "Beyond the routine chores of correcting spelling and punctuation, we made some cuts in the manuscript, I feeling that Ernest would surely have made them himself. The book is all Ernest's."

Although he doesn't specify his fictional sons' ages in the novel, Hemingway makes each of them a bit older than his true self. Thus, in the "Bimini" section of Islands—which is really the only place that they appear as breathing characters, since all three are dead by the time of the succeeding sections—young Tom Hudson seems about fourteen or fifteen, Davy Hudson about ten, little Andrew Hudson perhaps seven. There are places where the author doesn't even alter the real names of the people he's portraying. Now and again the main character addresses his oldest son as Schatz.

The longest descriptive passage about the main character's youngest son occurs on page 53. Gregory Hemingway told me that, when he first read that page, the shock of recognition was so great, the words so stabbingly right, he decided, right there, if he ever wrote his own book about his father he'd use it as his epigraph.

The smallest boy was fair and was built like a pocket battleship. He was a copy of Thomas Hudson, physically, reduced in scale and widened and shortened. His skin freckled when it tanned and he had a humorous face and was born being very old. He was a devil too, and deviled both his older brothers, and he had a dark side to him that nobody except Thomas Hudson could ever understand. Neither of them thought about this except that they recognized it in each other and knew it was bad and the man respected it and understood the boy's having it. They were very close to each other although Thomas Hudson had never been as much with this boy as with the others. This youngest boy, Andrew, was a precocious excellent athlete and he had been marvelous with horses since he had first ridden. The other boys were very proud of him but they did not want any nonsense from him, either. He was a little unbelievable and anyone could well have doubted his feats except that many people had seen him ride and watched him jump and seen his cold, professional modesty. He was a boy born to be quite wicked who was being very good and he carried his wickedness around with him transmuted into a sort of teasing gaiety. But he was a bad boy and the others knew it and he knew it. He was just being good while his badness grew inside him.

Gregory did indeed use that as an epigraph for Papa: A Personal Memoir, which was published in 1976. Papa, only a little more than one hundred pages long, continues to stand on the top rung of all Hemingway family memoirs, no matter its inaccuracies and omissions and distortions and deeply embittered tone. In the preface, Norman Mailer wrote, "For once, you can read a book about Hemingway and not have to decide whether you like him or not. He is there. By God, he exists." When his book appeared, fifteen years after his father's suicide, Hemingway's youngest son was in the fractured middle of his third marriage. He was a medical doctor, a semi-secret cross-dresser, a manic-depressive, an alcoholic, a largely neglectful father of eight (one of whom was an adopted stepson). And for all of that, and in another way because of all that, there were many people around who wouldn't have blinked to call him a very loving man. This is Gregory's opening sentence: "I never got over a sense of responsibility for my father's death and the recollection of it sometimes made me act in strange ways."

Among other things that a widened, shortened, middle-aged, pocket battleship of a man with an incredibly old-looking face said in a ninety-five-degree Coconut Grove night was this:

He always had this tremendous need to have a son who would do well, please him inordinately. But how we felt so compelled to do all these things to make him love us. Look, my brother Patrick went off to Africa to be a professional hunter. So did I for a time. That's no way for an adult to spend his life, taking people out with guns to destroy animals. But this was the kind of person I consciously and unconsciously knew he admired. And so did my brother Pat. Pat would have been so much happier being a curator in a museum.

Gigi shook his head. He was quiet for a minute.

I don't know exactly how it was done, the destruction. You tell me. What is it about a loving, dominating, basically well-intentioned father that ends up making you go nuts? I mean, the anger you feel—at what, exactly? Because he got so large, did that mean the rest of us had to diminish? None of us have amounted to very much. You can be angry at a man's overpowering unconscious, I guess. But was that unconscious malevolent? Did he wish to hurt us by it? I don't think so, not really. He was trying to do his work. His own insides were a wreck. My brother Pat, who was a brilliant kid, who really could have been something, was absolutely destroyed by my father to do anything in the outside world.

OUTSIDE WORLDS

From left, Mike Strater, Baroness Blixen, Pauline,
Ernest, and Bror Blixen, Bimini, early summer 1935

TO READ the Bimini letters from the middle of 1935 is to think of someone almost not bothering with sleep, such was the exuberance for a new
place he'd never been (as Hemingway said a bit tautologically in the May
1935 *Esquire*).

Among the first visitors to arrive (not counting his spouse) were Mike
Strater and the Blixens—the voluptuous Eva and the legendary Bror, out
of Africa by way of Sweden. Strater didn't know the Blixens. Everybody
slept on board. In those tight, rolling quarters, with Hemingway's bulk and
ego in the middle, it made for a combustible, eroticized mix. In between
the sexual anxiety was the fishing tension, a constant implicit competition
of its own.

Actually, you can feel the sexual tension just from looking at the photographs that were taken. It's so sybaritic-looking on his boat—the sunbath-
ing at the stern, the towels and tennis shoes flung here and there, the bare
bodies coated with tanning lotion.

Strater, of course, was the six-foot, two-hundred-pound, Princeton-bred amateur boxer and tennis player and painter with the hawk nose and slight stutter and girlish middle name of Hyacinth whom Hemingway had first met at Ezra Pound's studio, thirteen years before, when he'd just come back to Paris from a reporting assignment to Constantinople for the *Toronto Star*. He and Hemingway were drawn to each other by their common interest in the sporting life. The two novices on the Paris climb—Strater once characterized their relationship this way—would talk painting and literature for hours and then go off to a Montparnasse gym or the pebbly tennis courts at the Jardin du Luxembourg to try to outwit and out-hit each other. (Neither was worth much of a damn at tennis, not then, but at boxing they were roughly matched, in both weight and skill.) Strater was the first artist ever to paint a portrait of Hemingway. In early 1924, when William Bird's Three Mountains Press published Hemingway's second book, *in our time* (in an edition of 170 copies), a printer's wood-cut from what Strater called his "boxer portrait" of Hemingway made up the frontispiece. It had him staring moodily downward, as if into his pain. The full-face portrait had pleased Hemingway. The thirty-two-page book itself, made up of a dozen and a half prose vignettes so brief that they felt like jewels resting in the cup of your hand, had been a sensation among the Left Bank expats, at least the younger ones.

Strater, three years older than Hemingway, was president of the Maine Tuna Club. In the summer of 1933 he had caught sixteen tuna off the coast of Ogunquit, which is where he'd built a permanent home and had spent six months of every year since coming back to America in the mid-twenties. None of his New England tuna catches had been of the monster variety; Bimini was meant to fix that. For the last two years, ever since reports of giant tuna and swordfish and marlin off Bimini had begun drifting through the world of big-game fishing, he and Hemingway had been talking up a trip to the Bahamas. In a July 1933 letter to Strater, shortly before leaving for the first leg of his African safari (which Strater, like MacLeish, had prudently decided to sidestep), Hemingway had spoken of "the run to beat hell and steadily off Gun Key and Cat Key and Bimini on the other edge of the gulf stream only forty-five miles from Miami. We <u>must</u> try them there." He meant bluefin tuna. The island, according to Hemingway's informants, had a "good harbor, no mosquitoes, lots of wahoo, big and small marlin and wonderful bonefishing if you want to bring your grandmother along." This last crack was meant to say that bonefish were all right in their way, hard to catch, spooky as rainbows, silvery flashes in the shallow aqua flats, but it didn't matter, because he was a convert to another church, and it wasn't the church of small.

In this same letter, misspelling and mistyping and stream-of-consciousness-ing as he went, Hemingway had told Strater of the boat he hoped to buy when he returned from Africa: "thirty eight foot, diesel powered." He'd "put in twinscrews, double rudders, proppeller and rudder guards so you can't foul line and yet can spin her on her ass with the twin screws. We can live on her, carry a cook and fish anywhere." Somewhere between the writing of this five-page letter and the cab ride to Cropsey, in April of the following year, he'd decide not on a diesel-powered boat, but on a gas-powered vessel, with a powerful main engine and a smaller trolling one. And the actual *Pilar*, the realized one, wouldn't run on twin screws, as he had envisioned and as numerous Hemingway chroniclers have claimed. She'd have *double* screws, owing to the size difference of the big Chrysler and the small Lycoming: technical—and important—distinctions.

On the morning Strater made it to Bimini—May 3, 1935—Hemingway was waiting for him in the harbor aboard *Pilar*, and Gertrude Stein was marching up Madison Avenue, taking his name in vain.

Pauline had just departed. So had Charles Thompson and Katy and John Dos Passos. (The Dos Passoses would be back for another brief stay in June.) Pauline, who'd been over for a long weekend, had come on the Pan Am seaplane flight that left twice weekly out of Dinner Key Airport in Coconut Grove, en route to Nassau, with a Bimini pit stop. (The actual stop was at nearby Cat Cay. Cat Cay was where the wealthy of South Florida were erecting their Depression-era hideaways, and so that's where the flying boats splashed down.) Pauline would be back and forth during May (usually sleeping ashore, not keen on *Pilar*'s nighttime seesawing), and then in late June would return with the family to rent a cottage for a month, bringing along her sister, Jinny Pfeiffer, a lesbian, whose bobbed hair, diminutive frame, and cheeky way of speech had always attracted Hemingway, perhaps even sexually (students of Hemingway have long speculated on the idea); that is, until their mutual hard hatred set in. This would have to do with many factors, not least the split from Pauline.

Blixen: the name is intimately bound up with that whole engauzed Hollywood-soaked region of the mind known as British East Africa in the years from, say, the beginning of World War I to the end of the 1930s. You say "British East Africa" and you link it with the word "safari," and latter-day imaginations begin filling with visions of caravans rumbling over the Serengeti, of people who look like Robert Redford mucking about in their shiny jodhpurs and bush jackets tricked out with cartridge loops. Hemingway, with his usual genius for showing up in the right symbolic place at the right time, had gotten in on the back edge of the great romantic safari myth in its so-called golden age.

Baron Bror von Blixen-Finecke was one of Africa's greatest white hunters in the 1920s and 1930s. He was also a world-class philanderer. Blix, or Blickie, as he was known, is said to have possessed an almost alarming stamina—in bed, in the bush, with liters of alcohol. His authentic love for Africa was something that fairly oozed from his pores. He wasn't Hemingway's African hunting guide, but the two had connected pretty quickly. So, it almost seems, did anybody who ever met him. "The toughest, most durable white hunter ever to shoot a charging buffalo between the eyes while debating whether his sundowner will be gin or whisky," the East African aviatrix and author and horse breeder Beryl Markham once said of Blixen. (She was also, by almost no one's doubting, one of his uncounted lovers.) He's often claimed to be a model, or one of the models, for the hunting guide Robert Wilson in Hemingway's "The Short Happy Life of Francis Macomber," which isn't as great a short story as "The Snows of Kilimanjaro" but is pretty great all the same. In the July 1934 issue of *Esquire* ("Notes on Dangerous Game: The Third Tanganyika Letter"), Hemingway got in on the Blixen mythmaking. He wrote that the baron could stop a rhino at ten yards, and then apologetically explain to his client, whose weapon had been taken back to camp by the gun bearer, " 'I could not let him come forever, what?' "

(The other white hunter whom Hemingway lionized—empurpled might be the better word—in that same *Esquire* nonfiction piece was Philip Percival, an Englishman and partner of Blixen's, said to have been an even greater hunter than Blixen, although far less of a Technicolor human being. Blixen's branch of the business was Tanganyika Guides, Ltd., while Percival, based in Kenya, looked after African Guides, Ltd. Percival, not Blixen, is the guide whom Hemingway chose to employ on his 1933–34 safari. In *Green Hills of Africa*, Percival appears as Pop. In his youth, Pop had been part of Teddy Roosevelt's epic 1909 safari to Africa, which had been avidly followed in Chicago newspapers by a TR-worshiping Oak Park ten-year-old. As for the prototype of Robert Wilson in "Francis Macomber," it's probably closer to the truth to say that both white hunters, Blix and Pop, as well as other males, were in Hemingway's mind by the time he'd finished the story in the spring of 1936.)

If the name has registered, it's likely not because of Bror, but rather because of the literary genius to whom he'd once been married: Karen Blixen, who wrote under the pen name Isak Dinesen, and who authored the haunting memoir *Out of Africa*, published in 1937. "I had a farm in Africa, at the foot of the Ngong Hills" is one of the great beginnings in modern literature. Karen was Bror's Danish cousin. They'd gotten married in 1914, on the eve of war, and gone to Kenya to begin their doomed marriage and hilltop coffee plantation outside Nairobi. Not long into both, the adulterous husband, ever hopeless with money, unable to keep himself from sleeping with Masai women or the spouses of friends, had infected his wife with syphilis. They'd separated in 1921 and a few years later had divorced. In Hollywood's seven-Oscar 1985 version of the story, Meryl Streep, as Karen, incants *Out of Africa*'s opening sentence three times in her pitch-perfect Scandinavian voice-over. In old age, the real Karen Blixen is claimed to have said, "If I should wish anything back of my life, it would be to go on safari once again with Bror Blixen." In author Judith Thurman's magisterial 1982 biography of Dinesen, Bror is described as a man almost "maddeningly without moods . . . one of the most durable, congenial, promiscuous, and prodigal creatures who ever lived."

No one gets to be durable and promiscuous and prodigal and maddeningly without moods forever. When Bror visited Hemingway's boat in the company of the third Baroness Blixen (CAN EVA AND SELF VISIT YOU THURSDAY, he had cabled Hemingway on May 6 from Miami), he wasn't far from fifty, and old-manness was setting in. You can see it in the pictures. By contrast, the newest baroness on his arm was almost twenty years younger. She was the former Eva Dixon (in some accounts, it's spelled "Dickson"), who had come out to Africa from Sweden a few years before mostly for the purpose of snaring Bror. She is said by her biographers to have been a woman ever out for the main chance, someone who loved causing a sensation, faintly ridiculous in her vanities and coquetries. There is apparently some question as to whether they were ever formally married. Friends of Bror's are said to have resented the way she seemed to relish dominating him. As things turned out, they would be together for only a handful of years. Three years after she sunned on Hemingway's boat for most of May 1935, she died in a car crash in India. She was barely thirty-three. By then Eva's union with Bror seems to have been all but finished.

In the JFK Presidential Library, there are numerous photographs of her. In her fetching two-piece suit, she primps, flirts, sticks out her tongue, tosses her humidity-frizzed hair. She cuddles up to just-landed fish. Pauline is in some of these photographs. (Her look is quite different: to please her husband, whose hair fetishes are not exactly a secret, she's become an ash blond, and the once boy-cropped hair is now thick and grown out.) In some of the pictures, Hemingway and Eva are standing shoulder to shoulder, pressed lightly against each other, while Bror stands several feet away, wearing a floppy sun hat and holding a box camera. In some of the pictures, the hirsute Hemingway wears only a pair of smeared shorts (leather belt outside the loops), while Strater, vying for Eva's attentions, looks positively jacked in his sleeveless white muscle T-shirt. So look again at the picture at the front of this chapter.

Strater claimed to Carlos Baker (fellow Princetonian) that Hemingway had slept that summer with Eva. Baker interviewed Strater in July 1964, on the third anniversary of Hemingway's death. He wrote up his notes from the interview—at least some of it—in narrative form, with no direct attribution to Strater, but there's no question that he was indirectly quoting Strater. Several copies of Baker's typescript ended up with his Hemingway papers at Princeton. The document contains the following paragraph:

> A few days after arrival at Bimini, a Swedish count and his blond aviatrix wife [she was actually a former rally car driver] reached Bimini (Baron VonBlixen?) and were bunked aboard Pilar. Bred Saunders and Mike Strater slept on deck. The countess was put in forward cubby, and the count on deck above her. Ernest slept in the cabin. It was generally supposed by the deck-sleepers that Ernest and the countess were sleeping together below decks. The blond was a tough adventuress type. Count approached Strater and indicated jealousy of Hemingway.

In Baker's *published* account (page 273 of *Ernest Hemingway: A Life Story*), the claims are handled differently. The biographer wrote that Hemingway, who had been "carefully excluding" Strater from his conversations with Blixen about Africa, "also seemed resentful when the Baroness showed signs of preferring Strater to himself."

Mike Strater lived to be ninety-one. He died in 1987. He'd had several wives and eight children. He had kept on painting, a minor American artist who'd nonetheless been there, at the Café du Dôme and the Select and the Rotonde and Les Deux Magots and La Closerie des Lilas, not just with Hemingway, but with Joyce, Pound, Fitzgerald, Dos Passos, MacLeish, Picasso, all the rest. Near the end of his life, with only bitterness seeming to be left in his voice for Hemingway, he told an oral biographer named Denis Brian, in an odd, compelling 1988 book titled *The True Gen,* that "Hem" was the kind of charming bully and artful sadist who sought to get you drunk in a bar and then take you out into the dark and sucker punch you. "We were friends, but he was a goddamned thankless friend," Strater said. The thankless friend and charming bully had left Strater out of *A Moveable Feast,* and stuck the fact in his face by mentioning it in his preface.

As for the baron (who had another eleven years left to him after his stay on Hemingway's boat): if he was resentful (enraged?) about what Hemingway may have been doing with Eva just a few feet out of his sight, that didn't keep him from admiring (empurpling?) Hemingway's fishing prowess in his 1938 autobiography, *African Hunter.* You could say, in fact, that he did Hemingway one better than Hemingway did him in "Notes on Dangerous Game" in the July 1934 *Esquire.* Blixen told how on their last day of Bimini fishing, toward the end of May 1935, Hemingway hooked into a monster. Wrote the baron: "With the big, strong Hardy rod quivering under the colossal forces at work on both sides, he slowly began to haul in. . . . Hemingway toiled at reel and line like a galley-slave at his oar. The sweat stood in drops on his bare back as he strained every muscle to tire out his quarry." What could it be? It was a hammerhead shark. "There was great disappointment and annoyance on board; when one goes out lion-hunting one is not pleased to get a hyena."

Eva struck poses with the shark as it lay dead and white on *Pilar*'s transom with the gaff still in its jaw. She pretended to be beating it with a club.

But it wasn't any possible cuckoldry that effectively finished the Hemingway-Strater friendship. Rather, it was because of something that happened just between the two of them: the "apple-coring" of a huge fish, and Hemingway's role in that coring, and the lie of omission he afterward told in *Esquire.* "Apple-cored" is a term fishermen use for a fish that gets eaten nearly whole by the sharks.

They were out on *Pilar* one day in middle May when Strater hooked into a trophy black marlin. In forty minutes, he managed to get the fish close to the boat. All hands were trying to get it on board when the first shark or two appeared. That's when Hemingway took out a tommy gun that he'd recently acquired from another Bimini fisherman and started spraying the water—which only had the effect of bringing packs of sharks to *Pilar*'s stern. They came for the blood, which at first was the blood of one of their own. Wasn't Hemingway trying to protect his friend's fish against those cannibals?

It took another hour to get the fish in. What got in weighed five hundred pounds. There are a lot of pictures of the fish, and most of its lower half isn't there. Whole, it might have weighed twice as much. In the July 1935 *Esquire*, in a piece titled "The President Vanquishes," Hemingway wrote: "There were two buckets of loose meat that were knocked off when we took him over the roller on the stern that were not weighed. You take a look at him and figure what he would have weighed whole, remember that all the meat gone is solid meat, that a pint of blood weighs little under a pound, and that the part weighing five hundred pounds was hollow."

The fish was nearly thirteen feet long (Strater later claimed over fourteen feet), with a sixty-two-inch girth and a forty-eight-inch tail spread. According to Hemingway's piece, "We hung him up and weighed him and took the pictures and eighteen jigs followed the President around singing a song." It went like this: "Mr. Strater caught a marlin / Tonight's the night we got fun / Mr. Strater caught a marlin / One thousand pounds."

There's some memorable writing in "The President Vanquishes," which purports to be a tribute to Strater's fishing courage. (In the middle of the fight, Mike's knee went out.) The opening:

> You write this at three o'clock in the morning lying at anchor outside of Bimini harbor. There is a nearly full moon and you dropped out of the harbor to avoid the sandflies. Everyone is asleep below and almost everyone is snoring and you are writing on top of the house by the light of the riding light. It is almost light enough to write by moonlight. Yes, you can do it; but the penciling shows so gray on the paper that you go back to the riding light. A breeze is coming up from the southwest, and you know that if we get a southwest blow now it will bring the big tuna.

Midway in the article: "And as he went off jumping high, clean, throwing himself long, slamming, and clear he seemed smaller all the time. But it was because he jumped out nearly four hundred yards of thirty-nine thread and we were looking at him from a long way away." Hemingway later told Arnold Gingrich that he had just slapped out the piece—fifteen hundred words, apparently most of it from the top of the house in that wan 3:00 a.m. light—and thus had felt a little guilty for collecting his $250 fee.

What he didn't tell Gingrich—or the readers of *Esquire*—was anything about grabbing the tommy gun at the critical juncture to begin reddening the waters. It was jealous rage that made him do it, or so Strater would always believe. For the rest of his life, he'd nurse this grudge.

Later that summer, Katy Dos Passos described for Gerald Murphy what it was like with Hemingway and sharks and machine guns on *Pilar*. (This was in a letter not connected to the Strater incident.) "They come like express trains and hit the fish like a planing mill—shearing off twenty-five pounds at a bite. Ernest shoots them with a machine gun, *rrr*—but it won't stop them—It's terrific to see the bullets ripping into them—the sharks thrashing in blood and foam—the white bellies and fearful jaws—the pale cold eyes—I was really aghast but it's very exciting."

From "The President Vanquishes": "What we landed of him weighed 500 lbs. and the pictures show what the sharks took." The pictures also reveal what Hemingway tried to take. You'd swear it must be his fish. He stands in closer than the man who's caught it. He holds on to the fish while Strater peers over his shoulder. In the photograph accompanying the *Esquire* piece, Strater and Hemingway are standing on either side of the marlin. Hemingway is reaching up and holding on to a partially eaten fin. He looks at the camera, while Strater, holding his rod, stares across at him with something like an incredulous expression. In Denis Brian's *The True Gen*, Strater said that Hemingway "stood in front of me every time the fish was photographed." Not quite true.

Strater was in New York when he read the *Esquire* piece. That September he wrote to Hemingway, who was back in Key West from the summer on Bimini. Strater said that his wife, Maggie, had been operated on for an infected sinus. His weight was down to 194. The kids were good. "You sure did me proud," he said. So why didn't he say what he truly felt, which must have been rage? I can only think that the force field of Hemingway's personality was too great for him to speak up, at least then. But to Carlos Baker, Strater said it unambiguously: Hemingway had helped ruin the largest fish Strater had ever hooked into, and in so doing had ruined something greater, their friendship, if not immediately, soon enough.

Nearly a quarter century after the Baker interview (in the 1980s) Strater told Brian that, on the night of the big marlin, they'd gone off to Bobby Cash's bar at the foot of Alice Town, and everyone in the place had insisted on buying him drinks, and he'd gotten loaded, and finally the place emptied out, which is when Hemingway slugged him in the stomach. Strater said, "You're getting weak, old boy. Can't you hit any harder than that?" (If you're dead drunk, how could you remember what you said?) Hemingway had been "tonguing the bottle," meaning that he'd been only pretending to drink, biding his time until Strater was too far gone to fight back.

In *For Whom the Bell Tolls*, published five years afterward, Hemingway, in the voice of Robert Jordan, makes a coded reference to Strater. Jordan is thinking of his friend, Anselmo, whom he has known only in these last four days of his life. "I know him better than I know Charles, than I know Chub, than I know Guy, than I know Mike, and I know them well." He did know them well. And in Mike's case, no less than with Archie MacLeish, he also must have known what he had wrecked.

The Egyptians are said to have provided the earliest written accounts of angling as we know it, that is, something done with a length of thread affixed to a bent piece of metal. That was four thousand years ago. It wasn't until 1898, at the Tuna Club of Avalon, on Catalina Island off Los Angeles, that the idea of big-game sportfishing, with codes of conduct urging conservation ethics and sporting behavior, arose in America. On June 1 of that year, the Associated Press rifled the news that a naturalist and author and professor named Charles Frederick Holder had landed, by rod and reel, a 183-pound leaping tuna, an event eclipsing "all previous achievements in the line of angling for the big Thoroughbreds of the deep." Holder (his father had been the first curator of the American Museum of Natural History in New York) had done it with a stiff stick that weighed sixteen ounces, with twenty-one-thread line made of linen and a seven-foot leader made of piano wire. The *Los Angeles Times* said the epitome of angling had just been reached. Dispatches from the Spanish-American War almost took a back seat that day.

Tuna dreams. The Gulf Stream, tearing with terrific force through the narrow gorge that separates the outer edge of the Bahamas from the east coast of Florida, is said to move more quickly than any other current in all the world's oceans. It's apparently the speed, in conjunction with the heat and stunning clarity of the water, that has historically brought the "granders" close to Bimini, not only the tuna, but the big billfish and marlin as well. Tuna, those so-called oceanic bison, passed yearly in the 1920s and 1930s between Florida and Cuba, but off the northern shore of Cuba they tended to stay deep and were impossible to see. By the time they got up near Bimini, they often swam in close to shore. You could target them. They were like dark torpedo shapes, sometimes in less than a hundred feet

WHEN SHE WAS NEW

of water. For about five weeks every year, starting in middle or late May, the bluefin came in pods past Bimini, on their migration toward the colder waters of New Jersey and Nova Scotia. But no one had been able to boat a tuna—of any size—in those warm southern waters without first witnessing its mutilation by the sharks. No one had been able to boat one, that is, until Hemingway. The standard angling histories are agreed: he's the first known angler to have ever gotten one in whole, clean, at Bimini.

Tuna dreams. Since at least the early twenties, Bimini had been on big-game maps. Recognized names in the sport, like Van Campen Heilner or George Albert Lyon (an inventor out of Detroit—he had something to do with perfecting the automobile bumper), had discovered the island. Zane Grey had fished there. But it wasn't until the thirties that numbers of fishermen and their boats and their guides began converging on Bimini. For a few years, in the middle of the decade, when much of the country was just trying to keep bread on its table, this slice of colonial earth, which you could fairly hurl a rock across, became the epicenter of big-game angling of the Atlantic and the Caribbean. Again, it's no wonder that Hemingway, with his sixth sense for locating himself, channeled his boat to the right symbolic place.

In February 1933, a Bimini angler with an international reputation, S. Kip Farrington, had taken a small blue marlin of 155 pounds. But the news went around: if the small marlins were there, the big ones must be as well. Two weeks later, a female angler, Betty Moore, had hooked and fought a 502-pound blue for four hours at Bimini. (When her arms gave out, another fisherman took over and got it on board, so it was a co-catching and not a pure record.) Bimini was officially the newest *it* place in a very small club. Historians say that there were possibly no more than seventy-five or one hundred truly superior fishermen and guides and charter captains on both coasts of America.

In a first-rate book titled *Profiles in Saltwater Angling*, fishing historian George Reiger makes the case that the mid-thirties represented such an age for deep-sea fishing, and that for many reasons, not least ecological, such a period probably won't be around again. The rise of the age very much had to do with the astonishing abundance of fish, but just as much, maybe more so, with the attitudes of the fishermen, who understood that they were doing something well and first, and were willing to share with one another what they knew. Big-game fishing wasn't a competition so much as a passion undertaken for its own sake. The waste and depopulation of these great nomadic creatures hadn't quite yet begun to haunt sporting consciences—the ocean was still thought illimitable.* There's a beautiful shipboard letter Hemingway wrote to a fellow Bimini fisherman named Michael Lerner several years later, on his way to cover the Spanish Civil War. He was crossing the ocean once again on the SS *Paris*. He longed to be on Bimini with his boat. He spoke of fishing as "a sport where the competition should be all inside yourself. . . . It's serious while you're doing it but we have to remember it's fishing." This was the idealist talking, willing to betray his ideals at nearly every turn. But also a man headed to the battlefront.

At Bimini, in the summer of 1935, you could run into Tommy Gifford, a charter captain, who, among other innovations, helped to develop the concept of the outrigger, for skipping the baits clear of the boat's wake. (Hemingway had never tried an outrigger until he came to Bimini—Mike Strater made a gift to *Pilar* for her first rather primitive pair.) You might run into Tommy Shevlin, whose family had vast lumber concerns in the Pacific Northwest, and whom Hemingway came to regard as his protégé. (They were fifteen years apart.) You could run into Farrington, a large egoist. You could, not least, run into Mike Lerner, the best of them all, in terms of his generosity and commitment to the values of the sport and also for the modesty with which he lived his life, no matter his wealth. He'd made his fortune in a chain of women's clothing stores. His wife, Helen, was as gracious and serious a fisherperson as he was. At the end of the thirties, both Lerners, but especially Mike, would become the driving force behind the founding and establishment of the International Game Fish Association, which remains the essential governing body for ocean fishing. (The first organizational meeting was held in an office of the American Museum of Natural History, in Manhattan, on June 7, 1939. Hemingway

---

*From his letters and other writing, it's clear that the waste and depopulation *had* begun to haunt Hemingway. In that same *Esquire* piece in which he omitted his use of a tommy gun, he wrote: "In Havana you give the meat away or you sell it for around ten cents a pound. In Bimini it is wasted scandalously. . . . [I]t is disgusting and sickening to see edible game fish slaughtered and wasted. . . . Killing fish for no useful purpose, or allowing their meat to waste, wantonly, should be an offense punishable by law." He urged the Bimini government to build a smokehouse. The fishermen could pay a fee for the curing and take the meat themselves; the rest of it could be sold at market or distributed free by the government. But, true to character, the sense of appalling waste wasn't going to keep him from catching every fish he could, from besting every fisherman in sight. This was the same cross-grained man who'd written to his friend Waldo Peirce in Maine and called their mutual friend Archie MacLeish one of the world's finer nose-picker poets and then added quickly that he wouldn't wish to hurt his feelings for anything and so "tear this part out and burn it." His remorse may have been eating at him, but not enough to keep him from mailing the letter.

had intended to be in the room but couldn't make it. In 1940, Lerner took over as IGFA president, and Hemingway became first vice president, in which office he remained, if in a mostly titular way, for the rest of his life.)

It was Hemingway's friend Lerner who built, in 1933, "solid as a ship," the great house at Bimini with the three-sided screened-in porch that sat on the tongue of land between the harbor and the sea, the one "shaded by tall coconut palms that were bent by the trade wind," the one that would end up lasting through not just three hurricanes, but through an aborted novel that was put into a Cuban bank vault in 1951 and that took another two decades to find its light of print. It was Lerner, who, three years after Hemingway's suicide, sat in a room of his great island house, speaking to Hemingway's most troubled son, no longer a dopey little guy with his rolls of baby fat. It was midday and the blinds were drawn. The house was in some disrepair. He didn't look well. He didn't go out on boats much anymore. "There are so many things I'd like to tell you about your father, Gregory," said Lerner. "God we had fun in those days." That's on page 37 of *Papa: A Personal Memoir.*

Tuna dreams. In the May 1935 *Esquire,* on newsstands and in mailboxes just as he had arrived at Bimini, Hemingway wrote that marlin have some-thing on or in their noses that sharks are afraid of, and consequently they never come for a big marlin until they know that it is tired or bleeding badly. But it's different with tuna, he opined. The main defense a tuna has against a shark is its speed. In this same piece he said, "Your correspondent is as ignorant of giant tuna as any man can be."

That was hardly true, but what was true was that until then, he'd never had one on the end of his line. In December 1921, on his way to France as a twenty-two-year-old freelancer (with Sherwood Anderson's letter of introduction to Gertrude Stein et al. in his hind pocket), he had witnessed giant tuna leaping on a curve of bay in Vigo, Spain. They'd come down and hit the water with the smack of a stallion. Hemingway had absorbed it all—the way the peasant fishermen baited their hooks with silvery mullet, the way schools of sardines seemed depth-charged out of the water when a bluefin rose. In the town's fish market, he and Hadley had gawked at an eight-hundred-pound tuna laid out on a slab. About two months later, in Paris, from the newly rented cold-water walk-up at 74, rue du Cardinal Lemoine, near the place de la Contrescarpe, where the drunks and work-ing poor of the Left Bank lived, workmanlike sentences got written for readers of the *Toronto Star Weekly:* "A big tuna is silver and slate blue, and when he shoots up into the air from close beside the boat it is like a blinding flash of quicksilver. He may weigh three hundred pounds and he jumps with the eagerness and ferocity of a mammoth rainbow trout. Sometimes five and six tuna will be in the air at once in Vigo Bay, shouldering out of the water." A tuna, wrote the stringer in his seven-paragraph color piece (for which he was paid at space rates, meaning not much), was "the king of all fish, the ruler of the Valhalla of fishermen."

The handsome little thirteen-foot sea skiff that had bobbed along to Bimini in *Pilar*'s wake was part of Hemingway's tuna plans. The skiff was a Lyman, about half as broad as she was long. Like Wheeler, that name instantly meant something in the thirties boating world. Founded by cabinetmaker Bernard Lyman in 1875, and eventually headquartered in Sandusky, Ohio, the company offered small and extremely durable vessels mainly of a lapstrake construction. Lapstrake planking has to do with the way the boards get attached to the frames and to themselves. In a lapstrake hull, the planks are "lapped" one edge over another, in contrast to conventional hulls where the boards get butted together at their edges in a batten-seam construction. This provides more stability and sea-kindliness than in a flat-bottomed boat, because each protruding lap serves as a kind of shock absorber to the force of the water, the more so at high speeds.

Hemingway's notion was, once he'd hooked into the giant bluefin of his fantasies, to pass off his rod to one of *Pilar*'s crew and then to get quickly into the little boat, where a fighting chair would be rigged up and ready. The rod would be passed over; he'd screw down tight on the drag. Somebody from the mother boat would get in beside him to help with the steering. They'd un-umbilical the Lyman. He would set his feet against the sides of the boat and try to hold on for life while the tuna took him like a hydroplane through the ocean. The lapstrake construction would afford him better odds against flipping over. Sooner or later the dumb fish would exhaust itself. He'd let it tow itself to death, and afterward they'd bring it over *Pilar*'s stern, no matter that a dead weight in a fish is just like a dead weight in a human. For nearly two years, Hemingway had this towing vision in his head—it's there in the letters. The plan never materialized.

But his theory of might-against-might did, and it changed the rules for tuna. Simply stated, the theory was this: from the instant the fish is on your hook, you have to dominate it. You must make the fish understand it's dealing with a superior force. Pump and wind without ever taking a break. Don't give a foot of slack. Don't play the fish, as you might a lesser species, but horse it in, right to the breaking point of both your rod and your back. It's a simple proposition: either defeat the thing or break it. It's your only chance against the sharks. If you end up losing your tackle in the bargain, so be it.

He got his first one in clean. He did it in about seventy minutes. It happened in the latter half of May, after he'd been on Bimini roughly a month.

He was fishing with the 14/0 Vom Hofe. The bait itself—a baby tuna—weighed almost eight pounds. His boat was heeling into a southwest breeze, when he saw "a big yellowish brown fish pass alongside the boat traveling with the swells." He thought it was a marlin. The fish hit the bait and the reel began "to scream in the special high register a man attains when he is dying of lockjaw." The rod broke off at the tip. The fish was still on the line; they managed to get another rod tip in its place. He worked the fish to the side of the boat. The sun was blinding his vision. It's a mako shark, he thought. Before they could get the gaff in, the fish pulled the leader free and sounded. In fifteen minutes Hemingway had the fish back up at the surface, belly side up. He saw now it was neither a mako nor a marlin but a tuna, with "a head that seemed made of chromium, a dark blue back, silver sides, was streamlined like a bullet and there were little bright yellow finlets that ran from his anal fin to his tail and still quivered when we got him in the boat." They covered the fish with canvas and put it on the deck. That evening, on shore, it weighed out at 381 pounds, hardly a one-tonner but nonetheless Bimini's first recorded unmutilated tuna. Writing about it that August in *Esquire*, in "He Who Gets Slap Happy" (the quoted lines above are from the article), Hemingway began with this thought: "It is all just as serious as you take it. Certainly a fish is only a fish while a man is more than often a sonofabitch. . . . What is a sportsman, anyway? In what does he differ from the average four letter man?"

Before that saw print, the news of his feat made the rotogravure of the Sunday *New York Times*. With a photo, on page 2 of the June 16 edition: "THE AUTHOR'S BEST FISHING STORY: Ernest Hemingway, With a Blue-Fin Tuna Weighing 381 Pounds, Which He Landed Intact Aboard His Cruiser Pilar Near Bimini, to Establish a South Atlantic Record for This Kind of Fish." The picture was copyrighted in his name.

Soon after, he got a second one in whole. It weighed 319 pounds and he boated it in forty-eight minutes. Pauline as well as the Blixens were aboard. He hooked into the fish late in the day on the way back from Cat Cay. Now other charter captains and their clients were bringing tuna in clean at Bimini, using the new concept of horsing rather than fighting.

Hemingway had shown the way, and he knew it. In a June letter to Max Perkins he'd say, "[W]e've changed the whole system of big game fishing by the way we work them. Anyone can catch the tuna here now since we've showed them how. . . . This sounds awfully bragging but only write it because you might be interested." Earlier that month, he'd written to Gingrich: "All the boats . . . had been fishing four years and nobody caught any. Have won 350 bucks betting we would with the rich boys. Plenty rich boys. But now no bets." In his August *Esquire* dispatch, the man who loved everything up to a point said of his long-awaited experience of fighting the ruler of the Valhalla of fishermen: "They are tremendously strong, run beautifully, do not jump, ever, after being hooked, and can and will bend your back and your rod plenty. But for enjoyment of the fight and for a thrill a marlin has them beat three hundred ways."

Plenty-rich boys. For nearly all of his life, the son of an Oak Park doctor and a socially pretentious mother hated and pitied and feared the very rich as a class no less than he did women. At bottom, the same instinctive belief: you get too close, these people will destroy your art, even if on another level all you wish is to get close, to have their approval.

On May 26, the queen's birthday, when the whole island was drunk, some "worthless sporting characters" with loud mouths and too much money were shooting off flares with Very pistols. "Worthless sporting characters"—that's a line from *Islands in the Stream*. A fight, such as it was, ensued, probably lasting less than thirty seconds—something like six shots: three pop-pop-pop left hooks, and then a couple of dirty clubbings behind the ear (this wasn't Marquis of Queensberry), and then the roundhouse finishing right. The clubbings behind the ear caused his victim's ear to swell up like a bunch of grapes, like an overripe fig. The fight took place in the dark with bare hands on the government dock. Hemingway devotes a twenty-eight-page chapter in the "Bimini" section of the novel to a thin fictionalizing of this half-minute brawl, which, in real life, instantly entered island myth. They still sing about it in the waterside bars of Alice Town. The tune's called "Big Fat Slob." The Biminite who wrote it, Nattie Saunders, said to have been on the dock that night, has passed. His lyrics go like this:

> Mr. Knapp called Mr. Ernest Hemingway
> A big fat slob

> Mr. Ernest Hemingway balled his fist
> And gave him a knob
> Big fat slob in Bimini
> This is the night we have fun.

Mr. Knapp, who got the knob on Queen Mary's birthday, was Joseph Fairchild Knapp. His friends knew him as Dodi. He was the son of Joseph P. Knapp, chairman of the board of Crowell-Collier, publisher of magazines like *Collier's*, *Woman's Home Companion*, and *The American Magazine*. Dodi had come over to Bimini with his wife from their winter home at the Isle of Palms in Fort Lauderdale in their fifty-three-foot trunk cruiser. He is said to have retired, at thirty-seven, in 1929, from his father's lithograph company, another branch of the family publishing empire. Not that Hemingway knew any of this when he put him into the big sleep. Not that he even knew his name. He'd find that out afterward.

It's been said that Hemingway was on *Pilar* when the excessively ripped Dodi appeared on the deck of his boat and began hurling invectives across the transom. But Hemingway wasn't on his own boat; she was tied up down the way. He was visiting on another boat belonging to yet another worthless sporting character with a pet WASP name and way too much money and time on his hands—Woolworth Donahue, called Woolie, descendant of the five-and-dime tycoon. That Hemingway was on the boat in the first place, among these idlers who weren't true sportsmen and for whom he would have had fairly undisguised contempt, only suggests he was spoiling for a fight. There had to have been quantities of self-contempt, too.

Apparently, the uniformed crew of Dodi's boat never made a move to intervene. That seems telling. In the fictionalized version, written at least a decade after the actual event, the mean drunk isn't given a name. He just appears out of the darkness from his stateroom in his white-duck trousers and begins calling over in a choking voice. " 'You slob.' . . . 'You rotten filthy slob.' . . . 'You big fat slob.' . . . 'You phony. You faker. You cheap phony. You rotten writer and lousy painter.' " Earlier the drunk had appeared in his pajamas and cried, " 'Listen, you swine! Stop it, will you? There's a lady trying to sleep down below.' " What's aroused him are the Very flares falling too close to his boat. It's not Thomas Hudson, but Hudson's writer friend, Roger Davis, who climbs up on the dock to take care of the drunk. As already noted, both Hudson and Davis are Hemingway manqué—barely manqué.

In real life, something about the way the back of his victim's head banged down, with his eyes rolling around like pennies in a doll's head, caused alarm in Hemingway—and this, too, plays out in the fiction. Remorse sets in. But Dodi was just out cold. His boat is said to have slunk out of town before dawn, bound, as Hemingway later put it, "for Miami for doctorage." According to Hemingway, Knapp admitted to a charter captain in Florida that he had it coming.

Nine days after the coldcocking, briefly back in Key West, to see his kids and clean up the mail, still terribly thrilled and unable to hide it, Hemingway told Arnold Gingrich in a letter:

> [C]lipped him three times with left hooks didn't understand why he didn't go down . . . backed away and landed Sunday punch making him hit ass and head at almost same time on planks. . . . On the other hand it is called limiting one's market. Still the son of a bitch never touched me once and he started it and weighed 200 lbs, had shoes on and I was barefoot. Lost 2 toenails. If you have any curiosity about this thing it is very easily verified. The nigger band that sings was on the dock, saw it all and have a fine song now that you can hear if you will come to Bimini.

Actually, Dodi didn't weigh more than 180. And he was no more than five-foot-eight or five-foot-nine. And he was forty-three to Hemingway's nearly thirty-six. In other words, he gave away about seven years, four inches, and twenty-five pounds to somebody whose haymaker right arm had been bulking up even more than usual due to the pulling in of some large fish. And as for Hemingway's line about limiting his writing market: not true. In World War II, he'd be credentialed as a war correspondent for *Collier's*.

In *Islands*, remorseful for the beating he's administered, Roger Davis says to Thomas Hudson:

> "I humiliated him and I ruined him a little. But he'll take it out on someone else. . . . You know evil is a hell of a thing, Tommy. . . . Being against evil doesn't make you good. Tonight I was against it and then I was evil myself. I could feel it coming in just like a tide. . . . I just want to destroy them. But when

, you start taking pleasure in it you are awfully close to the thing you're fighting."

Ever the cross-graining.

The first draft of "The Snows of Kilimanjaro" was written at the end of Hemingway's first summer on Bimini. Of course, it's a tale about the corruptions of wealth, and of what those corruptions have done to a man named Harry, who once thought of himself as a serious artist. Now he's just full of his poisons.

The toxins he had, but also their opposite, and often those opposites would come out quickly, and in letters, when a child he loved was at risk—or past risk. One such letter was written not to a threatened child, but to the child's parents, Gerald and Sara Murphy. The child himself had died two days before, at fifteen, of spinal meningitis. The illness had seemed to erupt out of nowhere, and this was a great part of the shock. A seemingly ordinary case of measles at prep school in Rhode Island after Christmas break had turned into a double-mastoid ear infection that had passed critically into meningitis. And then Baoth Murphy, with all that life in him, was gone. The letter sent from Key West, trying to make sense of it, was eight paragraphs long and had an elaborate Pilar metaphor at its end. Hemingway wrote it up in his second-floor writing room on Tuesday, March 19, 1935, so about three weeks before that abortive first try for Bimini, when he wounded himself. He had tried to write the day before but found he could only go around his house in grief. "Dear Sara and Dear Gerald," he began. "You know there is nothing we can ever say or write. If Bumby died we know how you would feel and there would be nothing you could say."

He went on: "It is not as bad for Baoth because he had a fine time, always, and he has only done something that we all must do. He has just gotten it over with."

He went on: "About him having to die so young—Remember that he had a very fine time and having it a thousand times makes it no better. And he is spared from learning what sort of a place the world is."

On: "It is your loss: more than it is his so it is something that you can, legitimately, be brave about. But I cant be brave about it and in all my heart I am sick for you both."

On: "Absolutely truly and coldly in the head though I know that anyone who dies young after a happy childhood, and no one ever made a happier childhood than you made for your children, has won a great victory. We all have to look forward to death by defeat, our bodies gone, our world destroyed; but it is the same dying we must do; while he has gotten it all over with, his world all intact, and the death only by accident."

On: "You see now we have all come to the part of our lives where we start to lose people of our own age. Baoth was our own age. Very few people ever really are alive and those that are never die; no matter if they are gone. No one you love is ever dead."

And then he came to his boat metaphor:

> We must live it, now, a day at a time and be very careful not to hurt each other. It seems as though we were all on a boat now together, a good boat still, that we have made but that we know now will never reach port. There will be all kinds of weather, good and bad; and especially because we know now that there will be no landfall we must keep the boat up very well and be very good to each other. We are fortunate we have good people on the boat.

Hemingway and Dos Passos had been out fishing on the Stream when the wire about Baoth had come from Massachusetts General Hospital in Boston. They hadn't caught much that Sunday afternoon, St. Patrick's Day. When they'd gotten up to the house from the navy yard, along toward dark, Pauline was in the doorway with the manila sheet, which had been addressed simply "Passos Hemingway." It was time-stamped 2:17 p.m. Its first four words: BAOTH DIED THIS MORNING.

The Murphys had three children—a daughter and two sons. Baoth, two months shy of sixteen, was the middle child. Hemingway had known and loved all three Murphy kids since they were tykes in buckled swimsuits on the Riviera, in the mid-twenties, when his own firstborn was building moats and castles beside them, and when he and Hadley, and Scott and Zelda, and Archie and Ada, and the rest of that supposedly luck-struck crew who were privileged members of the Murphy expat circle, watched from beneath big striped umbrellas poked into the sand.

The other part of the shock of Baoth's dying was that he was the supposedly healthy son. If one of the Murphy kids was figured to die, it would have been his little brother, Patrick, who'd been struggling against tuberculosis for nearly six years.

Decades later, in a 1982 memoir about her family called Sara & Gerald, Honoria Murphy Donnelly, the eldest child, would say that of all her parents' famous friends from the twenties and thirties—and the unfamous ones as well—it was Hemingway who'd paid the closest attention to her and her brothers, who'd seemed to care for and understand each of them as if they were his own. In late summer 1932, the Murphys, save for Patrick, who was too frail to go, had joined Hemingway and his family for two weeks at the L-Bar-T Ranch in Wyoming. Hemingway, who had to catch more rainbows than anybody, who'd recently finished the final proofs for *Death in the Afternoon*, made big campfires at night and sat around with the kids in a goofy Tyrolean hat, roasting marshmallows, telling scary stories.

When Baoth took ill, in mid-February of 1935, his mother was in the Keys with Ada MacLeish, visiting the Hemingways and the Dos Passoses. Sara hadn't really wanted to go south that winter. Her husband had urged her to go. Sara's nerves had become badly frayed, and being around Hemingway always seemed to be a kind of tonic. (They spent hours alone with each other on Pilar through the years; no one knows for sure if they were lovers.) Instead of going to Florida with his wife, Gerald had stayed back to tend to the family's ailing Mark Cross leather business, but more importantly to be close to Patrick, who'd suffered a relapse. As scholar Linda Patterson Miller has put it, the double tragedy of Baoth Murphy's death was that "it coincided with the period of Patrick's worst relapse."

Six months before, in the fall of 1934, during a checkup, Patrick's doctors had discovered a patch on his good lung, on which he'd been principally breathing since he was nine. So instead of being able to go off to prep school, like Baoth, the youngest Murphy was now in his bed at Doctors Hospital in Manhattan, with his wood-carving set and his stamp collection. He had the bed faced toward the window, so that he could look out and see the boats going up and down the East River. This has been told vividly in *Sara & Gerald*.

When Hemingway first heard about Patrick's relapse, he'd been finishing up the first summer in Cuba with his new boat. On September 30, 1934, he'd written to Sara and Gerald from Havana and said he'd like to give Patrick one of his trophies from Africa—a Grant's gazelle or an impala, whichever he wanted. He had a hunch Patrick would love the impala.

Five months later, in Newport, at St. George's School, when Patrick's brother went to the infirmary with an earache and some red splotches on his face, no one was particularly worried—at first. From New York, Gerald had kept track of the situation. In a wire to Florida on February 20 he'd told Sara that their otherwise healthy middle boy was nicely on the mend, that she should just try to enjoy herself down there.

When it was clear the case of measles was spiraling in on itself, Gerald wired Sara to come north as fast as she could. In the middle of a late February night, Hemingway cranked up his boat and, with both engines going full out, roared Ada and Sara along the Keys, landing them on the Florida mainland in time for a flight to Boston.

For the next several weeks, the Western Unions had come to Key West about Baoth's condition. You can sit now at a polished table in the clinical quiet of a university archive and read the telegrams in sequence, and they might strike you as their own kind of cryptic novel, with a novel's cruelly false springs. They might strike you as their own kind of rebuke to that whole Lost Generation lie about living well always being the best revenge. On March 1, a wire time-stamped 10:10 p.m. arrived: BAOTH STILL UNCOM- FORTABLE BUT IMPROVING ALL SEND LOVE YOU ALL MURPHYS. Four days later: BAOTH MAY HAVE TO HAVE SECOND OPERATION DECISION WILL BE MADE TODAY. March 12: BAOTH HAD ANOTHER EMERGENCY OPERATION LAST NIGHT CONDITION NOT HOPELESS PRAY FOR US LOVE SARA GERALD. On the fourteenth: BLOOD TRANSFUSION TOMORROW TO COMBAT TOX- EMA AND REPLENISH CONDITION STOP HOLDING HIS OWN WE ARE HOPE- FUL STOP WE FEEL YOUR PRAYERS MUCH MUCH LOVE SARA AND GERALD. The next day: SECOND TRANSFUSION THIS EVENING RESISTANCE MIRACU- LOUS STRONGLY HOPEFUL KEEP PRAYING. And then that final one, on the seventeenth, sent by a family friend: BAOTH DIED THIS MORNING SARA GERALD WONDERFULLY BRAVE DETAILS UNDECIDED.

Two days later, Hemingway had been able to write his own words.

Here is another Hemingway letter. He wrote it on April 5, 1935, two days before the Sunday-morning shove-off for Bimini. It's a letter to a child about an imminent adventure, and it's as if it's being written from one Boy Ranger to another. It's nearly three pages long, typed, single-spaced, something like two thousand words. It's to Patrick Murphy. The fevered and bedridden boy, who's lost his brother, who's lost his appetite, whose breathing comes with great difficulty, can't go on this adventure with his fellow Ranger. And so the Ranger, in his writing room at Key West, in the midst of his packing and boat-loading, has come up with the next-best idea: he'll make his pal a virtual participant from his bed. He'll go into loving detail about all the things a fellow Ranger wants to hear about: nautical charts and hickory rods with twenty-three-ounce tips; the wahoo and big sails and giant tuna they'll hope to snare; the sea skiff he intends to use as a pair of water skis when he gets a tuna on the hook; and, oh, yes, the movies they'll make along the way, and of how these movies will be developed and sent to him straightaway.

"If your father will order the chart showing Florida and the Bahamas you can tell just where we are and where the places are that I will refer to," he says.

"I will send the films from Miami with your address on them. So you will be the first to see them. Then we can get copies from them later," he says.

He confides: "I have been feeling very gloomy with too many visitors and haveing to take the treatment for my amoebic dysentery that makes me over three quarters goofy. But now am cured, I think, and want to wash myself out clean with the Gulf Stream and the best soap I know—which is excitement or whatever you call it. Anyway we will try to can some of it on the films and send it up to you."

Trying to sign off: "Well Bo if there is anything you want to know about the trip. . . . Well So Long old Timer. Write me to Bimini will you? . . . Well, So Long again." He signs it, "Your friend Ernest."

Ernest's friend Patrick Murphy lived not quite another two years, until a few months past his sixteenth birthday. He spent much of the last part of his life at Saranac Lake in upstate New York, where it was thought that the cool Adirondack climate and treatments at a sanitarium might cut back the disease. Patrick's friend Ernest came to see him there in early 1937, at the point at which he'd entered into his adulteries with the woman who'd eventually become his third wife. In her beautiful memoir about her parents, Honoria Murphy Donnelly describes how Patrick saw him and said, "Hello, Ernest," and of how his friend had said, "Hello, Patrick, how are you? I hear you're doing well." He stood on the right side of the bed. They talked of boats and fishing and the sea. "I think I can come back later to say good night, Patrick, but I don't want to tire you out," he said. Quickly he left the room. In the corridor, he began to weep—"openly" as Honoria wrote. "He looks so sick. I can't stand seeing that boy look so sick," Honoria remembered Hemingway saying.

Patrick died on January 30, 1937. The wires went out. The next evening, from Tryon, North Carolina, F. Scott Fitzgerald said in a letter to Gerald and Sara, "Fate can't have any more arrows in its quiver for you that will wound like these." As for the toxic artist, he, too, wrote a letter, but it got lost in the mail. We'll never know what he attempted to say.

EXUBERATING,
AND THEN THE JACKALS OF HIS MIND

Bimini, summer 1935

FIVE DAYS AFTER the knobbing of Mr. Knapp, the puffed-up pugilist, accompanied by his wife (she'd just been over to Bimini on a conjugal visit), paid his twenty-two dollars and flew on the seaplane to the Florida mainland, then trained home down through the Keys. It was great to be with the kids—the Irish Jew, meaning Gigi, was causing hell's own havoc and making his father secretly pleased about it. (The repairmen were fixing hinges on the doors, and the Gig-man helped himself to their carpenter's glue and painted all the knobs with it. Soon enough, he'd be painting a pair of Persian cats green.) There was a month's worth of magazines to unwrap. Included in that pile was his piece about shooting himself, just out in *Esquire,* and also Arnold Samuelson's story in the current issue of *Outdoor Life* about the 420-pound blue marlin Hemingway had caught the summer before in Cuba. There was continuing business with the coming Africa book. There were consultations to hold with Pauline about improvements to the house: porches were being reinforced at 907 Whitehead, and a new wide one had just been built at the back of the master bedroom, and he and his wife were talking about a backyard pool (it wouldn't happen for two more years), and then, too, they wished to get going as quickly as possible—or he did—on the first edition of some kind of fence or wall to keep the world out. Toby Bruce had just arrived from Piggott, Arkansas. They'd put him on the job. Hemingway was damn tired of people peering in at him through the gate like a zoo animal. The city fathers had put 907 Whitehead at number 18 on the list of tourist attractions, behind Johnson's Tropical Grove, ahead of the lighthouse and the aviary. Even if he raged for his privacy, being only number 18 would have smarted like hell.

It's amazing to see what close attention the man with the genius for detail could pay to the dreariest household matters. From a Hemingway archive: "Isabel gets 8.00 Borrowed $1.50. So gets $6.50. Wants to borrow $2.00. So next week will get $6.00." That's from a little later in 1935. Isabel—the more accepted spelling of her name seems to have been Isabelle—was keeping the family fed, for eight dollars a week. There are letters in which Hemingway writes to Perkins, asking him to deposit funds into one of his New York accounts. He'll provide the precise address: City Bank Farmers Trust, 22 William Street, New York City—as if Max lived in Afghanistan.

Home two days, on June 2, having gone to Sunday Mass with the family at Saint Mary Star of the Sea, he's writing to MacLeish about his new-found sporting paradise:

> [N]ever took my clothes off for a month. To go to bed just take your pants off and roll up in a blanket and in the morning peel off your shirt and dive off the top of the house. It is the clearest water in the world and the islands are right in the center of the gulf stream with the goddamndest fish on earth a quarter of a mile out. . . . Have a fine house there on the sea on a high ridge with a seven mile un-walked sandbeach for 20 dollars a month. . . . The water is so clear that youn think you are going to run aground when you have fifteen fathoms under the keel. You can see bottom at one hundred fathoms. . . . Finest sand beaches you ever saw.

He signs it "Pappy."

Top of the week, Pappy was itching to get back. The wires were coming from Bimini about new runs of tuna. Instead of waiting for the Friday seaplane, maybe he could hitch a ride over on Captain George Kreidt's Tuesday mail boat. On Tuesday, still home, he wrote to Gingrich, telling him all about the trimming of Dodi Knapp, hectoring him as well: "I wish to hell you would come. I will be fishing alone there from June 7 to June 25.... I wish to hell you would come down. It is really a fine place and that kind of fishing is a hell of a lot better with two guys than one." He told Gingrich he was leaving for Miami on Wednesday the fifth. (He didn't.)

Meantime, he arranged by wire and letter for Carlos Gutiérrez to come to Bimini for the rest of the summer. Carlos would fly over from Havana. They'd meet in Miami, spend the night, go over together the next day, on Friday the seventh. Carlos was to be sure and bring with him for Pauline four or five bottles of Camomila Intea, which was the hair-lightening lotion she'd been lately using to turn herself into a bottle blond. (The lotion could be had absurdly cheap from the Havana *mercados*.) Pappy was also exuberating down at Josie Grunts' saloon on Greene Street.

Thursday night Hemingway took the train to meet Carlos. They bunked into the Miami Colonial Hotel, on Biscayne Boulevard. It was his regular Miami stopping-over place, seven blocks from the main rail terminal, with a good view of the turquoise bay itself and the speedboats plying it. The hotel, vaguely Moorish, was fronted by a row of royal palms and inside there was an adequate dark-paneled bar for a body to have a drink. Hardly the Hotel de Crillon, overlooking the place de la Concorde, where Jake Barnes waited at five o'clock for Lady Brett, but the joint would do.

Back now, he brawled on, sported on, fished on. He adopted as his protégé twenty-one-year-old rich boy Tommy Shevlin, telling people of how Tommy, a serious sportsman despite his family's preposterous wealth, had lost six marlins in a row until he'd personally begun coaching him, and then, what do you know, here's kid Tommy hauling in a world's record blue at 636 pounds. Shevlin did it on June 18 aboard a boat called *Florida Cracker II*. Same day, the instructor, working from his own boat, brought in a 785-pound mako shark, which was only twelve pounds shy of a world's record. He got it in within thirty-five minutes, using his might-against-might technique. The jumping had been spectacular. Come September, *Outdoor Life* would publish an item about it in one of their columns: "New American and Atlantic Record. Mako, 786 lb. by Ernest Hemingway, at Bimini, aboard his own boat the Pilar."

Pauline and her sister and the boys came on June 24. The Mexican Mouse began browning like a real Mexican. The Irish Jew was getting over his fear of water and learning to swim. Bumby was gone from his bed by every dawn, fishing from the docks or out in the shallow flats from a leaky outboard with his newfound black pals. All of this got told, no, exuberated over, in letters to friends. On the beach he and the kids built a cabana out of thatched palms. Fresh fish got cooked on open-pit fires on the sand, using driftwood bone-whitened from the sun and scoured by the wind. (This image would appear in the opening pages of *Islands in the Stream*.) Sometimes, after dinner, he'd lead expeditions through the town cemetery, studying the mix of English and African names, calculating the life span of the community. Sometimes he'd go over to the jewel box–size Wesley Methodist Church, with its miniature belfry and board-on-batten walls and sit alone in that perfect architectural space. Later, the limp bars, with their cold beer and sand flooring.

Early in July, *Pilar* needed an engine overhaul, a new strut bearing, and a copper painting on her bottom parts. It didn't dent his spirits. He fished off the docks. He wrote letters. He read proofs of his Africa book. To Perkins, he said: "This is a lovely spot—The kids are crazy about it. Swimming on a wonderful sand beach in the middle of the gulf stream—a fine cool house with ocean on both sides of it for 20.00 a month—servant 20.00 more." He was betting on *Green Hills* selling more than twenty thousand copies—okay, fifteen. "[I]t's the best writing I've ever done and the more often I read it the more I think it gets that extra dimensional quality I was working for." He meant the extra dimension in the landscape, that ineffable, Cézannesque quality. He had to turn the last page of the letter upside down to get his signature in: "Best luck to you—Ernest." He drew a circle and wrote inside it: "My best to Scott."

Four and a half months before, in February (the Maestro would have been just striking off for the cold north and the rest of his life), he hadn't been so magnanimous. He and his editor had had a set-to over money, specifically about the price Scribner's was offering for serialization of the new book. Fighting about money was always the worst. He'd wanted $10,000 for the first-serial magazine rights; Perkins had said the company could offer only $4,500. Hemingway had gone down to the Key West Western Union office close to midnight on the day he got the offer and fired off a night letter of 150-some-odd words, starting with this: LETTER JUST RECEIVED SORRY UNABLE UNDERSTAND YOUR ATTITUDE PRICE UNLESS YOU MEAN YOU WANT ME TO REFUSE IT TO RELEASE YOU FROM PURCHASING STOP. The master of cable-ese had made "New York" NEWYORK—probably saved him a penny. It's true that his mood hadn't been helped by those horse doses of emetine the doctor had him quaffing for the latest flare-up of his amoebic dysentery, which had never completely gone away since Africa. (Some mornings there'd be a cupful of blood in his stool.) Then, too, the semi-devout Catholic had made the mistake of giving up serious drinking for Lent. He'd limited himself to one drink a day. Christ, how long was Lent anyway? But that was then, wintertime. All was summer light now. Or mostly.

Eight days later (it's July 10), he writes to Sara Murphy, and again the manic onrush of sentences:

> You would love this place Sara. It's in the middle of the
> Gulf Stream and every breeze is a cool one. The water is so
> clear you think you will strike bottom when you have 10 fath-
> oms under your keel. There is every kind of fish. . . . There is
> a pretty good hotel and we have a room there now because
> there have been rain squalls at night lately and so I cant sleep
> on the roof of the boat. That's not a very nautical term but a
> fine cool place to sleep. . . . Tell Patrick I have a Thompson
> Sub Machine gun and we shoot sharks with it. Shot 27 in two
> weeks. All over ten feet long. As soon as they put their heads
> out we give them a burst. . . . I don't know any more news. . . .
> You can catch snappers, tarpon, and 25 kinds of small fish
> right from the dock here. About 400 people live in the town.
> Mostly turtling boats and spongers. Bonefish are common as
> grunts. . . . There is no kind of sickness on the island. . . . It
> is under the British flag. . . . We have celebrated the Queen's
> Birthday, the Jubilee, the Prince of Wales Birthday, the 4th of
> July, and will celebrate the 14th of July, getting drunk on all of
> these.

Ten days later, he brings in his tenth and eleventh catches of the season and puts them up on the dock along with two other marlin and then poses for many photographs. The next day, the gods arrange for him to land, on his birthday, a huge blue, 540 pounds, in thirty minutes. At the end of the month, he inventories the recent bounty for his various correspondents, sometimes listing weights and times with little arrows between the respective numbers, lest there be any confusion. To Gingrich: "540 on my birthday—Big current now and another run due in next 10 days. Sure—540 was 12 feet 8 inches—jumped 18 times—ran out 450 yards of line twice." To Perkins: "Only thing have piles from lifting them—it is work to take one that size up over the stern!" To both editors, he describes the newest island pastime. He says it's called "Trying Him." He's offered 250 bucks in

U.S. currency to anybody who can stay with him for three rounds of boxing. "Since the Knapp thing when anybody is tight here or feels dangerous they ask me to fight. . . . Have fought 4 times in last 2 weeks—twice with bare fists, twice with gloves—all knock outs—Don't know whether it is working the fish has built up my shoulder muscles or what but can <u>really</u> hit now."

A thirty-six-year-old light-heavyweight in peak condition, Hemingway had issued an island-wide open challenge, with serious money attached. Some Hemingway chroniclers—not least his youngest son—have worked hard to debunk these old fight stories on Bimini. Was Willard Saunders—whom Hemingway claimed to have fought bare-fisted on the dock, finishing him off in something over a minute—really able to carry a piano on his head? Probably not, even though you can go into the waterside bars of Alice Town right now and hear that claim. Even the debunking son could acknowledge in his *Papa:* "And you know, it is something to issue a challenge to an island, and ultimately to the whole Bahamas, that you could knock out anybody before the end of three rounds. Sure, it was Hemingway, the twentieth-century Byron, overcompensating for being dressed as a girl for the first two years of his life." In a letter to Gingrich on July 31, two weeks before he took *Pilar* home, Hemingway said, "Bimini is just about the size place that I could be heavyweight champion of!" But that sounds feigned, like an amateur fighter's too-obvious feint.

A week or so earlier, from Manhattan, on the engraved hotel stationery of the Waldorf-Astoria, Baroness Blixen had written. On the envelope: "Ernest Hemingway Esq. 'M.S. Pilar' Bimini, Bahama Islands." From the letter: "Darling fat Slob! I read a terrible story in the newspaper this morning about a marlin which had the cheek of weighing more than yours. Ernest you really can't have that!" Eva was leaving for Sweden—whether with Blix or without him wasn't clear from the letter—but she planned to return to Africa at summer's end. "Do come clown in the autumn," she said. Nope. His book was coming out. The pub date was now set, October 25.

Somehow, it was as if once he stepped off the island, and back into America, everything in his life had to change, to foul. It began with *Pilar* herself.

He aimed his boat toward Key West just after midnight on August 14. He made it in twenty-six hours, arriving at about 2:00 a.m. on the fifteenth. That afternoon he could read about himself in the *Citizen:* "Ernest

Hemingway the author who, when not writing intensely interesting novels and articles, seeks to capture prize specimens of the larger denizens of the deep, arrived in port this morning on the Cruiser Pilar." Oh, the hackdom.

The plan was to get the boat back, clean her up, rest her up, then hire a crewman or two to help him steer her over to Havana for the first two weeks of the September blue marlin runs. (Carlos Gutiérrez would rejoin the boat in Cuba.) The previous year they'd been "thickest" in the first three weeks of the month. But on the way down from Bimini, *Pilar* had begun to burn serious oil, and by the time he'd angled her through the little cut at the northwest corner of the submarine pens at the navy yard, the big Chrysler was smoking two quarts an hour. He ordered a new set of piston rings from Detroit, only to learn the best mechanic was not in town. Havana began to look seriously off.

Almost no sooner was he back than out-of-town guests descended, staying five days. He was trying to get a story started. On August 25, the day after the company was gone, he took *Pilar* out on the Stream around Key West and tried to kid himself into thinking he could make Havana anyway. The next day he told Gingrich: "If it would not have been any worse would have left tonight at midnight. But it is plenty worse." He meant the fouled rings. Cuba was now out for sure.

A few days later, over the Labor Day weekend, a killer hurricane. It is said to be the first recorded Category 5 event in the country's history. Although it struck all the Keys, the storm directed its full fury—an eighteen-to-twenty-foot surge—at the CCC (Civil Conservation Corps) camps occupied by World War I veterans on Upper and Lower Matecumbe Keys, near Islamorada, about forty-five miles from Key West. Hundreds died. Key West was only nicked. All the same, it was the closest Hemingway ever came to losing *Pilar*. He wrote about that and about the storm itself in a famous piece titled "Who Murdered the Vets?" which was published in *New Masses*. Even though Hemingway had no use for the magazine's Marxist agenda, he did the piece (after the magazine's editor had wired, fairly pleading) mainly because of his own fury at how the vets at Matecumbe had been left criminally in harm's way by the bureaucrats in FDR's Washington—or this is how he saw it. They could have been evacuated in time. If his report was scant on hard journalistic fact and documentation, it was long on his passion.

In the early part, he reports on *Pilar* herself, telling of how, on foot and with a flashlight and with the wind howling and trees falling and the rain in sheets and wires lashing down around him, he fought his way to the navy yard in the middle of the night. (His car, which he'd left in front of the house, because he feared for the rickety garage, was flooded out.) Earlier, in Sunday daylight, he'd done what he could, shifting *Pilar* to the safest part of the sub pens, securing her with fifty-two dollars' worth of new ropes and cables, wrapping the lines themselves with heavy canvas as a ward against the fraying. The Coast Guard had recently seized a rum-running boat, and this scow was tied up next to his own. The boat was secured to the dock by lines tied to ringbolts in the stern, and he knew that they'd jerk right out when the storm came, and that the "booze boat" would then come smashing right into *Pilar*, busting her into pieces. He told himself: *If my boat goes tonight, I'll never get enough money in one place again to get another.*

The remainder of "Who Murdered the Vets?" is about what Hemingway saw at Camp No. 5 at Lower Matecumbe, after he and some other volunteers from Key West had gone up to be part of a rescue effort. Eight out of 187 vets at the camp had survived. Bodies were strung high in trees, "beginning to be too big for their blue jeans and jackets that they could never fill when they were on the bum and hungry." Corpses everywhere: "Hey, there's another one." He's got "low shoes, copper-riveted overalls, blue percale shirt without collar, by Jesus that's the thing to wear, nothing in his pockets. Turn him over. Face tumefied beyond recognition." Hemingway seems to have written the piece in one sitting, five days after the storm was gone and he was home in Key West. On the same day, he told Perkins that he'd not seen such death since the lower Piave in 1918. Five days later, in another letter, he told Sara Murphy he was refusing payment. He wanted the editors to print a disclaimer to the effect: "We disapprove of Mr. H. and do not want anyone to ever be sucked in by anything else he may ever write but he is a very expensive reporter who happened to be on the spot and because he does not believe in making money out of murder he has written this for us for nothing."

His own inner hurricane of anxiety and bitterness, driving him deep into a new round of sleeplessness and old thoughts of self-destruction, came with the reception of his book by those angleworms in New York. He'd called them that on page 21 of *Green Hills of Africa*. Not quite a hundred pages onward, he'd spoken of book reviewers as "the lice who crawl on literature." It was as if he was begging for it, and they, the lice, the worms in the bottle, obliged.

Hemingway and his wife were booked into a suite at the Westbury Hotel at Sixty-ninth and Madison. He'd not been in Manhattan before when one of his books came out and he was doing so now against his better judgment. On the official day of publication, the two most prestigious papers in the city, *The New York Times* and the *New York Herald Tribune,* creamed him.

On A-1 of the *Herald Trib* is a pair of three-deck headlines, the head on the left about the British being cool to a peace bid by Mussolini, the one on the right about the cooling of mobster Dutch Schultz. (He's just been gunned down in New Jersey.) His review's on page 17. Just as Max has promised, there's an ad for the book opposite the review: "Published Today. *Green Hills of Africa.* By Ernest Hemingway. The story of a month's big-game hunt in Africa told with the movement, beauty and suspense of a fine novel." Lewis Gannett's syndicated Books and Things goes down the left side of the page. There's a line about "the increasingly thin books of Ernest Hemingway," a writer who seems to be evincing "the tired passion to escape, the sinking into contentment with the odor of mere blood—the farther from home the better." Shit.

The *Times* review is on page 19, alongside the headline "Needlework Art Seen in 2 Exhibits." The critic is John Chamberlain, who's not much over thirty, but who looks twenty, a stringbean New Deal liberal. Chamberlain, who's fairly new to the paper, is the first daily reviewer in *Times* history. He produces five columns a week, and his alive prose in the staid old girl has become a morning must-read for all the park-bench intellectuals who both wish and don't wish they had a job to go to. John Chamberlain can't abide Hemingway's book:

> Sometimes dispensing with grammar, Mr. Hemingway decimates the fauna of Kenya, Tanganyika, Northern Rhodesia and the Belgian Congo along with Emerson, Hawthorne, Whittier and Thoreau. The carnage is frightful. . . . For all his talk about seeing things "truly," he is not really interested in the underlying aspects, the fundamental meaning, of the human comedy— or tragedy. His book is all attitude, all Byronic posturing. . . . It is simply an overextended book about hunting, with a few incidental felicities and a number of literary wisecracks thrown in.

In the first paragraph, Chamberlain has quoted in full the offending "angleworms" passage, in which the "I" of the story opines: " 'Writers should work alone. They should see each other only after their work is done, and not too often then. Otherwise they become like writers in New York. All angleworms in a bottle, trying to derive knowledge and nourishment from their own contact and from the bottle.'"

The next day, in the *Saturday Review of Literature*, Bernard DeVoto, a critic with an even larger reputation, says of *Green Hills:* "A pretty small book for a big man to write."

Some good reviews appeared that weekend, both in New York and across the country. On Sunday, October 27, he got what amounted to a qualified rave in *The New York Times Book Review*—and that was far more important than any daily review. (He didn't make the cover, though. He made page 3. Mark Twain's notebooks and a Twain critical study got the cover.) But the damage had been done, certainly in Hemingway's view. The initial press run of 10,550 copies proved sufficient. He would later tell Perkins that the three things that ruined his book were its high pricing, his remarks about the critics, and the company's failure to push back at the early bad notices with sustained advertising.

The most wounding review was Edmund Wilson's, in *The New Republic*. It was in the issue of December 11, 1935, leading the Winter Book Section. It was lengthy and uncompromising, and seems to mark the moment when Wilson turned on Hemingway more or less for the long haul.

> [S]omething frightful seems to happen to Hemingway as soon as he begins to write in the first person. In his fiction, the conflicting elements of his personality, the emotional situations which obsess him, are externalized and objectified; and the result is an art which is severe, intense and deeply serious. But as soon as he talks in his own person, he seems to lose all his capacity for self-criticism and is likely to become fatuous or maudlin. His ideas about life, or rather his sense of what happens and the way in which it happens, is in his stories sunk deep below the surface and is conveyed not by argument or preaching but by directly transmitted emotion: it is turned into something as hard as a crystal and as disturbing as a great lyric. When he expounds this sense of life, however, in his own character of Ernest Hemingway, . . . he has a way of sounding silly. Perhaps he is beginning to be imposed on by the American publicity legend which has been created about him.

In the nearly two months since he'd left New York and come back to Key West, Hemingway had been consoling himself with afternoons on *Pilar.* The natural world itself is always there, the refuge. To read his letters of November and December to Max Perkins and F. Scott Fitzgerald and John Dos Passos and Sara Murphy and a handful of others is to gain new feelings about what would overtake Ernest Hemingway, under some mountains, far from salt water, on a Sunday morning a quarter century later.

On November 20, he wrote to the young Spanish American writer Prudencio de Pereda, whom he'd befriended in the past few years and whom he regretted not being able to get together with in New York. "[T]he thing to do is write and keep on writing," he said. "Am feeling a little discouraged myself knowing that I've written a good book and having to read that it is shit etc. but then I always feel discouraged in the fall along with the trees and everything else."

In early December, he's telling Sara that the mince meat she'd sent was marvelous. He talks of his "late age," and of how he seemed to be made up of two Hemingways: the one who could stay out all night and drink, and the other with an atavistic midwestern conscience who somehow needed to keep on working and try to get to bed—if not to sleep—by ten o'clock, and hopefully not doing it alone. He and his boy Patrick had been out shooting the day before and "never saw a dove nor snipe nor plover so finally shot 2 buzzard, 1 chicken hawk and a large crane." He closed, "With very much love much love and love also with love."

In mid-December, Fitzgerald wrote to Hemingway. We don't have that letter, only Hemingway's reply of December 16. Scott must have registered small notes of reservation about *Green Hills.* "You know you are like a brilliant mathematician who loves mathematics truly and always gets the wrong answers to the problems," Hemingway said. He went on: how is it that every time you meet an old friend, you have "to get stinking drunk and do every possible thing to humiliate yourself." Despite it, his friends still love him, he said. Why, up in Saranac, he and Sara had spent a whole afternoon talking about how much they cared about him, he wrote. But then, softening, the bully goes away: "The more I think back to it the better book Tender Is The Night is. This may irritate you but it's the truth. Why don't you come down here?"

The next day, Hemingway wrote to Perkins. (It's the letter where he cites the three things that killed his book.) He'd only heard about Wilson's review. His books were no longer being judged on whether they were good or lousy on their own merits, he wrote, but on how they stacked up against "A In Our Time B The Sun Also Rises C A Farewell to Arms D Death in the Afternoon. You may have noticed how this last which was hailed as lousy when it came out is now referred to with the hushhushes. It all gives me a pain in the ass." Toward the close: "I feel sort of bitter about a lot of things but I always get over that."

That same day he writes to Dos Passos, making cutting remarks about Fitzgerald. He and his family have $300 to get through Christmas, he says. A page or so later he's on Wilson again (although he still hasn't seen the review): "After all Bunny Wilson did speak well of me once so he has a right to try to put me out of business." Goddamn it, he'd written a good book. He'd like to get the tommy gun he shot the sharks with on Bimini and go up to New York and spray the offices of *The New Republic* and a few other places just to "give shitdom a few martyrs." Next three words: "and include myself."

Four days later, he writes again to Fitzgerald. Scott has answered his of the sixteenth. (This second Fitzgerald letter is also lost, but in it he must have spoken about a list of health problems.) Hemingway's reply has a bit of the usual bullying and condescension, but his dominant tone is solicitous. It's the caring of someone redeemed by his own suffering—momentarily. "And you with a bad liver, lung and heart. That's damned awful," he says.

> I mean what does the Doctor say? Non-sleeping is a hell of
> a damned thing too. Have been having a big dose of it now
> lately too. No matter what time I go to sleep wake and hear
> the clock strike either one or two then lie wide awake and hear
> three, four and five. But since I have stopped giving a good
> goddamn about anything in the past it doesn't bother much
> and I just lie there and keep perfectly still and rest through
> it and you seem to get almost as much repose as though you
> slept. This may be of no use to you but it works for me. If I get
> exercise and go out in the boat sleep like a log.

If he wakes on the boat, he can generally go right back to sleep. But even if he can't, just lying there on *Pilar* makes it all right, somehow. He can just consider his life and *"not give a damn*—it's a hell of a help."

Seven years before, in and around the time he'd first visited Key West, working on *A Farewell to Arms*, he has Lieutenant Frederic Henry, who's been blown up on the Italian front, alone in the American hospital in

Milan. He says, "I slept heavily except once I woke sweating and scared and then went back to sleep trying to stay outside of my dream."

Sleep and fright. Outside his dream. On either the final day or the second to the last day of 1935, the insomniac wrote again to his editor, and again he railed against the critics—he could bring out *Hamlet* and they wouldn't like it if his name was on it. "[A]s I say I was never around N.Y. when a book came out before and certainly never will be again." The bastards who write the columns hate his guts because they think he's loaded, and because they know he despises *them*, and all they can remember is "how wonderful Lady Brett was in the sun also rises." And yet at the close, this small redemption: "Caught a sailfish yesterday and one the day before. First two decent days to fish in a month. Good luck to you and all your family. Say Happy New Year for us."

The next summer, Hemingway returned to Bimini for almost six weeks. (His family was with him for most of it.) The year after that, 1937, he took *Pilar* to Bimini in late May, hoping to fish for most of the summer but found he could spend only a fractured run of days there—the world kept intruding on him. The Spanish Civil War was a year old by then, and his involvement in it, specifically with a film, *The Spanish Earth,* supporting the Republican cause, was one of the things taking him away. His affair with Martha Gellhorn was six months old by then, and this was an even greater thing taking him away, and not just from Bimini. Indeed, I've long wondered whether he already knew, by the late fall of 1935, when he had come back from New York and was deep inside his sleep fright, that an entire way of life was cracking beneath him—Bimini, Key West, all of it— and that something farther-shored was going to take its place.

By the time he took his boat to Cuba at the end of 1939, he had lived in Key West for the better part of nearly thirteen years. A place that was less than four miles long and less than two miles wide had held him all that while—well, if not held him, home-based him. In Key West, or at least in the Key West years, he completed a huge body of work. A partial listing: *A Farewell to Arms, Death in the Afternoon, Winner Take Nothing, Green Hills of Africa, To Have and Have Not, The Fifth Column,* "The Short Happy Life of Francis Macomber," "The Snows of Kilimanjaro." When he motored away on *Pilar,* at Christmas 1939, his marriage over, Key West over, he had one hundred thousand words down on *For Whom the Bell Tolls,* which, the next year, would be taken by the hateful critics as his finest novel yet.

And yet. Many of the critics of his day may well have missed the point of *Green Hills*. That's how it seems now. The book was an experiment, postmodern in nature, in which a too-full-of-himself author wished a platform to discourse—call it *flatulate*—on any number of subjects, not least the state of literature and the tensions of the artist. In many ways, as has been said by several influential latter-day critics, it's as much a book about the pursuit of art as it is about big-game hunting. I think Hemingway himself would have conceded he was serving an experimental literary purpose more than a reportorial or documentary one. In a brief foreword (added, it seems, after he had written the book), he had said: "The writer has attempted to write an absolutely true book to see whether the shape of a country and the pattern of a month's action can, if truly presented, compete with a work of the imagination." Did the experiment work? Did he compete with a work of the imagination, his imagination? Did he locate the shapes of the country and the patterns of action of, say, *A Farewell to Arms*? No one in his right literary mind would argue that. And yet there are unforgettable Africa passages. Max Perkins understood *Green Hills* for the lesser work it was. In a letter to Fitzgerald, a month before the book came out, the editor to both men, who could write to each in a confidential voice about the other's anxieties, had said: "Every writer seems to have to go through a period when the tide runs against him strongly." At least it was happening "when Ernest was writing books that are in a general sense minor ones." I prefer to think of *Green Hills* in the way Lincoln Kirstein— an acute critical mind of the thirties—thought of *Death in the Afternoon*, another nonfiction experiment commonly "explained" as a failure, as an early marker on the trail of Hemingway's supposed long decline. To Kirstein, the merits of *Death in the Afternoon* superseded its flaws. Kirstein believed that "however irritating," the "sum of the book stands head and shoulders above his worst self; it is his best self." Yes. "In the terms of his limits, he can best be explained." Yes again. Isn't that a kind of Hemingway epitaph?

In April 1933, a little more than a year after he and his family had moved into 907 Whitehead, Hemingway had written to an old pal from his Paris days, Janet Flanner. "We have a fine house here and the kids are all well," he'd said. "Also four coons, a possum, 18 goldfish, three peacocks and a yard with fig tree, lime tree. Very fine the way Pauline has fixed it. We have been (and are) damned happy. I could stay here damned near all the time and have a fine time watching the things grow and be happier than I understand."

There's a term in typesetting known as the "widow." It refers to a word or two hanging alone at the end of a paragraph. In the old days of newspapers, desk editors were always trying to squeeze the reporter's prose in the lines immediately above so as to eliminate the widow and save a line of type. Sometimes, in magazine work, chunks of white space remain at the end of a page, and so editors will sling in some filler. If it's a highbrow magazine, they might put in a verse. At the end of Edmund Wilson's take-apart of Hemingway in *The New Republic,* on page 136, there was an inch-and-a-half of white space. The magazine's literary editor, Malcolm Cowley, filled it with a recent eight-line poem of his own, titled "Hunter." Later, when he included it in a collection of his poetry, Cowley altered its form slightly and retitled it "Ernest." Why be obscure? Why not name his subject, whom he got to know, the decade before, in the cafes of Paris?

> Safe is the man with blunderbuss
> Who stalks the hippopotamus
> On Niger's bank, or scours the Veldt
> To rape the lion of his pelt;
> But deep in peril he who sits
> At home to rack his lonely wits
> And there do battle, grim and blind,
> Against the jackals of the mind.

The jackals of his mind. Only to grow more jackaled.

PART THREE

BEFORE

What did I know best that I had not written about and
lost?

—From *A Moveable Feast*

Because when you like to shoot and fish you have to move
often and always further out and it doesn't make any difference what they do when you are gone.

—*Esquire*, February 1935

They were seated in the boat, Nick in the stern, his
father rowing. The sun was coming up over the hills. A
bass jumped, making a circle in the water. Nick trailed his
hand in the water. It felt warm in the sharp chill of the
morning.

In the early morning on the lake sitting in the stern of
the boat with his father rowing, he felt quite sure that he
would never die.

—From "Indian Camp"

The child is standing on the bow of a small, wooden rowboat pulled up into the weeds. It's the summer of 1903 at the family cottage in Michigan. He's about to turn four. Behind him is an open field—so Windemere and the woods and the beach and Walloon Lake itself must be somewhere in the foreground, which you cannot see. What you see is the smiling little boy. He's got on fringed cowboy pants. Pitched on the back of his head is a wide-brimmed cowboy hat. Cradled in his arms is a gun. It doesn't look large enough to be a shotgun. It could be an air rifle. Just the way he holds it suggests a level of confidence and comfort. If it's only a play gun, this in itself would seem a little curious, because Ernest Miller, as his mother often calls him, is all but done with make-believe weapons. He's already been on hikes of up to seven miles through the forest with his daddy, toting a real shotgun on his shoulder. Doctor Hemingway had taken his son into the woods and allowed him to fire a rifle at two and a half—the thing had kicked like a mule but the child had loved it. We know so because the event was recorded in a family album kept devotedly by his mother. She calls them scrapbooks. She's going to fill up five for Ernest Miller, her second born, documenting the story of his life from birth into his high school years.

This picture and its caption are on page 54 of Album II. Beneath the glued-in image, in her bold, Palmer-perfect hand, with the big loops on the tails of several letters, Grace Hall-Hemingway wrote:

" 'Can cock my own gun.' "

EDENS LOST AND DARKNESS VISIBLE

Horton's Creek, northern Michigan, summer 1904.
An unidentified family member wrote on the back,
". . . Ernest Hemingway in Horton's Creek—near Walloon Lake,
Mich. 5 years of age. . . . Taken by his father Clarence Hemingway."

THERE ARE UNCOUNTED BOATS and streams and ten-foot Sears, Roebuck cane fishing poles of childhood and boyhood and young manhood that prefigured the life of *Pilar*.

In the cold Illinois spring of 1917, two months before their high school graduation and in the same week America entered World War I, Ernest Hemingway and a stubby five-foot-six-and-a-half classmate named Ray Ohlsen took a five-day camping-and-canoeing trip down the Des Plaines River and the Illinois River to Starved Rock State Park. Hemingway sat in the stern, his mate in the bow. In three months the stern paddler would be eighteen. In six months he'd be a cub on *The Kansas City Star*. In fifteen months he'd be blown up on the Italian front.

The Des Plaines River was a mile and a half west of the Hemingway front porch, straight out Chicago Avenue. Oak Park historians, with forgivable hyperbole, like to say that the "river of the prairies"—sluggish, sediment-filled, home to carp and bullhead, paddled by Marquette and Jolliet in 1673, known to native peoples for something like ten thousand years—is where the eastern woodlands of America meet the western grasslands. Winters, Hemingway skated on the frozen sloughs of this river. In the spring he hunted jacksnipe in the forest-preserve woods along its banks. Once—it's a well-known incident—he illegally shot a pheasant at a game farm just north of the North Avenue Bridge of the Des Plaines. Years later he wrote about this poaching moment in *Esquire*, of how "you can feel the bulk of him still inside your shirt with his long tail up under your armpit, walking in to town in the dark along the dirt road that is now North Avenue where the gypsy wagons used to camp when there was prairie out to the Des Plaines river where Wallace Evans had a game farm and the big woods ran along the river where the Indian mounds were."

If the Des Plaines was never an aesthetic thing—nothing like the alder-banked, swift-running, icy trout streams of northern Michigan—it was nonetheless Hemingway's "home river," the one a suburban teenager could get to fastest when he was dreaming his escaping dreams in the middle dormered room wedged under the eaves on the third floor of the big house at 600 North Kenilworth Avenue. It was a link, vital link, in that great chain of "highways" in the middle of landlocked America that rolls right down to the sea. Which is to say: the Des Plaines merges with the Kankakee River southwest of Joliet, Illinois, to form the Illinois River. And the Illinois traverses most of the state for which it is named before emptying itself into the Mississippi River above St. Louis. And the Mississippi flows into the Gulf of Mexico, collecting so many other rivers as it goes. If you lived on the fringe of Chicago in the shank of the century, and were mad for the outdoors, and were squirming in your confinements, parental and otherwise, that thought might well thrill you. The yearning for the short-water route to freedom, wide-open freedom, that would have been there. Call it Huck's yearning. To go riding on the spine of time, toward salt water. *Pilar* one day would provide the means.

The explorers left on a Monday, first day of their spring vacation, from the North Avenue Bridge. The temperature was in the mid-forties; the trees on the bank didn't yet have a leaf on them. In Washington, DC, Woodrow Wilson was asking Congress for a declaration of war against Germany, because the world had to be safe for democracy. "WAR RESOLUTION READY" ran the eight-column banner head on page one of the *Chicago Daily Tribune*. Someone took a photograph as they shoved off. On the back of the image, the doctor's son, with his mother's sense of history, and the impulse to record his place in it, would later write: "Start of Oak Park–Starved Rock canoe trip. April 2, 1917. Stern Ernest Hemingway (Stein). Bow Ray Ohlsen (Cohen)." It's what they called each other, Stein and Cohen. It was a running joke that had to do with a pretend pawnbroker business conducted out of their school lockers on the ground floor at Oak Park and River Forest Township High School. Actually, the two are said to have made *real* small-time book on local sporting events with their schoolmates and with students from other area high schools, collecting and paying off under an arc light half a block from their school's grounds, never getting caught. For the rest of his life, the one in the stern would keep up his unthinking Stein name-joke, referring to himself in letters and conversation as Hemingstein or Stein the Antique Brute or the Great Steinway or Hymenstein or the Stein or any of a half dozen other variants.

They were in their mackinaws and long underwear. In their borrowed canoe (Hemingway owned his own canoe, but for some reason they weren't using it on this trip) were tallow candles, army blankets, toilet paper, Swiss Army knives, a mess kit, extra pairs of socks, a lean-to tent, and cans of pork-and-beans. Their destination, several counties downstream, was a state monument thought to be home to humans as early as 8000 BC. The rock from which Starved Rock gets its name is a sandstone outcropping on the Illinois River. Once, peoples of the Potawatomi and the Fox, subtribes of the Ottawa nation, trapped their enemies from the Illinois tribe atop this cliff, starving them to death.

That first day out was pretty miserable. So was the second. Because of dams and shallow water, no matter the spring runoffs, they had to make numerous portages. There were boulders in their path that sent them hopping out of the canoe and into the cold, brownish water to try to protect the sides of the boat. Near a town named Riverside they climbed a local landmark called the Hoffman Tower. They came down and took pictures on the bridge. Hemingway, wearing a couple of shirts and an outer jacket, has a large pack on his back. In his right hand is his blade—if they would have left their paddles in the canoe, somebody might have come along while they were in the tower and stolen their boat. He's taking some of the weight off his shoulders with a tump-line harness at his forehead—he could almost be a French voyageur from the old fur-trading days on the river, no matter that he's still in the clutch of suburbia. Seven years from now, in Paris, nursing his *café*, his baby boy in the pram beside him, a voyager in literary modernism will write: "Nick walked back up the ties to where his pack lay in the cinders beside the railway track. He was happy. He adjusted the pack harness around the bundle, pulling straps tight, slung the pack on his back, got his arms through the shoulder straps and took some of the pull off his shoulders by learning his forehead against the wide band of the tump-line." That's from "Big Two-Hearted River."

Toward the end of the second day, when the landscape looked a little wilder, they decided to put the boat into the Illinois and Michigan Canal, which parallels the Des Plaines—but this meant they had to lug the canoe, with all the gear inside it, around a series of locks. Soldiers of the Illinois National Guard, protecting the canal, now that America was at war, came up and pawed through their things. That night it rained, and the water ran into their tent. In the morning they swirled their coffee in a skillet, having forgotten to bring a coffeepot. They hunched over their cups by the fire. The collars on their coats were turned up, their woolen caps pulled down over their ears. In the pictures, they look stiff and cold, their paddles against a tree, their boat upside down on the bank.

"Dear Dad," the stern paddler wrote in a postcard dated "5 April 1917" (it was actually Wednesday, April 4, their third day out). "Am writing from Chanahon [he misspelled it], a little village on the sleepy old canal about 10:30. This morning the river was absolutely black with ducks, bluebills, pintails, mallards. Weather is warm and are getting some good pictures. Fine eats." Despite their troubles, the canal and the river were quite scenic, he wrote. "We go into the Illinois River this aft. Have made about 50 miles, many portages. Ernie." In town, they saw a large sign the town fathers had just put up: AMERICA FIRST, THEN CHANNAHON. Hemingway stopped in a hardware store and bought a piece of railroad chalk. Cohen wondered what Stein was up to. Hemingway walked up to the sign, looked over his shoulder, scrawled on it: "And then God Almighty." Roaring, they tore for the canoe.

A day later, at the town of Ottawa, in La Salle County, they went to a freight office to send the boat back to Oak Park by rail. They hiked the fairly brief distance to Starved Rock. There, they climbed around on the monument, mildly terrorizing some local Boy Scouts on a camp-out. They skipped stones in the river, slept one more night on the ground, saw great blue herons and egrets and a kingfisher, watched a couple of smallmouth bass leap to bugs, hiked to a train depot, and then rode home to their families.

End of trip, end of story. Except it's not. There's a postscript.

Forty-three years afterward, on January, 11, 1961, a time-punching employee at Caterpillar, Inc., in Peoria, Illinois, heard on the radio that the most famous writer in America, if not the world, had been a patient for the last six weeks at Mayo Clinic in Rochester, Minnesota. The announcer said something about hypertension, about Ernest Hemingway having entered the hospital in late November under an assumed name, about his condition now being judged "satisfactory" by his doctors, with a release expected in the next two weeks. There was no mention of the twice-a-week electric shock treatments the patient had been undergoing since mid-December for his depression, for his paranoid delusions about the FBI combing through his bank accounts late at night with their flashlights.

Cohen hadn't talked to Stein in four decades. He knew almost nothing of Hemingway's life except its fame. The boy who'd paddled from the bow on that spring vacation trip down the Des Plaines drove to a drugstore and bought a get-well card. He wrote a few sentences and mailed it off. Would Stein even remember him? Several days later came a small envelope to the modest house with the 120 rosebushes in the yard at 1013 North Frink Street in Peoria. The note, dated January 15, 1961, dictated to a Mayo medical secretary, was signed and slightly amended by the patient. It said: "Dear Cohen. It was worth going to Rochester to hear from you, kid. Will be out of here soon. Let me know how you are and any news of the old gang when you get time." It closed, as if not quite wanting to close: "It certainly was wonderful to hear from you, and remember that trip we made in the canoe down past Starved Rock. Best always, Ernie."

Six months later, Ray Ohlsen again turned on the radio in his living room to hear the news of a suicide, which wasn't being reported as a suicide, not then.

Actually, there's a second postscript—you can find it in the endnotes.

When he was two and a half, Hemingway picked up some sheets of his father's medical stationery and began to draw. It was a Saturday morning in Oak Park. One of the first things he drew, along with a giraffe, was a sailboat. It was just a couple of abstractionist scribbles on the page, in pencil, but, yes, you could make out a big sail and a horizontal platform below it. His mother wrote on the first page of this, his first "book": "Ernest Miller made this book all himself. Illustrated it and named all his drawings at 2 years 7 months. March 8, 1902." Beside the sailboat "chapter," Grace Hemingway wrote: "Sailing in the sea."

Antecedents. The first boat Hemingway was ever on was most likely a mini–ocean liner named the SS *Manitou*. In the first week of September 1899, when he wasn't quite seven weeks old, the vessel carried him and his parents and nurse (the nurse's name was Katherine Love Norris, and not much is known about her) across a blue expanse that could almost have been the Atlantic itself, Lake Michigan, fifth-largest lake in the world. Is it possible a rocking sway indelibly imprinted itself? Did the deep love of ocean travel on big liners in adulthood have its conception in this over-night voyage?

It was a transit of approximately twenty hours, from a pier in downtown Chicago late on September 5 to a resort town in northern Michigan the next day called Harbor Springs, near the tip of the Lower Peninsula, close to the Straits of Mackinac, on Little Traverse Bay. The year before, Ed and Grace Hemingway had purchased an acre of land fronting a Caribbean-colored inland lake, close to another resort town called Petoskey, and they were going over now to check on the construction of their backwoods home. What was being built for them, in Windemere's first incarnation, on the shore of what would soon be renamed Walloon Lake—it was still known as Bear Lake at this moment—was little more than a twenty-by-forty-foot box, made from locally cut white pine, with an outhouse in the rear and a screened porch off the front. A $400 house. Later would come additions and improvements, although never indoor plumbing.

When the travelers landed at Harbor Springs, they had to transfer their luggage to a commuter local of the Grand Rapids & Indiana Railway, ride it around the curving horn of the bay for eleven miles to Petoskey (with passengers being let off at various resorts and whistle-stops along the way), switch at Petoskey to an even smaller commuter spur rail line (known in local parlance as the Dummy Train because it didn't really go anywhere—just back and forth), take it down to the depot at the foot of the lake that would soon be renamed Walloon, and load their belongings onto a small steamer that finally delivered them to their destination, which was an inn called the Echo Beach Hotel, about a mile from the property they had purchased. For the next two decades, this was the normal pattern of travel and intricacy of schedule for the ever-increasing Hemingway family in its summer relocations to Michigan. In late August, they'd reverse the process.

Sometimes, depending on which steamer they rode, the family was able to land directly at Petoskey, at the bottom of Little Traverse Bay, thus saving a link in the connecting chain. And there were several years when the Hemingways, or some of them, came to the woods via train from Union Station in Chicago, and in those instances there wasn't quite so much getting on and getting off. And in 1917, four Hemingways, including a restless and just-graduated high school senior, who'd recently been on a canoe trip to Starved Rock, rode to the family cottage in Ed Hemingway's Model T touring car. (The four girls in the family had gone ahead by boat.) That was a five-day adventure, with flat tires and sinkholes and nights under the stars and panfried trout in the morning out of the stream that they'd camped beside. Grace sat in the back with baby Leicester, wearing an ankle-length duster and a rail engineer's cap.

But what of the *Manitou*, Hemingway's maiden boat? If she was hardly the *Paris* or the *Île de France*, she was awfully grand in her own Great Lakes way. Her lines were long and sleek. Her name was an Indian word for God. She could carry four hundred passengers. She was made almost entirely of steel. She was 275 feet in length, with a forty-two-foot beam. She could cruise at nineteen and a half knots. Her dining room was trimmed in Mexican mahogany. On her upper deck was a promenade for late-night strolling. She was built during the Chicago world's fair in 1893, and her shipwrights had given her a rakish shear from bow to stern, with tall spars and a sharply slanting black stack. That stack, which you could apparently see from half a mile off, had a big white *M* painted on it. For three decades into the twentieth century, until the *Manitou* burned in a fire and was reduced to a barge and ultimately got scrapped for junk in World War II, she slashed up the lake several times a week in the summer months, bound for Mackinac Island with only two or three ports of call beforehand, one of which was Harbor Springs. You can study photographs of this proud old ship gliding from her stall in early-evening summer light at the foot of Rush Street and North Water Street in downtown Chicago, looking so tubular and graceful, ready for the race to the other side, and say to yourself: Damn, that could almost be *Pilar*, writ large.

In the summer season of 1907—Hemingway would have turned eight—the *Manitou* was offering three round-trip sailings weekly from Chicago. A one-way fare between Chicago and Harbor Springs was six dollars, not including meals or berths. There were six Hemingways in 1907—four kids and the two parents—so this would have amounted to something. If the boat departed Chicago at 6:30 on a Friday evening, her passengers could expect to be in Harbor Springs at 2:30 the next afternoon.*

Antecedents. There are something like eleven thousand interior lakes in the water-surrounded state of Michigan, but none is more distinctively colored, arguably, than Walloon Lake, which is located nine miles south of Petoskey, framed by wooded hillsides and ringed by coves and bays and points and beautiful beaches. If so many other Michigan lakes are a cast of rich blue, Walloon has the greens and jades and turquoises of the Caribbean. The tropical hue may have to do with sunlight reflecting off the calcite particles in the deeper portions of the lake. (At its deepest, the lake, which has about twenty-seven miles of shoreline and a surface area of about seven square miles, is one hundred feet deep; it is said to be the twenty-second-largest lake in the state.) It may have to do with the unusual number of springs and runoffs that feed Walloon. It may have to do with its gray clay bottom, once you are away from the shore. (The gray clay is really something known as marl, which again has to do with the calcite particles. The calcite particles themselves are said to arise from the groundwater that supplies the lake.) Whatever the cause or reason, the extraordinary color is just there. When Hemingway first saw the bonefish flats of Key West, did he think he was back home in some way? Home? By 1928, when he first saw those flats, he'd left northern Michigan far behind him, at least physically, even if a different northern Michigan was much alive in his invented memory. "Of the place where he had been a boy he had written well enough. As well as he could then," thinks the dying writer, eaten up by his poisons, in "The Snows of Kilimanjaro." That's from an

---

*And of course this doesn't even speak to all the prep and travel time at the *front* end. For instance, there would have been days in Oak Park devoted to the packing of trunks, certainly among the females in the family. And it's known that Ed Hemingway used to spend hours by late-night lamplight making lists of things to purchase by mail order from the Montgomery Ward catalog. Ward's, or Monkey Ward's, as practically everybody in Chicago called it, even sold staple groceries. The paid-for larders of flour, sugar, bacon, cocoa, coffee, hardtack, and candy would arrive by rail at Petoskey. A son, who'd grow to be brilliant at his own planning and list-making in advance of extended journeys, had to have been watching. On the great day of travel, teamsters would have appeared at Kenilworth Avenue to deliver the steamer trunks the eight miles to the river. I don't know it for sure, but I think of the family—with each member lugging his or her own suitcase and knapsack, his or her own canoe paddle or fly rod or badminton racquet—taking the "L" into Chicago. The L was the city's elevated rapid transit. Oh, maybe they went by horse-drawn taxi. But all of it must have felt so epic. And the doctor's authority in all the small matters of leaving must have been enormous, just as his son's eventual authority in all the small matters of getting ready to command *Pilar* somewhere—over to Havana, up to Bimini, out to the Tortugas—would be enormous.

early draft of the story, probably late 1935, when Hemingway was back from that first summer on Bimini.

The wedge of Walloon that belonged to the Hemingway family was on the north shore, with a wide beach, on a small bay. The acre of sloping field and sandy beach was protected from the stiff wind that sometimes came in from Lake Michigan by a point of land half a mile away known as Murphy's Point. Before a split-plank fence went up around Windemere, Holsteins from a neighbor's farm used to wander down onto the Hemingway beach, cooling their ankles in the shallow water.

In the story "Fathers and Sons," written in 1933, which is a psychologically layered tale about the inability of fathers and sons to understand each other, Hemingway has his Michigan alter ego, Nick Adams, remembering:

> He would be standing with his father on one shore of the lake, his own eyes were very good then, and his father would say, "They've run up the flag." Nick could not see the flag or the flag pole. "There," his father would say, "it's your sister Dorothy. She's got the flag up and she's walking out onto the dock."
>
> Nick would look across the lake and he could see the long wooded shore-line, the higher timber behind, the point that guarded the bay, the clear hills of the farm and the white of their cottage in the trees but he could not see any flagpole, or any dock; only the white of the beach and the curve of the shore.

Antecedents. In his childhood, Walloon's waters throbbed and pulsed and lapped and feathered and oared and wind-puffed with almost every kind of floating craft imaginable—including a small armada of Hemingway family boats. There were gaff-rigged racing sailboats out on the lake. There were smart little runabouts tricked out in gleaming chrome. There were rowboats. There were canoes. There were primitive launches driven by one-cylinder, two-cycle gasoline engines, known as one-lungers, whose spark came from a battery or from a magneto activated by a breaker switch connected to a flywheel. There were noisy tubs, powered by multicylinder four-cycle engines. There were sloops flying the flag of the Walloon Yacht Club. All of them, no less than the water itself, were framing a child's earliest field of vision, fueling the incipient literary imagination. Is it any wonder that *Pilar* seems inevitable?

There were also Walloon service boats operating as a public transportation system, making circuits of the lake four and five times a day, dropping off goods and mail and passengers at the docks of hotels and individual cottages. These boats were crucial to the life of the community. There were few roads then. The lake was the road.

Only occasionally does Walloon Lake appear as a place-name in Hemingway's Michigan writing. The point is that down at the shoreline is where the world opened up. Down at the water, boundaries and limits and, in a way, even horizons appeared to fall away. You lived in your cottage set back in the trees, amid beautiful cedars and beeches and maples and big-toothed aspens. But fifty yards off was a wholly different perspective. The water gave recreation, transportation, after-dark bathing, food for the table. Walloon was rich in northern pike and black crappies and pumpkin-seed sunfish and bluegills and walleyes and yellow perch and smallmouth bass. Not so many trout, though. They darted in the nearby streams. They craved colder water. The boy would find them.

Down at the water on the night of the Fourth of July, Doctor Hemingway would set off skyrockets and Roman candles. He'd nail pinwheels to the flagpole at the end of the dock and let his children light them. The rickety dock fingered out into the dark lake, and suddenly the darkness was ablaze.

Down at the water, after dark, Ernest Miller, as his mother so often called him, liked to spear fish with his sisters. He'd take long cattails that he'd gotten from the woods and soak them in kerosene and use them for jacklights.

If Walloon doesn't often appear by name, lakes are nonetheless present in some of Hemingway's finest Michigan stories. Sometimes their presence is ghostly, and at other times you can smell the dried fish guts and smeared night crawlers wedged down into the floorboards of a rowboat making its way across the unnamed water. The first four words of "Indian Camp" are "At the lake shore." The water is a kind of proscenium to the storytelling tension. The oars are creaking and groaning in their oarlocks. "Nick went back from the edge of the lake through the woods to the camp. He could hear the oars of the boat in the dark. His father was rowing and his uncle was sitting in the stern trolling. He had taken his seat with his rod ready when his father shoved the boat out. Nick listened to them on the lake until he could no longer hear the oars."

Actually, those lines are from an eight-page handwritten fragment Hemingway decided to *cut* as an opening, or maybe a precede, to "Indian Camp," which is one of his best and tautest Michigan stories. "Indian

Camp" is about a squaw having a baby. Nick's father, who's a doctor, has taken his son across the lake with him in the middle of the night, allowing him to be present during the delivery. The doctor's brother is also along. The operation is performed with a jackknife, and the incision is sewn up with a nine-foot tapered gut leader from a fishing line. The mother has screamed during her successful breech birth, and afterward it's discovered that her husband, lying in an upper bunk, has slit his throat from ear to ear. On the way home, the child asks, "Why did he kill himself, Daddy?" And the father answers, "I don't know, Nick. He couldn't stand things, I guess." The child asks, "Is dying hard, Daddy?" And the doctor answers, "No, I think it's pretty easy, Nick. It all depends." Hemingway first published "Indian Camp" in 1924, in Ford Madox Ford's *transatlantic review.*

In 1972, eleven years after Hemingway's suicide, that discarded but not destroyed fragment appeared in a somewhat controversial book titled *The Nick Adams Stories,* assembled by a Hemingway scholar at Pennsylvania State University named Philip Young, who, two decades earlier, had published a landmark—and far more controversial—Hemingway study. Young arranged the Nick Adams stories in their chronological sequence, which is to say he put them in an order conforming to the seeming age of the protagonist, as he went from boyhood to adolescent to soldier to veteran to writer and parent, as opposed to the way Hemingway had written and published the pieces in his own lifetime. Young postulated that the cut fragment represented the earliest known Nick "story," and because it was the earliest, it deserved to see the light of print, no matter Hemingway's discarding of it. Young placed it just ahead of "Indian Camp" and made it a separate piece, titled "Three Shots." Hemingway would have doubtless loathed him for it.[*]

---

[*]The earlier book, published in 1952, is *Ernest Hemingway.* Along with Carlos Baker at Princeton and Charles Fenton of Yale, Young was one of the earliest academic critics to write penetratingly—and in this case psychoanalytically—about Hemingway. He's considered a founding father in modern Hemingway studies. Hemingway had great distaste for what Young was purported to be doing, and at first had tried to stop his book, but in the end gave him permission to quote in full from his works. "[D]o you know it can be as damageing to a man while he is in the middle of his work to tell him that he is suffering from a neurosis as to tell him he has cancer?" Hemingway wrote in early 1952. Two months later he wrote to Young again: "I am very sorry, kid, if you are up the creek financially. I can let you have $200. if you need it. . . ." Young's study was much about what came popularly to be known as "the wound theory," which is to say the traumatizing effects of Hemingway's experiences in World War I. The wound theory "explained" Hemingway. Later in his life, Young would say, with a certain rueful humility, "All theses distort the work in some degree."

The first boat, of about half a dozen ultimately, to come into the family at Walloon as their own possession was *Marcelline of Windemere*. She was a lowly rowboat, around for decades, much loved, with her name handsomely lettered in black on both sides of her white bow. She arrived in the summer of 1900, taking her name from the family's firstborn, with whom Hemingway was to get famously "twinned" by his mother in dress and haircut and other ways for the first several years of his life. There are many photographs from Hemingway's first birthday at the lake, July 21, 1900, and *Marcelline of Windemere* is in them. The birthday boy clambers in and out of the new boat, which is pulled up on shore, its rope anchor tied to a rock. He sits in the bow, two tiny arms holding on to both sides. He's got on bib overalls and a frilly blouse, and his older sister is dressed identically. He's the captain of this ship, the name on the boat be damned. Thirty-four years later, there he is, in Key West, the real captain, waving from the cockpit of his own newly arrived motor cruiser, with her name lettered handsomely just below the window out of which he's leaning.

(*Twinning.* If one were trying to make something of something, there would be an entirely different way to think about the word "antecedent," as it is being employed here. There are photos aplenty, in Oak Park, of Ernest the he-man toddler, kept by his mother in gingham gowns, black patent Mary Janes, girly hats with flowers on them. As for the laden idea of getting "twinned" with his sister, Grace held Marcelline back for a year from entering first grade, so she and her little brother could start together and go side by side up through their senior year of high school.)

After *Marcelline of Windemere* came *Ursula of Windemere*, another rowboat, much loved and long-lasting, named for the second girl (and third-born) in the family. Then came *Sunny*, named for the fourth-born girl (whose christened name was Madelaine), and after that *Carol*, named for the last daughter in the family. These second-generation boats were motor launches. Because they were more costly craft, they got stored in the winter months at Ernie Culbertson's boathouse in the west arm of the lake. (The Hemingways had a small boathouse of their own, although not in the early years.) *Sunny* arrived in the summer of 1910, when Hemingway turned eleven. She was an eighteen-footer in a dory style, meaning that she had a flat bottom and fairly high sides and a sharp bow. She was powered by a sputtery Gray Marine inboard motor that was perpetually hard to start and leaked rainbows of oil on the surface of the lake, which made the head of the family sputter mild oaths—like "Oh, rats." *Sunny* had cushioned seats in her stern and a kind of small cockpit in her middle.

She flew a pennant with her name at the bow. She's *Pilar* in miniature. When the doctor was piloting her, he sometimes wore what looks in the photographs to be a canvas pith helmet.

There were usually canoes around, borrowed or owned. When the shiny mail-order red canvas canoe arrived from Old Town, Maine—this was in the summer of 1917—the family nicknamed it *Bonita Pescada*, their version of the Spanish for "beautiful fish." That winter the family stored the beautiful fish in Windemere's living room, protecting it with a bed quilt.

No sailboats—the Hemingways were rowboaters and canoeists and stinkpotters. Sailing was a different culture. This fits with the link between Hemingway and *Pilar* and Hemingway and fishing. You could formulate it like this: a sailboat will always be to a motor launch as fly-fishing is to night crawlers.

It was probably *Marcelline of Windemere* or *Ursula of Windemere* that Hemingway was referring to in 1937 when he wrote a bilious letter to his older sister from Bimini. By then, Windemere belonged to him—Grace had deeded him the house and property, which included the family boats. Even though he hadn't gone to Windemere in years, he wasn't keen on Marce or her family using the place. Some of his other siblings, okay. Marcelline and her husband and children had their own cottage at Walloon Lake in 1937. We don't have the precipitating letter from Marcelline that set Hemingway off, only his reply.

> Dear Marce—
> Thanks for your charming letter. Reading it made me slightly sick. . . .
> The keys to Windemere are in my workroom in Key West. The workroom is locked and I am here at Cat Cay B.W.I. where your letter took ten days to reach me. . . . If Sunny is *not* there you may use the row boat but I do not want you to use the house or anything else. . . . I expressly forbid you to enter or use it in any way except in the matter of using the row boat which you offer to repair and return in good condition in return for this use. If you go into the house for any other purpose, except if you go there as a guest of any of the people that I have given the right to use it, I will regard it as trespass and proceed accordingly. Your always, Ernest.

Something bitter got said between brother and sister at Ed Hemingway's funeral in December 1928, but what it was isn't clear. (It may have centered on the breakup of Hemingway's marriage to Hadley.) This is: after 1928, Hemingway and Marcelline never saw each other again, although they did communicate, and sometimes warmly, or at least with a surface warmth.

A year and a half later, in December 1938, Hemingway wrote to his sister and said, "Much love and Merry Christmas. Am awfully sorry I wrote you such a rude and boorish letter about Windemere that time." The usual pattern of remorse and self-recrimination, which must have set in long before that.

In 1962, a year after Hemingway's suicide, Marcelline, just as her kid brother Les, published a book about her family. Like Les, Marcelline had been working on her manuscript in not-quite secret for several years. *At the Hemingways: A Family Portrait* is a mostly sanitized view of the family epic. On the other hand, it's more reliable in its chronologies and facts and timelines than *My Brother, Ernest Hemingway*, even though Les's book is the far better read. According to Gregory Hemingway, in *Papa*, his aunt Marcelline, whom he barely knew, was intensely taking notes on the small plane that ferried family members and friends into Sun Valley for Hemingway's funeral. Gigi, sitting on the plane next to his aunt, had been hoping for some conversation. "She had a serious look on her face, almost evangelical, as if she finally believed that [Ernest] might amount to something," Gigi wrote. Within two years of her book, Marcelline Hemingway Sanford herself was dead. The doctors said natural causes, but several in the family suspected otherwise. She wasn't quite sixty-six. Three years later, in the fall of 1966, the third-born Hemingway child, Ursula, whom Hemingway called Ura, and who was probably his favorite sibling, and who was suffering from cancer and depression, took an overdose of drugs at her Hawaii home and stopped her life at age sixty-four. So, formulate it like this. In a Christian midwestern nuclear unit of eight—mother, father, six children—four (and possibly five) of the members would end up dying by their own hand: Clarence, Ernest, Ura, Les, maybe Marce. What flows from the father . . .

Antecedents. In time, a child's watery field of vision widened out from Walloon, and nowhere did it widen for the better, in terms of fishing and fiction, than at the crossroads of Horton Bay. Horton Bay, and more specifically Horton's Creek, which lies just outside the town, and which is a tiny thing, quite beautiful, quite cold, quite alive with trout, is where Hemingway first learned the thrill of horsing a rainbow trout out of the water and flying it over his head and into the cool green ferns somewhere behind him, with the lovely thing quivering and throbbing and gasping for its breath. Listen:

> When we first fished, as boys, we did not believe in flies. Horton's Creek, where we fished, was a beautiful, clear, cold stream but so covered with logs and brush that casting was impossible. We used angle worms, looped several of them on the hook with the ends free and dropped this bait under the logs or in any open places in the brush. We used a long cane pole, long enough so you could keep out of sight on the bank and swing the bait on the end of the line out and let it slink into the water. The difficult part was to keep out of sight so not even your shadow fell on the water and swing the bait with the long pole like a pendulum to drop it exactly in the small opening in the dead cedar branches. If it hit the water and the bait rolled with the current under the log and the trout struck, if they struck instantly, then you swung the long pole back, it bent and you felt the line fighting heavily pulling trout in the water and it seemed you could not move him. Then the unyielding fighting tension broke and the water broke too and as you swung the trout came out and into the air and you felt the flop, flopping of him still fighting in the air as he swung back and onto the bank.
>
> Sometimes he was back in the swamp and you heard him thumping and crashed toward him to find and hold him still thumping, all his life still moving in your hands before you held him by the tail and whacked him so his head struck against a log or a birch tree trunk. Then he quivered and it was over. . . .

That's from a fragment, unpublished in his lifetime, that Hemingway probably wrote in Paris in the mid-twenties. In this same journalistic piece, he says:

> This way of fishing I learned to look down on and it was not until long afterward that I knew that it is not the duration of a sensation but its intensity that counts. If it is of enough intensity it lasts forever no matter what the actual time was and then I knew why it was that I had loved that fishing so. Because in no other fishing was there ever anything finer than that first

sudden strike that you did not see and then the moment when you swung with all your force and nothing gave.

Yes, he'd grow into a much more sophisticated angler, would put his line in some far streams and oceans, would come to own expensive reels, custom-made rods, hand-tied flies, and deep-sea lures the size of a tennis shoe. But a core part of Ernest Hemingway would always be the five-year-old night-crawler fisherman with the overlong cane pole flying them over his head at Horton's Creek. The hell with fly-fishing—it was too dainty, too effete. (Which isn't to say he didn't get awfully good at it.) The might-against-might tuna theories on Bimini have their font in the cane-pole horsing at Horton's. Indeed, Horton's explains so much of the fishing part of him—his addiction to it, the primitive joy he got from it. If the sensation has enough intensity, it'll last forever.

But Ed Hemingway gave that, too, it needs be added. In "Fathers and Sons," the author has Nick Adams meditating on how "someone has to give you your first gun or the opportunity to get it and use it, and you have to live where there is game or fish if you are to learn about them." Nick "loved to fish and to shoot exactly as much as when he first had gone with his father," says the narrator. "It was a passion that had never slackened and he was very grateful to his father for bringing him to know about it."

Regarding the flying of them into the air over your head: in a long unpublished fragment of a novel—which Hemingway worked on through the fifties but could never finish, and which was posthumously published in *The Nick Adams Stories* as a lengthy short story titled "The Last Good Country"—Nick Adams says to himself, having just caught a fat trout on worms: "Damn, didn't he feel like something when I horsed him out though? They can talk all they want about playing them but people that have never horsed them out don't know what they can make you feel. What if it only lasts that long? It's the time when there's no give at all and they start to come and what they do to you on the way up and into the air."

There's a wonderful passage in *A Moveable Feast* when Hemingway describes going down to the Seine to watch the old Parisians working their long cane poles.

> At the head of the Ile de la Cité below the Pont Neuf where there was the statue of Henri Quatre, the island ended in a point like the sharp bow of a ship and there was a small park at the water's edge with fine chestnut trees, huge and spreading,

and in the currents and back waters that the Seine made flowing past, there were excellent places to fish. . . . [T]he fishermen used long, jointed, cane poles but fished with very fine leaders and light gear and quill floats and expertly baited the piece of water that they fished. They always caught some fish, and often they made excellent catches of the dace-like fish that were called *goujon*. They were delicious fried whole and I could eat a plateful.

Toward the end of the passage, the author says, as if trying to get down a truth of his life in eight words, "I could never be lonely along the river."

The fine chestnuts are still there, below the Pont Neuf, and the head of the Île de la Cité still comes to a point as sharp as the bow of a ship, and you still go down a stone stairway to get to the little park, and the old fishermen, who might be the great-grandchildren of the ones Hemingway watched and felt himself bonding with, are still there, working their long cane poles, trying, as Hemingway wrote, to take "a few *fritures* home to their families."

Take another look at the photograph at the start of this chapter: The helmet-haired five-year-old at Horton's with the straw sombrero and comically large wicker creel, clad in his favorite fringed cowboy get-up, is eyeing the lens at an off angle while he waits to swing with all his force. That left hand isn't holding lightly the stick in front of him. He's ready. And he's got that flat-lipped expression, as if to say: Go away, you're much in my way. This cedar-fallen and hemlock-strewn little stream belongs to me.

Horton Bay sits on Lake Charlevoix, which is west of Walloon and is a much larger body of water than Walloon. (It's the third-largest lake in the state and was known in Hemingway's time as Pine Lake.) Lake Charlevoix drains into Lake Michigan, just as Horton's Creek flows into Lake Charlevoix. Lake Charlevoix's color, as opposed to Walloon's, is deep blue, stunning in its own right. Horton Bay, which is on the lake's north shore and is the only real "town" between Boyne City and Charlevoix, used to be listed on Michigan maps as "Horton's Bay." In his writing Hemingway calls the place "Hortons Bay." Sometimes he refers to the creek as "Horton's Creek" and at other times he'll leave out the apostrophe. No matter how they're written, town and creek, and no matter how the current locals themselves tend to confuse the issue, both village and stream thread through some of Hemingway's finest Michigan stories. They are just in his imagination in a way Walloon isn't. In the Nick Adams story "The End of Something," Hemingway begins: "In the old days Hortons Bay was a lumbering town. No one who lived in it was out of sound of the big saws in the mill by the lake. Then one year there were no more logs to make lumber." By the third sentence he has you hooked like a fish. He's already reached the swing point of the story.

As a teenager, Hemingway usually got to Horton Bay and its creek by oaring one of the family rowboats across Walloon. He'd tie up on the opposite shore, directly across from Windemere, hide the oars in the weeds, then walk the three miles into town through open fields and along the sandy Sumner Road. By then his family knew a lot about the opposite shore, because, in 1905, a forty-acre farm was being sold at auction for back taxes across the lake, and Grace Hemingway had bought the place with her inheritance. They named it Longfield Farm. A tenant was put on the land to manage things, with Ed paying the bills and earning the right to a third of the crops. But all the Hemingways pitched in to farm the place. To say it mildly, Ed and Grace's second-born preferred to be fishing in Horton Creek or idling with friends in the village rather than to be digging potatoes or harvesting peaches or cutting alfalfa in twelve-hour workdays out at Longfield. In "Fathers and Sons," the narrator says: "His father had frost in his beard in cold weather and in hot weather he sweated very much. He liked to work in the sun on the farm because he did not have to and he loved manual work, which Nick did not." Hemingway spent a lot of his adult life avoiding manual work.

Horton Bay is where Hemingway met and grew to be fast friends with Bill Smith and his sister Katy (who became the wife of John Dos Passos). Horton Bay is where he married Hadley Richardson at the Methodist church on Saturday afternoon, September 3, 1921. Horton Bay is where a writer in Paris, still an apprentice, placed his bawdily titled 1923 story "Up in Michigan," which Gertrude Stein famously called *inaccrochable*, unpublishable, like a painting not to be hung. The story is about a drunken seduction/rape on the rough planking of the dock that reaches out into Lake Charlevoix. That "vulgar, sordid tale" is the way his moralizing sister Marce spoke of it, so many years later, in her family memoir, which was only an echo of her moralizing parents.

The little hop-across trout stream at Horton Bay, the one flowing fast and sure down into Charlevoix, can be thought of as the primal Hemingway trout stream. The following passage is from the Nick Adams story "Now I Lay Me," written in 1927, nine years after Hemingway was wounded in the war. Nick is lying in his Milan hospital bed. He can't sleep. Just the thought of closing his eyes in the dark fills him with terror. In his waking nightmare, the blown-up man tries to comfort himself with the memory of boyhood trout streams. Hemingway doesn't name Horton's but he's at Horton's Creek, all right. We know this because he talks about the mouth of the creek; where it comes into the lake is where Hemingway always found some of his best fishing.

> I had different ways of occupying myself while I lay awake. I would think of a trout stream I had fished along when I was a boy and fish its whole length very carefully in my mind; fishing very carefully under all the logs, all the turns of the bank, the deep holes and the clear shallow stretches, sometimes catching trout and sometimes losing them. . . . I would fish the stream over again, starting where it emptied into the lake and fishing back up stream, trying for all the trout I had missed coming down. Some nights too I made up streams, and some of them were very exciting, and it was like being awake and dreaming. . . . But some nights I could not fish, and on those nights I was cold-awake and said my prayers over and over and tried to pray for all the people I had ever known. . . . If you prayed for all of them, saying a Hail Mary and an Our Father for each one, it took a long time and finally it would be light, and then you could go to sleep, if you were in a place where you could sleep in the daylight.

A decade before "Now I Lay Me," the first American to be wounded in Italy in World War I wrote a four-page letter to his parents from his bed at the American Red Cross hospital in Milan. This was August 4, 1918. Hemingway, whose career as an ARC ambulance driver was over almost before it had begun, was sleepless, very scared. But he didn't focus on this. He said: "The rainbow trout up in Hortons Bay can thank the Lord there's a war on. But they will be all the bigger next summer. Gee, I wish I was up there fishing." Hemingway told his parents he'd been recommended for a medal. And as we know, he got it—and wore it on his tunic as he limped around Oak Park after he got home, telling fantastic stories about his bravery. It was the Silver Medal of Military Valor from the Italian government. The total wartime experience of the silver-medaled lieutenant Ernest Hemingway had lasted eight months, and six of those months had been spent in the hospital. But the intensity of the experience was enough. It's not the duration of a sensation but its intensity that counts. And if it is intense enough, the sensation will last forever.

It was most likely Horton's Creek Hemingway had in mind when he wrote, in a Nick Adams story called "On Writing," "All the love went into fishing and the summer. He had loved it more than anything. . . . It used to be that he felt sick when the first of August came and he realized that there were only four more weeks before the trout season closed. Now sometimes he had it that way in dreams. He would dream that the summer was nearly gone and he hadn't been fishing. It made him feel sick in the dream, as though he had been in jail."

Horton Bay, Michigan, is still just a wide spot in the road, with a couple of fine old country houses sitting under spreading trees. Long ago they paved the main road that runs through the town. The old Methodist church, where the wedding was, isn't there (a new church has taken its place on the east edge of the village), but the combination general store and post office is, right in the middle of the town. It's the same wooden building, with the same high front cement steps and "high false front" that Hemingway spoke of in "Up in Michigan." East of the store, there's still a side road, no longer sandy, paved now, running down through the trees to the blue bay, and on the left of this side road, as you go down, are two old white-frame cottages, Pinehurst and Shangri-La. A wedding breakfast was held for the just-married Hemingways at Pinehurst resort cottage.

But best of all, Horton's Creek is still there, still just the little hop-across thing not quite half a mile out of town, as you're heading west on the Charlevoix–Boyne City Road, still icy cold, clean as silver, riffling over stones, alive with fat, pulpy rainbows. I know this for a fishing fact.

Antecedents. Eventually, before he forsook the state, there were many other Michigan trout streams in his life and imagination: the Boardman and the Rapid and the Bear and Schultz's and the Manistee and the Minnehaha and the Sturgeon and the Pigeon and the Black and the Murphy and the Brevoort and, not least, the Two-Hearted, which is a river that Hemingway most likely never fished but only appropriated its storybook name for the water in Michigan's Upper Peninsula that he *did* fish, the Fox.

The writer in Paris took the Two-Hearted and put it where the Fox geographically is and added on the word "Big" and then proceeded to make the river immortal in a story.

Some Michigan trout rivers are finely pebbled at their bottom, almost as if you're stepping not on stones but birdshot. Some are sandy-bottomed and pancake-soft under your shoes, and their imperceptibly swift-moving water will sweep and circle around you, suctioning your waders to your thighs. Some are dark brown and yet exquisitely clear, almost as if they'd been put through a strainer. "Tea water" is what such streams are sometimes called. They get their color from their high iron content.

The Black is such a river. It's part of what's now known as the Pigeon River State Forest and is about a ninety-minute drive southeast of Horton Bay and Walloon. I've driven deep inside this forest; have skinned into my waders at Tin Shanty Bridge; have rodded up; have tied on a dry fly with trembling fingers; have coated it with the ointment that'll make the fly float on the surface; have attached one end of my old hickory net to the magnet clip that's hanging down between my shoulder blades on a lanyard (so that I'll be able to reach around and snap the net free from the clip with my left hand when I've got my dreamed-of defeated fish close to my boots); have walked into the stream and tried to feel something of what Hemingway might have felt in the summer of 1919, when, home from the war, he fished it with pals for two extended periods. In Hemingway's time, this region was known as the Pine Barrens. It was woods and swamp and lake and ponds in the process of making its way back from the ravages of the nineteenth-century loggers—"wild as the devil and the most wonderful trout fishing you can imagine," as Hemingway wrote in a letter to a fishing partner. That summer, recovering his legs, his mind, he'd fished the Black and the Sturgeon and the Pigeon in the Barrens, catching them by the hundreds, sometimes landing two fish simultaneously. (On one hook was a wet fly, on the other a grasshopper.)

I remember the day I drove to the Upper Peninsula to see the Fox, at Seney. Hemingway's Big Two-Hearted. On the way up, I spotted some wild turkeys, a pheasant, a couple of hawks, sandhill cranes. I arrived about four in the afternoon. The sun was brilliant. It was early fall. The town was very small. There was a burnt oil smell on the railroad ties. The railroad bridge was right where it was supposed to be, and the river was there, flowing under the bridge, and its surface was still "pushing and swelling smooth against the resistance of the log-driven piles of the bridge." I looked down to the sandy bottom, and just as he had said in the story, the trout were "keeping themselves steady in the current with wavering fins." Just as he had said, they "changed their positions by quick angles, only to hold steady in the fast water again." I stood there for a long while watching these probable descendants of the trout Ernest Hemingway had watched.

Antecedents. In June 1915, in his sophomore summer of high school, not quite sixteen, Hemingway and an Oak Park schoolmate named Lewis Clarahan got their parents' permission to go on a hiking and camping trip in Michigan. They rode the *Manitou*'s sister boat, the *Missouri,* across the lake, disembarked at the town of Frankfort, and then spent the better part of a week hiking through the northwest corner of the Lower Peninsula to Walloon Lake, past little towns and bigger burgs, through woods and fields, but especially via trout streams they'd plotted out ahead of time on their maps. They were living on fish and beans that get simmered in a saucepan till they bubble. It all went so well that the following June, start of his junior summer, when he was almost seventeen, Hemingway and Clarahan did it again. This time, to make their trek last even longer, they disembarked farther down the Michigan coast, at a port called Onekama. This time Hemingway kept a detailed journal and took rolls of pictures. In them are two blissful boys wearing dress shirts and ties on their way across the lake on the steamer. Two boys, shed of city clothes, hanging from boxcars in a rail yard, or walking through the woods with their packs and hiking sticks, or leaning over a rock and dangling worms and flies into the current, or standing up to their waists in the middle of a stream, with the water swelling smooth against their trousers.

Four decades ago, in the biography from which every Hemingway biography descends, Carlos Baker used a small part of the journal to sketch an account of the trip. Two decades ago, the executive director of the American Museum of Fly Fishing, which is in Vermont, wrote a much longer account of the 1916 hike, again using the journal, but this time in full. Donald S. Johnson, an angler, got the permission of the Hemingway family to reproduce the diary in the museum's journal, *The American Fly Fisher,* along with some of the photographs. It was an obvious labor of love.

Hemingway entered his notes in a pocket-size ledger book whose pages bore the imprint of the Old Hartford Fire Insurance Company. On Saturday, June 10, the starting-out day, he'd written down the time that he and Lew had agreed to meet at the Hemingway home ("4 O'clock here") in order to catch the L into the city ("Avenue Station at 5") for their overnight ride to the Michigan shore. In the days before leaving, the doctor's son had made a long list of things to gather and bring on the hike, and these got entered in the Old Hartford ledger book: matches, an ax, a can opener, postcards, a pedometer, adhesive tape, and so on. There are checkmarks beside many of these items. "Dig worms" was on the to-do list, but there's no checkmark beside the entry. The crawlers got dug in Michigan instead of Oak Park.

"Creek clean and must be waded. Caught 4 trout. 1 that was 14½ inches long and 1 that was 18 inches long. Great fighters. Took 15 minutes to land the big one," he wrote at 2:30 p.m. on Monday, June 12, on the second day out. They'd camped the night before at Bear Creek. Through the week, he wrote down where they camped, when a thunderstorm came up, where they stopped in for dinner, what the cost was of supplies bought along the way. "Dinner .30." "Sat. Eve. Post 0.5." "Chocolate .15." "Fare Mayfield to W.J. .25."

"Great fun fighting them in the dark in the deep swift water," he wrote on Friday the sixteenth. It could almost be a sentence out of "Big Two-Hearted River."

At Kalkaska, Michigan, the fishing partners said good-bye: Clarahan was catching a train south, to return to Oak Park, while Hemingway was continuing north by rail to Petoskey and Walloon and friends at Horton Bay. The family would be up later in the summer. That Saturday night, in Petoskey, the boy who'd been roughing it took a room at the Hotel Perry, which was right across the street from the railroad terminal. "Bed at Perry's .75," he entered in the journal.

"Good night's sleep," the journal keeper had written as part of the recap of his first day. "Had a good sleep," he said of an afternoon nap the next day. "[S]lept well Tues. night," he noted the following day. "Slept well at Dilworths," he reported on the following Monday, having arrived at Horton Bay.

Insomnia, as already discussed, is a deep swift current running through most of Hemingway's life—it's there in the fiction, the nonfiction, his correspondence. But we tend to connect his sleep anxieties, or the rise of them anyway, to his experiences in World War I. Sometimes, as in "Big Two-Hearted River," the water is so swift and dark and deep that you almost aren't aware of it as an anxiety having to do with sleep per se, and at other times the current is named for what it is, as in the Nick Adams stories "A Way You'll Never Be," "In Another Country," and "Now I Lay Me." Each is about the suffering of the blown-up man. "Imagine a young fellow like you not to sleep," Nick's bedmate says in "Now I Lay Me." The bedmate himself is in terror about his sleep. Nick answers, "I'll get all right. It just takes a while." And the bedmate responds, "You got to get all right. A man can't get along that don't sleep." But I've come to think that some kind of deep worry about sleep was inside Ernest Hemingway well before the war—which then got magnified to nightmarish degrees by what happened to him during the war. He seems very glad to say in his camping journal that he'd slept well. Just casual mentions? Maybe. To me, the mentions suggest that even or especially up in Michigan, even for an exuberant boy who's not yet seventeen, getting your sleep is critical, and not only for physical reasons. Without it, darkness is already visible, if just barely.

Edens lost. Nearly the entire upper half of Michigan was lost to the clear-cutters by the time the Hemingway family arrived at Walloon Lake at the start of the twentieth century. The slaughter of the Michigan forest had started in the 1840s, and the saws didn't really cease their whine until about 1925. The peak years of the decimation were probably between 1860 and 1910. Yes, the second- and in some cases third-growth timber had come, and the old pine and hardwood forests were reclaiming themselves, and there were genuine wilderness areas, such as the Pine Barrens, that you could get to—but Michigan was nothing like it used to be, and it would never be so again. The scholar Frederic Svoboda, who has spent many years studying Hemingway's Michigan life, has put it eloquently:

> While the Hemingways planned their cottage to be an Eden-like retreat, nearby were destitute Indians, once lords of the woods, now living in an abandoned lumber camp. All about Windemere lay the evidence of an orgy of clear-cutting that had raped the Michigan woods and sent its forest products through Chicago to build settlements on the prairies. [Hemingway] may have imagined a pristine north woods, but the evidence around him told a far different story.

What I think Svoboda is saying is that the writer at those marble-topped tables in Paris, re-creating Michigan in his invented memory, was caught somewhere between the Michigan he wished it to be and the Michigan he knew it was—or that a lot of it was.

In the photographs of Hemingway's camping trips, you begin to notice the open fields. You see all the stumps, the cut-over woods, the strange emptiness. The Barrens wasn't called the Barrens for nothing. He put the raped woods in the stories, even as he was re-creating the more primitive Michigan he wished it was or could be. In "Fathers and Sons," for instance, the narrator has Nick bitterly thinking about the waste of it all—of how the loggers in some cases weren't even really interested in the trees themselves: "[T]he peeled logs lay huge and yellow where the trees had been felled. They left the logs in the woods to rot, they did not even clear away or burn the tops. It was only the bark they wanted for the tannery at Boyne City; hauling it across the lake on the ice in winter, and each year there was less forest and more open, hot, shadeless, weed-grown slashing." And yet, for all that, you hear the hope. In the next sentence the narrator says: "But there was still much forest then, virgin forest where the trees grew high before there were any branches and you walked on the brown, clean springy-needled ground with no undergrowth and it was cool on the hottest days."

The word "slashing" is a Hemingway obscenity. He uses it several times in "Fathers and Sons." In "The Last Good Country," Nick Adams is talking to his kid sister, whom he calls Littless. They've escaped into the woods, like Huck and Jim down the river. "We have to go through some long bad slashings," he says. "All this beyond was hemlock forest," he says. "They only cut it for the bark and they never used the logs." Two pages later: "This is the way forests were in the olden days. This is about the last good country there is left."

In *A Farewell to Arms*, the lieutenant in Italy who's hiding in a barn, about to make his separate peace with war, is thinking about far-off Michigan, although Michigan isn't named: "The hay smelled good and lying in a barn in the hay took away all the years in between. We had lain in hay and talked and shot sparrows with an air-rifle when they perched in the triangle cut high up in the wall of the barn. The barn was gone now and one year they had cut the hemlock woods and there were only stumps, dried tree-tops, branches and fireweed where the woods had been. You could not go back."

If you can't go back, is your only real alternative to go farther out? As already said, that's one core way to understand *Pilar*.

In "Big Two-Hearted River," the first image, in the first sentence, is of something burnt and lost, something going away: "The train went on up the track out of sight, around one of the hills of burnt timber." Two sentences later: "There was no town, nothing but the rails and the burned-over country."

A lost Eden. For at least two decades before the Hemingway family arrived, Walloon Lake had been a summer resort for families from lower Michigan and Illinois and Indiana and Ohio. After the clear-cutting orgy was done, or the bulk of it, the railroads understood that the new way to dollars lay in recreation and tourism. Starting at midcentury with the development of Mackinac Island, the Michigan tourist industry had taken rapacious hold of the northland. So the boardinghouses and the tourist hotels got erected on the rim of the beautiful lakes in the northwest corner of the Lower Peninsula, and the railroads—which came in the 1870s—began hauling up the downstaters, the Chicagoans and Indianapolitans and Cincinnatians. The lake-crossing steamers joined in the gold rush to the region of beautiful water and cool summers. "TO HAY FEVER AND ASTHMA SUFFERERS. THE CLIMATE OF NORTHERN MICHIGAN! SPEEDY AND PERMANENT RELIEF FOR YOUR AILMENT!" So ran the rail advertisements for the Grand Rapids & Indiana. Following the tourist hotels, there came, in the new century, the rise of the family cottage. Again to quote Professor Svoboda: "Cottaging was a new and modern idea at the beginning of the twentieth century, replacing an older style of vacation that centered on resort hotels where all needs were provided for by a professional staff. Cottagers expected to be more involved with the requirements of everyday life . . . more directly engaged with the natural world."

Hemingway kept out of his fiction Walloon's resort hotels and yacht clubs and two-decked service boats delivering groceries to the family dock because they didn't represent the Michigan he wanted it to be. It wasn't the Michigan that jibed with his imagination. To quote Professor Svoboda once more:

> [W]hen Hemingway sat down to write about his Michigan summers, what emerged was not a snapshot. Neither was it an exact recreation of the Petoskey or Walloon Lake that existed between 1900 and 1920. The northern Michigan Hemingway created was something different: it often evoked feelings similar to those people still express today when they talk about their trip "up north." At other times Hemingway recreated the older, rougher Michigan of loggers and rail men that he knew partly by experience, partly through the tales of those who had lived the pioneer life. Neither sort of story was precisely journalism, but each one represented the spirit of the place more accurately than could any strictly historical account.

I suppose that's another way of saying he told beautiful lies about the place he put behind him when he was twenty-two.

But there is another and more personal sense in which Edens were already lost and darkness visible—and not so barely. By Hemingway's teens, his father was a man starting to go down, yielding to his nerves, his wife, his freezing and polarizing mind. It was evident by Hemingway's teens that Ed Hemingway had mostly lost the battle of wills to Grace. The marriage had always been grievously mismatched, if nonetheless respectful and loving, at least in the beginning. In 1912, the doctor who ministered to Oak Park's sick had to go away for his own "rest cure." His son had worshiped him as a boy—and withdrew from him as a teenager, which is what many teenagers do. But mixed in with this withdrawal, it seems clear, were condescension and pity and a certain anxiety, even amid the love; anxiety that he, too, might turn out in such a way. The Nick Adams stories are full of conflicting filial emotions, none more so than "Fathers and Sons," which is written from the vantage point of Nick's own fatherhood. There is such love and gratitude in the story for what his father has bequeathed in terms of the natural world. "His father came back to him in the fall of the year, or in the early spring when there had been jacksnipe on the prairie, or when he saw shocks of corn, or when he saw a lake," Hemingway says toward the back of the story. But the paragraph concludes coldly, "After he was fifteen he had shared nothing with him." At the front of the story, Nick thinks: "Like all men with a faculty that surpasses human requirements, his father was very nervous. . . . [H]e was both cruel and abused." His father "had died in a trap that he had helped only a little to set, and they had all betrayed him in their various ways before he died." That is a sentence about Grace as much as about Grace's husband.

One manifestation of how badly Ed Hemingway was being taken down by his fraying nerves was his propensity to erupt into red rage and physical violence during Hemingway's teenage years—and earlier, too. It wasn't uncommon for the Hemingway children to be razor-strapped and then commanded to get down on their knees and ask God for forgiveness. Children in moralistic, faith-heavy midwestern households of the early and mid-twentieth century were known to be strapped by their parents. But the degree of *this* corporal punishment, which is what it was often called, by ministers in the Sunday pulpit and by sleeve-rolling fathers reaching for the belt, seems beyond the common and the civilized by any standard. In her family memoir, Hemingway's sister Marcelline wrote about the beatings—it's one of her moments of true candor. She calls her father a "strict disciplinarian." She insists he "was never cruel." But in the same paragraph she contradicts herself. The behavior she describes sounds like incipient—or even arrived—bipolarism.

> [M]y father had another side to him. . . . He kept a razor strap in his closet, which he used on us on some occasions. . . . My father's dimpled cheeks and charming smile could change in an instant to the stern, taut mouth and piercing look which was his disciplinary self. Sometimes the change from being gay to being stern was so abrupt that we were not prepared for the shock that came, when one minute Daddy would have his arm around one of us or we would be sitting on his lap, laughing and talking, and a minute or so later—because of something we had said or done, or some neglected duty of ours he suddenly thought about—we would be ordered to our rooms and perhaps made to go without supper. Sometimes we were spanked hard, our bodies across his knee. Always after punishment we were told to kneel down and ask God to forgive us.

In 2002, a now-deceased Oak Park Hemingway scholar named Morris Buske, in a piece titled "Hemingway Faces God," published excerpts of manuscript passages that Marcelline had omitted from her book. She'd written about the beatings that became "more violent" if you refused to give the doctor "the satisfaction of saying, 'I'll be good' or 'I'm sorry.'" She spoke about her father becoming "so angry that he slapped at me with the strap." She remembered him standing over her with the strap after he'd earlier discovered she'd been dancing at school. "My father awaited me in the living room, his back to the fireplace. His hands were clenched. His face red. Mother was there too, with a handkerchief in her hand. 'I have told you I will not have dancing in my home. You are to promise me now that you will never do this wicked thing again.'" Marcelline tried to protest that she hadn't even been dancing with a boy, just with another girl in her class who felt sorry for her because she didn't know how to dance. "'But you wanted to dance. . . . I will not have it. No matter what your mother says. You will now get down on your knees and ask God to forgive you.' I knelt. I repeated the dictated words. . . . When I rose to my feet I saw my mother sobbing quietly in a corner of the room. She wouldn't look at my father."

In "Fathers and Sons," Hemingway writes of Nick coming home from a day's fishing and getting whipped for lying. "Afterward he had sat inside the woodshed with the door open, his shotgun loaded and cocked, looking across at his father sitting on the screen porch reading the paper, and thought, 'I can blow him to hell. I can kill him.' Finally he felt his anger go out of him."

You read that and you know why Hemingway couldn't whip his own children—all three Hemingway sons told me that. Once, when Jack Hemingway was about ten or eleven and was visiting his father and stepmother and half brothers in Key West, he did something horrible. Maybe he had filled the mosquito sprayer with tooth powder and sprayed one of his brothers. Maybe he'd spit at the maid because she had a land crab in her hat and was trying to terrify the bejesus out of them. He had to have a whipping—Pauline had said so. His father led him into the bathroom and sat him on the hopper and took down his own pants and proceeded to give himself whacks with a hairbrush. He motioned for the boy to fake some loud crying and pleading. "When we come out," he whispered, "Mother will know you were punished."

Hemingway's letter in *Esquire* in 1935, "Remembering Shooting-Flying: A Key West Letter," is the one where he speaks of needing to move farther out and it making no difference what they do after you are gone. He remembers Oak Park and the gone prairie and the illegal pheasant he shot at the Evans game farm along the Des Plaines and of how "I came by there five years ago and where I shot that pheasant there was a hot dog place and filling station and the north prairie . . . was all a subdivision of mean houses, and in the town, the house where I was born was gone and they had cut down the oak trees and built an apartment house close out against the street. So I was glad I went away from there as soon as I did."

He doesn't say so, but he is talking about the last time he ever saw Oak Park, at least that we know of. It was in December 1928, at his father's funeral. It wasn't true that they'd torn down the house where he was born. It's a wholly forgivable Hemingway lie, built on deeper truths, about loss, about fathers and sons.

Fathers and sons. In the fall of 1939, the father of Jack, Patrick, and Gregory Hemingway came out for the first time to the new mountain resort of Sun Valley, Idaho, and caught some feisty rainbows and cutthroats in the Lower Cottonwoods section of the Big Wood River. The next fall he came out again, arranging for his boys to join him and his bride-to-be, Marty Gellhorn. He drove across the country with his friend Toby Bruce but shipped all his fly-fishing gear ahead of him on Railway Express in an old metal footlocker. Almost every piece of trout tackle he owned was in that trunk. Some of it went back to Michigan. Peering inside the footlocker when you were a kid was like looking into King Tut's tomb. There were Hardy reels and silk leaders and any size hook and just boxes and boxes of flies—Royal Coachmen, McGintys, pale evening duns, yellow wood-cocks, gold-ribbed hare's ears. One of his rod cases had his name writ-ten on it in tiny black script: "Ernest Hemingway. Hardy Brothers Ltd., Alnwick, England." The custom-made rod itself was a thing of wonder: a three-piece traveling rod, with a soft cork handle and green silk wrappings on its thin-wire British guides. It weighed three ounces. You lifted it out of its chamois-soft cloth rod sack, and jointed it up, and held it in front of you, and felt it quivering to your heartbeat. It was an indescribable thrill when your papa had picked you, over your brothers, to be the first one to get to open the King Tut trunk when that year's family vacation had finally commenced.

When Hemingway got out to Idaho that year, fall of 1940, the people at the depot told him the footlocker had been lost. Railway Express couldn't find it.

Jack Hemingway recounted this story. He was sixty-three, and his coarse mustache was straw yellow, like the bristles of an old shaving brush. He talked of many things, not all of them sad. But at the memory of the lost footlocker, his voice caught. "I think it just broke his spirit for trout," he said. "He was stricken. He never really fished streams much after that."

This was in the late eighties. Our paths didn't cross again. But some years later I heard the following story about Jack himself: Not long before he died, at seventy-seven, of a sudden complication from open-heart sur-gery, the former Mr. Bumby and his second wife were visiting Heming-way places in northern Michigan. They drove into Horton Bay and parked their rental car. Jack went into the general store, shyly introduced him-self, bought some postcards with his father's photograph on them, and then walked the half mile or so down the road to the creek. He'd never seen it before. He walked into the meadow on the north side of the road, where the stream passes underneath the road, through a corrugated cul-vert. There's a small nature preserve on that side of the stream. It's a little swampy in there, squishy on your street shoes. The water is fairly deep and is cut with mossy banks and moves with a kind of deceptive listlessness.

Jack creaked down onto all fours. A grasshopper appeared in front of him. He reached over and imprisoned it gently between his first two knuckles. He stood up, walked back out of the meadow, came up into the light, crossed to the other side of the road, then edged down the steep bank to the south side of the creek, where the water, very much alive again, comes sluicing out of the culvert on its way into Lake Charlevoix. Jack got down on all fours again and leaned out over a rock worn smooth by all the water that had been rushing over it for who knows how long. The hopper was in his knuckles. He waited. He set it on the riffled surface. In an instant, a trout came up and took it.

This was in early September 2000. Three months later Jack was dead.

PART FOUR

OLD MEN
AT THE EDGE OF THE SEA:
ERNEST/GIGI/WALTER HOUK,
1949–1952 AND AFTER

. . . all sorrows can be borne if you put them into a story or
tell a story about them.

—Isak Dinesen, author of *Out of Africa,* in a 1957 interview

We stand at the prow again of a small ship
anchored late at night in the tiny port
looking over to the sleeping island: the waterfront
is three shuttered cafés and one naked light burning.
To hear the faint sound of oars in the silence as a rowboat
comes slowly out and then goes back is truly worth
all the years of sorrow that are to come.

—Jack Gilbert, "A Brief for the Defense"

On October 2, 1951, at 6:10 p.m., a man in Cuba unable to sleep or work wrote a four-paragraph letter to his publisher in New York. His handwriting was shaky. Thirty-six hours earlier, at three o'clock in the morning, West Coast time, his ex-wife had died of shock on an operating table in Los Angeles. A few hours before she died, this man had had a screaming argument with her on the telephone. The argument was over the conduct of their son, a troubled, gifted boy. The newest trouble was that Gigi Hemingway—then nineteen, newly married, due to become a father in two more months, living on the West Coast and working in an airplane factory (he'd dropped out of college)—had just been arrested for entering the women's restroom of a movie theater in drag. It was the first such arrest, though hardly the first such expression of a compulsion that Pauline and Ernest Hemingway's son seemed unable to control. The news about the dressing up in women's clothes was a shock only in the sense that a public space had been involved, and that the police had come.

No one can say for sure what terrible words passed between Gigi's parents on the telephone that Sunday night. (It was a little after 9:00 p.m., so just past midnight in Havana.) The gist of it from the Havana side of the staticky connection seems to have been: It's all your fault, you bitch, see how you've brought him up, you're corrupt and he's corrupt. According to Pauline's sister, Jinny, who is said to have been in the room in LA that evening with Pauline, but who can hardly be thought of as an impartial witness, Pauline was soon "shouting into the phone and sobbing uncontrollably"—those are words from Gregory Hemingway's memoir, Papa. Pauline was trying to defend herself against someone so very wicked with words. The conversation broke off. Pauline went to bed.

Sometime after midnight she awoke with severe abdominal pain. The pain got worse. They got her to St. Vincent's Hospital. Doctors worked furiously, bewilderingly. Her blood pressure crashed from 300 to zero. Three hours later Pauline was dead, at age fifty-six. "Hemorrhage into adrenal," the attending surgeon would pen into box 19 of the single-page certificate of death. Pauline's ex-husband found out by cable from his former sister-in-law at about noon that day, his time. All the rest of that day and into the next he is said to have stalked around Finca Vigía, evincing an exterior toughness. His present wife, his fourth, told him he was behaving appallingly. So of course they fought and of course the wicked words flew, almost impossible to defend against when the one attacking was Ernest Hemingway. According to Mary Hemingway, her husband followed her into her bathroom and spit in her face.

So now it was Tuesday evening, October 2, thirty-six hours after the death, and the sleepless, unable-to-work Hemingway, still in recoil, was writing to Charles Scribner, with whom he'd become very close, the more so in the four years since Max Perkins's death. In fact, this was the second letter he wrote to Scribner that day, which only suggests the level of his anxiety, the level of his denials.

Bad storms had been through—the letter writer had spent a lot of that day watching the barometer. His phone had gone out.

He not only put down the date, which he often forgot to do on his letters, he also set down the exact time. His mind had to have been very concentrated.

"Dear Charlie," he said. "The glass is lower; now 29.30 but the sky looks as though the storm were going away. It is a very strange storm. But this has been the strangest year for weather that I have ever known. I certainly would like to see the glass start to rise."

Three paragraphs down: "The wave of remembering has finally risen so that it has broken over the jetty that I built to protect the open roadstead of my heart and I have the full sorrow of Pauline's death with all the harbour scum of what caused it. I loved her very much for many years and the hell with her faults."

No, it wasn't him, of course not, it was his harbor scum of a son. It almost sounds obscene to say it, but the sea metaphor is so perfectly Hemingway when all the emotions are sounding at their deepest levels: the wave of remembering, the roadstead of his heart, the jetties getting breached.

There's a lot more to tell here, not just about Hemingway, always, of course, about Hemingway, but about Gigi, and about the price Gigi paid until the day he died, which came fifty years to the day of his mother's death, early on the morning of October 1, 2001, in a third-floor cell of a women's detention center on the edge of downtown Miami, about a mile from beautiful Biscayne Bay. The inmate, who'd been in jail for five days on charges of showing his sexual organs in public and resisting an officer without violence, was trying to get a bulky leg into a pair of too-tight underpants, which were women's panties, when he just fell over dead. He was six weeks from his seventieth birthday. This was the two-sentence lead that went out on the AP wire once the death was made public: "Gregory Hemingway, the youngest son of macho novelist Ernest Hemingway, died a transsexual by the name of Gloria in a cell at a women's jail, authorities said. He was sixty-nine." Weren't all the savage ironies instantly clear?

MOMENTS SUPREME

Walter and Nita Houk on their wedding day,
April 30, 1952

Why do old men wake so early? Is it to have one longer day?

—ERNEST HEMINGWAY, *The Old Man and the Sea*

AN OLD MAN in California, who wakes early, is drawing a picture
of Hemingway's boat. He's working with a sharpened pencil and an
old-fashioned clipboard to which he has attached a single sheet of unlined
white paper. Morning light is coming in through a window just to his
right, filtered and refracted by big coast redwoods that he has watched
grow from saplings into majestic trees. He's very intent. This is Walter
Houk's way, trying to get things right. It's as if he's talking out loud to
himself but in another way to the twenty-six-year-old incredibly fortunate
sapling self that once, in the early 1950s, got invited out for long cruises on
Ernest Hemingway's boat.

"See, the outrigger lines came around like this, amidships, out from the sides, in sort of a catenary curve," he says. "The whole point of outriggers in the first place is to keep your lines from tangling, so you can have several rods going at once." But he's already erasing. "No, I don't quite have this curve right," he says. He draws the lines again, extending them out further, in a wider loop. He puts in a whitecap or two. At the end of one of the outrigger lines he draws a mullet—or maybe it's a cero mackerel or a squid or a needlefish, all of which *Pilar*'s captain tended to keep in his bait box at the stern. The artist—who actually once was a working artist—labels the little pencil smudge "Bait."

"Okay," he says. "Better."

He's putting in the flying bridge on the topside. He's trying to get these angles and cross-hatches exactly right—from memory. "The roof over the cockpit was a little bit curved, like this, so Papa had a flat platform made that he could stand on up there," he says. "It was made of slats." He draws the flat, slatted platform over the curved sedan topside. Then a Lilliputian ship's wheel. Then a passable rendering of a slightly bulky figure standing at that wheel. It's more or less a stick person, but it's clear who it is. "I took a photograph of him once up there," he says. "Well, it wasn't just any old once, it was his fifty-second birthday. July 21, 1951. My first time on the boat. So of course all my senses were heightened. I guess I'd known him for about seven months. I wrote about it in my journal. We were out most of the day. I remember the sense of being apart from the world—the drift, the serenity. Anyway, I had my cheap old Argus C3 rangefinder with me. I climbed up on the bridge, or maybe I was on the ladder just a little bit below, trying to get the right angle. I said, 'Papa, would you mind?' He was standing at the wheel. He's in a blue tropical shirt and his hair is slicked back from the heat and he's got that reddish and almost blotchy skin. He really had a fair complexion, you know, and the sun and of course all the booze could make him florid. So I'm framing him in my thirty-five-millimeter camera, catching his right side in profile. The boat is rocking and I'm trying to hold the Argus steady so it won't blur. Those huge shoulders, that's what I remember. His beard wasn't a full white yet—it was kind of scraggly and flecked with white and not fully grown in. It looked itchy underneath. Anyway, my wife, Nita—what I mean to say is, she's not my wife just yet, but I guess I maybe had an idea she was going to be my wife—was up there, too, just a couple feet away. He said, 'Okay, Walter.' I remember how just before I snapped, he took off his glasses and held them in his right hand and sort of broke into a squinty smile and sucked in his stomach. That amused me."

From Walter Houk's journal entry of that day: "Around noon we pulled into shallows off the beach of Santa Maria del Mar, into that fantastic green water, clear as glass and cool after the beating sun. We had a swim, lunch, a siesta, another swim and then headed back toward Habana. It was Papa's birthday and the lure of celebration was drawing him back to the wicked city, I would soon realize."

Regarding lunch, and not just that first one: "We started with alligator pears. Papa's name for avocados. He used to pick them fresh from the hillsides of Finca Vigía, or get them in a little bodega at the foot of the hill, on his way in town in the car to the harbor. They were fat and juicy and we'd scoop out the flesh with a spoon or a fork. They'd be seasoned with vinaigrette dressing. We'd toss the seeds over the side. In the seed cavity was your little puddle of vinaigrette. You could practically eat a half avocado in three scoops, you'd get so hungry out there in the salt air. We'd all be gathered around that little folding table in the cockpit, with the cushioned bunks on either side. We'd eat the avocados and wash them down with cold beer. That was the first course, the salad, a side dish, if you will. For a second course, we'd have fresh fish."

He has looked up again from his artwork, and is gazing out toward the trees, or through them, as if trying to recover a sensation on the back of his tongue.

Regarding the fishing: "Ha. One strike all day. Papa said, 'Okay, you take it, Walter.' I didn't especially want to take it, but I got in the fighting chair. I knew a lot about the sea, since I'd gone to the naval academy, but I knew next to nothing about deep-sea fishing. Total amateur. It wasn't a big fish, although it seemed like it when he came to the top. It was about a forty-pound dolphinfish, they told me later. The word Hemingway would have said was dorado, not dolphinfish. People would call it mahimahi today. The point is, I lost it. Not a very good performance in front of somebody I would have liked to impress. I didn't know what I was doing. I jerked the rod upward. I could feel the line go dead."

An old man in California has just reflexively jerked upward on an invisible piece of big-game tackle, causing him to erupt in a laugh.

"Hemingway came over and said, 'Now, here's what you did wrong, Walter, and here's what you should try to do next time. Basically, you didn't slack to him.'"

Then: "The whole idea was to be instructional. He was trying to teach me something. People don't tend to know what a great teacher he was. He was always teaching you something, one way or another. In this case I think he needed to hang back and let me make my mistakes first, then he could come in and show me the right way."

Walter Houk, who keeps insisting he won't be around too much longer, has set down his pencil. The words "right way" may have tripped something in him. He's growing weary and needs to nap. At dinner tonight, stoked with a vodka martini and a glass of wine, he'll say: "You see, for a long time in my life, I avoided a consideration of all the negatives about Hemingway. It was just so politically correct to dislike the man. I didn't know what to argue against, or where to start arguing. I didn't want to be bothered. It wasn't going to change anything I knew. My whole experience with Ernest Hemingway is the conventional *dis*wisdom. He didn't wreck my life. It was a hugely positive experience to be around him, for those several years in the fifties, getting to go out on the boat and all the rest. I was half his age. He treated me kindly. He treated my wife, Nita, kindly. It was as if we were sort of the kids around the place, and I think he liked that, because his own kids so often weren't there, and he missed them. He wanted to help us out with our lives. The vultures have long ago gathered around the Hemingway corpse and rendered their judgment. But their judgment's wrong; at least it's incomplete. I don't think the terrible vile side defines him. It was a facet of his character. He was a great man with great faults. We should not allow the faults to overshadow the accomplishments. He said in a letter once—I think it was to one of his children—that 'a happy country has no history.' I'm paraphrasing, but that was his point. You could say a happy man has no biography—who'd want to read it? I think of him as a Beethoven, for the way he changed the language. He's Gulliver surrounded by the Lilliputians. He threatens all the little academics sitting at their computers. Somehow or other you've got to try to help rescue him from all that."

What kind of blind luck did it take to find Walter P. Houk of 21439 Gaona Street in Woodland Hills, California? Pretty blind is all I can say.

Walter Houk is an authentic living Hemingway witness, with his faculties mainly intact; with his memory, at least his long-term memory, still razor keen—and even now, after seven years of knowing him, talking to him, the thought still has the power to raise on my forearms what Hemingway used to call "the goose-flesh."

Not counting Hemingway's surviving middle son, there aren't two or three people left on the earth who can authentically say, as Walter Houk can, that, yes, they used to get invited out on Hemingway's boat; that, yes, they once took swims in Hemingway's soapy-soft pool (it was fed by rain collected in a cistern, and it was so refreshing you almost felt you were paddling in mountain lake); that, yes, they got to borrow books from Hemingway's personal library; that, yes, they got to attend lubricated, rollicking, multicourse dinners with Ernest and Mary Hemingway at their favorite Havana Chinese restaurant (El Pacífico, about ten blocks behind the Capitolio, next door to a nudie stage revue and porno theater called the Shanghai; the funky eatery sat beneath a canvas awning on the rooftop of a seven- or eight-story building, to which you ascended via the world's slowest and smallest iron-cage elevator, passing on the way a bordello and opium den and cacophonous Chinese orchestra, but never mind, because once you were on the roof, in the open night air, the view was amazing, and so was the food, starting with the shark-fin soup and the first bottle of Tavel rosé, Papa's favorite).

But there's no one else on the earth who can claim, as Walter Houk can, that Ernest Hemingway, in a pinstriped suit and clean white shirt and shined shoes (he even put on socks), stood up for him and his wife on their wedding day. He not only stood up, he gave the bride away and signed his name to the official documents. Later, on that same, indelible, swamp-hot April afternoon, both Hemingways, Mary and Ernest, hosted on the west terrace of their hilltop home in the village of San Francisco de Paula, Cuba, a champagne brunch–reception before the just-marrieds drove off in a rain squall of rice for the start of their four-day honeymoon to a place down the Cuban coast called Casa Happiness. To borrow a line from Arthur Miller's *Death of a Salesman*, doesn't attention have to be paid?

Appreciating the uncelebrated life of Walter Houk has helped me to appreciate all over again and in new ways the myth-swallowed life of Ernest Hemingway. It's as if he's single-handedly brought him back around—the goodness, in and amid all the squalor. In astronomy there's a technique known as "averted vision." The idea is that sometimes you can see the essence of a thing more clearly if you're not looking at it directly. It's as if what you're really after is sitting at the periphery rather than at the center of your gaze. Something of this same hope and principle was at work in telling Arnold Samuelson's story. But the Maestro's life was a mirror opposite.

Walter Houk is in his mid-eighties, as I write. He is a small, trim, learned, meticulous, and sometimes fussy and nitpicky man, a widower, an accomplished former journalist, a failed painter, an ex-outdoorsman and naturalist, an ex–Foreign Service officer, a once-and-long-ago midship-man, who lives alone, has long lived alone, quietly, unobtrusively, a little sadly, in a comfortable house, on an ordinary street, in a tucked-away corner of greater Los Angeles. That house, which is kept as tidy as the officers' quarters on a submarine, is full of old Hemingway photographs, nautical charts, unpublished book-length Houk manuscripts, Esso highway maps of Cuba in the 1950s, Havana bar menus, Christmas cards with Hemingway's greeting on them—and a lot more. Entering his house is like walking into a hidden Hemingway museum.

I'm certain I'd have no chance to do what Walter has so often urged me to do—namely, to try to help rescue Hemingway from his seemingly set-in-stone image of immortal writer and immortal bitch of a human being—had I not accidentally pulled down from a high shelf in a university library on the East Coast about eight years ago the wrong volume of an academic quarterly. The volume I'd been searching for contained some obscure reference to *Pilar* that probably would have helped me in my understanding only minimally, if at all. The one I inadvertently pulled down had a twenty-one-page article in it titled "On the Gulf Stream Aboard Hemingway's *Pilar.*" I stood there and stared at the title. What was it doing in an academic journal? Was the man who wrote it still alive? (The article in question was six years old.) Within an hour I had Walter's address and phone number, although I didn't muster the nerve to call until the next day. "I don't see why not," he said in that hearty voice that belies its age, the more so if you're first encountering it on a telephone. "That is, if you want to bother to come all this way."

It wouldn't be accurate to suggest that Walter Houk is an unknown figure in the scholarly Hemingway universe. He has published a handful of Hemingway-related pieces, contributed to online Hemingway chats and websites, spoken at an international Hemingway conference. But what I am suggesting is that so much of that scholarly Hemingway universe, as it stands, as I've encountered it, doesn't really seem to get it about Walter, namely, that he is still *here* just as he was once *there*. I've mentioned his name now and again to respected Hemingway scholars and critics, and the response has tended to run along these lines: "Oh, Houk. Rose-colored glasses." There are the exceptions, of course. But the general view seems to be that his testimony, which is breathing testimony, must somehow be tainted, even invalid, because he insists on viewing Hemingway in such a human light.

Up above I described him as a somewhat sad man. In fact, there is a great sadness about him, a kind of nimbus of sadness, which has little to do with the reality of someone facing his sooner-than-later extinction. Indeed, Walter has often said that it's not the dying itself he fears so much as the process, and that he would just as happily get it over with. (But I wonder, for all his infirmities, how many other octogenarians in California or anywhere else could find the will to get out of bed in darkness and lace on tennis shoes and get the walking stick that sits on the canvas deck chair by the front door and then go for about a mile and a half on up-and-down surfaces. Until just recently, this was Walter's almost daily regimen.)

No, the sadness that suffuses this man's life, not to say this man's spic-and-span sixties-modern California home, has to do with the absence of his wife. Nita's been gone since Christmas Eve, 1991—"at seven past noon and a part of my life ended" is the way he once put it. She died a hard death, and he was there through all of it, taking her out even toward the end to neighborhood parks in her wheelchair, tending to her meals and liquid oxygen tanks at home, which is where she tried to stay, until the last four or five days, when things were clear. Then it was just waiting in a chair beside her bed at the hospital until her vital signs flatlined in digital green on the overhead monitors. "She didn't say good-bye," Walter told me. "She just went to sleep." It was many things that killed her, but mostly it was a combination of virulent diabetes and lungs that were so eaten up with scar tissue that she could hardly breathe.

Nita had her own deep relationship with Ernest Hemingway. In fact, she knew Hemingway before Walter did. In fact, she's why Walter knew Hemingway at all: she got there ahead of him, and pulled him in, after she and Walter were sweethearts. Nita's real name was Juanita, although no one really called her that, certainly not Hemingway, who was fond of calling her "daughter" and Miss Nita. She used to take his dictation and transcribe some of his less poisonous letters off a wire recording spool that Hemingway called his "talk machine." (The truly awful ones he saved for his own typewriter.) From mid-1949 to about February 1952, Juanita Jensen worked part-time for Hemingway while she held her regular clerical government job at the American Embassy in Havana—which is where her future husband also worked, as a high-ranking diplomatic officer.

It's not uncommon for the still-grieving spouse to set a place for his wife at Saturday dinner—and always on their wedding anniversary. He'll make her a martini.

Perhaps you have a sense of him as a talkative person. The opposite is true. He possesses the knack of reticence. Because he's comfortable with the flat spaces between conversations, he can make other people at ease with them, too. Some of the inclination to silence comes from his long-ago training and experience as a seaman. There's a passage in *The Old Man and the Sea,* which Walter admires, where Hemingway writes, in the mind of the aged Santiago, who has now gone his famous eighty-four days in the Stream without taking a fish: "When he and the boy fished together they usually spoke only when it was necessary. They talked at night or when they were storm-bound by bad weather. It was considered a virtue not to talk unnecessarily at sea and the old man had always considered it so and respected it. But now he said his thoughts aloud many times since there was no one that they could annoy."

Walter and Nita were married for almost forty years. They raised two children. Walter's son, Paul, and his daughter, Tina, late-middle-aged now, have long been on their own with their own lives and, in truth, are somewhat distant from their father. There are no Houk grandchildren. It's the loneliness for Nita that seems to supersede everything.

Hemingway once saved Miss Nita from a shark attack when she was swimming off *Pilar*'s stern. He once made a semi-clunky pass at her when he'd taken her out on his boat alone for the purpose of trying to bed her. He once took personal charge of dyeing her shoulder-length brunette hair into a bleached blond, and then, about a week later, took further command of shearing it into a boyish cut, sides severely short, ears exposed. Yes, some of that sounds more than a little provocative. And I'll get to it. But wouldn't you rather hear just now about one of the most nonprovocative and unambiguous and *sweet* moments of a long and well-lived life?

Walter and Nita's wedding day. April 30, 1952.

Drift your eye back to the image at the beginning of this chapter. An eight-by-ten copy resides in an album that usually sits by the raised hearth in the middle of a Woodland Hills living room. There are probably two dozen surviving images from Walter and Nita's wedding reception at Finca Vigía. This one's not a great picture in any aesthetic sense, just the human one.

Here they are, the five-foot-nine groom, who's twenty-six, shortly to be twenty-seven, and his thirty-two-year-old bride, who has a twenty-six-inch waist, poised on the first step at the wide, main, portico entryway to the Hemingway home. It's right around two thirty. (Those lengthening shadows over on the left are from the giant ceiba tree that grows right up through the steps and part of the foundation of the house.) The newly minted Mr. and Mrs. Walter Houk, wed ninety minutes ago in a civil ceremony in downtown Havana, have just rolled up the *finca*'s long private drive and come around the circular driveway and stepped from their boat of a car. They've arrived, the guests of honor, in their squinty semi-daze.

Twenty or twenty-five people have gathered at the steps. Some of them, the women in their floral-print dresses and sling-back pumps, the men in their haspel suits and white shirts with moons of sweat growing beneath their armpits, are breaking into applause. A little bronze saluting cannon, a *lantaka,* is firing off blanks, sending out mini–sonic booms and puffs of sooty smoke. The cohost of the party, who's standing maybe ten feet *this* way from the lower edge of the frame, is orchestrating the firing, although he's left the actual firing to the black-robed figure beside him: don Andrés, an old exiled Hemingway priest-compatriot from the Spanish Civil War. The padre lives on another part of the island and comes on a bus every Wednesday for supper and nostalgia. Since today is a Wednesday, that makes the timing perfect.

Walter has recounted for me how much Hemingway loved his personal cannon, which sat up on wheels, and had been rolled into saluting position at the top of the steps. Mary Hemingway described it in her memoir of her fifteen years with Hemingway, *How It Was,* which was published a decade and a half after his death. (It came out the same year as Gregory Hemingway's *Papa.* It's about six times as long—exhausting to read and yet with startling and sometimes almost inadvertent revelations. Scholars and biographers have been mining it for years.) Her husband had purchased the cannon from a catalog for his fiftieth birthday in 1949. According to Mary, he owned *two* cannons, "no more than twenty inches long which fired real shells with impressive sound effects and backfired a mist of black soot which nestled snugly in the ears, eyebrows and hair of the artillerymen." Actually, they didn't fire real shells, but you can imagine the things firing up Hemingway in some delicious, atavistic, bad-boy way. The booms were said always to scare the bejesus out of the *finca*'s fifty-two cats and sixteen dogs, not to say its domestic staff of nine.

That boat of a car in the background: It's a four-door, pea-soup-green 1950 Buick Special with whitewalls (you can catch a glimpse) and Dynaflow automatic transmission and a three-panel window in the rear and a "bucktooth" vertical grill attached to the front bumper and, the pièce de résistance, an indicator on its "pilot console" dash that reports speed in kilometers instead of miles per hour. Two years ago, Walter bought the beast, on which he likes to keep a high Simoniz, and in which Hemingway has ridden a time or two, at a Foreign Service discount in a showroom in Manhattan. It was billed as the International Edition. Walter drove it to Miami, had it ferried to Cuba. It's only one of the accoutrements that give him a kind of diplomatic dash and bachelor-about-Havana aura. That should go in the past tense. He has just renounced bachelorhood.

"The whole thing was rather unnerving," Walter told me once. "And I just don't mean the cannon. I mean going to his house for the reception, the whole party in our honor. What I remember is how much Papa was enjoying himself. He was in full bloom."

Regard the groom in full bloom. That cock-combed, Beau Brummell up-gleam of hair. (A little dab'll do ya, as the jingle says.) And those Ray-Ban shades in his right mitt. And that too-short tie. (Okay, it was the fashion then.) And that big-as-your-fist flower in his buttonhole. Not to say the suit itself, gone sad-sack in this infernal humidity. One of Havana's better tailors made it for the occasion, but it looks as if Walter's tropical-weight threads could have stood at least one more good nip and tuck.

Regard his bride: this peachy-plain, all-American-looking tootsie, with her gloved right hand clutching her new husband's left, with her rope of pearls (they're real, but they belong to Mary Hemingway, who wants them back right after the reception), with her filmy blue organdy dress that's got its bib collar locked chastely at the throat, with those sensible white pumps, with that ridiculous, flower-bedecked yellow hat that looks almost mashed on the back of her head, with that nosegay knotted at her midriff.

It was almost exactly a month ago that the lovebirds drove out to the *finca* with their surprise news. Nita, who didn't quite have Hemingway twisted around her little finger, had said that evening: "Papa, won't you please come? Papa, will you be one of our witnesses? Papa, would you give me away?" "Done, daughter," he'd answered. And almost in the next heartbeat: "Would you like to have the reception here?" And then hugs and awkward laughing and the breaking out of booze.

On Monday, March 10—so roughly six weeks back of this moment—General Fulgencio Batista, the iconic military thug who in one way or another has had his way with power in Cuba since the mid-thirties, had regained the country in a coup against the elected government of President Carlos Prío Socarrás. When that happened, Walter realized that life is momentary. After the takeover, Batista's troops had been circling the city with blaring horns on the tops of cars and tanks: "*Batista, este es el hombre para Cuba.*" Batista is the man for Cuba. Walter, in his post as second secretary (about fifth in the hierarchy of command), had been thrust into new responsibilities, intelligence responsibilities, in the embassy's political section. As he went about his expanded duties, he kept thinking of Nita, whom he'd been dating for something like a year and a half. He felt seized with romantic excitement. Six days after the coup, Walt, as Nita calls him, popped the question. She said yes.

But they hadn't been able to come out to tell Ernest and Mary until the end of March, because on the same day Batista drove Prío from power, the Hemingways had slipped out of Havana on *Pilar* at 9:40 a.m., motoring over the next two days some ninety miles westward down the coast to an uninhabited island off Pinar del Río province that they'd nicknamed Paraíso Key: their little paradise hideaway key. Hemingway had told friends and correspondents this would be an "austerity vacation." For two and a half weeks, while a new government lowered its calming iron fist on the country, he and his wife had fished and swum and drunk and eaten like kings and tried to forget about the world's problems, not to say their own. They'd loaded up with barracuda, cero mackerel, horse-eye jacks, red hinds, speckled hinds, red snappers, mangrove snappers, amberjacks, and needlefish. A big storm had delayed their return. Hemingway had come home in a restored mood, and sitting in his metaphorical back pocket was the uncorrected typescript manuscript of 26,531 words that he'd now all but decided to go ahead and publish as a separate work. He'd settled on its title: *The Old Man and the Sea*. The manuscript had been ready for almost a year, but he'd been hesitant to publish it as a stand-alone fiction, believing it to be the coda or epilogue to the great Sea Book that a blocked writer had been trying to make right in his head and on paper, on and off, since the postwar forties. More accurate to say great *mess* of a Sea Book that in turn was an intended part of the even greater and unwritten trilogy mess in his head known as the Land, Sea, and Air Book.

As he'd said in a letter to a Scribner's official just before shoving off: "I am tired of not publishing anything. Other writers publish short books. But I am supposed to always lay back and come in with War and Peace or Crime and Punishment or be considered a bum. This is probably very bad for a writer and I will bet it did more to wreck poor old Scott than anything except Zelda, himself and booze." From this last sentence alone, you could understand how good he must have felt: gratuitously kicking Scott, dead now eleven years, once more.

Anyway, right after their return, Nita and Walter had driven to the *finca* with the good news. The benevolent, reigning monarch of all he surveyed had said, "Done, daughter." Hell, he'd even wear a suit, although he wouldn't put on one of those damn wedding-party boutonnieres because he'd feel like he was attending "the Saturday-night taxi-driver's ball." (Walter remembers this remark, but says he has never quite understood its meaning. In the greenhouse climate of Cuba, lapel flowers could grow to a ghastly size—regard again Walter's.)

The actual ceremony probably hadn't lasted ten minutes, which suited everybody fine, since it was so damn hot. It was scheduled for noon in an attorney's office, but nothing in Cuba happens particularly on time. Hemingway handed off Miss Nita to Walter in a small, florid, grinning flourish. It was pretty obvious to the bride and groom that he was giving away the daughter he knew he'd never have. Afterward, three witnesses signed their names to the documents. The lawyer told the newlyweds that the official certificate of marriage wouldn't come in the mail for another month or so. (It did, although it took longer than a month, and it's pre-served now in an album in California. Beside Hemingway's name, penned by some Havana bureaucrat lost to history, are the words "*ocupación escritor.*")

After the hitching, the stand-in father drove the thirty minutes home in his own car. Walter and Nita lingered in town for a while, so that their guests might arrive ahead of them and so that Mary Hemingway could get everything arranged. (She'd skipped the ceremony on this account.) The cohost of the party got out of his monkey suit and into a white guayabera, a pair of white flannel trousers, a pair of loafers without socks—which is how he's standing now, in the nick and click of time, drink in his paw, spectacles slightly sliding down his nose, as "the kids" arrive and step from the Buick and don Andrés loads in another charge. Up north today, Harry Truman is nationalizing steel mills, and Dwight Eisenhower is mulling a run for the presidency, and Ringling Brothers is running two shows a day at Madison Square Garden.

Let it roll. The iced champagne gets served in Mary Hemingway's best stemware. (She's in an off-the-shoulder dress and no brassiere—pretty racy.) There's much delicious food. Roman candles and skyrockets get lit on the west terrace, off the dining room. A two-tiered cake gets sliced into, but not before a statuette, of a hooked-together bride and groom, with angel wings on their backs, and with a black netted veil hanging down over the bride's tiny plaster face, are removed for keepsaking. The slicing is done with a big blade that the head of the house is said to have lifted off the corpse of an SS officer in World War II. Who knows, maybe it's true.

Nita, probably feeling a bit of the "champers" (it's a Hemingway word), drops her elaborate garters to her ankles and prances around in her bare feet on the *finca*'s cool red tiles. There's no doubt the host is having a good and semi-sloshed time—and he doesn't even cotton to parties of this size. Walter sheds his suit jacket while the bride goes into another room to change from her wedding dress into more comfortable traveling garb. She makes sure to hand back personally to the hostess the choker of pearls. Mary Hemingway can be such a nasty woman, nearly the equal of her husband in a fight, especially when she's a little liquored herself, and yet in other ways, just like her husband, when you scratch her you find a deep traditionalist and sentimentalist. A few days before the ceremony, she'd asked Nita if she'd made sure to gather the four essential things any bride must wear on her wedding day: you know, "Something old, something new / Something borrowed, something blue." When Nita answered she hadn't thought to borrow anything, Mary ran to her jewelry drawer.

It's time for the newlyweds to load up their loot and to make their good-byes and to run hand in hand down the steps to the Buick. So much rice gets hurled from the *finca*'s steps—Papa's said to be right in there, with the best of the hurlers, even chasing after the car for ten or fifteen yards as it eases off down the hill—that several of the kernels lodge in the corners of the backseat and up on the upholstered ledge by the rear window. A year from now, when the Houks are in Tokyo (it's Walter's next diplomatic post, although he has no clue of it today), some of the kernels will end up sprouting in the wet climate of Japan.

Their destination is Varadero, eighty-some miles east of Havana by way of the Vía Blanca. Most Yankees living in Cuba know Casa Happiness by its informal name: Happy Pete's. That's because its proprietor is a jovial Greek American immigrant named Peter Economides. The resort is really just a two-story cement block of rooms with a restaurant and one little cottage whose front door opens practically onto the water. But the sand is blindingly white and is so fine that it feels almost sugary. "Heaven on Earth," proclaims Happy Pete's letterhead. "American Management."

Tomorrow, May 1, is a national holiday. So they have the rest of today, all of May Day, plus Friday, Saturday, and half of Sunday, before they must return to reality on Monday. At Happy Pete's, they'll be doing what honeymooners do, emerging from their bedroom for not much more than martinis and cool-offs in the ocean. Happy Pete will have put them in the suite that fronts the ocean.

So click the shutter once more, forward, to *real* time. "Our little cottage by the edge of the blue sea," an old man in California is saying aloud, but once again as if talking to himself. He's in his chair by the fireplace. The word "blue" has emboldened me.

"Is it possible we could look at Nita's dress, Walter? Is it packed away?"

His left thumb jerks over his left shoulder. "Why not? Right behind me."

He gets up and goes over to a large and ornately carved wooden chest. He opens the lid. A clean woody scent is perfuming the room. "Camphor," he says. "Teak on the outside, camphor wood inside. Far better than cedar." He lifts out a cardboard box with "Amazon.com" printed on it. On top of some folded tissue there's a yellow card, and written on the card, in ink, in his hand: "Nita's wedding dress and slip." He separates the tissue, lifts out a white silk slip. "I don't think girls wear slips like this much anymore. Do they wear them at all?" He refolds the slip, in halves, sets it in another compartment of the chest. He lifts the dress from the box, holds it out in front of him, by the shoulders, allowing it to swing open and fall downward. The blue of the organdy has faded almost to the hue of an oft-washed denim shirt. It looks so sheer and small and beautiful.

Softly, but smiling broadly: "Well, the moths haven't quite gotten you yet, have they, babe?"

Where she tried to stay, until the final four or five days, when things were clear, when her breathing through the oxygen tubes in her nose was such a labored sound, is a small, shade-drawn room down the hall from Walter's living room. In this room now are some fine old photographs of Havana in the fifties. There's a picture of Pilar. A bareheaded Hemingway is up on his boat's flying bridge, his flimsy spectacles in his hands, which are resting on that polished dinner plate of a steering wheel. The photograph is in color, the blues of it very blue, an unnatural blue; it's the close-up of Hemingway (with a sunsuited Nita a few feet away) that Walter took with his Argus on July 21, 1951, Hemingway's fifty-second birthday, Walter's first outing on the boat. "I used to be able to steer twelve hours *every day* on my feet without leaving the bridge and have many times steered 18 hours," Hemingway had boasted in a letter not long before Walter took the shot. "Plenty people know about this and it is not a delusion on my part. I can steer 12 hours now but the sun is bad for my head."

The first time Walter opened the door to this room for me, he didn't enter, only stood in the doorway. He turned on the overhead light. "So, yes, this was the infirmary for Nita's last days—hospital bed, and so forth," he said. The "and so forth" trailed off.

Sitting on a shelf above a TV in this room is the little hooked-together plaster bride and groom from their wedding reception. The wings have come off the backs of Walter and Nita, but otherwise the ornament is intact, including Nita's netted wedding veil. Next to the statuette is a small, squat, ornate, triangular-shaped, and heavy-looking glass bottle with a thick stopper. On the front are the words "Jean Patou" and "Moment Suprême." The contents now look purply, bruise-colored. The bottle is maybe a third full.

"French perfume," Walter said. He was still standing at the door. "A two-ounce bottle. Moment Suprême, by Jean Patou. Pretty fashionable fragrance in its day. Probably not as expensive as that packaging suggests. Papa and Mary brought it back as a gift from Paris for Miss Nita in 1950. She'd been working for him on and off for about a year by then. The color used to be amber. That's the air that's turned it black. That's the evaporation you're looking at over—what?—half a century. I suppose she opened it once or twice, maybe even dabbed a little on, you know, just to try it out, but she was never a perfume kind of girl."

He turned out the light and closed the door and headed back down the hallway. Suddenly his leg buckled. He grabbed the wall. "Oh, trick knee," he explained.

FACET OF HIS CHARACTER

Up on the flying bridge, Ernest and Nita Jensen,
July 21, 1951

The world is charged with the grandeur of God.
It will flame out, like shining from shook foil;
It gathers to a greatness, like the ooze of oil
Crushed.

—Gerard Manley Hopkins, "God's Grandeur"

He wears a mask, and his face grows to fit it.

—George Orwell, "Shooting an Elephant"

OPENING A DIFFERENT TRUNK, not camphor scented:

On Thursday September 7, 1950—three months and one week before Walter Houk met Ernest Hemingway for the first time—Charles Scribner's Sons published *Across the River and into the Trees*, its most important author's first novel in a decade. The cover price was three dollars, and the first printing consisted of seventy-five thousand copies. If all his novels were autobiographical, this one was Hemingway's most autobiographical, more than any critic could know.

To say a lot was riding on the moment would be like saying that whenever "the great DiMaggio" came up with the bases loaded and the score tied in the bottom of the ninth, it was a big moment.* *Everything* was riding on the moment, or at least it seems hard not to make that conclusion after you've read Hemingway's letters and tracked his day-to-day movements of this period. He was poised at a near-equidistant moment: a little less than ten years since his triumph with *For Whom the Bell Tolls*, a little more than ten years before his shotgun destruction.

In the previous decade, Hemingway had been divorced (from his second wife), married (to his third wife), divorced (from his third wife), married (to his fourth wife)—indeed, all of this had occurred in the first half of the 1940s. (He and Mary Welsh were married in Havana on March 14, 1946; on their wedding night, they got into a terrific row at the *finca*, causing her to pack her bags, only to relent the next morning.)

His stomach, like his face and fame, had grown round now—florid, you could say. (Despite the full belly, his waist was surprisingly slender.) He wasn't a tight end anymore, as he'd looked in certain photographs at certain moments in the early and mid-thirties; rather, an overweight fullback, with very tanned calf muscles, and with that old and still very visible pulpy welt on his forehead above his left eye (his right, as you look at him in photos), about the size of a Brazil nut, caused by that accident in Paris in 1928, when he'd come home from dinner with Pauline and had gone to bed and had risen at 2:00 a.m. and had stumbled into the loo and yanked at the cord for the opened skylight instead of the cord that controlled the flush box, thus pulling the entire faulty thing down on top of him, the glass shards breaking over him like crinkling cellophane or maybe like the ocean opening up when a huge fish comes to the surface. Anyway, nine stitches, sewn in by an intern at the American Hospital at Neuilly at three o'clock in the morning.

---

*Hemingway, who fancied himself an aficionado of baseball almost as much as he regarded himself as *the* American expert of the bull ring, often referred to the Yankee Clipper in these years as "the great DiMaggio," and indeed the phrase appears just that way, with the "great" lowercased, several times in *The Old Man and the Sea*—which wasn't quite written yet, not now, in the early fall of 1950, except maybe in the author's mind. "I would like to take the great DiMaggio fishing," the old man tells the boy at his side. "They say his father was a fisherman." As for the game itself, Hemingway was always peppering his correspondence with baseball metaphors, such as this one, to a New York critic who was in his pocket, and written two months before *Across the River* came out: "Naturally being a writer, the pitch is my own works: high and inside and see whether you can turn his fucking cap around. Ok he is spooked but he is mean. I give him the nothing ball, with the same motion, and he gets a little piece of it in his anger and desire to knock it out of the ball park, and he is OUT to short."

He drove a royal-blue Buick Roadmaster convertible with a red leather interior now—or rather a member of the household staff named Juan Pastor drove it for him. His coat size was a 48 now, although he still liked to try to fit into a 46. He was "half a hundred years plus one" now, as he liked saying on the eve of publication of his fourteenth book (depending on how you counted), which he professed to be his best yet, a three-cushion shot, slow poison, higher math, capable of breaking "my fucking heart" every time he let himself sit down and read it in page proof. "But I have read it 206 times to try and make it better and to cut out any mistakes or injustices and on the last reading I loved it very much and it broke my fucking heart for the 206th time," he told a reviewer-interviewer for *Newsweek* two weeks before *Across the River* appeared.

He combed his hair straight back now, on both the sides and the top, not quite in the way of a Roman senator. His hairline had receded, but on top his hair was still fairly black and thick. (At the back of his head, where he wore it long, his hair tended to curl up in silvery ringlets.) He wore a mustache, as he'd worn one through the years, except that now its color was something like salt-and-pepper. He wore steel-rimmed spectacles, as he'd long worn them, only now, funnily enough, at least judging from photographs, there always seemed to be a wad of paper stuck in their nosepiece. He wore a wristwatch with an expandable gold band now—sometimes well up his left arm.

Max Perkins was gone now—heart attack and pneumonia and overwork taking the good man down, at not quite sixty-three, three years before. The reserved and blue-blooded Charles Scribner III, who'd headed the firm since 1932, and who'd become, by default, his new Max, had cabled on the day it happened (June 17, 1947), and that evening Hemingway had wired back with a thirteen-word response. Eleven days later, he'd written to Scribner and said, "Dear Charlie: Don't worry about me kid. . . . The bad was for him to die. I hadn't figured on him dying. . . . One of my best and most loyal friends and wisest counsellors in life as well as in writing is dead."

Many other literary friends as well as enemies were gone now, too. Fitzgerald, James Joyce, Gertrude Stein. Scott's last letter to Hemingway, in November 1940, had thanked him for the inscribed copy of *For Whom the Bell Tolls*. "I envy you like hell and there is no irony in this," he'd said. He'd died two months to the day after Hemingway's book had come out, and by then sales were at 189,000 copies and the movie deal had closed for a big number.

Although at fifty-one he still projected much virility, Hemingway was not a well man now. In truth, he was in a deep holding action, and had been for four or five years, against ringing ears, migraines, hypertension, diabetes, kidney problems, depression, and paranoia—and all these ailments, and others, were not only aging him at what seemed a far faster rate than his chronological age, but each was prone to balloon up wildly and almost virally before subsiding again. It was as true of his high blood pressure—it could surge like that to 225 over 125—as of his bouts of paranoia. The insomnia was always simmering below his surface, like malaria, kept at bay by bottles of Seconal. When the insomnia was on him, everything seemed lost. "Shit on hope," he'd said one night to his wife not long before the first finished copy of the book had come into his hands. "I'm just a desperate old man." The next morning he and his wife had gone down the coast on *Pilar*, to the place he and Mary called Paraíso. The fishing in paradise was lousy.

To add to his history of strange illnesses and accidents: The year before, 1949, while at the back end of an extended sojourn in Europe, the corner of one eye began to feel funny. Was it a dust infection in a small scratch at the cornea? There was some belief he'd been accidentally hit by the end of an oar by a hired boatman while going into a duck blind in the marshes of greater Venice. Later he'd say the dust-mote infection had stemmed from riding in an open car over gravelly roads. Later still he'd blame fragments of wadding from his shotgun that had come powdering up into his eye— that was the explanation he favored. Whatever the cause, the results were spectacular: Both eyes swelled shut and his already meaty face puffed up like the Elephant Man's. His neck began to bulge. He broke out in a rash. Doctors diagnosed erysipelas, which is a contagious disease of the skin and subcutaneous tissue. They told him they were worried that the infection might spread to his brain. He entered a hospital at Padua and stayed for ten days. They slathered his face in ointments. He tried to tape one eye open so he could write some letters—he did, and it was as if the characters were standing up three inches high on the page. Along with penicillin, he took many sulfa drugs, and this made his kidneys nearly shut down. Several million units of penicillin got injected. (He'd later claim sixteen million.) Somehow, though, the old capacity for bouncing back had bounced back. The fever subsided, the neck and facial swellings went down, the rash disappeared. The erysipelas, streptococcus, and staphylococcus hadn't been fatal.

He'd been going so good at his writing when it happened, working on what he'd imagined to be only a fairly concentrated short story about a Venetian duck hunt and an embittered infantry army colonel who's been busted down from brigadier general. But between his recovery and the journey homeward by sea to Cuba, the piece had grown longer and fuller in his mind—the old pattern. "I couldn't stop it," he later said. For six months in Cuba, he had put aside his on-again, off-again work on the so-called trilogy of war novels that had been tormenting him through the postwar forties so that he could work in a head-long fury toward this new thing. In the end, the Venetian duck shoot became the framing device, a pair of bookends, for a love story about the demoted fifty-year-old Richard Cantwell, fatally ill with heart disease (he has survived four heart attacks when *Across the River* opens), and an eighteen-year-old Italian contessa named Renata. If Colonel Cantwell seemed almost a dead ringer on the fictional page for the man of the same age who'd been creating him, in the spring and summer and fall of 1949, then the countess seemed a dead ringer for the real-life Vene-tian teenager whom the author had met only a few months before his erysipelas and Padua hospital stay, and with whom he'd become fool-ishly, wildly, infatuated. Her name was Adriana Ivancich. In real life, as in the fiction, the author had met her about two and a half weeks before her nineteenth birthday. In real life, as with her counterpart in the modest-size novel just now showing its face to the world (and which those lice-crawling angleworms feeding in their New York literary bottle were going to treat as though it had Elephant Man disease), she had pale, almost olive skin, green eyes, a thin Roman nose, jet-black hair falling down over her fair shoulders.

And *Pilar,* that other narrow beauty and deepest material love?

She was more than sixteen years old now. His hard-worked fishing cruiser might be thought of as having entered her late middle age. Heming-way's love for her had only deepened. They'd come this far together. If *Pilar* wasn't a named presence in the new book, she was nonetheless there. No one would say *Across the River* is a story about boats and the sea—and yet the word "boat" appears nine times on its first page. Early in the novel, there's a passage when Colonel Cantwell arrives by water at Venice's Gritti Palace Hotel. "The motor boat came gallantly up beside the piling of the dock. Every move she makes, the Colonel thought, is a triumph of the gallantry of the aging machine. We do not have war horses now like old

Traveller. . . . We have the gallantry of worn-through rods that refuse to break; the cylinder head that does not blow though it has every right to, and the rest of it." Isn't that really about *Pilar* rather than about some old Venetian service boat?

She'd undergone uncounted overhauls and several engine replacements now. She'd survived many squalls and tropical storms and full-blown hurricanes. She'd endured uncounted stays in dry dock for repaintings and rescrapings of her bottom. (In *How It Was*, Mary Hemingway wrote that *Pilar*'s "care and feeding," in the early 1950s, "reached to about three times the maintenance costs of the Finca.") She had a different registry number lettered in black on a little wooden plate on both sides of her bow now. A high-tech swivel fighting chair had come to *Pilar*, bolted and centered aft at her stern. She had a new pair of Samson posts on either side of her stern. (These are strong square bitts to which lines can be tied for mooring or for towing a dingy.) She had a new pair of sockets in the corners on either side of the transom for holding fishing rods. She had a new searchlight with a blinker device for sending Morse code—it was up on the flying bridge. She also had a one-foot-long board up there next to the wheel, with two holes cut into it, to hold her master's tumblers of tequila while he steered through the swells.

Although she still possessed no ship-to-shore radio, *Pilar* now had a portable shortwave Zenith receiver usually balanced on a ledge in the cockpit near the stuttery phonograph. She also had a second-generation set of outriggers, just installed. They were sturdy and dainty and quite beautiful all at once—they looked a little like the varnished ribbings of an airplane wing, and they gave the old girl a little extra glamour as she glided out of the harbor toward the fishing grounds. When the riggers were in use, they slanted out to the sides, like gull wings.*

Pilar's first mate now was Gregorio Fuentes. *Pilar*'s original mate, Carlos Gutiérrez, had been gone since 1938, when Hemingway had replaced him with Gregorio. The received story about the aging Gutiérrez (whose name has seemed to slip into the folds of Hemingway history) is that Jane Mason (Hemingway's reputed lover from the early and mid-thirties) had

---

*But to explain it a bit more, at least the way they worked on Hemingway's boat: the lines controlled by the riggers were connected to the two rods held in the stern sockets. At a strike, the line that had just been hit would snap free from a clothespin breakaway catch at the tip of the outrigger. The rod in the stern socket—or, rather, the fisherman trying to jerk free from his reveries and grab hold of that rod and reel—would try to take up the slack in the belly of the line, hopefully before the fish could spit the hook.

been furious over Hemingway's love affair with Martha Gellhorn, and that she thus stole Carlos away from *Pilar* to be the mate on her own boat. It happened while Hemingway was off at the Spanish Civil War. Hemingway himself aided and abetted this version of the story in vague ways through the years, but I think the closer truth, as with almost every Hemingway truth, is more ambiguous. I think Hemingway was psychologically ready to cut Carlos adrift not too long after he had employed him. Yes, he arranged for his mate to come to Bimini in the second summer of the boat (where on at least one occasion Hemingway had reduced him to tears in front of others on the boat), and, yes, he continued to praise him in print for a good while after. But to paraphrase Les Hemingway, in that line from *My Brother, Ernest Hemingway:* he loved everything for a small time, and then nothing was any good anymore.

It was Carlos who told Hemingway the real-life story that became the basis for the fictional *The Old Man and the Sea*. In the eighteenth paragraph of his October 1936 *Esquire* piece, "On the Blue Water: A Gulf Stream Letter," Hemingway gave us the germ of his novella. The actual writing was still a decade and a half in the future.

> Another time an old man fishing alone in a skiff out of Cabanas hooked a great marlin that, on the heavy sash-cord handline, pulled the skiff far out to sea. Two days later the old man was picked up by fishermen sixty miles to the eastward, the head and forward part of the marlin lashed alongside. What was left of the fish, less than half, weighed eight hundred pounds. The old man had stayed with him a day, a night, a day and another night while the fish swam deep and pulled the boat. When he had come up the old man had pulled the boat up on him and harpooned him. Lashed alongside the sharks had hit him and the old man had fought them out alone in the Gulf Stream in a skiff, clubbing them, stabbing at them, lunging at them with an oar until he was exhausted and the sharks had eaten all that they could hold. He was crying in the boat when the fishermen picked him up, half crazy from his loss, and the sharks were still circling the boat.

The first mate on *Pilar* now was a native Canary Islander, born in 1897, who'd come to Cuba with his parents when he was ten. Gregorio Fuentes, who spoke little English, was going to live through the entire twentieth century and serve Hemingway and his boat loyally from 1938 to the Idaho suicide.* When he hired out on *Pilar*, he was forty-one, two years older than Hemingway, almost two decades younger than Carlos.

He and Hemingway had met in 1931 in the Dry Tortugas. (Max Perkins had come down from New York to be part of that fishing trip.) They'd run out of Bermuda onions for the sandwiches. Hemingway had gone aboard Gregorio's fishing smack to see if he could get some. Gregorio had refused money, and gave Hemingway rum as well. Hemingway remembered. He'd also been impressed by the shipshape boat Gregorio kept.

In October 1944, when Hemingway was overseas reporting the war, Gregorio had stayed with *Pilar* during a hurricane that, according to Hemingway, "blew 180 mph true, and small craft and Navy vessels were blown up onto the harbor boulevard and up onto the small hills around the harbor." Hemingway loved his loyalty.

Now, in 1950, Gregorio was fifty-three and hale and earning $155 a month—three times what any Hemingway household employee got paid. He was the mate and cook and all-around best hand. He knew his place. When he didn't have work to do, he liked sitting alone at the bow, amid the anchors and throw-off lines, staring into the sea, with a smoke. Like Carlos, he was a bony welterweight, only instead of wearing ball caps with the brims turned around, he favored old straw or felt fedoras.

One more piece of *Pilar*'s myth from the decade that had flowed beneath her hull. For approximately fourteen months in the wartime forties—from late November 1942 to late winter 1944—*Pilar* got converted by her master into a patrol boat, armed with light machine guns, hand grenades, bazookas, and satchel charges of explosives. In the early stages of the war, German subs had been sinking tankers in the North Atlantic convoy routes almost at will. The Gulf Stream and its surrounding waters had fairly crawled with U-boats. The idea—authorized by the new American ambassador to Cuba, Spruille Braden—was that *Pilar* and her crew might be able to lure a Nazi boat to the surface and get in the first blasts before escaping. *Pilar* would be disguised as a scientific vessel conducting experiments for the American Museum of Natural History. A wolf

---

*He lived until January 13, 2002. He made almost 105. Four decades after Hemingway was gone, there he was, the old man of Cojímar, with his rheumy eyes and mottled skin that looked scaly as the hide of a defanged rattler, sitting daily in his rocker outside his small pastel house, smoking a cigar and allowing the Hemingway shrine-goers to snap his picture—for maybe ten bucks, collected by a nephew. Cojímar is the little seaside village about seven miles east of Havana where Hemingway used to moor *Pilar* when he wasn't stabling her in town, at the Club Náutico, at the foot of the San Francisco wharf.

in sheep's clothing, she'd patrol with her concealed armaments along the north Cuban coast. If Hemingway and crew could draw a U-boat close, they'd pull the covers off their weaponry and open fire and even try to get a grenade down the sub's conning tower. Nothing like this ever happened. Hemingway's Q-boat (as such civilian decoy vessels were known in World War I) never encountered an enemy ship, although there was one occasion when a U-boat was in sight. (The boat was going too fast in the other direction, and *Pilar* couldn't close on her.) Hemingway's motley and revolving band of volunteers consisted of a local jai alai player, a merchant seaman, a wealthy playboy sportsman, a machinist, and military men on loan from the government. (Gregorio Fuentes was also involved.) The whole enterprise earned the contempt of Hemingway's third wife, Martha Gellhorn, who was convinced her husband was trying to avoid, or at least delay, going to the war in Europe as a correspondent, as well as trying to get in some free fishing with his hangers-on, meanwhile burning up gasoline courtesy of the American government. (Briefest recap of his briefest marriage: After nearly four years of adultery, Hemingway and Martha Gellhorn had wed on November 21, 1940, in Cheyenne, Wyoming, before a justice of the peace, in the dining room of the Union Pacific Railroad, sixteen days after the divorce from Pauline was finalized. Not quite three years later, early fall of 1943, when Martha left to report on World War II, the marriage was all but done, even if the actual divorce didn't come until December 1945.)

Gellhorn was wrong. While Operation Friendless (Hemingway had named the reconnaissance patrols for one of the cats at the *finca*) often got polluted in the usual Hemingway manner with far too much alcohol and ego, there were, at base, courageous motivations at work. Hemingway and his boat performed needed—and dangerous—picket duties, keeping watch on uncounted inlets, bays, uninhabited keys. This, the director of the FBI (never mind Gellhorn) could never buy or stomach. The abstemious and paranoid J. Edgar Hoover had little use for Hemingway, going back at least to the Spanish Civil War, when he became convinced that Hemingway was either a Communist or a sympathizer—and no question a drunk and womanizer. In the early forties, Hoover had his agents in the American Embassy in Cuba monitoring Hemingway, and indeed Hoover himself, as evidenced from an FBI file on Hemingway that's nearly as long as your arm, was writing his own paranoid memoranda about Hemingway from his desk in Washington. Hoover's and the bureau's paranoia about Hemingway—and Hemingway's paranoia about Hoover and the bureau—

would keep up for the rest of Hemingway's life, right to the locked doors of Mayo Clinic.

In the long history of Hemingway's boorish behavior toward other human beings, the middle and late months of 1950 mark a special moment. The anger just flamed outward, a kind of spectacular shining of his rage, in the weeks and months leading up to the publication of *Across the River*, and in the weeks and several months immediately following—which was right when a young embassy officer was coming to know him and experiencing him as something wholly opposite.

If, on the front end, this rage was tied chiefly to his anxieties over the quality of what he'd produced, after so long a publishing absence, then, on the back end, it was linked mostly to his rejection by the critics, which was a rejection unlike anything he'd yet suffered. But the rage was also connected in more general ways with mortality, dropping broader and broader hints, as well as connected to his idealized love for a green-eyed Italian girl whom he knew he'd never have, not sexually, for lots of reasons. He was more than twice Adriana Ivancich's age, and he wasn't even half a decade into his own fourth marriage, which, for all its shipwreck, would be the marriage he'd stay in, for better and worse, through much sickness and occasional patches of health, until that morning in Ketchum, when he'd leave behind, for his spouse to be the first to find, running from her bedroom at the sound of it, what you might regard as his last and most splattering expression of anger.

Some glimpses of these electrified displays, fore and aft.

On Friday May 5, four months and two days ahead of official publication of *Across the River*, Hemingway, having lit himself up with frozen double daiquiris at his favorite Havana bar-restaurant, the Floridita, collected a nineteen-year-old whore, whom he'd nicknamed Xenophobia, and brought her down to the boat to have lunch with his wife and her sixty-five-year-old visiting cousin, Bea Gluck, a reserved Chicagoan. Xenophobia was crisp and beautiful, but the trouble was she didn't like going to bed with her clients—so he liked to say. The occasional client who owned *Pilar* claimed she wouldn't have eaten that day if he hadn't invited her to the boat. That morning, Mary Hemingway and her cousin had gone out for a short cruise in and around the harbor with Gregorio. They'd come back at noon and tied up at the Club Náutico and were waiting for Hemingway to arrive so that the three could sit down to a prearranged lunch on board. He showed up more than an hour late, with the tart on his arm, rocking and reeling down the boards, doing introductions all around. Mary's cousin had never met a designated whore before and tried to see the humor in it. The next morning, Mary handed her husband a lengthy typed letter. He went back to his own bedroom to read it. "As soon as it is possible for me to move out . . . I shall move," she said. Further down: "If there were any sign of remorse after such bouts of behavior on your part, I could believe we might try again and make things better." In *How It Was,* quoting her letter, Mary records no apology from Hemingway. "Stick with me, kitten. I hope you will decide to stick with me," she says he said. She goes on to say that he kept her so busy with beautifying projects at the *finca* that she sort of plumb forgot she intended to leave him.

On the same day that his wife handed him the letter, he was banging out several of his own on his old portable Royal. One was to his publisher. He told Scribner he was in the doghouse again, in part because he was dead on his ass from work on the galleys for the new book. Okay, his Italian girl, too. "I miss who I miss so badly that I do not care about anything," he said. "Loveing two women at same time is about a rough a sport as you can practice." (In subsequent days, he'd reprise the bit with Xenophobia. To Scribner: "I wouldn't do it again. But I would do something worse, I hope.")

It was certainly true he'd been exhausting himself on the galleys. They'd just come at the top of that week. He'd started in on them by first light on Monday, May 1, and by that Saturday he'd finished number seventy-seven, out of a total of eighty-eight. His plan was to make all the corrections, to write his inserts (three pages of inserts got written on Saturday and Sunday) and then to get the package back in the mail to New York early in the next week so that the typesetters at Scribner's could send first-pass page proofs to Cuba by early summer.

The galleys had been waiting, along with the stack of other mail, on Sunday night, when he and Mary had come in from a three-day weekend on *Pilar.* Since February, a paler version of the novel had been appearing in installments in *Cosmopolitan,* but this was the one for keeps. He'd even slept well that Sunday, although some of that must have been owed to how bushed he was from fighting a big marlin the day before. He described it to Charlie Scribner on Monday afternoon. "Am tired from yesterday. Fought two marlin, one big, and the second one whipped the shit out of me. He threw the hook when he jumped and it caught just under his fin and he could then (being foul hooked) keep his mouth shut and pull sideways like a nine foot sea anchor. He could also sound, run and do anything he wished. He never had it better except when he was a free fish." As for his wife, quite beautiful and browning up with the sun, well, "truly I do not mean to be a shit about Venice and all." He meant Adriana.

He'd also spoken in his Monday letter about something else, which goes a long way in explaining his need to humiliate his browning wife at week's end: Lillian Ross's lengthy profile of him in *The New Yorker*. It, too, had been waiting, along with the galleys and the rest of the mail, when he and Mary had walked into the house on Sunday night. The piece wasn't a surprise in that sense—the author had sent it to Hemingway ahead of time to check it for factual error. And yet to see the story in its published light in arguably the best literary magazine in America had to have been a different experience, its own small shock. Hemingway liked Ross a lot—she was another "daughter"—and he would keep up a correspondence and friendship with her for years. All the same he had to have known she'd made him out—he'd made himself out—to sound like a horse's ass, not to say a drugstore Indian in a Hollywood B movie. ("Book start slow, then increase in pace till it becomes impossible to stand. I bring emotion up to where you can't stand it, then we level off, so we won't have to provide oxygen tents for the readers.")

The previous November, Ross, who was one of the magazine's star reporters, still in her twenties, had followed Hemingway around Manhattan for two days. The Hemingways were en route to Europe and had stopped over at the Sherry-Netherland hotel with fourteen suitcases. The manuscript of his novel, now on its "jamming" back end, was in his battered and travel-stickered old briefcase—sort of spilling out of it, in fact. Ross goes shopping with Hemingway at Abercrombie & Fitch. She's in his hotel suite when room service arrives with caviar and champagne, and then here comes the Kraut. That's Marlene Dietrich. "The Kraut's the best that ever came into the ring," Hemingway tells the reporter, who is gimlet-eyeing it all. One of his tics is the way her subject raises his fist to his face, like a fighter, and rocks in silent laughter.

So much has been written over the last six decades about Ross's profile, a precursor to what we think of as New Journalism. It ran on May 13, 1950, and is titled "How Do You Like It Now, Gentlemen?" which is what Hemingway keeps saying aloud in the story—but to whom, and why, it isn't wholly clear. Horse's ass—yes. Hemingway used that term in his letter to Charlie Scribner of May 1. Four days later, the horse's ass, beat from the galleys, wishing to even the score for some public embarrassment he has just suffered in *The New Yorker,* parades a prostitute in front of his wife.

Three days later (the finished galleys are either in the mail or about to be), Senator Joseph McCarthy of Wisconsin is the target. McCarthy is in his moment of fame as the great Red-baiter of America. Hemingway dictates the letter, and his young secretary, Nita Jensen, types it. "[Y]ou are a shit, Senator, and would knock you on your ass the best day you ever lived," he says. Some of his sentences don't quite track. "[I]f we can take off the part of the uniform you take when you go outside, and fornicate yourself." He signs it twice. (This letter may never have been sent.)

Two days later, he's typing a letter to Charlie Scribner on a piece of plain white paper. There's concern on his publisher's part whether some of the "fictional" things he's said in the new book about his third wife are actionable. Listen, Charlie, Miss Martha would be well advised not to try to pick a fight with me, he writes—I hit too hard. She's a phony who tried to run in the social register, he says, who neglected to tell him before they got married that her insides were gone for childbearing, who lied about the fact of her Jewish blood. Let's drop it there, Charlie, he says, before I get really serious. "I would fix her up for posterity, or whatever they call the place, like a trussed pig on a wheel-barrow in China." He ends: "Better stop writing this." He means before he really gets worked up. He signs it in a smeared hand, "Yours always Ernest," and writes beside his signature, "Broken pencil lead." Was he jamming down so hard that he snapped the pencil itself?

Seven weeks later, no page proofs, goddamn it. He's out on the boat. Through May and June he's soothed himself with short vacations on *Pilar.* He and his wife and one of his Havana hangers-on, Roberto Herrera, intend to stay out again for a couple of days. Late in the day, they put in behind the reef at Rincón, east of Bacuranao. He's climbing the ladder to the flying bridge to relieve Gregorio at the wheel. Just then Gregorio swings the boat broadside to enter the channel. The captain, with one leg over the guardrail, pitches backward and headfirst into the hooks and clamps securing the gaffs. "*Yodo y vendas,*" Gregorio is yelling. Iodine and bandages. Mary is trying to stanch the wound with rolls of toilet paper. Hemingway is going woozy. The deck slats are turning red and sticky. While Mary gobs, he's thinking about Adriana. They get the boat turned around and headed home. They have him wrapped in a cashmere blanket on the long cushion on the starboard side in the cockpit. At the wharf, they load him into a taxi. Back at the *finca,* his doctor closes the wound while the rebounding patient drinks a gin and tonic in a leather desk chair. It wasn't an S.I.W., he'll tell friends in coming days, you know, a self-inflicted wound.

Some of these details are in *How It Was*. What isn't in Mary's memoir is something Walter Houk's wife told her husband not long before she died. One morning, possibly a week after Hemingway's non-S.I.W., Hemingway's young secretary went into his bedroom with a stack of dictated letters ready to be signed. "Oh, daughter," he said, taking off his belt and sliding his khaki shorts to the knees. "Forgive me for exposing myself, but I wanted you to see what happened to me. Look here at my right thigh." His thigh was a mass of red scabs. He told Nita how he'd pitched into the clamps, which had not only opened his head to the bone and severed an artery but had done a serious job on his leg, too. Nita put the letters down and backed out of the room. A little later, she encountered Mary in another part of the house. Mary had overheard the exchange in the bedroom. Nita: Terrible, isn't it? Mary, venomously: "He was drunk." A man in a reeling state trying to take over the wheel of his boat with his wife and others aboard might be thought of as acting out some rage, yes.

July 9. A Saturday. Like a fool, he's waited all morning for proofs to come. No chance they'll be here now till Monday. *Pilar* is in temporary dry dock and he can't even go fishing. Thirty-two years ago yesterday, they blew him up at Fossalta. In commemoration he went into town last night and rounded up Xenophobia and another fond whore, much older, whom he calls Leopoldina. He's writing these things this morning to Scribner, who's been hospitalized with heart problems. He's typing on *finca* stationery. It's a long letter, and he won't finish till tomorrow. You gotta take care of your ticker, Charlie, he says, because we get only one of those in this life. Soon enough Charlie's ticker problems are off the page. He's on to Henry James, and by the way, "fuck all male old women anyway." Just once he'd have liked to see him on a mean bucking bronc or trying to hit a ball out of the infield. "What did he do when he was a boy do you suppose. Just jerk himself off into Fame and now Fortune like T.S. Eliot." His mind goes to the general subject of sports and his own kids. Jack's a hell of an athlete and can play anything except baseball. Patrick's a terrible athlete, at least of the kind that involves hand-eye coordination, but such a fine kid. Gigi, well, he can play any damn thing, ride any damn thing, shoot any damn thing. Course, the girls are after the Gig-man now. "But I wish there had never been a divorce and loss of control and discipline (not harsh as I rebelled against when I was a boy) but just sound control." Much further down (it's Sunday, and he's finishing): "You know that on today July 10th 1950

I have still not received the original duplicate page proofs. I would shoot on that anywhere any time." The salesmen won't do their job, he says, the critics will have their own time with it, there won't be any copies in the stores. "I would never go with any other publishing house; but Jesus Christ I would like to put yours in order." Don't let your lousy people fuck my book—this is the refrain. "Sometimes I get discouraged, Charlie. Today is one of the days." He signs it "Ernest," postscripting, "How do you like it now, Gentlemen?"

Ten days later, July 19, the same laments and rage: "My dear Charlie: Your fucking page proofs (first series) turned up yesterday. That ought to be almost a record." Eight paragraphs down: "The hell with it all." Next paragraph: "There is nothing for me to do now. The horse is under the starter's orders." I am a bad boy, Charlie, and not proud of it. "You are older than me and I should be respectful." Toward the end: "We are going fishing today." He and Mary will leave in an hour. At least he's got *Pilar.*

On August 3, a hurricane passes through—the *finca* was on its eastern edge. Another storm is due in four days. He's scared for the boat. "Send me any reviews you have," he writes. "They won't bother my nerves."

On August 9, he writes again to Scribner, the first part of it by hand. He can't sleep, he says. He logs in the time at the top: "0415." He's still waiting to receive the first finished copy. "It's all sorts of things wake you. This morning it was bad cramps in the left leg and bad nightmares. Detailed nightmare in which gigi had killed seven people and then himself. Waiting now for the morning papers to see it isn't true." Sorry about my bad handwriting, Charlie, he says—no clipboards are handy, they're on the boat. "Maybe I can get some sleep now it is daylight." He doesn't finish the letter until afternoon. "Book didn't come." Shit on hope.

But finished copies do come, within two days. Even in the fourth decade of writing books, there is the wild thrill to tear open the lid and pull the first one from the box. That afternoon he signs a copy for Marty Gellhorn and dictates a letter, which his secretary neatly types: "Quite a few people came into Venice from the country to see you when you were in that town. The summing up was; 'She must have been quite beautiful then. So you can't really blame Ernesto for having married her.' They also read your articles and found them without style nor much talent; but conscientiously and honestly written." Nine days later he writes to his old army pal, Buck Lanham. "Am scheduled to be on the cover of Time." Six days later, another letter to Buck: "Believe the reviews will be mixed. Cover stories are off." It's August 26, 1950, twelve days before publication. His fucked horse is in the gate. He has so little idea—or maybe he does.

Here's what the *Saturday Review of Literature* was putting on the presses. (Their review would come out on Saturday.) "It is not only Hemingway's worst novel; it is a synthesis of everything that is bad in his previous work and it throws a doubtful light on the future. It is so dreadful, in fact, that it begins to have its own morbid fascination and is almost impossible as they say, to put down." Here's what *Commentary* was getting set to run. (They were a monthly, so it would be a few weeks.) "The first thing to be said about this novel is that it is so egregiously bad as to render all comment on it positively embarrassing to anyone who esteems Hemingway as one of the more considerable prose-artists of our time." Here's what *The New Yorker* had in the can. (It was by Alfred Kazin, it was called "The Indignant Flesh," and it, too, would come out that weekend.) "[I]t is hard to say what one feels most in reading this book—pity, embarrassment that so fine and honest a writer can make such a travesty of himself, or amazement that a man can render so marvelously the beauty of the natural world and yet be so vulgar. . . . [I]t is held together by blind anger . . . a rage that is deflected into one of the most confused and vituperatively revealing self-portrayals by an American I have ever seen." Even so lowly and obscure a publication as *The Yale Review* (certainly lowly and obscure in Hemingway's eye) would chirp in with the *E* word, although not immediately: "In spite of some good writing, it is an embarrassing book to read." Embarrassing? When was the last time the chicken-shitters used that word to describe his stuff? You mean because he had written such sentences as " 'Oh you. Would you ever like to run for Queen of Heaven?' " (The dying soldier is tête-à-tête with Renata in the bar of the Gritti Palace.) Or: "They stood there and kissed each other true."? Or: "The Martinis were icy cold and true Montgomerys, and, after touching the edges, they felt them glow happily all through their upper bodies"? Or: " 'I love you and I love you and I love you' "?

The only review he saw on the day of publication was *Time*'s, and they, too, spoke of his book as an embarrassment. Hemingway was a subscriber to *Time,* and his copy nearly always arrived on Thursday, having been published four days earlier in New York. He'd have liked going out on the boat to celebrate the day with a fish or two, but he'd stayed home to see what the bastards would say. In his gut he must have known, since there'd been that earlier talk of a cover story, now quashed. I picture him turning to page 110 and seeing the small blocky head ("On the Ropes") and reading the sarcasm of the first line ("Hemingway was the champ all right") and jumping into the second column ("never wins a round") and then flipping to the end ("a bore who forfeits the reader's sympathy"), and then tossing the rag down, all of it happening in eye-blinks of time, about as reflexively as some jerk of an amateur angler might jerk from a marlin's jaw an 8/0 Mustad hook with a Japanese feather squid and strip of pork rind on it.

Beneath the review was an interview the editors had recently conducted with him via telegram. It was bordered in wavy red lines and immediately drew the eye. They'd asked him in a phone call to keep his replies tight—to about twenty-five bucks worth of international cable tolls. So wasn't the hero of his book a pretty bitter man? And weren't the colonel's personal history and even his characteristics startlingly parallel to the author's? And might he be willing to concede he may have rushed things a little to get this one out? "We concede nothing, and what we take we hold" was one of his answers, and "Hemingway is bitter about nobody" was another. At the end, the editors included this: "Anything Mary told you over the phone I deny." Mary Hemingway used to be a reporter for *Time*. What a double cross.

He went into town before noon, hoping airmail letters from in-house friends at both *The New York Times* and *Newsweek* might be at the post office and he could get them before Friday's delivery. The letters weren't there. Nor did any telegrams of support from his publisher arrive that day or the next or the next. Mary Hemingway wasn't around—she'd recently gone over to the States to help get her aging parents settled into a new residence in Gulfport, Mississippi. Xenophobia had contracted some kind of crud in her chest and was on penicillin—couldn't even distract himself sexually. Did he wander the *finca*, take laps in the pool, kick at an underfoot cat or two?

On Saturday he got up and went to his desk to write to his publisher. Reviews were appearing everywhere in the country (and also in England, where *Across the River* was being published simultaneously), and some weren't half bad and a few were damn good—although he knew nothing of them. On the day of publication, both *The New York Times* and *The New York Herald Tribune* had run prominent, if hedging, notices, and his publisher had done right by him and placed large ads. But the only thing he knew of so far was that dirty double cross in *Time*.

"Dear Charlie: When the hell you been, boy?" (He had to have meant "where," perhaps the smallest index of his distracted fury.)

> Did you read the *Time* review and take off for the wilds of Jersey to launch your counter-attack from there? Well everybody has their own way of doing things. But isn't it sort of customary to inform an author about how things go and what people say when a book comes out that he has bet his shirt on and worked his heart out on nor missed a deadline nor failed to keep a promise. . . . Do you think maybe I am not old enough to be told how my horse broke and what he is doing?

Eighth paragraph: "I'm going to take a dry martini now and the hell with it." Next sentence: "Later: Got the Newsweek review which they sent me; also Times daily and Sunday which Juan, the chauffeur bought in town." He means *brought from* town. What apparently happened is that he took the martini and in the meantime Juan arrived from town with the airmail packets from New York. The *Times* Sunday review, which wouldn't be out until the next day, was a rave from fellow novelist John O'Hara. About a month earlier, he'd been tipped by his friendly inside source at the *Times* (it was a critic named Harvey Breit) that O'Hara was doing it. The editors had put the review on the cover. "The most important author living today, the outstanding author since the death of Shakespeare, has brought out a new novel" was the first sentence. That's about all he needed to see. *Newsweek* published—on the same day as *Time*'s review—a long and mostly admiring piece, a kind of feature-cum-review. It was written by the magazine's book editor, Robert Cantwell, whom Hemingway had known casually from years before, in Europe. No double cross there. "I don't think you backed the wrong horse: if you backed him," he told Scribner, when he took up the letter again later that afternoon.

The lift couldn't last. He wrote a letter to Harold Ross, editor of *The New Yorker.* He didn't date it; he may not have sent it.* He wrote it aboard *Pilar,* plowing through a rough sea as he was trying to steer. Was he zonked to his eyeballs? If you study the handwriting—never mind the content—you'll believe so. It almost looks as if he used an auger instead of a pencil, for the way the words were bored into the page. Some of them

---

*So far as I know, this letter has never seen print until now, and it wouldn't be seeing print now were it not for the diligence and generosity of a Key West writer and Hemingway researcher named Brewster Chamberlin, who uncovered it and provided me a copy.

were written in cursive, others were printed. He wrote the letter on the pages of an old Warner's Calendar of Medical History. He had used parts of this calendar to keep a log of his 1939 fishing season. (Had he grabbed the partially filled-in logbook from a desk drawer at home that morning on his way to the boat?) He wrote the letter across four sheets of old dates: September 10, 11, 12, 13; 1939 dates. He probably wrote it in mid- or late September, after some of the earliest reviews had reached Havana. Ross was a friend; the letter was intended for Alfred Kazin, who'd said he'd made such a travesty of himself. Kazin was really only the stand-in— for *Time*, for *Commentary*, for the *Saturday Review*, for every bad notice his eye and fury were coming across.

> Dear Mr. Harold:
> Please excuse my bad orthography in hurricane months. We have had six only one hit here but not badly.
> Please inform Mr. Alfred KAZIM (or KAZIN) or however the poor shit spells it that he can stick (STICK) his review up his ASS repeat ASS and that I will send him the grease (GREASE) Repeat GREASE (any time he preffers).
> It is not dishonorable to fight for your country (OR CUNTRY) but when phonies with names like *THAT* write the criticism of a TRADE (OVER) that you have ACTUALLY Practised for Better or Much Worse (Much Movement on Ship and Me Steering.)
> Please TELL KAZIN (if that is his real name) TO GO HANG HIMSELF (Will Furnish Worn Out Rope From the Boat STOP Adequate to hang repeat HANG shits, LIARS and MENTAL and Physical and *Moral* JERKS repeat JERKS. Best always Ernest Hemingway

In comparison to the rest of the letter, the "Best always" and his signature are almost neatly executed—which would make you think he signed it after he was home, having read it over to his satisfaction.

Mary Hemingway returned from the Gulf Coast to find that the path of the storm had violently turned. His treatment of her in late September and early October gathered to a kind of crushing greatness. On October 12, five weeks after publication, Mary wrote to Charles Scribner. She said, "At various times in the last several months he has called me, and repeated the names, rolling them around juiceily on his tongue: whore, bitch, liar, moron." The night before, with half a dozen guests at the dinner table, she had made a rather innocent remark that she didn't intend to bet on a pigeon-shooting contest that was being planned for the next day on the grounds of the *finca*. "So Ernest denounced me several times as 'cobarde' (coward) but the Spanish is somehow stronger and more insulting in meaning." She said, "At table his favorite and frequent means of protesting any word, glance, gesture or food he doesn't like is to put his full, freshly served plate on the floor. The other day he dumped the entire plate of bread and crackers on top of my plate." She told of the Xenophobia incident in May. She said, "It is more than a year since he actually hit me." She wondered whether her inability to conceive a child had something to do with his behavior. "He taunts me with this." She said she feared "the disintegration of a personality." She said she had decided again she must leave him—did Scribner know of any writing jobs in New York? She asked that he not reply directly—"Ernest is inclined to open my mail before I see it."

Incidentally, in a letter of his own to Scribner, written on the day before Mary's letter, Hemingway had put everything on his wife's menstrual period. "She was quite happy yesterday and the day before," he said. "About writing to Mary: please lay off any references to problems I may have. I have not been married 29 years and not learned I am a son of a bitch every twenty-eight days or so." In an earlier letter, he'd told Scribner that his wife was talking to him "like a fishwife before everyone, and I have to keep my temper." I can believe the fishwife part. It was as if two adults, acting like children, were running to a parent to tell on the other, the parent here being not quite a decade older than Hemingway. Several times in these weeks Scribner wrote to Hemingway and asked that he treat his wife more respectfully. In one of his replies, Hemingway said, "Thanks for the morality lecture."

Incidentally again, E. B. White of *The New Yorker* had just finished—and the magazine had set immediately in type, to go in that week's issue—his hilarious little ditty titled "Across the Street and into the Grill," mentioned previously. It began:

> This is my last and best and true and only meal, thought Mr. Pirnie as he descended at noon and swung east on the beat-up sidewalk of Forty-fifth Street. Just ahead of him was the girl from the reception desk. I am a little fleshed up around the rook of the elbow, thought Pirnie, but I commute good....
>
> What a stinking trade it is, he thought. But after what I've

done to other assistant treasurers, I can't hate anybody. Sixteen deads, and I don't know how many possibles.

If that public mockery had to press hard on a nerve when Hemingway read it in the magazine a few days later (he was a subscriber), it should be noted here, although not as any kind of excuse, that something had been literally and badly pressing on one of his nerves, making his right leg swell up and go ice-cold. His Havana doctor determined that old encysted shrapnel dating from 1918 had been knocked loose by the July 1 headfirst fall into the hooks and clamps holding the gaffs.

No amount of rage from Hemingway and no amount of vituperation from his critics were having any apparent karmic effect on the sales of *Across the River.* The book had torn through its first printing before September was out, and the publisher had ordered another twenty-five thousand. At the moment of his wife's October 12 letter to Scribner, the novel that had been dedicated "To Mary with Love" was landing at number one on *The New York Times Book Review* best-seller list.

The day following her letter, the weather was too stormy for fishing. Hemingway couldn't go out on his boat. He said he was going to take a car trip down the island with his driver, Juan. He had no idea how long he'd be gone or where he was staying. He packed books, medications, glasses, land clothes. His wife went to her desk and wrote a quick poem called "For the Road." She handed it to him and kissed him and then stood with the servants on the terrace and waved as the two men pulled off down the drive. She went down to the pool and did about a half mile of laps in the nude and came up and took lunch. By midafternoon, there he was, back in front of her, "well-filled with frozen daiquiris." This story is in *How It Was.* Apparently there were no brutalities on October 13. But a few days after, according to entries in her journals as well as what's in the memoir, Hemingway turned to her and said, "You camp-follower and scavenger." A couple of days further on, he said, "You have the face of Torquemada." (She went to a dictionary to look up Torquemada: Dominican monk in the Spanish Inquisition who tortured thousands of Jews and suspected witches.) She walked into her rose garden and sat under a lychee tree to cry and conduct a self-interview about why she didn't have the guts to leave him. From *How It Was:* "Wild Mary: 'What about your pride? Haven't you any pride? You're too craven.' Mild Mary: 'My pride? It's wounded. It stings.'" Shouldn't she have known what he could do when the demons were on him? He'd shoot at anything. In early 1945, in Paris, at the Hôtel

Ritz, about nine months after they'd first met, he had put into a toilet bowl, and begun firing away at it, a photograph of Mary's Australian journalist husband, Noel Monks, from whom she was separated but not divorced. That display flooded their room.

On October 28—now seven weeks since the critics have been firing away—an Italian cargo-passenger ship named the *Luciano Manara* arrives in Havana Harbor, and Adriana Ivancich and her widowed mother, Dora, are aboard. They've come to Cuba for what'll turn out to be a three-month visit. Adriana's older brother, Gianfranco, has been living in Cuba for more than a year, and this fact lends propriety and moral plausibility to the visit—which had been hatched, the previous spring, in Venice, near the end of a second consecutive lengthy Hemingway stay in Europe. More obsessed than ever with the girl whom he'd known at that point for roughly a year and a quarter, Hemingway had told his wife that he wanted to invite Adriana and her mother to Havana, and to stay with them. Mary, feeling helpless to stop it, had nonetheless demanded that if it was going to happen, the invitation should be a joint one—for the sake of propriety. "You're right, my kitten. You fix it up then," Hemingway had told her. A couple of weeks after the invite, Hemingway had had a reunion with Adriana in Paris. This was mid-March 1950. Hemingway and his wife were about to sail for America. On the day before the Hemingways caught the boat train to Le Havre, Hemingway and Adriana had gone for a walk along the boulevard Saint-Germain. They'd stopped at a sidewalk table and sat under a striped umbrella at the Les Deux Magots. Florid-faced, Hemingway had made a fumbling declaration of his love. In a roundabout way, he'd even brought up the subject of marriage. "I love you in my heart and I cannot do anything about it," he said. "But you have Mary," Adriana had said, feeling paralyzed. "Ah, yes, Mary. She is nice of course, and solid and courageous," he'd answered. Two days later, Hemingway and his wife were on the *Île de France,* and five days later, at noon on March 27, they were easing into New York Harbor. They spent ten days in New York and had then entrained for Florida and ferried onward to Cuba, arriving home on April 8. Within two days, he had written to his love: "I missed you every minute of all the time since Havre." A few days later: "I do not, and cannot, ever love anyone as I love you." Such letters had kept up through the summer. Sometimes he had addressed her as "Adriana Hemingway." Sometimes he had signed himself "Ernest Ivancich."

So here they were, at the *finca,* this strange quartet: the Venetian mother and widow, whose aristocratic family had fallen on hard financial times; the not-quite-twenty-one-year-old daughter; the forty-two-year-old rebuked wife; the fifty-one-year-old rejected novelist (in his own mind)—all breathing the same coolish autumn air on a hill outside the city where, when the day was clear, you could look down through the mangoes and poincianas from the west terrace and see the Capitolio and also the glint of the blue harbor, although not quite an aging, elegant, faithful fishing boat nodding in it.

One night, there was a planned outing in town for dinner and a film. Mary chose a dark dress. "Your hangman's suit. Your executioner's suit," her husband told her. But she loved that dark dress and until that moment felt he'd been fond of it, too. "You've sabotaged it," he said, meaning the outing.

One night he shot out a lamp. One night he said, almost from nowhere, "You slut." One night, after Mary had brought her typewriter out to the living room, he came in, picked it up, and slammed it to the floor. Later that evening he took exception to some "incautious" word she'd used and threw wine in her face. She ducked and most of it went staining down the white plaster wall behind her. These stories are in *How It Was*.

As is this one: Mary went looking for some business papers she kept in a drawer beneath the window seat in an anteroom just off the master bedroom. She kept personal letters in there, too, including copies of hers to him, as well as originals of his to her. The personal letters were gone. "I've put them in the bank," he said.

A photograph. He's in one of the matching and deep-cushioned floral-print armchairs in the *finca*'s long living room. He's wearing a tux and French cuffs with cuff links. He's got his legs crossed—you can see a bit of his hairy shin. He looks a little like a dressed-up Einstein—with a haircut. There's a floor lamp shading him—its scalloped and crinkly shade is decorated with toreadors. At his elbow, positioned between the two easy chairs, is a table holding maybe a dozen bottles of liquor. Adriana, in evening wear, a shawl around her shoulders, is right there, too, kneeling, with her chin on her clasped hands, which are in turn resting on the arm of the easy chair. She's sleek-skinned, Mediterranean, aquiline, bejeweled. She's not looking at him so much as past him, as if taking in something he has just said, tête-à-tête. Have the four just come from a candlelit dinner in the dining room? Was this the evening they'd gone into the Vedado district of the city to hear Arthur Rubinstein playing Chopin? Where is Mary? Seething, on the far other side of the room?

In mid-November, the foursome was out on *Pilar*. They were down at Puerto Escondido. More than a year before, in the summer of 1949, he'd taken his old Royal typewriter to Puerto Escondido and had worked furiously and contentedly for six days aboard *Pilar* on *Across the River*, averaging better than a thousand words a day. But now, with the *real* Renata aboard, the weather at Puerto Escondido began to seethe. Hemingway said later that *Pilar* took the wind at "maybe a touch over 95 in the gusts," and that the thing had "hit like a cleaver. We still had the hurricane months gear on board and had four anchors out and two lines made fast to the shore." They saw an Italian freighter smashed up on the rocks like a toy. *Pilar* got coated with a rime of sea salt, but otherwise came through fine. Hemingway evacuated his guests and wife to shore, where they caught a train back to Havana. He and Gregorio brought the boat home and caught another load of good fish for the freezer. He described the fury of it all in several letters.

What he didn't tell was how, before it had come lashing, Adriana had cut her finger on a fin of a fish, and of how he'd bent over her to suck out the blood, and of how Mary, sickened at the sight, had turned her face and gone to another part of the boat. All of them arrived back at the *finca* for a belated and relatively quiet Thanksgiving dinner. Not quite three weeks later, into the lee of these becalmed gales, knowing next to nothing of them, not then, came an alert and highly educated young Foreign Service officer with important duties at his nation's embassy. His girlfriend, whom he'd been dating since October, brought him out about an hour before dark on that Thursday afternoon.

"I know what I know. I don't think I had blinders on. I would have been reacting closely to everything. I know how warm he was. I know how we just seemed to hit it off from the first—what's wrong with that? I never really saw the kind of behavior all these books love to describe, and if I had witnessed some of it for myself, then I might have carried across the years a wholly different feeling," I've heard an old man in California say. Sometimes, though, and more often lately than formerly, I've heard sentiments like those being expressed less with a conviction and defiance than with a small, weary note of apology seeming to be tucked inside them—which has made me feel almost dirty, as if I've flown across the country once more to goad Walter Houk into saying things he not only doesn't wish to say but is incapable of saying.

Walter Houk's gray-painted wood and stucco house in the foothills of the inland slope of the Santa Monica Mountains is shaded by eucalyptus trees and river birches and seventy-foot-high coast redwoods and, most immensely, a two-hundred-year-old live oak that comes right up through the deck. That California live oak in the back of Walter's home always puts me in mind of the immense ceiba that used to shade the front of Ernest Hemingway's home and which came right up through the front steps and part of the Finca's foundation. A ceiba is a silk-floss tree, native of Brazil and Argentina, with greenish bark and with spring and summer blossoms that range in color from white to pale pink to deep pink. (Hemingway's used to swoon into pink in mid-February.)

In 1985, Martha Gellhorn traveled back to Cuba for the first time in four decades. Afterward she wrote a lyric piece, laced with bitterness and regret. The story was published in Granta magazine in January 1987 and was titled "Cuba Revisited." The opening: "The first morning in Havana, I stood by the sea-wall on the Malecon, feeling weepy with homesickness for this city. Like the exile returned; and ridiculous. I left Cuba forty-one years ago, never missed it and barely remembered it. A long amnesia, forgetting the light, the color of the sea and sky, the people, the charm of the place."

She wrote of the village that was right below her old home, and of how she really had known nothing of it in the years she lived there, except that San Francisco de Paula had a post office and many ragged children, at whom she would wave when she rode into town in the car. "I did not say to myself: it isn't my country, what can I do? I didn't think about Cuba at all. Everything I cared about with passion was happening in Europe. I listened to the radio, bought American newspapers in Havana, waited anxiously for letters from abroad. I wrote books, and the minute I could break free, I went back to the real world, the world at war."

She wrote about how she used to swim in the sea, wearing motorcycle goggles—"masks and snorkels had not been invented." She must have been so fetching.

She managed in the piece to pull off the feat of not uttering the despised Ernest Hemingway's name until the last pages. She collected Gregorio

Fuentes from his little house in Cojimar and went out with him to the finca, which was now the Museo Hemingway, property of the state. Gregorio was almost eighty-eight. They rode up the long driveway flanked by its huge royal palms and hibiscus and jacaranda trees—she remembered nothing so grand when she'd lived there. They came around the curve. There was the "pleasant old one-story affair," a limestone villa with its six airy rooms, only now the house was standing "glaring white and naked." When she lived at the finca, she had it painted a dusty and pale pink, to pick up the colors of the ceiba's blossoms. "It looks like a sanatorium," she said to Gregorio. And then, her shock. Why, yes, no wonder it's so naked-looking. "What did they do to the ceiba?" she asked. Gregorio told her the roots were pushing up the floor; the tree had to go. "They should have pulled down the house instead," she replied, which must have meant more than it literally said.

From the piece:

> Forty-six years ago [it was in the spring of 1939], I found this house through an advertisement and rented it, for one hundred dollars a month, indifferent to its sloppiness, because of the giant ceiba growing from the wide front steps. Any house with such a tree was perfect in my eyes. Besides, the terrace beyond the steps was covered by a trellis roof of brilliant bougainvillea. Flowering vines climbed up the wall behind the ceiba; orchids grew from its trunk.

I once asked Walter when we were standing beneath his live oak how far away the ocean was. "Oh, I suppose about ten miles, as the crow would fly, if you got up high and rode the ridges, and then came swooping down the other side," he said.

For many years now, this old eagled widower has been walking the slopes and ridges of his side of the Santa Monica range. He can begin literally at his front door. Usually he does his workout in the 5:30 or 6:00 a.m. hour. He's almost always awake by 4:00. Old men wake up early. He'll lie there for a while in the darkness. Possibly some memory of Nita or something about one of his children will float into his mind. He'll listen for the soft thump of the newspaper hitting the front step. He'll get out of bed, put on the coffee, come back, make the bed, get dressed, do his exercises, retrieve the paper, go out the front door. He loves taking his walks in the early winter, when the hills are turning green with the oats the Spanish planted two centuries ago. He's got about half a dozen routes, and he likes to vary them so that he won't get bored. Few people will be out at this hour—the dog walkers, some joggers padding by. Two or three of his routes take him up pretty high, nearly to the top of the ridges, just as a bird would go, to crooked little streets named San Blas and Iglesia. On the inland slope of the Santa Monica range, the ascent is much steeper than on the seaward side. On the seaward slope, long, gentle canyons support clear-running streams, at least one of which, Malibu Creek, is still alive with steelhead and rainbows. The predawn fragrance of so many California blossoms, summer and winter, cannot help but remind Walter of predawn fragrances on an island he said good-bye to in the early fall of 1952, bound for new adventures and a new diplomatic assignment in Tokyo.

"I just don't wish to go back," he has said often. "I'm too old to go back now, but even if I weren't, I wouldn't go."

"You kind of prefer to hold it all inside you?"

"I guess."

"It's a philosophical notion?"

"I don't know if it's that lofty."

When his workout is through (the distance is closer to a mile and a half, but he permits himself to round it off at an even two miles, because of the inclines he's negotiated, and, by the way, one of his curvier routes takes him right past a young and still green ceiba), he comes back to the house for his mug of black coffee and a page-by-page read of the Los Angeles Times. He takes his meds. He checks his e-mail. He eats his breakfast. "This gets me to about eight o'clock," Walter told me once. "The rest of the day is pretty flat." There was quiet resignation in it. I tried to shift the subject. He shook his head. "What you're not quite seeing is the memory failure. My ancient memory is still there. Thank God. It's the recent things. What can be done? Nothing. You outlive it. Except you don't. You just go on."

Years ago, starting out on this book, I used to go into a small soundproof booth at the Library of Congress and listen to Ernest Hemingway's voice on old wire recordings. The material on the preserved spools had long been transferred to audiotape, but the voice I heard was the one that had been captured magnetically by lengths of wire in a house in Cuba in the late forties and into the early fifties. In August 1949, as a way of trying to help him beat back his mountain of mail, Hemingway's publisher had presented him with a new wire recorder. He was said to be very tentative with it at first, and I can picture him holding the mic like a man holding something that's about to bite. Six decades later, I could go into a room and hear the disembodied self of Ernest Hemingway spookily speaking in my ear in a thin, precise, high-timbered pitch. Actually, according to Walter and others, his voice wasn't thin or high-timbered at all—it was just the primitive technology of the day.

On October 20, 1949, deep inside the writing of Across the River, about to go out for a long weekend on Pilar with his wife, Hemingway was using his new talk machine to write to his youngest son. Gigi, whose troubles were hardly unknown in the family, was then almost eighteen and in his freshman year at St. John's College in Annapolis, Maryland, but soon to drop out, much against his parents' wishes, and head for an abortive stay on the West Coast and a half-century spiral of psychic pain. In a month, Hemingway and his wife would sail for Europe on the Île de France, stopping over in New York, where among other things he would permit comely and ambitious young Lillian Ross to follow him around with her notebook. As for the new book, whose title hadn't really come to him yet, he told his son that he was at fifty-four thousand words and coming like a racehorse down the stretch. "We are ahead by about eleven lengths as of this morning," he told his boy. He'd been "averaging close to 1,000 a day keeping the quality as it should be." Damn, he wished Mr. Gig could read it right then. Next paragraph: "Please don't ever let them sell you on that powerful personality line which is evidently the thing on which my sons are sold now. I would not believe it myself because do not run as a powerful personality but rather as an instructor, never a professor, and am only fond of my children and try to tell them the truth. If there is any such thing." Next came a revealing sentence: "Understand all your problems within the limits of my intelligence and back your plea all the way." Further down: "[I]f you want to come up to New York to talk anything over . . ." Toward the close: "It's a beautiful morning, Schatz, with the mist laying in the hollows and over the hills as gray as Monet ever painted it." Signing off: "So long, Mr. Gig, and try not to worry. It never got anybody anywhere. Much love from all your friends here, And from Papa."

Four nights later, Sunday, late at night, Gigi's papa was back from the sea and dictating on the machine to Charlie Scribner. He said it had been a wonderful trip, and not least because of how rough the weather had been. They'd all taken it fine, including Pilar. They'd caught enough fish to fill up the deep freeze for weeks. He felt ready to go back at it hard again. "Want to clear everything up so as to sleep good and pitch good tomorrow." A few sentences down: "Mary is fine and says she had the finest trip on the ocean that she ever made. For once it was almost rough enough for her. . . . At one time we had to have five anchors out and heard the surf cannonading on the reef all night. I like it very much but very few women do and I have been extremely lucky to find one who does." The way "cannonading" came off his tongue and rolled through the mesh speaker in the darkened booth at the LOC was its own sweet onomatopoeia. It would be another four years before I discovered that the woman who took that letter off the magnetic spool and put it down in shorthand with a fountain pen in a tan marbleized stenographer's notebook and then transferred it by typewriter to a piece of onionskin airmail letterhead that was surely limp with Havana humidity was Walter Houk's wife—who wasn't his wife at that point, who, in fact, hadn't even met Walt yet. But Nita Jensen would, and eventually they'd get to California, beneath a gallant old live oak.

THE GALLANTRY OF AN AGING MACHINE

Motoring from Havana Harbor, August 26, 1951.
Twenty-six-year-old Walter Houk is at the stern with his foot up.

> Everything about him was old except his eyes and they
> were the same color as the sea and were cheerful and
> undefeated.

—ERNEST HEMINGWAY, *The Old Man and the Sea*

HE WAS BORN to working-class folk in Mission Hospital, on June 14,
1925, in a little nondescript community on the eastern edge of Los Angeles
called Walnut Park. That was the summer of *The Sun Also Rises*—its seeming miraculous, falling-out-whole, first draft, which in effect was the final
draft. Another story of that summer, not nearly so well known, might be
thought of as the first node of connection between someone destined to
be very famous and someone who'd achieve a startling lot in his life, even
if none of it was destined for the front page, which is only the story of all
the rest of us.

Two days before Walter Houk was born, and half a world away, on the Left Bank of Paris, twenty-five-year-old Ernest Hemingway and thirty-three-year-old Hadley Hemingway, who lived so reputedly broke and happy with their baby boy above the high whine of a sawmill, had gotten into their gladdest glad rags and gone to a major art opening. It was the first one-man show at the Galerie Pierre for the Spanish Catalan surrealist painter Joan Miró. Hemingway got seized that evening to own a canvas called *La Ferme* (*The Farm*). For some months he'd glimpsed the painting as a work in progress in the artist's studio. The next day, saying that he wished it as a birthday present for his wife, he put down a five-hundred-franc note as a down payment, with the balance due in the fall. A small complication was that the gallery owner had already promised the painting to Hemingway's friend Evan Shipman, the sometime American poet and lover of the horses at Longchamp and Auteuil. The day after that, at Shipman's urging, the two nonheeled writers decided to do the sporting thing and roll the dice. Biographers disagree on whether the painting's full price was thirty-five hundred or five thousand francs, but either figure would have represented something mountainous to Hemingway. (The lower figure would have been $175; the higher, $250.)* In another two weeks, he and his wife would leave for Spain and the festival at Pamplona, and within little more than a year he'd no longer be poor or unknown or living with Hadley—one of the self-admitted biggest mistakes of his life. But the connecting point here is that he'd thrown the dice and held his breath and won his Miró on the same day that Walter was born—and twenty-five years later, in an impromptu tour of his home, Hemingway would be showing off that painting to Walter, whom he'd met about twenty minutes before, and who, in his own way, would feel transfixed by *The Farm*, as he'd be struck by the other modernist oils hanging casually throughout the house: the Paul Klee, the Juan Gris, the Georges Braque, the André Massons. But most especially the Miró, hanging on the south wall of the dining room. "You see," Walter said once, knowing nothing of the dice story, "I'd never met anyone before who owned paintings of this quality. And since I was a

---

*For the balance, Hemingway and Dos Passos and Shipman (who must have been a hell of a sport), went around Montparnasse that fall, scrounging the dough with IOUs to friends and barkeeps. They brought the big canvas home in a taxi, and when it began to billow in the wind like a sail, Hemingway made the driver slow to a crawl. In 1926, when he and Hadley separated, Hemingway moved the painting to her new apartment. In 1931 he asked to borrow it back for five years. He never returned it. Today *The Farm* hangs in the National Gallery of Art, its value in the millions.

painter myself, doing it in my spare time, trying to put together a show at a small gallery in Havana, this was eye-opening. Looking at those paintings with him that first day, listening to him talk about them with such pride, especially the Miró, with its technical precision, may have been my first real clue that there was some other kind of man here."

His father, E. J. Houk, was a draftsman and master machinist out of Ohio with an incurably restless bone—which made him perfect for the rootlessness of California, but especially of Los Angeles, a place that seems always to have been invented yesterday. In the 1920s, Los Angeles was the fastest-growing city in the world. In Walter's boyhood, his family—it was just himself and his parents and one brother sixteen months older to whom he would never really be close—moved something like nine times, in and around greater LA. At first, the family lived in rental apartments, and then in cheap little stucco bungalows without any shade, and finally in some substantial dwellings on modest lots. His folks would buy a fixer-upper, fix it up, apply for the next FHA home loan late at night at the kitchen table (it was his mother, Philippina "Bena" Houk, who was the brains of this operation), move to the new place in a slightly leafier neighborhood. The family's path of migration was generally westward, toward the ocean; and northerly, out toward the San Fernando Valley, for this is the way the city was growing in the thirties and forties. "I grew up with no sense of roots or extended family," Walter wrote once, in an unpublished memoir, which qualifies as an understatement. He said once, "I guess all that early dislocation is the reason I've never been a joiner—and pretty much of a loner."

Those nine relocations during Walter's growing up were *in* greater Los Angeles. But there were other uprootings—of a transcontinental kind. Before he was even five, Walter and his brother, Lawrence, had been transported by their parents from LA to Northern California (there was shipyard work for E.J. up there), back east to Akron (where their folks had started out their married life), and back once more across the country to the city of Walter's birth (where the new Goodyear Tire and Rubber plant was promising steady work for the family's breadwinner). That return to Southern California, on the eve of Walter's fifth birthday, in the late spring and early summer of 1930, was made in a Dodge sedan, green with black trim and a flat black roof that needed coating every now and then to keep it from springing leaks. The car had a push-out windshield, to allow a breeze to get in, and you could adjust the angle and degree of tilt to suit conditions. The windshield got secured on either side of the window posts with two clothespin-like hinges. Once, when he was looking at some photographs of *Pilar*—Hemingway was standing at the wheel in the cockpit with no shirt on and his stomach popped out and his hair looking quite greasy—Walter pointed at one of the popped-out windshield panels, secured with clothespin-like hinges at what looked like a 45-degree angle. "See, Papa's letting the breeze come in on his boat, just like we'd do with our old Dodge sedan, minus all the dirt and grime, when we were coming across America that time in 1930."

He began talking excitedly about that trip. There was a terrible heat wave. The Dodge broke down in Garden City, Kansas. The two-day forced stopover had allowed the family to take in the big Decoration Day parade, where firemen pitched toy whistles and candy bars at the kiddies from the tops of their hook-and-ladder trucks. When I got back to my room that night, I consulted my Hemingway chronologies, and, sure enough, it turns out that the Hemingway family, in the early summer of 1930, about five weeks behind the Houk family, had made its own heat-choked transcontinental motor trip. Only instead of aiming south by southwest, from Ohio to California, the Hemingways (Ernest, Pauline, Bumby) had gone north by northwest, from Piggott, Arkansas, to the Yellowstone country of Montana and Wyoming. And, as opposed to traveling in a Dodge with a leaky roof that had been purchased on the installment plan, the Hemingway trip was made in a Ford roadster that had been presented as a gift by Uncle Gus Pfeiffer two years before. En route to the mountains (it was his first trip to that country, which he'd make his own in one way or another for the rest of his life), Hemingway had written several perspiring letters about the infernal temperature of the plains. The Houks would have come through Kansas City just before the end of May. Hemingway and his family were in KC over the Fourth of July weekend—where they took in the big parade. Hemingway gave an interview to a reporter for his old paper. Not much of an interview, not much of a story—five paragraphs on page 3, no byline. "The novelist, who was a member of the editorial staff of The Star prior to the war, in which he was wounded while in the service of the Italian army, will leave tomorrow for Wyoming to continue work on his next novel, which will have bullfighting as its background," the story said. *Death in the Afternoon* wasn't a fiction, but maybe he'd said so, or the reporter had scribbled it wrong.

Scribbling and tromboning through Walter's history: In high school, he used to usher at the Hollywood Bowl, and so got to see—and hear— Rubinstein and Barbirolli and Rachmaninoff in the flesh. At Manual Arts High, he came under the spell of a literature teacher named Edna

Joy Addison. Miss Addison led him to Tolstoy and Dostoyevsky and T. S. Eliot and the Brontë sisters—not to Ernest Hemingway. In the fall of 1940, when Walter was an eleventh grader, with *For Whom the Bell Tolls* outselling every novel in the country, Miss Addison took a look and pronounced the book trash. (Too much sex in a sleeping bag.) The following year, Miss Addison, a Victorian spinster, took her favorite pupil down to the Olvera Street Market in Los Angeles where you could buy authentic Navajo and Mexican crafts. It was a one-on-one outing, lunch included, with the gloved Miss Addison piloting her black Buick with the dignity with which she controlled a classroom. She told Walter she just wanted him to have the experience of other cultures. That day his eye fell on a tiny sterling silver box with an ornately worked and hinged lid. It was about one inch by one inch. He said he wouldn't know to what use he'd ever put such a receptacle but that he loved the look of it. "Then you shall have it, you don't need to use it for anything, it can just *be*," Miss Addison said. It took Walter almost seven decades to find a practical use for this piece of saved art, whose silver is now tarnished but whose hinged lid still has a clean snap to it. Walter keeps the box in his left front pants pocket. Before he goes to bed, he puts into the box four large yellow pills, so that the next day he can swallow them, one at a time, with a glass of water, two before lunch, two before supper. They're a hedge against what he has been told by his doctors is no longer a general old-age "forgetfulness," but rather an advancing Alzheimer's disease. The four gelatinous, horse-choking yellow pills fit perfectly inside the Navajo jewel. "I haven't started putting the mail in the refrigerator or watering the plastic plants yet," he said one evening at dinner, in a deflecting shrug.

On nearly the day he turned seventeen, Walter graduated from high school (he had skipped a grade in elementary school), and a week later he was enrolled at UCLA. The war was on; everything was at double time. After six months, he joined Navy ROTC and soon became captain of about a five-hundred-man brigade. The midshipmen lived in a converted dorm and wore brass-buttoned uniforms and marched every morning to class. Attending class year-round, and excelling, Walter completed three years of academic work in less than two. He majored in the sciences, with a minor in art, bonding (just as he had with Miss Addison) with an internationally known abstract painter of patrician cast named Stanton Macdonald-Wright, who told Walter that he might have a future as an artist. (He was wrong.) On summer sailings, clad in navy dungarees, the science-cum-art student learned steering, sextant-reading, knot-tying, deck-swabbing, watch-standing. The pull of the sea had always felt magnetic to him. As for the pull of Ernest Hemingway, not so magnetic. He read *A Farewell to Arms* and a few of the short stories, and thought them okay, but, clearly, Miss Addison's shadow was lingering. "I can hardly believe it now," Walter once said, "but I'd never heard of *The Sun Also Rises* when I was in college—and I was a pretty damn literate fellow. I'd read *Ulysses* and a whole lot else. How did I miss *The Sun*?"

The literate fellow, athletic, with his shock of dark hair, not quite nineteen, on the short side, but with a way of projecting both confidence and jauntiness, decided to take the national examinations for an appointment to the United States Naval Academy. He won one of the ten seats. Essentially he'd be starting college all over again, which was fine by him, since he loved learning and wasn't especially keen to go to war. He left Union Station for the East Coast on the *City of Los Angeles* on the day before D-day, June 5, 1944.

Annapolis now. An even larger gaining of cockiness. "The academy conditions you to think that way about yourself," Walter told me once. For the first time in his life, he's older than his peer group. He's a two-pack-a-day man now—Chesterfields, "short and mean," as he likes to say. He likes to roll his sleeves up well past his elbows. He's thinking of taking up a cigarette holder to combat the tar in nicotine. His mates have nicknamed him Vladimir. Vladimir barely goes anywhere without his gunmetal-gray Zippo lighter, which he can flick into fire on the first try. Walter's is the last of the academy's sped-up, three-year wartime classes—he and his mates of 1948A (the *A* stands for "accelerated," and they will finish in June 1947) have to cram it all in. Summers are given over to a short leave home and then six weeks of classes and six weeks of cruises. One summer, he's out on the *Savannah*, a light cruiser with six-inch guns; the next summer, he's a gun captain on the *North Carolina*, a big battleship from the recent war, whose artillery pieces had bombarded Iwo Jima to soften up the dug-in Japanese before the marines got there. Walter gets to see the Panama Canal Zone and Cap Haitien and Guantánamo Bay, where he marvels at the idea of cactus and desert on a Caribbean island.

In that final year at the academy, Christmas 1946, forgoing a holiday at home (it would have meant three days each way by rail), the loner decided to seek the tropics, or at least the subtropics. He rode the Seaboard Air Line Railroad to Miami, thumbed down to Key West on the Overseas Highway. (Even though the war was over, if you were in uniform, you were golden for a ride.) He wasn't Arnold Samuelson on the rackety top of a sooty freight, but the freedom he felt—not to say the sight of an almost surfless green and blue sea on either side of him that looked so unlike his California ocean—was exhilarating. He got to the bottom of the Keys about three days before Christmas, took a room on the third floor of La Concha Hotel (Max Perkins used to stay there when he came to see his star author), made some pencil sketches of the view out his window (one, dated December 23, 1946, is hanging in the small room in Woodland Hills where Nita spent her last days), sat on the docks, slipped into a bar or two, made entries in his journal, talked to no one. He didn't ride the elevator down to the lobby, walk out onto Duval Street, go to the corner, go one block, turn left onto Whitehead, and then proceed four blocks down the street to number 907—that might have taken all of five minutes. He wasn't even aware Ernest Hemingway had once bestrode this town.

And the bestrider himself? He'd just gotten home from New York. Hemingway and Mary had trained down to Miami and then caught a Pan Am DC-3 over to Havana's Rancho Boyeros Airport in the same time frame that Walter was training and hitching to Key West—so paths had been vaguely crisscrossing again. The Hemingways arrived in Cuba on the twenty-third ("Got in here today," he began a typed letter to Buck Lanham), the head of the house having recently made a boor and inebriated bully of himself at the Stork Club—twice. (Both occasions involved Ingrid Bergman, who'd been dining at a nearby table with a male companion. She'd played Maria in the 1943 movie of *For Whom the Bell Tolls*, and so the cameo-skinned beauty, who was appearing in a play in New York, in his mind belonged to him in proprietary ways, and so naturally he was compelled both times to begin tossing loud, insulting comments at her escorts.) He'd told the *New York Post Week-End Magazine* some silly lies, but also that he'd "like to write a good novel and ten or fifteen more short stories and not go to any more wars. I'd like to raise my kids." Perhaps he'd said the last part with momentary quiet in his voice.

In the spring of 1947, not long from graduation, Walter Houk, midshipman, did something on his nerve and impulse that would change his life: he requested permission to resign from the academy following graduation. He wished to renounce his commission and his anticipated assignment to a light cruiser named the *Pasadena* in the western Pacific in favor of directly entering the Foreign Service. He sat for the exams, passed in style, attended graduation with his mates (his academic ranking was number 75 out of a class of 500), sailed his white hat into the air, got a little time off, got commissioned to the Foreign Service, and went to Washington to study for six months at the Foreign Service Institute. The navy was behind him.

They sent him to Ecuador. He hated the fevered backwater. At the end of 1949, he was posted to Havana as third secretary. Instantly, things got better. He liked the coffee, the food, the women, the architecture, the music, the casinos, the nightclubs, the sunsets, the air of gangsterly intrigue. The embassy was right in the heart of the old city, bordering the Plaza de Armas. The embassy didn't have its own building, but rather it leased space in a building that housed an American importer of farm equipment. Walter got a good office with a good view, and eventually he'd get an even better one—with a shuddering air-conditioning box. Some months into the next year, he bought himself a snazzy car. That fall he took an apartment that opened out onto a terrace that looked out over the rooftops to the Gulf—he enjoyed coming home after work, with or without dames, to pour a drink and to watch the big pearly Cuban moon roll up over his railing. He got assigned to the desk of the agricultural attaché. Eventually he took weeklong trips to inspect rice crops at places like Santiago de Cuba, at the far eastern end of the island. Cuba is the seventeenth-largest island in the world—the "long green lizard," as a famous Cuban poet put it. It's really a vast archipelago, and the curving coastline of its main island—something close to eight hundred miles on an east–west axis—is washed by the Atlantic, the Caribbean, and the Gulf of Mexico. It's only an island, yes, but it feels like a whole nation, which it is. It's got the mountains, the seashore, big cities, villages stuck in colonial time. It's the "little" nation that's the "big" island that we have made this last half century into one of our larger Western Hemisphere myths, going back, at a minimum, to New Year's 1959, when Batista fled and the Bearded One, as his worshipers liked to call Fidel, came down out of the Sierra Maestra to ride like Jesus into Jerusalem on the tops of tanks and on the hoods of jeeps. In Walter's time, the not-yet myth of Cuba and the world was only a high-pitched, stringbeanish, rabble-rousing law student at the University of Havana, and then, following that, an agitating lawyer with his own scrabbling one-man practice in Havana.

The third secretary was in his post about ten months when he stopped by an embassy party one October night and was taken by a perky brunette standing in a group of male admirers. She was a typist and confidential secretary in army intelligence—those offices were housed in the embassy, on another floor. Her name was Nita Jensen, and she'd been born in

Tacoma, Washington, but raised in the Canal Zone, where her father had held various quasi-governmental jobs. She'd gone to business school and had then begun working in government herself—a way to see the world. She'd worked in Guatemala and Madrid (where she'd fallen headlong for the bullfights and had read *Death in the Afternoon* as a kind of Baedeker) and Washington, DC. There seemed something charmingly naive and deceptively sophisticated about her. If she didn't confide her age, she did confide that she was moonlighting, with the embassy's okay, at the home of the great Ernest Hemingway. "I'll take you out," she said, the sentence sort of turning Walter on. It was clear to Walter how deeply enamored she was of the old guy.

Old guy in California talking. He's got a liquid cough. Small, red, chapped, and blue-veined hands are riding the morning air. A lusty grin is easing up, making Walter Houk's eyes, not quite the color of the sea, seem brighter, younger. "I was interested because *she* was interested. If she wanted to take me out to the *finca*, that was fine. I didn't have that much invested in it. It's true I'd bought a copy of *Across the River* that fall—he lived right there in Havana. Why not? I liked the book."

December 14, 1950. The light was dimming. Out of the corner of his eye, the studly young government officer could see a wide, bulky vision in bagged-out khaki shorts and thatched sandals and with a deceptive lightness in his step coming toward him. The man was walking at a tilt, and on the balls of his feet, as if it were a half-conscious calf-strengthening exercise. He was carrying a clipboard. *My God, what bulk* was the first thought that entered Walter's head. Hemingway looked old enough to be somebody's grandfather. Walter saw a high center of mass culminating in a thick chest and shoulders that seemed twice as broad as his own.

Walter and Nita had been on the Hemingway premises for maybe forty-five minutes. Mary Hemingway had greeted them at the door. At first, the three had talked down by the pool and the tennis court. Mary, who hadn't met Walter till now, had been cool toward him; polite, but formally aloof. And yet it wouldn't be long, perhaps on the very next visit, that the *finca*'s mistress would draw Walter aside. "You know, young man, this almost never happens, my husband accepting another male in his home so readily. I don't quite know why it's happening here, but if I were you, I'd just go with it."

After some time by the pool, Mary had led Walter and Nita up to the main house. "My husband will be by shortly—he's been working late this afternoon," she said. She was pointing out flowers, talking about gardening and house projects. Nita knew all that Mary was saying, but had been trying to pay attention. In this year and a half of her part-time employment, Nita had learned to work around Mary's moods and envy and profanities. The two had established an uneasy peace, the more so now that Mary had stopped fearing Nita as any kind of romantic rival. They'd even been to town together on a few Saturday afternoons for shopping or the movies.

Before Walter could fully get him in profile, the vision coming toward him had seemed almost to bound up onto the west terrace. Maybe an hour before, the sun had broken through, after what had seemed like weeks of gray skies. The *finca* was now cast in a dusky glow. That sounds too hokey, but Walter noted this in his journal entry for December 14, 1950, and Havana newspapers of the day confirm it.

Hemingway extended that enormous hand. Across the bow and foam of six decades, Walter can still hear the first words. "Hello," he said, "my name's Hemingway." He said it softly, with shyness. The handshake turned out to be like that, too—solid, for sure, but with a surprising gentleness. He was looking directly at Walter, but even in the directness, there was something almost vulnerable.

"I think he was trying to put me at ease," Walter told me. "I think he was trying to say he wasn't assuming I had to know what he looked like, even if the whole world *did* know. I think he was trying to signal in some way that we were sort of equal here, man to man." Indeed, it almost sounds as if Hemingway had made up his mind to like Walter almost before Walter had a chance to open his mouth—something akin to the moment sixteen years before when a gawky, earnest boneyard just off the rails from Minnesota presented himself at 907 Whitehead Street. Had Hemingway done some reconnaissance on Walter? Was he embracing Walter because he so liked Walter's girl? But turn that thought around. Why wasn't Hemingway taking instant, vicious, proprietary *exception* to Nita Jensen's new beau? Walter: "This will sound egotistical, but he was an astute judge of character. That was his business, right? I was dumb enough, and not just that first time, to try not to be a phony."

From a journal entry: "Still handsome with a reddish complexion (erysipelas? probably booze), he speaks slowly, with an odd turn of phrase that commands attention. His sincerity and humanity are very real, and almost astonishing in view of the tone of some parts of his writing."

The conversation got on to cockfighting. Hemingway said he hadn't

figured out the morals of it, only that he liked it well enough, and was raising gamecocks himself. He said the moralizers should understand that the
birds are never made to fight and are not interfered with once they've been
put into the pit. "It's just in their blood to do it," he said. Might Walter like
to go with him sometime? Sure. (Was it some kind of test?)

Suddenly, Hemingway had turned, lightly taken Walter's arm, and said,
"C'mon, kid, I'll show you the joint."

A voice lifting, still astonished: "We left the women behind us."

Actually, the kid had already seen the joint, not that he was about to let
on. A month before—when he and Nita had been dating for only three or
four weeks—Nita had brought him out to the *finca* unannounced. But the
Hemingways had been down the stormy coast with their Italian house-
guests. Nita had asked the servants if it was okay to show Walter through
the house. He'd surveyed the paintings, the animal heads coming out of
the walls, the shelves of books, the typewriter sitting on a small Indian rug
on a high chest in a bedroom at the south end of the house, the stacks of
opened mail twined into packets on the double bed in that same room, the
bee swarm of phone numbers written in pencil on the wall on both sides of
the hand-crank phone in the pantry. (Walter had sealed the number in his
memory: Cotorro 17-3.) His eye, the trained naval eye, was fairly recording the place. Standing in the long living room, he'd counted seven doors
and arch openings leading directly to the other rooms, without hallways in
between. Architecturally, the entire house flowed from that sunny room.

And now he was getting a personal *finca* tour from the *finca*'s owner,
which included several minutes of standing before Miró's *The Farm*.

From a journal entry: "The Venetians . . . made a brief entrance and
vanished. She [Adriana] gracefully saluted me with a handshake, but the
glimpse was too fleeting to decide if she is beautiful or merely attractive."

"Are you sure you wouldn't like to borrow some books?" Hemingway
said as the couple was leaving. He was leaning in through the darkened car
window. That huge head.

"My boat," he said. "We'll be getting you out on *Pilar*." As it turned
out, this wasn't going to happen for seven more months. But there were
reasons, which you'll hear about in a moment. Meantime I have a theory:
Was there something in Hemingway right then, after all the recent beast-
liness, which longed to intersect with someone wholly new, whom he'd
perceived, in the usual heartbeats of recognition, to be a decent person, and
with whom he could make a fresh start at being his own good man again?
Could such a need have been operating in half-conscious ways? And if so,

wouldn't this desire speak in a fundamental way to the man he truly was, down deep, which he seemed to wish always to betray, sabotage? In the novel the critics had just savaged, the dying colonel asks himself: "[W]hy am I always a bastard and why can I not suspend this trade of arms, and be a kind and good man as I would have wished to be. I try always to be just, but I am brusque and I am brutal. . . . I should be a better man with less wild boar blood in the small time which remains. . . . God help me not to be bad." On the next page, the narrator writes: "He went out, walking as he had always walked, with a slightly exaggerated confidence, even when it was not needed, and, in his always renewed plan of being kind, decent and good. . . ."

That's fiction, of course.

For decades, a wonderfully humane writer and editor named William Maxwell worked at *The New Yorker*. Not long before he died (in 2000), in a piece called "Nearing Ninety," he wrote, "I have liked remembering almost as much as I have liked living." That's Walter Houk, too. It's true that he got to go out on Hemingway's boat only about half a dozen times in the two years he knew Hemingway. But somehow he seems to have sealed inside him every last square inch of not just *Pilar*, but of that entire, exotic, long-ago Hemingway-cum-Havana-cum-Nita dream. One shard of Cuban memory, whether nautical or emotional or geographical, will splinter off another, and this in a person claimed to be on the path to Alzheimer's.

He said once that the kitchen galley, belowdecks, directly opposite the head, had a metal sink and cupboards and dish racks and an ice-box and a *three-burner* enameled alcohol stove. (It did.) He was talking once about her length. *Pilar* was listed in the old Wheeler catalogs as a thirty-eight-footer—not *Pilar*, of course, but the stock model on which Hemingway put down his money when he went to Cropsey Avenue. Hemingway himself tended to speak of her as a thirty-eight-footer, but he was also known, especially in later years, to round her off at forty. "True enough on the thirty-eight," Walter said once, rifling for some papers in his basement. "Her waterline length was thirty-eight. But her overall length was thirty-nine. Thirty-nine and one inch, to be precise—so, hell, you might as well say forty. Her registered length was thirty-five feet. No, thirty-five feet, five inches, to be precise. That's what the certificate of admeasurement says." He explained that "admeasurement" was a nautical term for hull measurement. He located a piece of his own writing on the subject. It said: "[R]egistered length is an internal measurement calculated by measuring between 'perpendiculars,' as from the stem or forward perpendicular aft to the stern post or rudder post. It of course has to be shorter than a water-line or overall length." Yes, sometimes Walter can sound more than a little like a pedant and one-upper.

Studying *Pilar* photographs, he once said, "Do you know how Papa used to signal for Gregorio to take the wheel when he was on the topside and Gregorio was down below? He'd stamp three times with his feet through the floorboards. Big nautical secret."

Another time he was looking at a set of close-ups of the flying bridge. "What is this object?" he asked. He was pointing to something affixed to the horizontal rack just behind the wheel. The object was covered with a rubbery-looking or maybe canvas-like hood. It was tied at its neck with a cord. Extending down below the object was a handle with a knob on it. "We know he had a searchlight with a blinker device for Morse-code signaling—he'd used it at night on his wartime patrols off the north coast of the island. I should know what this thing is. I was on that bridge. Why is it covered? Well, that's easy. You cover anything you can cover at sea to keep it from corroding in the salt air. Anything metal will start to corrode. Brass will start to turn green. You're going to have me obsessing on this thing. We know *Pilar* had a compass. Course, it could also be a pelorus." The following week there came in the mail a lengthy explanation of a pelorus, something about circular horizontal rings and 360-degree markings and the "intersection of two lines to two different landmarks whose position is known from a nautical chart." But he'd decided the object was a searchlight, after all.

Another time we were looking at a set of photographs that I'd brought with me from the JFK Presidential Library. He fixed on *Pilar*'s bow. "Mmmm," he said. "He's under way with the fenders out. That's not good. It says that not everything's shipshape." I had just walked back down the hall from the bathroom, where there was a cube of unused soap in a meticulous soap dish, and beside it a row of three perfectly folded hand towels.

Once, gazing at the photograph that begins this chapter, Walter began labeling parts of the boat with his No. 2 pencil. He drew a line with an arrow to himself and wrote, printing the words, "I am standing at the after end of the 'sedan.'" (Why didn't he just write "stern"?) He said, "This would have been August 26, 1951. A Sunday. I know because Nita was away, up in the States, on home leave, with her folks in Baltimore. On Monday,

I wrote her a letter and told her to hurry back and described the outing the day before. That's Mary and Felipe in *Tin Kid*. We didn't catch any fish. Actually, our main goal was to get some good photographs for an article Mary was writing for a magazine." He talked about *Tin Kid*, Mary's sweet little twenty-foot launch, crafted from Cuban cedar, a gift from Papa. She was meant for local cruising, in and around Havana Harbor, although *Tin Kid* had been up as far as the lower Bahamas, in convoy with the big sister in whose wake she's bouncing in this picture. Her open cockpit was five by seven. Walter said that Felipe was a *joven* from Cojimar. Hemingway didn't like him much, but he was good at his job, which was to pilot *Tin Kid*. Walter said that in Cuba *joven* tended to be reserved for someone still a little green. Suddenly, as if standing up from a slice of emulsion, Walter said, "Wait here." He came back with a copy of his two-page letter to Nita. (It was a carbon copy.) Typed at the top was "La Habana, August 27, 1951." In the last paragraph, smitten, six months away from proposing matrimony, he had written: "I'll be there with bells on Sunday, in lieu of a brass band." It was signed, "Love, Walt."

It's inarguable that right at the moment when Walter Houk was being led—literally—by the arm into Hemingway's home and life, Hemingway had begun one of his most prolific writing streaks ever. It was the last great writing streak. As biographer Michael Reynolds has succinctly written: "Fifty-one years old, sicker than most knew, and eleven years without a successful novel, Ernest Hemingway seemed to have reached the end of his career." Except he hadn't. The Manhattan angleworms had written him off, said he was through, but what did they ever know? What they didn't know in this case is that in the final three weeks of December 1950, and for five months into 1951, the written-off man could hardly be halted. It was almost as if he'd reverted to that seeming autodidact of twenty-five years before, back from the bulls, writing out of his head on *The Sun*. By Christmas Eve (two weeks after Hemingway and Walter had met, and not quite four months since *Across the River*), Hemingway "finished" what he was then calling "The Sea When Absent," which was one part of his big Sea novel, which, in turn, was one leg of the never-to-be-completed trilogy about the Land, Sea, and Air. "The Sea When Absent" is what we today know as the middle "Cuba" section of *Islands in the Stream*. Scholars have determined that he probably began working on what became "Cuba" in the summer of 1948; that he had shelved the pages; that he had taken them up again in the summer of 1950 (in those flashing-outward, baiting weeks before *Across the River*); and that now, with many friends and family filling up the house for Christmas, and after twenty-one straight days of work, he'd brought the manuscript to its satisfactory end. It wasn't satisfactory. "The Sea When Absent," along with other parts, would go into a bank vault, or at least a microfilm copy, there to remain for the rest of a downward-sloping life. The author of the manuscript knew in his bones it wasn't ready.

In the first week of January 1951, after the noise from the holidays had subsided (Walter and Nita had been a minor part of the noise), Hemingway sat down in a relatively empty house on cool mornings and began his apparently simple, declarative story about a boy and a fish and an old man. He'd been saving himself, fearing himself, to write this story since about 1935. The title long in his mind was "The Sea in Being." "It's about an old man and a fish. . . . But it is about everything in the world that I know," he said in a letter on January 17, after he'd been at it for about eleven days. He had six thousand words down, almost a quarter of the whole. Thirty-one days later, on February 17, he finished the first draft of what we know as *The Old Man and the Sea*. On February 6, in the middle of the torrent, he'd said in a letter that he had put down never less than a thousand words a day for sixteen days running—except twice.

Sixteen days after finishing the Santiago story, on March 5, he began, apparently from scratch, what became the final section of *Islands*. It's the part we know as "At Sea." (His working title was "The Sea Chase.") It was the story of Thomas Hudson's pursuit of the crew of a sunken German sub, and of the painter's own death in the process on the deck of his converted fishing cruiser as he listens to the "lovely throb" of her engines against his shoulder blades. On the starting day itself, he managed 1,578 words. Two and a half months later, on May 18, the story was done (not really). In the middle of the stretch, he had told Charlie Scribner that he was eating three rye crisps for breakfast, a couple of carrots, radishes, green onions. For lunch it was a peanut butter sandwich or nothing. "Will swim fifty laps in the pool so that I'll sleep good and hit the book tomorrow. I'll still go over 5000 for the week," he said. He didn't mail that letter for another day, which allowed him to do a count and put in a postscript: 5,267 words. This was in early April, and he was taking a day off. "My God it is fun not to be working for a day. I love to write. But it can be really tough too," he said, like that boy in Paris writing to Miss Stein about a new fish story and, gee, isn't writing such hard work, though?

The commonly held view is that the writing frenzy had come about because of the presence of the green-eyed Italian girl who'd been living beneath his roof. (Actually, Adriana Ivancich and her mother slept in the little guesthouse down the drive from the main house.) As Carlos Baker put it, "He was neither the first nor the last of the romantics to elevate a pretty girl to the status of a muse while managing to remain in love with his wife." In *Papa*, Gregory Hemingway, who was at the *finca* for the Christmas holidays in 1950, quotes his father as telling him: "God, I feel strong and I don't think I even need to sleep, but Adriana is so lovely to dream of, and when I wake I'm stronger than the day before and the words pour out of me. They come so fast I can't keep up with them and I don't want to stop, but force myself to, after five hours, because I know I must be getting tired. . . . But the juices are flowing again, pal. No, not the seminal juices, you lecherous little bastard." A few months later, in a letter to Adriana (it's undated but he probably wrote it in late March), Hemingway alluded to the muse idea. By then Adriana and her mother were back in Italy. "Please give your mother my love and tell her how happy I was when we were a family here. We had the problems of a family and all the small worthless quarrels of a family which no family ever was without. . . . I was always happier while you and she were here than I have ever been. . . . Why aren't you here now to come in with your shining loveliness when it is such a beautiful day?"

The effect of Adriana cannot be discounted. But is it also possible to imagine him just flipping the bird at the world once more?

Walter: "He'd talk of his work a bit when we were there for dinner in those first months, and we were there a fair amount. It was kind of in code. I knew he was elated. I guess I thought this is how things are around here all the time—lots and lots of work getting done. I had no understanding of his psychic ups and downs, not then. But I'm convinced this is why it took so long for me to get out on the boat—he was too consumed and then exhausted afterward. He wanted it to happen, but couldn't find the time."

Once, early on, at a lunch or a dinner, Hemingway said something about the "C" section of a three-part overarching work, or at least this is what Walter thought he said. "You mean, like A-B-C?" he asked. Hemingway laughed. No, like "sea, as in S-E-A."

On another visit, Walter said he'd been on subs in his academy days. Suddenly, Hemingway was leaning across the table and asking questions about layout, equipment, procedures during drills. He would have been at work then on "A Sea Chase."

Could Walter have been just the beneficiary of a soaring mood? Did the relationship flint-spark into being because his timing was so unwittingly good? While there must be some truth in that thought, it can't possibly be all of it.

Because in this same belle epoque of supposed new good feeling toward mankind, Hemingway was writing some of the vilest letters of his life. The same day that Hemingway had started "The Sea Chase" and had gotten down his 1,578 words, he typed a letter to Charlie Scribner. Recently, his publisher had mailed him the new Scribner's war novel, *From Here to Eternity*, by James Jones, thinking he might like it and be enough outside himself to pass along a good word for a new kid on the literary block. Jones, a late discovery of Max Perkins's, was another small-town Illinois boy, son of a medical man. How unthinking of Charlie Scribner.

> About the James [Jones] book . . . It is not great no matter what they tell you. . . . To me he is an enormously skillful fuck-up and his book will do great damage to our country. Probably I should re-read it again to give you a truer answer. But I do not have to eat an entire bowl of scabs to know they are scabs; nor suck a boil to know it is a boil; nor swim through a river of snot to know it is snot. I hope he kills himself as soon as it does not damage his or your sales. If you give him a literary tea you might ask him to drain a bucket of snot and then suck the puss out of a dead nigger's ear. . . . How did they ever get a picture of a wide-eyed jerk (un-damaged ears) to look that screaming tough. I am glad he makes you money and I would never laugh him off. I would just give him a bigger bucket of the snot detail. He has the psycho's urge to kill himself and he will do it. Make all the money you can out of him as quickly as you can and hold out enough for Christian Burial. Wouldn't have brought him up if you hadn't asked me. Now I feel as unclean as when I read his fuck-off book. It has all the charm and trueness of the real and imitation fuck-off.

He signed it, "Mary sends her love to you and to Vera. Best always, Ernest."

On the day I handed this letter to Walter, he was wearing a V-neck cotton sweater, khakis, denim shirt, sneakers, thin-stemmed stylish glasses—an old man clad like a hip, athletic young man. He doesn't weigh 140 pounds now. He was sitting in near darkness in his usual chair. He'd never known of the letter. He coughed a couple times, nodded slowly, kept reading, didn't speak, handed it back.*

Nita had been working for Hemingway for about ten days. She'd been nervous enough, on that first night they'd met (he'd insisted she stay to supper), to blurt, after one or two glasses of wine, that she'd always had a secret desire to be a blond. "Well, I can help you with that, daughter," he'd said. Next thing Nita knew, Mary Hemingway had shown up at the embassy to tell her that things were all set for the following Wednesday. She rode the bus out from town that day, and Papa greeted her at the door and led her to the bathroom. He sat her on a stool and draped her in towels and sheets. Mary was close by. So was a Cuban beautician named Lili who regularly worked on Mary's nails and hair and who'd come out from town especially for this. He told her to relax. He said he'd had personal training in hair-blonding from the folks at Alberto Culver VO-5 in Los Angeles, when he and his ex-wife, Martha, were on their way to China in 1941. He was standing over her, working from behind. She could feel the stuff, cool and gelatinous-seeming, seeping in. It felt like soapsuds, but thicker. He told her the job would take a little while, so she should just sit there, he'd

*For two months, Hemingway couldn't get rat-faced James Jones out of his spleen. On April 11, to Scribner (it's the letter in which he's telling of his breakfast of rye crisps and of how enjoyable it is to take a day off), he says, "All I hope is that you can make all the money in the world out of him before he takes that over-dose of sleeping pills or whatever other exit he elects or is forced into. In the meantime I wish him no luck at all and hope he goes out and hangs himself as soon as plausible." Next paragraph: "All this written by a boy who resolved to be a good Christian all day today anyway before biteing on the nail tomorrow." Nine days earlier, Walter and Nita have been out to the *finca* for a swim. "Black Dog lay nobly and serenely at his master's feet," Walter records in his diary. "The afternoon was calm. We left with an armful of books." Six weeks later, May 18, 1951: Hemingway is boiling again. Just yesterday, he's completed *A Sea Chase* and so has laid in a couple of big steaks to celebrate. He's typing letters this afternoon with his usual jumpy spaces. On his desk is a letter from Scribner accusing him of "malice." Look, Charlie, he writes, very sorry I got you so angry. I get exhausted after a day's work. No malice against the Jones boy. When's it okay not to bet on another horse? Three paragraphs down: "Malice is a rough word to use in a letter." It's as if that word has lit the fuse: "Max was Max with five daughters and an idiot wife. Tom Wolfe was a one book boy and a glandular giant with the brains and the guts of three mice. Scott was a rummy and a liar and dishonest about money." He postscripts twice in pencil: "Please don't be offended by any of this and remember I am writing from fondness. Glass OK. with usual pm decline. Hurricane seems to be petering out."

be back shortly. He said, "I think I better warn you, daughter, that sometimes these first bleach jobs turn out to be . . . orange."

Nita's hair didn't come out orange at all. "Oh, daughter," he said, "it's beautiful, look at yourself." She stayed to dinner and rode the bus happily back to her boardinghouse and walked in the door to hear her roommate scream.

A week or so later, again at supper, Hemingway said she should complete her new look and have her hair sheared off like a boy's. No worries, he had shaped his wife's brown hair into its fine boy-blondness. Mary was away from the *finca* that night. Again he led Nita to the master bathroom, sat her on the stool, began to scissor it off in clumps.

I remember the first time this story came up between Walter and me. We were looking at a family photo album. I was new in my visits to Woodland Hills. Walter turned the page, and there was his late wife out on *Pilar,* in the fighting chair, turning toward the camera, wearing a plaid blouse and a huge smile, with her wrinkly shorts hiked up her raised thigh. She was so young and attractive. Even in monochrome, you could tell how blond her hair was. It looked almost white. It was a helmet of hair, with the sides cut very short, streaked-looking, wind-blown, limp from the salt air. The caption said: "On board Pilar—after I caught my first fish. Summer 1949."

Walter said, not exactly in a rush, and in a voice I hadn't quite heard before, "And that's Nita. With bleached hair. Papa dyed it. Then he cut it. I didn't know her yet. It stayed that way until family members saw it when she was home on a visit and didn't approve and then she got rid of it and let it grow out."

A day later, he supplied additional details, warily. I kept nudging. He shrugged, and there was irritation in it. The shrug was saying: *It's somebody else's problem. I don't have to worry about it. It doesn't concern me.* In the years I've known Walter, I've come fully to know this shrug, and the small silences that follow. There's a line I know I can't cross.

Still, it seems impossible there wasn't some kind of deep erotic gratification playing out in the fingers and mind of the man standing behind his new secretarial daughter and kneading and massaging in the bleaching formula. You can't read Ernest Hemingway even half-seriously without becoming aware of his fixation with hair. Scholarly forests have been clear-cut in the service of explaining his so-called fetishes, but most especially his hair fetish. In *A Farewell to Arms,* Hemingway wrote: "Catherine was still in the hair-dresser's shop. The woman was waving her hair. I sat in the little booth and watched. It was exciting to watch and Catherine smiled and talked to me and my voice was a little thick from being excited." (Relatively speaking, that lustrous novel is full of hair fetishism.) In the story "The Last Good Country," a little sister, who has always wanted to be a boy, and who has run away to the woods with her hero-brother, has taken off her hair in clumps. Her brother is getting their supper in the trout stream. When Nickie comes up to the lean-to, Littless is lying on her side. "Do I look like a boy?" she asks. "It's very exciting," she says. "Now I'm your sister but I'm a boy, too. Do you think it will change me into a boy?" In *The Garden of Eden*—the novel the psychobabblers fairly salivate over, without stopping to ponder what kind of courage, literary and otherwise, it must have taken for someone to attempt such a book in the first place, knowing that one day, when he wasn't around, it would get so dissected—the narrator says early in the story: "Her hair was cropped as short as a boy's. It was cut with no compromises. It was brushed back, heavy as always, but the sides were cut short and the ears that grew close to her head were clear and the tawny line of her hair was cropped close to her head and smooth and sweeping back." Catherine Bourne has just been to a hairdresser and is now showing her husband what she's secretly done. "You see," she says to David, "That's the surprise. I'm a girl. But now I'm a boy too and I can do anything and anything and anything." That night, in bed, something very strange and vague and apparently role-changing happens between these honeymooners, who've come down on the train from Paris with their bicycles and are now in the seaside village of le Grau du Roi. The strange "changing" thing happens again, several nights later. After, Catherine whispers, "Now we have done it. Now we really have done it," and her husband thinks to himself, yes, "Now we have really done it." But what exactly *has* this deeply tanned couple—who'll soon be getting twin haircuts and dying their hair to the same whiteness and dressing in their lookalike peasant fisherman shirts and linen trousers and espadrilles—done? Again, forests have been slain to "answer" that question.

In real life, in 1947, in a period of extraordinary stress, here's something that novel's creator did: he took a bottle of shampooing dye and turned his hair red. He did it sometime during the night of May 13–14. His wife was in the States, tending to her infirm father. He started on a "test piece" of his scalp, went for the whole head. "So I thought, what the hell. I'll make it really red for my kitten, and left on 45 minutes . . . and naturally in the morning I was spooked shitless—and then thought what the hell." This is from a letter to Mary Hemingway in the daylight of May 14. Hemingway told the startled servants he'd mistakenly used an old bottle of Miss Martha's shampoo. But the letter gives the lie.*

In the late summer of 1949, wondering how she might give the lie to her family, Nita Jensen was about to go on home leave. Her part-time employer, for whom she'd been working for roughly three months, convinced her she needed a retouching. But this time the blonding came out ghastly. She felt like a floozy. At home her sister introduced her as Harpo Marx. Her mother came crying into her bedroom to beg her to go back to what she was. She went to a Baltimore hairdresser, who tried to make her hair brown again, but that only made things worse. Meantime, she got a letter from Cuba. "Don't let anybody bluff you out of what colour your hair is," Hemingway said. Outdoing himself with his quirky spelling, he said that "my eye-seight having been blinded at an early and late age by looking at Miss Mary, Miss Marlene and Miss Ingrid," but he was still pretty sure, "through my astygmatic, bi-focallism that you look lovely." When she got back, her hair was in three colors. She began to let it grow out and to return to its natural color, although that took some months and plenty of jokes around the office. Hemingway allowed—just once—that he was disappointed she'd been talked out of her boy-blondness. The subject never came up again.

A seduction try: It happened after Nita had been taking his dictation and typing his letters for perhaps a month (before that trip home to Maryland). Mary had seemed to grow testy around her. At lunch Hemingway said, "I have an idea. We'll go out on the boat this afternoon and work from there. We'll take a pile of mail." Great, Nita said, turning to Mary to ask, "What time will we leave?" Mary said, "I'm not going." Hemingway seemed in a hurry to finish his food. Nita felt growing panic. Juan drove them to the waterfront. Gregorio was waiting at the boat. Hemingway steered out of the harbor. He stamped his foot three times so that Gregorio, up top, would know to take over. Hemingway came over and

---

*Re the stress: Patrick Hemingway, eighteen, had suffered an undiagnosed concussion in a car crash in Key West (Gigi was driving), and shortly after, on a visit to Cuba, he complained of headaches and went into deliriums and turned violent. He was given shock treatments. For a month, his father slept on a mat in the hall outside his room. Others, including Pauline, over from Key West, helped with the nursing, too, but Hemingway, assuming charge, took most of the midnight-to-dawn shifts. For something like forty-six days, Patrick had to be fed rectally. Hemingway said he averaged two hours sleep in twenty-four. His blood pressure spiked. To escape, he drank—and red-coppered his hair.

sat down beside her on the wide padded cushion on the starboard side. From her purse she took out her steno pad and fountain pen. "Daughter, I have a better idea," he said. "Why don't we just enjoy the Stream?" He moved in closer. Silence. His voice was gentle. "Daughter, has anyone ever made really good love to you?" She felt herself trembling. "I don't know, Papa," she said. Neither spoke. After a little while, Hemingway got up and stamped three times and took the lower wheel and turned the boat around. They were back at the *finca* in about an hour.

Only when Walter's wife was becoming an invalid, in the late 1980s, did Walter learn this story. "Isn't the Catholic Church set up for sinners, not saints?" he said once. "That's my assessment. If anything, he grew more protective of her, paternal. To me it's all pretty much in character—both the trying and the not holding a grudge." He said he was almost certain that Mary was testy with Nita before the try because Hemingway had told his wife he wanted Nita, and intended to try, and Mary could like it or lump it. When they arrived back at the *finca* so soon, Mary knew Nita had passed a test. "Nita wasn't inexperienced sexually," Walter said. "But she wouldn't try that, for many reasons. He was 'Papa.' To her, Papa was old." The seduction try never came up again.

The shark story. Nita has known him for not quite a year. "Beautiful Nita, my Secretary" is the way he has just described her in a letter typed by his own hand. He and his wife and Nita are out on *Pilar* today and have come into a cove for lunch and a swim and a siesta. Nita gets up and dives off the stern and swims to shore. She sees a dark shadow in the green shallows and screams. Hemingway, stretched out on his daybed with a book, jumps up, tears off his shirt and glasses. He puts his hunting knife between his teeth. He reaches Nita, places himself between her and the shadow, and together they swim very fast back to *Pilar*. Gregorio is on the bow with one of the rifles. But the shark has already finned away. "Nothing nasty he ever could have done or said to his wife in Nita's presence could have bothered her after that," Walter told me once. It wasn't long afterward that Nita witnessed a fight on *Pilar* between Hemingway and his wife. Mary was throwing plates and screaming, Hemingway ducking and cursing back. Nita hid this story from Walter for years. "She needn't have," he said.

On Sunday evening, August 24, 1952, with most of their belongings already packed, Walter and Nita, married for four months, drove out to the *finca* to say good-bye. In nine days they'd be leaving for a new diplomatic assignment. In eight days, editors at *Life* would be putting into circulation more than five million copies of *The Old Man and the Sea*, having paid $40,000 for first serial rights to be able to publish the entire novella across twenty pages of their September 1 issue; the magazine would sell out almost instantly. That night, Hemingway gave the Houks one of his ten advance copies of the book—the box had just come from Scribner's. (The first printing of fifty thousand copies was going to sell out, too.) He wrote on the flyleaf, "To Nita and Walter, Wishing them good luck in Japan or wherever. Affectionately, Ernest Hemingway." Half a century onward, a California widower, living on Social Security and a small pension, would offer that book, and two inscribed others, for sale through Sotheby's auction house in New York. "It's okay," the widower would say. "You can't take it with you. Besides, my fixed income needs fixing." (The auction brought far less money than Walter had dreamed.)

Home that night, Nita went tearfully to sleep, while Walter, on the other side of the bed, angled the gooseneck lamp down low and read the story to its end. He cried.

They rode the Havana car ferry to Miami, drove northward to Maryland, visited family, turned west, headed across the country to Los Angeles to visit family again. They drove on to San Francisco, loaded the Buick onto the SS *President Wilson,* sailed for Honolulu, called on Hemingway's sister Ursula (fourteen years from her suicide), tossed leis into the water (so that they'd come back), continued on their thirteen-day sea voyage to Yokahama. From there they made their way by land to their new home in Tokyo.*

Walter's now the junior man in the political section of the American Embassy, a much larger operation than Havana's. It's not that he doesn't enjoy the work, or that he and his wife aren't stimulated by the Orient, but an old family gene of restlessness seems at work. Within a year their son, Paul, is born. Within another year, Walter, who's begun to wonder about the viability of a diplomatic career, and who's never quite gotten out of his system the itch to see if he can make it as a painter (there had been at least one show at a gallery in Havana, but it wasn't terribly successful, and the Hemingways had meant to attend that night, but didn't, and were very apologetic afterward), has convinced his wife he should resign from the

---

*In one of their steamer trunks was a book called *The Joy of Cooking,* a wedding present from the Hemingways the previous April. The inscription: "For Nita and Walter, hoping the new joy of cooking won't over-shadow the old. Love from Papa."

government and that they should head home. They land in Menlo Park, California. (Nita has family in Northern California.) Now Walter's in a rented detached garage with his oils. He has allowed himself a year to see if he can make this thing work. He holds a show at a department store, but there's little critical notice and fewer buyers. His semi-abstracts have boldness and a technical precision, and maybe that's the problem: it's as if a humanist is at war with a technocrat. His year is up. It's 1955. He needs a job. From a family friend, who's in personnel at *Sunset* magazine—the great bible of western living—he hears of an opening for a travel writer. *Sunset*'s headquarters are nearby. For the rest of his working life, he'll function as a West Coast journalist, for a long while as a salaried employee, later as a freelancer. He's an extremely meticulous journalist. The rage to get it right to the last comma of every fact must have something to do with the scientific side of his brain, but often, it must be said, this rage costs him any real storytelling emotion. In any case, in short order Walter is writing authoritative pieces about homes and homeowners. He becomes the magazine's building editor. He and his family relocate—from Menlo Park to Redwood City to an old farmhouse in a onetime prune-plum orchard. A second child, Tina, has joined the family.

After eight years at the magazine, and a proven record of productivity, Walter gets the okay from his bosses to transfer to the Los Angeles office. His parents, aging, are in Van Nuys, out in the Valley, and this has something to do with the urge to get south. Walter hears about a hillside house, three thousand square feet, across from a golf course, twenty-five miles from downtown LA. It has overhead radiant heat, lots of glass, soaring ceilings. It's not a custom design, rather a "builder home," sort of like a long-ago stock boat that came sliding off the banana-greased wooden ways at Coney Island Creek, and whose original proprietors have only recently given up the family's proud boating ghost.

Always something of an outdoorsman, Walter becomes a nature writer as well as an expert on western homes. No question his journalism helps raise a consciousness for preservation of Southern California's natural resources. Things go along—except they don't: In 1976, after he's been running the Los Angeles office for thirteen years and has been at *Sunset* for twenty-one years, he's fired. The loner had become openly disdainful of corporate politics and risen too high up on the pay scale.

He decides not to fight it legally. He has lots of contacts and in short order converts himself into a successful freelancer. He specializes in travel stories about Mexico and particularly about Baja California. He gets stand-

THE GALLANTRY OF AN AGING MACHINE

ing assignments with in-flight magazines, with *Travel-Holiday*, with *West-ways* (West Coast organ of the American Automobile Association). To Mexico alone, he makes something like sixty reporting trips. He turns himself into a good photographer. He becomes expert on the whale lagoons. He has to be his own bookkeeper. Constantly, he's pitching editors. He's his own travel agent. There are lengthy absences from home. The strains seem more or less manageable until Nita's health begins to decline. Her decline, starting in the mid-eighties, well after the kids have left the house, more or less coincides with the decline of Walter's career. In her great essay about New York City, "Goodbye to All That," Joan Didion writes about how it's impossible to lay one's finger "upon the moment it ended, can never cut through the ambiguities and second starts and broken resolves to the exact place on the page where the heroine is no longer as optimistic as she once was."

Editors stop calling, sources dry up, magazines change hands. Walter's brand of utterly trustworthy, fact-driven copy doesn't seem to be what editors want anymore. And Nita's decline? More or less the same slow attrition.

In the last two years of her life, when Walter's new job became that of tending her full-time, Nita was seeing six specialists in addition to her internist—almost weekly. Sarcoidosis in her lungs. Insulin-dependent diabetes. A failing heart. Then it was the liquid oxygen tanks standing in a corner of the living room with their long plastic tubes running along the baseboards into the sickroom.

And Ernest Hemingway? In those first few years after Havana, Walter and Nita would get cards at holidays with brief messages from both Hemingways. But Walter and Nita had their lives. They were raising their children. As the years passed, Nita also grew to feel very possessive of Papa—she'd been there first, hadn't she? Wasn't it her Papa truly cared about? Would Hemingway even remember him? Nita had never read many of Papa's books, nor did she need to. Walter, on the other hand, could now recite Hemingway passages by heart. But in a curious way, a husband and wife, in their loving marriage, found themselves nearly unable to talk about the man or even the country that had so touched their lives. To their kids, yes, they could talk about Hemingway and Cuba, but to them it was ancient history.

In 1964, three years after the suicide (Walter can't remember where he was when he got the news, only that he was shocked and yet somehow wasn't), Nita had gotten a letter from Professor Carlos Baker at Princeton. He was working on his Hemingway biography, and did she have any of Hemingway's correspondence? In a shoe box in the garage, Nita found three of her old steno notebooks. The pages were soft as lanolin, and the blue and black ink of her shorthand was very faded but she could read the words. She remembered how, in that first week or two, Papa's dictation had been pretty stilted. Then, stopping, he said, "Daughter, do you mind if I use four-letter words here?" After that, his letters loosened up considerably. She'd always worked sequentially through her notebooks, filling up the pages, one side at a time. She'd get to the end of the book, come back the other way. After she had transcribed a page, she'd draw a big X through the sheet. Here was a letter from October 1949 that she'd taken off the talk machine and put down first in shorthand. Papa was writing to an insurance agent regarding a mink coat he'd just bought for his wife. "Mrs. Hemingway wants to insure a mink coat which she has just purchased from Marshall Field & Co., natural wild mink, 43 inch length, with cuffs three pelts deep for $4,735.00 against all risk (sea, air and land) including theft, any form of damage, etc., good for all countries. The coat is at present in cold storage in a fur cold storage house here in Cuba." That was Papa, all right, with his beautiful detail. Did Nita know that Operation Mink Coat, as Hemingway called it, had come about as a makeup present to his wife for the terrible things he was saying to her in the spring and summer of '49 during the writing of *Across the River*? Mary had come back from Chicago in early October with the coat on her arm. Her husband met her at the airport with frozen daiquiris, and they had downed them in the backseat on the ride to the *finca*. But the reunion had fouled when Mary discovered that, in her absence, Hemingway had had his teenage whore, Xenophobia, out to the house about three times.

In that same shoebox in the garage, Nita had found an old, yellowed single sheet of white paper with Hemingway's signature on it in four forms—for her to use to sign letters if he wasn't available. There was "Mister Papa," "Ernest," "Ernest Hemingway," and "Ernie." She'd become a pretty skilled signer.

She had opened another box of her Cuba things that had survived all the years and moves, and there were some of her old letters to *him*. This one, for instance, typed on Papa's portable. It's February 26, 1950, and the Hemingways are abroad, and she's been helping to hold down the fort at the *finca*. He has sent her a list of questions, and she's answering them in numerical order: "We have had several good rains which have helped considerably. The garden is beautiful and all sorts of vegetables are on hand. The boat is completely rejuvenated and Gregorio told me several weeks ago that everything is in applie-pie order (I mean to say apple-pie)." Next page: "Papa, please don't forget to send Abercrombie & Fitch a check—they just sent another bill with a gentle reminder." And a month later, March 28, 1950, catching the travelers up on all the news, and adding a word about Papa's youngest son, who's been on a visit: "Will certainly miss Gigi when he leaves. He's a sweet boy and will have no trouble breaking a few female hearts."

That same year, 1964, when Nita had first heard from Professor Baker, she had also gotten a letter from Mary Hemingway, who was living at 27 East Sixty-fifth Street in New York. "We're letting Pilar rot away in Cuba because I know Papa couldn't bear the thought of anyone else being her 'commander,' " Mary had said.

In the late eighties, when it was clear that his wife was dying, Walter gently suggested they should try to produce a joint memoir of their time in Cuba, with Hemingway at the center. Nita nodded. Walter wrote the text, interpolating long Nita passages set off by quotation marks. In the way that she had found several of her old steno books, he rooted around and found some of his old Havana diaries. But the pages were badly disintegrating, so he retyped selected portions without editing or otherwise polishing them. The manuscript that emerged, from both memory and documents, was modest in size and titled "Havana and Hemingway: A Mid-Century Memoir." Walter sent it to a dozen publishers. He was dreaming of getting it into print before Nita died. Every publisher sent it back with notes to the effect of, we don't really do regional stuff, or, sorry, it's a little too narrow for our needs. I've read this manuscript, and what seems closer to the truth is that there just wasn't enough Hemingway dirt.

After Nita died, Walter tended to stay in more and more. He'd never joined clubs or attended churches. Widows and matchmaking friends of widows were calling up, but he wasn't interested. He liked going to the Saturday morning organic farmers' market down in Calabasas. Avoiding the freeways, he'd cruise at forty miles an hour in his spotless 1984 Honda Accord, which he otherwise kept in his locked and spotless garage. He took his walks. He obsessively cleaned the house. He organized his old travel slides. He created a rack by the front door where he lined up dozens of old *Sunsets* and in-flights with his pieces in them. More than once, giving fits to neighbors, he got up on his roof via a stepladder and started whacking away at tree branches with a pruner. From a neighbor, who tended to look after him, he got a cast-off Ping-Pong table and brought it to the basement and cut down the legs and spread out huge nautical maps. He wanted to begin charting Thomas Hudson's submarine pursuits in *Islands in the Stream*. With his exquisitely sharpened pencil, he'd bend over the maps for hours, with the deeply annotated text beside him. On the maps he'd enter his calculations: "Soundings in Fathoms. Soundings in Meters." This work eventually led to a nearly book-length manuscript, "A Sailor Looks at Hemingway's Islands," which got into academic print. Other manuscripts—about growing up in Los Angeles, for instance—got drafted and put into neat red binders with clear plastic covers. Walter didn't bother to send them out. He was writing these manuscripts for himself, or his children.

They came to visit, though not all that often. Who can ever know from the outside all the tensions that root up inside families as they seek to nourish and wound each other? The core explanation here seems to be that Paul Houk and Tina Houk feel they were emotionally deprived of a dad when they grew up. Walter was too involved with his career, and, in another way, with his spouse. There were and are other issues, too. All of it is sad, and none of it is nefarious. One night, on the way back from dinner, Walter said softly, almost from nowhere: "I'm inclined to say I wasn't very good at parenting. Nita was so much better. You don't get another chance at that. It's not coming back." After a while: "I just wasn't made for the twenty-first century."

In these widowed years, Walter had ventured out once to a Hemingway conference, in Colorado Springs. By chance he'd found himself seated at a dinner next to the editor of *North Dakota Quarterly*. It was as if Robert Lewis (that was the editor's name) understood completely about Walter. "Why don't you try contributing something to one of our special Hemingway issues?" he asked. This offer turned into the 1998 memoir piece, "On the Gulf Stream Aboard Hemingway's *Pilar*," the one I accidentally pulled down from a library shelf in Philadelphia six years after its publication. Several other *NDQ* pieces followed, including the long one about Hemingway's islands. In modest ways, Walter, the breathing witness, had begun to feel himself "drawn in," as he likes to say, to the scholarly Hemingway universe.

One afternoon Walter and I were on a walk in the neighborhood when we ran into a friendly girl from Cleveland with a big dog. Determined to check my hunches, I asked, "Did you know Walter was once an intimate of Ernest Hemingway?" I thought she was going to hyperventilate. "But, Walter, you never told me this!" she cried. Although he pretended otherwise, I think Walter was pleased.

On July 23, two days after Walter had been on *Pilar* for the first time, he wrote in his journal: "I climbed aboard Pilar Saturday (July 21) for the long-awaited fishing trip."

In the previous seventeen days, Walter and Nita had been guests at the *finca* three times—on two Sundays and on the Fourth of July. Those were lubricated times, punctuated by cooling swims in the pool, and by the boisterous mood of the head of the house, but they weren't anything like an outing on *Pilar*. The sailor-diplomat was just dying to be on *Pilar*. The day before he got his wish, Hemingway had written to Charlie Scribner. He'd been distinctly nonboisterous; mortality seemed the underlying note. He'd talked about the Sea book, and its various parts, semi-complete. (He still thought of it as a four-part story, with the Santiago tale a kind of coda to the whole.) He'd said he wanted Scribner to know what was in his publishing mind "in case of my death." Several paragraphs down: "My chances of living to complete the book are excellent according to my doctor. However, I have worked so hard in the last six months that I know I need a rest." It had been a searing July, with the temperature above ninety almost every day, and he now had a case of permanent prickly heat. At the end of the letter he'd spoken of not being able to "get away from the book." But he'd also noted that he'd been able to put 250 pounds of dolphin and kingfish into the Deepfreeze. In his postscript: "Tomorrow is my birthday and I am going fishing." He hadn't told Charlie of the two "kids" he was taking fishing.

It was relatively cool that Saturday morning as the small boating party, in a gently rolling sea, and with a line of thin cirrus clouds on the horizon, stood down the channel past the Morro Castle. Mary wasn't aboard—she was once again up in the States. Rains had come in the night before, sending sheets of fresh water across the top of the waves. The man at the wheel, who'd just made fifty-two, told Walter and Nita that he was going to take her out farther than usual, because that's where the fish would be. (They weren't.) Gregorio rigged the baits. Soon they were in deep blue water, with the drifts of sargasso coming by. Walter's words about that day, from that first piece in *North Dakota Quarterly:* "Out here and sufficient to ourselves, large questions of world destiny, high art or philosophy were less absorbing than the need to watch a squadron of flying fish planing above the water. Those in-transit butterflies flitting above the billowing surface, expending as much energy in vertical as in forward movement, fixed our attention."

As they were purring through the channel, with the Morro Castle in the background, Walter climbed up to the flying bridge with his Argus and asked Hemingway if he could make a picture—the one you've already seen. Walter's girlfriend was on the bridge, too, in a red-checkered sunsuit and a white tennis hat.

There were several swims in the turquoise cove at Santa María del Mar, where they lay at anchor for three hours, and that wonderful lunch of alligator pears and fresh fish washed down with wine and beer at the folded-down table in the shade of the cockpit, and the naps, and long periods of semi-wakefulness, and just gazing out over foamy blue hills of ocean with very little being said by anyone. At length, they pulled in the anchors and glided back toward "the wicked city," as Walter wrote in his diary entry. From that diary: "It hit with a bang that evening in the Floridita, when we were suddenly surrounded by mobs of people saluting him. A large part of the mob was Marita, Marchesa de San Felice, of the Italian Embassy, abandoned and wild. Quantities of champagne and caviar flowed—enough, in fact, that taken on top of the three double-sized daiquiris I had just had, I didn't stay to see the party over." Walter has a memory of Hemingway stumbling toward his station wagon, the Italian diplomat's wife on his arm.

The next day, Sunday, Hemingway rang up Walter very early at his apartment in Vedado. He was ready to go out on the boat again. Still hungover, Walter picked up Nita at her boardinghouse and drove to the waterfront. This time the Marchesa was on board and her presence more or less ruined the mood, at least for Walter.

Fifty-three years from that birthday weekend, on my second visit to Woodland Hills, Walter and I decided more or less on the spur to go on a picnic in a little park close to his home. At Gelson's Market on Mulholland Highway, we bought Santa Fe chicken sandwiches, which the clerk put into pre-molded plastic containers. Walter had brought a small cooler from home with Cokes in it. He'd packed carefully into a wicker picnic basket real silverware and glasses and cloth napkins. The park was very hot. Some kids off a school bus, on an outing, were making too much noise up on a hill. We looked for shade and, unable to find any, took a cement table in the middle of a brown field. We spread out our lunch. Nearby was a trash barrel being picked at by large green flies. Walter said he used to bring Nita here in her wheelchair. Mangy-looking squirrels came close; Walter eyed them in disgust. He fell quiet. We ate the sandwiches. We weren't dining on alligator pears on Ernest Hemingway's boat with a marlin leaping off the stern; no, we were at this ugly picnic table in this too-hot park in greater Los Angeles.

I said something about his need not to talk. "Well, I guess it's my way," he said, "or at least my way now. But it also comes out of the tradition of sailing ships—spending three months at sea, and you've said it all to your mate. And you save the talk for the tense moments of instruction—if a line breaks and you need a rope and have to act fast. It becomes a matter of luck almost. A superstition. That's how the connection is made. If you talk too much, you divert attention from other things that may need attention."

Suddenly, I said, with no idea I was going to say it: "Fuck all those critics who wouldn't accept him after 1930." I added quickly I was sorry for my profanity.

"It's a good Anglo-Saxon word. Why not?"

At length we packed up and went back to Gaona Street.

This was in 2004. I now know so much more about this proud, lonely old man, with his disposition to silences and emotional containment. The secrets have come out, or many of them. I've heard him talk of his regrets, most of which have to do with family. Not too long ago, as I write, I got an e-mail from Walter that made me sad. He said he could no longer afford to "overlook accumulating indications. Am trying not to make this just the old codger wailing gloom-and-doom for the next decade or so. Mortality just now seems not as fearsome as the scrambling of the mind. I think. I don't speak of this because no one knows how to respond except to say nonsense, you'll live to be 105 and I don't need that. Or pity."

Too many times, on visits to Walter's, I've found myself exclaiming, "You *knew* the man." And he'll shrug and say something like, "I arrived at my own conclusions. I didn't know about this Hemingway industry. I was a young man in Havana in love with a young woman and it just happened." He'll invariably add: "I know what I know."

On a recent visit, he talked about being depressed. He said he was afraid of what he might do at the end—"you know, breaking down or something." He said he'd begun to feel almost panicky.

"Do you ever think about suicide, Walter?" I wanted to stuff the words back in.

"Of course. Often there doesn't seem very much point to hanging

375

around. I've fantasized going out in one great burst—right through that plate glass behind you, after the tenth martini." The glass window and sliding door to which he was pointing led out onto the deck and to the live oak. He erupted into a laugh. "Don't worry, I don't think I would. Too much of a mess."

Three weeks before he took Walter for his first cruise on *Pilar*, Hemingway's mother died in Memphis at age seventy-nine. Grace Hemingway was an old, bewildered woman who'd lost her mind and was often found wandering around her daughter Sunny's house in the middle of the night. They'd stuck her in a convalescent home, and when the staff there could no longer abide her, she'd ended up for several weeks in the mental ward of a county hospital. Although Hemingway had paid the costs, and had arranged for the church bells in the village below his house to toll on the day of the burial, he'd not attended the funeral. In a letter at the end of August, Hemingway made an accounting of the amount of recent death and dying: his mother; his father-in-law's losing battle with prostate cancer; his first grandson (Bumby's child), dead five hours after delivery; four of the *finca*'s dogs poisoned by thieves; four cats lost or killed but in any case missing.

If July had been hot, August was hotter yet. Writing to Charlie Scribner on September 9, he talked of how there were just no damned fish in the Stream. It had to be the heat. Ordinarily he'd be out on the boat today, a Sunday, but, shit, why not stay home and save some gas and bait? Later in this letter, circling back to some of those who'd died, including Max Perkins, four years before: "But I have been so conditioned about it that I think of death now like a possible blow-out on a tire on a transcontinental motor trip. It is only something that has to be figured in."

A letter of September 19 to Scribner: "There have been no dolphin, albacore, small tuna or bonito. There are only the very big marlin now which, with the heat, are down deep and should be drifted for with boats about 80 and 100 fathoms down. I did this Sunday but caught nothing. Picked up about a 30 lb. wahoo trolling home when it was almost dark." Writing again to Charlie the next day, a watery reprieve: "Caught one 200 lb marlin just before it got dark. He was foul hooked near the vent and jumped very wildly (as who wouldn't). The leader finally caught around his tail and with a straight pull he ran off about 300 yards of line. I killed him in less than 15 minutes but when I had him on top of the water comeing into the boat with a big sea running a shark hit him." Toward the end of this typed letter of September 20, 1951: "The paper said this morning that the last three days were the hottest in the history of Cuba."

No fish to speak of. Unrelenting heat. Death at every turn. It was almost as if he understood by these omens what was coming, ten days hence, middle of a Los Angeles night, and of his own role in it, which he'd deny for the rest of his life.

That Idaho night, the trouting took place in a moonrise, on the Henrys Fork of the Snake, with the Centennial Mountains rising on one side and the Tetons on the far other and with lodgepole pines standing up on the near bank like spooky sixty-foot stalks of corn. Suddenly, after a 9:00 p.m. dinner, Ernest Hemingway's middle son said, "So why don't we go out?"

I remember how we walked single file, in our waders and fishing vests, down a silvered path, and how Patrick entered the stream so noiselessly. The water was very cold and up to our waists. Everything was so quiet, so absent of urban sounds. Patrick fished with a black graphite rod and a beautiful antique reel and a peach-colored line to which he had knotted a size 16 elk hair caddis dry fly. A No. 16 is tiny enough that three of them would sit handily on your thumbnail.

In the gathering dark of that mid-June 1987 evening, the water seemed to lie around us like glass. We stood about fifteen yards apart. Fat, pulpy rainbows began rising to our casts. You couldn't quite see them but you could hear them sipping and slurping and breaking the water. Patrick worked his rod like a wand, sending his line in great noiseless loops far out onto the stream. We fished for about an hour and barely spoke. But at one point, after he'd reeled in a particularly beautiful rainbow and held it at the surface of the water in one hand and had expertly removed the hook with his other hand and had then studied his prize for an instant more before delivering it back to the inkiness from which it had come, Patrick called over in the softest voice, "I love fishing after dusk. It's called fishing off the mirror."

Earlier that day, this same Hemingway son, about to turn fifty-nine, who had on fire-engine-red L.L.Bean suspenders and an Orvis fishing shirt and a big outdoorsy watch that kept slipping around on his wrist, had leaned across a booth in a crowded noontime café and said in a very warm voice able to be heard by everyone in the room:

"Killing. Now that's something I know quite a lot about, actually. Killing. Big-game hunting is very good training for war. I've never had any experiences in war. But I feel if I lived in a country that didn't have hunting, I'd be drawn irresistibly to be involved in a war. War is about organization and terrain and supply. So is hunting. I've shot many wild animals, and you wouldn't believe how many people have said to me in my life, 'But, Pat, you don't seem like the killing type.' Oh, no? Let me tell you a little story. I've seen packs of wild dogs in Africa literally killing an animal by biting it to death on the run. The animal is trying to escape and the dogs are taking out whole chunks of him, as they go. This seems truly horrible, being eaten alive while you're trying to get away. And yet these same canine fellows can be quite wonderful to each other in a different context. They can nurse each other, they can make their camp while one of their number is recuperating. Now, would you ever think that your little Fido eating his Alpo there on your kitchen floor—would you ever think he's capable of doing something like this? But he's descended from these boys, isn't he?"

The dirty, scary, toothsome Hemingway grin had come all the way up. "Well, I am descended directly from Ernest Hemingway."

The good and the affectionate and the just Patrick Hemingway, which is how his father fictionally described him in Islands in the Stream, said many startling and seemingly performance-based things before we'd gotten tired of talk and gone fishing.

A day and a half later, in Ketchum, I was with the eldest son, Jack. That encounter, too, had its soft and anything-but-soft moments. And then, on the fifth day of the trip, when I was still in Idaho, the phone in my room rang and there he was on the other end: Gigi. For more than two weeks, I'd been trying to reach him. I'd left many messages at numbers in Montana, Florida, New York City. They weren't his phone numbers, but the numbers of people who were said to know him and to be in sporadic touch.

He sounded very up. He said he was in Coconut Grove. He'd gotten my messages and was very sorry he hadn't been able to find the time to call back. "Lots of things going on," he said. I asked if I could come. "Of course you can come, I'd enjoy talking about it, you know, life with Papa and all that, by the way, how are Jack and Pat, you've already seen them, you say, I'll bet the weather's great up there in Idaho, isn't it, you'll find it's hot as Christ down here, are you sure you really want to come?" He had seemed to say this in about two breaths.

Within twenty minutes I had checked out of my hotel room and was driving very fast the four-plus hours it takes to get to Salt Lake City. I couldn't get on a flight to Florida until late the next morning. We didn't meet until after eight o'clock that evening. By then his mood had crashed. Everything seemed seeping toward gloom and depression. But even in the gloom and depression, I'd encounter flashes of the old famous Gigi charm. The one in the family who fell like Lucifer possessed an extremely likable and caring side, which, from everything I know, he managed to hold on to, right up to the end, in pod 377 of cell 3C2 of the Miami-Dade County Women's Detention Center, which came fourteen years after that night.

BRAVER THAN WE KNEW

Gigi, sitting watch on bow of *Pilar*,
Cayo Confites, Cuba, June 1943

I sometimes fantasy about what it would mean if a child . . . never had to disown his feelings in order to be loved. Suppose his parents were free to have and express their own unique feelings, which often would be different from his, and often different between themselves. I like to think of all the meanings that such an experience would have. It would mean that the child would grow up respecting himself as a unique person. It would mean that even when his behavior had to be thwarted, he could retain open "ownership" of his feelings. It would mean that his behavior would be a realistic balance, taking into account his own feelings and the known and open feelings of others. He would, I believe, be a responsible and self-directing individual, who would never need to conceal his feelings from himself, who would never need to live behind a façade. He would be relatively free of the maladjustments which cripple so many of us.

—CARL R. ROGERS, *On Becoming a Person*

A TV WAS ON in an upstairs room, flickering patches of silver against the stucco walls of the stairwell. A copy of *M* magazine ("How to Feel GREAT") was on the coffee table in the living room. So was a huge book of *Bartlett's Familiar Quotations,* opened in the middle and propped up like a missal at Mass. Spread out on the sofa was an old green flannel blanket, as if the physician, or former physician, had been trying to warm himself in the airless night. On the rug was a picture postcard, its face turned upward. Gregory Hancock Hemingway, MD, didn't pick up the card, just stepped over it.

Hanging down from the ceiling were some carved Haitian masks—scary as hell, the more so because it was so damned dark in the place.

"Let's go out back," he said. "Perhaps a breeze will come in tonight."

I was eyeing the masks. He laughed, a big, guttural, liquid laugh. Patrick's loud, high, and almost girlish laugh, and the way he'd stuck it in at weird moments, was still echoing. Of Gigi, Patrick had said, fairly breaking up: "The devils in him. There is something molten in him, demons roasting in fiery pits." Jack's laugh, by contrast, which had seemed to punctuate every other sentence, was chiefly about his nervousness. This laugh had its own disconcerting Hemingway quality—something sardonic, for sure.

"Something, aren't they?" he said. "They're not mine, of course, they belong to the people who own this house. I'm just staying with them. I stay with a lot of people. By the way, I went to Haiti once. I remember walking into a hospital there, the pediatrics unit, and seeing twenty babies convulsing. It was an awful sight. At birth their mothers had rubbed their cords in cow dung. And no neonatal tetanus. It's a ritual." It was as if the caregiver in him was repulsed, but the symbolist in him, the symbolist's son, was savoring the image.

He had on running shorts and sneakers and a white T-shirt with "Unicorn University" printed in orange on it. His stomach was heavy; the nails of his fingers were long and shiny. He had very muscular legs. His neck seemed hammered into his brawny shoulders. The huge, wide, dark eyes were sunk deep in the pouchy face. His hair was long and stringy, oily-looking. His stylish red-stem glasses were almost dainty. That morning, while I was flying to meet him, he'd broken off a tooth right at gum level.

All night he drank Scotch, just pouring it in over the top of the water and not even stirring it with his fingers. "I've had seven nervous breakdowns," he said at one point. Very low, almost as if he were trying to *whish-whish* it through the back of his mouth, in the way that a naturalist, son of a naturalist, might call to a shore bird: "I've tried so goddamn hard my whole life to get free of it."

Earlier: "Yes, I had the most talent, I was the brightest, I could do so many of the things he loved most." The statement hung. "I've been a doctor, that's something. I've written a little. That's something. And of course I guess you know that his father was a doctor, so a lot of people have drawn the point that I was only trying to please him."

He kept crossing and uncrossing his legs—ladylike. The shorts would ride up high. It was almost seductive. Once, he crossed his legs, took off his glasses, plowed his hand through his hair like an old torch singer, and sighed. "He got into everybody's unconscious with his symbols. That's part of what he's about, you know."

Just ahead of this: "Let's face it, any kid reaches a certain age where he wants to destroy his father and have his mother sexually. But this was impossible if you were a son of Ernest Hemingway. He was too large. I mean, on a basic psychological level, there was a time when you were just terrified of your old man because he was so much bigger than you were. In one sense, this never leaves you."

With almost no pause: "I've spent hundreds of thousands of dollars trying not to be a transvestite. It's a combination of things. The problems are twofold—no, they're threefold. First, you've got this father who's supermasculine, but who's somehow protesting it all the time, he's worried to death about it, never mind that he actually is very masculine, more masculine than anybody else around, in fact. But worried about it all the same—and therefore worried about his sons and their masculinity. Secondly, you start playing around with your mother's stockings one day when you're about four years old. Maybe it all starts with something as seemingly innocent as this. And why do you do this? Who knows? But it must have something to do with the fact that your mother doesn't seem to love you enough. Or that's your perception of it. Her maternal instincts just aren't very strong. . . . You think she loves your older brother Patrick more. So maybe you're putting on her clothes in the first place because you somehow think you'll be able to win her that way, get close to her. But then, you see, it starts to feel sexy for its own sake, just to have those things on. It's erotic, it arouses you. The third thing is your own heightened awareness to everything around you. You're a writer's son, after all. You take in a lot more." He had said it all slowly, with his head slung a little off to the side, the way a child will do when he's trying to puzzle out something.

His hand moved into a long, wrinkly, narrow white sack of French bread on the table in front of him. The hand seemed to hold inside the sack, and then began to probe it. It was as if he was examining beneath a sheet. The hand pulled off a large chunk of the bread, came out of the sack, and the image was gone. He popped the bread into his mouth.

"You know, he said to me one time, he was trying to help me, I knew it, no matter how it was killing him, he said, 'Listen, Mr. Gig, I can remember a long time ago seeing a girl on a street in Paris and wanting to go over and kiss her just because she had so much damn red lipstick caked on. I wanted to get that lipstick smeared all over my lips, just so I could see what that felt like.' The other thing about him—and, funny, with me too—is he really needed to be in love with a girl to bring about this unexplainable chemistry that could produce the words in the right combination, you know, the whole artesian outflow. Hell, I'd love to be in love with a woman right now. Maybe I could actually be a doctor again. There's been this one woman, lately. I can make out with her, all right, but the trouble is she's fat and I can't fall in love with her."

Later: "None of my mistakes were in medicine. All my mistakes were social."

Toward the end: "If I could only sleep well."

The laugh, stuttering from him: "Course I need a 'fixed address.' If only I had the goddamn 'fixed address.' "

His voice all the way back down: "I just can't concentrate like I used to."

Coming in close: "Everything finally comes home to roost, doesn't it?"

Saying it twice: "Not much malevolence, you see. But an absolute destruction."

He walked me to the front of the house. Suddenly, he seemed anxious. "Listen, there's no place for you to turn around here, you'll have to back out, and these maniacs come flying down this street after midnight trying to kill people. You get in and back out very slowly, I'm going to go halt the traffic." He broke into a trot. I rolled down the driver's-side window and started to creep out. In the rearview mirror I could make him out, the fireplug figure in the unicorn T-shirt and satiny running shorts, arms extended outward, like a traffic cop without a whistle. He was standing in the street yelling at headlights: "Slow down, slow down, goddamn it, slow down, I gotta guy pulling out here!" I backed into the street, threw the car into forward. He ran over and slapped at the doorpost. "You know where you're going, right, you go get a good sleep now, huh?"

There's a Hemingway letter from early 1936 that's extraordinary for its fatherly affections and momentary wisdom about family life. It was written when Gigi was newly four, so, yes, in the same time period when he'd first begun stealing to his mother's closet to put on her nylons—and allowing the tinglings from that to travel upward. By Gigi's testimony, he wasn't to get caught at what he was shamefully doing for about another five or six years. He said it happened when he was "nine or ten," on summer vacation in Cuba, when he and his brothers were visiting their father and his new wife—on whom all three Hemingway sons, though especially the younger two, had their large crushes. (It was almost as if Marty was their big sister and not their stepmother. Gellhorn was nine years younger than Hemingway and from the first had shone on all three boys, but especially the younger two, the beam of her loving attention.) He said his father just walked in on him, stood there frozen, with this look of horror and disgust, turned, and left the room. Who knows if it's true: Gigi could be a wild distorter and exaggerator and misrememberer and often bald liar about his own history. Wouldn't he have learned the trade at the master's knee? If it did happen that way, then the catching must have taken place in either the summer of 1941, when he was nine, going on ten, or in the summer of 1942, when he was ten, going on eleven. By then the dopey little guy with the pudgy fingers and rolls of baby fat (go back to that photograph of him on page 201, taken with his brothers and papa on the docks of Bimini in the summer of '35, when he was three and a half, with Pilar in the background) had grown into a mop-haired, freckle-faced, pug-nosed, Key West imp working hard on his altar-boy card, so that he could get up early during the school year and serve at daily Mass at Saint Mary Star of the Sea. Going into the fifth grade, the imp still stood barely four-foot-six.

My own belief is that it happened in June or July of 1941, his fourth-grade summer, for reasons I'll detail in the next chapter.

But this earlier Hemingway letter, with its transcendent note, written on a Sunday afternoon, up in the writing loft, two and a half months after Gigi had turned four. It's a long letter; Pilar and the sea are much in it. It was as if once he'd gotten going, in his bighearted way, the letter writer couldn't stop. (As he notes toward the end, he went on so long he missed the special Sunday afternoon airmail pickup.) Hemingway is writing to his mother-in-law, Gigi's maternal grandmother, Mary Pfeiffer, and his chief purpose is to thank her and her husband for their once-again generous Christmas gifts (a fat check and a bunch of new stocks). But soon enough the letter is getting off onto the letter-writer's kids, onto his loving and decent wife, onto all the family's amusing, mundane doings. It's as if a man, lately wounded, has awakened to what's important in this life, not the lusting after fame, but your own family.

Hemingway, of course, had been creamed that fall on *Green Hills of Africa*. Afterward, the sleeplessness and thoughts of suicide had come on hard. He wishes to say here they're passing off, but it isn't so. His night terrors will be with him through much of 1936, and indeed are now probably what a clinician would term chronic. In any case he doesn't nearly name them for the stark things they are, but rather codes and masks them to "Mother" Pfeiffer, whom he likes a lot, as his recent "spell."

"Had a spell when I was pretty gloomy, that was why I didn't write first, and didn't sleep for about three weeks," he says. "Took to getting up about two or so in the morning and going out to the little house to work. . . . Had never had the real old melancholia before and am glad to have had it so I know what people go through. It makes me more tolerant of what happened to my father."

As to the kids, and how they've unwittingly been rescuing him: "It is only in this last year that I have gotten any sort of understanding or feeling about how anyone can feel about their children or what they can mean to them."

He's been taking them out separately in the boat. The day before he had Pat out. "I was steering and saw him throwing up over the side and heard him, in the midst of it, shouting 'Papa! Papa!' I jumped to him to see what was the matter and he said, 'There's a sailfish jumping over there. I just saw him while I was throwing up!'" The Mouse-man, seven now, has even come up with a little ditty to fortify him against all his puking. It goes: "You put the chowder down. The stomach goes round and round hydeeho hydeehay and it comes out here."

And the Gig-man? This damn kid can do addition in his head up into the hundreds. He can multiply by fives and tens. "You will say to him 'What's 240 and 240 Jew?' and he will put his head on one side and say 'I think its about four hundred eighty.'" A few days before, when Mousie was in school, he had Gigi in the boat, "and there were some friends down here and we harpooned a porpoise and put the harpoon on a rod and reel so the porpoise was making a monkey out of the man who was trying to catch him and when we would shout suggestions to him in the bow Gregory would repeat these all and add new ones of his own."

The letter's date is January 26, 1936. In less than a year Hemingway was in adultery with Martha Gellhorn. As for the so-called spell of recent melancholia, this is what it was really like: "I felt that gigantic bloody emptiness and nothingness like couldn't fuck, fight write and was all for death," Hemingway said in a letter to Dos Passos, three weeks after the one I've been quoting. As for the cutest one in the family, who had a way of slinging his head off to the side when you posed him a riddlesome question, who could stand in the bow of his papa's boat and shout instructions like a good first mate, who may have already entered the thing from which there seemed no turning back, why, they'd recently given him this humongous birthday party in the backyard of 907 Whitehead. That was on November 12. There'd been pony rides and a hired clown and neighbor kids, both black and white, from up and down the street. Not least there'd been a four-layer cake with four candles on it that the Gigster had stood over and whoofed out nifty as you please.

IN SPITE OF EVERYTHING

Gigi, Havana, summer 1945

Doctors did things to you and then it was not your body any more.... The head was mine, but not to use, not to think with, only to remember and not too much remember.

—Ernest Hemingway, *A Farewell to Arms*

The 5 foot 7 inch, 189 pound body is white with an overall male body habitus and some female phenotypic features. The gray scalp hair is thin with anterior male pattern balding. The face has sparse mustache and beard stubble. The irides [*sic*] are brown. The corneas are clear. The conjunctivae are pale and free of petechial hemorrhages. The upper teeth are in good repair with porcelain restorations. The mandible is edentulous. The ears, nose and mouth have no abnormalities. The earlobes are pierced one time each. The neck is symmetrical and free of palpable masses. The torso is symmetrical and of normal configuration. There is slight female breast development, with the left breast larger than the right. The abdomen is flat. The back has a normal contour and the anus is without lesions. The external genitalia are phenotypically female with labia, urethra and vagina. The extremities are symmetric and the joints are not deformed. All digits are present. The fingernails are long and painted pink. The toenails are thick and painted pink. The skin is free of icterus.

> —The first paragraph of Gregory Hemingway's autopsy report, Case No. 01-2325, Miami-Dade County Medical Examiner Department, October 2, 2001, the day after the death. There were four "findings," including this: "Severe coronary atherosclerosis with 90% stenosis of right coronary artery and 75% stenosis of left anterior descending artery."

I'LL WHOOF *this* straight out: a lifelong shamed son was only acting out what a father felt, which is why they couldn't forsake each other, no matter how hard they tried. Firstly, they were father and son. But past this, they recognized they were yoked more deeply and darkly than anybody ever knew. Didn't Hemingway himself signal it on the page? Go back to that passage in *Islands in the Stream*. "[H]e had a dark side to him that nobody except Thomas Hudson could ever understand. Neither of them thought about this except that they recognized it in each other and knew it was bad and the man respected it and understood the boy's having it."

"Things may not be immediately discernible in what a man writes, and in this sometimes he is fortunate; but eventually they are quite clear and by these and the degree of alchemy that he possesses he will endure or be forgotten," Hemingway wrote to the Swedish Academy upon accepting his Nobel Prize in 1954, the ceremony for which he was much too ill to attend.

In those 1987 *Washington Post* pieces, "Papa's Boys," I had made the same general point I am making here, but I had phrased it as a question and more or less slipped it in at the back of the Gigi portrait. I wrote, equivocally: "There are Freudians afoot—especially in light of so much of the recent Hemingway scholarship, and the publication last year of his novel *The Garden of Eden*, which is awash in transsexual fantasies—who would raise this question: was the son merely acting out what the father felt?" I was doing what journalists do when they don't quite have the courage of their convictions—or enough facts. Namely, hedge the bets. Put it off onto others.

No longer. I've come to think of both of them, the one who exploded himself into infinity, the one too long regarded as the genetic blunder of the Hemingway family, as far braver human beings than anyone ever knew. Which is why, in spite of everything, there is uplift in their separate and bound stories.

It happened, if it did, the first catching, by his father, in the early summer of 1941, and I'll base my conviction on an important Hemingway letter, written in a kind of code.

It's a short letter, misdated, three paragraphs long. Hemingway wrote it to his ex-wife possibly around August 1. He was thanking Pauline for letting him know that the boys, Pat and Gigi, had arrived safely back in the States from a shortened stay in Cuba. Since their divorce, their feelings toward each other had begun to mend. But they were still finding their way. As with any divorced parents of young children, their communication was often taken up with mundane logistical matters, hence the first sentence of this one: "Thanks for the wire about the kids arriving o.k."

In the second paragraph: "Giggy is better all the time *I think* [my itals]. He has the biggest dark side in the family except me and you and I'm not in the family. *He keeps it so concealed that you never know about it* [my itals] and maybe that way it will back up on him. But *maybe too it will disappear* [my itals] as nearly all talent does along with youth and all the perishable commodities that shape our ends. (Sic)"

These hedgings and codings are enough to make me believe Gigi's father had only recently found him doing something horrid. We will never know for sure. The letter writer can't say that horror's name, not even (or especially), to his own former spouse.

That night in Coconut Grove, I should have pressed Gigi for more details about this moment. Maybe a mind-fogged man wouldn't have had them. What I do know is he told me his father opened the door of the *finca's* master bedroom and came in while he was putting on "Marty's white nylons." But almost as soon as he said this, Gigi's mind went to something else.

So why don't I believe it would have happened during the next summer's vacation at the *finca*, when he was ten, going on eleven? Two reasons. First, because the summer of 1942 constituted one of the largest triumphs of Gigi's boyhood; and, second, and as a direct result of the triumph, Hemingway's correspondence of that summer, as it concerns Gigi, seems unambiguous in its fatherly pride. The codings and shadings are largely absent. (With Hemingway, you have to insert the word "nearly" or "largely.")*

In 1942, Hemingway taught his youngest son how to shoot. Next to fishing, shooting was the supreme outdoor Hemingway manly value. Within weeks of learning how to fire a gun, the vest-pocket Hemingway was going up against grown men in live-pigeon shooting competitions at the Club de Cazadores del Cerro, and doing so as if he possessed "built-in radar." Actually, he was competing against some of the finest marksmen in all of Cuba, including the great Rodrigo Díaz and the almost-as-great Antonio Montalvo. The pint-sizer was using a .410-bore against professionals with 12-gauges. Gigi had never picked up a shotgun until that summer. He just seemed to understand in his veins about shooting. In no time he could place his weight on his back foot and lean forward with just the right bead; could swing and lead the birds, and keep swinging and keep leading after the recoil. He was like that other natural, the one who'd sat down at the iconic tables in the iconic city by the Seine and written an ostensible fish story titled "Big Two-Hearted River." And wouldn't that former phenom, watching this phenom, have been trying to convince himself that things were turning out just fine with his youngest, even if something disturbing had happened the summer before?

---

*If there's muddiness here, what can be said with certainty is that the pieces in *The Washington Post* marked the first time Gigi's lifelong semi-secret was revealed in a national publication. Two years later, in 1989, Gigi spoke again of his cross-dressing, and of that first catching, to an interviewer for a short-lived celebrity magazine named *Fame*. It was as if the floodgates to his torment had opened. The title of the article was "The Sons Almost Rise." Gigi told the interviewer that "[W]hen I look back on it—maybe I'm reading more into it than is there—the look of horror on his face may not just have been, 'What's wrong with my boy?' Maybe it was 'What's wrong with the family? My God! Is he doing this too?'" The last sentence of this quote strikes me as a kind of provocative Gigi add-on—he knew it would make great copy. According to the son, the father had said, a couple weeks after the catching, "Gigi, we come from a strange tribe, you and I." In 2007, that phrase, "strange tribe," would become the title of a brave and moving and unjustly ignored book about the Hemingway family by Gigi's own eldest son, John Hemingway, whom you'll hear more about later. As for the questions of whether it really *was* his father who'd caught him, that first time, and at what age, Gigi told a noted Hemingway scholar named Donald Junkins, who'd become a good friend and the best man at his fourth marriage, that, yes, it was his father, and that he was about ten.

Built-in radar: about a decade and a half after Gigi's first summer with a gun, Hemingway used this image in a deeply bitter story titled "I Guess Everything Reminds You of Something." It's not a very well-known piece in the Hemingway canon, and wasn't published in his lifetime. It was probably written in 1955. By then, it would have been too painfully clear to the author of "I Guess Everything Reminds You of Something"—or so all the surface evidence would seem to argue—that the "fictional" boy who'd shot with the coolest hand and the built-in radar for the National Live Pigeon Championship of Cuba "had never been any good." He was just vile. "His vileness came on from a sickness." The specific sickness isn't identified.

Am I confusing fiction with real life? Yes, deliberately, riskily.

That boy, called Stevie, son of a man called Papa, "never took a shot out of range nor let a driven bird come too close." His father would watch him with the "heel of his right foot lifted gently as all of him leaned behind the two loads in the chambers."

> "Ready," he said in that low, hoarse voice that did not belong to a small boy.
> "Ready," answered the trapper.
> "Pull," said the hoarse voice from whichever of the five traps the grey racing pigeon came out, and at whatever angle his wings drove him in full, low flight above the green grass toward the white, low fence, the load of the first barrel swung into him and the load from the second barrel drove through the first.

"I Guess Everything Reminds You of Something" is centrally about plagiarism, committed by a somewhat older schoolboy, the same one who'd shot so magically against adults. Part of the story's brilliance, though, is the way Hemingway collapses time and connects two events that happened in real life. Hemingway altered these events only minimally, which is one reason why, aesthetically speaking, it's a lesser story.

On June 26, 1942, with America seven months into world war, the three Hemingway sons flew together to Cuba on a Pan Am Clipper from Miami to visit their father. They arrived in time to celebrate Patrick's fourteenth birthday, two days hence. Jack, eighteen, who'd joined the Marine Corps Reserve, could stay for only ten days. He'd just finished his freshman year at Dartmouth and was scheduled to take summer classes, in the hope of earning a college degree in two and a half years before shipping off to Quantico, Virginia, for officer's training. The plan was for Gigi and Patrick to remain at the *finca* for the remainder of the summer. Actually, Gigi, going into sixth grade, ended up staying into the fall, while Patrick, who was about to enter his freshman year of high school at a Catholic prep school in Connecticut, had to get ready to go north by mid-September. Among other pleasures of that summer, in addition to the pleasures (if occasional puking) aboard their father's boat, two largely unsupervised kids, away from their mother's more puritanically Catholic eye, were able to sleep as late as they pleased; to take made-to-order breakfasts on trays brought to their bed by servants; to drink all the Cuban beer (and Bloody Marys for the next morning's hangovers) they could suffer; to ride to the cockfights and the jai alai fronton in the back of their father's chauffer-driven car. (When they got there, they'd wager with their papa's money.)*

There was also baseball. Two summers before, their father had built them a makeshift diamond just inside the *finca's* front gate, where the slope of the hillside wasn't so steep. The "diamond" was really a home plate and two bases set about seventy feet apart. The kids from the village came up again to play ball, sans shoes. Sometimes Papa pitched. He declined to run the bases. That summer, the team's sponsor and player-manager went into town and not only bought another round of balls, bats, and gloves but, this time, real uniforms (including cleats) with a team name stitched in royal blue across the flannel fronts of the shirts: Estrellas de Gigi, Gigi's Stars. That's because Gigi was the natural of the lot. The caps of the Estrellas de Gigi were emblazoned with a star, in the way of the Cuban national flag. There's an old sepia snapshot of Gigi, circa 1942, taken with his ball-playing pals. Their arms are slung around one another. They could be in an "Our Gang" movie.

But the shooting of that summer was best, at least for Gigi. The Club de Cazadores del Cerro (Cerro Hunters Club for English speakers) had been going since 1909. Its grounds were spacious and country-club colonial. In its early days, male members used to shoot in ties and shirts and suspend-

---

*At prep school, Patrick would go out for freshman football, and make the team, greatly pleasing his slow-of-foot and semi-clumsy ex–interior lineman father, who'd only made second-string varsity in his final year at Oak Park and River Forest Township High. In a letter to his son about a month after he had arrived at Canterbury School, Hemingway said, "About football—always remember to swing your arms wide when you tackle. Open them <u>wide</u> before you make the tackle and then slam them together <u>hard.</u> Like slapping them together across your chest. Try always to fall sideways so as to protect your balls as in boxing. Wear a jockstrap when you play."

ers and boater hats, while their ladies watched from rockers and sipped drinks on the clubhouse veranda. In Hemingway's time, the Cerro catered to American industrial magnates and Cuba's intellectual bourgeoisie. It offered trap, skeet, rifle, live pigeons. Hemingway, who could show up in shorts and penny loafers, shot there for years.

On Sunday, July 26, 1942, three Hemingways competed for the national championship. That morning, the *Havana Post* ran a small story: "Cuba's 1942 competitive shooting season will be formally closed at the Cerro Hunters Club with holding of the National Live Pigeon Championship, third and last of the big three title shoots. . . . One of the largest fields to enter a 1942 shoot is expected to participate in today's live bird competition, to start at 9:30 a.m."

Four days earlier, the chief shooter of the family talked of the upcoming match in a letter to his first wife. His present wife wasn't home—Martha had gone off on a Caribbean journalism assignment, in a thirty-foot sloop, for *Collier's*. Two days earlier, he had turned forty-three. Perhaps this is why Hemingway was so sentimental for the times he and Hadley had known when they were just kids in Paris. The night before, he couldn't sleep. So he lay awake trying to "remember the races out at Enghien and the first time we went to Pamplona by ourselves." He addresses Hadley as "Miss Katherine Kat." He tells her he loves her very much, and feels it's all right to say this, because "it is just untransferable feeling for early and best Gods." Damn, if he doesn't love fishing and the sea and his boat—"I would hate to die, ever, because every year I have a better time fishing and shooting. I like them as much as when I was sixteen." As for his boys, he is trying to be a good father. Gig, who is "a better boy all the time," is "known in the papers as el joven fenomeno Americano and day before yesterday a reporter called him 'el popularissimo Gigi.' So now we say go down to the post-office and get the mail popularissimo or time for bed, popularissmo. But inside himself he is very happy to be the popularissimo and he shoots like a little angel."

The little angel didn't win, but he scored a huge moral victory, not to say earned his father's bursting pride. He even beat his dad. And there was no way Hemingway would have eased off. He would have been shooting for his life at the all-day event.

The author of *Papa* devotes most of a chapter to the contest, and exaggerates what happened. Gigi didn't tie for first place; he finished fourth. He didn't knock down twenty birds in a row, as he said; he got twelve straight, partially got his thirteenth, hit six more dead on, which finished him just out of the money. There weren't 150 shooters entered, as he wrote; there were 30. But by any measure, his performance was a triumph. The great Diaz, who'd been shooting for decades, *did* end up winning, and Carlos Quintero and Antonio Montalvo fought to a tie and went into a shoot-off. These were possibly the three best marksmen in the country and, by extension, the hemisphere. "Havana" is one of the most beautifully written chapters in *Papa*, but amusingly the author (not to say the author's father in his letters) didn't get his own age right:

> At age eleven, I'd just tied for the shooting championship of Cuba against some of the best wing shots in the world. Minutes later at the bar I was explaining to a group of newly acquired admirers that it was really nothing if one had my 20/10 vision, fabulous reflexes, co-ordination, guts and stamina. After listening to this as long as he could, papa took me aside and said:
>
> "Gig, when you're truly great at something, and you know it, you would like to brag about it sometimes. But if you do, you'll feel like shit afterwards. Also, you never remember how a thing really felt if you talk about it too much."

He got that part exactly right.

The day following the championship, Hemingway typed a two-page letter to his absent wife. She was somewhere down the Caribbean. "Dear Pickly," he began. You would have been so proud yesterday. Gigi never once let his nerves get to him. Poor Patrick blew up after a good start. But Gigi was hitting them all—"drivers to the right, to the left, high screamers and two slanting incomers." He was "almost like that girl who won the Grand National in National Velvet. Imagine him not blowing up after that thirteenth and when they robbed him he came over to me and said, very quietly, 'Papa they lied and they stole from me and watch me kill this pidgeon now to show them.' It was a high one and he hit it and it seemed as though it were going outside the wind and then he chopped it right down against the inside base of the fence." Hemingway told Martha how he'd taken his sons into town for dinner, and of how they came home and lay down in a bed together and talked to the ceiling in the dark about what had happened.

Two weeks later, on August 14, Hemingway wrote again to his wife. She was still at sea. The letter's addressed to "Muki." He said, "Think all the time have put in with them (children) hasn't been wasted. Childies take lots of patience as they go through the damdest things but these childies are comeing along all right now. The shoot was the turn of the corner for Giggy.... He's just got what he did that day inside of him like the vault of a bank full of o.k. securities."

The last few pages of the "Havana" chapter have to do with the Stream and *Pilar*—a particular incident. The fishing had been lousy that day. The youngest boy was out into the water, near a reef, with his spear gun. He was after yellowtail and snapper and grunts. Gregorio was nearby in a dinghy, while Gigi's father, and maybe Patrick, stayed on the main boat. Suddenly, there were three sharks.

> I took the grunts off my belt and tossed them toward the sharks. Papa was about forty yards away, and although I wasn't much of a swimmer, I must have made it to him in near-record time. He lifted me up on his shoulders and then thrashed through the water to the dinghy.... I can't say with certainty that my father was very brave that day. He seemed cool enough, but I could tell he was frightened, too.... I never felt more like his son than I did that day.... I hadn't realized how much he really cared until he hoisted me on his own shoulders, which were barely out of water, and swam back across that reef with most of his own body still exposed under the surface.

Four summers later, a precocious fourteen-year-old, going into his sophomore year at the same Catholic prep school in New Milford, Connecticut, from which his older brother Pat had just graduated, stole a pair of French underpants and some other lingerie from the closet of his newest stepmother. Mary Hemingway, who'd been Hemingway's wife since March, accused her Cuban maid of the theft. The maid, in tears, said she was innocent, but Mary dismissed her. After Gigi had returned to the States and to Canterbury School, the garments were found—by Gigi's father—under the mattress of the bunk bed in the room in the little guesthouse where the boys had slept that summer. Gigi later tried to lie his way out of it. His father knew. Eventually he'd own up to it. In a sense, Mary never forgave him this incident. That was part of her character: holding grudges.

Two years later, the son who'd been so gifted with guns at the Cerro Hunters Club was trying hard to fashion himself into a writer—wouldn't this have been the best way of all to win his father's approval? There are a number of photographs around of Gigi from the summer of 1948, when he was about to enter his senior year at Canterbury. He was sixteen. All the baby fat was gone. He was taller, handsomer. There was something soft, though not unmanly, about him. He didn't seem impish any longer so much as deep, inward. He seems rarely to be smiling in the pictures. The cinnamon-colored freckles dotting his high cheekbones and the ridge of his nose are still there. You can see him instantly appealing to girls—they'd want to protect him.

That previous school term, his junior year (or "fifth former," as it's known at Canterbury), Gigi had become an associate editor of the school's magazine, *The Tabard.* He'd won first place in a campus-wide competition for a historical essay. This was announced in the June 1948 issue. He apparently won first place in a fiction contest as well. The piece was said to be about seagulls. But the June issue makes no mention of a short-story prize. What seems to have happened is that a committee designated a prize, and the winner was informally told, who then told his parents, who of course were thrilled (there are letters documenting their thrill), but then someone on the faculty discovered the story was a rank plagiarism. The prize was rescinded and the scandal hushed up. At least this is what the current dean of faculty at Canterbury, Lou Mandler, surmises. (Mandler has done first-rate research on the history of the Hemingway family at Canterbury. One of the things Mandler's research has uncovered is that Hemingway, the devoted father, seems never to have once set foot on Canterbury's grounds, not even for his sons' graduations—Patrick's in 1946, Gigi's in 1949. Both graduated with honors, near the top of their classes. Hemingway hated the school—for its perceived New England elitisms and parochial rigidities.)

In *Papa,* Gigi says he was eighteen when he committed the plagiarism. He couldn't have been eighteen; he was gone from Canterbury by then. He claims to have written the seagull story on his father's typewriter, on summer vacation.

> That summer in Havana I read papa's favorites, from *Huckleberry Finn* to *Portrait of the Artist as a Young Man:* like him, I sometimes had two or three books going at the same time. Then papa steered me to the short story masters, Maupassant and Chekhov. "Don't try to analyze—just relax and enjoy them."
>
> "Now," papa said one morning. "Try writing a short story yourself. And don't expect it to be any good."
>
> I sat down at a table with one of papa's fine-pointed pencils and thought and thought. I looked out of the window,

and listened to the birds, to a cat crying to join them; and to the scratch of my pencil, doodling. I let the cat out. Another wanted in.

I went to papa's typewriter. He'd finished with it for the day. Slowly I typed out a story and then took it to him.

His father read it and then slowly took off his glasses. According to Gigi, the stunned man said: "I've wanted to cut down for a long time. The writing doesn't come so easily for me anymore. But I'll be just as happy helping you as doing it myself. Let's have a drink to celebrate." From *Papa*:

Only once before can I remember papa being as pleased with me—when I tied for the pigeon-shooting championship. And he was confident that there was another winner in the family when I entered the short story for a school competition and won first prize.

Turgenev should have won the prize. He wrote the story. I merely copied it, changing the setting and the names, from a book I assumed papa hadn't read because some of the pages were still stuck together.

From "I Guess Everything Reminds You of Something":

It was seven years later that his father read the prize-winning story again. It was in a book that he found in checking through some books in the boy's old room. As soon as he saw it he knew where the story had come from. He remembered the long-ago feeling of familiarity. . . . In the last five of the seven years between the summer of the prize-winning story and the day his father ran onto the book the boy had done everything hateful and stupid that he could, his father thought. But it was because he was sick his father had told himself. His vileness came on from a sickness. He was all right until then. But that had all started a year or more after that last summer.

There are no time frames in the fiction. But, as noted earlier, a good guess for the date of the story's composition is mid-to-late 1955—which would have been "seven years" from the 1948 discovery of Gigi's plagiarism in his fifth-form spring at Canterbury. In the last five of those seven years—that is, from 1950 to 1955—the boy in the story and the boy of real life had done every hateful and stupid thing. The fiction doesn't specify what they were. In real life, nothing a youngest son would have done in this interval, after leaving prep school and dropping out of college and getting his girlfriend pregnant, was stupider or more irresponsible, certainly in his father's mind, than an incident involving a movie theater—because that public incident had led directly to the middle-of-the-night death in a Los Angeles hospital of the youngest son's mother.

The final three sentences of the story: "Now he knew that boy had never been any good. He had thought so often looking back on things. And it was sad to know that shooting did not mean a thing."

And yet here is a characteristic Hemingway switchback. In 1955, four years after Pauline's death, Gigi's father was working overtime to try to be a supportive father. Hemingway hadn't abandoned Gigi, or vice versa. They had said horrible, unconscionable things to each other. But in a way, wouldn't that just prove how much they cared?

Things written in a kind of code. Things exposed under the surface.

Hemingway wrote four stories about homosexuals and lesbians. The most psychologically layered and surprisingly sympathetic ran to five and a quarter pages in its first published form, in the 1927 Scribner's collection Men Without Women. (It's really a very brief story. The book was compact in design, with large type, making the piece seem deceptively longer than it is.) The story is called "A Simple Enquiry." The irony starts there, for there is nothing simple in the enquiry the story turns on. A homosexual Italian major is reclined on his bunk in his hut at the snow-blinded front. He announces he is going to take a little sleep. Outside, the March sun is thawing the mounds of snow, which are piled higher than the hut's windows. Signor Maggiore, as his subordinates address him, has been at his desk in the other room, oiling his swollen and blistered facial skin that has been badly burned by the sun's glint off the snow. Very delicately he's been "stroking" his forehead and cheeks and nose. Now, reclined, with the door half-open, his head on a rucksack, he tells his adjutant to send in the orderly. The orderly, whose name is Pinin, is nineteen. The officer, it hardly needs saying, has every advantage. "Come in," he tells the boy, "and shut the door." The orderly comes across the room and stands beside the bunk. The major wishes to know if Pinin has a girl, if he's ever been in love, in love with a girl, or whether, in fact, he is—"corrupt."

" 'I don't know what you mean, corrupt.' "

The major tells him he needn't be "superior." Pinin studies the floor. The major is eyeing him up and down.

" 'And you don't really want—' the major paused. Pinin looked at the floor. 'That your great desire isn't really—' Pinin looked at the floor. The major leaned his head back on the rucksack and smiled. He was really relieved: life in the army was too complicated. 'You're a good boy,' he said. 'You're a good boy, Pinin. But don't be superior and be careful some one else doesn't come along and take you.' "

The boy stands there. He hasn't been dismissed.

" 'Don't be afraid,' the major said. His hands were folded on the blankets. 'I won't touch you.' "

The piece ends with the orderly walking out awkwardly, stiffly. "Pinin was flushed and moved differently." As for the relieved Signor Maggiore, who will not be acting on his erotic urges today, he is still on his bunk, thinking aloud. That's the story's final sentence: "The little devil, he thought, I wonder if he lied to me."

For decades, Hemingway scholarship largely ignored "A Simple Enquiry," and it is hard to understand why, for it has the terseness and precision and subsurface swirls of the best of Hemingway's work. It seems to be suggesting that moral and sexual dilemmas are deserving of our deepest human understanding—not of our rejections and bigotries. Archibald MacLeish read the story and told his touchy friend in a February 20, 1927, letter: "I think its in your real manner, a fine, cool, clean piece of work, sure as leather, & hard and swell." In the margin, he added: "Ten things 'said' for every word written. Full of sound like a coiled shell. Overtones like the bells at Chartres. All that stuff you can't describe but only do—& only you can do it."

Twenty-four years later, on October 2, 1951, a sleepless, denying, lashing-out man employed the same semi-coded word, "corrupt," in a letter to his publisher regarding his ex-wife's death. Hemingway, remember, wrote an earlier letter to Charlie Scribner, on the day following Pauline's death, in addition to the letter he wrote at 6:10 p.m., in which he called his son "harbor scum." Here's part of what he said in that first one, in respect to his late-night phone talk with Pauline, two nights previous, that, from all that can be known, had gone very cruelly: "I was sympathetic and kind although I did not feel that way since she had the boy in her charge and I had been writing her registered letters about how he was doing and asking for details and receiving no answers. . . . But this boy Gigi was not brave as Patrick always was. He was only terribly skillful and corrupted. His mother, and her sister being corrupt did not help him much."

Corrupt, as in general moral deviance, not corrupt in the narrower sense he'd employed it in "A Simple Enquiry." Hemingway's son wasn't a homosexual, and he knew this. His sister-in-law was an open lesbian, yes, and it's also true that his ex-wife had drifted by now into some lesbian relationships of her own (including one with the poet Elizabeth Bishop), and that he generally knew about these, or suspected as much, or had heard talk about such. But if you're newly married, as Gigi was; if you have a child on the way, as Gigi did; if you go into a ladies' room of an LA movie theater in drag, as Gigi did, thus willing to risk arrest and public shame and damage to your family's decent name, then aren't you damn well "corrupt"? Not that the lashing-out man writing to his father-figure publisher spelled out any details of the corruption. He just used the code word. "[A]nd the story was sordid and bad" is the way he put it.

Once again, Hemingway was trying in any way he could to fling blame from him, scapegoat others: a lifelong pattern. But he had to have known in his bones that not all the perfumes of Arabia could sweeten his complicit hand.

"NECROTIC"

Ernest with his sons, Havana, June 1945.
On back: "Pigeon Hunting Club, Cazodores del Carro."

WE DON'T KNOW the name of the movie theater he entered. We don't know the day it happened (although Saturday night, September 29, seems probable). We don't know who called the cops, or what police substation they took Gigi to, and whether they carted the kid in drag directly downtown to the central jail. We do know they held him through the rest of that weekend, while his distressed mother flew in from San Francisco, and while he awaited a scheduled hearing on Monday afternoon, October 1. But records of that hearing, if there was one, as well as any record of the arrest itself, have disappeared. What may have happened is that, once word had come that his mother had died on an operating table overnight, the authorities let him go. And records eventually got tossed.

Gigi and his wife of five months were living in a one-bedroom concrete-and-stucco apartment two blocks in from the Lincoln Highway, in the seaside community of Venice. The unit was part of a complex of two-story, look-alike postwar pastel housing spreading itself over eight or ten LA acres. Their flat was about a half-mile walk to the beach. But neither Gigi nor his wife, the former Shirley Jane Rhodes—who was even younger than he was, who was descended from Cherokee Indians on her mother's side (which gave her stunning high cheekbones), who'd worked a bit as a Powers agency model, who is said to have held a recent job taking tickets at an LA movie house—would have much free time to go to the ocean. They were both holding down sixty-five-dollar-a-week jobs at Douglas Aircraft in nearby Santa Monica, and in addition Gigi was enrolled in a night class or two at UCLA Extension. (The two are said to have met on campus.) There had to have been pressures beyond the pressures of a new marriage between teenagers.

He was six weeks shy of twenty and an expectant father. He'd quit college back east, just one more hardheaded and ill-advised and impulsive thing he'd done. The quitting, as noted earlier, was at the end of his freshman year, from a college only a few blocks from the naval academy, where Walter Houk had finished up four years before.

What else to say of him? He was getting a hundred bucks in the mail every month from his father as part of Hemingway's divorce agreement with Pauline. He'd become a semi-disillusioned believer in the gospel of L. Ron Hubbard; it's what had gotten him out of college and to the coast in the first place—Hubbard and the pseudopsychiatry of Dianetics. The year before, he'd been so certain that Hubbard's claims about "auditing" your unconscious were going to rid him of the compulsion he despised and yet curiously craved. (All his life he would talk about the cross-dressing having this strange calming effect on his nerves, even as it was thrilling him.) At about the time Gigi had come to swallow Dianetics whole, Hubbard had come up with this crazed idea about Benzedrine, vitamins, and glutamic acid: the "Guk" treatment. It was a chemical way of auditing yourself, without the need of a partner. You self-administered huge amounts of vitamins every two hours for twenty-four hours. Might Gigi have been high on the Guk on the night he entered the unknown movie house? It's only one more of the unknowns.

From *Papa:* "In 1951, when my father was fifty-two and I was nineteen, I got into some trouble on the West Coast for taking a mind-stimulating drug before such things had become fashionable." This is how he speaks of it (three times) in that beautiful, slender, distorting, omitting book—"the trouble." The troubles. In relating the story of his mother's death, he never mentions the movie theater, or the cross-dressing, or the arrest.

Some fifteen months before, in the early summer of 1950, right after quitting school, Gigi had enrolled as a student-researcher at the Hubbard

Dianetics Research Foundation in Elizabeth, New Jersey. There were six Hubbard foundations in America, and the New Jersey Board of Medical Examiners was trying hard to shut down that branch first, perhaps as a lead for the rest of the country. Gigi knew that prophets aren't understood in their own time. On July 15, 1950, he'd written to his father from Elizabeth: "Dianetics has proven high blood pressure to be psychosomatic in origin and can cure it. That buzzing in your ears . . . has been proven to be the result of pain received while you were inside your mother's womb." Five months later, on December 7, 1950, still in Elizabeth, Gigi wrote to say that his current girlfriend's dad, a high official in Hubbard's empire, wished to come to Cuba to visit Hemingway to explain firsthand about Dianetics. Hemingway answered his son's letter one week later—which was the day, December 14, when a third secretary from the American Embassy drove out to the *finca* with his new girl to meet her part-time employer for the first time. "Dear Gig: Thanks for the letter. . . . The Dianetics king never sent the book so I bought one, but Miss Nita borrowed it and it is still outside of the joint. So have not been able to practice jumping back into the womb."

In early January 1951, right after Gigi had come back from a Christmas visit to the *finca* with his New Jersey girlfriend (to whom Hemingway took instant dislike), Hubbard had summoned him and another student-researcher in Elizabeth and told them to pack all his personal possessions—Hubbard's, that is—into Hubbard's black limousine and to leave for LA as soon as possible. The New Jersey authorities had begun proceedings against the Elizabeth office for practicing medicine without a license. Gigi and his partner flew across the country in the overstuffed car.

He soon broke up with his Hubbard girlfriend, got classified 1-A for the draft, enrolled in night classes, began dating Shirley Jane Rhodes, impregnated her, married her before a JP (on April 29), and informed his father of the news after the fact. It was just the "logical thing to do if we are going to have a child," Gigi wrote in a letter on the day following the marriage. She was such a beautiful girl, "one of the most beautiful women I have ever met (really!). Mother was crazy about her and so was Aunt Jinny, although I am afraid that this may not be of much comfort to you." The same day, April 30, 1951, Hemingway had wired from Havana: HAVE RECEIVED NO LETTERS FROM YOU SINCE YOU LEFT HERE IN JANUARY STOP GIVE ABSOLUTELY NO CONSENT NOR APPROVAL TO YOUR MARRIAGE WITHOUT FULL DETAILS AND OPPORTUNITY TO CHECK STOP LOVE PAPA. But it was too late.

He and Jane, working at Douglas, living at 1056 Doreen Place, unit 4, with a high-walled patio off the front of their unit, drove an old beater. Sometimes he'd put on his wife's girdle, ruby his nails with her polish, strut behind that high wall. Was it "her" movie theater he walked into on that Saturday night? Gigi's first wife, who had a tragic history, is dead; we'll never know.

Pauline had recently returned to California from a quick trip to Key West, which was still her principal place of residence. For years she'd been coming to California, both Northern and Southern. She preferred San Francisco and often had leased apartments there for stays of several months, or else lodged with old family friends, the McEvoys. She'd known Jay McEvoy, a wealthy art dealer, since the 1930s. On the weekend of her death, just before she got the news about Gigi, Pauline had been staying with unmarried Jay McEvoy and his sister in their big house on Russian Hill. She was planning a trip to New York. She thought she might go down to Los Angeles first to see her sister, Jinny, with whom she'd been staying on and off for the last two months. She seemed in high spirits, although it's true she'd been complaining of headaches and poundings of the heart and a general feeling of anxiety. Soon she intended to go for a full checkup at Mayo Clinic.

Jinny Pfeiffer and her longtime lover, Laura Archera, lived in a beautiful home high in the Hollywood Hills, on a hairpin curve, practically beneath the famous HOLLYWOOD sign. (To yank the story out of time: Not quite five years from this tragic 1951 moment, Archera—a onetime concert violinist who'd been born in Italy, a professional film-cutter and producer of documentary films, a lay psychotherapist, a breeder of poodles, an investigator of LSD—would marry widower and novelist Aldous Huxley in a drive-up wedding chapel in Yuma, Arizona. It would mostly be a marriage of convenience and companionship for the famous author of *Brave New World*. From the mid-fifties on, Jinny and Laura and Aldous would all more or less live together, each caring for the one as much as the other. At the end of Huxley's life—he'd die of cancer in November 1963, on the day of John F. Kennedy's death, and toward the end Laura would be injecting him with LSD and reading to him from the works of Timothy Leary—they'd literally be living together, these three, because their separate but nearby houses on Deronda Drive had earlier burned to the ground, and afterward these three, plus Jinny's two adopted children, would have moved into Jinny's new rented home on Mulholland Drive. Jinny herself would die of cancer, in 1973, and afterward Laura Huxley would take in and raise Jinny's granddaughter, Karen Pfeiffer. I once spent part of a pleasant afternoon with Karen Pfeiffer, who lives in the San Fernando Valley, and who's in her thirties, and who's a New Age woman, and whose explanation of everything you've read in this parenthesis made utter California sense.)

Sometime on that Sunday, September 30, probably before noon, Pauline received a call telling her that her son was in jail, and the basic reason why. Was it Gigi himself who put in the call to his mom? It seems so, but again there is so much in his memoir that's either elliptical or false. From *Papa:* "My mother . . . did not seem at all alarmed by my predicament but thought my father should be notified. When I said that it would be simpler if papa were not brought in she said, yes . . . a lot of things would be simpler if you had only one parent. But she wasn't really at all upset. I can remember this as clearly as if it were yesterday." *Predicament.* Put it in code.

Pauline apparently sent Hemingway a cable sometime that Sunday (I've never been able to find it) to the effect that their son had been arrested, and that the circumstances were messy, and that she was flying down to gather more of the facts and to try to get him out of jail and to keep the story from the papers. She'd be in touch from Jinny's house at nine that evening, her time. This basic chronology is in Hemingway's first letter to Charlie Scribner of October 2. What can be said for certain is that the story got kept out of the papers. And that Pauline *didn't* succeed in getting him sprung—her son was in jail when she died. There would be another way to look at this: she *did* get him sprung, but she had to die for it first.

Despite what Gigi writes in his memoir, Pauline was very upset as she flew south. Jinny met her at the airport that Sunday afternoon. Pauline told her she wasn't feeling well, that she had a sharp pain in her stomach. They drove to Deronda. Pauline made phone calls to lawyers and others. Laura came home from a swim at the house of one of her film producers. Laura and Jinny fixed a dinner for Pauline, but she couldn't eat. She went upstairs to bed. The pain in her abdomen grew worse. Jinny and Laura called a doctor who said she might have to be taken to the hospital. Did Pauline force herself from bed at nine to make the call to Havana that she had promised in the earlier wire? Many years later, when she was almost eighty-seven, Laura Huxley would remember some of these details in an interview with Professor Ruth Hawkins of Arkansas State University, a Pfeiffer family scholar to whom I am much indebted. Laura would say there were several Hemingway calls that night. *He* was the one who placed the calls. Whether that's true seems far less important than the fact that

Pauline felt sick even before she got on the phone. And what did Hemingway, in full lashing-out mode, say to his weakened wife? To repeat Gigi's words: "My aunt, who hated my father's guts and who certainly couldn't be considered an unbiased witness, said the conversation had started out calmly enough. But soon Mother was shouting into the phone and sobbing uncontrollably."

Sympathetic and kind, according to Hemingway, in his letter to Scribner the next day, which was the day after he'd spit in Mary Hemingway's face. A year later, he'd say in a letter to Archie and Ada MacLeish: "It was a terrible thing having Pauline die that suddenly. I had talked with her, both very lovingly, an hour before she died on the coast." (It wasn't an hour before she died.)

Sometime after midnight, the house came awake with Pauline's screaming. Jinny and Laura got her dressed and into the car. St. Vincent's Hospital, at Third and Alvarado Streets, on the edge of downtown LA, was a good half hour away—in daylight. Tearing down those hairpin curves from the Hollywood Hills in the dark must have been terrifying. St. Vincent's was run by the Daughters of Charity, and the sisters themselves worked as RNs on the floors. The Catholicity of the place had to have given comfort.

Once they'd gotten her into the hospital, and in the hands of the emergency room staff, Jinny and Laura decided not to stay. Jinny wasn't feeling well herself. So Laura drove her back to the house on Deronda, and they went to bed.

Henry Randall Thomas was an attending surgeon at St. Vincent's. He and his fellow physicians did regular sleepover shifts at the hospital, and this was one of his nights. In four days he'd turn thirty-six—so he was twenty years younger than Pauline. He was lean and soft-spoken, with residues of a calming southern accent. He was a man who enjoyed literature. He'd grown up in an Alabama family of nine and had studied medicine at the University of Pennsylvania on a scholarship and had surgical training at Mayo. He was a native of Montgomery, and had graduated from Sidney Lanier High School, which is where Zelda Fitzgerald had graduated fourteen years ahead of him. Did the name "Hemingway" on the medical chart register in any way that night as he and his surgical team worked furiously to stanch a hemorrhage from an unknown origin?

His medical office, where he saw patients on a nonemergency basis, was a couple of blocks from St. Vincent's. He'd only recently located to 630 South Bonnie Brae, on the corner of Bonnie Brae and Wilshire Boulevard, from an office a little farther down, at 1930 Wilshire. The reason for noting such an inconsequential fact here is because, the next day, on the second, when he was filling in, in his own handwriting, Pauline's certificate of death, he started to write down in box 23d the wrong address for his office. He wrote "1930 W"—and then drew a line through it and wrote "630 S. Bonnie Brae St." Was his mind still reeling from his failure, even as another reeling mind, half a continent away, was trying, that same day, in two letters, to push it all away?

From *Papa:* "I can imagine the wild frustration of the surgeons as they searched for a bleeding point in the abdomen, where Mother had originally felt the pain." Those are a fellow doctor's words.

It was apparently Dr. Thomas himself, at four o'clock, who awoke Jinny and Laura to tell them Pauline had died of shock on the operating-room table. They'd tried everything. (Virtually every Hemingway account lists 4:00 a.m. as the time of death. She died at three. It's on the certificate.)

The body was taken to Pierce Brothers Funeral Home on Santa Monica Boulevard in Hollywood. The mortuary was across the street from Hollywood Memorial Park Cemetery. In daylight, Jinny put in the calls to family members. (To repeat: she cabled Hemingway at 9:00 a.m., her time.) From *Papa:* "But Aunt Jinny told me nothing of the details of the phone conversation the next morning [he is referring to the Sunday night call at 9:00 p.m. with Hemingway], just that Mother was dead. . . . My mother's face looked unbelievably white at the funeral, and I remember thinking through sobs what a barbarous ritual Anglo-Saxon burial is." But there wasn't a funeral, per se. Gigi has to be referring to the viewing, which was private, in the parlor of Pierce Brothers.

The next day, October 2, on page 20, the *Los Angeles Times* ran a small story under this headline: "Hemingway's Second Wife Dies In Hospital."

The Wednesday funeral was a brief graveside ceremony, casket closed. There were five mourners—Gigi, his aunt, his aunt's partner, Jay McEvoy, and Garfield Merner, who was a first cousin of Pauline and Jinny's. Patrick Hemingway was in Africa and it wasn't possible for him to get home fast enough. Did a priest say prayers? Pierce Brothers in those days had on call a cleric from the archdiocese who made it his personal act of mercy to offer prayers (a little bit out of the eye of the archbishop) at the secular burials of Catholics, especially Catholic out-of-towners, whose families might have had few other options. A burial Mass in a local Catholic church was out of the question: Pauline was a divorced Catholic. Jinny badly wanted to rest Pauline in a Catholic cemetery, but there was no chance of that, either, and so the path of least resistance was chosen: the nondenominational cemetery across the street. The plot cost the family $350. And a stone? It's a hard and strange fact that, all these years later, there is still no marker of any kind at Pauline Hemingway's grave. She's there, anonymously, at what is now known as Hollywood Forever Cemetery, two rows in from the pavement, down from Nelson Eddy Way, under a spongy piece of ground, alongside the modest markers of Lydia Bemmels and Leiland Irish, in almost the literal shade of Paramount Studio's main lot, just a few yards from a man-made lake with a fountain, not far from the tombs and stones and marble mausoleums of Tyrone Power and Douglas Fairbanks (both junior and senior) and Bugsy Siegel and Rudolph Valentino and Fay Wray and Peter Lorre and Cecil B. DeMille and Jayne Mansfield and Johnny Ramone of the Ramones—to cite only ten.

I've deliberately held back the medical specifics of Pauline's death, so that I could go into them in more detail here, quoting the words of a deceased doctor-writer-son.

Gigi's mother died of a rare and undiagnosed tumor in the core of her adrenal gland called a pheochromocytoma. Each of us has two adrenal glands, one just above each of our kidneys. Our adrenal glands produce hormones that give instructions to almost every organ and tissue. If you have an undetected pheochromocytoma, your adrenal glands can produce too much of certain hormones, raising your blood pressure and heart rate. Such a sleeping tumor can explode in times of emotional stress. As Gigi explains in *Papa*, a tumor like this doesn't kill by attacking vital organs, but by secreting huge amounts of adrenaline—"which then make the blood pressure rise to incredible heights, often causing a rupture of an artery." Gigi explains that there are generally two types of the tumor—"the intermittent and the constantly secreting types." After reading the autopsy report (more on that in a moment), he was pretty sure she'd died of the intermittent type. Something as slight as standing up, or being jostled in a crowd, or a bad dream, could make the tumor "fire off."

From *Papa*: "The tumor had become necrotic or rotten and when it fired off that night, it sent her blood pressure skyrocketing; a medium-sized blood vessel, within or adjacent to the rotten area, had ruptured. Then the tumor stopped discharging adrenaline, her blood pressure dropped from about 300 to 0, and she died of shock on the operating table."

But Gigi didn't know this for almost a decade. He'd thought his mother had died of a heart attack and ruptured artery of an unknown origin. In

1960, after many false starts, Gigi began medical school at the University of Miami. One of the first things he says he did was "to write the hospital where Mother had died and ask them for an autopsy report." The report showed there was "no blood in the abdominal cavity and the autopsy showed only 500 cc. of blood in the space around her right kidney." It was as if the patient, dying of shock, had bled out invisibly before the attending surgeon with the calming attitude and residues of Alabama speech.

Why, nine years after the fact, had Gigi sent for a copy of the autopsy? Well, he was a medical student and would have been medically curious. But it was much more than that; in a way it was *everything* more than that. About a month and a half after Pauline's death, no longer a wage-earning aircraft mechanic, but rather an inheritor of fifty thousand dollars (it was true he didn't actually have his mother's inheritance in his pocket yet, but he had advances on it from the estate lawyers), Gigi and his much-pregnant wife flew to Havana to meet his father. There was wary distance between father and son, but Jane helped bridge it. Toward the end, Gigi let down his guard.

From *Papa:* "Referring to the trouble I'd gotten into on the Coast, I said, 'It wasn't so bad, really, papa.' "

" 'No? Well, it killed mother.' "

That paragraph goes on: "Whatever his motives were the yellow-green filter came back down over my eyes and this time it didn't go away for seven years. I didn't say anything back to him. He'd almost always been right about things, he was so sound, I knew he loved me, it must have been something he just had to say, and I believed him."

He claims that the yellow-green filter didn't go away until after he'd done many unconscionable things—such as going to Africa and slaughtering eighteen elephants in a single month. The yellow-green filter didn't go away until after a twenty-eight-year-old first-year med student at the University of Miami had written to a Los Angeles hospital and gotten an autopsy and read the specifics of his mother's case and then done his own research on a ghost of a disease called pheochromocytoma.

Gigi says in his book that a year before his father committed suicide, he wrote him a letter (I've never been able to locate it), confronting him with the facts of the autopsy, as he interpreted them. It wasn't what *he'd* done that weekend that had brought about his mother's death; no, far more likely, it was the brutal conversation at 9:00 p.m. on Sunday night that had caused the somnolent tumor to fire off.

From *Papa:* "According to a person who was with him in Havana when he received my letter, he raged at first and then walked around the house in silence for the rest of the day." Next paragraph: "About three months later his first noticeable symptoms of paranoia began, with the worries about the FBI chasing him for income tax evasion."

In about nine more months, Hemingway was dead.

Several pages earlier, Gigi recounts something else his father had said, as he and his wife were at the doorstep of the *finca*, heading for the airport, at the end of that visit after Pauline's death: "I remember papa remarking, 'Well, don't take any wooden trust funds.' I could see the humor and I smiled as we were parting." Then Gigi writes, "I never saw my father again."

But he *did* see his father again, at least once, at a critical juncture when Hemingway was trying with everything in him to help his hospitalized son. Despite how he seeks to portray their relationship in the years after Pauline's death, the letter trail proves they were in touch far more often than they were not. There were periods of silence and of rage, no question. But their mutual need to be connected, at least until toward the end of Hemingway's life, when he'd lost touch with nearly everyone and anything around him, trumped everything.

As for what Hemingway had said—"No? Well, it killed mother"—that got said, at least the first time, in a phone conversation immediately after Pauline's death. There's a letter of Gigi's documenting this. Why did he alter the facts? Perhaps because he wished to enhance the storytelling tension. He rearranged the truth from real life just as his father had been doing for his whole writing life. And no matter how devastating it had to have been to hear those words on the phone right after Pauline died, it wasn't devastating enough to keep Gigi from traveling to Cuba a short while later to see his father. To me, it's one more proof of how large the parental approval needs were—like any child's. And who is to say, for that matter, that his father didn't repeat some version of it in Havana.

So is Gigi's beautiful book built on a tissue of lies? No, it is a memoir, with a memoir's faults, and then some. The essence of the story is all there, but it's clear how he elided and omitted and rearranged and misremembered to suit his purposes. One of the reasons I've been able to become a sadder but wiser man about all this is because I've closely read John Hemingway's *Strange Tribe* (published, as noted earlier, in 2007), to which high tribute must be paid for correcting the record. Straightening out a record from what Gigi wrote in *Papa*—John was able to draw on and quote at length from previously unpublished letters between Hemingway and his son—is just one of the contributions Gigi's eldest son has made in a memoir–cum–family biography that is a deep act of honoring: loving someone for who they are.

Dr. Thomas himself apparently ordered Gigi's autopsy on the day after the death. But St. Vincent's no longer has any records of Pauline's death. Nor does any California government repository have a copy of the autopsy. Nor does any Hemingway family member, at least that I am aware of, possess a copy. What exists as documentary evidence of Pauline's death is the one-page death certificate. What happened to Gigi's copy? Who could say? Metaphorically, if not quite literally, he was a man who lived most of his life in the five decades after Pauline's death from the trunk of his car.

But back to the first sentence of *Papa:* "I never got over a sense of responsibility for my father's death and the recollection of it sometimes made me act in strange ways." Like the best of openings, it's a sentence conveying so much more than it tells. What Gigi is really telling us is that he never got over a sense of responsibility for *both* his parents' deaths. No matter the terrible cruelty of his father's words, no matter the seemingly exculpatory thing he later found in an autopsy report, he had to know, in some deep necrotic pocket of himself, that his father was exactly right; that by going into that movie theater in women's clothes, he had set off—call it fired off—the chain reaction of sorrowful events. And the double guilt over two deaths would end up pursuing him right to pod 377 of cell 3C2 on Monday, October 1, 2001, when a shamed child, former doctor, with his surgically altered genitals, with his pink-painted toenails, scheduled for a hearing later that morning on indecent exposure charges, was awakened by a corrections officer, rose, and five minutes later pitched down dead on his face.

In Islands in the Stream, *late in the story,* Thomas Hudson *is dreaming on the sand in a cove. He'll get up shortly and go back to his armed fishing cruiser. He'll steer through the night. He'll run the boat in a "heavy beam sea" and it'll come to him that steering her like this, trying to roll her as little as possible between the waves, is like riding a horse downhill. "It is all downhill and sometimes it is across the side of a hill. The sea is many hills and in here it is a broken country like the badlands."*

That's later. Right now the captain of the cruiser is on the beach, asleep, dreaming of his former wife and three dead sons. They're alive. The war is over. Young Tom's mother is sleeping on top of him, as she used to like to do. Hudson, who'll never complete another canvas, can hear himself speaking to his ex-wife.

"You," he says. "Who's going to make love to who?"

"Both of us," she responds. "Unless you want it differently."

After a couple more exchanges: "Should I be you or you be me?" He answers, "You have first choice."

"I'll be you."

"I can't be you. But I can try."

There is an earlier section of the Islands *manuscript that Hemingway marked for setting aside. Hudson's first wife has cut off his hair, to match her own, so that "we'll be just that same."*

"Now kiss me and be my girl," she says. He answers, "I didn't know you wanted a girl." She says, "Yes I do. Now and right away and my girl is you." He protests, "I don't know how to be a girl."

The notion of not knowing how to be a girl: toward the end of A Farewell to Arms, *Catherine Barkley and Frederic Henry, about to have their baby, are talking of cutting their hair to the same length. One can be blond, the other dark. This is Catherine's idea. "Then we'd both be alike. Oh, darling, I want you so much I want to be you too," she says.*

"You are. We're the same one."

"I know it. At night we are."

"The nights are grand."

"I want us to be all mixed up."

Mixed up? In late 1953, when he and his wife were in the fifth month of their safari to East Africa, Hemingway wrote in Mary Hemingway's diary:

> She has always wanted to be a boy and thinks as a boy without ever losing any femininity. . . . She loves me to be her girls, which I love to be. . . . In return she makes me awards and at night we do every sort of thing which pleases her and which pleases me. . . . Mary has never had one lesbian impulse but has always wanted to be a boy. Since I have never cared for any man and dislike any tactile contact with men except the normal Spanish abrazo or embrace which precedes a departure or welcomes a return from a voyage or a more or less dangerous mission or attack, I loved feeling the embrace of Mary which came to me as something quite new and outside all tribal law. On the night of December 19th we worked out these things and I have never been happier. EH 20/12/53.

Something quite new and outside all tribal law. In The Garden of Eden, or rather in the drastically cut-down published version of about seventy thousand words and thirty short chapters that appeared in 1986, after a decade of innuendo and psychosexual speculation, there's a passage at the start where something role-changing occurs in bed between the newlyweds honeymooning in the south of France. David has shut his eyes. He can feel the slender weight of his spouse on top of him. "He lay there and felt something and then her hand holding him and searching lower and he helped with his hands and then lay back in the dark and did not think at all and only felt the weight and the strangeness inside and she said, 'Now you can't tell who is who can you?'"

He answers, "No."

"You are changing," she tells him. "Oh you are. You are. Yes you are and you're my girl Catherine. Will you change and be my girl and let me take you?"

He answers. "You're Catherine."

She answers, "No. I'm Peter. You're my wonderful Catherine. You're my beautiful lovely Catherine. You were so good to change. Oh thank you, Catherine, so much."

The sentence that follows is the most significant in the whole passage: "Please understand." Couldn't it be a son's cry, from real life? Or a father's?

In light of these passages—and there are others—it might reasonably be asked: How did we, meaning the world, read Hemingway's work so wrong, for so long? How did we read the man himself so wrong, for so long? Well, he misdirected us with the mask. The mask wasn't false, a lie, a fraud, as so many detractors have wished to say. The hypermasculinity and outdoor athleticism were one large and authentic slice of him. But beneath the mask was all the rest, which is why his work endures, why his best work will always have its tuning-fork "tremulousness," as it's been called. And, incidentally, where did this beautiful nervousness come from in the first place? No one will ever answer that definitively. Maybe everything goes back to the foot and feet of Grace Hemingway in Oak Park, and maybe it doesn't. "Pressure under Grace" is a too-clever phrase that was the headline on a rather brilliant piece some years ago in The New York Review of Books, by a critic named Frederick C. Crews. He was reviewing Kenneth S. Lynn's psychoanalytic (and often ridiculous) biography of Hemingway. All the essay lacked, no less than did Lynn's nearly six-hundred-page text, was a sense of compassion—for how much someone suffered in his life.

Hemingway was working on the semi-secret and cross-gendering manuscript of The Garden of Eden in the period, the early and mid-fifties, when his bitched baby son, with all his recklessness and irresponsibility and manic behavior, was disappointing and embarrassing and worrying and angering him most. "Please understand." Could you think of not just that sentence, but a passage like that, a whole book like that, as a father's testament of sympathy, support, love, for his child?

One more thought: If Hemingway's therapeutic release from all the things he felt inside was in his writing, where was Gigi's? Could you say he was writing out his novel with his life, that it was what he had?

WHAT HE HAD

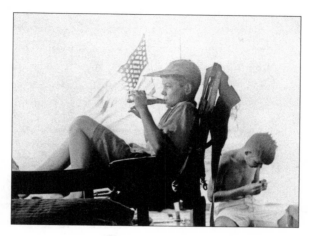

Gigi in the fighting chair, Paraíso Key, July 1945.
His brother Pat is behind him.

> She changes from a girl into a boy and back to a girl care-
> lessly and happily.
>
> ERNEST HEMINGWAY, *The Garden of Eden*

AT 8:55 A.M. on February 11, 1952, *Pilar* eased out of Havana Harbor
and turned westward with fifteen hundred pounds of ice and newly laid
Philippine mahogany planking on her outsides and insides. Running to
port as she chucked against the sea, with Hemingway at the helm, was
Mary Hemingway's launch, *Tin Kid*, manned by Felipe, the skilled but
unlikable *joven*. Another *joven* was tending to his duties that Monday at
the American Embassy; in thirty-four days he'd be proposing marriage
to Miss Nita. Still another *joven*, Gigi, in whose head had to have been
echo-chambering five words (no matter when exactly they'd been uttered),
was back in LA, following a recent visit to his father's home in the wake of
his mother's death.

The plan was for Hemingway to spend a couple of weeks recharging the
batteries down at Paraíso Key—this is how he put it in letters. "All I have

is over-work and over-worry," he'd say in a letter ten days later, after the battery-charging had been aborted.

There weren't any mosquitoes on that first night, at Bahía Honda. The next morning, coming past Punta Gobernadora Light, Mary Hemingway watched a loggerhead turtle devour a Portuguese man-of-war. She and her husband marveled at three dolphins—they guessed them to be papa, mama, child—sunning on their backs in a kind of dolphinesque dog paddle. That evening, having made it to their private vacation island, they had a supper of soup, watched the moon roll up, drank moderately, read, turned in at nine. They woke with the sun. "Papa sweet and happy," Mary entered in her diary. As she wrote in *How It Was*, the source of many of these details:

> We were living in a world of twenty shades of blue, wind from some seventy different directions, sunlight and moonlight ever changing on the water, sounds varying from the gentlest slurp of finger-sized wavelets against the hull to banging thunder of heavy seas against the outer reefs, the fishy smell of the beach at low tide and the lung-scouring cleanliness of the north wind to the sophisticated tastes of Gregorio's simple, exquisite food. We were caught in a web of endearments to our senses.

In the next paragraph, she tells of how her husband seldom invited her to his own (and larger) bed belowdecks during their extended cruises— "and I thought I understood why. In our mutual sensory delights we were smoothly interlocking parts of a single entity, the big cogwheel and the smaller cogwheel, I felt, with no need for asserting togetherness. Maybe we were androgynous." Maybe so.

Six days out, the outside world broke in—with news of the death of Charlie Scribner. He'd died of a heart attack on the day they had left Havana. But it wasn't until Saturday the sixteenth, when Mary and Gregorio went with the skiff, after a morning's fishing, to buy ice and gas in a village called La Mulata, that they found out. Mary had telephoned the *finca* to see if things were okay with the staff and the property. René the houseboy read her the telegram. Mary and Gregorio motored back to *Pilar* before dark with the supplies and bad news. "We'll have to leave here," her husband said. But he'd heard on the shortwave a norther was coming, so they remained for a few more days.

That Monday, Hemingway wrote a letter to Scribner's wife, Vera, at the family estate in Far Hills, New Jersey. "At sea," he wrote at the top.

Mary asked me if I couldn't tell her something that would help her to reconcile herself or anything to console both of us because it was very bad. I told her the best thing was to think of how you and Charlie loved each other and how kind you were to each other when you were here and how proud he was of his children and his work and of you. How fortunate Charlie was to have the good fortune to be a Christian and how you had said your prayers together when you were down here.

A week later, at home, Hemingway wrote to Vera and Charlie's son, Charles Jr., who'd now be coming out of the navy to take over the firm: "Since he had to die at least he has gotten it over with." It's what he'd said, seventeen years before, to Gerald and Sara Murphy, when their son Baoth had died: *he has gotten it all over with.* That's the letter with the elaborate *Pilar* metaphor: "It seems as though we were all on a boat now together, a good boat still, that we have made but that we know now will never reach port. There will be all kinds of weather, good and bad." *Pilar* was so new then.

A couple of days before his letter to Charlie Junior, Hemingway had written to his own sons—Nita Jensen typed the letters from the talk machine. He'd been back on shore for two days. Patrick's was longer and kinder. In the five months since Pauline's death, Hemingway had been talking about many business matters to both his children by Pauline. One of these was the question of selling or renting out the Key West property, whose ownership had reverted to Hemingway and also to his sons. At least on paper, his sons had become well-off young men. Why should he be obligated to pay further child support to Gigi? "If Gregory is receiving the amounts of money which you told me you were receiving, or had received in the month of January, it seems a little incongruous for me to send him $100 a month," he told Pat. "It seems almost hopeless for me to write a letter to Gregory, since he does not answer them. But I will write one anyway." He did—it's the next letter on the tape belt, two paragraphs, mailed to Doreen Place in Venice. "This type of letter probably bores the shit out of you but it certainly bores the shit out of me to have to write them. Charlie Scribner died a week ago Monday and so it will be rather difficult for me to borrow money from him against my loan account paying two percent to send you a monthly check until you attain the age of 21 years."

Gigi wrote back four days later, using the bottom half of his father's letter: "I am not only tired of this type of letter but offended by everyone you write. If you were a shit as this type of letter would lead anyone to believe, I wouldn't mind, but I don't think you are and I love you very much and this is why I am offended."

Hemingway read it and wrote right back: "For your information I never took or received a dime from my family from the time I was 16. I paid my father's debts and supported various relatives and have supported Mary's father and mother since we were married. I do not relish being called a shit by any teenage delinquent at the safe distance of several thousand miles."

Two weeks later, the vacation got taken up again. The day before, on March 9, trying to repair relations with his son, Hemingway wrote: "Charlie Scribner dying so suddenly made things pretty complicated. . . . I was trying to skip burdening you with any of this when I wrote you that I would omit personal problems or whatever the phrase was. Have been busy trying to work them out and I have them worked out so that there is money for your hundred dollars a month until you are 21. So please never worry about that."

He and his wife were heading down the driveway on the morning of the tenth when Juan the chauffeur said, "¿Has oído lo que pasa en La Habana?" Have you heard what's happening in Havana? Fulgencio Batista was happening. Hemingway (he always sat in the front seat, Mary in the rear), reached over and switched on the radio. The army had surrounded the presidential palace. The road to town was clogged with convoys of canvas-roofed trucks, with soldiers sitting on the rims and riding on the running boards. But they got to the harbor and aboard *Pilar* and out to sea and rode against the wind to Bahía Honda. From *How It Was:* "One night we set the bright gas lantern on the stern fishbox, watched sardines in droves congregate toward it just below the surface." Gregorio netted them for bait—which, the next day, netted for the fishermen some tasty Nassau grouper and turbot and rock hind. They stayed out until March 29 and then came home with the fish hold loaded to its brim. Two days later, an awkward, giddy couple drove out to see them to tell them of their news—and, to their surprise, got offered on the spot the use of the *finca* for their wedding reception. "It will add a romantic touch to the formalities," Walter put in his journal entry of March 31, 1952.

It's later that same summer, nine months since the death at St. Vincent's, two months from publication of *The Old Man and the Sea*. Gigi's finishing premed exams at UCLA, hoping to be admitted to the university's med school. In four months he'll turn twenty-one. He's seeing a psychiatrist. This letter's date is July 3. At its end: "Give my love to Miss Mary and tell her if I see her again I sure as hell would like all to be forgiven. I did a terrible thing in lying about that clothes business and I make no excuses for it (except to say that the whole business is my least rational aspect) but everyone's life is not simon says." He's talking about the French underpants theft from Mary's closet—six years ago. Has it swum upward in some recent therapy sessions?

Listen to the rage of four months onward, right around the time of his birthday: "You ever write another letter like that and I'll beat the shit out of you," he says to his father on November 3, nine days before his birthday. Several paragraphs later: "When Mother died and I first called, you accused me of killing her. . . . If we see each other again and you act nastily, I will fight and I will beat the shit out of you."

Ten days later, on the thirteenth, the day after he turns twenty-one, he calls his father a "gin-soaked abusive monster." He tells him he "will die unmourned and basically unwanted unless you change, papa." He says, "When it's all added up, papa it will be: he wrote a few good stories, had a novel and fresh approach to reality and he destroyed five persons—Hadley, Pauline, Marty [Gellhorn], Patrick, and possibly myself. Which do you think is the most important, your self-centered shit, the stories or the people?" He says, bringing up his mother:

> You accused me of killing her—said it was my arrest that
> killed her. For your information, a heart condition is incurred
> over a period of time. Do you think that little scene did her
> any good? I would never think of accusing you of killing
> her . . . but you accused me, you cocksucker—you wonder if
> I don't forget all and kiss your sickly ass when you send me
> a birthday greeting? You think you can repair a break in the
> damn with a telegram? God have mercy on your soul for the
> misery you have caused. If I ever meet you again and you start
> pulling the ruthless, illogical and destructive shit on me, I will
> beat your head into the ground and mix it with cement to
> make outhouses.

There's a PS to the letter that amounts to a letter in itself.

Next day: "I suppose you wonder what has happened to all my filial respect for you. Well, it's gone Ernestine, dear, it's gone!"

Ernestine, dear.

Further down: "Little goody-goody Miss Mary, for instance, who's taken more shit from you than they dump in Havana harbor. But we know better, don't we, you'll never write that great novel because you're a sick man—sick in the head and too fucking proud and scared to admit it. In spite of the critics, that last one was as sickly a bucket of sentimental slop as was ever scrubbed off a barroom floor."

Four days later, Hemingway answers:

> Your threats to beat up your father are comic enough.
> Ordinarily I would ignore such nonsense. But obscene threat-
> ening letters sent through the United States mails are not
> comic at all. . . . I am not a gin-soaked monster going around
> running people's lives. . . . Your mother wrote me before she
> died that she did not believe that you were taking drugs but
> that you had simply deteriorated mentally so that you were
> unable to accept any discipline and that even any suggestions
> angered you. . . . Right now I could use a good flash of your
> old charm and decency. I cannot use any more obscene or
> threatening letters. Mary can do without your thefts and your
> insults.

He signs it, "Your father, E. Hemingway."

Three days later, Gigi replies, and *please understand* is all over the page, as is the need for a cease-fire. "The clothes business is something that I have never been able to control, understand basically very little, and I am terribly ashamed of. I have lied about it before, mainly to people I am fond of, because I was afraid they would not like me as much if they found out. It has been a terribly destructive influence on my life and is undoubtedly responsible for a lot of moral disintegration."

About four days later, a father, who must have had nearby a work in progress about sex-twinning honeymooners and their fears of moral disin-tegration, wrote across the front of Gigi's envelope: "No answer."

In *Papa*, Gigi wrote: "My mother made her absences in the early and most formative years of my life readily explicable later on, when she admitted, 'Gig, I just don't have much of what's called a maternal instinct, I guess. I can't *stand* horrid little children until they are five or six. . . . But I loved you, darling, I really did, though I guess I didn't always show it.'" This

paragraph ends: "Understood completely and forgiven. But not originally."
Did he ever really forgive? It's hard to believe that.

In late September 1945, back from war, trying to heal, to begin serious
writing again, Hemingway said in a letter to his future wife, Mary Welsh:

> 13 years since Gigi was born and twenty one since Bum but
> don't believe the basic problems have changed much. . . .
> Went to Africa after Giggy was born. He born in Oct., went
> abroad following July and didn't come back until the next year
> after May or June. Along about April (ten months) Pauline
> said, "I think I ought to see my Baby." . . . I love them but
> learned from haveing to take all care of Bumby that anybody
> *good* you hire can take better care of them at the start than
> I can and no reason to have the drudgery wear out husband
> and wife or split them apart and no sense ever have baby
> drive you crazy.

Hemingway and Pauline went to Africa in 1933, when Gigi was two, so
he's off in his dates by about a year. Nor are other time frames right. But
it isn't that; it's the casual claim that a mother, who couldn't stand horrid
little children, had more or less yawned near the end of the long absence
and said: *Mmmm, guess I oughta see my Gig.* Not that her husband was any
less accountable. (They'd left their baby child in the care of a shadowy
woman named Ada Stern. For at least part of the time away, five-year-old
Patrick was put with relatives in Piggott. The Dickensian-named Miss
Stern, from upstate New York, had begun watching over Gigi when he was
three months old—and she tended him until he was twelve. In *Papa*, Gigi
describes how, when he was a toddler, she'd threaten to leave him when he
was bad. "She would pack her bags and go hobbling down the stairs with
me clinging to her skirts, screaming, 'Ada, don't leave me, please don't leave
me.'" And Ada would say, "All right, I'll stay, you little shitsky." He loved
her, though, in spite of everything.)

In *Papa*, Gigi makes it sound as if he might not ever have spoken again to
his father had Hemingway not suffered those two back-to-back airplane
crashes in East Africa (near Murchison Falls in January 1954) from which,
as we now know, he never really recovered in either his body or mind. Gigi
writes: "The first headlines announced that the wreckage of the plane had
been sighted and that there was no sign of life. Thinking he was dead, I

realized how much I still loved him. When I found out soon afterward that he had survived, I resolved to patch up our differences. After he won the Nobel Prize that October, I sent him a congratulatory wire."

What he doesn't say—once again, John Hemingway in *Strange Tribe* fills in the record—is that there was a quiet letter of apology nearly six months before that wire. He'd said, "I didn't mean to say those things. I was crazy at the time, just as crazy as Mouse was when he used to swing at you during the shock treatments [of 1947]. If you don't ever want to see me again, O.K., but I hope you will change your mind when you find out over a period of time that I am on my feet again." Over the next several months father and son talked of business matters, family matters. In early August 1954, Hemingway wrote a letter any child would crave to have.

> I've digested what you told me about you not feeling ok when you were writing those bad letters. I know, beside accepting what you told me, that it is true on acct. of the penmanship. Now everything is straight. Not chickenshit like forgiveness. Rubbed out. Any time you want to show up: show up I am working hard now and not seeing anybody. . . .
>
> This is not a cry towell letter. It is just to give you the gen. In the aircraft nonsense I got smashed really bad. I never had a broken back before, certified anyway, and it can be uncomfortable and shitting standing up, while not a difficult feat, can get to be a bore. . . . I went 22 days when I couldn't unlock the spincter. Then shat a species of white hard nobby rocks about ball size. . . . One time when I missed from my berth to the can Miss Mary said, "Don't you know that no gentleman ever shits on the floor?"

Soon they were talking about the possibility of Gigi going to Africa to visit his brother Pat. Gigi wanted to take his wife and child, and also his old governess. His father thought it a terrible idea to take a child and a sixty-seven-year-old woman to Africa—the risk of infection would be enormous. Gigi made a budget and asked his father for $2,500. Hemingway promised to send it—and more, if he won the Nobel, which was shortly to be announced. "About dough again," he wrote on October 12, sixteen days before he got the prize: "I have $6,046.81 in the bank. $33,000 income tax paid this year. . . . I pay $320 a month for Mary's mother and father in the nursing home, which adds up to $3,840 per year, plus extra expenses, and is a little more than half of my total income from all securities which I had originally intended to be a reserve fund for when I was sick. My basic income, if I were ill and could not work, is about the same as yours and Mouse's."

The next day, talking again of Africa's danger: "There are all sort of things there are no serums against."

Gigi did go to Africa with his family in early 1955, and about all of it was a disaster. He departed with $5,000 in his pocket from his father—"right off the top of the tax-free bounty of Sweden," he says in *Papa*. He had an affair with the wife of a plantation owner. He threw down money from his inheritance on a coffee farm. But he had no real interest, let alone know-how, in managing a coffee operation. In Nairobi bars, he drank himself into stupors. In the bush, he wouldn't come out of his tent for days. He got into quarrels with his brother Pat, who was trying to establish himself as a guide and white hunter in Tanganyika. In December, his wife gathered up four-year-old Lorian and flew back to America, to her sister's place in Arkansas. In a few months, there was her husband on her doorstep, crying, drunk, making threats, eventually getting himself arrested. None of this appears in *Papa*. What appears: "I felt guilty about Mother's inheritance, thought that since I had killed her it was blood money, and I got rid of it incredibly fast. My marriage finally broke up and I was drafted into the army."

On the page before this: "I shot eighteen elephants one month, God save my soul. But it's no use running when you're sick, because when you finally stop, you find you're just as sick as when you started." Such beautiful ellipsis.

It was apparently somewhere in here—mid-to-late 1955, maybe into early 1956—that Gigi's father wrote an elliptical story about a boy and wing shooting and plagiarism. Its first sentence: " 'It's a very good story,' the boy's father said." Its last: "And it was sad to know that shooting did not mean a thing."

About the army, into which he was sworn, on the fifth anniversary of Pauline's death, October 1, 1956: they sent him home before he completed basic training. The ex–buck private, judged psychologically unstable, turned up in Miami, unloading trucks. His father, just across the Straits of Florida, hadn't heard.

From *Papa:* "After an undistinguished career in the peacetime army, I went back to Africa to do more killing. Somehow it was therapeutic. Although the yellow-green emotional filter was still in place, the focus of my mind was sharpening."

About the killing and the elephants: years later, in Montana bars, when he was a doctor, and a damn fine one (until everything got bitched again), the fleeing man used to tell friends, in various states of melancholy and rage, "Those assholes, they believed what I wrote about the eighteen elephants." He meant the readers of his best-selling book, and all the subsequent Hemingway chroniclers who'd passed the story on.

In the approximately five years between the end of his army "career" in 1956 and his father's death in 1961, Gigi did little but disappoint and often disgust his father. The reverse could also be said. More manic trips to Africa, more depressive ricochets back home, with Hemingway paying many of the bills, including hospital bills. On August 15, 1957, Gigi ended up in a Miami medical center, where they gave him shock treatments for what was diagnosed as schizophrenia. "I'm sorry that I got into this shape, but I will be out of here soon," he wrote to his father, five days after he was admitted. Hemingway wrote back, in a softened key:

> Thanks very much for your two letters. I've talked to
> Dr. Jarrett and to Dr. Anderson and arranged to handle the
> hospital bills and the cost of your treatments as you asked in
> your letter of August 20. . . . They say that treatment cannot
> possibly do your brain any harm. . . . We want to do everything
> that can be done to make you well, Gig. . . . Do you have a
> good radio? If not, ask the hospital to rent you one. I will pick
> up the bill with the regular bill. The same holds true for maga-
> zines and books. . . . [T]ake it as easy as you can and know that
> for once we are getting something constructive accomplished
> on these worries that have bothered you for so long.

These worries. Keep it in code. And yet the caring—undeniably.

When Gigi was let out, in mid-October, Hemingway flew over to Miami to meet him and they drove down to Key West in a rented car, stopping at various bridges to look at the sea. So far as anyone seems to know, this is the last time they were ever physically together. Two months later, Gigi was back in the same hospital.

A couple of months later, he got this letter from his father: "Times are really rough now and going to be much rougher. . . . When I have to worry about you I can't write. It knocks everything out of my head and this is the time I have to work or else. . . . Have been lashing myself to work for so long under difficulties, bad financial problems, no chance to get out on the boat for nearly two months with this godawful weather." The letter's date is February 4, 1958. The black-sheep son was still two and a half years from starting medical school (Gigi got admitted to the class of 1959 at the University of Miami School of Medicine, but dropped out almost immediately); two and a half years from reading his mother's autopsy; two and a half years from writing a letter in his bad penmanship to his wrecked father that said, no, it couldn't have been me, it was you.

In July 1968, seven years after the Idaho suicide, four years from finishing med school, a thirty-six-year-old bipolar doctor, who'd become a doctor, in spite of everything, took his daughter, Lorian, on a fishing trip to Bimini. Gigi was now the father of five children, by three women. He was also a medical resident in anesthesiology. (He wouldn't finish this residency, at Jackson Memorial Hospital in Miami, as he hadn't completed an earlier orthopedic fellowship in Boston.) Gigi's wife now was Valerie Danby-Smith, from Ireland, who'd been raised in a convent boarding school. He'd met and picked her up (literally, in a borrowed station wagon) at his father's funeral. For a brief time, Valerie had worked as his father's last secretary and fantasy love projection. (Hemingway met her in Spain, in 1959, when she was nineteen.) She'd soon be giving birth to Gigi's sixth child.

Actually, Gigi had married this third wife twice by this time—first in Mexico City, in September 1966, when he wasn't yet unmarried from his second wife, Alice, who, a few months before, in March 1966, had given birth to Gigi's fourth child. (His name is Patrick Hemingway.) Gigi had taken care of these complications, and had married Valerie again, in Miami, in November of the succeeding year, that is, 1967, with a champagne toast at Uncle Les's house in Miami Beach.

Has that confused you? At almost any point where you try to pick up Gigi's story, its zigs and zags will drive you nuts.

The fishing story isn't confusing at all. It amounts to a chapter in Lorian Hemingway's *Walk on Water*, a slim, beautiful book about all kinds of angling and all kinds of legacies. Lorian is Gigi's first child, another writer in the family, like her younger half brother, John. She's a small woman with dark-socketed eyes, an old soul, older than her years, who has lived a life of pain, much of it self-rendered. *Walk* was published in 1998, three years before Gigi died. The two never got to spend very much time together. Of Gigi and his lifelong gender tortures, Lorian writes: "The truth is, I never had a clue until my mother told me that he sometimes wore her girdle and painted his nails a bright, clean red. Not until, say, the change of life had become a foregone thing. I've seen pictures. He looks like Ethel Merman. Around Mother's Day, in the Hallmark section, I am tortured. There are no greeting cards that read, 'Thinking of you fondly, transvestite Dad.' Or, 'On your special day, Whatsit.'" That would sound mean if you didn't understand how much hurt it's filtered through.

Lorian was sixteen when her dad took her over to the speck of sand and coral that his own dad had conquered in the thirties aboard *Pilar.* Lorian hadn't seen Gigi in more than ten years. Still, she wished to think of him as a father. She needed a real father: in tenth grade, she'd been expelled twice. Against her mother's advice, she'd located Gigi, wrote to him, got back in the mail a plane ticket to Miami. On the way to the Bahamas, they stared out the scratched windows of the Grumman Goose at the twenty shades of blue, trying to think of things to say. "Marlin," Gigi told Lorian. "We are going for the great blue marlin. Four hundred pounds, five hundred pounds, six hundred pounds in these waters. Monsters, huge, their bills like swords, their girth massive. You hook into one and they walk on water."

They chartered a boat from Captain Bob Smith, famous Bimini guide. Out of sight of Gigi, Captain Bob made a gagging reflex with his finger: he was telling Lorian that her dad always got sick on boats.

" 'You say he never catches fish,' I asked, feeling vaguely ashamed.

" 'No fish, mon, sure. I tell you right.' "

Except that this time they hooked into a monster. "The rod butt was wedged securely in the gimbal on the belt around my father's waist, his left hand white knuckle as it clutched the grip on the butt. . . . I looked at my father, at the pure fear that washed his face. . . . The panic in his eyes, the strong need to not screw up, was all over him like a rash. I could even smell it on him."

The fish dived and Gigi didn't slack to him. The line snapped.

"My father looked broken. There is no other word for it. He sat crumpled in the chair, folded in on himself, his face an odd off-white, and I couldn't help myself. I reached out, touching my fingertips lightly to his forehead."

Lorian said, "Sorry, Greg."

Her dad: "You're a pretty girl." He reached over and drew his fingers along the side of her cheek. "A very pretty girl. Call me 'Father,' would you?" In a minute Gigi got sick over the side. As he pulled himself up,

Lorian saw the nail polish, "a slash of it on two cracked and dirty nails . . . a red bright as the inside of the marlin's hooked jaw."

The chapter ends: "The next time I saw him was twenty years later, in a photo, a glossy eight-by-ten, and in that picture he is a woman, a stocky, bowlegged brute of a woman but a woman nonetheless. His hair is frosted in a bouffant style, his nose bobbed and straightened, and he grins to show two even rows of capped teeth."

The saddest line in Lorian's sad, beautiful book appears several pages before: "How did it feel, exactly, to keep losing?"

In the late sixties and into the back half of the seventies, Gigi lived mainly in New York City with his third family. These years amounted to something like stability—not that there weren't hospitalizations, and shock treatments, and much self-medication (lithium was the new hope, although he tended not to self-prescribe it), and crazed sprees in the women's department at Saks Fifth Avenue. (The pattern was to wear the stuff once, stuff it in a Dumpster. The pattern was also to take from his wife's closet, return the things stinking of cheap perfume and caked around their stretched-out necks—if they were dresses—with dime store makeup.)

He held a string of jobs that bored him, working as a part-time in-house physician at corporations like Standard Oil, General Motors, and McGraw-Hill publishers. He took his kids on Saturday mornings to a playground in Central Park called Little Egypt. He wrote *Papa*, not without alienating editors and switching publishing houses and offending many others, including his uncle Les, who'd helped raise several of his children, and who'd agreed to help out in some of the writing of the memoir, but who'd ended up getting stiffed for any fee or percentage of the royalties. (They went to court but then settled and didn't speak again.) Still, the book must have brought to him all he dreamed of: toasts from Norman Mailer at Elaine's restaurant, cover of *The New York Times Book Review*, alternate selection at the Book-of-the-Month Club. It was almost as if he were beating the subject of the damn book, not that the feeling could last.

It was also in this period that Gigi began talking out loud about the possibility of turning himself surgically into a woman. The esteemed British travel writer James Morris had altered himself sexually in Morocco in 1972. If James could become Jan, why couldn't Gigi become Gloria? "If I had a sex change, could we still be friends? Could we continue living together as girlfriends, going out to lunch, shopping and to the beauty par-lor? Wouldn't it be fun?" Gigi said one night to his wife, after the kids were in bed in the family's two-bedroom apartment on East Eighty-seventh Street. Valerie Hemingway has told this story, and so many others, in her brave Hemingway family memoir, *Running with the Bulls: My Years with the Hemingways,* which, like *Strange Tribe,* got unjustly ignored when it appeared in 2004. Her directness and unpretentiousness and honesty are what move the reader, and yet, having said that, it also needs to be said that, in 2002, when *Rolling Stone* magazine did a long piece on Gigi ("The Good Son"), publishing it close to the first anniversary of his death, Val-erie Hemingway was quoted as saying, "He was a very smart, very with-it, all-together person. And we had a lot of fun together. I never, ever saw him cross-dressed." Was the embarrassment over her husband's life too much to own up to, at least initially, at least in the pages of *Rolling Stone,* in the way the embarrassment and horror of what Ernest Hemingway did on that Sunday morning in Ketchum was too much for *his* wife to admit to, at least in the immediate aftermath? At the close of *Running with the Bulls,* having quietly told so many Gigi stories, Valerie says, "[H]e suffered far more than anyone I have ever known." She would have been including in that statement Gigi's father.

Montana is a very large part of the Gigi Hemingway story. It's where he lived on and off for the last quarter century of his life, where so much hope and hard work and honest doctorly trying came to dust.

In the summer of 1976, when he was forty-four, and on the heels of his literary triumph, Gigi secured his first Montana medical job. His brother Pat lived in Bozeman; Jack was one state over, in Ketchum. Under that big tent of western sky, near his siblings, he hoped to save himself. He worked as a general practitioner in the old fur-trading town of Fort Benton. It was a good job, but after a year or so he walked off.

By the late seventies, with Valerie and the kids still living in New York, Gigi had signed on as a country doctor in Jordan, Montana. This was his best moment in medicine, and he made the moment last for almost five years, until the spring of 1983. The town, in the far eastern part of the state, had a population of six hundred; the county, fifteen hundred. Garfield County's four-bed hospital, with its adjoining nurs-ing home, was said to be the remotest hospital in the lower forty-eight. Gigi, with his ratty little red Subaru hatchback, was the sole MD in an area a little smaller than Connecticut. He seized on the work and the place and the life. When I was writing the pieces for *The Washington Post*, four years after Gigi had lost his practice in Jordan, I spoke on the telephone to about a dozen Garfield Countians. What they wished to remember was all the good, even though they told me eventually of some of the bad. "I'll tell you what, you never saw a guy work like this," John Fitzgerald, the town pharmacist, said. "Everything from headaches to delivering babies. Hell, the next nearest town from here is Miles City, and that's eighty-three miles away. He was a little rusty when he first came here—I don't think he'd practiced in a while—but, boy, did he work. He rode in the ambulance, he stayed up all night with sick old women. He never once tried to dine out on his name."

Gigi lived in a county-provided ratty trailer a block or two from the hospital, which was located in the center of town. Ratty because of the way he kept it. He'd pile up TV dinners and half-eaten pizzas on the floor by the couch, stub out half-smoked cigarettes on the wall and let them fall where they wanted to fall. Forget about making the bed, which always seemed askew of its frame. Forget about flushing the toilet, as long as it was just his pee. But there he was by eight the next day over at the hospital, with his lab coat and stethoscope and amazing energy: Doc, as everybody knew him. Doc Hemingway loved to arm-wrestle townsmen over the counter at the admissions desk—not somebody sick, but maybe a cowboy half his own age who'd brought in his ill wife or young child. Almost always, you could take him. "That's the funny part," John Fitzgerald told me. "This muscular little fireplug guy, who thought he was tough, was easy to take. And yet I think Greg was trying to become a man out here again in Jordan. He'd give you twenty-four hours straight, if you had to have it." Fitzgerald, twelve years younger than Gigi, his closest friend, who'd consult with him on the phone three or four times a day, didn't tell me about the arm wrestling in our 1987 conversations. He said it a few months ago, as I write. It was twenty-odd years onward from the last time we'd spoken, and Fitzgerald was still the county's only pharmacist, and Gigi had been dead for almost a decade. The Jordan Drug Company was closing down—Fitzgerald and his wife were about to retire. Jordan's population was less than three hundred; the county's below twelve hundred. The high school had forty-four kids—and a six-man football team.

I also got back in touch with several of the county nurses with whom I'd talked before—they were still there. Jana Olson was getting set to leave Montana, to go over toward Oregon and semi-retirement. Last time, she'd said, "We were doing all we could to try and understand Doctor Hemingway. He had a lot invested here." This time, in and amid the still-tender mercies, Olson began remembering something else: Gigi's need to keep his patients alive. "I've thought a lot about this," Olson said. "It was something way beyond. Doc just wouldn't let people die. Elderly people who needed to be allowed to die. Their veins so fragile. He'd demand another IV. They'd be so edematous. It was like water under their skin. I'd say to myself, 'Why are we doing this IV antibiotic on someone who should be allowed to die?' There was this one woman—her third vein blew. I told him I wouldn't try again. He'd just come in. He grabbed her chart. He screamed at me, 'We're keeping this woman alive, do you hear me?'"

I told Olson about Pauline. The line fell quiet.

Valerie and the family came west on July 4, 1980—Gigi's pleading had finally paid off. (Their youngest child, Vanessa Hemingway, whose name he'd already tried on a time or two, in his trailer, along with the corsets and girdles, was ten.) But the family didn't settle in Jordan, rather in Bozeman, 320 miles to the east. Bozeman was a city, with a university. He and Valerie bought a house on Bridger Canyon Road, up by Bridger Bowl, in the ski basin. The plan was for Gigi to go back and forth every other weekend. He had worked hard to get everything in place before the family arrived: horses for the kids, camping equipment, ski equipment, fishing gear, rubber rafts for river running, a snowmobile. He'd gotten the snowmobile secondhand from John Fitzgerald, who tried to help him wedge it into the back of his hatchback. They roped it in and let a quarter of it stick out the back. Just as he was leaving town, it started to snow—heavily. Gigi pulled his ski cap down over his ears, turned the heater up full blast, and drove the six hours to Bozeman with a near blizzard filling up the back of his car. Years before, when he was a med student, trying to make it back to Miami from Bimini in a hurricane on a Sunday afternoon in his fifteen-foot open skiff with its two twin Johnson outboards, he'd been warned by the locals not to go. He went anyway—gunning the Johnsons like a madman, trying simultaneously to bale out the skiff with a bucket.

For the next several years, things went along, sort of. From *Running with the Bulls:* "The weekends passed. Sometimes Greg came home, sometimes not. He always arrived late and it was clear he had stopped at a motel on the way to indulge his habit. He became increasingly careless, arriving with obvious lipstick stains, eye makeup, ears bloody from self-piercing, traces of nail polish. During the weekends he was distant and quarrelsome or weepy and apologetic." Okay, but how exhausted must he have been:

640 miles, round-trip, by car, every other weekend, and all that doctoring—to a Connecticut-size county—in between?

There were two bars in Jordan. The Hell Creek was the cowboy bar. It was the "uptown" drinking establishment. You could make a movie there—cane chairs with swirled backs, big mirrors behind the bar, polished old dark wood to lean your elbows on and order up. Into the Hell Creek one Friday night came Doc in drag. He had on a blond wig and heels. His unshaven face was smudged with makeup. He ordered a drink. He took out a little coin purse. There wasn't enough money in the purse, so he pulled up his dress and fished out a bill from inside his pantyhose. On Monday he was on the job. "That was the thing," Fitzgerald said. "Everyone knew; no one said a word. We needed him here; hell, we loved him here. He worked so hard. Too much damage to this man."

One day Gigi called the hospital administrator a "cocksucker" and chased him upstairs. One day he got one of the nurses by the neck, pinning her on the wall, holding her up by the V fold of her scrubs. "Don't you ever question my authority," he yelled. One weekend—it was spring of 1983—he didn't come home. The telephone rang on Bridger Canyon Road. The police department in Ketchum was calling. With his wife's identification, Gigi had gone into Sun Valley boutiques and tried on women's clothes, smearing them with lipstick and makeup before he came out of the dressing stall. He'd ruined $1,000 of merchandise.

The newest mania—already in full swing—was winning the Boston Marathon that April. The country doc from Montana began telling anyone who'd listen he was going to make history by winning the Boston Marathon at age fifty-one. "He'd run twenty miles in the wind around here," John Fitzgerald recalled. "He sent away and got every map there was of the course layout. He'd sit with me for hours and go over the route. I think he had the whole course memorized—a thirty-one percent grade here, a wide turn there. He had to win that damn race—or place very high."

To this day, people in Jordan and Bozeman believe he competed, but Valerie Hemingway says in *Bulls* that he never flew to Boston, didn't check into his reserved room at the Copley Plaza, but rather hid out somewhere else. He'd arranged for a leave of absence from the county commissioners and the hospital administrator, and he stayed away far past his leave. John Fitzgerald got a call maybe two weeks after the race. *Listen, John, I fought hard, but couldn't finish. Listen, John, need a favor—would you go down to the hospital and make up some story about why I'm not back?* Fitzgerald said he wouldn't do that. Gigi slammed down the phone. A week later, he drove into town, stopped at the drugstore, went to his trailer, threw some things together, and drove out of town on the same day.

He came back once, maybe a year and a half later. He was living in Missoula by then, in another medical job. He'd served Valerie with divorce papers. (The divorce would drag on for three and a half years—until October 1987.) Into the pharmacy one summer day tottered this wide, short figure wearing a cockeyed wig and a fire-engine-red two-piece suit and matching high heels. No female in the historical memory of Garfield County had ever shown up downtown in a red suit on a summer's day. The person sat down at the old 1937 soda fountain, asked for a Coke. Fitzgerald: "I was down the way filling prescriptions. None of us knew what to say. We pretended not to know it was him. I guess it was our embarrassment. He had the Greg voice. He made the ugliest woman you ever saw. I think he wanted us to recognize him. I think I see now we weren't giving him the one thing he wanted most—to be recognized, to be addressed as Greg. We did not do this." Gigi finished his Coke, got up, and left.

So he was in Missoula, home of the University of Montana, with a writer or would-be writer under every rock, sleeping in his car, living in an upper room in an alley off Spruce Street, or booking himself for weeks at a time into room 102 at the Thunderbird Motel. For the rest of his life, Gigi would make this room and this motel, with its big red western neon welcoming sign, one of his safe havens. Years later, after his sex change, he'd come back to 102 during his recovery and say to the motel owner, Thelma Baker (to whom he'd once proposed), "Thelma, you're my only friend."

He moved into a two-level apartment just out of Missoula, on Rattlesnake Creek. His bedroom window looked out on the rushing stream, which supported populations of cutthroats and rainbows. On the other side of the creek was a narrow little park with benches, and he'd go across just before dark and sit and look at the water. In late June 1985, his second child, John, who was in his mid-twenties and had been living in Italy, came to visit. Gigi left him a key beneath the doormat. John opened the door to rank odors, broken furniture, gouges in the walls. Gigi was working as a doctor over in Deer Lodge—although not for long.

One morning, Gigi, who'd been out all night, stuck his head in the apartment. From *Strange Tribe:* "Greg was wearing a blond wig, a knee-length, cream-colored sequined dress, and matching high-heeled shoes. His cherry-red lipstick was smudged, and he reminded me of a four-year-old who's decided to play with his mother's cosmetics." This was the first time John had witnessed his father in women's clothing. Gigi went up to his room and put on khakis and a polo shirt and they went out to pancakes at the Four B's restaurant. The father tried to explain to his son about his lifelong need to wear nylons and dresses and makeup.*

Not long after, John and Gigi drove up to Canada to pick up John's girlfriend, Ornella (who today is John's wife and mother of his two children). On the way down to Missoula, Gigi began flirting with Ornella. He plucked her flowers from the roadside and handed them over like a smitten boy. Back at the apartment there was an ugly scene. This was Friday, July 12, 1985. Gigi banged out of the place and stayed out all night. At dawn, drunk or high or both, he tried to invade a woman's aerobics class at the Missoula Athletic Club—in bare feet and a sports bra and red hot-pants. Later that morning he showed up at the Four B's, and when they wouldn't serve him because he was in drag, he kicked out the glass in the front door. (He was wearing shoes by then.) The manager called the cops, but Gigi beat it in his car over to East Missoula, where he stood at a pay phone outside a liquor store and called up a writer named William Kittredge. "Bill," he said, in an oddly dignified voice, "I need a keeper. Might you be that person?" Kittredge wasn't, but he helped out with some money and a cheap motel room. But Gigi was too agitated. About midnight he came back to the apartment on Rattlesnake Creek and fell into his water bed, and early on Sunday the police were at the door to arrest him. He went without incident, with a sad little wave at his son and his son's girlfriend. On Monday, John was in the courtroom when his father shuffled in wearing an orange jumpsuit. Gigi wrote furious notes, which he kept trying to hand over to

---

*At an international Hemingway conference in Kansas City in 2008, John Hemingway and I met and became friends. We talked of the Missoula incidents and others like it. John was almost forty-eight and lived in Montreal with his wife and two children. *Tribe* had come out the year before. I asked why he wrote the book, but I knew why—the answer was implicit on nearly every page. He said, "It made me angry that a lot of people thought of my father as some kind of circus freak. As if there was no explanation or logic for all his torments. As a son, who loved him, even though I'd gone years without talking to him, I found this personally insulting. See, there was a time when I was blaming my father for everything bad that had ever happened in my life." John wore jeans and sneakers and carried a knapsack. He was short and compact and muscled. The Hemingway grin was there. He spoke in a softly charged voice. If he was emotionally generous, he was also self-protective. He'd jump backward as he spoke. He'd say something, and then the quick little hop back. It was like a fighter, feinting. I asked if he got together much with his seven siblings. "No, no," he said, laughing. I asked about the order of Gigi's kids. He answered slowly, needing to think it through. Lorian was first; he was second. He tabbed on his fingers: Maria, Patrick, Sean, Edward, Vanessa—and Brendan, who was out of the order, because he was Valerie's son by the Irish author Brendan Behan. "Yeah, that's all of us," he said, pleased.

the court. Municipal Judge Wallace Clark, who knew Gigi and liked him and was an old military type, sentenced him to six months. A day or so later, Gigi put in a collect call to Larry Howell, the police reporter for the local paper, the *Missoulian*. He told Howell that the only reason he'd pleaded guilty was because he thought the judge would be lenient. He said he'd been dressed as a woman when he kicked out the door of the Four B's because he was the son of Ernest Hemingway and was doing research for a novel. He told the reporter to go over to the public library and take out a copy of *Papa*, and to look at his jacket photograph, and then to come to the jail to talk to him. Howell did this and wrote a small story with this headline: "Hemingway Lands in Jail." Two weeks later, Gigi got released to the custody of a psychologist at a clinic in Butte, where he dodged treatment. But word was out now in wider ways. His story was making the papers, at least locally.

Nine months later, on April 9, 1986, this *Missoulian* headline: "Hemingway Jailed on Criminal Mischief Charges." The story, by the same reporter, told how Gigi had kicked in another door and thrown a rock through a window while dressed as a woman. The manager of the Rancho Motel said Gigi had been making sexual advances toward two employees. The police report said he was writing himself prescriptions and was drunk. They transferred him to the psychiatric wing of St. James Hospital in Butte. After this—not immediately—he'd lose his license to practice medicine in the state. After this, he'd request permission to enter a sanitarium in Atlanta for addicted doctors. According to Valerie Hemingway, when the plane landed in Atlanta, Gigi walked up to a ticket desk and got a flight to Miami, which is where he mainly stayed for the next few years. Through the efforts of a pal with whom he'd been in med school, and who was now director of a pharmacological department at the University of Miami, Gigi got a chance to reenter his profession. He told anyone who'd listen he was going to reapply himself and work doubly hard. He studied intensely for the Florida boards. And then one day he didn't show up at Jackson Memorial Hospital. It was the last medical try. After this you could find him hanging out in an up-from-hippie Coconut Grove alehouse called the Taurus; or sleeping in Peacock Park down by the waterfront with its whipping sailboat flags; or sitting all day in the woody little library across from the park, reading fiction, biography, newspapers—anything that hit the line of vision.

In early summer 1987, there was a family wedding in south Florida.

Much of the extended Hemingway clan came. Gigi wasn't invited, not that anyone knew where he was, exactly. He was within a causeway or so. And it was right in here, with me knowing practically none of this, just as I was getting set to leave Ketchum and fly back east to try to write a story for my newspaper with a hole in its middle, that the phone in my motel room rang. I remember one of the first things he said, that next evening, when I got into that dark Coconut Grove house with those scary Haitian masks hanging down from the ceiling. It was about fishing. It was about water. He said, "I was down in the Keys the other day. I went bonefishing out in the flats. I used a crab. You put a pole in a holder and then you doze off and then the line jerks you awake."

Telescoping the next fourteen years in a life that's too often been misreported, sensationalized, circus-freaked; telescoping them, in order to tell more closely the last several weeks.

In 1988, Gigi had a breast implant. This was the first surgical feint. But he still tended to dress as a man far more often than as a woman. He liked Lacoste polo shirts, and to see that bulge on the left side of his chest, behind the green alligator, was disconcerting for friends and dates and strangers alike. (A woman he was dating told him he was trying to be two ideas at once, which was more or less true.) Three years after the implant, in February 1991, a busty, brassy Florida blond named Ida Mae Galliher followed Gigi into the ladies room of the Taurus, on the edge of downtown Coconut Grove. Galliher, who knew how to drink and swear, and who was ten years younger and a head taller than Gigi, drove a Mercedes convertible. She talked a passable game at literature and politics and real estate. "You look like a Hemingway," she'd told him, as they primped before the mirror in the bathroom. Twenty-one months later, on November 21, 1992, they were married. Fifty guests came to the garden of Gigi's boyhood home, and sat on white chairs, while cats wandered in and out the many doors of 907 Whitehead and rubbed up against stockings or pant legs. His old boyhood home had been a museum since the early 1960s, a National Historic Landmark since 1968.

Money? That night in Coconut Grove, I had asked Gigi about the fact that Hemingway had disinherited his children, but that a negotiation had eventually been reached over the will and with Mary Hemingway. It was clear he didn't want to talk about money. But I had been able to find out that royalties from foreign book sales currently being shared by the three sons almost always came to at least $120,000 annually for each, except that Gigi's part was under the control of a court-appointed conservator.

In August 1994, Hemingway biographer Jeffrey Meyers looked up Gigi out west with one of Gigi's sons. A decade earlier, Meyers had interviewed Gigi and Valerie for his work in progress. Gigi had recently bought a house on Airport Road in Ennis, Montana. He and his fourth wife were in the midst of a divorce, and he'd trashed the new place almost before he'd moved in. "Are you still fucking my wife?" Gigi asked, trying to punch Meyers in the stomach. Gigi offered his guest a beer and sat across the table from him, jabbing the opener in his direction. Meyers described the encounter in a 1999 piece for the *Virginia Quarterly Review*. Wrote Meyers: "Transposing his own fantasies onto his father, he claimed that Hemingway couldn't sleep at night because he dreamed he was a woman.... I tried to look suitably pious as we drove off, but our calm was soon shattered as Gregory, reckless as ever, chased us in his car, forced us off the narrow dirt road and passed us in a cloud of dust at high speed."

Late that year, Gigi checked into Dr. Stanley Biber's sex-change clinic in Trinidad, Colorado. Over the next few months, into early 1995, he underwent the series of operations that provided him a woman's sexual organs. (The surgery is said to have cost $20,000, paid in cash.) His divorce from Ida became final in 1995. He came back to the Thunderbird in Missoula, where his friend Thelma Baker, who'd once been a nurse, looked after him. Gigi's son, Edward, who was living in Bozeman, also came to help with the care. (He'd left the clinic too early and was experiencing hemorrhaging.) Gigi's son, Pat, and Pat's girlfriend came to Missoula and knocked on the door of 102. Gigi, feeling better, was swinging in and out of identities, talking to his boy in a growl about where the beer was, turning to Pat's girl and speaking in a trilling voice about makeup and how to cross your legs. Weekly, bundles of women's clothing bought over the QVC channel would arrive at his doorstep.

In the summer of 1995, Gigi, sixty-three years old, attended the First International Hemingway Colloquium in Havana. He came dressed as a man. The conferees found him warm, charming, and witty. One day he and some of the scholars went out to see the *finca*, and walking up the drive, he stopped, overcome. Later, when he met up with some of his old ball mates from Estrellas de Gigi, he wept again. "We were just boys," he said.

Five months later, on December 14, back in Florida, staying with his ex-wife at the home they'd purchased the first time around at 3558 Royal

Palm Avenue in the Grove, Gigi climbed early one morning onto a city bus. He was in black culottes, nylons, pumps, and a wig. He made sexual advances to the driver. He harassed a female rider. He told the driver that if he turned around one more time, he'd break his jaw. The driver pulled into an Amoco gas station on Southwest Twenty-Fourth Street and called the cops. It wasn't yet 8:00 a.m. "Let me show you that I'm a woman," he yelled at the officers. "Are you going to make me put down my skirt? You can get hurt that way." It took three policemen to subdue him. (They hit him in the shin with an ASP baton, but not before he'd gotten one of them in the groin with the spike of his high heel and had put another on the ground with a bloody mouth.) They booked him as John Doe; later, he told them to put down Gloria Hemingway. He was charged with aggravated battery to a police officer, resisting arrest with violence, and simple assault. He got out on a six-thousand-dollar bond. In *Strange Tribe,* John Hemingway says that his kid brother, Pat, was in Miami close to the time of Gigi's court date (which had been set for April 16, 1996). Gigi got his son to meet him at an old Coral Gables motel. From *Tribe:* "My brother drove over there with a brown paper bag full of the things Greg had asked for. . . . When Greg finally came out of his room, Pat saw him walk around the block twice. . . . Patrick said that he was wearing a dress and wasn't exactly inconspicuous as he tottered along in his high heels. . . . [I]t was his intention to flee the state. He didn't want to go to jail and was starting to panic."

A bit ahead of the court date, on March 26, the police had been called at 3:30 in the afternoon to the wooden-gated house on Royal Palm Avenue. Ida—who had said to friends that she had allowed Gigi back in because he had nowhere else to go, and, anyway, they still loved each other—told the officers that Gigi had stolen her car, had returned, had thrown a glass of Coke at her head, had declared, "I'll see you dead." What's astonishing in these incidents is how he kept managing not to serve real time.

That July, in Herb Caen's Monday gossip column, in the *San Francisco Chronicle,* there were the usual three dozen or so banalities for the morning transit riders, including this item: "The youngest son of one of the most macho American writers has just had the complete sex change operation and I guess that's showing Ol' Hairy Chest."

Still, there were moments of the old calm and decency. On July 4, 1999, the Hemingway-Pfeiffer Museum and Educational Center opened in Piggott, Arkansas. Gregory and Ida Hemingway were the guests of honor; they'd gotten remarried, before a judge, two years earlier, in Washington

State. Gigi wore a suit and cut the ribbon at the ceremony. It was 102 in the shade. He went over to the parlor of his aged aunt Matilda, who was Pauline's sister-in-law, and sat holding her hand. And yet, three weeks later, in Oak Park, at a party marking the one hundredth birthday of his father, Gigi was a wreck. His two brothers had come for the celebration. "I can't go in there," he said to an organizer, sitting on a step, crying. Inside, the crowd was singing, "Happy Birthday, Dear Ernest."

Six months later, in January 2000, he and his wife showed up in Bimini for another Hemingway conference. He was fine, if distant, company. There were no crackpot ravings or schemes for winning a Nobel Prize in science. He went out fishing with several of the scholars. The sessions were held in the same little white clapboard Wesley Methodist chapel his father used to slip into, after a day on *Pilar,* to watch light shaft across the wooden pews. Mostly, Gigi sat by himself up front, in a white guayabera. He was very round now. He had a bad left hip and clogged arteries and high blood pressure. There was something waxy and not quite real about his features. But you could have studied him from behind and almost convinced yourself: it's *him.* The other him.

It's the last photograph, so far as I know, ever taken of Ernest Hemingway's youngest son while he was still alive: a police mug shot, recorded, along with a right thumbprint, at about 1:05 p.m. on Wednesday, September 26, 2001, Gigi's last day as a free man (well, he was free only for part of that morning, until his 12:15 p.m. arrest), five days before his heart went into cardiac arrest on a cement floor.

If you knew nothing of his life, would you ever guess, from looking at this picture? I'm not talking about his surgical alterations but about his apparent devil-may-careness. Why does he appear so . . . untroubled? This can't be somebody living his life in deep shame. It's just some middle-aged, or maybe late-middle-aged, semi-androgynous guy with beach-boy hair and a toothy smile and what looks like a reddened nose and a gaze going straight at the lens. (That choker necklace was bought in a Key West trinket shop a few years earlier.)

That's a white hospital gown bunched around his shoulders.

I think I know exactly why Gigi looks so untroubled, or wishes to appear that way. He's trying to cover all the rottenness he feels inside, has always felt inside.

When the police had picked him up fifty minutes earlier, when he had been sitting bewildered and seemingly drunk on a strip of median curb at 1121 Crandon Boulevard in Key Biscayne, right outside the entrance to Bill Baggs Cape Florida State Park, he'd had the hospital gown wrapped around his shoulders, but was otherwise naked. In one hand were a red jumper and black high heels. He looked like a man, although his toenails were painted, and he was wearing makeup and two rings.

As Officer Nelia Real of the Key Biscayne Police Department drew up in her cruiser, Gigi was on the curb trying to put on a flowered thong. A few minutes before, a park ranger named Nelson Mompierre had noticed him stumbling along, north on the boulevard's southbound lane. When the police officer got out of her car, Gigi was sitting down, as if pooped, or possibly trying to get his bearings. He was grinning.

From Officer Real's typed report: "Mr. Hemingway (defendant) had he/her genitals (Mr. Hemingway is a transsexual and had his male organs removed) exposed to the public. The defendant had a hospital gown

444

wrapped around the shoulder area exposing the breasts. The defendant refused to be handcuffed and refused to enter the police unit. He was screaming and resisting our requests to leave." Despite those last two sentences, the officer wasn't really exercised about Gigi. Neither she nor her backup, Officer Ben Torres (she'd radioed for assistance, just in case), thought him dangerous in any real sense. He was just some confused old gay or bi or trans, possibly homeless. As Officer Real said later, "At times he was very coherent, but at other times he didn't make any sense." In the squad car, after he'd calmed down, Officer Real had a pleasant talk with Gigi. Once she'd discovered who he was, or who he was the son of, she told him that Ernest Hemingway was just about her favorite author. Her own people were from Cuba. At the Key Biscayne station house (before he was transported across Rickenbacker Causeway to Miami's main detention center for women), Gigi offered to autograph the back of her arrest affidavit. She took him up on it. He was plying the old Gigi charms. He must have been hoping it would do him some good. He told her he was going to come back and take her out to lunch. The whole thing must have made some impression on her, for after his death, Officer Real told an Associated Press reporter: "I feel really bad that that happened. He was a very nice guy." She repeated that sentiment throughout the week.

No one has ever been able to explain with any certainty how and why Gigi came to be where he was, that day, September 26, 2001, with his clothes off, in the midday sun, immediately outside the entrance to a state recreation area at the southern tip of Key Biscayne, which itself is more or less at the southern watery end of greater Miami. I can't explain it for certain, either, but I do have a deeply held theory about it.

REENACTMENT

Gregory Hemingway,
September 26, 2001

Because I could not stop for Death—
He kindly stopped for me—

—beginning of an untitled poem by Emily Dickinson

No one has explained what the leopard was seeking at that altitude.

—ERNEST HEMINGWAY, "The Snows of Kilimanjaro"

THE BUILDING where Gigi died sits under a swirl of raised freeways on the edge of the Miami skyline. The Dolphin Expressway and I-95 and I-395 come together here. It's a four-story, monolithic, concrete, beige box, with little slits for windows and some concertina wire wrapped around the perimeter. The people inside can't see out the windows, though—they're covered over. The jail is on the corner of Northwest Seventh Avenue and Northwest Fourteenth Street, which is also known as Tornado Way. The roar of cars and trucks overhead goes on day and night, although it's doubtful the inmates think very much about freeway noise. They make their own noise. It comes from blaring TVs in the common spaces to clanging doors to yelling of all kinds.

"A lot of the guards would still remember him," said Janelle Hall, a public affairs officer from the corrections department, when I visited the jail. "Very interesting case. We had him in here several times. People liked him. Highly intelligent. He didn't cause us trouble. He went by this other name—"

"Gloria," I said.

"That's right. Sometimes he'd be Greg, sometimes we'd have him as Gloria."

Cell 3C2 was a safety cell, she explained. It's for inmates with psychiatric or other problems who need to be segregated from the general population.

Gigi's pod in 3C2 was and is about a ten-foot-by-ten-foot room. They let me look through the window. The room had a steel bunk, a metal sink, a hopper, a ledge for toiletries. Gigi's and the four or five other pods of the cell were arranged in a semicircle, fronting a common area. There were two TVs going, and the sound was being piped into the pods. There was also a telephone in the common space, and it was on a rolling pedestal. It looked like a payphone outside a 7-Eleven. Attached to the pedestal was a length of cable tethered to the phone's receiver. The way it worked, I was told, is that when an inmate wished to make a call—and, really, there were few restrictions on calls, as long as the party on the other end was accepting charges—the inmate signaled the guard, and the guard rolled over the phone and fed in the receiver via an opening in the locked door.

I can't report how many phone calls Ernest Hemingway's son made—or whether he made any at all—in the five days he lived in 377 of 3C2 of the Miami-Dade County Women's Detention Center in the last week of September 2001. The jail doesn't have those records. The only person in his immediate or even extended family who apparently knew where he was that week was his wife, Ida, who was at their home back in Montana. Once she found out (on the second full day he was there), she declined to get him out. His bail was $1,000, which means $100 would have sprung him, because all you need is a tenth. John Hemingway feels huge regret about this. He writes of it in *Tribe.* "Christ, even I would have had a hundred bucks," he said to me once. "If one of us kids had known, maybe we could have gotten him out of there and into some serious medical care in a hospital." As to why he thinks his father didn't tell any of his children where he was, ask them for help, John said, "I don't know. Maybe there was no place for us in what he had to go through. This was a reenactment. He was reenacting it all over again, and there wasn't room for anybody else."

. . .

Gigi had had a rough summer. He'd gotten his hip replaced at Miami Heart Institute. In both Florida and Montana, he'd been getting around with a walker. He was taking too much Percocet, mixing it with too much alcohol, talking morosely about the fact that he was closing in on seventy. He was fighting more than ever with his wife.

In early September he called his old friend Thelma Baker in Missoula. He was three hours away, in Bozeman. He was going to leave Ida, this time for good, but he was scared about it, too, because he didn't know if he'd be able to take care of himself. He didn't know what Ida's reaction would be. She was physically stronger than he was. "Let me come over to my old room at the motel, so you can take care of me," he said. Through the years Thelma had held money for him, barked at him, done laundry for him, mothered him, big-sistered him. Gigi had gotten to be friends with her three grown sons, who helped their mom with the motel. They'd played tennis together, and hunted and fished, although one of Thelma's sons couldn't abide his sex change. (Thelma herself had tried hard to talk him out of going through with it.) Gigi and Thelma were almost the same age. Once they'd gone out on a sort of date, but their relationship had never really been romantic, despite that he'd once proposed. He'd spent all day worrying about where to go for dinner, arranging for flowers, getting his car washed, his clothes cleaned. The evening turned out to be a big success. He was a nervous gentleman.

Through the years Thelma had listened to Gigi's crazy ideas about making some kind of scientific breakthrough on chelation therapy, which has to do with the removal of heavy metals from the body. He was going to apply chelation's methods to getting plaque out of the arteries and curing heart disease once and for all. He'd be world famous.

"If you come to Missoula, Greg, I won't be here," Thelma said. She was going out to Hawaii with a friend for the University of Montana's opening game of the football season against the University of Hawaii. Gigi begged her not to go, but after she was in Honolulu, he had called to see if she had arrived okay and was having a good time. This was probably on September 7, 2001. Four days later, two taken-over airliners arrowed into the World Trade Center. Thelma and her girlfriend couldn't get off Maui. Gigi called again. "Please, I need you," he'd said. She told him, "I'll be there soon." He said, "If you aren't coming back now, I won't be coming to Missoula at all."

By the third week of September, in Miami, he was raging. The newest breakthrough was to sink all his money into airline stocks—and then sit back and watch them rise in the aftershock of 9/11. He'd make a fortune and leave the money to his kids. His wife was a money-grubbing alcoholic, he told some friends and at least one of his children. (In his manic state, he couldn't find phone numbers; pieces of paper spilled from his wallet at telephone stands outside gas stations.) He had come down to Florida from Montana with barely a change of clothes. Mostly, he was sleeping in those clothes at the house he and Ida owned in the Grove.

On Friday night, September 21, in drag, he tore through a local Borders bookstore. He was yelling and pulling down off the shelf his father's novels, scribbling his own name across the title page. Three days later, he dialed his third wife in Montana. He and Valerie hadn't spoken in a long while. When she didn't pick up, he left a lengthy message. He wished to thank her for the good years they'd had together, no matter all the bad, far more his fault than hers. "You did a wonderful job with our children," he said. Valerie Hemingway writes about this call on the second-to-last page of her memoir. "I did something I never did before, I taped it," she says. Did she somehow understand he was telling her good-bye? She doesn't say that, exactly.

That same evening, Dick Edmonston held his regular Monday-night open house at his home on Park Drive in the Grove. Gigi was a casual friend of the host's, and he tended to turn up at these standing parties when he was in town. Edmonston, a Miami playboy with a thing about cats, wandered around talking to his guests, who were smoking weed but not really snorting things. Gigi spent about two hours on a stool just outside the kitchen, stroking a cat in his lap and sipping from a glass of red wine. He was in a black cocktail shift and a brown wig. He held his unshaven legs crossed in a modest way. His wide feet were in a pair of spiky heels that looked at least a size too small. His friend Peter Myers, an Australian journalist, was at the party. He'd never seen Gigi as a woman. Myers thought to himself that Gigi was in better spirits than he'd seen him in a long time. He seemed damned healthy. Maybe he was like a lightbulb that incandesces the moment before it's going to go out. "Hello, Greg," Myers said, trying to be casual. "No, it's Vanessa," Gigi said evenly. "Oh, right, okay, Vanessa," Myers said. The party broke up about midnight and Gigi drove off in a 1995 blue Ford.

The next afternoon, September 25, at 4:25 p.m., Vanessa or Gloria or Greg or Gigi or whoever he was at that moment was found by the police barging his way through a security gate at the entrance to a high-end high-rise apartment on Crandon Boulevard in Key Biscayne, quite close to Bill Baggs Cape Florida State Park. There was said to be a woman in this complex whom Gigi had dated from time to time. From the arrest complaint: "When the def. was confronted, he refused to cooperative [sic], refusing to give his name and D.O.B. and attempted to walk away several times from this officer." They booked him on a double charge of resisting arrest without violence and failure to possess a valid Florida license. (He seems not to have had any license.) The bond for each charge was set at $500. He was kept in jail overnight, posted the $100—Ida, in Montana, terrified, and not wrongly, that he was going to blow all their money on crazed stock investments, had had their bank accounts frozen—got out by ten the next morning. Was it his last $100? I don't know.

The legal documents account for nothing between the time of his release on the morning of the twenty-sixth and his second arrest, two hours and fifteen minutes later, very close to the site of the previous arrest. Officer Real came along, with her flasher going, and there he was, the pathetic old guy with the streaked and almost whitish hair, clothes bunched in one hand, flowered thong in the other, and that white hospital gown covering his sun-burning shoulders.

Two days later, as mentioned, on Friday the twenty-eighth, his spouse learned where he was. Ida later claimed to friends and the press that she'd spent hours on the phone from Montana calling hospitals and jails, trying to find him. And once she did find him, why didn't she try to get him out? "He would've been on the street," Ida said, a year later, to a reporter for *Rolling Stone*. "I wanted to get him into a hospital. I sent a psychiatrist to see him, but they wouldn't let him in." Four days after he was dead, she told *The Miami Herald*, "He would not be dead if he had gotten the medical attention that he needed. I called constantly, constantly. I don't know if they ever gave him his high blood pressure medication." And yet on the day after his death, on October 2, at 12:30 p.m., Gigi's wife would tell a medical examiner investigator on the phone from Montana: "He was not under any medication, but took Percocet until 4 months ago."

On the same day that Ida found out where Gigi was, an entry was made in a jail log about his general behavior. Later, after his death, in an all-capped synopsis titled "TERMINAL EVENT," an official of the detention center would write: "On September 28, he appeared forgetful and confused at times. His vital signs were taken and were as follows; b/p 140/90, pulse 80 and he was also afebrile. He complained of pain and was given two Tylenol tablets. By September 29, 2001 [that was Saturday], he appeared to be calmer than initially. He remained in a calm state with appropriate behavior." Ahead of this: "He was advised that his doctor had called and ordered him to take lithium; however, he refused stating that he does not take lithium and had not taken lithium in 3 years." (The doctor's name is Floyd Rosen. He's still a practicing psychiatrist in Miami. He declined to talk with me because, as he said in a phone message, he just couldn't violate the patient-doctor code of privacy, even if Gigi was long dead. "First, do no harm," he said, "and even now talking about it could do harm to the family." There was a pause. And then the disembodied voice said, even more quietly, "You see, this was a man who suffered very much, and he was a . . . *doctor.*")

The prisoner stayed calm through the weekend. On Monday morning he was awakened at 5:50 a.m. for his scheduled early court hearing. Fifty years before, another Monday, in Los Angeles, he'd had another hearing scheduled for another court. Now Gigi asked Corrections Officer Chandra Christin, who had just come on duty, if he could have some "slippons"—his toes were cold. Christin left to get the paper-like shoes. Within five minutes she was back at pod 377. She looked through the window and saw Gigi facedown on the floor, wedged against a leg of the bed. She yelled to a fellow guard, Rosa Echevarria. They unlocked the door. They called out his name. No response. They turned him over. In the words of the Investigation Report summary, they "found him without a pulse or palpitation. C.P.R. was administered until the arrival of paramedics. Paramedics arrived and pronounced him deceased." One of the documents ("Natural Death Investigation Continuation/Supplementary") gives the time of death as "Approx. 5:55 a.m." Fifty years before, at nearly the same moment, if you factor in Pacific time, Doctor Henry Randall Thomas was pronouncing Pauline Hemingway dead.

On a form titled "Deceased's Valuables and Personal Property Record," there was a space provided for a listing of clothing at the time of death. "None" was written across it. There was another space for a listing of "Valuables" at the time of death. Written across it: "None."

Did he somehow know this was the end? For fifty years, every end of September and beginning of October, to lesser or greater extents, the old sorrows and shames and manias over his mother's death had been clicking in for Gigi—only this time something in the gears slid and shifted and took him all the way over. This is the way I understand his story. Unlike his own father, Gigi didn't take the "family exit," to use John Hemingway's expression in *Tribe.* In that sense, Gigi was braver than his own father—he let death find him. But to repeat what I said earlier: I consider them both far braver than we ever knew. Hemingway always had the gift and release of his words—until he didn't have them. Gigi, without such a gift or outlet, ended up sparing his own children the burden and guilt of a parental suicide. The spiral ended. Two generations down from Ed Hemingway in Oak Park, something hopeful, in spite of everything, had happened for future generations of Hemingways. God knows, though, how Gigi must have dreamed and longed for death for so much of his life. Dream? On the last page of *Papa,* Gigi has his father telling him, "Atoms can't dream, Gig. No use deluding yourself, old pal."

So what would a person with no clothes on have been doing outside the entrance to Bill Baggs Cape Florida State Park at 12:15 p.m. on the Wednesday before death came stopping? I prefer to believe this: Gigi was sitting on that median curb, trying to regain his breath and courage, to climb Cape Florida Lighthouse, which was about a mile away. It sits at the bottom of Bill Baggs, surrounded by sea grapes and palms and a wild stretch of beach. It's one of the most famous landmarks in all of South Florida. Gigi liked going there. As a med student, he had climbed it with friends. It is 109 hard-breathing iron steps to the top, or at least to the watch tower. Gigi used to sit with friends at the little café near the base of the lighthouse. He liked the Cuban food and one of the old waiters, who was from Havana. At least once, in drag, he got his heel caught in the wedge between the slats of the café's outdoor deck and took a humiliating header.

Up there, on a clear day, it's possible to see all of watery metropolitan Miami. You can face southwest and cup your eyes and look down the flat curving necklace of the Florida Keys as far as your vision will allow. If you were able somehow to look nearly 155 miles down the blue-green necklace, to its last bead, you'd see another lighthouse, the one that stands catty-corner across from Gigi's boyhood home, the one at 938 Whitehead, the one around whose grassy base he and his brother Pat used to sometimes play cowboys and Indians while their father, across the street, worked on *Green Hills of Africa.* When the mood was right, when the writing had gone good, their dad would knock off early and go find them and walk with them the eighty-eight circular steps to the top, sometimes carrying the younger one in his arms or on his back, telling them both on the way up rich stories about the old, lonely nineteenth-century keepers who used to spend the nights fueling their lanterns and positioning their big reflectors for lost ships trying to make home. Making home, such a complicated notion. I want to believe that a lost son, who'd decided to shed all his clothes so that he could feel lustful and lawless in the salt air, was intending to climb the lighthouse at Key Biscayne that noonday so that he could see, at least pretend-see, the lighthouse of his Key West boyhood, so he could *see,* way off in the distance, his father, his mother, his two brothers, Saint Mary Star of the Sea (where he served early-morning Mass in the middle years of grammar school), the P&O Steamship dock, the dance floor at Sloppy Joe's, his father's workroom, all the cats, his old bedroom up on the second floor, his maroon Sears, Roebuck bike, and, not least, down at the navy yard, bobbing so loyally, gassed up and good to go, his papa's boat.

Perhaps I came too soon. I was a painter of your generation more than my own. . . . You are young, you have vitality, you can imbue your art with a force that only those with true feelings can manage. As for me, I'm old. I won't have time to express myself.

—CÉZANNE, to a young artist in 1896,
ten years before his death

. . . all stories, if continued far enough, end in death, and he is no true story-teller who would keep that from you.

—from *Death in the Afternoon*

The old man knew he was going far out and he left the smell of the land behind and rowed out into the clean early morning smell of the ocean.

—from *The Old Man and the Sea*

We looked and there it all was: our river and our city and the island of our city.

"We're too lucky," she said.

. . .

Standing there I wondered how much of what we had felt on the bridge was just hunger. I asked my wife and she said, "I don't know, Tatie. There are so many sorts of hunger. In the spring there are more. But that's gone now. Memory is hunger."

—from *A Moveable Feast*

EPILOGUE
HUNGER OF MEMORY

Under way, in her newness, that first summer 1934

IN NATIVE AMERICAN CULTURE, there is a belief about "blood memory." It's tied up with ancestral connection to language, song, spirituality, tribal teaching. If you lose the blood memory of your people's language, you've lost your center. What happens if you are a writer and you've lost your center? In *The Garden of Eden*, Ernest Hemingway wrote of his frozen writer protagonist:

> When he finally gave up writing that day it was afternoon. He had started a sentence as soon as he had gone into his working room and had completed it but he could write nothing after it. He crossed it out and started another sentence and again came to the complete blankness. He was unable to write the sentence that should follow although he knew it. He wrote a first simple declarative sentence again and it was impossible for him to put down the next sentence on paper. At the end of two hours it was the same. He could not write more than a single sentence and the sentences themselves were increasingly simple

and completely dull. He kept at it for four hours before he knew
that resolution was powerless against what had happened.

We know what happened on Sunday morning, July 2, 1961. A
writer who'd lost the prairies of Oak Park, the Michigan woods, the
illimitable-seeming riches of the Gulf Stream, and now, or so he
was convinced, the center of who and what he was, stepped inside a
five-and-a-half-foot-by-seven-and-a-half-foot space at the entryway of
his house and destroyed himself. He aimed for just above the eyebrows
and nothing went awry. He'd been home from Mayo Clinic for two days,
having been driven back to Idaho in a Hertz rental car in the company of
his wife and an old boxing friend in whose Manhattan gym he used to take
workouts. Mary Hemingway had gone to bed the night before in the big
bedroom that occupies most of the upper floor; he'd taken the small room
that's down the hall. From their respective quarters, as they readied for
sleep, they'd called out to each other snatches of an Italian folk song. At
about 7:25 a.m. Mary was brought awake to what sounded like two muffled
thumps. It was, she later said, like the sound of bureau drawers pulled out
too far and falling to the floor. She rose on one elbow and called out her
husband's name. She threw back the coverlet and ran down the hall. One
of the twin beds was mussed, but he wasn't in it. She reversed direction,
went to the head of the stairs, held for half a second, and tore down the
twenty-odd steps, across the living room to see, or get a glimpse of, what
her spouse had done.

At 7:40 a.m. the telephone rang at the home of Dr. Scott Earle, who was
on call that weekend for the Ketchum hospital. The hospital operator told
him there'd been an accident at the Ernest Hemingway home. Earle pulled
on his clothes and was in the Hemingway driveway by 7:45. Mary signaled
to him from a second-floor window not to come to the front entryway but
around the other way. She met the doctor at the kitchen door. While she
stayed behind, he went across the kitchen, stepped down into the living
room and over to the vestibule, and saw on his own from the inner doorway the fragments of strewn bone, teeth, hair, flesh. The walls and ceiling
and floor of the boxlike space were "speckled," the doctor said, with a yellowish red. Hemingway's legs were "flexed," and between them, resting
against his chest, was the double-barreled 12-gauge. In place of a head, the
doctor saw a "disc-shaped and empty skull."

For the rest of her life, Mary Hemingway never used that entryway.

At the funeral, three days later, the pastor of Our Lady of the Snows

Catholic Church in Ketchum read from Ecclesiastes: "One generation cometh and another passeth away, but the land abideth forever." He mistakenly stopped short of the words "The sun also ariseth."

The stone the family picked was flat to the ground, and wide, as if to accommodate the special bulk beneath it. This half a century on, the stone is there, unchanged, except by the wear of time, in the town cemetery just north of the village center, set between two pines more than thirty feet high, and there is a rough-made white wooden cross at the head of the smooth gray marble. There is only the name, Ernest Miller Hemingway, and his dates, 1889–1961, cut carefully in.

If you go to the other end of town, northeast, about a mile up past Sun Valley Lodge, off Trail Creek Road, you'll find a small Hemingway memorial. It's in a grove of aspens and willows with clear running water. There is a bust of him, mounted on a stone pedestal. Inscribed at the base are some words edited by his wife that he once wrote for a Sun Valley friend, who'd died in a hunting accident:

> *Best of all he loved the fall*
> *The leaves yellow on the cottonwoods*
> *Leaves floating on the trout streams*
> *And above the hills*
> *The high blue windless sky*
> *Now he will be a part of them forever*

It's heartbreaking to read Hemingway's letters of his last few years and see how *Pilar* and the sea were slipping from him, no less than his mind was. For all the years he'd had her, Hemingway always knew he could stop what he was doing and drive to the waterfront and meet Gregorio and unfasten the ropes and climb up onto the bridge and step on the starters and glide his boat out of Havana Harbor toward the Stream. In the midday heat, he used to love to lie on his back on the long bed on the starboard side in the cockpit and watch the rod tips make sawing arcs against the puffy clouds. Gregorio would have the wheel then. Hemingway would prop himself against a reading pillow with a book and drink. Soon he'd be asleep. Often during these siestas, Mary wedged herself in beside him on the inner side of the leather bunk.

"You know you love the sea and would not be anywhere else," Hemingway wrote in *Islands in the Stream*. "She is just there and the wind moves her and the current moves her and they fight on her surface but down below none of it matters."

By the end, none of it was mattering in a different way. On April 21, 1961, in Ketchum, four days before Hemingway was flown again in a Piper Comanche four-seater to Saint Marys Hospital at Mayo Clinic for more shock treatments and locked rooms, Mary found her husband standing in the same vestibule off the living room where, two and a half months hence, he would succeed in killing himself. He was wearing his Italian bathrobe. It was midmorning. He was holding a shotgun. On the ledge in front of him, he had set two shells upright. From *How It Was:*

> "I was thinking we might go to Mexico," I said softly. "Gregorio might be able to get *Pilar* over there." Ernest turned and looked at me, but my message didn't connect. "I read somewhere that there's marvelous fishing off the Yucatán peninsula. We really haven't discussed Paris, either. We could sublet a little flat there. We've been awfully happy in Paris, lamb."

He stepped past her and went into the living room and looked out one of the windows at the mountains. The spring melting hadn't yet come. He was holding the gun. Mary sat down on a small sofa. "Honey, you wouldn't do anything harmful to me as well as you," she said. In a little while, George Saviers, his doctor and good friend and hunting companion, was at the house; he'd been scheduled to come by to take his patient's blood pressure but was a little late. He tramped into the house in his boots, saw what was happening, and said: "Hang on, Papa, I want to talk to you." Saviers called a colleague, and the two doctors got Hemingway into the car and over to the Ketchum hospital, where they sedated him. When the weather cleared, the patient was taken back to Rochester. Mary Hemingway tells this story and then says, "Years later, reconsidering, I wondered if we had not been more cruel than kind in preventing his suicide then and there."

In truth, the receding of *Pilar*, the slipping from him of the Stream, had been happening for a long time—maybe from the mid-fifties on. On January 31, 1958, eleven months before Fidel entered Havana, fourteen months before Hemingway paid $50,000 in cash for the charmless, two-story block house where he'd end his life, he wrote a lengthy letter to Adriana Ivancich's brother, Gianfranco. "Fish have disappeared from the ocean and the fishermen in Cojimar are desperate with the fish never comeing," he said. "Havana is more like Miami Beach all the time. I do not know where to go. Do you?" That "Do you?" is so uncharacteristic. All his life, people had asked *him* about the next best symbolic place to go. At the end of that year, writing from Ketchum, he wrote to his middle son: "Cuba is really bad now, Mouse. . . . Might pull out of there. Future looks very bad and there has been no fishing in Gulf for 2 years—and will be eventually no freedom coastwise and all the old places ruined."

"When you have loved three things all your life, from the earliest you can remember; to fish, to shoot and, later, to read; and when, all your life, the necessity to write has been your master, you learn to remember," he wrote in *Esquire* in 1935. Twelve years later, he said in a letter to William Faulkner: "My own country gone. Trees cut down. Nothing left but gas stations, sub-divisions where we hunted snipe on the prairie, etc." In a sense, all his life had been a hunger to get back what he'd only briefly known.

As noted earlier, what seems inarguable now is that Hemingway never recovered mentally or physically from those back-to-back plane crashes in early 1954 in Africa. The world, of course, wished to believe otherwise— he was Ernest Hemingway; he'd cheated death once more. Biographer Michael Reynolds has put it best: "Between 1955 and 1961 Hemingway's life alternated between ever-shortening cycles of euphoric writing and paranoia-ridden depression." And yet, in the face of all his illnesses, he kept on writing, or tried to—that's the heroic part. In 1955 he spent the entire year in Cuba. In April 1956 he flew to Peru to help out the movie-makers on the film version of *The Old Man and the Sea*. (They couldn't get the thousand-pound marlin they'd wanted for Spencer Tracy's fight with the fish that got cannibalized by the sharks.) Later that year, Hemingway attended the *corridas* in Spain, and then he was in Paris at the Ritz. In the rotogravures, he was still his own kind of Hemingway hero, man of action and movement. If that was false, what was true was that he tried to find a writing desk, wherever he was: for work on his trilogy, on *The Garden of Eden* manuscript, on a series of sketches about being a young man in Paris. These he had started in July 1957, a month or so before his youngest son, back from a manic trip to Africa, got hospitalized in Miami and wrote to his dad apologizing for getting "into this shape." *Pilar* is always there, in the backwash of these letters and emotions, but less and less.

In 1959, he was back in Spain, to spend the summer covering for *Life* the mano a mano bullfights between Antonio Ordóñez and his older and more famous brother-in-law, Luis Dominguín. There was a big sixtieth-birthday party for Hemingway that started on the twenty-first and went till breakfast the next day. But his mood shifts were frightening. In October he began to write his nonfiction piece for *Life,* an agreed-upon ten thousand words. He wrote five thousand words in five days and said he'd hardly begun. At the end of the month, Hemingway sailed to America on the SS *Liberté.* A biographer of F. Scott Fitzgerald's, Andrew Turnbull, watched him touring the deck in a plaid shirt and sleeveless leather vest, speaking to no one, avoiding eye contact. Turnbull wrote him a note and had a steward deliver it. He asked if they might meet, and on the last day out Hemingway consented. They sat in the ship's bar and Turnbull was struck by Hemingway's "sad mask of a face," both "shy and wistful, with something inexpressible in his glance." The biographer held this apparition inside him and eight years later wrote a piece recalling it for *The New York Times Book Review.* Turnbull couldn't avoid the feeling that at some indefinable point, probably back there in the mid-thirties, as the critics turned and the talent appeared to ebb, that the mask had become the face, and the face had become the mask, and Hemingway "ate his publicity and became a travesty of his former self. Never completely, though, and that was his pathos and his grandeur. Part of him knew what was happening." Turnbull quoted from *Richard II:* "For you have mistook me all this while."

The *Liberté* docked, and Hemingway went to his publisher and deposited the incomplete manuscript that would become *A Moveable Feast.* He flew to Cuba. Reporters were at the airport. They asked what he thought of America's hardening attitude toward the Castro revolution. Hemingway answered that he thought of himself as a true Cuban, and to prove it he kissed the national flag. An account of this got back-channeled to Washington from Havana and put in his FBI file.

A week later, Hemingway departed from Florida for Idaho in a nearly new Buick, provided by the sponsor of CBS's *Buick Electra Playhouse.* Doing most of the driving was Roberto Herrera, an old Havana retainer, and also in the car were Antonio Ordóñez and his wife, Carmen, who were seeing the great American landscape for the first time. (Hemingway had invited them to Cuba and to Idaho without consulting Mary; she'd gone ahead to prepare the newly purchased Ketchum house for the Spanish guests.) Hemingway rode in the front passenger seat and kept a frightening log of the mileage and the gas—frightening if you read it now. He made his entries in a palm-size spiral notebook. On the starting-out day, November 12, he wrote: "Key W. 1420—2605." This meant the group had departed at 2:20 p.m. with the odometer reading 2605. At "1510" (ten after three) they got to Marathon, Florida, and the odometer was 2656. The next entry: "1515—Leave." Three days later, it was: "Leave—New Orleans 0830—3718." Each gas stop got recorded—to the fractions of fill-up. Slidell, Louisiana: "15 3/10 gal." Alpine, Texas: "16 0/10." Jackpot, Nevada: "14 8/10." On and on and on, nothing but numbers and the names of places, some abbreviated or misspelled. On November 18, Hemingway entered: "Arriv Ketchum 2315 6643," which meant they'd made it to their destination at forty-five minutes to midnight on the seventh day out, having gone 4,038 miles and having spent $106.78 on gas and oil. (He'd totaled both.) It was as if the observer of the natural world, whose emphasis had always been on what can be seen and felt, never noticed a bird, a sunset, a tree, a dog, a mountain, let alone a passing car, or another human being. And yet Hemingway wrote some fine letters about the trip afterward.

Early in the New Year, the Hemingways went to dinner at the home of old Ketchum friends, Lloyd and Tillie Arnold. Powder was drifting down in saucer-size flakes and the foursome watched it from the windows. Hemingway saw the lights on in the local bank. "They're checking our accounts," he said. "That's just the usual cleaning women," Tillie Arnold said. "They're trying to catch us," Hemingway said. "They want to get something on us." Mary Hemingway said, "Who's they?" Hemingway answered: "The FBI." This story is in *How It Was*. Of course, anybody would have said it was an insane notion that FBI agents were going through Hemingway's bank accounts on a January Saturday night. (They weren't.) Totally paranoid—except in some weird, other clairvoyant sense, not so paranoid an idea at all.

Unreasonably plagued by his bullfight article, Hemingway became convinced he'd work better at his old standing place (using the top of the bookcase in his Havana bedroom), so, having only recently come to Idaho, he and his wife packed and rode the train back across the country to Miami. His boat would be there in Cuba to ease the writing strains—except all that spring, the weather was lousy ("peevish," Mary called it), and the fish didn't come, and, anyway, it was as if, with all his work, which he felt so behind on, he could barely find the time to take her out. Too much energy required.

Hemingway paid for nineteen-year-old Valerie Danby-Smith, whom he'd met in Spain the summer before, to come to Havana to help him on his bullfight article, swelling beyond all control. "How's it going?" his wife asked one afternoon. "It's hell. I can't get it all down," he answered. "Could you summarize, or digest, or something?" He said, "I don't see how I can do it." Again, this is from Mary's memoir.

On March 31, he wrote to Charles Scribner Jr.: "We are finally getting some decent weather here and I am going to try to fish two days a week to get some juice back." But he didn't fish two days a week and the juice in him was all of the wrong kind. By summer, a *magazine* article had grown to twelve times the length of what he had initially agreed to write. The goiter-like thing was at something like 120,000 words. "Fishing been lousy due heavy rains from two tropical depressions. Haven't been in boat since May 19," he said in a June letter to George Saviers. (Saviers had visited in April to fish and to check on his patient, but there had been only a few afternoons on *Pilar.*)

He had to get at least 70,000 words out of the article—and managed 530. At the end of June, Hemingway pleaded with A. E. Hotchner to come down from New York to try to help him with "The Dangerous Summer," as he'd titled the piece. Hotchner took the first hundred pages of the 688-page manuscript and began to read it in a terrible heat and a kind of terrible panic: so much of it was numbingly repetitious. The following afternoon, he gave Hemingway a list of eight cuts in the first hundred pages. The next morning they conferred in Hemingway's bedroom. On a lined pad of paper Hemingway had jotted his reasons for rejecting each of the proposed cuts.

Finally, though, over the next several days, the two got the manuscript down by 54,916 words; Hemingway had caved. The *Life* editors paid him $90,000 and ran portions in three installments that fall. The issues sold well; the name "Hemingway" was attached.

Before this, on July 6, he'd written to Scribner that he'd "not had a day off from work nor been out in the boat from May 19 to July 4." The final sentence of this letter: "The big fish have not come yet but are over-due and I would like to pull on a couple of big ones before I leave." He didn't pull on them. There is no record I can find that suggests Ernest Hemingway was ever out on his boat again after May 19, 1960.

The Hemingways were foreign residents in a nation held in increasingly hostile regard by their own country. Hotchner had helped find a small rented apartment at 1 East Sixty-second Street in Manhattan. Hemingway told his wife he would not consider the idea of leaving the *finca* for good—Cuba was their home. He was insistent on returning to Spain to write codas and postscripts to the manuscript he'd already surrendered to *Life's* editors, and to which they'd already allowed a greater length. Mary refused to accompany him. On July 25, the Hemingways and Valerie Danby-Smith got on the ferry from Havana to Key West. From *How It Was:*

> We had left at the Finca all its silver, Venetian glassware, eight thousand books, a number of them autographed first editions, and Ernest's small collection of paintings, one Paul Klee, two Juan Gris, five André Masson, one Braque and several good, lively paintings of bulls by Roberto Domingo. At my bank in Havana we had left reams of unpublished manuscript.

She might have added to the list *Pilar.* He would never see his boat again; he would never see Cuba again.

On August 15, in Spain, he wrote to his wife about his panic of a "complete physical and nervous crack-up." It was as if she didn't hear him, not to judge by most of her correspondence. Five weeks later, from Madrid, he told Mary in a letter he needed her "to look after me and help me out and keep from cracking up. Feel terrible and am just going to lie quiet now and try to rest." Two days later he wrote and said, "Must get out of this and back to you and healthy life in Ketchum and get head in shape to write well." Mary quotes from these letters in *How It Was* and says, "I failed totally to evaluate the importance of these successive warning signals." A couple of weeks earlier she had tried to evoke *Pilar:*

> I wish I could give you something wonderful and refreshing and renewing—3 weeks of our old-style holidays at Paraiso in an air-mailable capsule—but containing all of it—the changing winds, the long view across the violet satiny water toward the sunset, the gay fun fishing in the mornings and then the welcome shade of *Pilar* at noon, and the long, cool starlit nights with us kittens sleeping as softly as Cristobal.

In October, back in the States, in the apartment on the Upper East Side, he stood at the door of the kitchen and watched as his wife made supper, as if for the first time. She tried to lure him out to the zoo in Central Park. "Somebody waiting out there," he said. As soon as she could, Mary got him west; she was praying the Idaho air would renew him. George Saviers met them at the train station in nearby Shoshone. Two men in overcoats came out of a café across the street. "They're tailing me out here already," Hemingway said.

In late November, he was taken by air to Mayo Clinic, where he registered under the name George Saviers. The covering story was that he was being treated for high blood pressure. He was being looked at for everything. The shock treatments began. We now know that his attending Mayo psychiatrist, Howard Rome, talked about him to the FBI. On January 13, 1961, the bureau's Minneapolis SAC (special agent in charge) wrote a report to Hoover. That declassified document still has its redactions, but it's clear that Rome was the agent's source. He told the bureau that his patient was "worried about his registering under an assumed name, and is concerned about an FBI investigation," and "inasmuch as this worry was interfering with the treatments of Mr. HEMINGWAY, he desired authorization to tell HEMINGWAY that the FBI was not concerned with his registering under an assumed name." It was as if a doctor was taking orders from men in overcoats.

Two days later, Hemingway dictated a note to his old high school pal Ray Ohlsen, with whom he'd once canoed to Starved Rock, that he'd be "out of here soon," and that it was almost worth having gone to Rochester just "to hear from you, kid."

He did get out. He went back to Ketchum. Briefly, he seemed better. But the irrational fears returned, and the writer who, a few months prior, couldn't control his writing now felt incapable of writing one sentence. He was taken back to Mayo in the Piper Comanche, and while there he wrote a letter of 210 words to a heart-diseased child, who was the middle son of his family doctor in Idaho. He convinced his Mayo doctors to release him again. He got home on a Friday night, on the last night of June, and on Sunday morning, before the sun was fully over the mountains, he was dead.

If you study original Hemingway manuscripts from the thirties through the fifties, you'll see numbers written above the lines on certain sheets. I first saw Hemingway's letter to nine-year-old Fritz Saviers many years ago, framed and hung in a hallway at Sun Valley Lodge. I never go to Ketchum that I don't take time to drive to the lodge and stand in the hallway and read the letter again. Amid so much ruin, still the beauty. There are no numbers written above the letter's lines, but I have counted the words many times. I say 210, but it's actually 219 "words," if you count the return address, and the numerals "15" and "1961" in the date, and even the number "2" written at the top of page 2. I've studied the letter with a magnifying glass—the way he made tiny x marks for periods in several places; the way he put that "2" with a not completely closed circle at the top of the second page; the half parenthesis after the "Mister" of "Mister Papa"; the second signature after the postscript, forgoing the Mister. Fritz had a dispensation to call him just Papa, and so I'm thinking that the desperately ill man remembered at the last second.

A month and a half after Hemingway's death, in its issue of August 25, 1961, *Life* ran a photocopy. The story, "Last Words Hemingway Wrote," told how, on the day before he killed himself, Hemingway put his arm around the nine-year-old and said, "Be a good scout." Dr. Saviers was about to take his child back to the hospital in Denver. The editors published a picture of the buzz-headed child. He's holding a .22 rifle, a gift from Mary Hemingway. He's in a short-sleeve white summer shirt, and his right arm is wrapped in gauze above the elbow. The watch on his other arm is sliding down his forearm—he's losing weight. Fritz gazes skyward and holds the gun with both hands.

On a recent trip to Ketchum, I read the letter and then went into town and sat for an hour talking to Fritz's brother, Pierre Saviers. It was a bright, blue, cold winter day, and the hard-packed snow of the day before squeaked on the sidewalk under my boots. Pierre Saviers is a psychotherapist. George Saviers had three sons, and Pierre, the youngest, is the only one alive. He's in his late fifties. There was a woven Indian rug on the floor, soothing light, classical music, framed photographs. The therapist sat facing me with his lanky legs crossed. I asked him about the letter.

"It's layered," he said. "My dad would have told Hemingway how congenitally sick Fritz was, that he wouldn't live long. Fritz couldn't run and exercise like other kids. He was angry about it. My dad would drive him regularly to the specialists in Denver. My dad had gone to Cornell and Berkeley, but he was a small-town doctor. He had a dying child. There's no question Hemingway liked and trusted my father, and there's no question my father knew Hemingway was a sick man beyond any power my father had to help him. Hemingway? He knew he was done. And he knows Fritz is done. But he still wants to save him, even as he wants to save himself. You know about the damsel in distress tied to the railroad tracks? Well, that's us. You recognize yourself there, and you want to save yourself."

He stood up. He was tired of talking about it. He had other things to do. "It's all layered. The way I see all this is that part of what we do in this life is conscious. And the rest of it is unconscious. Maybe this is the best we can ever say."

ACKNOWLEDGMENTS

In the following Essay on Sources, and also in parts of the text, I have tried to name as many of those as I could who aided on this project, and to whom I am very grateful. Here, I'll express my gratitude to a narrower and simultaneously more arcing group of individuals: those who helped keep *Hemingway's Boat* afloat for these last seven or eight years, more than they knew, and even when I wasn't in touch, and in some cases in ways that don't even relate to books and book-making.

The Hemingway Women, as I like to think of them. Almost from the start I was struck by the fact that I seemed to be gaining more from female Hemingway scholars than from their male counterparts. It was the first cue things would not necessarily be as they seemed with the famous misogynist, Ernest Hemingway. There are many such female Hemingway authorities I could name, but the two who've become close associates—and I hope friends for life—are Sandra Spanier and Linda Patterson Miller. The best of what these two Penn State university professors have taught me has come by indirection—a chance remark dropped (which must not have been so chance at all), a piece of writing (not necessarily their own) passed on at a timely moment.

Brewster Chamberlin, to whom I made reference in a footnote. He and his wife, Lynn-Marie, live and work in Key West. Once we lived unaware of each other on the same block on Capitol Hill in Washington, DC. We found each other through our separate (then informally joined) research on Hemingway. For the last half-dozen years, Brewster has been compiling and wonderfully annotating and continuously updating what amounts to almost a daybook calendar of Hemingway's life. No other previous Hemingway chronology comes close to what is now well over 150,000 words of manuscript—and cries out for publication by a major publisher.

The Ernest Hemingway Foundation of Oak Park. Every time I went back to Hemingway's hometown, both to do research and to touch a spiritual base with my own Illinois roots, I found myself treated with midwestern kindness by Barbara Ballinger and Ginie Cassin, but most especially by Redd and Mary Jo Griffin. They, and other foundation members, just opened the doors—and drawers. In northern Michigan, members of the Michigan Hemingway Society were similarly welcoming, though none more so than president Michael Federspiel.

I cannot list all the librarians and staff historians and audiovisual experts at all the archives and museums and research libraries—from local and county institutions to federal and university ones—who gave of their time and help, but these must be named: Susan Wrynn, James B. Hill, Laurie Austin, and Maryrose Grossman at the John F. Kennedy Presidential Library and Museum in Boston; Tom Hambright at the Florida History Room at the Monroe County Public Library in Key West; and Gail M. Morchower of the International Game Fish Association in Dania Beach, Florida. I also feel special gratitude to the entire library staff in manuscripts and archives at Princeton.

At the university where I am privileged to conduct nonfiction seminars with very smart twenty-two-year-olds, I wish to thank, for their steadying belief, my colleagues Al Filreis and Greg Djanikian, who run such a fertile creative writing program out of a woody two-story Victorian dream set back from the main campus walk and known as Kelly Writers House. I am also deeply indebted to three former students—Jessica Lussenhop, Allison Stadd, and Jessica Yu—who served as intern-apprentices at various points in my writing and research. It isn't everyday someone gets to go from one world-class institution (*The Washington Post*) to another (the University of Pennsylvania), but that happened to me.

These, too—former students, a friend I have known since first grade, my oldest pal in journalism, Penn colleagues, former *Washington Post* colleagues, a couple of fellow authors, four siblings, and so forth—I would like to acknowledge here, in no particular order, for their support and friendship: Mike Woyahn, Bill Gildea, John Moody, Wendy Steiner, Jennifer Conway, Jim English, Nancy Bentley, Tim Corrigan, Loretta Williams, Elizabeth Anderson, Ann Marie Pitts, Stephanie Palmer, Mingo Reynolds, Gabe Oppenheim, Elaine Wong, Josh Pollick, Jenna Statfeld, Caroline Rothstein, Tom Rankin, Hiram Rogers, Bob Hansman, Douglas Brinkley, David Maraniss, David VonDrehle, Shelby Coffey, Wil Haygood, Mary-Jo Adams, Bobbye Pratt, Claudia Pennington, Dink Bruce, Charlie Clements, Gigi Wizowaty, James Godsil, Kirk Curnutt, James Meredith, Scott Schwar, Robert Coles, Sunita Nasta, Robert Fry, Elaine Chiang, Richard Toof, Kathy Milton, Marty Hendrickson, Eric Hendrickson, Mark Hendrickson, and Jeannie Snider.

With particular thanks: my longtime agents, Kathy Robbins and David Halpern, wise counselors who let me do the work but were ever there at crucial moments of decision.

Also with particular thanks, for all his computer and moral help, whenever I needed it, my Penn colleague and friend Brian Kirk.

At Alfred A. Knopf, I owe my deep respect and gratitude to several floors of gifted book people, but especially to Sonny Mehta, Anke Steinecke, Carol Devine Carson, Peter Andersen, Paul Bogaards, Nicholas Latimer, Michelle Somers, Ellen Feldman, Patricia Flynn, Jenny Pouech, Joey McGarvey, and, rising above them all, my editor, Jonathan Segal. In a business of revolving doors, ours is a relationship, both professional and personal, spanning thirty-two years. Jon waited for this book far longer than he should have; I think I knew before I wrote my first sentence I would dedicate the book to him.

And, finally, my family: Ceil, John, Matt and his dear Jennie. More than any of the above, they were the true sustainers. Over and over, my spouse listened to all the fears as the bedroom lights were going out. As for my now-grown sons, I am prouder than I dare say that they've followed me, each in his way, into the world of working in media. The future is all theirs.

ESSAY ON SOURCES

[T]he best way out is always through.

—ROBERT FROST

I've long believed books find their writers, more than writers find their books, and sometimes the finding can be a half-alert thing winding on for years. The origins of this book go back at least through three decades and four intervening books. I've told in the text how I met Les Hemingway on the way over to Bimini in a Grumman Goose seaplane in the winter of 1980—perhaps this was the original seeding moment, or splashing one. (My spouse was with me, and all I knew then was that I was trying to write my first book, a seminary memoir.) If we didn't go out in a Bimini boat with Hemingway's little brother that weekend, if the name "Pilar" didn't surface (I don't remember), boats and water and fishing were everywhere around us. Indeed, outsize black-and-white images of *Pilar* and her master were on the walls of the bar and in the iron-gated museum room of the Compleat Angler, that perfect, small, funky hotel, in the center of that perfect, small, funky island, that is, alas, no more—the Angler, that is. Before dawn on January 13, 2006, the twelve-room inn burned to the ground.

A year following that 1980 encounter with a living Hemingway, I purchased at a discount bookstore in a strip mall on Rockville Pike in suburban Washington, DC, a copy of the just-published *Ernest Hemingway: Selected Letters, 1917–1961,* edited by Carlos Baker. This couldn't have been accidental—all that Les had told me, including incredible-sounding stories about his nephew Gigi, was still jouncing around inside. I still have my beat-up brown copy of Baker's 948-page book— the Princeton scholar had brought into print the door-stopper letters volume twelve years after he'd brought into print his door-stopping *Ernest Hemingway: A Life Story,* which I've now run out of ways to describe, in terms of its being first and being essential. Reading the letters book, was I making dim connections to the idea that Hemingway's boat might serve as some sort of structural frame and organizing principle for my own Hemingway book? I don't know, but I will say it seems almost impossible to read the letters book—at least from about page 404 onward—without registering the name *Pilar.* At page 404 he's had her just days and is raving her beauties to Arnold Gingrich—I've quoted from this letter in the text.

Six years from the letters book, in the early summer of 1987, I searched out the three Hemingway sons and wrote about them for *The Washington Post,* my employer. By then, I think the idea of something on Hemingway between hard

471

covers was actively taking hold, not that I yet recognized it. I remember thinking at a later date, when I did recognize it as a possible book, and one involving *Pilar*, that if the project actually got launched, I wouldn't want it to be a story only about *Pilar*'s owner. And further, I'd want it to be far less a biography than an interpretation, an evocation, with other lives streaming in. I'd worked this way previously, and what was the point of another biography after so many—the good, the bad, the ugly—having marched before?

The material for *Hemingway's Boat* has been gathered in three ways. First, from my own interviewing and reporting. Since I come proudly from a journalistic rather than an academic background, the notion of being able to go out and talk to sources, which is to say anybody and everybody who might know something about the central subject, has always provided immediate and stabilizing comfort. Here, given Hemingway's birth date, I understood there'd not be that kind of ballast. Sure, there would be plenty of people to talk to, from Walloon Lake historians to restorers of vintage boats to old Key West hangers-on, but no one, or almost no one, who'd ever known the man himself. So I am only stating again my gratitude for having stumbled, all but blind, on Walter Houk.

The second way I obtained information was from documents—letters, manuscripts, old *Pilar* logs, photographs, newsreels, eight-millimeter films, tinny wire recordings converted to audio recordings. There are Hemingway repositories—or repositories of Hemingway-related materials—all over this country. I have written books about civil rights and Vietnam, but the sea of Hemingway documentary materials still seems deluging, no matter my gratitude that they exist. I have been in most of the Hemingway or Hemingway-related archives (and will name some of them as I go along here), but the archive where I have spent the most time in these last seven or so years of research and writing is Firestone Library at Princeton. The university is an hour and ten minutes from my front door; the car knows the way. I doubt I would have been able to complete this project at all were it not for the Carlos Baker papers, properly known as the Carlos Baker Collection of Ernest Hemingway at the Department of Rare Books and Manuscripts. The Baker-Hemingway archive, along with the university's Scribner's files (its proper name is the Archive of Charles Scribner's Sons), became my centripetal research force. Nearly all the letters I quote from or make reference to in this book I have sat and held and read in the chapel-like Dulles Reading Room at Firestone, in most cases a photocopy, but sometimes the original document.

The largest Hemingway archive in the world, of course, is at the John F. Kennedy Presidential Library and Museum in Boston; its Hemingway Room is banked by windows looking out onto wind-whipped Dorchester Bay. I always felt welcome there.

There were other, more specialized kinds of museums and archives I traveled to—those having to do with boats and boatbuilding or big-game fishing—and some of them I will also name in their relevant places.

The third way I gathered material was from so-called secondary sources, which in many ways became primary. I've stood on the shoulders of a lot of giants (and some pygmies, too). I am referring to the authors of books, monographs, theses, dissertations, magazine articles, newspaper pieces, studies in scholarly journals. Once again, the amount of Hemingway literature in all its forms and guises felt swamping, and often I knew I had to get out of a library almost as soon as I got into one, no matter if I had just journeyed some distance.

There was also the Hemingway-related material held privately. To cite three über-sources: What would I have done had Arnold Samuelson's daughter, Dian Darby, in Austin, Texas, not been willing to share what she had of her father's life with a stranger who came knocking, just as the Maestro had once come knocking at Hemingway's door? (I have never been able to talk to Dian's brother, Eric Samuelson.) Same with Wes Wheeler: when he took me down to his chaotic basement in Stamford, Connecticut, I knew I'd hit documentary gold on the proud, defunct shipyard his father and grandfather and uncles had run for decades. And Walter? Yes, there was a sense in which he had all the Hemingway-related paper and miscellany in the world waiting inside 21439 Gaona Street in Woodland Hills, California. But the real thing Walter had waiting, it goes without saying, was his own life. Paper is only paper next to human beings. (I am happy to report Walter has recently given his entire collection of Hemingway materials, including his own writing, to Princeton—it's there for future Hemingway scholars.)

The two biographies I carried like talismans over the length of the project were those of Baker and Michael Reynolds; the full citations of their books appear in the selected bibliography. Reynolds's work, rigorous and novelistic (in the way Baker's is exhaustive and academically straitlaced), is in five volumes; it stretches over something like twenty-five years of scholarship, almost right up until his early death in 2000. I am indebted to his widow, Ann Eubanks Reynolds, also now deceased, who allowed me into her Durham, North Carolina, basement to open boxes and boxes of her husband's research. I found several key things connected to *Pilar*.

If Baker and Reynolds (pride of place always to Baker) are the gold standard, I'll pay tribute to four other biographers and biographies I regularly consulted, and roughly in this order: Bernice Kert's *The Hemingway Women;* Jeffrey Meyers's *Hemingway;* Kenneth S. Lynn's *Hemingway;* James R. Mellow's *Hemingway.* (Again, for full citations, see the Selected Bibliography.) I should also add Denis Brian's quirky *The True Gen* and Mary Hemingway's *How It Was.* The first is oral history, the second—well, I am not entirely sure what it is. Memoir, biography, inadvertent confession, score settler: all of that, and then some.

And as long as I'm making lists, and using the word "quirky," the following books and articles and critical studies and popular essays rose up out of the great sea of Hemingwayana to speak in a particular way—call them my private Hemingway satchel. Baker and Reynolds are again on the list, namely Baker's

Hemingway: The Writer as Artist and Reynolds's "Ernest Hemingway, 1899–1961, A Brief Biography," which is what its title indicates: a thirty-five-page piece charting the arc of the life. (It appears in *A Historical Guide to Ernest Hemingway.*) The other works, in no particular order: "Hemingway: the Old Lion," in Malcolm Cowley's *A Second Flowering;* "A Quarter-Century Later, the Myth Endures," by Lance Morrow, in the August 25, 1986, *Time* magazine; *Coffee with Hemingway,* by Kirk Curnutt; *Notes from a Sea Diary: Hemingway All the Way,* by Nelson Algren; "Reading Hemingway Without Guilt," by Frederick Busch, in the January 12, 1992, *New York Times Book Review; Letters from the Lost Generation,* edited (and wonderfully annotated) by Linda Patterson Miller; "Hemingway the Painter," in Alfred Kazin's *An American Procession;* "Last Words," by Joan Didion, in the November 9, 1998, *New Yorker; Classes on Ernest Hemingway,* by Matthew J. Bruccoli; "Braver Than We Thought," by E. L. Doctorow, in the May 18, 1986, *New York Times Book Review; Ernest Hemingway and His World,* by Anthony Burgess; "Punching Papa," in Norman Mailer's *Cannibals and Christians;* "Pressure Under Grace," by Frederick C. Crews, in the August 13, 1987, *New York Review of Books;* "For Ernest Hemingway," in Reynolds Price's *A Common Room.* These are the ones I always came back to, when I wasn't coming back to the writing of the man himself. (Again, see bibliography.)

What follows isn't meant to be an all-inclusive line-by-line source-noting; rather, a kind of prose-form road map, both essay and citation, not every citation, no, but ones I judge the reader will be curious to know about, and also ones where I am directly indebted to my predecessors. Truth be told, these notes are also a way of telling some side stories I couldn't fit into the main frame. I use "EH" fairly often; other abbreviations and shorthand will be evident. When citing page numbers for quoted passages from Hemingway's novels and book-length nonfiction, I refer, unless otherwise specified, to the original hardcover editions of those works. No page numbers are given for the short stories. For the EH journalism, just title and date and name of publication.

PROLOGUE: AMID SO MUCH RUIN, STILL THE BEAUTY

"In hunting" quote: "On the Blue Water," *Esquire,* April 1936. "He can see" quote: "Out in the Stream," *Esquire,* August 1934. "Once you are out of" quote: "On the Blue Water." Conduct being "a question of how the good professional" quote: *Time,* July 14, 1961. The passage from *Holiday* appears in "The Great Blue River," July 1949. The Norman Mailer quote is in "Punching Papa," collected in *Cannibals and Christians.* The Edmund Wilson quote is on p. 802 of *The Sixties.* The Ella Winter quote is from a letter to Carlos Baker, February 10, 1962, and the original document is in the Carlos Baker Collection of Ernest Hemingway, Manuscript Division, Department of Rare Books and Special Collections, Princeton University Library. The Algren quote is from *Notes from a Sea Diary,* pp. 88 and 93. EH letter to Sara Murphy is April 27, 1934.

Sanctity, or yearning for it. The first time I began to think seriously about Hemingway and this absurd notion was when I read Reynolds Price's essay "For Ernest Hemingway," cited above. (It's in a 1987 Price collection, but I had discovered it some years before.) Price, a literary hero of mine, used the word "saintliness" and put it in italics. It jolted me. This became a new line of thinking and feeling, its own governing principle. In 2004, perhaps four or five months after I'd begun the book, Linda Patterson Miller, mentioned above, and of whom you've read earlier, picked up on the same idea. "I warned you that working with Hemingway would be a spiritual quest—totally life-affirming," she e-mailed. I could almost hear her laughing—at my turmoil, already considerable.

PART ONE. GETTING HER

Wagner's quote is in a 2002 monograph, *Blanchard Built,* published by the center.

AMERICAN LIGHT

Precede. Grace Hemingway's "I will take care of it for you" is in her letter of March 24, 1929. The Lance Morrow quote is in his August 25, 1986, *Time* essay. Nearly all of Hemingway's major biographers have written of this wavery fable, as I like to think of it. On the key question, that is, of Grace's intent, judgment seems divided. But I believe something chilling had to be going on between mother and son. Grace had gone twice to the coroner to try to retrieve the .32. On February 24, in a ten-page letter of gratitude to her son for his financial support in the wake of her husband's death, a letter with much seeming forced gaiety in it, she said she had "secured" the weapon. "Do you want me to send it down to you. Les wants you to leave it to him, when you are through with it—but you have first choice." *When you are through with it. First choice.* As I say, loaded, at least to my ears—and eerily premonitory of two suicides. In May 1965, writer Dawn Powell told Baker what she knew of the runny cake and the mailed gun. Baker then wrote to Dos Passos, citing Powell's account. Dos supplied his own inaccuracies—in blue ink over top of Baker's letter. We'll never know the truth of the matter.

Chapter. Going to the New York Public Library to read the April 4, 1934, newspaper accounts of EH's arrival on the *Paris* of the day before gave me the idea for how to frame the chapter. Interestingly, of the city's big dailies, the New York *Daily News,* circulation 1.5 million, skipped Hemingway—they went with Hepburn. She kept moving up in the various editions, and in the four-star final made p. 3. I tried in vain to find out whether she and EH had met on board, or even at the publicity rail. But the bigger mystery is how the shipboard reporters would have missed Dietrich. Her story re meeting Hemingway, written twenty-one years later, ghosted or not, is in the February 3, 1955, *New York Herald Tribune*.

E. B. White's parody is in the April 14, 1934, *New Yorker*. Re cost of the safari: the figure has ranged over the years from $25,000 to $33,000; I'm going with a round-off. Mark Stevens's quote is in a February 7, 2000, essay in *New York* magazine. "It is awfully easy to be hardboiled" quote is on p. 34 of *The Sun Also Rises*. "I sat in a corner" passage is on p. 76 of *A Moveable Feast*. EH quote about remembering when and where he wrote *A Farewell to Arms* is dated June 30, 1948, and is in the introduction to an illustrated 1948 edition of the novel. "I was always embarrassed" passage is on pp. 184–85. Max Eastman's review is in the June 7, 1933, *New Republic*. MacLeish's "I have always suspected" quote is in his letter to Baker, August 9, 1963. "Before these rich" passage is on pp. 209–10 of *Feast*. "We had tried" is on p. 86 of *Green Hills of Africa;* "What did you get?" passages are on pp. 291 and 293.

Re EH and Frank Lloyd Wright: Oak Park historians say there's no evidence the egomaniacal architect and future egomaniacal author ever met or talked in their overlapping years in that manicured place of broad lawns and reputedly narrow minds. (There's also no evidence Hemingway ever said that, even though you hear the claim all the time.) But it would be accurate—albeit fanciful—to go this far: had he wished to, Wright, from a high stool in his octagonal drafting room, in, say, 1906 or '07 or '08, could have looked out his window, catty-corner across Chicago Avenue, and observed the elementary-school children of Oliver Wendell Holmes School at their noon play, one of whom could have been one of his own children, and another of whom could certainly have been Ernest Hemingway. It's not literary or architectural scholarship—just fun—to squint and picture a roughly forty-year-old visionary gazing out on a fairly typical-seeming schoolboy named Hemingway, still in single digits, whose family name Wright may or may not have known. (I'm pretty sure he did: EH's mother and Wright's wife Kitty were casual friends who came together to paint, to talk books and the suffrage movement at Oak Park's Nineteenth Century Club.)

Re the retyped letter of EH to Fadiman, and the loss of the original: After his October 28, 1933, *New Yorker* review of *Winner Take Nothing*, Fadiman's editorial assistant, Miss Bert Hunt, bet her boss he'd hear from Hemingway. Fadiman said he doubted it. Hunt said she'd put a hundred bucks on it, but that the bet would have to run six months, in case EH was on the high seas or in a jungle somewhere. When the letter came in, Hunt grinned and collected her hundred. After Fadiman had read it and yukked, he had wanted to toss it, but his assistant, recognizing its worth to future scholars, remembered that she stuck the letter in a folder marked "Important Letters to Keep." Just to be on the safe side, she typed out a duplicate copy for herself. Twenty-five years later, Fadiman confessed to Hunt he'd sure like to have that old Hemingway letter. She was then retired in Palm Beach. Apparently she couldn't find the original, but retrieved the copy she'd typed out and squirreled away. These details are in a Hunt letter to Baker of March 25, 1962, eight months after the suicide. A few years ago, I decided to try out the story on Fadiman's daughter, Anne Fadiman, herself a respected author. She said the way her father always told it was that he just threw out the letter. In any case, all praise to the faithful and posterity-minded Miss Hunt.

Re EH and Ned Calmer: I decided to expand on Baker's account on pp. 257–58 of his bio, and did so by using two letters from Calmer to Baker and by conducting my own research. As I say in the text, I think the story is emblematic of the contradictory man with softness for those who are ill too early in life, women and children, especially.

THAT BOAT

Precede. The passage from *Green Hills* is on p. 49. The boat descriptions are from 1934 Wheeler catalog copy.

Chapter. "Horsing Them in with Hemingway" appeared in the September 1965 *Playboy* and is collected in *The Well-Tempered Angler.* Gingrich's words for EH after the suicide are in the October 1961 *Playboy.* The master carpenter's certificate is in the *Pilar* papers at JFK.

To write this chapter, but even more the one that follows, I talked to boating and fishing historians, read books and magazines devoted to wooden boats and big-game fishing, went to maritime museums and libraries (and also to one latter-day shipyard specializing in vintage boats), but mostly I went to Wes Wheeler's Connecticut basement. He had ancient issues of the *Rudder,* dozens of old Wheeler catalogs, photographs, record books, family albums, court transcripts, bankruptcy notices. He's a walking Wheeler encyclopedia, and fine company to boot. On what he knows: the reason *I* know that Howard E. Wheeler himself had addressed the 1933 fold-over pamphlet to EH is because his grandson—Wes—instantly recognized the handwriting.

I am also more generally in the debt of four wooden boat authorities: Dick Wagner, Dana Hewson, Llewellyn Howland, and Anthony Mollica Jr.

Wagner gave me a personal tour of his Seattle center a few years ago and talked offhandedly for three hours about the mystique of wooden boats.

Hewson is vice president for watercraft preservation and programs at Mystic Seaport in Connecticut—more about his crucial help at the end of these notes.

Howland, around boats his entire life, who once wrote a piece in *Wooden Boat* magazine titled, "Why People Own the Boats They Do," said that the three finest

American boatbuilders of the golden age of boating—commonly understood as the first half of the twentieth century—were Herreshoff in Rhode Island, Lawley and Sons in South Boston, and Henry B. Nevins on Long Island. But those shipyards, in the main, were custom builders, producing lavish yachts for high society. To compare their silk-stocking wares to the humbler (and perhaps far sturdier) wares of a Brooklyn production yard seems an apples-and-oranges argument. When I asked Howland if he didn't think a Wheeler was the right boat, right maker, for Hemingway, he said: "A Wheeler was a good bargain at good workmanship. You see, pleasure boats and sportfishing boats of the kind Hemingway got from Wheeler are to real yachting as Miller High Life is to Chivas Regal. Okay, Howard Wheeler built an adequately competent boat, a good boat, at a good price. I'm not saying it was the wrong choice at all for Hemingway. It apparently fit the man. It's what he needed and wanted." We spread out some pictures of *Pilar*, from that first season of the fishing, with her master's catches strung up on the dock beside her. "The phallic nature of the thing," Howland howled. "It's pathetic." Later, though, he said, softening: "Every day on a fishing boat it's a little theater. There's blood. It's a self-enclosed world. It's womb-like. Time is different. Time begins at dawn and ends at sunset. Here is a perfect time on a boat: you've had a long, hard day, you've caught your fish, and now you're purring home, toward your mooring."

Mollica, a prolific boating historian, said of Wheeler: "For a boatbuilder to turn out stock boats every year, using the same hull, is a remarkable thing. I have a lot better feeling than some people would about production-yard boats, and that's because they have been tested and tried. They will last. Look at *Pilar*."

Finally: On November 23, 1933, when a native midwesterner was on the Mediterranean en route for Mombasa, Vincent Astor was writing a letter to the Wheeler shipyard about his custom-built *Little Nourmahal*—which was then gracing the cover of the current *Rudder*. Old money versus new; custom versus stock; eastern blue blood versus Oak Park middle blood: while Astor was oozing with noblesse oblige ("I am delighted with her performance, and want you to know that she has proved herself to be a fine sea boat, most comfortable, and ideally suited to my purposes"), EH was raging on his French scow of a liner with its upchucking toilets. In three days he'd be upchucking to Kip Fadiman of *The New Yorker*. But who really gives a damn nowadays about Vincent Astor? And has his white-hulled beauty gone to firewood? Not so *Pilar*.

GONE TO FIREWOOD

Precede. The wild letter to Wilder is dated May 26, 1929, and I located it in the Wilder papers at Beinecke Rare Book and Manuscript Library, Yale.

Chapter. The passage from *Islands* is on p. 359. The Historical Index to *The New York Times* was helpful, as was a Wheeler file at the Brooklyn Public Library, as were general files at Mystic Seaport; the Mariners' Museum in Newport News, Virginia; and the International Game Fishing Association outside Fort Lauderdale.

What I love about the boom-to-bust Wheeler story is how self-made American it is—family and company. Wes Wheeler told me that in the early days of the company his father and uncles and aunts, along with Ma and Pa Wheeler, all used to live at the family boatyard. When the younger sons finished Brooklyn's Erasmus Hall High, they put on aprons and got knee-deep in shavings in the mold loft, even as they took college engineering and drafting classes by night. Chris-Craft may be the Coca-Cola of American boating, but this boat-crafting family went for its Loop-O-Plane ride in Coney Island's shade. I noted that no one seems to know the total number of Wheelers that were built—in a real sense the company was always too busy just trying to survive to worry about counts for future boating historians. In a presentation he once made before the Society of Naval Architects and Marine Engineers, Wes Wheeler said his grandfather's company had produced somewhere between four hundred and five hundred boats during World War II for the army, navy, Coast Guard, and War Shipping Board. Buried in a legal document from the fifties was the following sentence: "Both before and after the incorporation of these companies, petitioners practically designed, built, sold, tested, and delivered to the owners, private of Government, substantially every Wheeler boat, the 2,247th such boat being in construction at the time of trial." That was written in connection with tax and bankruptcy hearings for the years 1946 and 1947, following the failure of the Sunlounge, and it's a fact that significantly more Wheelers were built after that. So probably three thousand is a good rounding guess.

And yet. Although Wheeler's accomplishment in American boatbuilding can never be denied or discounted, consider nonetheless Chris-Craft's numbers. The company existed, in its original incarnation, roughly from 1922 to 1960, and in that time it is said to have made over one hundred thousand wooden boats. A Chris-Craft was ever about eye appeal, about what you could see on the outside, all the high-gleam brightwork. Apparently, Hemingway never wanted or needed that. Two years before Hemingway's death, the chairman of Chris-Craft, Hansen Smith, made the cover of *Time.* By then, spring of 1959, Hemingway's boat was a quarter of a century old and still sturdy as a tree, even as the company that had made her was on its final legs, at least in terms of involvement by Wheeler family members.

Boom to bust: Just recently (as I write), I went by the foot of Cropsey Avenue for yet another look. Alas, the Hopperesque diner sharing the pocked parking lot with the Pathmark Super Center was boarded up and had a chain-link fence around it.

Precede. In 1991, Michael Reynolds published *Hemingway: An Annotated Chronology,* the first serious attempt by a scholar to calendar EH's life. He cited Wednesday April 4, 1934, as the date EH went to Brooklyn to buy his boat, and so many behind him have followed that lead. But here's why I am convinced the date is wrong: Gingrich wrote to EH, with the $3,000 check enclosed, on Monday the second. The airmail letter wasn't officially on its way until the following morning—the postmark on the envelope says "APR 3, 11 AM." So before noon on Tuesday (about six hours before EH was entertaining the press at the rail of the *Paris*), the letter was somewhere between Chicago and New York. It's possible it could have landed at Scribner's by the next day, and that EH was there when it did and opened it and seized on its contents and went straightaway to Brooklyn with his wife. It seems far more likely, though, that it took a minimum of two days for the letter to get into EH's hands. Even that sounds fast, but it's a fact that mail in the 1930s traveled with surprising speed. (Hemingway often received mail in Key West from New York in two days—this can be tracked through his own replies.) EH and his wife couldn't have gone to Brooklyn any later than Thursday the fifth, because we know (from coverage in *The Key West Citizen,* for one thing) that Pauline arrived home in Key West by rail at midday on Saturday the seventh. This means she had to have left New York on Thursday night. (It was always "two nights out" to Key West from New York, as the rail advertisements put it.) So assuming Pauline went with her husband to Brooklyn—and I know of no evidence to the contrary—it could only have happened on Wednesday or Thursday. I say Thursday, April 5, 1934.

And as long as I am disagreeing with esteemed predecessors, I'll point out that Baker, on p. 259 of his bio, got three-in-a-row small and yet not-so-small facts wrong as regards the acquiring of *Pilar.* She wasn't diesel-powered, and she didn't have twin screws (but rather double screws), and the down payment wasn't $3,300. (In *Selected Letters,* on p. 405, he corrects that figure.)

Chapter. Both the purchase order and bill of sale are in the *Pilar* papers at JFK. EH letter to Balmer: August 3, 1934. Alfred Kazin's defense of Fitzgerald is in an essay titled "Retrospect, 1932: The Twenties and the Great American Thing," in his *An American Procession.* Edmund Wilson's quote is on pp. 301–3 of *The Thirties.* Matthew Bruccoli's surmise about Fitzgerald and the notebook entry re "the authority of failure" is in his *Fitzgerald and Hemingway: A Dangerous Friendship.* EH letter to MacLeish re "have to shoot myself" is September 26, 1936. "The Art of the Short Story" is in the spring 1981 *Paris Review.*

The Academy of Natural Sciences in Philadelphia—in its Ewell Sale Stewart Library—has a lush, if small, Hemingway file, and going there marked the first time I ever had the thrill of holding an original handwritten EH letter. In a glassine folder there's a tiny, elegant business card, manila-colored, not much larger than a Band-Aid. The card says, in caps, "Mr. Ernest Hemingway." Below that, in italics: "Key West, Florida." Re the original telegrams from EH in the library: holding them marked the first time I ever felt the palpable truth of Malcolm Cowley's remark about "cabelese" (as he spelled it) being an exercise for EH in "omitting everything that can be taken for granted." (Cowley says this in his *A Second Flowering*.)

To construct EH's trip home, I went to the New York Public Library and found old Havana Special timetables, as well as photographs of that kind of lost American travel.

Re *Tender Is the Night:* If there's a way to think about Fitzgerald heroically as well as tragically, in April 1934, when EH held every emotional advantage, there might also be a way to read the descriptions of the main character in *Tender* and form a mental image not of Gerald Murphy—upon whom Dick Diver is unquestionably modeled—but of EH. I'm not suggesting FSF deliberately painted EH into the shadows of his novel; I'm only saying I have been put in mind of EH when I read passages from that poetic and great and uneven book. "Did you hear I'd gone into a process of deterioration?" Diver says to the young American socialite, Rosemary Hoyt, whom he's falling for, as he is "in love with every pretty woman he saw now." "Oh, no," Rosemary responds. But the doctor is insistent. "It is true. The changes came a long way back—but at first it didn't show. The manner remains intact for some time after the morale cracks."

Re *The Snows* and the riddle of the "Dark Lady," as I'll call her: yes, a lot more to tell, and here would be a bit of it: the Whitney family personal papers are held privately within the family and are not for looking into by pesky journalists. And yet, several years ago, when I asked about the possibility of any correspondence between EH and Helen Hay Whitney, Kate Whitney, who is Jock Whitney's adopted daughter, was very gracious and seemed faintly amused by the prospect of it all. (We spoke on the phone on the day she turned seventy—I got the idea she'd lived long enough to be amused by such things.) She said she'd never heard about her grandmother inviting EH to tea, but that the idea was plausible enough on its face. "Not all the stories are recalled," she said. She told me she'd do a quick check among her father's personal papers. She called back a few hours later to say there was nothing there. As for the papers of HHW herself? Off-limits to researchers. But Kate Whitney did say: "Look, if we had a framed Hemingway letter that was once hanging on a wall somewhere, I think we'd tend to know about it." HHW died in 1944, at age sixty-eight, in a New York City hospital her family had financed almost single-handedly. I'm wondering if Kate Whitney's rich old eccentric granny didn't choose to take with her to heaven any correspondence between herself and EH, having read *Esquire* eight years before and recognizing herself, unhappily.

I believe Baker knew her identity, and I further believe, even if I cannot prove it, that the identity was confirmed for him by Buck Lanham, as well as one or two others, and yet for one reason or another, the biographer decided not to name the name. Baker's endnotes relate how EH, during the war, had told the story to Lanham. Wouldn't the spoken accounts, in wartime, have been lubricated by alcohol and thus a tad more indiscreet than the later written ones? According to Baker's notes, Lanham and another World War II officer wrote to Baker in the course of his research to tell him what they could remember of EH and the Dark Lady story. On p. 611, Baker writes of Lanham's memory of the telling: "He [EH] explained that 'The Snows of Kilimanjaro' was based in part on his imagination of what would have happened had he accepted the woman's offer." Baker cites a particular correspondence: "Lanham to author, June 1963." I felt sure HHW's name would be in that letter, but when I went to look, the letter wasn't there. There are folders of letters at Princeton between Lanham and Baker, all arranged in chronological order; this one's missing. In 2005, when I queried the curator of manuscripts, Don Skemer, about what might have happened to it, he graciously responded, in part, in an e-mail: "I've heard it said that not all of Carlos Baker's files came to the Library. Carlos Baker's daughter—or at least one particular daughter—is supposed to have retained some files. Acting on this rumor, early in my 15 years as Curator of Manuscripts, I telephoned his daughter and asked if she had any related files. But she said most definitely that she had none—that what she had at home was personal, not part of her father's files, and that she wouldn't let anybody see anything." That daughter is deceased.

PART TWO. WHEN SHE WAS NEW, 1934-1935

"If I Had a Boat" is the lead track on Lovett's second album, *Pontiac*.

HOME

Precede. "The rooms on the northeast corner" passage is from "Marlin Off the Morro: A Cuban Letter," in *Esquire*'s inaugural issue, autumn 1933.

Chapter. The April fishing log is in the *Pilar* papers at JFK. EH letter to Waldo Peirce is circa May 26, 1934. (He didn't date.) If the item in *The Key West Citizen* is to be trusted (and I do trust it), then EH departed for Miami to collect his boat on Tuesday afternoon, May 8. (In the mid-Depression, rail service between Miami and the Keys was down to two runs a day.) The May 9 item doesn't say Pauline and Bra Saunders were with him, but they were. (It's referenced in various letters of Pauline's and EH's.) On April 30, EH had said in a handwritten postscript at the end of a long typed letter to Max Perkins: "get the boat May 9—Then I can work in the morning and go out in the boat in the pm." This supports the May 8 departure timeline. The three must have slept over at a Miami hotel and gone excitedly on Wednesday morning to collect the boat—EH the most excited. We know from various sources that *Pilar* and company arrived back in Key West late on Friday afternoon. It's a fairly easy two-day cruise from Miami to Key West—roughly 130 nautical miles. The actual "driving time" would have been about thirteen hours, based on a steady-as-she-goes ten knots. My guess is EH and Bra and the Wheeler rep spent Wednesday getting the boat in the water, checking out her equipment, running her around Miami a bit—and then on the tenth began steering her south. Pauline, meanwhile, rode the train home ahead of them, and late on Friday was waiting at the navy yard with her children and friends when *Pilar* tooted round the bend. The reason I am going into this at all is because it's one more example of the way Hemingway researchers disagree on dates. These struggles for timelines are almost always compounded by the contradicting testimony of witnesses—in this instance, Les Hemingway and Arnold Samuelson, both of whose memoirs have been crucial to my own research, but neither of which can be really trusted for its chronology.

SHADOW STORY

Precede. The "If you go" dictum, which I've tried to live by, belongs to the late Shirley Povich of *The Washington Post*.

Chapter. I couldn't have done it had Dian Darby not taken a leap of faith and offered family letters, journals, diaries, photographs, scrapbooks, newspaper clippings, tapes. Even more, she gave so much of her personal time. Several others in the extended Samuelson family also helped, notably Sunny Worel, in St. Paul, Minnesota, who has a library background and thus a natural archival sense; she made available Arnold's journal from the summer of 1932. I am also indebted to the residents of Robert Lee—only two are named in the text, but a dozen or more people on my three visits added little bits.

The epigraph from *Death in the Afternoon* is on p. 506. "Road brings in every son of a bitch" quote is in EH letter to Thomas Shevlin, April 4, 1939. The passage about Pinky is on p. 228 of *Death*. Fitzgerald's remark about a writer not writing is quoted in Andrew Turnbull's bio, *Scott Fitzgerald*. "Just start with the canoe" passage is on p. 77 of *Islands*. Robert Lacy's "Icarus" essay is in the Fall 2003 *North Dakota Quarterly*. EH's desperation to Hotchner is quoted by Hotchner on pp. 285, 297, 298 of the updated 1983 Quill edition of his *Papa Hemingway*. "As full a life in seventy hours" quote is on p. 166 of *For Whom the Bell Tolls*. "I did nothing" passage is on p. 148 of *Green Hills*.

Would the Maestro have ridden a rail to EH's door had someone offered him a crystal ball about the rest of his life? I'd bet yes. In a letter I quoted from in the text, written on April 28, 1936, little more than a year after he'd left EH and *Pilar*'s company, the lost boy, already sounding lost, said: "It is Sunday morning and it makes me drowsy listening to the church music on the radio." That strangely moves me, like all of his life.

HIGH SUMMER

Precede. I suppose it's fair to say that these several pages represent what I've learned, physically, about *Pilar* after some seven years of riding her in my head as metaphor and motif and storytelling structure. Would that I could have had one real ride on her and felt her under me in a wholly different way.

As I noted in an earlier part of the text, the handwritten manuscript of *Green Hills* resides at the University of Virginia—at the Albert and Shirley Small Special Collections Library. "I saw the faces" passage is on p. 211 of *A Farewell to Arms*. "Loosening" letter is to Arnold Gingrich, June 21, 1934.

Chapter. Reading EH's back-to-back Saturday and Sunday letters to Gingrich of July 14–15, 1934, gave the idea of how to construct the chapter. For instance, the reason I know Bumby came in with the mail while he was writing the Saturday letter is because EH said so in the letter.

For the start, that is, the ride over, Samuelson's memoir was crucial, along with his February 1935 *Motor Boating* piece, "Marlin Fishing with Rod and Reel." The clearance and manifest papers are in the *Pilar* papers at JFK. EH letter to MacLeish with "Why don't you come down here sometime" is April 4, 1943. "My right arm broken off short" passage is on p. 148 of *Green Hills*. MacLeish's letter to Baker re the terns is January 31, 1965, and his earlier one re "most profoundly human and spiritually powerful creatures" is August 9, 1963. "Completely happy" passage is on p. 55 of *Green Hills*. "Cool in the shade" passage is on pp. 107–8.

Timelines (again): Although the clearance and manifest papers are dated July 18, suggesting that as the date of departure, I am convinced he didn't go until the following day. Why? Because of an old wire I came upon in the Hemingway archives at JFK. On Tuesday evening, the seventeenth, at 8:36 p.m., EH cabled his Havana boatman, Carlos, at his home at 21 Vives in Havana: LLEGAREMOS JUEVES TARDE. We will arrive late on Thursday. Which is to say, the nineteenth. (Gutiérrez had lately moved from 31 Zapata, and for some reason Hemingway seemed to be very fond of that address—he even put it in the *Esquire* piece of the year before, when Carlos's name came up.) What I think happened is that EH went down to the customhouse on Wednesday and filled out the departure papers, in order to be ready for the next day's early going. This tracks with events on the Havana side. It also tracks with the A-1 story in the *Havana Post* on July 21 that EH and *Pilar* "entered Havana Bay Thursday night." It also tracks with a front-page story in the *Citizen* on the eighteenth that Hemingway "will leave tomorrow on his cabin cruiser Pilar for Havana waters."

Re the tension to get down the words: As noted, on May 26 EH advanced his safari story by less than two hundred words. Three were "strawy dung piles." At some point between ms. and galley and published book, the phrase became "strawy piles of dung." Above and below "piles" on the ms. sheet, he wrote the numbers 118 and 472. What they referred to, other than a toting up of some kind, is anybody's guess.

Finally, re the new issue of *Esquire* that Bumby brought to his dad's workroom on that Saturday morning: Three small pen-and-ink drawings illustrated the piece. One has Hemingway tilted back with his rod in his fighting chair, draining a bottle of booze, with a dozen other liquor or beer bottles beside him. On the jump page, two baby fish stare at a very large marlin. This is the caption: "Confidentially, he's a she." In light of all we posthumously know, or think we know, or are all too eager to speculate, about Hemingway's psychosexual conflicts, his hair fetishes, his fascination behind the bedroom door with sexual role reversals, as these themes and fetishes and half-concealed desires seem to speak to us so loudly now from his grave, it's a little disconcerting—even startling—to go to a library and pull down from a dusty shelf a bound copy of the August 1934 issue of *Esquire* and come on that cartoonish illustration.

CATCHING FISH

Precede. "One Trip Across" first appeared in the April 1934 *Cosmopolitan.* The passage from *Islands* is on p. 110.

Chapter. I cross-referenced a dozen sources: among others, Samuelson's memoir and his two journalism pieces of February and June 1935, EH letters, the *Pilar* logs, EH's fishing letter in the October 1934 *Esquire,* and Havana newspaper accounts. What such cross-referencing mainly gets you is headaches. The Maestro is only too happy to contradict himself all over the place. For instance, re the catching of Pauline's pint-size marlin on Hemingway's birthday, he reports in *With Hemingway* the fish weighed sixty-four pounds and was gaffed in seven minutes. But in his *Motor Boating* piece (written closer to the actual event, and under the editing eye of his mentor), he says the fish weighed forty-four pounds and was gaffed in fourteen minutes. The *Pilar* log entry, which was surely written within hours of the catch, must be nearest the truth: a forty-four-pounder, landed in twelve minutes, length "six feet eight." Bit of pedantry, I know.

The passage re water color is on p. 107 of *Islands*. The quote re David lifting and reeling is on p. 110. Linda Patterson Miller's essay about the *Pilar* logs is titled "The Matrix of Hemingway's *Pilar* Log, 1934–1935," and is in *North Dakota Quarterly*, 64, no. 3 (1997). Bruccoli's comment about EH as restaurant critic is in his *Classes on Ernest Hemingway*. Doctorow's quote about EH and food is in his "Braver Than We Thought." The passage from *Green Hills* re "cold sliced tenderloin" is on p. 111 and the "chop box" passage is on p. 110. EH letter to his mother-in-law is August 14, 1934. EH letter to Gingrich re trying to write a novel part-time is August 18, 1934. Second letter to Mary Pfeiffer is August 20, 1934. *The Sentence* is on pp. 148–50 of *Green Hills*. EH letter to Murphys re coming back across is November 7, 1934. *New Masses* smackdown of EH is November 27, 1934.

Portrait of the scientificos: largely from my own reporting. Re the big catch of August 6: writing of that day in his "Genio after Josie" letter in the October 1934 *Esquire*, EH gave the technical data, as if only the facts, the names of things, had dignity: "This fish was hooked on a trolled cero mackerel bait, on a 12/0 Pflueger swordfish hook, No. 13 piano wire leader, Hardy 20-oz. tip and Hardy 6-inch reel with 500 yards of 39-thread line and was taken on board in one hour and twelve minutes from the time he was hooked." From the logs of that day: "No. 2 of 1934. 12 feet 2 inches. 420 pounds. Girth 4 feet 8 inches. Head 3¼ inches."

Re the *Pilar* logs: As noted, in the late 1980s, the JFK library acquired a carbon copy from the Samuelson estate—some ninety-five pages of gapped text, with a first full entry of July 28. (There was a partial entry ahead of this, thought to be from July 27.) It was assumed that this was all there was. But in the last few years, another eleven pages have come forth, found in the family archives of Toby and Betty Bruce in Key West. So the extant if still incomplete logs are now an even more valuable 106-page document, commencing on July 21, 1934.

ON BEING SHOT AGAIN

Precede. Time review of Les Hemingway's novel is November 2, 1953, and EH letter about it six years later is September 14, 1959. EH's yelling at his little brother aboard *Pilar* is described in Vernon (Jake) Klimo and Will Oursler's *Hemingway and Jake*. As said in the text, the passage from *Islands* forms that novel's perfect first paragraph. EH's letter to his brother re forbidding publication of any kind of book about him while he was alive is September 14, 1959.

I am staring at a curling photograph of Les and me taken by my wife with Les's camera, a Polaroid; it's more than thirty years old. Les and I are saying good-bye at the Chalk's seaplane ramp. A bright red hibiscus petal is stuck in the buttonhole of my denim shirt—Les has reached over and put it there. He has on his black horn-rims, a plaid woolen shirt. He could be my best older friend, or the favorite uncle always looking out for me. I can't really see his brown eyes—they're obscured by his thick lenses. The man who did what he could. The apparition, free of the disease.

Chapter. I drew on EH letters, accounts of others (John Dos Passos, e.g.), EH pieces in *Esquire*, logs, film footage. (A cache of footage is housed at the museum-library of the International Game Fish Association in greater Fort Lauderdale.) First epigraph is from letter to the very ill Patrick Murphy, April 5, 1935. Second epigraph is from EH's "a.d. Southern Style" in May 1935 *Esquire*. Letter to Gingrich re "Here is the piece" is April 12, 1935. Stein in America: details were culled from news accounts and several biographies, including Janet Hobhouse's *Everybody Who Was Anybody*. Re EH and eight-millimeter home movies: In one of the sequences of *Pilar* getting away from the dock en route (on the first try) to Bimini, you see the boat turning around. The figures on shore are waving; the figures on the boat are waving back. But now *Pilar's* making a long, slow curve in the navy yard harbor. EH needs to retrieve the movie camera. What's this about? He wishes to document his leaving, and somebody on land has obliged him, but he's now coming back to collect the camera for all the anticipated catches on Bimini.

Re size of EH's reels: A few years ago, in Jupiter, Florida, I spent a happy afternoon with one of America's foremost antique tackle experts and collectors. Ed Pritchard not only had the tackle, he had the vintage catalogs from Abercrombie and Hardy. He owned both a 14/0 Vom Hofe and several of the larger Zane Greys. He took one of the latter from a cabinet—I think it was a seven-incher—and set it in my hands. It felt like a bowling ball—I was worried I'd drop the thing. I played with the spindle and listened to the oiled whir and click of its wheels and bearings. "How much do you want?" I joked. "Oh, give me fifteen or twenty thousand," he said.

OUTSIDE WORLDS

Precede. July 20, 1935: The JFK library has many photographs, which aren't dated but are unquestionably from that day. Extremely helpful was the eight-millimeter footage donated to the International Game Fish Association museum by legendary Bimini angler Mike Lerner. Lerner's footage has these old-timey title cards: "That Memorable Day July 20. Four big blue Marlin on Bimini's Dock."

"And meanest" quote is on p. 10 of *Islands*. "Something about him" quote is on p. 144. "Smallest boy" passage is on p. 53. Re the never-completed trilogy of war novels, and re scholars still trying to sort out time frames of composition: I am not alone in thinking that the best work done on this entire period is by Rose Marie Burwell in her *Hemingway: The Postwar Years and the Posthumous Novels*. I am not only indebted to her 1996 book, but to the time she gave to me in an interview at her Oak Park home several years ago, with elegant refreshments.

Re EH's use of title page of *The Magic Mountain* for a fishing log: Literature professor and bibliographer James D. Brasch, retired now from Ontario's McMaster University, sent a close-up slide of that title page, and he was also generous on the phone and in correspondence with what he knew. In 1977, shortly after New Year's, Brasch and a fellow McMaster professor, Joseph Sigman, went to Cuba to work in Hemingway's library as part of an ongoing effort by bibliophiles to try to gauge how many books Hemingway had owned through the moveable feast of his life, from Oak Park to northern Michigan to Paris to Key West to Havana to Idaho, and all the Hemingway places in between. (Essentially, Brasch and Sigman were concerned with the personal libraries of Key West and Cuba.) The truth is we'll never know the total number of books EH owned in his lifetime. Like people, he left too many behind. According to the Boston-based Finca Vigía Foundation, which works privately with Cuban conservators to preserve Hemingway's home (including *Pilar*—see the end of these notes), there are about nine thousand items—books, magazines, pamphlets—in his personal library, and it's estimated that about 20 percent have something written by Hemingway in their margins.

Chapter. I charted the timelines by again cross-referencing letters, movie footage, logs, EH pieces in *Esquire, Islands in the Stream,* books about Bimini in the thirties and the years beyond. As for broader history, about Bimini and also big-game fishing, I've mentioned in the text George Reiger's *Profiles in Saltwater Angling,* but mention should also be made of Ashley Saunders's two-volume *History of Bimini.* Saunders is the nephew of the composer of "Big Fat Slob," and I have pedaled a bike with him up-island from Alice Town to another little clot of Bimini life called Bailey Town, to dine on a late dinner of fry bread and plantains and deep-fried grouper at a wobbly table covered with oilcloth—and listened to Nattie's nephew, on the way home, through the starry midnight blackness, singing verses of his uncle's song.

Re EH letter to Mike Strater of July 1933 re hoping to go eventually to Bimini for tuna, and of the boat he hoped to buy on his return from Africa: it's a pity we don't have an exact date for this letter, for it's important in the history of *Pilar.* I think it's primarily from this letter—ten months before *Pilar* was in EH's possession—that a lot of misinformation about her has barnacled itself to biographies.

Passage from *For Whom the Bell Tolls* re coded reference to Mike Strater is on pp. 380–81. Shipboard letter to Lerner re competition should "be all inside yourself" is March 4, 1937. EH *Toronto Star Weekly* piece is February 18, 1922. Letter to Perkins re how he's "changed the whole system" is June 19, 1935. Letter to Gingrich re "plenty rich boys" is June 4, 1935. The "slob" passages in *Islands* are pp. 35–39. Letter to Gingrich about "clipping" Dodi Knapp is June 4, 1935. Quotes re "I humiliated him" etc., appear on pp. 46, 47, 48 of *Islands.* A Knapp researcher named Ken Spooner has done invaluable work on the real-life Dodi, as opposed to the EH fictional creation, and I am grateful to him for making some of it available to me.

Re the question of EH's first-ever tuna catch: On p. 272 of his bio, Baker describes a different and much larger tuna that he didn't hook but fought for hours. The suggestion is that *this* was EH's first battle with a bluefin, and that the fight occurred in May. But Dos Passos, who witnessed the fight, wasn't on Bimini anytime in May. He and his wife were there the month before, but then left and didn't come back to the island (and then only for a week), until the second week of June. Katy and Dos watched the battle from the top of *Pilar*'s cabin, and Dos describes it in *The Best Times*. So I think that the tuna catch I've told of—and that EH wrote of in his August *Esquire* letter—was his first one, as well as Bimini's first-ever recorded bluefin that was brought in unmutilated. In the *Esquire* piece Hemingway says, "I was steering into the sea with a big southwest breeze blowing when we hooked *the first one*." (Italics mine.) He then tells of this 381-pounder with the head that seemed made of chromium. EH doesn't give a date for the historic catch, and neither do his letters, but, as I say in the text, it had to have happened in the latter half of May. Incidentally, the *other* fish was hooked by a local named Charlie Cook, caretaker of Cat Cay. The fight lasted something like ten hours and ended in darkness with a circle of boats shining their searchlights on *Pilar*'s stern. By the time they got the fish into the boat, only backbone, head, and tail remained: apple-cored.

Finally: The original document of Baker's Strater interview is in the Carlos Baker Collection of Ernest Hemingway, Manuscript Division, Department of Rare Books and Special Collections, Princeton University Library.

EXUBERATING, AND THEN THE JACKALS OF HIS MIND

Precede. Re question of whether EH and Sara Murphy were ever lovers: my own hedge is yes. Nearly from the start, they seemed to have connected with each other powerfully, and you can get it from their letters, in coded and less-coded ways. Such as this one, of April 27, 1934, a fortnight before he claims *Pilar:* "Dearest Sara: I love you very much, Madam, not like in Scott's Christmas tree ornament novels but the way it is on boats where Scott would be sea-sick."

Chapter. Letters, logs, diaries, movies, photographs, oral histories. Also works by other Bimini anglers as well as of some general Hemingway hangers-on. In the former category, S. Kip Farrington's *Fishing with Hemingway and Glassell* was helpful, and in the latter Ben Finney's *Feet First.* (Both are self-aggrandizing.) Letter to Max re "lovely spot" is July 2, 1935. EH midnight wire to Max is February 18, 1935. Letter to Gingrich re birthday catch is July 31, 1935, and one re his "piles" to Max is the day before—July 30. Letter re "the Knapp thing" is to Gingrich, July 31. "Who Murdered" piece is in *New Masses,* September 17, 1935. "Writers should work alone" quote is from p. 21 of *Green Hills,* and Mark Twain quote is p. 22. EH's letter to Janet Flanner is April 8, 1933.

PART THREE. BEFORE

Quote from *A Moveable Feast* appears on p. 76.

EDENS LOST AND DARKNESS VISIBLE

Precede. Grace's family albums are too fragile to be examined any longer in the original. But a transcript and reproduction of their contents will give new awe for her will, energies, abilities, suffocations, egotisms, loyalties. Her son's second album charts his life from age twenty-three months to five years, five months. On p. 8, a picture of EH fishing on a log at Windemere, with this caption: "Gonna cats a big back bass." (He's in overalls, boots, straw hat.) On p. 11, he's naked on a boat, pointing to a tree, with this caption: "little mercury, quite unconscious." On p. 30, seated in a chair with his newly born sis, Ursula: "I wuv her to pieces."

Chapter. I have stood on the shoulders (metaphor I used earlier) of more than a dozen Oak Park and Michigan historians. For the canoe trip down the Des Plaines, the family of Ray Ohlsen was crucial. His three daughters and one son, all proud midwesterners in upper age, had vivid memories of their dad. So did several middle-aged midwestern grandsons and grandnephews. The Ohlsen family provided a copy of a 1974 tape recording that Ohlsen made with his grandson, Steve Rae, and also a transcript. The historians and archivists at the Ernest Hemingway Foundation of Oak Park, housed in the Oak Park Public Library, had a copy of EH's January 15, 1961, letter from Mayo. The foundation also had photographs of the canoe trip; JFK as well. After I had studied these photographs for a while, a dumb question occurred to me: Who took the photographs of EH and Ohlsen along the stream bank and at their campsites? It must have been their fellow high school buddy, Toy Ullman, who joined them briefly on the trip. (Ohlsen speaks of Ullman in the tape recording, but makes no mention of how he caught up with them and if he had his own canoe.) I'm guessing he came overland, perhaps on the train, camped out with them for at least a night, and then went on his own back to civilization.

I said in the text I had a second postscript: Ray Ohlsen himself. What was the rest of his life like? At Class Day in graduation week, Hemingway had delivered the class prophecy and said that Cohen—he called him by his real name—would end up president of Harvard. What I ended up learning about the history of the real man moved me. If his story—and I can only suggest the bare outline of it—sounds ordinary, un-Hemingway-like, sane, decent, midwestern, banal even, well, that's pretty much my point.

His grandkids—sixteen at his death, twelve great-grandchildren—used to call him Dad-o. In retirement Dad-o drove this rancid old 1964 Rambler station wagon, and he loved loading up the kids on an airless Peoria summer night and carting them off to Velvet Freeze, "Home of the Wonder Dog."

He was married to the same good woman for sixty-two years, not without heartache and temporary separations due at least in part to his difficulties in holding steady work. Instead of getting hitched in Illinois, he and Angeline had run off in 1925 to a justice of the peace at the Lake County Courthouse in Crown Point, Indiana, because that's where Rudolph Valentino got married.

In his retirement from Caterpillar, Dad-o became something of a rose fanatic. He gave up cigarettes just to have the money for new bushes. Weekends, he'd go around to juried shows with one of his favorite grandsons, Andy Rae. They'd get up early on a Saturday morning and go to the backyard and snip a just-blooming "Peace" rose or a bright red "Mr. Lincoln." They'd put the prizes in a Styrofoam cooler and then light out for Illinois burgs like Pekin and Decatur and Mattoon, hoping to snare a best-of-show medallion. Late in the day, grandfather and grandson would pull into the driveway at 1013 North Frink—"Stinky-Frinky," the grandkids called it—beat and happy.

At age seventy-five, the idea came up to make a tape recording about his memories of his boyhood friend. In his flat midwestern drawl, he read into the machine Hemingway's letter from Mayo. His voice lilted just a little on the word "kid." The kid was on his way to eighty-nine when the massive stroke took him off in the early fall of 1987. His family had him cremated. The roses in the backyard and along the side of the house had come in beautifully that summer.

EH letter to Philip Young is March 6, 1952. Young's statement re "All theses" distorting the work is in his 1966 *Ernest Hemingway: A Reconsideration*. EH's undated letter to Marcelline re use of Windemere is circa July 1937, and his apology is December 22, 1938. The quote from *Feast* re the fishermen of Paris is on p. 43. EH letter from the Pine Barrens is to Howell Jenkins, July 26, 1919. Marcelline's passage about her father's "disciplines" is on p. 31 of her memoir, and Morris Buske's "Hemingway Faces God" is in the Fall 2002 *Hemingway Review*.

Re travel on the *Manitou* and other Great Lake steamers to the northland: William Lafferty of Wright State University in Dayton, Ohio, had the old timetables—and much else. (His website, Lake Michigan Maritime Marginalia, was very helpful.) George Hilton's *Lake Michigan Passenger Steamers* was useful, as was a July–September 1946 article, "Chicago to Mackinac: Story of the Northern Michigan Transportation Company," by Thomas Dancey, in *Michigan History Magazine*.

The *Manitou*, which I think of as the primal Hemingway boat, changed ownership several times during her career—but her cut-above service didn't alter. Her longest operator was the Northern Michigan Transportation Company, referred to by almost everyone as the Northern Michigan Line. Just the name is said to have enlivened the pulses of Illinoisans dreaming through hard winters. In the *Chicago Tribune* and other dailies of the city, you'd see the NMTC's display ads for their flagship boat, the one "equipped for people who travel right."

For the northland itself: Clarke Historical Library at Central Michigan University in Mount Pleasant has an extensive Hemingway collection (and an angling one, too). In 2003, the Clarke mounted an exhibit called "Hemingway in Michigan, Michigan in Hemingway," and the catalog was valuable. In 2007, the library helped put on an exhibit at the Crooked Tree Art Center in Petoskey (*Up North with the Hemingways and Nick Adams*), and again the companion booklet-catalog was helpful. (The two quotations in the text from Professor Frederic Svoboda are in that publication.) The Petoskey District Library's History Department has much northland material. Constance Cappel Montgomery's 1966 study, *Hemingway in Michigan,* was helpful—and still up-to-date in its own way. Walloon Lake has its own library—the Crooked Tree District Library—with works on the history of Walloon, particularly a lavishly illustrated local history–oral history titled *Walloon Yesterdays.* Speaking of lavish: JFK has hundreds of pictures of the Hemingways in Michigan, and boats are in half of them, or so it seems to me. And, of course, Grace's exhausting albums, word and photo. Also: Jim Sanford, Marcelline's son (and EH's nephew), in Petoskey, was generous with his memories about water, about boats, about family disputes, and so was his brother, John Sanford, in California, who said in an e-mail: "I wish there were sailboats as I am a sailor myself." Both brothers remembered the canoes. When EH was in high school (long before the Sanfords were alive), he gave his kid sister Sunny, five years his junior and the tomboy of the four girls, a picture of himself paddling a canoe. He wrote on the back: "Me trusty Bitch Bark viacle. Length 9 feet wt 20 lbs. Just as sturdy as a church, like hell. You have to part your hair in the middle to balance it." Years later, Madelaine Hemingway Miller (Sunny) reproduced the picture in her adoring memoir, *Ernie.* The paddle her bro's using is made of ashwood, given to him by an Indian who lived in the woods behind Windemere. Finally: in the text I spoke of Hemingway forsaking northern Michigan. But we do know he went back as a rolling spy at least once—September 1947, in his new royal blue Buick Roadmaster, with Toby Bruce doing most of the driving, the two of them en route from Miami to Ketchum via Walloon Lake. The last look.

PART FOUR. OLD MEN AT THE EDGE OF THE SEA: ERNEST/GIGI/WALTER HOUK, 1949–1952 AND AFTER

Isak Dinesen's oft-quoted line, misquoted through the years, seems to have first been said in a telephone interview, and published in *The New York Times*

Book Review, November 3, 1957. Jack Gilbert's poem is collected in his *Refusing Heaven.*

MOMENTS SUPREME

Precede. Re the level of his anxiety and of how concentrated his mind had to have been: In the first letter of October 2 to Scribner, written by hand, three pages long, Hemingway starts in on the same line as the greeting, as if he can't take the time to skip down a line. At the end, in a PS without the "PS": "Times are bad general but we've seen worse." The last four words are going up the side of the page. I first saw this letter, a photocopy, in the Baker files at Princeton. There's a red line drawn through the sentences "But this boy Gigi was not brave as Patrick always was. He was only terribly skillful and corrupted. His mother, and her sister being corrupt did not help him much." In the left margin, in what looks like Baker's handwriting, are four words I've wondered about: "delete without indicating deletion."

Harbor scum: In *Islands,* in the middle "Cuba" section, there's a passage about the diseased upper end of Havana Harbor. Thomas Hudson, having lost all three sons, is getting ready to go into town to make a report to a military attaché at the American Embassy re his submarine patrols. He's trying not to think about it, and the "it" seems to be almost anything and everything in his recent and not-so-recent life. "It wasn't the sea you wanted to forget," he thinks to himself. Dressed now, he comes out of the long, bright living room that still seems so enormous to him. He comes down the stone steps. Some dead branches have fallen from the great ceiba. He climbs into his car with a drink of gin and bitters in his hand and his driver takes him down the long drive and unchains the gate and turns onto a side street of the dirty village below. They maneuver onto the old stone highway of Cuba, the Central Highway, cracked and cobbled, running downhill for three miles. A man drinking and self-pitying for things he can't fully articulate, gone children, gone wives, destroyed friendships, squandered opportunities at his art, gazes from the window. He hates this part of the ride the most. "I drink against poverty, dirt, four-hundred-year-old dust, the nose-snot of children, cracked palm fronds, roofs made from hammered tins, the shuffle of untreated syphilis, sewage in the old beds of brooks, lice on the bare necks of infested poultry, scale on the backs of old men's necks, the smell of old women, and the full-blast radio." Now the approaching smokestacks of Havana Electric. Now the upper limit of the harbor, where the stagnant water is "as black and greasy as the pumpings from the bottoms of the tanks of an oil tanker." The gates of a railroad crossing come up and the car is moving again and there on the right are the old wooden-hulled ships of the merchant marine. They "lay against the creosoted pilings of the wooden docks and the scum of the harbor lay along their sides blacker than the creosote of the pilings and foul as an uncleaned sewer." This old colonial harbor, with its scum, has been like this for three or four hundred years.

As I note, scholars generally agree EH finished the "Cuba" section on Christmas Eve, 1950. Nine months later, early evening of October 2, 1951, he called his own child "harbor scum." I think he reached into his recent fiction and found what he needed.

Re the spitting at his wife: Mary entered in her journal, "News of Pauline's death. Alto came over. They talked like vultures and I said so. E. followed me to my bathroom and spit in my face. Next day he gave me $200, which I gravenly accepted." She must have meant *cravenly.*

Chapter. The epigraph quote is on p. 26 of *The Old Man and the Sea,* and the passage about silence is on p. 43. Walter's piece is in *North Dakota Quarterly* 65, no. 3 (1998). Letter to Wallace Meyer at Scribner's is March 4 and 7, 1952. The chapter represents a distillation of all I know and feel about a proud, honorable old man whom I first met in 2004—and continue visiting to this moment.

FACET OF HIS CHARACTER

Precede. EH letter re steering prowess is to Charlie Scribner, May 18–19, 1951.

Chapter. Since I quoted or referenced a lot of EH letters in this chapter, I've tried to give dates and days in the text itself as a way to help keep the reader chronologically steered. But here are several dates and citations (not only to the letters) I didn't provide: Quote from *Old Man* re DiMaggio is on pp. 23–24. The New York critic EH wrote to on July 9, 1950, with his baseball conceit was Harvey Breit. EH's "shit on hope" is in *How It Was.* The motorboat passage from *Across the River and into the Trees* is on pp. 55–56 of the softcover edition, and the lovebird passages are on pp. 81 and 89. *Time*'s review is September 11, 1950. E. B. White's parody is October 14, 1950. Letter re *Pilar* taking the wind at 95 is November 28, 1950, to E. E. "Chink" Dorman-O'Gowan.

Re *Pilar*'s wartime patrols: I could have, and possibly should have, written much more on this period, but I had another aim for the chapter, namely, documenting EH's rage. Of all Hemingway's full-length biographers, Michael Reynolds has done the most original work on *Pilar*'s submarine hunts, and so I admiringly direct readers there.

THE GALLANTRY OF AN AGING MACHINE

Precede. In her 1987 "Cuba Revisited" piece in *Granta* (researched in late 1985), Gellhorn writes: "Gregorio was interested in two large cement cradles, placed where the tennis courts used to be. The *Pilar* was his inheritance, he had cared for it and given it to the state, and it was to be brought here and placed on these cradles." See my coda at the end of these notes re the curious afterlife of *Pilar*—and the question of "bogus *Pilars*."

Chapter. Epigraph quote is on p. 10 of *Old Man*. Re Walter's old UCLA paint-ing teacher, Stanton Macdonald-Wright: art historians regard him as the most important twentieth-century figure on the West Coast to have taught and pro-moted Cézanne to his students. Since Hemingway's indebtedness to Cézanne is both profound and self-acknowledged, this seems just one more unwitting node of connection between Walter and EH. Interview in *New York Post Week-End* is December 28, 1946. "Why am I a bastard" passage is pp. 66–67 of *Across the River*. Letter to Scribner re his diet during his writing tear is April 11–12, 1951. Gigi's quoting of his father re Adriana is on p. 111 of *Papa*. EH's letter to Nita in Baltimore is September 1, 1949. Walter's nearly book-length piece about *Islands* is in the Winter–Spring 2006 *North Dakota Quarterly*. Re forests being clear-cut to "explain" EH's "fetishes": One of the earliest and bravest and yet probably most "out there" works done on this whole subject is by Carl Eby, in his *Hemingway's Fetishism: Psychoanalysis and the Mirror of Manhood*. The book has sentences such as these: "To say that Hemingway *was* a transvestite would mistakenly give the impression that such fantasies dominated his erotic life; yet within the domi-nant field of his fetishistic fantasy, the transvestic position was one to which he returned repeatedly." I first met Professor Eby—who teaches at the University of South Carolina–Beaufort—in Key West in 2004 at an international Hemingway conference. I was prepared to dislike him instantly, but in fact he was disarmingly friendly, not to say a little self-mocking. Early one morning he was on a panel, and the advertised title of his paper was " 'He Felt the Change So That It Hurt Him All Through': Sodomy and Transvestic Hallucination in Late Hemingway." I ran into him in the hallway as the audience was gathering. "Uh, little bit grabby for 8:30 a.m., wouldn't you say?" he sort of hooted-cum-winked. I heard one of the old guard say afterward, "That man is *dangerous*." Actually, I don't think so.

Re Walter's old Havana journal in its retyped, incomplete state: I take on faith it's a document undoctored in any way—but would that we had it all.

Finally, re EH telling Nita he'd had lessons in hair-dying from the Alberto Culver company in LA en route to China in 1941: I don't believe it. The timelines would argue against it. He and Martha were in LA for barely two days in late January 1941. They stayed at the Gary Coopers' and were feted at parties. Could he have gotten away for blonding tutoring?

BRAVER THAN WE KNEW

Precede and chapter. I wrote the two-part, nine-thousand-word piece called "Papa's Boys," which was published in *The Washington Post* on July 29–30, 1987. Three years later, on May 13, 1990, I wrote "Rainbow Chaser" for *The Washington Post Magazine*. That was a piece about fly-fishing, and I began it with a memory of my night of having gone trouting with Patrick Hemingway. This precede, as well as this chapter, are a reworking and abridgment of those previously published pieces. But here's a story connected with the publication of "Papa's Boys" I've not told till now: About two weeks after I'd returned from Miami in late June 1987 and was trying to write a first draft for my editors, the phone rang. It was Gigi. He said he'd changed his mind and now didn't want me to "put anything in" about his cross-dressing, the more so since he planned to make a "comeback" in medicine. I was startled—only I wasn't. This kind of thing happens to journalists all the time, especially if they live and work in Washington, DC, where politicians try to backpedal after they've told you something for the record. I reminded Gigi he'd spoken to me willingly, and that for me to try to write around the fact of his cross-dressing, which was the central story of his life, would be a lie. Even though I knew I was within my rights, journalistic principles don't sound so grand on the telephone when you're talking to someone with both pleading and rage in his voice. He said I'd ruin his life if I wrote the stories. I reminded him that some of his arrests in Montana connected with his transvestism had already made local papers there. We argued. I said again he'd laid down no preconditions about his cross-dressing. He cursed and slammed down the phone. A little shaken, I went in and told my editors what had happened and that maybe we should include some of the phone call in the pieces themselves. No, that would be a bad idea, they said. That would raise more questions than it answered, would make me seem defensive. "Papa's Boys" came out. The same day, I nervously sent tear sheets and a cover note to all three sons. Patrick thanked me for sending them, but his letter then went into a strange tangent that had nothing to do with the pieces. Jack wrote and said he thought the series was well done, if in extremely poor taste. Gigi wrote and said my ambition "overcame" my sense of decency and that with "such malleable principles you should go far in journalism." He wrote twice on the same day, August 1, 1987, addressing me as "Dear Paul," using an ink pen, starting out in fairly smooth penmanship, the words getting larger and larger. "[A]nd your editor will probably credit you with a first, ie, a journalistic autopsy on a living human being," he ended. And yet I heard later from one of his children he'd changed his mind and thought the pieces were pretty fair to him, after all. Which only suggests to me once more his decent-hearted and forgiving nature—in spite of everything.

IN SPITE OF EVERYTHING

Precede. Re "Marty": I can recall all three sons, if Jack not so much, talking about their leggy stepmom with an almost unconscious and faintly sexual schoolboy longing.

Chapter. Epigraph quote is on p. 231 of *Farewell.* Re "I Guess Everything Reminds You of Something": the story first saw print in the 1987 *The Complete Short Stories of Ernest Hemingway.* The three sons signed their names to the foreword—so, again, praise to Gigi. A perceptive analysis of the story (even though his article contains several important errors of fact) is Robert C. Clark's "Papa y el Tirador: Biographical Parallels in Hemingway's 'I Guess Everything Reminds You of Something,'" *The Hemingway Review,* Fall 2007. Lou Mandler, named in the text, was particularly helpful re Canterbury School—her two-part "The Hemingways at Canterbury," published in the school magazine, *Pallium,* Fall 2008 and Winter 2009, and a later version, in *The Hemingway Review,* Spring 2010, is the definitive study.

"NECROTIC"

Precede. Again, a perceptive analysis is Charles J. Nolan Jr.'s "Hemingway's Complicated 'Enquiry' in 'Men Without Women,'" *Studies in Short Fiction,* Spring 1995. The three other EH stories with homosexuality and/or lesbianism as the central subject: "Mr. and Mrs. Eliot" (from *in our time*), and "The Mother of a Queen" and "The Sea Change" (both in *Winner Take Nothing*). Re the need to fling blame from him: in the October 2 letter to Scribner, he said of Pauline, "Her get, and her families get, do not do well after adolescence. But you don't know about that when you marry a woman."

Chapter. If much of it is the product of my own digging, I could hardly have proceeded without the help of Ruth Hawkins, named in the text. Hawkins— director of Arkansas Heritage Sites, which includes the Hemingway-Pfeiffer Museum and Educational Center in Piggott—has done more work on the Pfeiffer family than anyone I know. Re Dianetics and L. Ron Hubbard: Russell Miller's 1987 *Bare-Faced Messiah* was helpful. Re Pauline and Jinny Pfeiffer and Laura Archera Huxley: both Huxley's *This Timeless Moment: A Personal View of Aldous Huxley* and vol. 2 of Sybille Bedford's *Aldous Huxley: A Biography,* contained their nuggets.

Re what Hemingway said to his son in Havana: *you killed her.* In *Papa,* on p. 7, Gigi says the trip was after Lorian was born, and that he took both his new wife and new baby to introduce them to his father. But Lorian wasn't born until December 15, and Gigi and Jane were back in the States by mid-November— there's a Hemingway letter of late November documenting this. So once again he either misremembered or misled. But the spiritual truth is there.

WHAT HE HAD

Precede. "Downhill" quote is on p. 345 of *Islands,* and "make love to who" passage is on p. 344. "Both be alike" passage is on pp. 299–300 of *Farewell.* EH's "outside all tribal law" entry in Mary's diary is quoted on pp. 369–370 of her *How It Was.* "Felt the weight and strangeness inside" passage is on p. 17 of *Garden.*

Re that oft-quoted passage, and also re the word "tremulousness": Frederick Crews used the word in his 1987 *New York Review of Books* essay ("Pressure Under Grace"), and the word put another image in my head: tuning fork. In his brilliant, bloodless dissection (disguised as a book review), Professor Crews quotes a passage from Mary's memoir that has been much taken up by the latter-day EH psychologizers. It's a mock interview that Mary's husband created in 1953 for her apparent enjoyment, and it appears on pp. 368–69 of *How It Was.* I've heard this passage referred to as "the famous sodomy passage," as if it were the smoking gun of smoking guns. EH is supposedly clowning with an imaginary interviewer. "Reporter: 'Mr. Hemingway, is it true that your wife is a lesbian?' Papa: 'Of course not. Mrs. Hemingway is a boy.' Reporter: 'What are your favorite sports, sir?' Papa: 'Shooting, fishing, reading and sodomy.' Reporter: 'Does Mrs. Hemingway participate in these sports?' Papa: 'She participates in all of them.' " Concludes Crews: "The manually sodomized partner, we can infer, was Hemingway himself." Well, maybe. And maybe not. Re Grace Hemingway and the psychic damage she may have inflicted on her child (not least by dressing him as a girl and twinning him with Marcelline), Crews writes: "In all likelihood what Grace wanted, beyond an enactment of some private cross-gender scheme, was a boy whose sexual identity would remain forever dependent upon her dictates and whims. If so, she gruesomely got her wish. The apparent effect of all that dolling and doting was not so much to lend Ernest a female identity as to implant in his mind a permanently debilitating confusion, anxiety, and anger." Which only makes me think of Gigi.

Chapter. I suppose the chapter represents my nearly twenty-five years of trying to think about EH's tormented youngest son, since that night in Coconut Grove. I've tried to name in the text key people I interviewed, but here's one source I didn't name: C. E. "Abe" Abramson, a Missoula, Montana, real estate agent and voracious reader and all-around intellectual gadfly. He befriended Gigi early in Gigi's Missoula years and stayed in touch with him until the end. Abramson and I have been talking about Gigi in one way or another since the *Washington Post* pieces. As is evident, I'm indebted hugely, and not just for this chapter, to John Hemingway and to *Strange Tribe,* and am proud to regard him as a latter-day friend and fellow searcher of unsolvable riddles. John has reproduced in his too-little-recognized book, at nearly full length in some cases, previously little-known correspondence between Hemingway and Gigi. Just as evident here will be my debt to Valerie

Hemingway's *Running with the Bulls*. Valerie and I know each other casually. I have heard her read from her memoir at Hemingway gatherings—the first time was at a Michigan Hemingway Society conference several years ago. She was in her late sixties then and seemed wise and exuded much dignity and was in the company of her son, Edward, a writer of, among other things, children's tales. He was friendly, if wary.

My indebtedness will also be evident to Lorian Hemingway's beautifully titled and written *Walk on Water*. Lorian and I have communicated somewhat elliptically through the years. After the *Washington Post* pieces, she called to say I hadn't gotten her father wrong, even if I had gotten some facts about him wrong. Like all of Gigi's children, she remains skittish to talk to outsiders about her father, and who could blame her, or them? Gigi's former wife, Ida, has also never consented to talk to me, even though our mutual friend Abe Abramson tried several times to intercede.

Jeffrey Meyers's piece in the Spring 1999 *Virginia Quarterly Review* was valuable, and I should also cite his concise reflections on Gigi in his *Hemingway: Life into Art*. *Rolling Stone*'s piece on Gigi, by John Colapinto, was published on September 5, 1992. E. L. Doctorow's review of *Garden*, "Braver Than We Thought," in *The New York Times Book Review* cited above, gave not only a line of thinking and feeling, but, as is evident, inspired one of my chapter titles. (He's referring, however, only to EH, not to father and son.) A perceptive analysis of Gigi vis-à-vis *Islands* is Fred Ashe's " 'A Very Attractive Devil': Gregory Hemingway in *Islands in the Stream*," in *The Hemingway Review*, Fall 2008. Court documents and arrest narratives and jail records, in both Montana and Florida, became their own little novels of textured detail. I was astonished to be able to obtain so easily the full record of Gigi's death and autopsy from the Miami-Dade County Medical Examiner Department. I just went to the offices, and there the file was, stamped declassified. I was even allowed to make photocopies. In that file is a handwritten note from a department official to the effect that on October 9, 2001—nine days after her husband's death—Ida Hemingway called and "stated that she would like to keep the file of her husband confidential." She was told the procedures for getting the file sealed. This was done. But in early 2003 the file was unsealed, in connection with disputes and legal proceedings between Ida and several of Gigi's disinherited children, including John Hemingway. (A settlement re the will was eventually reached, with terms kept secret.)

Re dates of letters not obvious from the text: EH letter to Vera Scribner is February 18, 1952. Letter to Charles Scribner Jr. is February 25. Letters to his sons are February 22. Gigi's reply: February 26. EH's reply: March 2. EH's letter to Mary Welsh re child-rearing is September 28, 1945. Gigi's letter of apology to his father is May 3, 1954. EH's letter re getting smashed in the "aircraft nonsense" is September 7, 1954. EH's letter to his hospitalized son ("Do you have a good radio?") is August 24, 1957.

REENACTMENT

Precede. I used arrest reports filed by both the Key Biscayne and Miami-Dade police departments; also newspaper clippings after Gigi's death. Officer Nelia Real of KBPD declined to be interviewed, but her partner, Officer Ben Torres, spoke briefly to me, on the telephone.

Chapter. Again, I used jail reports and medical-examiner documents and arrest affidavits, as well as secondary sources. Inevitably, there are time conflicts and other contradictions in the documents. If it isn't possible to know the moment he died, 5:55 must be very close—within just minutes, apparently, of his mother's death, half a century before, if you factor in the time differences, here to there, Eastern Standard Time to Pacific Standard Time. What a mystery.

EPILOGUE: HUNGER OF MEMORY

The Cézanne quote was in exhibit materials at a 2010 exhibition, *Cézanne and American Modernism,* at the Baltimore Museum of Art. *Death in the Afternoon* quote is on p. 122. *Old Man* quote is on p. 31. *Feast* quote is on pp. 55–56. *Garden* quote is on p. 239. The account of Hemingway's death is from various sources, including my own Ketchum reporting, previous EH studies (bios and otherwise), and newspaper reports of the time. But I also crucially employed two pages of handwritten interview notes, and a typed document, from Baker, that I found at Princeton. Baker had interviewed Dr. Earle and Mary Hemingway as well as others, but in his bio made a more limited use of the materials. A valuable roundup of some of the contradictory things the press said at the time is John R. Bittner's "Dateline Sun Valley: The Press Coverage of the Death of Ernest Hemingway," collected in *Hemingway and the Natural World,* edited by Robert E. Fleming (see bibliography).

The words on the Hemingway memorial at Sun Valley are from a eulogy delivered by Hemingway after the death of his friend Gene Van Guilder, who died in a hunting accident (in October 1939). The eulogy was published in the *Idaho Statesman* on November 2, 1939. "You know you love the sea" quote is on pp. 239–40 of *Islands.* Letter to Patrick Hemingway is November 24, 1958. Letter to Faulkner is July 23, 1947. Michael Reynolds's quote is in his "A Brief Biography," previously cited. Turnbull's reminiscence is in the January 16, 1967, *New York Times Book Review.* The account of EH's kissing the Cuban flag, entered in his FBI file, was sent to Washington as a Foreign Service Despatch and titled "Ernest HEMINGWAY Gives Views on Cuban Situation." It's dated November 6, 1959, which was two days after he'd landed in Havana and kissed the flag. The log of EH's cross-country trip is at JFK. Letter to George Saviers re not being able to be on his boat is June 14, 1960. Story of trying to get the swollen manuscript down to some kind of palatable size is in Hotchner's *Papa Hemingway*. Re no record I can find that EH was ever on *Pilar* after May 19: four days before, at the annual Hemingway marlin-fishing tournament, Fidel and EH met for the first and only time. It sounds incredible, but *el commandate*, no deep-sea fisherman, won the two-day tournament without having rigged the outcome—or so the history books say, as well as my own research. From *How It Was:* "[H]e followed precisely the big-game fishing rules, hooking the fish and playing them, and his boatman made no attempt to gaff before he could grasp the leader, rather than the line. . . . [T]he combined weight of his fish earned him Ernest's silver trophy cup, which he presented that evening at the dock. On the way home in the car Ernest murmured, 'He said he'd read *The Bell* in Spanish and used its ideas in the Sierra Maestra.' " In several of the photographs of the two giants shaking hands, EH looks terrifyingly cracked. EH's letter to Mary from Madrid re "just going to lie quiet now and try to rest" is September 23, 1960.

Finally: a note on the picture captions. In some cases, I am certain, down to the day, down to nearly the minute, of the time and place an image was recorded. In other cases, I've been able to supply only approximate information. Hemingway, meticulous in so many ways in his record-keeping, was often curiously lax when it came to documenting photographs—and sometimes he was flat wrong. The audiovisual specialists at JFK were very helpful—and, like me, often exasperated in trying to fix a date and place.

CODA
ON THE CURIOUS AFTERLIFE OF *PILAR*

On September 17, 1955, at his Havana home, Ernest Hemingway set down in blue ink on a sheet of onionskin letterhead stationery a last will and testament, in which he left his entire estate and property to his wife and nothing to his children. "I have intentionally omitted to provide for my children . . . as I repose complete confidence in my beloved wife Mary to provide for them according to written instructions I have given her," he wrote. The instructions were said to be in a letter, dated the same day as the will. The letter is blacked out, so it is impossible to know what he said.

On August 25, 1961—roughly eight weeks after the suicide—a facsimile copy of the handwritten will appeared in *The New York Times*. The day before, Mary had submitted the document for probate. The day before that, she wrote a signed and dated statement of her own that contained several errors of fact and included this: "Following the instructions of a letter—which was accompanied by his will . . . I have given Ernest's yacht, the *Pilar* to Gregorio Fuentes." Through the years, Gregorio maintained to interviewers and friends that he had been bequeathed the boat.

I'm not so sure. As noted in the text, there exists a letter that Mary sent to Walter and Nita Houk, from New York, in February 1964, in which she said, "We're letting Pilar rot away in Cuba because I know Papa couldn't bear the thought of anyone else being her 'commander.'" It doesn't sound from that as if she'd made the boat Gregorio's legal property.

In *How It Was*, Mary's 1976 memoir, she describes how Gregorio had come to the *finca* shortly after the suicide to talk about what might happen to *Pilar* now that her master was gone. Mary writes that she told Gregorio to remove the rods and reels and outriggers and other paraphernalia and then "take her out and sink her in the current." Gratefully, that didn't happen. Mary concludes this section of her memoir: "As it turned out, the Cubans used *Pilar* as a workboat for a while, and then installed her (poor thing) as an exhibit on the Finca lawn, so I was told."

In 2005, when I saw *Pilar* in Cuba, an officer at the *finca* handed me a two-page document titled "Yate El Pilar" (The Yacht Pilar) in which there was this sentence: "Gregorio kept it in Cojimar until he decided to give it to the Revolutionary Government. It was moved from Cojimar to Finca Vigía, as the Museum's main exhibit." No dates are provided. The document, which is an overview history of the boat during and after Hemingway's ownership, is riddled with errors. But there the boat sits.

So much for ownership issues. But there is a stickier question: Is the boat sitting on Hemingway's old tennis court at the Museo Hemingway the *real* boat?

At least four times through the 1970s and 1980s the boat said to be *Pilar* was removed from the property and taken away to shipyards for repairs, hauled overland to Casablanca and Cárdenas and other places. The restorers would do their work, cosmetic or more substantive, and then she'd be brought back to the *finca* at the village of San Francisco de Paula on wide-load trucks. The comings and goings fueled rumors of a "fake" or "replica" boat. *Somebody has switched the boats.* It's what I heard said almost as soon as I had begun working on this book in earnest about seven years ago.

It's true that you can look at certain photographs of the displayed boat that were made, say, in the mid-seventies, and see that some things are off from the boat Hemingway had been master of. She looks too bulky and upright—or might this be because of the angle from which the shots were taken? The flying bridge is wrong—but could that just be a result of quick repair work? Other and more superficial things, including insignia and the lettering of her name, are also incorrect.

The rumors of a fake boat intensified among American Hemingway watchers in 1984, when the book publisher Lyle Stuart brought out an English edition of a Spanish work titled *Hemingway in Cuba* by a young Havana journalist named Norberto Fuentes. (The nonfiction book had been published that same year in Cuba.) Valuable in many respects, *Hemingway in Cuba* nonetheless contains numerous errors, some of which can probably be attributed to translation. In a section on *Pilar,* there is this: "In the famous Chullima shipyards on the city's waterfront, an exact replica of Hemingway's yacht was built. The work is of such precision and high quality that not even Gregorio Fuentes can tell which is the original. . . . Neither Gregorio nor anybody else can explain the reason for the new replica. The captain of the *Pilar* will often wistfully ask his friends at Cojimar, 'Why a double for my boat—why?' " Fuentes reportedly later said that he hadn't really meant "replica" and "double," that the passage got bollixed up in translation.

The boat at the *finca* clearly has only one screw—I verified this for myself. There's no question *Pilar* ran two engines and two screws in her day. Hemingway speaks of this in many letters. As was noted in the text, the purchase order specified a small "4-cylinder Lycoming straight drive engine" that was to be used for trolling purposes and that was "to be installed as a unit entirely independent of main power plant, and all controls and instruments are to be at steering position." In *With Hemingway,* Arnold Samuelson tells of taking a *Pilar* guest for a swim beneath the boat as she lay at anchor to see both propellers, the smaller of which was at "the side." In another passage, he describes *Pilar* bucking headlong into the waves, with both engines hooked up, "and sometimes she rolled so much we heard the side propeller thrump when it came out of the water." The Maestro doesn't mention whether the little one was located at port or starboard, only the thrumping.

An identification number for the hull can't nail the case because, as was noted in the text, *Pilar* was built from a stock Wheeler hull. At Wheeler and many other boat manufacturers of the thirties, especially at the stock production yards, a "builder's plate" made of bronze or copper, with the hull number listed on it, got affixed to the boat after a boat was built and was ready to be given to her owner. Often the plaque got attached in the cockpit by the steering controls. The hull number on the boat at the *finca* was and is 576. I have never been able to find a piece of Wheeler paper that verifies 576 as the manufacturer's hull number of Hemingway's boat. The number is not on the original purchase order or bill of sale or various boat registry papers from the Department of Commerce. And even if there were such a piece of paper, or even if Hemingway had referenced this number in a letter (why would he have done so?), what would it really prove? For who is to say that somebody in a back shed at a Havana shipyard didn't make a lookalike builder's plate with that number on it and affix it to the boat? That's the problem: the hull number wasn't built into the hull itself, but rather attached— and thus detachable.

And yet: there seems no question that the boat on display at the *finca* is built from an authentic Wheeler hull. Some years ago a Wheeler family member went to Cuba and verified this. But is it possible that what is there is some *other* Wheeler from the thirties, some "cousin," not the actual one Hemingway owned? You can make the argument go on and on.

It's a fact that *Pilar* had two main-motor replacements in her seagoing life. The flying bridge was added. Her outriggers got built and rebuilt. She underwent wartime alterations—the head in the main cabin got preempted for radio gear, for instance. Hemingway's boat is a metaphor for endurance, but changes were always being made to her in her owner's lifetime.

Regarding the issue of lookalike boats: Until a few years ago, there was a thirty-eight-foot Wheeler Playmate, built in the mid-thirties, looking very much like *Pilar,* anchored outside the International Game Fish Association museum near Fort Lauderdale. "Pilar's Sistership" announced the plaque beside it, with three errors of fact in its seven lines of type.

At Islamorada, in the Florida Keys, as you head toward Key West, there is a giant fishing outfitter store called World Wide Sportsman, and sitting inside on the main floor is a vintage sportfishing boat with the name *Pilar* lettered on it. "PILAR—the half-sister ship to Hemingway's famed 'Pilar,'" a handout sheet proclaims. It goes on to say that this *Pilar* was built at a different Brooklyn shipyard a year before Hemingway's *Pilar.* Only in superficial ways do the two look alike.

Several months ago, as I was writing this, I went to Mystic Seaport in Connecticut, and spent most of a day with Dana Hewson, arguably the foremost wooden boat expert in America, who, as I've noted in the preceding Essay on Sources, is vice president for watercraft preservation and programs at Mystic. He is also a member of what was formerly known as the Hemingway Preservation Foundation Advisory Board and is now the Finca Vigía Foundation. As noted, the foundation is a private group, based in Boston, seeking financial ways to preserve, in cooperation with the Cuban government, Hemingway's home and property. The day I spent with Dana brought me all the way over in believing that the boat on Hemingway's hill is the real *Pilar*. Actually, I had believed it for a good while.

In November 2002, Dana had traveled to Cuba as part of the American delegation that participated in a formal signing of a document (Fidel himself was at the signing table) to begin the process of preserving Hemingway's home and property. The day after the signing, Dana examined the boat closely. He was allowed to get on board, comb her cabins, open her hatches, make sketches and measurements. After he returned home, he wrote up a brief condition assessment, with recommendations for *Pilar*'s repair. Dana was sure the Cuban government would never allow the boat on Hemingway's hill to leave Cuba, and he was right.

Several years went by. The Finca Vigía Foundation did what it could to raise money. It wasn't that Dana's urgent recommendations for *Pilar* were being ignored—just that the bureaucratic wheels turn very slowly in a socialist country that often doesn't have the money to provide basic needs for its people and that furthermore is in a suspicious standoff with what it regards as imperialist America. Both the Cubans and the American group were working hard to come up with a feasible plan for restoration. Meanwhile, in June 2005 Finca Vigía was named to the National Trust for Historic Preservation's list of America's 11 Most Endangered Historic Places (even though Hemingway's home wasn't *in* America). The next year, the *finca* was listed on the World Monuments Watch of the 100 Most Endangered Sites on the globe.

That same year, 2006, in April, Dana went again to Cuba with members of the Finca Vigía Foundation. He again studied the boat on the hill, to see what temporary changes might have occurred, and while there he and others from the foundation got the news that the Cuban government would provide the funds for a complete restoration. The work would be done by preservation experts at Marina Hemingway in Havana.

And it has been done, and well. *Pilar* is now shiny as a new penny. Dana is pleased.

Through the years, Dana has heard talk of the "bogus boat." One of the first things he told me in our day together is that when he opened the hatches on that first visit in 2002 and looked inside, he saw two engines. "No question," he said. The main engine and its shaft came down the center; the secondary engine was at the port. "There was no second shaft installation, but there were two engines; I take that as just something that happened during one of the temporary restorations through the years. It would have been cheaper. They got rid of the second screw to save money. They would have done other things like that in the various inadequate restorations."

We spread out a couple dozen photographs of the boat that had been taken through the years. He said, "I just don't see any way to prove that the boat there now isn't Hemingway's boat, given the amount of changes and restoration work this boat has undergone. Let me put that another way. Everything that seems 'wrong' about this boat—and by that I mean everything that's not necessarily true to the Wheeler tradition or the look of the boat that Hemingway bought in 1934, or the boat that he made adjustments to through the years—can be explained by whatever restoration processes she has undergone."

He said, "When does a boat begin to deteriorate? When they chop the tree down. George Washington's ax—the head has been changed twice. The handle has been changed twice. Is it still George Washington's ax? What's the answer to that? I don't think there is one. You are always working on a boat, fixing her, making repairs, doing changes."

He said, "Did the Cuban government take her into a back shed sometime back there and in the process of starting to repair her say, 'Oh, it's too damn hard, we'll just build a replica and pass her off as the real boat?' Yes, governments lie. Ours does. Theirs maybe more. Ernest Hemingway means an awful lot to the Cuban people, and so does his boat. His boat means an awful lot to American literature. But does any of that translate to the fact that somebody in Cuba pulled a fast one? From everything I've studied, I believe she's the real boat. Or at least I say it cannot be proven she isn't the real boat. That's where I stand."

Me, too. To tell the truth, I am sort of secretly glad we can't know for certain; that she resists knowing, as her captain himself finally resists knowing. Which makes *Pilar* a better metaphor and storytelling vehicle than I ever bargained for.

—P.H., January 2011

SELECTED BIBLIOGRAPHY

Along with this list, interested readers are invited to consult the Essay on Sources, for not everything cited there is included here, and vice versa. Also, I've omitted in this list bibliographic information on Hemingway's own works, based on the idea that those works are easily accessible on their own, although in the source essay I've listed the dates and titles and places of publication for the Hemingway journalism that comes up in the text itself.

Algren, Nelson. *Notes from a Sea Diary: Hemingway All the Way.* New York: G. P. Putnam's Sons, 1965.

Arnold, Lloyd. *Hemingway: High on the Wild.* New York: Grosset & Dunlap, 1968.

Ashe, Fred. "A Very Attractive Devil: Gregory Hemingway in *Islands in the Stream.*" *Hemingway Review* 28, no. 1 (Fall 2008).

Baker, Carlos. *Ernest Hemingway: A Life Story.* New York: Charles Scribner's Sons, 1969.

———. *Ernest Hemingway: The Writer as Artist.* Princeton, NJ: Princeton University Press, 1972.

———, ed. *Ernest Hemingway: Selected Letters, 1917–1961.* New York: Charles Scribner's Sons, 1981.

Bedford, Sybille. *Aldous Huxley: A Biography,* vol. 2, *1936–1963.* London: Chatto & Windus, 1974.

Beegel, Susan F., ed. *Hemingway's Neglected Short Fiction: New Perspectives.* Ann Arbor, MI: UMI Research Press, 1989.

Benson, Jackson J., ed. *New Critical Approaches to the Short Stories of Ernest Hemingway.* Durham, NC: Duke University Press, 1990.

Bethel, Rodman J. *Flagler's Folly: The Railroad That Went to Sea and Was Blown Away.* Key West, FL: Slumbering Giant Publications, 1987.

Bigelow, Gordon E. *Frontier Eden: The Literary Career of Marjorie Kinnan Rawlings.* Gainesville: University Press of Florida, 1966.

Brasch, James D., and Joseph Sigman. *Hemingway's Library.* New York: Garland Publishing, 1981.

Brian, Denis. *The True Gen.* New York: Grove Press, 1988.

Broer, Lawrence R., and Gloria Holland, eds. *Hemingway and Women: Female Critics and the Female Voice.* Tuscaloosa: University of Alabama Press, 2002.

Bruccoli, Matthew J. *Classes on Ernest Hemingway.* Columbia: Thomas Cooper Library, University of South Carolina, 2002.

———. *Fitzgerald and Hemingway: A Dangerous Friendship.* New York: Carroll & Graff, 1994.

———. *Scott and Ernest: The Authority of Failure and the Authority of Success.* New York: Random House, 1978.

Burgess, Anthony. *Ernest Hemingway and His World.* New York: Charles Scribner's Sons, 1978.

Burrell, Rose Marie. *Hemingway: The Postwar Years and the Posthumous Novels.* New York: Cambridge University Press, 1996.

Busch, Frederick. "Reading Hemingway Without Guilt." *New York Times Book Review,* January 12, 1992.

Buske, Morris. "Hemingway Faces God." *Hemingway Review* 22, no. 1 (Fall 2002).

Clark, Robert C. "Papa y el Tirador: Biographical Parallels in Hemingway's 'I Guess Everything Reminds You of Something." *Hemingway Review* 27, no. 1 (Fall 2007).

Colapinto, John. "The Good Son." *Rolling Stone,* September 5, 2002.

Comley, Nancy R., and Robert Scholes. *Hemingway's Genders: Rereading the Hemingway Text.* New Haven, CT: Yale University Press, 1994.

Connett, Eugene V., ed. *American Big-Game Fishing.* Lanham, MD: Derrydale Press, 1935.

Cowley, Malcolm. "Hemingway's Wound—And Its Consequences for American Literature." *Georgia Review,* Summer 1984.

———. "A Portrait of Mr. Papa." *Life,* January 10, 1949.

———. *A Second Flowering: Works and Days of the Lost Generation.* New York: Viking Press, 1973.

Crews, Frederick C. "Pressure Under Grace." *New York Review of Books,* August 13, 1987.

Curnutt, Kirk. *Coffee with Hemingway.* London: Duncan Baird Publishers, 2007.

Curnutt, Kirk, and Gail D. Sinclair, eds. *Key West Hemingway: A Reassessment.* Gainesville: University Press of Florida, 2009.

Dancey, Thomas B. "Chicago to Mackinac: Story of the Northern Michigan Transportation Company." *Michigan History Magazine* 30, no. 3 (July–September 1946).

Didion, Joan. "Last Words." *New Yorker,* November 9, 1998.

Doctorow, E. L. "Braver Than We Thought." *New York Times Book Review,* May 18, 1986.

Donaldson, Scott. *By Force of Will: The Life and Art of Ernest Hemingway.* New York: Penguin Books, 1977.

———, ed. *The Cambridge Companion to Hemingway.* New York: Cambridge University Press, 1996.

Donaldson, Scott, in collaboration with R. H. Winnick. *Archibald MacLeish: An American Life.* Boston: Houghton Mifflin, 1992.

Donnelly, Honoria Murphy, with Richard N. Billings. *Sara & Gerald: Villa America and After.* New York: Times Books, 1982.

Dos Passos, John. *The Best Times: An Informal Memoir.* New York: New American Library, 1966.

Eby, Carl P. *Hemingway's Fetishism: Psychoanalysis and the Mirror of Manhood.* Albany: State University of New York Press, 1999.

Erb, Mary Whitfield, Cynthia Beadell Hermann, and Charles E. Schloff. *Walloon Yesterdays: A Glimpse of the Past Through Photographs and Memories.* Petoskey, MI: Mitchell Graphics, 2003.

Farrington, S. Kip, Jr. *Atlantic Game Fishing.* New York: Kennedy Brothers, 1937.

———. *Fishing with Hemingway and Glassell.* New York: D. McKay, 1971.

———. *Sport Fishing Boat.* New York: W. W. Norton, 1949.

Federspiel, Michael. *Picturing Hemingway's Michigan.* Detroit: Wayne State University Press, 2010.

———. "Up North with the Hemingways." *Michigan History* 91, no. 5 (September–October 2007).

Fenton, Charles A. *The Apprenticeship of Ernest Hemingway: The Early Years.* New York: Farrar, Straus & Young, 1954.

Finney, Ben. *Feet First.* New York: Crown, 1971.

Fleming, Robert E., ed. *Hemingway and the Natural World.* Moscow: University of Idaho Press, 1999.

Fuentes, Norberto. *Hemingway in Cuba.* Secaucus, NJ: Lyle Stuart, 1984.

Gellhorn, Martha. *Travels with Myself and Another.* New York: Dodd, Mead, 1978.

Gingrich, Arnold. *Nothing but People: The Early Days at Esquire; A Personal History, 1928–1958.* New York: Crown Publishers, 1971.

———. *The Well-Tempered Angler.* New York: Alfred A. Knopf, 1965.

Griffin, Peter. *Along with Youth: Hemingway, the Early Years.* New York: Oxford University Press, 1985.

Heilner, Van Campen. *Salt Water Fishing.* New York: Alfred A. Knopf, 1946.

Hemingway, Gregory H. *Papa: A Personal Memoir.* Boston: Houghton Mifflin, 1976.

Hemingway, Jack. *Misadventures of a Fly Fisherman: My Life with and Without Papa.* Dallas: Taylor Publishing, 1986.

Hemingway, John. *Strange Tribe.* Guilford, CT: Lyons Press, 2007.

Hemingway, Leicester. *My Brother, Ernest Hemingway, Memorial Edition.* Sarasota, FL: Pineapple Press, 1996.

Hemingway, Lorian. *Walk on Water: A Memoir.* New York: Simon & Schuster, 1998.

Hemingway, Mary Welsh. *How It Was.* New York: Alfred A. Knopf, 1976.

Hemingway, Valerie. *Running with the Bulls: My Years with the Hemingways.* New York: Ballantine Books, 2004.

Hotchner, A. E. *Papa Hemingway.* New York: Random House, 1966.

Jobst, Jack. "Gone Fishin'." *Michigan History* 79 (November–December 1995).

Johnson, Donald S. "Hemingway: A Trout Fisher's Apprenticeship." *American Fly Fisher* 15, no. 1 (Summer 1989).

———. "Hemingway's Fishing Apprenticeship." *Outdoor America*, Summer 1987.

Kaplan, Moise N. *Big Game Anglers' Paradise.* New York: Liveright Publishing, 1937.

Kazin, Alfred. *An American Procession.* New York: Alfred A. Knopf, 1984.

———. *On Native Grounds.* New York: Harcourt Brace Jovanovich, 1982.

Kemp, Tom. "The Fishing Life of Ernest Hemingway." *Fisherman*, January 1958.

Kennedy, J. Gerald. *Imagining Paris: Exile, Writing and American Identity.* New Haven, CT: Yale University Press, 1993.

Kert, Bernice. *The Hemingway Women.* New York: W. W. Norton, 1983.

Langley, Joan, and Wright Langley. *Key West: Images of the Past.* Key West, FL: C. C. Belland and E. O. Swift, 1982.

Langley, Wright, and Stan Windhorn. *Yesterday's Key West.* Miami: Seeman Publishing, 1973.

Lea, Lawrence H. *Prowling Papa's Waters.* Marietta, GA: Longstreet Press, 1992.

Lynn, Kenneth S. *Hemingway.* New York: Simon & Schuster, 1987.

Macrate, Arthur. *History of the Tuna Club.* Avalon, CA: 1948.

Mailer, Norman. *Cannibals and Christians.* New York: Dial Press, 1966.

Mandler, Lou. "The Hemingways at Canterbury." *Pallium* 25, nos. 1 and 2 (Fall 2008 and Winter 2009).

Marek, Ken. *Hemingway's Michigan: A Driving Tour of Emmett and Charlevoix Counties.* Mount Pleasant, MI: Clarke Historical Library, 2007.

Matthews, Bruce, and Ed Pritchard. *Fin-Noir: The Legacy Years.* Tulsa, OK: W. C. Bradley/ZEBCO, 2007.

McIver, Stuart B. *Hemingway's Key West.* Sarasota, FL: Pineapple Press, 2002.

McLendon, James. *Papa Hemingway in Key West.* Key West, FL: Langley Press, 1990.

Mellow, James R. *Hemingway: A Life Without Consequences.* Boston: Houghton Mifflin, 1992.

Meyers, Jeffrey. *Hemingway: A Biography.* New York: Harper & Row, 1985.

———. "The Hemingways: An American Tragedy." *Virginia Quarterly Review*, Spring 1999.

Miller, Linda Patterson, ed. *Letters from the Lost Generation: Gerald and Sara Murphy and Friends.* Gainesville: University Press of Florida, 2002

———. "The Matrix of Hemingway's *Pilar* Log." *North Dakota Quarterly* 64, no. 3 (1997).

Miller, Madelaine Hemingway. *Ernie.* New York: Crown Publishers, 1975.

Miller, Russell. *Bare-Faced Messiah: The True Story of L. Ron Hubbard.* London: Michael Joseph, 1987.

Mizener, Arthur. *The Far Side of Paradise: A Biography of F. Scott Fitzgerald*. Boston: Houghton Mifflin, 1951.

Montgomery, Constance Cappel. *Hemingway in Michigan*. New York: Fleet Publishing, 1966.

Morrow, Lance. "A Quarter-Century Later, the Myth Endures." *Time*, August 25, 1986.

Nagel, James, ed. *Ernest Hemingway: The Oak Park Legacy*. Tuscaloosa: University of Alabama Press, 1996.

Nagel, Jan. "They Remember Hemingway." *Inside*, July 2, 1975.

Ohle, William H. *How It Was in Horton Bay*. Horton Bay, MI: n.p., 1999.

Oliver, Charles M. *Ernest Hemingway, A to Z*. New York: Checkmark Books, 1999.

Ott, Mark P. *A Sea of Change: Ernest Hemingway and the Gulf Stream: A Contextual Biography*. Kent, OH: Kent State University Press, 2008.

Price, Reynolds. *A Common Room: Essays, 1954–1987*. New York: Atheneum, 1987.

Reiger, George. *Profiles in Salt Water Angling: A History of the Sport—Its People and Places, Tackle and Techniques*. Englewood Cliffs, NJ: Prentice-Hall, 1973.

Reynolds, Michael. *Hemingway: The Final Years*. New York: W. W. Norton, 1999.

———. *Hemingway: The Homecoming*. Cambridge, MA: Blackwell, 1992.

———. *Hemingway: The 1930s*. New York: W. W. Norton, 1997.

———. *Hemingway: The Paris Years*. Oxford: Blackwell, 1989.

———. *The Young Hemingway*. Oxford: Blackwell, 1987.

Ross, Lillian. "How Do You Like It Now, Gentlemen?" *New Yorker*, May 13, 1950.

Rovere, Richard R. "End of the Line." *New Yorker*, December 15, 1951.

Ruhlman, Michael. *Wooden Boats: In Pursuit of the Perfect Craft at an American Boatyard*. New York: Viking Penguin, 2001.

Samuelson, Arnold. *With Hemingway: A Year in Key West and Cuba*. New York: Random House, 1984.

Sanford, Marcelline Hemingway. *At the Hemingways: With Fifty Years of Correspondence Between Ernest and Marcelline Hemingway*. Moscow: University of Idaho Press, 1999.

Saunders, Ashley B. *History of Bimini*, vols. 1 and 2. Alice Town, Bimini, Bahamas: New World Press, 2000.

Scafella, Frank, ed. *Hemingway: Essays of Reassessment*. New York: Oxford University Press, 1991.

Spanier, Sandra, and Robert W. Trogdon, eds. *The Letters of Ernest Hemingway: Volume 1, 1907–1922 (The Cambridge Edition of the Letters of Ernest Hemingway)*. New York: Cambridge University Press, 2011.

Spilka, Mark. *Hemingway's Quarrel with Androgyny*. Lincoln: University of Nebraska Press, 1990.

Svoboda, Frederic. *Hemingway in Michigan, Michigan in Hemingway*. Mount Pleasant, MI: Clarke Historical Library, 2003.

———. *Up North with the Hemingways and Nick Adams.* Mount Pleasant, MI: Clark Historical Library, 2007.

Svoboda, Frederic, and Joseph J. Waldmeir, eds. *Hemingway: Up in Michigan Perspectives.* East Lansing: Michigan State University Press, 1995.

Trogdon, Robert W. *Ernest Hemingway: A Literary Reference.* New York: Carroll & Graff, 2002.

Turnbull, Andrew. "Perkins's Three Generals," *New York Times Book Review,* January 16, 1967.

———. *Scott Fitzgerald.* New York: Charles Scribner's Sons, 1962.

Wagner-Martin, Linda, ed. *Ernest Hemingway: Seven Decades of Criticism.* East Lansing: Michigan State University Press, 1988.

———, ed. *A Historical Guide to Ernest Hemingway.* New York: Oxford University Press, 2000.

Watson, William Braasch. "Hemingway in Bimini." *North Dakota Quarterly* 63, no. 3 (1966).

Wilson, Edmund. "Letter to the Russians About Hemingway." *New Republic,* December 11, 1935.

———. *The Wound and the Bow: Seven Studies in Literature.* Boston: Houghton Mifflin, 1941.

Young, Philip. *Ernest Hemingway.* New York: Rinehart, 1952.

———. *Ernest Hemingway: A Reconsideration.* University Park: Pennsylvania State University Press, 1966.

INDEX

Page numbers in *italics* refer to illustrations.

Abercrombie & Fitch, 327, 371, 487
Academy of Natural Sciences, 84–7,
    149, 173–5, 480–1
Across the River and into the Trees
    (Hemingway), 30, 216, 316, 317*n*,
    320–1, 325, 332–6, 339, 343, 353, 358,
    359, 370, 494, 495
"Across the Street and into the Grill"
    (White), 335–6
Adams, Richard "Saca Ham," 212
Addison, Edna, 348–9
Africa, 29, 30, 35–6, 95, 153, 154, 160, 161,
    179, 188, 223, 417, 425–6, 427–8
African Hunter (Blixen), 226
"After the Storm" (Hemingway), 35
Algonquin Hotel, 211
Algren, Nelson, 17, 474
Ambos Mundos Hotel, 75, 92–3, 167,
    173–4, 180, 181
American Broadcasting Company,
    67–8
American Fly Fisher, 285
American Museum of Fly Fishing,
    285
American Museum of Natural
    History, 231–2, 323
American Society of Ichthyologists
    and Herpetologists, 175
Anderson, Dr., 428
Anderson, Sherwood, 210, 232
Anita, 150, 157
Aphrodite, 49

Armstrong, Dick, 181
Arnold, Lloyd, 461
Arnold, Tillie, 461
"Article" (Samuelson), 119
"Art of the Short Story, The"
    (Hemingway), 82–3, 480
Associated Press, 229, 445
Astor, John Jacob, IV, 50
Astor, Vincent, 50, 478
Atlantic, 35, 213
At the Hemingways: A Family Portrait
    (Sanford), 277
Autobiography of Alice B. Toklas, The
    (Stein), 35

Bahamas, 152–3, 202
Baker, Carlos, 70, 77, 158, 190, 225,
    228, 274*n*, 285, 360, 370, 371, 471,
    472, 473–4, 477, 480, 481–2, 492,
    500
Baker, Thelma, 436, 440, 448
Baldwin, James, 104
Batista, Fulgencio, 309, 422
Beach, Sylvia, 43, 50
Behan, Brendan, 437*n*
Best Times, The (Dos Passos), 208
Beyond the Street (Calmer), 44
Biber, Stanley, 440
"Big Fat Slob," 235–6
"Big Two-Hearted River"
    (Hemingway), 33–4, 267, 284, 286,
    288, 392

Bimini, *59,* 82, 96, 98, 138, 150, 170, 176, 182, 194–9, 201–3, *201,* 204, 205, 209, 212, 213, 220, *220,* 221, 225, 226–7, 230, 231, 232, 233, 234–8, 243, 245, 250–1, 257, 272, 279, 322, 386, 429–31, 434, 442, 471
Bimini News, 194, 198
Bird, Josephine, 127
Bird, Ulmer, 127, 129
Bird, William, 221
Bishop, Elizabeth, 403
Blixen, Bror, 220, *220,* 222–3, 224–6
Blixen, Eva, *220,* 224–5, 226, 250
Blixen, Karen (Isak Dinesen), 224, 295, 492
blood memory, 455
Bollo (cook), 187
Bonita Pescada, 276
Boss shotgun, 18–19
Bozo (horse), 122–3
Braque, Georges, 346
Brasch, James D., 488
Brave New World (Huxley), 408
Breit, Harvey, 333
Brian, Denis, 226, 228
Bridge of San Luis Rey, The (Wilder), 57
"Brief for the Defense, A" (Gilbert), 295
Brontë, Charlotte, 349
Brontë, Emily, 349
Brooklyn Daily Eagle, 43, 66, 67
Brothers Karamozov, The (Dostoyevsky), 118
Brown, Harcourt, 198
Brown, Ossie, 198
Bruccoli, Matthew, 76, 179, 474, 480, 486
Bruce, Benjamin, 190
Bruce, Toby, 191–2, 246, 293, 486
bullfights, 9, 32, 459–60

Bumby (dinghy), 188
Burns, Joan, 125
Burwell, Rose Marie, 487
Buske, Morris, 291

Cadwalader, Charles, 84–5, 86, 173–5, 178, 182, 183, 187
Caen, Herb, 441
Calmer, Alden, 44
Calmer, Edgar "Ned," 43–5, 190, 477
Calmer, Priscilla, 44, 45
Calmer, Regan, 45
Canby, H. S., 35
Cantwell, Robert, 333
Cash, Bobby, 228–9
Castro, Fidel, 91, 92, 458, 461, 506
Catalog of World Fishes, A (Fowler), 175
CBS Radio News, 44–5
Center for Wooden Boats, The, 21
Cézanne, Paul, 454, 495, 500
Chamberlain, John, 253–4
Chamberlin, Brewster, 333*n*
Chaplin, Charlie, 210
Charles Scribner's Sons, 32, 40, 51, 53, 76, 83, 248, 310, 316, 367, 472
Chekhov, Anton, 398
Chicago Tribune, 43, 265
Chris-Craft, 61, 62, 479
Christin, Chandra, 451
City of Los Angeles, 350
Civilian Conservation Corps (CCC), 251
Civil War, 120
Clarahan, Lewis, 285
Clark, Wallace, 438
"Clean, Well-Lighted Place, A" (Hemingway), 35
Club de Cazadores del Cerro, 394–5, 397, 405
cockfighting, 354–5
Cojo (mechanic), 167, 178, 181

Colapinto, John, 499
Collier's, 236, 237, 395
Cook, Charlie, 489
Cooper, Gary, 495
Cosmopolitan, 97, 107, 326
Cowley, Malcolm, 86, 158, 259
Crane, Stephen, 112
Crews, Frederick C., 418, 474, 498
Cuba, 6–7, 12–13, 85, 91–3, 105, 125, 157,
     166–92, 340, 352–3, 369, 370, 376–7,
     393–4, *405,* 414, 458–9, 461, 500
"Cuba Revisited" (Gellhorn), 340–1
Culbertson, Ernie, 275

Darby, Dian Samuelson, 102, 121, 122,
     123, 125, 127, 128, 130–2, 168, 483
Davis, Joan, 124–5
Death in the Afternoon (Hemingway),
     31, 35, 75, 104, 109–10, 169, 257, 258,
     348, 353, 454, 483, 500
Deux Magots, Les, 337
Dianetics, 406–7
Díaz, Rodrigo, 392
Dickinson, Emily, 103, 446
Dietrich, Marlene, 26–7, 327, 476
DiMaggio, Joe, 317, 494
Dinesen, Isak, 224, 295, 492
Dixon, Eva, *see* Blixen, Eva
Doctorow, E. L., 179, 474, 486, 499
Dominguín, Luis, 459
Donahue, Woolworth, 236
Donnelly, Honoria Murphy, 241
Dos Passos, John, 52, 57, 88, 96, 105, 151,
     156, 158, 206, 208, 213, 222, 225, 241,
     255, 256, 281, 346*n*, 388, 475, 489
Dos Passos, Katy, 88, 96, 105, 208, 213,
     222, 228, 281, 489
Dostoyevsky, Fyodor, 349
Dreiser, Theodore, 52, 97
Dudek, Al, 98
"Dumb Ox, The" (Lewis), 43

Earle, Scott, 456, 500
Eastman, Max, 31, 35, 39
Eby, Carl, 495
Echevarria, Rosa, 451
Economides, Peter, 312
Edmonston, Dick, 449
Eliot, T. S., 329, 349
"End of Something, The"
     (Hemingway), 281
Ernest Hemingway: A Life Story
     (Baker), 70, 225, 471
Ernie (Madelaine Hemingway Miller),
     492
Esquire, 72, 150, 220, 261, 265, 459, 484,
     485, 488, 496
  Ambos Mundos described in, 92
  EH advanced money by, 12, 53, 72,
     83, 95, 97
  EH's letters to, 148–9, 153–4, 292, 489
  EH's piece on fishing in, 8–9
  EH's proposed safari piece for, 50–1
  Hemingway's payment agreement
     with, 52
  "He Who Gets Slap Happy" in, 234,
     235
  inaugural issue of, 151
  "Monologue to the Maestro" in, 105,
     106, 113
  "Notes on Dangerous Game" in,
     223, 226
  "On Being Shot Again" in, 203–4,
     205, 207, 209, 211
  "On the Blue Water" in, 322, 474
  "One Too Many" in, 121
  "Out in the Stream" in, 151, 152, 474
  "A Paris Letter" published in, 35–6
  "The President Vanquishes" in,
     227–8, 231*n*
  Samuelson's piece in, 119
  "The Snows of Kilimanjaro" in, 80,
     120, 481

Estrellas de Gigi, 394, 440
Eubanks, Lois, 122
Evening Journal, 25

Fadiman, Clifton, 39–40, 476–7, 478
Fame, 392n
Farewell to Arms, A (Hemingway), 34,
    38, 57, 112, 113, 144, 211, 256–7, 258,
    288, 350, 362–3, 389, 416, 476, 484,
    498
Farrington, S. Kip, 230, 231, 489
"Fathers and Sons" (Hemingway), 35,
    272, 279, 281, 288, 290, 292
Faulkner, William, 459
FBI, 268, 324–5, 461, 464, 500
Federal Emergency Relief
    Administration (FERA), 154
Felipe (*Tin Kid* pilot), 358, 419
Fenton, Charles, 274n
Ferme, La (Miró), 346, 347, 355
Feurer, Anne E. J., 198–9
Fifth Column, The (Hemingway), 257
First International Hemingway
    Colloquium, 440
fishing, 8–9, 10–11, 13, 38, 51, 85, 98, 105,
    221, 264, 292–3, 378, 429
  by EH as a child, 277–85, 286, 490
  EH's lessons to children on, 7, 14–15
  in EH's writing, 162–5, 278–9, 282
  history of, 229–31
  see also Pilar, fishing on
Fitzgerald, F. Scott, 32, 52, 75–7, 80,
    123, 156, 241, 244, 256, 310, 318, 460,
    480, 483
  EH's destroyed friendship with,
    159–61
Fitzgerald, John, 433, 435
Fitzgerald, Zelda, 76, 156, 241, 310, 410
Flagler, Henry, 86–7
Flanner, Janet, 258, 489
Flaubert, Gustave, 112

Florida Keys, 14
Ford, Ford Maddox, 274
Forsythe, Robert, 189–90
"For the Road" (Mary Hemingway),
    336
Fortune, 156
For Whom the Bell Tolls (Hemingway),
    135, 199, 229, 257, 317, 318, 349, 351,
    483, 488
Fowler, Bonnie, 176
Fowler, Henry, 84–5, 173, 175–7, 180,
    182, 187
Franco, Francisco, 120
Franklin, Benjamin, 185
Franklin, Sydney, 75, 180, 182
From Here to Eternity (Jones), 361–2
Frost, Robert, 471
Fuentes, Gregorio, 321, 322–3, 324, 325,
    328, 339, 340–1, 357, 365, 371, 397,
    457, 494, 503, 504
Fuentes, Norberto, 504

Gannett, Lewis, 253
Garden of Eden, The (Hemingway),
    364, 390, 417, 418, 419, 455–6, 459,
    498, 499
Gar Wood firm, 61
General Metzinger, SS, 38, 39
Gilbert, Jack, 295, 493
Gingrich, Arnold, 35, 50–2, 53, 74, 149,
    155, 156, 161, 189, 204, 209, 227–8,
    235, 237, 247, 249, 250, 251, 471
  EH advanced money by, 53, 72, 83,
    95, 97
  EH's copy not tampered with by, 97
  on EH's suicide, 123, 477
  novel attempted by, 184
Gluck, Bea, 325–6
Goddard, Paulette, 210
"God's Grandeur" (Hopkins), 316
Granta, 340, 494

Great Depression, 48, 49, 60, 61, 62, 63, 76, 87, 107, 158, 222, 482

Great Gatsby, The (Fitzgerald), 32, 76

Greco-Turkish war, 86

Green Hills of Africa (Hemingway), 41–3, 46, 93, 157, 158, 211, 223, 248, 252, 253–5, 257–8, 476, 477, 483, 486
  EH's jealousy in, 41–2
  manuscript of, 484
  stream sentence in, 135, 185–6
  writing of, 41, 151–2, 160–1, 177–8, 179, 185–7, 188–9, 387, 452

Grey, Zane, 230

Gris, Juan, 190, 346

Gulf Stream, 8, 9, 12, 46, 140, 142, 144, 185–6, 197, 202, 211, 229, 243, 244, 248, 322, 323, 376, 456

Gutiérrez, Carlos, 148, 151, 166, 167, 171, 172, 173, 179, 181, 182, 183, 186–7, 212–13, 247, 251, 321–2, 484

Hall, Janelle, 446–7

Hall-Hemingway, Grace, 23, 65, 197, 235, 263, 270, 276, 290, 475, 476, 498
  death of, 376
  EH's childhood writing and, 268–9
  EH sent father's suicide pistol by, 23
  farm purchased by, 281
  husband's suicide and, 196
  intelligence of, 85

Hammett, Dashiell, 210

Happy Pete's, 312

Harcourt, Brace, 44

Havana, 6–7, 12–13, 91–3, 105, 135, *405*

"Havana and Hemingway: A Mid-Century Memoir" (Houk), 371

Havana Electric, 149

Havana Post, 169–70, 173, 180, 485

Havana Special, 87, 88

Hawkins, Ruth, 409, 497

Hawkshaw, 98

Hay, John, 81

Heilner, Van Campen, 230

Hellman, Lillian, 210

Hemingway, Alice, 429

Hemingway, Clarence E. (Ed), 235, 264, 267, 269, 270, 271*n*, 273, 279, 452
  as abusive, 290–1
  as boat pilot, 276
  debts of, 422
  EH taught shooting by, 263
  funeral of, 276–7, 292
  scientific passion of, 85
  suicide of, 23, 34, 57, 194, 195–6, 277, 387

Hemingway, Edward, 437*n*, 440

Hemingway, Ernest, *104, 166, 201, 316, 405*
  affairs and attempted seductions of, 51, 225, 226, 242, 257, 365–6, 489
  on Baoth Murphy's death, 240–1, 421
  book sales of, 35, 248
  bullfighting article of, 459–60, 461–3
  bulls killed by, 42
  bullying and fights of, 226, 228–9, 235–6, 245, 247, 250, 256, 298, 334, 335, 338, 410, 494
  as Catholic convert, 28
  childhood book of, 268–9
  childhood camping trip of, 265–8, 285–6, 287–8
  critical views of, 31, 35, 38, 39–40, 93, 160, 189–90, 253–4, 256–7, 259, 317, 325, 331–4, 375
  destroyed friendships of, 37, 155–61, 228–9
  divorces of, 36, 191, 277, 317, 324, 406
  drinking by, 16, 17, 51, 329, 485

Hemingway, Ernest *(continued)*
  dysentery of, 30, 248–9
  early hunting by, 263, *264*, 265
  electric shock treatments received
    by, 268, 458
  film footage of, 206–7
  generosity of, 44
  Gigi's cross-dressing and, 386, 391,
    392, 397, 400, 403–4, 423, 493
  hair fixation of, 225, 307, 362–4, 485,
    495
  health problems of, 319
  inability to whip children, 292
  injuries of, 110, 135, 156–7, 203–4,
    207–8, 264, 317, 328–9, 336
  mental problems of, 16, 252, 268, 319,
    387, 388, 414, 424, 459, 460, 463–4,
    494
  Michigan stories of, 272–4
  Miró painting purchased by, 346, 347
  myth of, 17–18
  Nita saved from shark by, 307, 366
  Nobel Prize won by, 7, 196, 390, 426
  in plane crashes, 196, 425–6, 459
  psychosexual conflicts of, 364, 390–1,
    417–18, 485, 495
  recording of voice of, 342–3
  reels of, 96–7, 205, 215, 234, 487
  Samuelson's first meetings with,
    110–12
  short stories of, 32–3
  stories about homosexuality by,
    402–3
  suicide of, 10, 12, 16, 69, 82, 98, 123,
    156, 194, 199, 218, 232, 277, 322–3,
    325, 369–70, 413, 414, 432, 451,
    456–7, 458, 465, 477, 500
  teenage camping journal of, 285–6
  trilogy planned by, 310, 358–9, 459
  will of, 439, 503
  writing advice of, 112–13, 184
  writing apprenticeship of, 31–2, 33

  writing style of, 13, 18, 19, 138, 144–5,
    151
  see also Pilar
Hemingway, Gregory (Gigi), 14–16, 24,
    191, 195, 215, 216, 217–19, 232, 292–3,
    343, 366, 371, *381*, 387–8, 389–400,
    419, 422, 423
  in Africa, 427–8, 459
  arrests of, 297, 298–9, 400, 405, 406,
    409–10, 423, 427, 437–8, 444–5,
    446–7, 449–51, 496
  athletic skill of, 329
  in author's *Washington Post* articles,
    14–16, 195, 379–80, 382–5, 496
  autopsy report of, 389–90, 415
  birth of, 34, 109, 425
  child support received by, 406, 421–2
  cross-dressing of, 15, 297, 383–4, 386,
    391, 392, 397, 400, 403–4, 405, 406,
    408, 423, 424, 429–30, 434, 435,
    436–7, 438, 440–1, 493, 496
  death of, 298–9, 444, 445, 446, 450,
    451–2
  as doctor in Montana, 432–9
  fishing by, 216, 292–3
  health problems of, 448
  interest in Dianetics of, 406–7
  shock treatment received by, 15, 428,
    431
  shooting and hunting by, 392, 394–6,
    427–8
  as transsexual, 299, 390–1, 415, 431–2,
    436, 439, 441, 444, 445, 448, 498
  writings of, 397–400
Hemingway, Hadley Richardson, 36,
    37, 80, 232, 241, 277, 281, 345, 395,
    423
Hemingway, Ida Mae Galliher, 439,
    441–2, 447, 448, 449, 450, 499
Hemingway, Jack (Mr. Bumby), 485,
    496
  athletic skill of, 329

in author's *Washington Post* articles,
14–16, 195, 496
birth of, 425
as character in *Islands in the Stream*,
171
as child in Paris, 37, 210
death of, 294
Esquire brought to EH by, 151, 152,
484, 485
fishing by, 215–16, 247–8, 292–4
laugh of, 382
on Leicester Hemingway, 198
in Marine Corps, 393–4
son's death and, 376
Hemingway, John, 392n, 414–15, 426,
429, 436–7, 441, 447, 451, 498
Hemingway, Leicester (Baron), 98, 99,
183–4, 194–200, 270, 277, 322, 429,
431, 471, 483, 486–7
Hemingway, Lorian, 427, 429–31, 497,
499
Hemingway, Maria, 437n
Hemingway, Martha Gellhorn, 36, 37,
45, 191, 257, 293, 322, 324, 340–1,
386, 388, 391, 395, 396–7, 423
Hemingway, Mary Welsh, 158, 310, 328,
332, 351, 353–4, 361, 363, 371, 373,
397, 417, 419, 423, 425, 426, 461–2,
463, 465, 494, 500
EH's abuse and mistreatment of,
298, 325–6, 334–5, 336–8, 339, 366,
424
EH's suicide and, 12, 456
EH's will and, 439, 503
at Houks' wedding, 304, 311, 312
Islands in the Stream edited by, 197,
217
marriage of, 317
in plane crashes, 196
sailing enjoyed by, 11, 326, 344, 358,
420
Hemingway, Ornella, 437

Hemingway, Patrick, 88, 191, 219, 249,
397, 398, 423, 425
in Africa, 427
athletic skill of, 329
in author's *Washington Post* articles,
14–16, 30, 199, 378–9, 496
birth of, 34
on bullfighting, 109–20
as character in *Islands in the Stream*,
164–5
courage of, 403
in Cuba, 391, 393–4
EH's letter to, 40–1
fishing by, 215, 216, 292–3, 378
on Gigi, 382
hunting by, 218, 255, 378–9, 411, 426,
427
shock treatments received by, 365n,
426
Hemingway, Patrick (EH's grandson),
429, 437n, 440, 441
Hemingway, Pauline Pfeiffer, 23, 38, 57,
72, 94, 100, 118, 151, 153, 167, 168,
169, 173, 180, 191, 207, 220, 222, 234,
247, 252–3, 258, 292, 317, 348, 365n,
391, 482, 483
birth of Gregory and, 34, 109
death of, 297, 298, 400, 403, 406,
409–13, 414, 415, 419, 421, 422, 423,
427, 429, 434, 451, 497
EH's adultery with, 9
EH's boat named for, 9
EH's passion for, 36–7
fishing by, 171, 178–9
hair dyed by, 225
marriage of, 36
on *Paris*, 25, 27, 29
purchase of *Pilar* and, 74, 85, 99
on safari, 40, 43, 46
Samuelson and, 113, 115–16, 173
in "Snows of Kilimanjaro," 80
Hemingway, Sean, 437n

Hemingway, Shirley Jane Rhodes, 406, 407, 413, 427

Hemingway, Ursula (Ura), 277, 367

Hemingway, Valerie Danby-Smith, 429, 432, 434, 435, 436, 437*n*, 438, 448, 449, 461–2, 463, 498–9

Hemingway, Vanessa, 434, 437*n*

Hemingway: A Biography (Meyers), 204

"Hemingway Faces God" (Buske), 291

Hemingway-Pfeiffer Museum and Educational Center, 441–2

Hemingway Review, 491, 497, 499

Hepburn, Katharine, 26, 475–6

Herrera, Roberto, 328, 460

"He Who Gets Slap Happy" (Hemingway), 234

Hewson, Dana, 477, 506–7

Hickok, Guy, 43

Hobhouse, Janet, 487

Holder, Charles Frederick, 229

Holiday, 11

Hoover, J. Edgar, 324–5

Hopkins, Gerard Manley, 316

"Horsing Them in with Hemingway" (Gingrich), 51

Horton Bay, 277–81, 282, 283, 284, 286, 293

Hotchner, A. E., 27, 133–4, 462–3, 483, 501

Houk, E. J., 347

Houk, Lawrence, 347

Houk, Nita Jensen, 301, 303, 309, 314–15, *316*, 353–4, 356, 357, 358, 359, 362*n*, 366–7, 372, 407, 419, 421, 495
    EH's attempted seduction of, 365–6
    EH's dying hair of, 362–3, 365
    health problems and death of, 351, 369, 371, 375
    saved from shark, 307, 366
    as secretary to Hemingway, 306, 328, 329, 344, 352–3, 365

wedding of, *300*, 304, 307–8, 309–13, 422

Houk, Paul, 307, 367, 372

Houk, Philippina "Bena," 347

Houk, Tina, 307, 368, 372

Houk, Walter, 300–313, 314–15, 316, 339, 340, 341–2, 343, *345*, 360, 362*n*, 363, 422, 472, 495
    background of, 347–53
    birth of, 345–6
    as diplomat, 306, 309–10, 366–8, 419
    EH's early meetings with, 316, 353–6, 359, 361–2, 366–7
    fishing by, 302–3
    journalism of, 368–9, 371–2
    Pilar drawn by, 300–1
    wedding of, *300*, 304, 307–8, 309–13, 422

Howell, Larry, 438

How It Was (Mary Hemingway), 326, 329, 336–7, 338, 420, 422, 458, 461, 462, 463, 473, 494, 498, 501, 503

Howland, Llewellyn, 477–8

Hubbard, L. Ron, 406–7, 497

Huckleberry Finn (Twain), 398

Hudnut, Richard, 30

Hunt, Bert, 476–7

"Hunter" (Cowley), 259

hunting, 18, 26, 28–9, 97, 158, 378–9

Huxley, Aldous, 408

Huxley, Laura Archera, 408–9, 410, 411

"Icarus," 133

"If I Had a Boat" (song), 89, 482

"I Guess Everything Reminds You of Something" (Hemingway), 393, 399, 497

Île de France, 27, 337, 343

"In Another Country" (Hemingway), 286

"Indian Camp" (Hemingway), 261, 273–4

In Our Time (Hemingway), 221, 256

insomnia, 252, 286–7, 319, 387

International Game Fish Association, 231

"In This Corner, Mr. Hemingway," 189–90

Isabelle (cook), 94, 246

Islands in the Stream (Hemingway), 59–60, 132–3, 170–1, 197, 201–2, 235, 237–8, 248, 358–9, 390, 416, 457–8, 478, 486, 488, 493–4, 498

    EH's sons in, 164–5, 171, 216, 379

    Houk's charting of pursuits in, 372

    as part of projected trilogy, 216

Ivancich, Adriana, 320, 325, 327, 328, 337–8, 339, 355, 360, 458

Ivancich, Dora, 337–8

Ivancich, Gianfranco, 337, 458

Jackson, Captain, 138

James, Henry, 112, 329

Jarrett, Dr., 428

Jenkins, Howell, 491

Jensen, Nita, *see* Houk, Nita Jensen

Jimmy (yardman), 94

Jock: The Life and Times of John Hay Whitney (Kahn), 84

John F. Kennedy Presidential Library and Museum, 47, 132, 168, 177, 224–5, 357, 472, 486, 490, 492, 500, 501

Johnson, Charles, 99

Johnson, Donald S., 285

Jones, James, 361–2

Joyce, James, 43, 112, 225, 318

Joy of Cooking, The, 367n

Juan (cook), 166–7, 172, 174, 187, 365, 422

Judd, Winnie Ruth, 109, 110, 124

Junkins, Donald, 392n

Kahn, E. J., Jr., 84

Kansas City Star, 109, 110, 264

Kazin, Alfred, 76, 92, 331, 334, 474, 480

Kerouac, Jack, 104

Ketchum, Idaho, 13, 439, 456–7, 458–9, 460, 461, 463

Key Largo, 213

Key West, 18, 38, 53–4, 56, 57, 70, 76, 83, 84–8, 94–100, *94*, 105–6, 110–14, 119–20, 147, 148, 149, 150, 154, 170, 176, 177, 179–80, 191–2, 200, 203, 251, 252, 255, 257, 271, 275, 276, 421, 480, 486

Key West Citizen, 88, 95, 97–8, 99, 105, 115, 155, 480, 482

Kirby, Gene, 67–8

Kirstein, Lincoln, 258

Kittredge, William, 437

Klee, Paul, 346

Knapp, Joseph Fairchild (Dodi), 236–7, 245, 247, 250, 488–9

Knapp, Joseph P., 236

Knox, Frank, 67

Kreidt, George, 246–7

Kronenberger, Louis, 35

Lacy, Robert, 133

Lafferty, William, 491

LaGuardia, Fiorello, 67

Lanham, Charles Trueman (Buck), 16, 79, 84, 197, 330–1, 351, 482

"Last Good Country, The" (Hemingway), 279, 288, 364

"Law of the Jungle, The," 29–30

leopards, 28

Lerner, Helen, 231

Lerner, Mike, 231–2, 487

"Letters from a Forgotten Boy," 106–7

Lewis, 94–5

Lewis, Robert, 372

Lewis, Sinclair, 52

Lewis, Wyndham, 43

Liberté, SS, 460
Library of Congress, 342–3
Life, 367, 459–60, 462–3, 465
Lili (beautician), 362
Lincoln, Abraham, 81
lions, 28, 50–1, 82
Little Nourmahal, 50
Loomis, Robert, 132
Loos, Anita, 210
Los Angeles Times, 229, 342, 411
Lost Generation, 16–17
Lovett, Lyle, 89, 482
Luce, Henry, 156
Lunn, Charles J., 147
Lust for Life (Stone), 190
Lyman, Bernard, 233
Lynn, Kenneth S., 208*n*, 418, 473
Lyon, George Albert, 230

Macdonald-Wright, Stanton, 349, 495
MacLeish, Ada, 96, 156, 158–9, 241, 242, 243, 410
MacLeish, Archibald, 34, 38–9, 82, 96, 100, 115, 152, 156–9, 183, 225, 231*n*, 241, 246, 410, 476, 480
Magic Mountain, The (Mann), 215, 488
Mailer, Norman, 16, 218, 474
Mandler, Lou, 398
Manitou, SS, 269, 270–1, 491–2
Mann, Thomas, 215
Marcelline of Windemere, 275, 276
Marita, Marchesa de San Felice, 374
Markham, Beryl, 223
marlin, 138, 150, 151, 152–3, 162–3, 167, 169, 170, 171, 172, 178–9, 182, 188, 214, 215, 226–7, 230, 234, 245, 250, 326–7, 430, 459, 485, 501
Martí, José, 168
Mason, Grant, 159, 172
Mason, Jane, 51, 159, 172, 178, 321–2

Masson, André, 346
Matthews, T. S., 35, 39
Maupassant, Guy de, 398
Maxwell, William, 356
Mayo Clinic, 18, 268, 325, 408, 410, 456, 458, 463–4, 490, 491
McCarthy, Joseph, 328
McEvoy, Jay, 408, 411
McGrath, Thomas J. S., Father, 99, 100, 154, 155
McKinley, William, 81
Men Without Women (Hemingway), 402
Merner, Garfield, 411
Merner, Ward Pfeiffer, 180
Mesquite Lumber Company, 121, 124, 127
Meyers, Jeffrey, 15, 204, 439–40, 473
Miami Herald, 155, 450
Michigan, forests of, 287–90
Miller, Linda Patterson, 177–8, 242, 474, 475, 486
Miller, Madelaine Hemingway (Sunny), 275, 376, 492
Minneapolis Tribune, 106–7, 108
Minot Daily News, 108–9
Miró, Joan, 346, 347, 355
Missoulian, 438
Mollica, Anthony, Jr., 61, 62, 477
Mompierre, Nelson, 444
Monks, Noel, 337
"Monologue to the Maestro" (Hemingway), 105, 113
Montalvo, Antonio, 392, 396
Moore, Betty, 230
Moore, C. Philip, 61
Morris, Jan (James), 431
Morrow, Lance, 24, 475
Motor Boating, 117, 173, 181, 484
Moveable Feast, A (Hemingway), 33, 37, 226, 261, 279–80, 454, 460, 476

Murphy, Baoth, 240–3, 421

Murphy, Gerald, 37, 75, 156, 187, 189, 228, 240–3, 421, 481, 486

Murphy, Patrick, 241, 242, 243, 396, 487

Murphy, Sara, 18, 37, 75, 96, 99, 156, 187, 189, 240–3, 248, 252, 255, 421, 474, 486, 489

Murrow, Edward R., 44–5

My Brother, Ernest Hemingway (Les Hemingway), 98, 199, 322

Myers, Peter, 449

Nairobi, 30

"Nearing Ninety" (Maxwell), 356

New Deal, 154, 184

New Masses, 189–90, 251–2

New Republic, 31, 254, 256, 259, 476

Newsweek, 318, 332, 333

New York, 476

New Yorker, 29–30, 39, 327–8, 331, 333, 335–6, 356, 476, 478

New York Herald Tribune, 27, 29, 67, 81–2, 252, 332, 476

New York Post Week-End Magazine, 351, 495

New York Review of Books, 418, 460, 498

New York Times, 35, 53, 68–9, 111, 210, 234, 253–4, 331–2

New York Times Book Review, 254, 333, 336, 431, 492–3, 499

Nick Adams Stories, The (Hemingway), 274, 279

907 Whitehead, 94–5, 98, 134, 156, 245–6, 258, 351, 353–4, 388, 439, 452

No. 5 Hardy hickory rod, 96

Norris, Katherine Love, 269

North Carolina, 350

North Dakota Quarterly, 372, 373–4, 495

Notes of a Native Son (Baldwin), 104

"Notes on Dangerous Game: The Third Tanganyika Letter" (Hemingway), 223

"Now I Lay Me" (Hemingway), 282, 286–7

Oak Park, Ill., 23, 36, 65, 144, 264, 266–9, 275, 282, 285, 290, 292, 418, 456

O'Brine, Jack, 169, 170*n*, 183

O'Hara, John, 333

Ohlsen, Angeline, 491

Ohlsen, Ray, 264, 266–8, 490–1

Old Man and the Sea, The (Hemingway), 192, 216, 300, 307, 317*n*, 345, 454, 494, 495, 500
   as based on real-life story, 322
   film of, 459
   first draft of, 359
   in *Life* magazine, 367
   as part of projected trilogy, 216, 310
   publishing of, 310

Olson, Jana, 433–4

On Becoming a Person (Rogers), 381–2

"On Being Shot Again: A Gulf Stream Letter" (Hemingway), 203–4, 205, 207, 209, 211, 213

"One Too Many," 121

"One Trip Across" (Hemingway), 51, 107, 138, 162–4

"On the Blue Water: A Gulf Stream Letter" (Hemingway), 322

"On the Gulf Stream Aboard Hemingway's *Pilar*" (Houk), 305, 372

On the Road (Kerouac), 104

"On Writing" (Hemingway), 283

Operation Friendless, 324

Ordóñez, Antonio, 460

Ordóñez, Carmen, 460
Orwell, George, 316
Outdoor Life, 118, 180, 181, 245
"Out in the Stream: A Cuban Letter,"
    151, 152
Out of Africa (Dinesen), 224, 295
outrigger, 231, 301

Pamplona, Spain, 32, 346, 395
Papa: A Personal Memoir (Gregory
    Hemingway), 232, 250, 297, 360,
    395–6, 398–9, 406, 411, 412, 413–14,
    424, 425–6, 427, 431, 438, 449
Papa Hemingway (Hotchner), 133–4,
    483, 501
"Papa's Boys" (Hendrickson), 14–16,
    390, 496
Paris, 16–17, 50, 57, 278
Paris, SS, 25–8, *25,* 30, 41, 44, 50, 102,
    231, 475–6
Paris Herald, 43
"Paris Letter, A" (Hemingway), 35, 36
Paris Review, 82–3, 480
Pasadena, 351
Pastor, Juan, 318, 333, 336
Patou, Jean, 314
Payson, Charles Shipman, 49, 82
Peirce, Waldo, 57, 75, 100, 152, 158, 159,
    231*n*
Percival, Philip, 223
Pereda, Prudencio de, 95–6, 212, 255
Perkins, Maxwell, 25–6, 32, 35, 52, 72,
    75, 97, 160, 185, 187, 188, 189, 211,
    235, 246, 248, 252, 253, 258, 298, 318,
    323, 351, 482–3
Peru, 459
Petoskey, Mich., 269–71, 286, 289
Pfeiffer, Gus, 30, 75, 94, 157, 348
Pfeiffer, Jinny, 222, 407, 408–10, 411
Pfeiffer, Karen, 409
Pfeiffer, Mary, 184, 187, 387, 486

Philadelphia Evening Bulletin, 175
Picasso, Pablo, 225
Pilar, 6, 8–9, 10–11, 30, 37, 46, *47,* 49, 56,
    58, 122, 144, 242, 252–3, 256, 272
    alterations on, 53
    author's visit to, 7–8
    busted water pump on, 148, 166, 167,
        178
    current version as possible fake,
        504–7
    design of, 9–10, 62, 138–41, 222,
        356–7
    drawing of, 300–1
    engine overhaul of, 248
    fishing on, 56, 82, 96–7, 99–100, 103,
        115–17, 138, 146–7, *146,* 149, 154–5,
        157–8, 161, 167, 169–73, 178–9,
        180–1, 187, 188, 200, 204, 205–6,
        214–15, 220, 226–7, 230, 234–5, 241,
        247, 276, 302–3, 310, 319, 326–7,
        330, 339, 343, 373–4, 376–7, 422,
        489
    flying bridge of, 10, 11, 139, 301, 314,
        316, 328, 374
    German subs hunted by, 7, 323–4,
        494
    Gregorio's alleged inheritance of,
        494, 503–4
    Hemingway's writing on, 41, 160,
        339, 343
    Houks on, 300–2, 303–4, 314, *345,* 373–6
    log of, 126, 131–2, 167, 177–9, 180–1,
        472, 485, 486
    outrigger for, 231, 301
    photos of, 110, 134, 167, 182, *345,* 348,
        357, 471
    price of, 12, 50, 70, 73–4, 95, 99, 480
    purchase of, 12, 18, 64, 70–1, 73–4, 76,
        85, 99, 159, 480
    purchase order of, 70–1, 73–4, 92, 480
    registration of, 53

Samuelson on, 102–3, *104*, 113–14,
126, 130–1, 140, 147, 157–8, 171–3,
175, 180–1, 186, 188, 485, 504–5
scientific excursion on, 173–7, 183
speed of, 8
steering wheel of, 10, 141, 301, 314
Pinder, Albert "Old Bread," 212
Pine Barrens, 284, 287–8, 491
Pioneer Press, 28
Playboy, 51
Plaza de Armas, 91–3
Porter, Katherine Anne, 43
Portrait of the Artist as a Young Man
(Joyce), 398
Pound, Ezra, 221
Povich, Shirley, 483
Powell, Dawn, 475
Prado, *166*, 167–9
"President Vanquishes, The"
(Hemingway), 227–8
President Wilson, SS, 367
Preston, John Hyde, 211
Price, Reynolds, 475
Prío Socarrás, Carlos, 309, 310
Pritchard, Ed, 487
Profiles in Saltwater Angling (Reiger),
230, 488
Prohibition, 150

Quintero, Carlos, 396

Random House, 132
Rashin, Morica, 107
Real, Nelia, 444–5, 450
Reiger, George, 230, 488
"Remembering Shooting-Flying: A
Key West Letter" (Hemingway),
292
René (houseboy), 420
Reynolds, Michael, 358, 473–4, 480,
494

Richard II (Shakespeare), 460
Rimbach family, 69
Robert Lee, Texas, 102, 120–5, 128, 130,
132, 483
Robert Lee Observer, 129
Roe, Fred, 120
Rogers, Carl R., 381–2
Rolling Stone, 432, 450
Rome, Howard, 464
Roosevelt, Franklin D., 88, 154, 158,
184, 251
Roosevelt, Theodore, 81, 223
Rosen, Floyd, 451
Ross, Harold, 333–4
Ross, Lillian, 327–8, 343
Rubinstein, Arthur, 338, 348
Running with the Bulls: My Years
with the Hemingways (Valerie
Hemingway), 432, 434, 435, 498–9
Russell, Joe (Josie Grunts), 150–1, 157,
247

safaris, 35–6, 38–9, 41–3, 44, 82, 417,
476
Saga, 49
Samuelson, Anders, 109
Samuelson, Arnold Morse (Maestro),
28, *104*, 105–36, 140, 147, 157–8, 167,
168, 171–3, 180–1, 186, 245, 304, 351,
483, 485, 486
background of, 106–8
death of, 102–3, 129
diary of, 134
eccentric behavior of, 122–31
EH's first meeting with, 102, 113,
483–4
log kept by, 126, 177
memoir of, 102, 110–11, 114, 117–18,
122, 130, 132, 170, 171, 173, 174, 182,
183, 188, 485, 504–5
pregnant lover of, 135–6

Samuelson, Eric, 121, 123, 125–6, 128–9

Samuelson, Hedvig (Sammy), 108–9, 124, 131, 132, 134

Samuelson, Marie, 109

Samuelson, Sam, 107, 123, 124, 131

Samuelson, Vivian Stettler, 120–1, 123, 124, 125, 126, 127

Sanford, Jim, 492

Sanford, John, 492

Sanford, Marcelline Hemingway, 275, 276–7, 281, 291, 491, 498

San Francisco Chronicle, 441

Sara & Gerald (Donnelly), 241, 242

Saturday Evening Post, 75

Saturday Review of Literature, 35, 331, 334

Saunders, Ashley, 488

Saunders, Bra, 98, 115, 157, 213, 482, 483

Saunders, Nattie, 235–6

Saunders, Willard, 250

Savannah, 350

Saviers, Frederick G., 18, 19, 464–5

Saviers, George, 18, 19, 458, 462, 463, 500–1

Saviers, Pierre, 465

Scribner, Charles, III, 298, 318, 326, 327, 328, 329–30, 333, 334–5, 343, 359, 361, 362n, 373, 376–7, 409, 495
death of, 420–1, 422

Scribner, Charles, Jr., 462, 499

Scribner, Vera, 361, 420–1

Scribner's Magazine, 57, 211

Sea Chase, A (Hemingway), 359, 360, 362n

September 11, 2001, terrorist attacks of, 448–9

Shakespeare and Company, 43, 50

sharks, 77, 116, 173, 204, 209, 226–7, 230, 234, 249, 366, 459

Shevlin, Tommy, 231, 247, 483

Shipman, Evan, 346

Sholtz, David, 154

"Shooting an Elephant" (Orwell), 316

"Short Happy Life of Francis Macomber, The" (Hemingway), 223, 257

Sigman, Joseph, 488

"Simple Enquiry, A" (Hemingway), 402–3

Skemer, Don, 482

Sloppy Joe's, 38, 150

Smith, Bill, 281

Smith, Bob, 430

"Snows of Kilimanjaro, The" (Hemingway), 16, 37–8, 79–81, 82, 84, 223, 238, 257, 271–2, 446
crack about Fitzerald in, 80
in *Esquire,* 80, 120, 481
mysterious lady in, 77–8, 81, 83–4, 481–2
origins of, 83

Sotheby's, 367

Sound of the Trumpet, The (Les Hemingway), 195–7

Spain, 459–60, 461, 463

Spanish-American War, 229

Spanish Civil War, 10, 95, 120, 135, 231, 257, 322, 324

Spanish Earth, The (film), 257

Spooner, Ken, 488

Stein, Gertrude, 114, 203, 209–12, 213, 222, 232, 318, 359
Hemingway attacked by, 35, 39, 42, 211–12, 222, 281

Stendhal, 112

Stern, Ada, 425

Stevens, Mark, 31, 476

Stone, Irving, 190–1

Stone, Julius F., 154

Strand, Mark, 216

Strange Tribe (John Hemingway),
  414–15, 426, 432, 436, 437*n*, 441,
  447, 451, 498
Strater, Henry (Mike), 39, 74, 156,
  157, 206, 213, 220–2, 220, 225, 227,
  228–9, 231
Strater, Maggie, 228
Streep, Meryl, 224
Stuart, Lyle, 504
Sun, 32, 358
Sun Also Rises, The (Hemingway), 32,
  34, 57, 143–4, 190, 256, 345, 350, 476
Sunny, 275–6
Sunset, 368, 371
Svoboda, Frederic, 287, 289

Tender Is the Night (Fitzgerald), 75–7,
  159, 255
Thomas, Henry Randall, 410–11, 415,
  451
Thompson, Charles, 38, 41–2, 43, 88,
  100, 115, 150–1, 155, 207, 213, 222
Thompson, Lorine, 43, 115, 207
"Three Shots," 274
Thurman, Judith, 224
Time, 10, 24, 196, 197, 332–3, 479
Tin Kid, 358, 419
To Have and Have Not (Hemingway),
  150, 257
Toklas, Alice B., 114, 209–10
Tolstoy, Leo, 112, 349
tommy gun, 226–7, 228, 231*n*
Toronto Star, 86, 221, 232–3, 488
Torres, Ben, 445
Tracy, Spencer, 459
transatlantic review, 274
Travel-Holiday, 369
True Gen, The (Brian), 226, 228, 473
tuna, 213, 221, 229–30, 232–3, 234, 235
Tuna Club of Avalon, 229
Turgenev, Ivan, 399

Turnbull, Andrew, 460, 483
Twain, Mark, 254, 489
Two-Hearted River, 283–4

Ullman, Toy, 490
Ulysses (Joyce), 350
"Up in Michigan" (Hemingway), 281,
  283
Ursula of Windemere, 275, 276

van Gogh, Vincent, 190
Van Guilder, Gene, 500
Vogue, 168
Vom Hofe, 205, 215, 234, 487
von Kurowsky, Agnes, 80

Wagner, Dick, 21, 477
Walk on Water (Lorian Hemingway),
  429–31, 499
Walloon Lake, 271–3, 275, 276, 277, 280,
  281, 284, 285, 287, 289
Warner Brothers, 210
Warren, William, 207
Washington Post, 14–16, 103, 132, 390,
  433, 471, 483, 495, 498
Washington Post Magazine, 496
"Way You'll Never Be, A"
  (Hemingway), 35, 286
Westways, 369
Wheeler, Edith Berentha Clayton, 65,
  479
Wheeler, Eugene, 68
Wheeler, Howard E., 47–8, 61, 65–6,
  67, 69, 477, 478, 479
Wheeler, Robert, 68
Wheeler, Wesley, 69
Wheeler, Wesley D., 61–2, 63, 477, 479
Wheeler, Wesley L., 61, 68
Wheeler Shipyard, Inc., 13, 30, 47–54,
  59–69, 72–88, 98, 99, 141, 213, 233,
  356, 483, 505

White, Bud, 151
White, E. B., 29–30, 335–6, 476
Whitney, Helen Hay, 49, 77–80, 81, 83–4, 481–2
Whitney, Joan, 49, 81
Whitney, John Hay (Jock), 49, 81–2, 84, 481
Whitney, Kate, 481
Whitney, Payne, 49, 78
"Who Murdered the Vets?" (Hemingway), 251–2
Wilder, Thornton, 56–8, 210, 478
Wilson, Edmund, 16, 42, 76, 152, 253, 255, 256, 259, 474, 480
Wilson, Woodrow, 265
Windemere, 272, 276, 281, 490
"Wine of Wyoming" (Hemingway), 35
Winner Take Nothing (Hemingway), 35, 39, 44, 257, 476, 497
Winnie Ruth Judd: The Trunk Murders (Dobkins), 124
Winter, Ella, 16
With Hemingway: A Year in Key West and Cuba (Samuelson), 105,
110–11, 114, 117–18, 122, 130, 132–3, 170, 171, 173, 174, 182, 183, 188, 485, 504–5
Wolfe, Thomas, 362n
Woodward, H. L., 149–50
Worel, Sunny, 483
World-Telegram, 29
World War, I, II, 16, 44–5, 64, 65, 80, 135, 200, 265, 274n, 282, 286–7, 323–4
Wright, Frank Lloyd, 36, 476
Wright, Kitty, 476

Xenophobia (prostitute), 325–6, 332, 335, 370

Yachts in a Hurry (Moore), 61
Yale Review, 331
Yardley, Jonathan, 132
Young, Philip, 274, 491

"Zane Grey" Hardy nickel-plated reel, 96, 205, 487

A NOTE ABOUT THE AUTHOR

Paul Hendrickson's previous book, *Sons of Mississippi*, won the 2003 National Book Critics Circle Award for nonfiction. Since 1998 he has been on the faculty of the creative writing program at the University of Pennsylvania. For two decades before that he was a staff writer at *The Washington Post*. Among his other books are *Looking for the Light: The Hidden Life and Art of Marion Post Wolcott* (1992 finalist for the National Book Critics Circle Award) and *The Living and the Dead: Robert McNamara and Five Lives of a Lost War* (1996 finalist for the National Book Award). He has been the recipient of writing fellowships from the Guggenheim Foundation, the National Endowment for the Arts, the Lyndhurst Foundation, and the Alicia Patterson Foundation. In 2009 he was a joint visiting professor of documentary practice at Duke University and of American Studies at the University of North Carolina at Chapel Hill. He is the father of two grown sons and lives with his wife, Cecilia, outside Philadelphia.

A NOTE ON THE TYPE

This book was set in a modern adaptation of a type designed by the first William Caslon (1692–1766). The Caslon face, an artistic, easily read type, has enjoyed over two centuries of popularity in the English-speaking world. This version, designed by Carol Twombley for the Adobe Corporation and released in 1990, insures by its even balance and honest letterforms the continuing use of Caslon well into the digital age and the twenty-first century.

Composed by North Market Street Graphics,
Lancaster, Pennsylvania
Printed and bound by Berryville Graphics,
Berryville, Virginia
Designed by Peter A. Andersen